HISTORY OF WESTE
VOLUM

Also available from Continuum:

History of Western Astrology, Volume I
Nicholas Campion

The Medieval and Modern Worlds

History of Western Astrology
Volume II

Nicholas Campion

continuum

Continuum UK, The Tower Building, 11 York Road, London SE1 7NX
Continuum US, 80 Maiden Lane, Suite 704, New York, NY 10038

www.continuumbooks.com

First published 2009

British Library Cataloguing-in-Publication Data
A catalogue record for this book is available from the British Library.

ISBN 978 1 84725 224 1

Typeset by Pindar NZ, Auckland, New Zealand
Printed and bound by MPG Books Group, Cornwall

Contents

Acknowledgements

I would like to thank Tony Morris for his faith in me, Kathleen Quigley for setting this project in motion many years ago, Wendy Buonaventura for her patience, my colleagues and students in the Sophia Centre and at Kepler College and all those other friends, students and scholars who have inspired me.

To Steve

Introduction: Origins and Background

Two things fill the mind with ever new and increasing admiration and awe, the oftener and the more steadily we reflect on them: the starry heavens above and the moral law within.

IMMANUEL KANT[1]

This book is the sequel to the first volume, which considered the history of astrology from the earliest prehistoric speculation and concluded with the triumph of Christianity in Europe in the fifth century CE. This volume runs from the fifth century to the present day and, together with Volume I, draws connections between prehistoric mentalities and modern. This is far from being a controversial statement for the evidence suggests that many modern people experience the cosmos as a potential source of order, meaning and significance, exactly as did their stone-age ancestors. The connection between widely separated times and cultures is possible if we adopt a broad definition of astrology. In this respect I follow Patrick Curry who argued that 'Astrology is the practice of relating the heavenly bodies to lives and events on earth, and the tradition that has thus been generated.'[2] It will be instantly clear that such a liberal view allows astrology to include not just the casting and interpretation of horoscopes, but calendar construction, archaeoastronomy (the creation of buildings embodying astronomical alignments, orientations or symbolism), astral religion, magical ritual and other forms of divination or inquiry into the cosmos which may use astrological symbolism or astronomical cycles.[3] I don't deal with calendars and archaeoastronomy, but a central theme of my narrative is religious. It is impossible to deal adequately with medieval and Renaissance astrology without considering the collision between astrology, which suggested that the individual has a direct relationship with the cosmos, and Christianity, which insisted that this must be mediated via the Church. The, as yet unresolved, argument between the two has shaped, informed, obstructed and encouraged the practice and philosophy of astrology in the West over the last 1500 years.

There is a simple narrative running through this volume. I am proposing that the period from the fifth to eleventh centuries was a period of collapse after the sophistication of the classical world. Few historians would disagree with this. There then followed half a millennium during which astrology was a central part of European culture. It rested on two fundamental hypotheses, with which it was impossible to disagree. The first was that God spoke to humanity partly through signs in the sky. This was an obligatory article of faith for every Christian. The second was that earth and heavens were linked in a series of interlocking natural influences. This was self-evident to anyone who experienced the heat of the sun or observed the relationship between the moon and the tides. The arguments and debates over astrology rested not on its fundamental premise. The first objection to astrology was theological, that only God could know the future. The second was evidential: some critics accepted the principle of planetary influence or significance, but doubted whether astrologers could speak in detail on all matters, great and small, with the precision which they claimed. The arguments against such practices intensified in the seventeenth century and, since around 1700, astrology has struggled to find a recognized role and has been largely excluded from educated discourse. The present situation finds astrology an accepted part of popular culture, but subject to ridicule and overt hostility from both religious and scientific arenas. The last three centuries have been more like an iron age than a golden one, so I offer simple narrative, with just a hint of repetition. In the fifth century astrology collapsed, in the twelfth it revived, and in the late seventeenth it collapsed again. Or did it? As we shall see, the truth is rather more complex, with some forms of astrology thriving and others disguising themselves behind other names. The book concludes with the question of whether astrology's current popularity in any way constitutes a second revival.

Astrology is not a single practice or idea; it includes multiple narratives about the nature of the world. If we examine its history carefully we can see that it is, variously, a form of magic, a system of prediction, a model for psychological growth, a science, a spiritual tool, a religion and a system of divination, definitions which are not mutually exclusive. It has competing rationales and a variety of technical systems. It may be directed towards sacred goals (the soul's union with the divine) or profane (the making of profit or seizure of one's enemy's castle), the trivial (the location of lost property) or deeply serious (the length of one's life). It depends on the blurring of the distinction between matter and consciousness, the distance between near objects and far-away ones, and on what the philosopher Ernest Cassirer called a 'grandiose, self-contained intuition of the spatial-physical cosmos'.[4] It provides a grand narrative, a 'meta-narrative', which it claims is capable of explaining anything from one's emotional state and destiny, to the fluctuations of popular culture, the condition of the stock market, the identity of the next US president and the quality of one's last incarnation. Within the community of astrologers there are vigorous debates over what the practice can actually achieve: for over 2000 years astrologers have argued over such questions as whether it can predict the future and, if so, in precise detail or in only general terms?

The astrological universe has been described as a 'cosmic state' or a 'republic of heaven', in which the 'up-there' and the 'down-here' are inseparable.[5] It offers a framework consisting of patterns within which otherwise random events may be interpreted as having a purpose. It also provides what the sociologist Max Weber calls a 'theodicy', in which apparently inexplicable events, good or bad, can be seen to make sense.[6] Its cosmos is beautiful and perfectly ordered – as in our word cosmetic – and, in its own terms, it enables people to develop survival strategies, negotiating with the heavens in order to better manage their daily affairs. It is 'imaginal' not in the sense of imaginary, meaning false, but in the sense that the cosmos is psychically as well as physically linked to the mind of every human being.[7] Astrology is, above all, difficult to pin down to a single set of ideas or practices, and this is a problem for historians. In the final analysis I follow Ann Geneva who, denying attempts to define astrology according to its relationship to scientific or religious mentalities argued that 'it is first necessary to locate astrology within its own universe of discourse before historians can attempt to compare it with other explanatory systems'.[8] So, the question before us is, what, exactly, is 'astrology's universe of discourse'? This is a question I explore largely through the claims of some of the leading protagonists, both sympathetic and hostile. And here we have to acknowledge our source problems. We can trace the literary tradition, but that might not conform exactly to the lived experience. We have astrological texts surviving from the Middle Ages which tell us the complex rules that astrologers could apply if they wished, but we do not know which ones were applied or how widely. No doubt itinerant fortune-tellers would have found it easier to refer only to the moon's position, perhaps, or rely on a form of geomancy, an oracular practice in which the casting of stones bearing astrological symbols negated the need for calculating a horoscope at all. Neither do we have much idea of what it might have been like to visit an astrologer.

All of the above suggests that we can analyse astrology according to its competing technical or philosophical schools – or its social contexts. This being a cultural history, I deal only peripherally with the development of astrological technique, which awaits an authoritative study. That does leave us with the question of what exactly constitutes 'culture', a word which Terry Eagleton described as 'one of the two or three most complex' in the English language.[9] Some definitions of the term are, though, particularly helpful to the history of astrology. The anthropologist Clifford Geertz served the subject well when he wrote that culture is 'an historically transmitted pattern of meanings embodied in symbols, a system of inherited conceptions expressed in symbolic form'.[10] Such a definition could function equally well as a description of astrology, which itself becomes a vital means of the transmission of knowledge seen as symbol rather than, as would be the modern view, factual information.

In the past, histories of astrology have tended to be 'external' in the sense that they have documented its social or political use. This is a perfectly valid exercise, and it is one in which I am engaged in this book. However, to try and understand astrology's appeal, which at times has been intense and widespread, we need to try and penetrate its inner language, the means by which its claims and practices were lived and experienced. One means of approaching the inner experience might be through the language and development of interpretative technique, a task which must be left until later. My concern is with philosophy, especially the ebb and flow of debates about fate, destiny and free choice that form, perhaps, the most consistent linking thread in arguments about astrology's role and legitimacy from the fifth century to the present day. The key issue for anyone engaging with astrology in a Christian context, which means most people in Europe from the early-Medieval to early-modern periods, then becomes the extent to which the reading of destiny in the stars is entirely compatible with the making of moral choice, or militates against it. The issue was profound, and confronts the user with two possible futures: an eternity of bliss in the former case, or of torturous damnation in the latter. The stakes could not have been higher.

As so often happens, the issue revolves around exactly what astrology is: a form of divination (and, if so, legitimate within a Christian context or not) or of natural philosophy (and, if so, counter to scripture or not). Central to such debates is a useful modern distinction made by some historians between 'natural' and 'judicial' astrology. Natural astrology required no more than the observation of natural influences deriving from the planets, and was universally accepted in the medieval and Renaissance worlds. Judicial astrology, requiring the astrologer's judgement, depended on complex deductions made from horoscopes and was widespread, but never entirely accepted by theological and sceptical opponents. This distinction is essential for understanding astrology's sometimes contradictory position in the West, especially denunciations of it, which invariably referred to the judicial variety, not the natural. I have also adopted Patrick Curry's hierarchical model of three forms of astrology forming a rough analogy with the three social groups, upper, middle and lower class.[11] The first, high astrology, is the astrology of the philosophers and theologians, concerned with speculative matters such as whether the theory of celestial influence leaves room for moral choice. The second, middling astrology, is characterized by the casting and interpretation of horoscopes, a practice requiring a considerable level of literary study and mathematical skill. The third, low astrology, is the astrology of street fortune-tellers, of almanacs (after the fifteenth century) and, in the modern world, newspaper and magazine 'sun-sign' columns.

Astrology's history presents us with certain terminological difficulties. J.R.R. Tolkein spotted this in his discussion of enchantment and magic. 'Supernatural,' he wrote, 'is a dangerous and difficult word in any of its senses, looser or stricter.'[12] The word's main problem, Tolkein saw, was its assumption that there is a world, a sphere of existence we might say, which is automatically and utterly distinct from the natural, a belief which then sets up a false view of the natural world itself as entirely physical, easy to weigh and measure and readily susceptible to scientific analysis. The supernatural is, by contrast, mysterious, remote and, quite probably, non-existent. Similarly, astrology is often described as 'occult', meaning hidden and, by inference, sinister. The word 'occult' in the meaning of hidden knowledge was promoted by Henry Cornelius Agrippa's sixteenth-century *Three Books of Occult Philosophy*, a summation of medieval astral magic, but seems to have entered the language as an umbrella term for the secret, mysterious and potentially dangerous after the French esotericist Eliphas Lévi published *Le Grand Arcane, ou l'Occultisme Dévoilé (The Great Secret, or Occultism Unveiled)* in 1868.[13] The word can be used simultaneously by occult practitioners to surround themselves with an aura of mystery, and by its critics to signify automatic condemnation.[14] I use the term 'occultist' in the final chapters because it entered the language of the people and groups I am discussing, but we have to be careful not to read pejorative meanings into it: the historian must remain methodologically neutral, observing, explaining and analysing, but neither condemning nor promoting.

The term esoteric, meaning inner wisdom, as opposed to knowledge of the outer world, also seems to have come into common use in the modern period, partly as a reaction to the increasing concern with a purely material view of the natural world.[15] Hedged about by such terms, astrology is removed from what it was – a central feature of European life – and is – a fundamental part of popular culture – into a fringe activity, in which its practitioners were deluded dabblers. What terms like supernatural, occult and esoteric try, but fail, to invoke is that sense of complete integration with the cosmos which I argued in Volume I was the goal of the astrological experience, namely Lucien Lévy-Bruhl's *participation-mystique*.[16] The nature of astrological knowledge-claims is often difficult to pin down and there is a slippage between ontology, the assumption that astrologers are really examining the real underlying nature of the universe, and the more modern notion of analogy, that the world is being described not as it is, but in terms of what it is like. An event which takes place under the planet Mars, for example, might no longer be essentially Martian in its character, but merely described by Martial qualities.

I have also tried to steer my way around the modern distinction between astronomy and astrology. The fact that the two terms were once interchangeable is acknowledged by most historians of astronomy. To consult a modern Latin dictionary we find that *astrologia* is defined as astronomy while the practitioner, the *astrologus*, is either an astrologer or an astronomer, while the first great text of medieval astrology was Guido Bonatti's *Liber Astronomiae*.[17] When Aristotle, whose work was the ultimate authority on such things in the Middle Ages, used the word *astrologia*, modern translations render this, with no explanation, as astronomy.[18] This might suit modern scholars, but completely obscures and distorts Aristotle's importance in the Middle Ages from the twelfth century onwards, when his prestige did so much to confer legitimacy on astrology. The most influential of medieval and Renaissance astrologers, those who served at court, were more likely to be known by other names entirely; in the 1600s Johannes Kepler was neither astronomer nor astrologer to the Holy Roman Emperor – he was the Mathematician. The medieval study of astronomy was more likely to be known as the study of the *sphaera*, the spheres on which the stars and planets revolved, than of the stars themselves. Various people have suggested solutions to the terminological problem: Edgar Laird suggested the term 'Star Study', Roger Beck 'Star Talk'.[19] I generally follow Claudius Ptolemy's second-century distinction in which astronomy is divided into two stages: the first measures the positions of the stars and planets, the second their effects.[20] So, Ptolemy's second form of astronomy is generally what we would know as astrology. Except, of course, 'effect' implies a causal relationship between planets and people, which is by no means necessary. For most of the period we are studying, the significance of astrological patterns, their ability to impart meaning to humanity via celestial signs, was equally important. The two rationales, influences and signs, went hand-in-hand as equal and complementary justifications for astrology. There are, though, forms of astrology that rely on celestial symbolism together with the general principle of divination – that by looking at one thing, a tarot card, for example – one gains an insight into another which is entirely unrelated. In the Middle Ages onomancy allowed the practitioner to construct a horoscope by converting the numerology of an individual's name into planets and zodiac signs, while in the 1980s one could purchase a set of astro-dice; by rolling the dice while asking a question, an answer was provided by the resulting combination of planet with zodiac sign.

There is a certain amount of information in this volume for which a full explanation is provided in Volume I. That said, it is necessary for me to give the briefest of brief summaries of the salient points of ancient astrology. The distant, textual origin of modern Western astrology lies in the cuneiform tablets of Mesopotamian civilization, which indicate that, from around 2000 to 500 BCE, astrological rules were constructed in two ways, whether on the basis of theoretical speculation about the nature of the cosmos, or direct, empirical observation of the coincidence between celestial occurrences and earthly events. The practice of astrology was based on the assumption that the cosmos was repetitive – that when the same astronomical pattern recurred in the future the corresponding terrestrial events would be similar in nature. The system was divinatory in nature in the sense that it required communication with divine beings, and destiny itself was negotiated via ritual acts designed to appeal to or propitiate such beings. A process of codification is evident from the fifth century in which the 12-sign zodiac was devised and the practice of casting birth charts (or horoscopes in modern terms) for infants was developed. From the fourth to first centuries BCE Mesopotamian astrology entered into a series of creative interactions with Greek, Egyptian and Indian culture which led to the development of the highly complex mathematical and interpretative system which survived in Europe until the seventeenth century and is still practised in India. A number of different systems of Greek thought fed into astrological theory and practice, fracturing the Babylonian model into different schemes. From the works of the seventh-century BCE poet Hesiod came the concept that the passage of the stars through the year is directly related to the seasons. Pythagoras (sixth century BCE) contributed the idea that the cosmos is constructed mathematically, its motions directed by numerical laws. Plato (fifth–fourth centuries BCE) followed Pythagoras in his belief in perfect mathematical order, but gave detail to the idea (which was already current) that the cosmos is alive and conscious, is created by a 'God' who is conceived of as good, supreme and conscious, and that the human soul originates in the stars, to which it returns after death, having an innate desire to reunite with its creator. Destiny might be negotiated and the future improved if one led an upright, moral, scholarly lifestyle. All things in the visible universe are based on 'archetypes', or 'Ideas', original models which inhabit an eternal, unchanging, perfect realm. Physically, the universe was structured in concentric systems of crystalline spheres, on which the planets orbited around a stationary, spherical earth. The soul travelled down through these spheres before birth and returned up through them, after death. Plato's student Aristotle retained some of his master's ideas, but emphasized natural influences and causation. God was reconceived as little more than a 'first-mover' who started the universe in motion, and the planets operated as 'secondary causes' which transmitted the intent of the prime-mover to earth. Other causal mechanisms might include light, as well as the archetypes, which manifested as 'formal' causes (form being a synonym for archetype). Also of significance for astrology was Aristotle's concept of the 'final' cause, the future condition which draws the present towards it: in a simple example, an acorn becomes an oak tree, the oak being the acorn's future state and final cause. Aristotle also argued that the earth and the area of space between it and the moon was imperfect, in a state of constant change and made of four elements – fire, earth, air and water. The space above the moon was perfect and filled with the fifth element, ether. Another of Plato's students, Eudoxus, took Plato's statement that all perfect movement must be circular and developed a model for planetary motion based on perfect circles, which was to have a direct impact on astrology much later: when the system was discredited in the seventeenth century, astrology, too, lost credibility. Plato's universe moved according to predetermined mathematical and geometrical laws but each individual could exert moral choice. Around the year 300 BCE the philosopher Zeno developed his fatalistic Stoic philosophy, in which moral choice was (almost) as predetermined as were planetary motions. The astrology which is evident from the first century onwards tended to be Pythagorean and Stoic, fatalistic in tone and assuming that people move like planets, in line with mathematical law. However, it is unlikely that such work existed independently of Greek religion, in which it was taken for granted that the future was negotiated by prayer and sacrifice. In addition, the so-called Hermetic texts, composed at the same time as the first Greek-language astrological works, laid the foundation for initiatory practices in which the soul was prepared for death by the acting out of rituals corresponding to the planetary spheres. We also know that astrology was used to cast spells and create talismans, familiar ways of influencing the future. The people who visited temples, participated in initiatory Hermetic rituals or wore talismans to enhance their love lives were the clients of the astrologers. We should doubt then, that the deterministic tone of the texts was reflected in the actual practice of astrology, and we may suspect a disconnection between the literary tradition and the lived experience. In the second century CE, a further development took place when Claudius Ptolemy, the leading astronomer of his day, reformulated astrology within a natural, Aristotelian context. Destiny was now to be negotiated not through propitiating the gods or leading a virtuous lifestyle (although neither activity was ruled out) but, for example, by taking care of one's body.

Ptolemy brought astrology down to earth. The final classical philosophers of interest were the so-called Neoplatonists (of whom the most significant for later European astrology were Plotinus and Iamblichus) who flourished in the fourth to sixth centuries and who were concerned with the reunification of the soul with the divine, either through the moral, scholarly lifestyle advocated by Plato, or through ritual magic. By this time Christian polemics against astrology were being written and circulated, culminating with its denunciation as satanic by St Augustine in the early fifth century.

By the end of the classical period we can distinguish different varieties of astro-logical theory and practice. Astrology might be justified according to a variety of explanatory models, either physical influence alone, a combination of psychic and material causes, celestial signs transmitted by superior powers or divinities, or the doctrine of 'sympathies'. The latter were relationships between all things in the universe, material and intangible, which were thought to be linked in a web of relationships through similarities or differences in their essential natures. For example, the zodiac sign Aries, the planet Mars, the colour red, blood, knives, angry people and feverish illnesses were all connected. A.O. Lovejoy called this system the 'Great Chain of Being'.[21] The cosmos was regulated mathematically, but was also moral and gendered (for example Venus was a benevolent planet and female). Another very important distinction was identified by Cicero in the first century BCE.[22] The horoscope, a diagrammatical representation of the earth's relationship with the heavens, usually calculated for a particular place, date and time, was the fundamental tool of astrology. Horoscopes could be cast to analyse an individual's future, answer specific questions, choose auspicious moments in the future and assess prospects for the coming year (known respectively as nativities, interrogations, elections and revolutions in medieval Europe). The rules for interpreting horoscopes were complex and based on ever-increasing levels of mathematical division and logical procedures which were designed to relate the living personality of the cosmos at any moment in time to earthly affairs. Horoscopes were not, though, essential and some disagreed with either their validity or usefulness. All forms of astrology, though, whatever their varying attitudes to fate, appear to have been directed towards a dialogue with destiny, negotiating the future through lifestyle changes, moral virtue, magical rituals or supplication and prayer. This takes us to the end of my Volume I.

This being a history of Western astrology, which I am defining conventionally as the astrology of the European/Christian world, there are certain areas that I am unable to include. The problem is acute in that for over half a millennium, from the fifth to eleventh centuries, astrology all but died out in Christian Europe while Persia and India remained centres of creative activity. Faced with the choice, I decided to explore the tenuous survival of at least some knowledge about the sky in early medieval Europe, from the fifth to tenth centuries. In this I was encouraged by Steve McCluskey's observation that this period is now seen to have contained much of interest, in contrast with earlier opinions.[23] Yet, a number of the astrologers and philosophers of the Islamic world were to be figures of great importance in medieval European debates about the nature of the cosmos, so a brief introduction is essential.[24] For the future, I am planning a more substantial account of astrology in Islamic culture.[25] But, for now the following must act as a summary.

In the first two centuries of the common era, and until the inauguration of the Persian Sassanian dynasty in 226 CE, we have little idea of how the astrologers of Mesopotamia or Iran conducted themselves except, perhaps, as intermediaries in the extension of trade in ideas between India and the Mediterranean. The Sassanians brought a much greater interest in foreign scholarship and the new monarchs set out to do what all self-consciously great rulers do, which is to patronize learning; they collected, translated and edited the great books of their own and neighbouring countries. According to the eighth-century scholar Nawbakht, who was one of the Islamic caliph Caliph Harun al-Rashid's astrologers, the Sassanian monarch Ardashir I (226–41) had commissioned the translation of the works of Greek and Indian astrological classics, including, from the Greek world, staple works by Claudius Ptolemy.[26] The Islamic conquest of Persia between 632 and 650 brought a brief hiatus in royal patronage of astrology, although not of scholarly activity and, certainly, public use of astrologers for all sorts of predictive and magical activities continued. It was the Abbasid caliphs, who took power in 750, who were responsible for this transformation of attitudes at the highest levels of society, and a succession of rulers established the conditions for what has come to be known as the golden age of Islam. Al-Mahdi (775–85) founded schools and patronized the arts; Harun al-Rashid (786–809) signalled his respect for pagan learning by ordering a collection of original Greek manuscripts. Caliph al-Mamun (813–33), building on the imperial library created by al-Mansur (754–75), set up the *Bait al-Hikma*, the House of Wisdom, in Baghdad, as a deliberate and very successful attempt to bring scholars together to translate Greek, Syriac, Persian and Sanskrit works into Arabic, and exchange ideas about the nature of the cosmos.

At the risk of ignoring many of the distinguished achievements of the scholars of the Islamic world, I will mention just five whose work was to be critical in medieval Europe. The first was Masha'allah, a Jew who was born in Basra, in modern Iraq, around 740 and died in 815. In the course of his life, Masha'allah composed around 25 astrological texts, a number of which were to become standards in medieval Europe, where he was known as Messahala. His work was continued by Abu Ma'shar; born in Balkh, in modern Afghanistan, in around 787, he wrote some 50 books in almost 100 years, dying in 886 after what was, by the standards of the time, an extremely long life. Under his Latin name, Albumazar, Abu Ma'shar was one of the the best known astrologers of the Middle Ages in both the Islamic world and the Christian West, rated on a par with Masha'allah and the second-century Greek polymath Claudius Ptolemy.

Abu Ma'shar had supposedly been introduced to astrology by Al Kindi, a scholar whose honorific title, the 'first philosopher', points to his reputation as the man who imported classical Greek thought to the Islamic world. Al Kindi was born to an aristocratic family in the city of Kufah, a major centre for Arab learning and culture, sometime around 795. In his long life – he died sometime between 866 and 870 – he became perhaps the seminal figure in the development of Islamic intellectual thought. He has been described as court astrologer (though of course there was no such official position) to the Caliph al-Mamun and headed the team in the House of Wisdom which translated ancient texts into Arabic. He was a synthesizer and he set out, on the basis of his readings of Aristotelian and Platonic theories, to provide a universal model, the sort of key-to-everything for which cosmologists are still searching. His interest for us, though, lies in his attempt to construct a mechanism for astrology. In *On the Stellar Rays* he attempted to identify a means by which the heavens might influence the earth through rays of cosmic sympathy.[27] The logic was fairly straightforward: all visible objects emit rays, otherwise, obviously, they'd be invisible. It was believed that each planet's rays extended a different number of degrees over the zodiac and if, to take one example, a planet was too close to the rays of one of the unfortunate planets, such as Mars or Saturn, the individual concerned would suffer ill fortune.[28] It was as if the light itself carried the nature of the planet. These rays can be seen as causal connections as long as it is remembered that all causal links in the world around us are, in fact, coordinated by rays emitting from the 'One', God. While Al Kindi's ideas play a part in the history of optics, we should always remember that he was working in the context of Hermetic teachings, in which light carries divinity: it does not just allow us to see, but enables us to be close to God.[29]

The last two thinkers were not practising astrologers, but they did lay the foundations for debates among medieval Latin scholars about the need to reconcile sacred scriptures, whether Islamic Koran, Jewish Torah or Christian Bible, with the classical philosophers, especially Aristotle. The former emphasized faith and divine knowledge, the latter, reason and inquiry into the natural world. The problems were serious ones, for the sacred texts insisted that the only authority for any kind of knowledge was God, and classical philosophy offered an alternative cosmology in which human beings could reason for themselves, and discover truth by independent logic. This challenge to the universal dominance of scriptural truth was to allow astrology to make at least a partial return to favour in medieval Europe. The first of these two scholars was Ibn Sina. Born in 980, possibly in the central Asian city of Bokhara, he is more usually known under the Latinized form of his name, Avicenna. By all accounts Avicenna was a prodigy who was, the stories say, an accomplished doctor by the age of 16 and, three years later, began a period of travel between the various courts of the Islamic world, until he died in 1037. Ibn Sina's views, which included the existence of angelic and spiritual hierarchies uniting angels, planets and humans, were challenged in the twelfth century by the Andalusian philosopher Ibn Rushd (1126–1198), better known under his Latinized name, Averroës. Born in Cordoba, Averroës lived in Marrakesh before becoming a judge in Seville and, through the accident of his geographic location, he was to have an impact on European thought as immediate as that in the Islamic world.[30] He attacked the 'cosmological argument' – that as all things must be caused by something else, there must be a supreme cause, a Creator – and argued that only physical arguments can explain physical things.

The scholars and astrologers of the Islamic world saved classical learning for Latin Europe, but there was to be a gap of at least 500 years between the collapse of the Roman world in the West and the beginning of the rediscovery of its intellectual splendours. And it's with those centuries that the story continues, beginning with the slow death of classical learning in fifth-century Europe.

The Latin West: Decline and Disappearance

From one beginning rises all mankind;
For one Lord rules and fathers all things born.
He gave the sun his light, the moon her horns
And men to earth and stars to grace the sky;
He clothes in bodies minds brought down from high
A noble origin for mortal men.

BOETHIUS[1]

In the winter of the year 531, some time towards the winter solstice and the shortest day, a group of the most distinguished pagan and Neoplatonic scholars in the Roman Empire set out on a journey to the court of the Persian emperor at Ctesiphon. Coming from the eastern part of the empire, in which pagan learning remained influential, they were in despair at the gradual closing down of intellectual inquiry in the Roman world, but hopeful that, in the East, they would find a more liberal environment, one in which scholarly inquiry into the nature of the cosmos would be encouraged. If any date marks the end of the classical world, this is certainly a prime candidate. For the philosophers of the Eastern Empire, Persia offered a possible safe home. But for their Christianized cousins in the West, there was no escape. They were left behind, struggling to save what they could of respectable pagan learning.

The long period in Western Europe following the decline of classical culture was characterized by an intermittent and fragmentary knowledge of the rich astrology and technical astronomy of the Greek and Roman worlds. Although it is no longer fashionable to talk about the 'Dark Ages', there is no doubt that the scholars and intellectuals of this period were increasingly deprived of the rich heritage of classical speculation on humanity's relationship with the cosmos. True, there were individual scholars of great ability, but the intellectual climate within which they operated was narrow and hemmed in by the narrow confines of Christianity and the scriptures and, by comparison with their contemporaries in Persia, say, or India, woefully stunted.

The fall of the Roman Empire is one of the legendary presiding events of Western culture. It forms one of those neat punctuation points in our evolutionary narrative that gives form and structure to European history. It defines the end of a golden age either of republican virtue or imperial splendour, however we choose to portray the character of the Roman state. Together with the democratic virtue and scientific genius of classical Greece, the Roman world comprises a mythical past which we can be forever trying to recreate. Yet, the truth, which is of direct relevance for the history of ideas, as well as of astrology, is that the Roman Empire never 'fell'; there never was a dramatic moment at which the barbarians destroyed classical civilization. Instead, there was an increasing dislocation between the Greek-speaking Eastern Empire, with its capital at Constantinople, which escaped Germanic domination, and the Latin-speaking West, which was overrun by German peoples. The speed and intensity of the process of decline varied from one part of the empire to another. In the West, the collapse of Roman culture in Britain was rapid in the early decades of the fifth century, but in Italy, France and Spain the disintegration of Roman civic life was much more gradual. In southern France, from 419 to 507, and then in Spain for 200 years until the Muslim conquest in 711, the Visigoths ruled as nominal representatives of the emperor in Constantinople, and the majority of the population, although deprived of large areas of land, continued to be Roman. In Italy itself, there was no resident emperor after 476, yet the Senate continued to sit in Rome until around 580, a century after the last Western emperor, Julius Nepos, was deposed. The new German rulers were not only nominal viceroys of the Eastern emperor, but had a high regard for Roman culture, and the greatest of the new monarchs, the Ostrogothic king Theodoric, who ruled Italy from 489 to 526, saw the Romanization of his people as one of his vital tasks and thoroughly in keeping with his political aspirations. He retained the administrative skills of the Roman civil service, along with a network of educated Greek speakers who could maintain close contacts with Constantinople. Theodoric's fine example was followed by his grandson and successor Athalric (526–34) who, Cassiodorus tells us, was something of a philosopher, having himself studied natural phenomena, which would have included, at least, naturalistic teachings about the stars. The Roman re-conquest of Italy itself, beginning in 535, ushered in almost another two centuries of close political contact with the court in Constantinople, although, ironically, the subsequent wars led to Rome's devastation in 537, when the Ostrogoths cut the aqueducts on which the city depended for its water supplies. In southern Italy, eastern political control survived until the ninth century and, in Sicily, the cathedral at Messina owed its allegiance to the Patriarch in Constantinople, rather than the Pope in Rome until at least the twelfth century. All of which should make us guard against simple notions of Europe as a whole being submerged by a barbarian flood. The shift from classical to medieval worlds was gradual and complex and the decline in knowledge of astrology and astronomy was similarly dependent on what texts were available in which places.

   Although the Greek and Latin speaking worlds remained on familiar terms, partly because theologians and Church authorities were obliged to talk to each other, knowledge of Greek in the West declined so sharply that Plato, Aristotle and the other classical philosophers were only accessible in what few Latin fragments were translated. The direct consequence was that the practice of astrology, together with most knowledge of astronomy, among the intellectual elite, collapsed.[2] Evidence concerning folk beliefs is scanty although we have to assume the existence of sky tales, such as those concerning the Great Bear, and lunar lore relating to fertility, medicine and herbal remedies. At all levels, astral and celestial theology was absorbed by Christianity and popular magic did not disappear; it was merely Christianized as saints replaced nature spirits. We should, though, question what we really mean by Christianization. There is a strong case to be made that a Christian is only distinguished from a pagan by dint of political allegiance to the Christian political structure, rather than a pagan one. The sharpest distinction between Christianity and its pagan rivals was found in their competing attitudes to sin, the physical body and eternal damnation, all three of which were equated. This, though, was the theology of the extremist, the evangelical. For most people, the shift from pagan to Christian affiliation was superficial and unthinking and, as we shall see, there is evidence that popular astrological fortune-telling survived. The astrology of the philosophers and elite practitioners, though, undoubtedly went into a steep decline. The question is why this should have been so. Astrology's parallel slump in fortunes in both the former Western Empire and the surviving Eastern half, suggests that there had to be a common factor which is not simply connected to the collapse of literacy, which only afflicted the West. Simply, Christianity allowed little space for the horoscopic arts. Christ was lord of the new cosmic state; he could be approached directly rather than via the stars; and, in any case, in the New Jerusalem, prophesied in the Revelation of St John, there would be no sun, moon or stars, and so no conceivable use for astrologers.[3] The heavens, which had once been a flourishing, active part of the world, populated by Platonic intelligences and other invisible beings, and the source both of political and individual affairs on earth, became a backdrop to God's splendour. True, the sky was still inhabited by a host of invisible beings, angels and demons, but, in an age when Psalm 19.1 – 'The heavens are telling the glory of God, and the firmament proclaims his handiwork' – was a more important cosmological text than either of the great classical works of astronomy and astrology, Claudius Ptolemey's *Almagest* and *Tetrabiblos*, the heavens were reclassified as a prop for the Christian church's claim to an absolute monopoly of truth.

Astrology's loss of function, rather than its condemnation as demonic, seems to have been the fundamental reason for its decline. The stars were, simply, no longer a path to salvation as they had been in the classical world. While astrology's pagan associations were undoubtedly problematic, for the Church Fathers had used them as a stick with which to beat astrologers, many Christian theologians had a high regard for aspects of classical teaching and actively absorbed Platonic thought, with its notions of an ordered, meaningful, purposeful, rational cosmos. St Augustine (354–430), bishop of the Tunisian city of Hippo and the single most important figure in medieval theology, had specifically singled out Platonists as the only pagans with whom one could have a decent debate.[4] Even so, it was Christianity which absorbed Platonism, not the other way round, and scripture was always to be the highest authority: Genesis trumped Plato's *Timaeus* every time as a source of information about the origins of the universe.

Typical of the sort of dilemma in which theologians found themselves was that posed by the Greek bishop Theodore of Mopsuestia, who died in 428.[5] As a Platonist, he believed that people should use reason to approach God but, as a Christian, he considered that this could be achieved through contemplation of God's celestial handiwork, as in Psalm 19.1. Plato himself would have been perfectly content with this, but the Platonic culture which had spawned Hellenistic astrology was to be of no value whatsoever if one was in constant and direct communication with God; one's horoscope, whatever truth was ascribed to it, became a matter of complete irrelevance. There was another, more emotional, advantage which Christians held over the Neoplatonic philosophers who had nurtured late classical astrology: their ability to communicate directly, at any time they chose, with God. The philosophers worked hard all their lives to achieve contact with the One through their intellects, or even through theurgy, or ritual magic, but might, as the Neoplatonist Plotinus admitted, achieve direct, ecstatic union with God once or twice in a lifetime.[6] But for devout Christians who had undergone a true conversion experience the dialogue with God was constant and intimate: he was in them and they were in him.

In many instances, Christians appropriated pagan space by converting temples into churches, but they also colonized pagan time. The Christian ceremonial calendar swallowed the pagan solar festivals, of which the most obvious example was the conversion of the festival of Sol Invictus, 25 December, into Christmas Day.[7] For pragmatic reasons, the magical powers of pagan deities were not necessarily denied, but could be defined as inferior to those of the true God. In one sixth-century account we read that when, in the early 490s, the Frankish queen Clotild was campaigning to have her husband, Clovis, convert, she didn't deny the power of the pagan deities, only its extent: 'What have Mars and Mercury ever done for anyone?' she is said to have asked, adding for good measure that 'They may have been endowed with magic arts, but they were certainly not worthy of being called divine.'[8] The Christianizers, though, met with limited success in their desire to erase the planetary day names.[9] Such planetary names might have been a matter of common usage in ordinary situations but, when it came to magic, it was vital to conduct a ritual on the required day. For example, a love-spell would work best if performed on a Friday, ruled by romantic Venus and, most likely, not at all if conducted on Saturday, ruled by Saturn, a notoriously difficult planet. In Latin only *dies Soli*, Sunday (which became the first day of the week because it witnessed Christ's resurrection[10]), lost its astronomical designation, becoming *dies Dominico*, the Lord's Day, and only in Portuguese were all the days renamed. Modern French maintains the complete sequence of planetary names following the Christianized Dimanche – Lundi (Moon), Mardi (Mars), Mercredi (Mercury), Jeudi (Jupiter), Vendredi (Venus) and Samedi (Saturn).

To turn to the question of the survival of cosmological literature, there were a number of classical texts which survived into the sixth century and were to become the basis of what has been called 'Romano-medieval astronomy', that body of rudimentary knowledge and practice which sustained Latin scholars for almost half a millennium, from around the year 500 until the flow of ideas from the Islamic world began to take effect in the twelfth century.[11] Among the surviving texts were the *Phaenomena*, Cicero's Latin version of the poem on the constellations by the Greek author, Aratus of Soli (c.315–245 BCE); Pliny's *De Natura Rerum*, dating from the first century BCE, which included basic information on planetary positions and influences; Columella's *On agriculture*, which was written around 60–5 CE and related the farming year to the heavens in the manner of Hesiod; and Calcidius's late-fourth-century commentary on Plato's cosmological text, the *Timaeus*.[12] With the exception of these, plus fragments of Aristotle, virtually all knowledge of classical cosmology was lost. And, with the possible exception of Julius Firmicus Maternus's fourth-century Latin text, the *Mathesis*, all the great works on horoscopic astrology were unknown to the early medieval world. Even the *Mathesis* did not surface definitively until the eleventh century. In the absence of both Claudius Ptolemy's *Tetrabiblos* and *Almagest*, the entire canon of classical cosmology was forgotten; when the sixth-century philosopher Boethius mentioned Ptolemy, it was quite clear that he had never read him in the original.

There is another class of late-Roman literature which should be seen as less a footnote to classical cosmology than the foundation of the medieval world-view by virtue of its wide dissemination in the Western Christian world from the sixth century onwards. The first of these texts was Macrobius's commentary on Cicero's 'Dream of Scipio', which dealt with the soul's journey to the stars. This work was complemented by the writings of three remarkable classically educated Roman Christians, Martianus Capella, Boethius and Cassiodorus, who were distinguished by their devotion to what they saw as the best of pagan learning, especially the curriculum of the seven liberal arts. Even though this model had provided the standard educational scheme in Rome for centuries, it was only formalized by Martianus Capella of Carthage around 410 to 439 in his *De nuptiis Philogiae et Mercurii*,[13] a book whose influence long outlived its author; it was to become reputedly the most widely read textbook of the European Middle Ages. The memory of a heliocentric – sun-centred – cosmos in Martianus Capella's account of the orbit of the sun (rather than of the earth, as was usually accepted) by Mercury and Venus, may eventually have influenced Nicholas Copernicus's revolutionary espousal of the sun-centred cosmos in the sixteenth century.[14] Martianus divided the curriculum into seven disciplines. The first part, consisting of three practical areas, grammar, rhetoric and dialectic (logic), was known as the trivium, from which our word trivial is derived. This was the smaller, less important syllabus, designed to teach critical thinking and effective communication, after which the student might progress to the more important quadrivium. In its standard version the quadrivium included the practical disciplines which Plato believed took the philosopher closer to God: geometry, arithmetic, music and astronomy/astrology. Martianus's account of the latter was what we would identify as heavily astronomical – concerned with the measurement of the stars rather than their meaning. Based on such authorities as the author of the major Greek star catalogue, Hipparchus (c.46–c.370 BCE), Pliny and Ptolemy, Martianus' work was mainly devoted to descriptions of the constellations, the rising times of the zodiac signs and the orbital period of the planets. This was material which was undoubtedly essential for the practice of astrology, but horoscopic astrology itself found no place in his account.

The central position of astronomy in medieval learning right through to the Renaissance was reinforced by the commentary on the 'Dream of Scipio' composed by the early-fifth-century scholar Macrobius,[15] a story which itself occurred in book VI of Cicero's *Republic*, composed in the first century BCE. Cicero's work was in turn a homage to the Myth of Er in Plato's *Republic*, with its detailed account of the soul's journey to and from the stars via the planetary spheres.[16] While both Plato's and most of Cicero's work was lost to the Latin West, Macrobius's survived, preserving the doctrine of the soul's descent from the stars. The construction of a physical journey by which the soul might journey from earth to heaven provided a literal explanation of just how the righteous might meet their salvation and, as long as the thorny problem of reincarnation (which had featured in Plato's theory) was ignored, this piece of pagan teaching presented very little challenge to Christian doctrine. Macrobius's God was the Platonic Creator, the One, the Good, *Nous* (or Mind), while his cosmos was structured according to Platonic geometry and regulated by numbers divided, as by Pythagoras, into their male and female parts. 'Seven,' he agreed solemnly with Cicero, 'is, one might almost say the key to the universe.'[17]

The most distinguished of the late-classical Christian scholars was Boethius, who was born in 476, the year that Romulus Augustulus, the last Roman emperor to live on the Italian peninsula, abdicated. Boethius was a member of an established aristocratic family and served Theodoric, the Ostrogothic king and imperial representative in Italy. He became one of the most distinguished statesmen of his time, served as consul in 510 and was also, for a while, quite a favourite of Theodoric, who appointed him *magister officiorum* – head of the civil service. The scholarly task Boethius set himself was to produce Latin translations and commentaries of the entire works of Plato and Aristotle, a deliberate attempt to preserve Greek teaching in the Western world, much as Berossus, the Babylonian priest, had tried to preserve Babylonian culture – and astrology – 800 years earlier. In this noble aspiration, Boethius failed, although he did succeed in producing editions of Aristotle's logical works and Porphyry's *Isagogē* (Introduction) to Aristotle, both of which meant that the philosopher's works were never entirely lost to the Latin world, and his commentary on the liberal arts was widely used in Medieval Schools, alongside Martianus Capella's. But, what do we know of Boethius's attitude to astrology in particular? He composed several works of theoretical relevance to the subject, including a treatise on music in which he discussed the music of the spheres, the harmonious sounds that the planets were believed to make as they rushed through space, concluding that, though real, they were inaudible to human beings.[18]

Boethius' major work on astronomy, though, has been lost for reasons which are not clear. The church historian Henry Chadwick speculated that the reason for its disappearance may have been that he 'prejudiced readers against him by dark hints about horoscopes, a study which . . . was not necessarily a matter of which a Christian was expected to be ignorant, but was certainly regarded as dangerous'.[19] Boethius, in Chadwick's view, may have included sufficient astrology in his work for subsequent devout Christian copyists to refuse to reproduce it. Whether Chadwick is correct, we cannot say: when Boethius turned to Ptolemy, it was to his astronomical work, the *Almagest* (probably Proclus's fourth-century paraphrase) rather than the astrological *Tetrabiblos*.

In the absence of any specific surviving work on astronomy and astrology, Boethius's enduring significance in the history of Western cosmology lies in his articulation of the Platonic cosmology within which astrology frequently found a safe philosophical home. While in prison awaiting execution on the, almost certainly false, charge of involvement in a conspiracy with the emperor in Constantinople, against Theodoric, Boethius composed his most influential and long-lasting work, *The Consolation of Philosophy*. This was the last major classical piece of theoretical speculation on humanity's relationship with the cosmos to be produced in the Latin speaking world, and was to join Martianus Capella's *De Nuptiis* and Macrobius's *Commentary* as an essential part of the medieval scholars' library. It is actually said to have been the most widely used textbook of the medieval Western curriculum, was translated by the Saxon king Alfred the Great, the English poet Geoffrey Chaucer and Queen Elizabeth I of England, and was praised by Gibbon, the eighteenth-century historian of Rome. Boethius's genius lay in his use of a Christian framework to carry pagan philosophy into a post-pagan world. *The Consolation* took the form of a dialogue between Boethius and 'Philosophy', the latter appearing in female form as his nurse, although the whole text is constructed as a journey of intellectual exploration, not unlike Scipio's and Er's journeys to enlightenment through the celestial spheres; in keeping with the traditions of celestial-journey literature, Boethius praised Philosophy as 'my leader towards the true light'.[20] The book bears comparison with Augustine's *City of God* in that it was similarly conceived in disaster and asked how a good God could permit such evil things to occur, although there were significant differences of detail between the two works. Augustine was concerned with the rise and fall of empires, Boethius with his own personal catastrophe. Augustine needed desperately to know just why God had allowed Rome, even though it had become a Christian city, to be sacked by the Goths in 410, while, for his own sake, Boethius tried to comprehend how, having been both a good Christian and a loyal servant to his king, God could have permitted him to be subject to blatant injustice. Both men found the answers in variations on Stoic and Neoplatonic conceptions of fate, which held that one's physical life is essentially determined and only one's soul is free. The point was well made by Boethius in his use of poems of praise for God's starry heavens. Clearly influenced by the *Timaeus*, he wrote:

O Thou who dost by everlasting reason rule
Creator of the planets and the sky, who time
From timelessness didst bring, unchanging Mover
No cause drove Thee to mould unstable matter, but
The form benign of highest good within Thee set
All things Thou bringest forth from Thy high archetype ...
The soul once cut, in circles two its motion joins
Goes round and to itself returns encircling mind
And turns in pattern similar the firmament.[21]

Boethius managed to merge two conceptions of God: on the one hand, the personal God of the Christians, who rewarded good and punished sin; and, on the other, the remote, impersonal Platonic 'First Mover' who, having started the planets in motion, allowed no appeal by prayer and no miraculous escapes from prison. Boethius the Christian had done his best to please the lord of the cosmos, but Boethius the Stoic had to submit to a cosmic law which took no account of his actions. 'The heavens,' Boethius concluded, 'are less wonderful for their foundation and speed than for the order that rules them,' an order that decrees that, if you want to be 'resplendent in the dignities of high office' as he had been, 'you will have to grovel before the man who bestows it'.[22] As the planets move on their inexorable courses, so do human lives. Boethius set out one of the most eloquent and enduring accounts of the Stoic–Platonic–Christian cosmos, ruled by God but administered by Fate. He even came close to choosing Platonic 'emanation' as the origin of the world, in which all things, including the entire plan for the cosmos, emerged out of what he called 'the unchanging mind of God, the high citadel of ... oneness', implicitly rejecting the conventional Christian notion of a deliberate act of creation, as set out in Genesis.[23] In Boethius's view, the plan for the cosmos, rational and pure as it was, was Providence, the cosmic order to which all human beings must gladly submit. Providence, though, was just the plan, and no more; it had no existence other than as a set of possibilities in the mind of God. But all possibilities have possible manifestations and, when Providence is implemented, it becomes Fate, which Boethius described as the 'ever-changing web, the disposition in and through time of all the events which God has planned'.[24] It had therefore always been in God's mind for Boethius to go to prison, no matter how much the poor man had prayed or led a good life.

So much for the theology. But, could Boethius identify a single mechanism by which Providence is converted into the 'chain of Fate'? Reasonable answers might include divine spirits, the power of angels, the obedience of nature or the celestial motions of the stars. All would have come within his philosophy. For his physical cosmology, Boethius adapted the model set out by Plato and Aristotle in which the world was surrounded by concentric planetary spheres, each contained within another, like the layers of an onion. Providence, which could be compared to perfection, ruled on the outermost sphere, that of the stars, furthest away from the earth and closest to heaven. As one descended from the outer sphere towards the earth, via the spheres, imperfection increased and one therefore became ever-more subject to Fate.[25] At least, this is one reading of the theory. Elsewhere, Boethius was more rigidly deterministic, and his view of the fated condition of the cosmos was uncompromising: from the movements of the sky and stars, to the motion of the four elements (fire, earth, air and water) out of which all material objects are made, together with the birth and death of all things, people, plants and animals, everything was ruled by Fate – with absolutely no exception. This state of affairs, Boethius wrote, was not just desirable – it was completely necessary if change was to be managed in an orderly fashion and if disruptive, random events, which might cause chaos and suffering, were to be avoided. The only reason, Lady Philosophy tells Boethius, that the world appears to be chaotic, is that men are too stupid to perceive the wonder of the divine order. On the universal level, Boethius has dealt with the problem of evil in the cosmos – it's all part of God's plan if only we could understand it. Specifically, his influence in the history of astrology was to be immense precisely because the wide circulation of *The Consolation of Philosophy* in medieval Europe provided a theoretical rationale in which fate, seen as the unfolding of God's providential plan, might be analysed and anticipated through the movements of the planets. This model, written into the cosmological narrative of Europe, was eventually to provide the foundation for the 'clockwork' universe often attributed to Isaac Newton.

Boethius's Stoic principles might open the door to astrology, especially, in theory, to a relatively recent astrological work like Julius Firmicus Maternus's fourth-century Latin text, the *Mathesis*. Firmicus's theology matched Boethius's almost exactly: Fate originates in the Divine Mind, he argued, and cannot be avoided – philosophers who insist that it can, such as the great Neoplatonist, Plotinus, Firmicus insisted, are just plain wrong.[26] No amount of philosophizing or ascetic practice can save one from the inevitable, and even the great Plato, Firmicus added, was sold out by a Fate he couldn't control. Yet astrology, simply, was no longer an integral part of sixth-century culture. In any event, whatever was contained in Boethius's lost work, the *Consolation* itself has nothing direct to say about astrology. Boethius's writings on the liberal arts curriculum would have implied strongly that the study of astrology was necessary, but left it open to the students to concentrate on such matters as the calculation necessary for fixing the date of Easter, rather than the prediction of individual lives.

Boethius may have largely failed in his self-appointed task of saving classical learning, but he did legitimize pagan thought within a Christian context, and he allowed generations of medieval thinkers to discuss classical philosophy as if it were a valuable counterpart to Christian theology. Much like Aristotle, he was even seen by later scholastic writers as being supportive of astrology.[27] To an extent, then, Boethius opened an alternative Christian attitude to astrology, neutralizing Augustine's angry denunciation of it. Whereas Augustine denounced astrology as demonic, the reader of Boethius might be led into thinking it was a harmless means of gaining insight into one's fate.

Boethius's aspirations were shared by his contemporary, Cassiodorus (c.480/

90–583), another great Christian Roman statesman; he served as consul under Theodoric, though four years after Boethius, in 514.[28] Cassiodorus believed devoutly that education was central to the good Christian life and when, in 538/40, the Pope failed to take up his vision of a Christian Academy in Rome, Cassiodorus retired from the civil service and founded his own school and monastery in southern Italy. This was where he composed the *Institutiones* – the *Institutes Concerning Divine and Human Readings* – which, along with Martianus Capella's work, was one of the most influential medieval commentaries on the liberal arts, including, naturally, astronomy. Cassiodorus, though, was less equivocal than Boethius when it came to the difficult subject of astrology. He reserved a special place for his caution against astrology, however seductive its charms, in the conclusion to Book II:

> Some have been led astray by the beauty and brilliance of the shining stars, and eagerly seek reasons for their own destruction. In their mental blindness they tripped over the motions of the stars and through dangerous calculations that are called astrology (*Mathesis*) they were sure that they could foresee the course of events. Not only men of our own language, but also Plato, Aristotle and other men of high intelligence, who are motivated by the truth of the facts, condemned, in full agreement, astrologers, saying that the only result of such a belief would be confusion. If the human race were forced by the inevitability of its birth to various actions, which would good behaviour gain praise or evil behaviour come under the punishment of laws? And although these men were not dedicated to heavenly wisdom, they nevertheless, to bear witness to the truth, rightly attacked the errors of those of whom the Apostle says: 'You are observing days and months; I fear for lest perhaps I have laboured among you in vain.'[29]

Cassiodorus opened another front in the attack on astrology: it was not evil, as Augustine would have said, merely foolish, which was the classical, sceptical view set out by Cicero in the first century BCE.[30] He also represented a completely different point of view on fate to that set out by Boethius, one which provided a context for his dismissive attitude to astrology. In his view, the inevitability of birth did not lead to unavoidable events in one's life and astrology is therefore, simply, illogical. This argument would break down, of course, if one were to practise an astrology based variously on medical treatment, magical manipulation of the world or liberation of the soul, all of which practices depended on the assumption that the future could be changed. The standard astrological texts, though, tended to be written in a highly deterministic style, allowing little or no room for personal negotiation with destiny, and this was certainly how astrology's critics saw it. But, if Boethius and Cassiodorus represented two possible scholarly attitudes to astrology in the sixth century, that still begs the question of whether, and to what extent, its practice survived the collapse of literacy and Christian censure.

There is evidence that, if any classical astrology was still practised in the Latin West while Boethius and Cassiodorus were writing, it was medical, an application of the art which might have a clear naturalistic rationale, often being based more on the seasonal rising of stars and the passage of the moon than the casting of horoscopes. We hear, for example, of a certain Aetius, who lived around the year 500 and who gave a list of times ordained by God for the rising and setting of stars which, in turn, were supposed to affect the air and cause disease in suitably susceptible individuals.[31] Aetius's contemporary, Alexander of Tralles, was rather better known.[32] He came from a distinguished family – one of his brothers was architect of St Sophia, the magnificent cathedral church of Constantinople. Alexander visited Italy, France, Spain and Greece before composing the great 12-volume medical treatise which was his enduring legacy; it was later translated into Hebrew and Syriac, and Latin manuscripts are known from the ninth to the sixteenth centuries. Alexander relied heavily on the doctrine of sympathies, through which all things in the cosmos were connected through their essential, underlying, natures, and made extensive use of magical remedies: to treat epilepsy, he wrote, one should use nails from a cross or a wrecked ship and the bloodstained shirt from a dead criminal or gladiator. The nails are then attached to the patient's arm, the shirt is burned and the ashes drunk in seven glasses of wine. If there's any doubt about cosmological participation in this chain of magical correspondence, the use of the number seven gives it away; as a timing measure seven evokes both the days of the week and the planets. More overt celestial factors might also be taken into account. One ligature, which was known as an effective treatment for feet ulcers, used the muscles from a wild ass, a wild boar and a stork and, for best effect, was to be applied when the moon was in the west or a 'sterile' sign, and approaching Saturn.[33] Astrological timing was also necessary for the creation of talismans or gathering of herbs. As a cure for gout, one should copy a verse from Homer onto a copper plate when the moon is in either Libra or Leo. Gathering of herbs for the treatment of bleeding hands or feet should take place when the moon is in Aquarius and under Pisces, an instruction which suggests that constellations were being used, rather than zodiac signs.[34] Sometimes, it was not necessary to treat a wound directly; instead one could create an image which healed at a distance. One remedy required the engraving of a lion, a half-moon and a star in a copper die which was then to be worn in a ring on the fourth finger. Incantations could be prescribed on the grounds that sometimes a word was most efficacious when it was spoken, rather than written, and the day of the month could also be significant; one healing oil, for example, was to be prepared on the fifth day of March. Taken in isolation there can appear to be a random quality about such measures, but they are better seen as systematic extrapolations from the notion of a complex, interconnected and interdependent cosmos in which words, smells, illnesses, remedies and stars are all part of a single time–space continuum.

Such work as Alexander's, though, and its survival, tells us something else. Certain applications of astrology might have died out, such as the use of horoscopes to make precise predictions about personal character and destiny, but disease and death were universal problems which required pragmatic solutions. Besides, it was self-evident that winter ailments occurred when the sun was low in the sky and particular constellations (Taurus, for example) were visible at night. And even the great Augustine, for whom astrology was demonic, had conceded the reality of planetary influences.[35] Who, then, could seriously deny that knowledge of the stars and planets could be used to treat such complaints?

Christian cosmology from Cassiodorus onwards was encompassed in a world in which theology was experiential, based on empirical observation (it was apparent to everyone that the earth was the motionless centre of the cosmos) and faith (evidence of God's power could be found everywhere in the otherwise inexplicable marvels of life). The study of astronomy as the physical structure of the cosmos consisted of a series of definitions of terms which emphasized the observation, identification and sometimes tracking of celestial bodies with little in the way of a coherent model. Cassiodorus's description of the west as 'the place where some stars set according to our vantage point' was typical of a discipline which seems to have completely abandoned the complexities of classical knowledge.[36] The level of mathematical sophistication required was variable, but always basic. If one was using the medical practices advocated by Alexander of Tralles, the only necessary calculation was of the moon's zodiac position, although other computations were required if one wanted to apply the complete range of remedies. Important for the theologians was *computus*, astronomical calculation with the primary aim of managing the liturgical calendar and daily prayer cycle, the latter from observation of the sun and stars. The date of Easter, the most important moment in the Christian calendar, might be worked out on the basis of mathematical tables, requiring no actual observation of the sky whatsoever.[37] It was not just that the twin studies of observational astronomy and interpretative astrology lost their former prominence, though. The entire liberal curriculum became largely redundant as, one by one, areas of the former Western empire lost the institutions and processes of civil society. Roman legal and administrative structures slowly gave way to Germanic practices, while the exemplary moral tales of Greek and Roman heroes lost their ability to inspire, and the functional value of the old educational system simply disappeared. This process was obviously much more pronounced the further one moved from Rome, and might have been imperceptible in parts of Italy which remained under Byzantine control until the mid-eighth or ninth centuries.[38] However, the problem was worsened by the fact that most of those who could read were priests, for whom scripture always took priority over classical learning. Astronomy's theoretical and conceptual framework, along with its geometrical spatial awareness, then, became essentially arithmetical and concerned primarily with calculating the ecclesiastical and sacred calendar.

While Boethius left no surviving writings on astrology, Cassiodorus dismissed it, and practitioners such as Alexander of Tralles avoided theoretical questions, it was left to Isidore of Seville, the last of the great classical compilers, to produce the definitive early medieval attitude to it; Isidore's encyclopaedia, the *Etymologiae*, was one of the chief sources for classical learning until as late as the thirteenth century. Isidore was born in Spain sometime between 560 and 570, at a time when Byzantine power was resurgent across the Mediterranean – the great emperor

Justinian had died in 565, having re-established temporary Roman control over the south-western corner of Spain. Isidore was descended from an old aristocratic family which now exercised its influence through the church rather than the state, and he was appointed as bishop of Seville in either 599 or 600. He embodied the old spirit of learning in that he was fluent in Latin, skilled in Greek and dedicated his literary works to the Visigothic king, Sisebut, as a means of reminding the political establishment of the virtues of true Christian education.

Isidore's notion of astronomy, though, was quite clearly impoverished. He may have possessed an expert knowledge of Greek but, if he read any of the most important Greek works, he either ignored or didn't understand them. It is likely that his knowledge of classical cosmology was second-hand and his astronomy is just a matter of random definitions and descriptions of celestial phenomena with, in Bruce Eastwood's rather harsh assessment, little concept of any physical or philosophical coherence.[39] Isidore knew of the notion that the planets orbit the earth on seven spheres, and thought that the constellations were figures burnt into the vault of heaven, and repeated the dates for the rising of different constellations throughout the year. And, to his great credit, in all the theories he outlined, he was very careful to keep an undogmatic, open mind. It was not the depth or accuracy of Isidore's knowledge which concerns us here, even though that tells us about the limited scientific knowledge of sixth-century Spain, but his influence on future thought. His discussion of astrology was brief but of immense significance. In a few short paragraphs he recategorized it in such a way that, although he appeared to condemn it, he simultaneously permitted it. The confusion, though, was not in his logic, which was perfectly clear, but its consequences. To start with, he followed Claudius Ptolemy in declaring that there were two parts to astronomy, the first which dealt with the laws of planetary motion, and the second which dealt with its effects. He named the first part *astronomia*, the law of the stars, and the second, *astrologia*, and, even though the two words were often interchangeable down to the seventeenth century, from Isidore onwards, it was possible to use them in different senses. However, he realized that it was not enough to follow Augustine's fudge by condemning astrology as demonic while simultaneously allowing for planetary influences, pretending unconvincingly that the latter were not astrological. Isidore therefore clearly separated astrology into two parts. The first, which was acceptable in a Christian context, was natural astrology, based on solar and lunar influences and seasonal changes in the positions of the stars. The second, which was emphatically not permitted, was superstitious. Elaborating on his theme, he wrote that mathematicians, by which he meant astrologers, should under no circumstances 'practice augury by the stars ... associate the twelve signs of the zodiac with specific parts of the soul or body ... or attempt to predict the nativities and characters of people by the motion of the stars'.[40] Such astrology was connected with magic, which he unequivocally condemned: even the magi, he claimed, had lost their astrological powers after the birth of Christ.[41]

Superstitious astrology was definitively condemned, but natural astrology was not, and that simple fact was bound to lead to later confusion. Isidore's words in his earlier work, *De natura rerum*, which dates from around 613, expose the difficulties of condemning astrology completely. He was clearly influenced by Pliny's book of the same name in his statement, for example, that Saturn is a cold star, or that everything in nature grows in accord with lunar cycles.[42] Such comments clearly belong under a natural rather than superstitious astrology, but an astrology nonetheless. Isidore also conceded that comets signified war, plague and revolution and suggested, following Ptolemy, that the differences between nations may be due to the stars, and that physicians should know astronomy. Isidore died in 636, leaving no scholar of comparable skill and stature to take on his mantle, but he did bequeath to later generations a clear idea that, while one might study the motions of the stars, and even their general influences, they should never be used to plan or predict the future, or inquire into the details of anyone's life.

We face the familiar question which always arises when we study the condemnation of particular practices. Was the person doing the condemning concerned with what was actually happening, or merely copying by rote from earlier accounts, as a warning to any potential back-sliders. Was Isidore merely paraphrasing Augustine, or were there astrologers practising in Visigothic Spain? In this respect, there's one interesting and potentially relevant anecdote in a twelfth-century reference to the supposed practice of astrology in Anglo-Saxon England. The story takes the form of a possibly fanciful concoction in Geoffrey of Monmouth's imaginative chronicle, *The History of the Kings of Britain*, which was probably composed around 1136. In book 12, Geoffrey relates the story of Pellitus, an 'astrologus' employed by King Edwin of Northumbria, who reigned from around 616 to 632, exactly at the time when Isidore was in his prime. Geoffrey's work is often highly romanticized, but the story is well worth repeating, as it does possess a certain plausibility.[43] Pellitus, we are told, came to England from Spain, and, according to Geoffrey, was 'extremely knowledgeable about the flight of birds and the courses of the stars'.[44] Edwin was at that time engaged in a war with a British confederation led by the Celtic leader Cadwallo, and Pellitus, sensing an opportunity, offered his services to the Northumbrian king. By employing Pellitus's skills in the divinatory and celestial arts, Edwin was able to anticipate Cadwallo's movements and so surprised him, defeating the British army and sinking its navy. Pellitus's success was such that, the story continues, he appears to have taken direct command of Edwin's army, but the astrologer's end came when he was later assassinated by Brian, Cadwallo's nephew, around 631. Pellitus's death appears to have been such a morale booster for the British that they attacked and defeated Edwin, killing him in battle in 632. Could Geoffrey's account contain a germ of truth? We just don't know, for while Geoffrey clearly embroidered many of his stories, there is no reason why an ambitious monarch such as Edwin, who was one of the great kings of Britain, should not have regarded it as a necessary status symbol to have employed an astrologer; Edwin was not only listed later as a Bretwalda, considered an 'over-king' over the other Anglo-Saxon monarchs, but was a pagan until 627, so still inhabited a world in which the flight of birds and appearance of the heavens was a matter of some significance, and he was therefore entirely unconcerned with Christian denunciations of pagan practices. Equally likely, though, is that the Pellitus story is of the same class as that which makes Merlin, King Arthur's fabled magician, an astrologer. Perhaps Geoffrey was deliberately providing authority for the practice of astrology in the mid-twelfth century, by relating past stories of its great success. There was also a distinct tendency, once horoscopic astrology had been re-established in the 1100s, to look back and see it everywhere; in the thirteenth century, Michael Scot, astrologer to the Holy Roman Emperor, Frederick II, presented both Boethius and Isidore as sympathetic authorities on the subject,[45] along with Hermes, Dorotheus of Sidon and Masha'allah. There also may have been another literary agenda at work, a widespread custom in the twelfth century to seek ancient authority for modern dynasties.[46] In the Arthur stories we see an example of the use of cosmological details in order to make a story more significant or meaningful. The chronicler Nennius, writing about 830, recorded that Arthur fought 12 battles, a number which was normal for Welsh heroes, and would have carried the same calendrical resonance as did Hercules' 12 labours.[47] Arthur, like Hercules, then becomes a solar hero whose exploits take him through the twelve months of the year. There are also suggestions that the name Arthur was derived from the star Arcturus, the third brightest star in the night sky. Arcturus means 'bear-guardian', so, if the connection is a genuine one, it would tie Arthur into archaic myths and rituals of the celestial bear.

While Isidore was struggling to preserve classical learning in Spain, a separate, flourishing centre of culture had become established in Ireland. Much of Britain had enjoyed the best part of a century of rule by Christian Roman emperors before it drifted into independence in the early fifth century and, by the sixth century, reverted to paganism. However, Christianity had been introduced into Ireland, which had never been part of the empire, following missionary expeditions by Palladius in 431 and Patrick in 432. There, Christianity both survived and flourished, benefiting from its distance from Rome, and developed a distinctive culture. The result was the remarkable flowering of Celtic Christianity, a marriage of Hellenistic and classical learning with the wisdom of the Irish Celts. That raises the question of what sky-lore the Irish may have possessed. When, for example, it is suggested that the monks in seventh-century Ireland were ignorant of astrology, what is really meant is that they had no knowledge of Hellenistic astrology or the casting of horoscopes.[48] It does not mean that they had no astrology of their own. We do know that one of the Druids' favoured methods of divination was to analyse the shape of the clouds, and the Celtic word for this, *naladoracht*, appears also to have been applied to astrology, which is reminiscent of the inclusion of all sky omens under the same heading in the Babylonian omen collection, the *Enuma Anu Enlil*. Certain references, which have been assumed to apply to astrology, exist in the Celtic literature of Ireland. One such story relates how a diviner scanned the heavens and told the father of

St Columkille – St Columba (521–97) – who introduced Christianity to the Picts of Scotland, that the time was propitious for his son to begin his lessons.[49] But the means by which the heavens would have been scanned, and what signs might have been considered significant, are lost to us, at least unless any of the many as yet untranslated Irish manuscripts reveals any clues. Forgetting textual evidence for a moment, ethnography can provide other evidence. A correspondent to *The Gentleman's Magazine* for February 1795 recorded how on 21 June 1782 he had been fortunate to witness, exactly at midnight, what he called 'the lighting of Fires in honour of the Sun'.[50] This festival, the witness recorded, was clearly ancient and pagan in origin, and there is no reason to doubt that this might have been the case.

The first great school of Irish Christianity was founded by Eudo (c.450–540) at Aranmore and, in the seventh and eighth centuries, Irish clerics exported their scholarship to northern Europe, establishing a series of foundations at such places as Luxeuil, Gall, Würzburg, Salzburg, Tarantum and Bobbio, and even founded a diocese of the Celtic Church in Galicia, in northern Spain. The Irish monks were in touch with discussions and debates in the rest of the Christian world. We have, for example, Old-Irish glosses on Theodore of Mopseustia's commentary on the Psalms, and Irish monks, in the eighth century, copied and disseminated Macrobius's *Commentary*, complete with its celestial journey, in France and Germany.[51] It was the Irish who reconverted northern England, establishing the great monastic settlement on Iona, off the north-eastern coast of the kingdom of Northumbria, from which several of the leading scholars of the early medieval period were to come. Chief among these was the Venerable Bede, who lived and worked between 671 and 735. Like Isidore, with whom he disagreed in many respects, uncharitably denouncing him for his 'lies', Bede was deeply influenced by the Roman scholar Pliny, for whom study of the natural world was crucial.[52] The world, for Bede, may have been presided over by God and his angels, but it could be understood in terms of natural processes and laws. Bede's great work on natural philosophy, the *De Natura Rerum*, compiled around 703, expanded considerably on the space allotted by Isidore to cosmology, but still remained broadly descriptive and more heavily based in scripture than the classics.[53]

Bede was probably aware of the existence of the rules for interpreting horoscopes from astrological passages in Books 9 and 10 of the Christian *Recognitions of Clement*, which were written some time in the second or third centuries.[54] But while he mentioned the *Recognitions*, he did not refer to the astrological passages which were, in any case, used to attack astrology. He only stopped at repeating the assertion that Venus was the nourisher of all things on earth, for this would have denied that task to God. He did, though, apparently repeat statements on thunder divination, relating it to the four points of the compass, the seven days of the week, and the twelve months of the year, possibly based on his own translation of a work by the sixth-century Greek astrologer John of Lydus; if thunder occurs in the east, for example, there will be bloodshed.[55] I say 'apparently' because the relevant text may have been attributed to Bede but not written by him.

Nevertheless, that an eighth-century monk should have had access to a Greek astrological work composed around 550 CE, and that this should have contained material traceable to the eighth-century BCE Babylonian omen collection, the *Enuma Anu Enlil*, is both evidence of the passage of astrological material from the Byzantine Empire to northern England, and remarkable testimony to the survival of specific astrological doctrines from the ancient Near East.[56] The advantage, though, of reliance on the more recent natural science approach to the stars epitomized by Pliny is that it made no mention of such practices as the use of incantations and talismans. Bede himself sought scriptural authority for his rejection of the notion that planets possessed psychological qualities which they bequeathed to humans, and instead relied on Ecclesiastes I.6 to justify his view that the sun gives heat to Mars, the light of wisdom to Mercury and the light of beauty to Venus, while Jupiter is balanced between Mars's heat and Saturn's cold.[57] In Bede's view, the only permitted symbolic connections between heaven and earth were strictly Christian: Christ himself was the 'Sun of Righteousness' and the Church, which he filled with his spirit, was the moon.[58]

The Church, paradoxically, was later to make use of Plinian astronomy to counter notions of a magical, miraculous universe, giving rise to a convenient alliance between theology and natural science. An opportunity for the theologians to defend the notion of a natural rather than miraculous world was provided a few hundred years later by the occurrence of an alarming eclipse while the Holy Roman Emperor Otto II was campaigning against the Byzantines in Calabria, one of the last enclaves of the Eastern Empire in Italy, in 968. Heraclius, bishop of Liège, who was accompanying the emperor, was able to cite the authority of the *astrologi* (astronomers) Pliny, Macrobius and Calcidius in order to argue that the eclipse was a purely natural event with a perfectly ordinary explanation, and nothing at all to be alarmed about.[59] Quite aside from the confusion this anecdote reveals about the use of the word 'astrology', it demonstrates the value of Isidore's distinction between natural and superstitious astrology. Bede himself, though, did appear to endorse the conventional view of comets. In his *Ecclesiastical History of the English People*, he recorded that:

> In the year of our Lord 729, two comets appeared around the sun, striking terror into all who saw them. One comet rose early and preceded the sun, while the other followed the setting sun at evening, seeming to portend awful calamity to east and west alike. Or else, since one comet was the precursor of day and the other of night, they indicated that mankind was menaced by evils at both times. They appeared in the month of January, and remained visible for about a fortnight, pointing their fiery torches northward as thought to set the welkin aflame.[60]

He then related the corresponding events; the Saracens launched a terrible incursion into France but were turned back (this was three years before they were decisively defeated by Charles Martel at Tours), and Egbert, the bishop who, in 716, had persuaded the monks of Iona to end the dispute with Rome over the date of Easter and other doctrinal matters, died, as did King Osric of Northumbria. It is actually unclear whether Bede was merely reporting popular beliefs about the momentous import of such celestial omens, and to what extent he shared them; he mentioned the comets of 664 and 678 almost in passing, as if they were of little interest.[61] And perhaps that tells us much about the concern with scripture rather than nature which so coloured early medieval thought.

2

The Carolingian World: Survival and Recovery

Man is not created for the stars, but the stars for man.
THE 'HOMILIES' OF AELFRIC[1]

Eighth-century Baghdad, the capital of the Islamic empire, was one of the most magnificent cities the world had ever seen. It was a cosmopolis in the true sense of the word, founded at an auspicious hour which was chosen by a team of the best astrologers the Caliph al-Mansur could find, and laid out in such a way that it would function as a talisman, harmonizing celestial principles.[2] In the Islamic world, which was then in the first flush of its intellectual glory, the latter part of the eighth century was a time when imperial patronage brought scholars together from Egypt, Persia and India, from all over the known civilized world, to exchange information and debate ideas from the natural sciences to theology, from matters of day-to-day survival to questions of ultimate truth. In this environment astrology was practised at all levels of society, from the street to the court, and was a matter of profound philosophical inquiry and theological concern. In Christian Europe, meanwhile, especially in the Catholic West, civilized living and learning had all but collapsed. Yet, as history so often reveals serendipitous parallels, so something similar to the Islamic discovery of ancient scholarship took place in the remote reaches of north-western Europe, even though the scale was far more limited and primitive. There, the Holy Roman Emperor Charles the Great – Charlemagne – king of the Franks, who presided over what has come to be known as the Carolingian Renaissance, undoubtedly saw himself as the equal of such rulers as Harun al-Rashid, his contemporary in the Islamic Caliphate.

The new curiosity about classical knowledge, and the secrets it might unlock, also appears to have affected the scholarly class in the Greek-speaking world, at least to judge from the evidence that the Byzantine Empire, by now shorn of its North African possessions and much of its Asian lands by the Arabs, experienced something of an economic and cultural revival around the year 800.[3] There seems to have been a fundamental shift in the attitude to classical pagan literature, which was no longer necessarily seen as a threat to Christian piety, but could be appreciated from a safe distance of time. Progress was slow. Plato was transcribed in the ninth century in Byzantium and Aristotle's writings published around 850, but neither appear to have been much studied until the eleventh century, when both philosophers, along with the Neoplatonists, attracted increasing numbers of keen advocates and commentators. There is, though, evidence that astrology was back in use in eighth-century Byzantium, partly thanks to one Stephanus the

Philosopher, a student of the caliph's astrologer, Theophilus of Edessa. Stephanus moved from Baghdad to Constantinople in 775, taking astrological manuscripts with him, and, by all accounts, found a receptive audience. It appears that military astrology of the type advocated by Theophilus was employed by the imperial astrologer Pancratius at the siege of the city of Marcellae by the Bulgars in the summer of 792.[4] We also hear of other practitioners, such as a certain Leo the Mathematician who lived from around 790 and died after 869. We can tentatively conclude that there appears to have been a textual tradition of astrology at Constantinople, and perhaps a little evidence of actual practice, surviving in the antipathetic atmosphere created by Christian orthodoxy.

In the West, Charlemagne ruled as king of the Franks from 768 and, from 800 to 814, as the first Holy Roman Emperor, and was to be the patron of learning who was to, at least in a limited way, galvanize scholarship in Catholic Europe. Charlemagne's realm extended across the whole of France, Germany and northern Italy, where he removed forever any Byzantine hopes of dominating the Pope, ensuring the separate development of eastern and western churches, and his lands shared a common border with the Islamic emirate of Cordoba in Spain. Charlemagne's motives in encouraging scholarship were devout and religious. He knew that his duty as a Christian ruler was to make sure that the rituals of the Catholic Church were celebrated properly, and that meant at the proper time. It was essential that he gather scholars who were competent in *computus* and the calculation of the correct date of Easter, but Charlemagne wanted to encourage all learning. His key ally in this aspiration was to be Alcuin, an English monk who was destined to become the leading scholar in the Latin West. Born in England in 735, the year of Bede's death, Alcuin studied with Bede's pupil, Egbert, and absorbed all the available surviving classics. His scholarly skills were widely recognized and he was appointed head of the Cathedral School at York, which was a major centre of the Irish-English curriculum, including the study of astronomy, cosmography and *computus*. In 780, on one of his visits to Italy, Alcuin met Charlemagne, and, in 793, the Frankish king invited him to join the cosmopolitan community of scholars at the unofficial palace school at his capital, Aachen. We read about Alcuin's intellectual qualities in the biographies of Charlemagne by Einhard, who described him as 'the most learned man anywhere to be found', and Notker the Stammerer, who praised him as 'a man more skilled than any other person in modern times'.[5] Einhard also reported that, under Alcuin's careful stewardship, 'the Emperor spent much time and effort in studying rhetoric, dialectic and especially astrology . . . [and] applied himself to mathematics and traced the course of the stars with great attention and care'. Alcuin himself wrote to Charlemagne that Pliny was the authority in astronomy, and the enthusiastic emperor gathered what material he could – new astronomical extracts from Pliny seem to have appeared – and encouraged the copying and dissemination of manuscripts; one of the most beautiful of surviving ninth-century manuscripts is the Leiden *Aratea*, an illustrated version of the *Phaenomena*, the famous poem about the constellations, composed by the third century BCE poet Aratus of Soli.[6] Platonic thinking seeped into Alcuin's cosmology through the Platonized Christianity of Augustine and Boethius, and copies of Calcidius's commentary on the *Timaeus* were also made. Alcuin was aware of the limited abilities of the priesthood, the literary class of the time. In 799, he composed his *Epistula 170* and shared with Charlemagne his concern that some scholars, for whom education meant learning liturgical chants and *computus*, might be bored by his astronomical work. The *Epistula*, which was composed at the emperor's request, was an attempt to explain the mystery of why the moon might appear smaller than expected on any given date. In the same letter, Alcuin displayed his overt allegiance to classical wisdom when he added that, if the emperor were to show his support for the study of astronomy, a 'new Athens' might be born in the Frankish realm.[7] The seven liberal arts, Alcuin told his pupils, had won lasting fame and glory for the pagan philosophers, who would all have known from the *Timaeus* that the planets were the keepers of God's divine time. Although we only have surviving tables for the sun and moon, we do know that all the planets were observed. Just as the priests of Pharonic Egypt had watched the stars to prepare for their dawn rituals, monastic communities had to do the same if they were to maintain the regularity of prayer.[8] And, if regularity was required, irregularity was a major problem, the sin of a cosmos out of control; this was precisely why *Epistula 170*, which explained an apparent anomaly according to the rules of mathematical order, was so important.

Charlemagne maintained the Plinian notion that astronomy is natural philosophy, and nothing to do either with the soul or the horoscope. In 811 he had a chance to make a public display of such views when he called for an explanation of the two solar eclipses of 810. He asked for advice from an Irish monk called Dungal, who appears to have come to France 25 years earlier and was well known at court.[9] Dungal responded not just with an explanation of eclipses, but with a summary of all contemporary astronomical knowledge, including such matters as different versions of the order of planets from the sun.

Charlemagne's prestige was sufficient to warrant a visit by envoys from the Caliph Harun al Rashid, who arrived in Aachen with gifts of spices, scents, medicaments, monkeys and an elephant. Notker the Stammerer's account of the visit emphasizes the problems that the Persian ambassadors encountered in finding the emperor, including a year in Italy being driven away by local people or given false instructions by various bishops.[10] Such problems would also have hindered the passage of scholarly literature. Although astrology had assumed a place at the Persian court almost as prominent as that it had held at the Assyrian, we do not hear of any astrological or astronomical manuscripts passing from Baghdad to Aachen. We do know that a group of churchmen with astronomical interests travelled to Charlemagne's court in 810 or 811 and, while their interest would almost certainly have been confined to *computus*, they may have been familiar with Ptolemy's *Planisphere*, and probably introduced the first Ptolemaic material to the scholarly environment at Aachen.[11]

The general scope of astronomical studies at the end of Charlemagne's reign, and hence of Alcuin's 'astrology', is indicated by anthologies which survive from around the years 810 and 818. Each one is based on the same general structure and includes a church calendar, lists of astronomical phenomena including the solstices, equinoxes and the sun's entry into each zodiac sign, seasonal phenomena such as weather and bird migrations, tables and instructions for calculation, followed by descriptions of the constellations from various ancient sources and extracts from Pliny. The Carolingian revival seems both to have encouraged the first signs of a theoretical, rather than purely descriptive, approach to astronomy, and initiated a revival of interest in astrology.[12]

So, when we say that astrology was studied at the Carolingian court, we need to be very clear exactly what this consisted of, and the failure, in spite of Isidore of Seville's plea, to fully distinguish acceptable astronomy from forbidden astrology. Steve McCluskey has identified five areas of early medieval astronomy: astrology itself; the literature on the seven liberal arts; monastic observations of the sun and moon for calendrical purposes; the observation of the sun on the horizon in order to orientate churches; and *computus*.[13] The rules of *computus* enabled the locations of the sun and moon in the zodiac to be found, but not the planets, which could be located only according to their average motion. If, for example, Jupiter took 12 years to complete one revolution through the zodiac, its location on any given date could be simply, though frequently inaccurately, estimated. In the ninth century, Hrabanus Maurus, who was to become archbishop of Mainz in 847, calculated the positions of the sun and moon to within a degree, but was able to compute the location of Mars, Jupiter and Saturn only approximately, within their zodiac signs.[14] In these circumstances, the casting of accurate horoscopes was impossible. Fortunately there were forms of astrology which had no need of precise astronomy and the types of divination available in the ninth century included practices based on planetary correspondence with numbers, with days of the week and with plants and herbs (for medicine and agriculture). One ninth-century *computus* included a numerological divining 'sphere of Pythagoras', an account of Egyptian lucky and unlucky days, performing a service not unlike modern horoscope columns, and instructions on divining from wind.[15] Divination based on the day of the month or lunar cycle was also common and *Lunaria*, or moon-books, designated favourable and unfavourable days. A volume ascribed to 'Saint Daniel' provided advice for babies born on the lunar day, while another treatise went further and offered a prognostication based on the day of the moon on which the patient fell ill.[16] There's an assumption behind advice on the best day to breed animals, buy or sell goods, send children to school, operate on a patient, build a mill or aqueduct, board a ship or enter a city, that astrology is a managerial system, designed to maximize one's prospects of success. Whether such ideas are derived from simplified versions of texts on electional astrology filtering through from Persia is not known. Neither can we tell whether they owed anything to the lucky and unlucky days of the Celtic Coligny Calendar, beyond the assumption that the broad tradition has roots that may go back to the second millennium or earlier.[17] The use of the word Egyptian suggests, literally, an Egyptian origin, although we are more likely looking at a composite tradition, drawing on a widespread belief that some days are better suited to certain activities than others. We also find simplified forms of interrogations (horoscopes cast in order to answer specific questions) – what chance there might be of recovering stolen goods on a particular day – and natal astrology – whether a boy born on one day will be astute, illustrious and intelligent, or a girl will be 'chaste, benign, good-looking and pleasing to men'. Scriptural support was invoked when the birthdays of biblical characters were given – Adam on the first day, Eve on the second, followed by Cain and Abel on the third and fourth – in much the same way as modern sun-sign guides include the birthdays of famous celebrities; readers were invited to compare themselves to their more illustrious astrological twin. That other astrological texts were making their way from the East is suggested by another ninth-century manuscript, the *Sphere of Petosiris*, which survives in Latin translation from the monasteries of Laon and Corbie.[18] The *Sphere*, of which that attributed to Petosiris was one of many, was a means of answering questions by the following method: the numerological value of the questioner's name in Greek letters is added to the number of the lunar day, and then divided by 29, the approximate number of days in the lunar cycle, from new moon to new moon. The answer can then be read from a circular diagram. An alternative method works from the days of the week, giving the numerical values of the planetary gods (moon for Monday and so on) rather than the lunar days. The evidence suggests that, while both philosophical debate on astrology and the casting of horoscopes almost completely died out, at the popular level an astrology which required neither sophisticated literacy, nor complex mathematics, flourished. While surviving sources date to the ninth century, it would be frankly unlikely if popular astrology had not survived through the fifth to eighth centuries. If it had died out, we would be faced with the remarkable prospect of a pre-modern society which had no sky-divination.

A great emphasis was placed on the observation of celestial phenomena, including such rare events as comets and eclipses, which could swiftly arouse popular feeling.[19] In the 840s, Habranus told how, on one occasion, he was able to chastize his congregation for their reaction to a lunar eclipse. At around sunset, when the moon would have been rising, the poor, ignorant people began blowing horns and shooting arrows at the monster they believed was about to devour it. Habranus's response, like that of Heraclius, bishop of Liege in the next century, was partly natural and Plinian, and partly scriptural; he pointed out that if genuine signs appeared in the sky then it would mean that the day of judgement had arrived, which it clearly hadn't.[20] His rejection of the miraculous, in which he is true to the early-medieval Plinian tradition, was a rhetorical device designed to save such events only for those sanctioned by the Church.

The ninth century itself seems to have marked a watershed in the study and practice of astrology in the West, which is not to say that it regained its former position, but that an interest in it was encouraged. It has been argued, though with little support, that within a very short time every Carolingian prince, duke and count had his own astrologer.[21] Equipped with such knowledge, we assume, the feudal lord believed he was in an ideal position to anticipate and outsmart his enemies. Astrology was as much a part of the technology of power as was the latest armour or cavalry tactics. Kings, councils and bishops recommended the study of astronomy to the clergy, the results of which were, it has been claimed, an enormous increase in the number of astrologers. This statement should be treated with a little scepticism, given that the terms astrology and astronomy were interchangeable, and that there is no evidence for any practical knowledge of horoscopic astrology. Perhaps the political crisis of the mid-ninth century encouraged a greater need to know the future. The combined effect of the fragmentation of the empire as Charlemagne's heirs struggled for supremacy, the incursions of the Northmen – the Vikings (who attacked all three of his successor kingdoms in 845 and came close to taking Paris in 885) – and continued Islamic raids (Rome was attacked in 846) encouraged the breakdown of central order in Italy, France and Germany, and the spread of local feudal powers.

There is some evidence that a sort of opulent courtly astronomy and astrology did indeed continue.[22] Charlemagne himself possessed a magnificent silver table which was decorated with the entire celestial sphere, including the stars and courses of the planets. After the emperor's death, his son, Emperor Louis the Pious (814–40), saved it for himself out of all the other treasures bequeathed to the Pope for charitable purposes. Within this context, then, in the year 837 the emperor, Louis the Pious was approaching his 60th birthday, when he asked a member of his court, known to us only as 'the Astronomer', about the significance of a comet – it was Halley's comet – that had appeared in the evening sky. Instead of being told that it heralded the death of princes (Louis died two years later), the nameless Astronomer told the emperor off, sternly quoting Jeremiah 10.2–3:

> Thus saith the Lord
> 'Learn not the way of the nations
> nor be dismayed at the signs of the heavens
> because the nations are dismayed at them
> for the customs of the peoples are false.'

However, other evidence suggests that the 'Astronomer' was alive to the significance of celestial portents, even if he was dismissive of Louis. In one example from an earlier chronicle, he had connected a lunar eclipse and an ominous group of comets in the constellation Auriga with the death of Pope Stephen II in 817.[23] Such events could be seen as signs from God, but were also perfectly explicable within a naturalistic context as the moon clearly exerted a physical effect on the earth, while comets were thought to stir up the atmosphere.

The anonymous Astronomer's condemnation was, perhaps, intended to prevent the king from straying into heretical territory, and was echoed by a treatise *On the Magical Arts* by Hrabanus. His attitude was essentially Augustinian – astrology is demonic, he claimed – but his limited knowledge of it was entirely derived from Isidore. However, the mood was changing. Apart from the many manuscripts, which represented the cosmos in geometrical form – evidence of increasing conceptual sophistication, perhaps – the other most remarkable item of royal stellar iconography was a magnificent ceremonial mantle, possibly inspired by Martianus Capella, and later owned by the Holy Roman Emperor Henry II (1002–24). Decorated with a combination of celestial and scriptural imagery, it showed the sun and moon on either side of Christ in majesty, the Virgin Mary described as *stella maris* (the star of the sea), the celestial sphere and the zodiac. Henry may have intended the robe as a clear political statement designed to demonstrate that he was more like the Byzantine emperor, was only subject to Christ himself as *cosmocrator* – lord of the universe – and was less dependent than papal theory held on the power of the Church. The robe, though, contained two clear astrological messages: 'where Scorpio rises, deaths increase' and 'This star, Cancer, brings evil things of the world,' alongside a cautionary sentence that warned 'There let the astrologer be careful.'[24] There is also one example of an astrological manuscript which may have been written in the ninth century, and certainly no later than the eleventh, the dating of which may be established by its complete ignorance of the astrology which was to flood in from the Arab world after 1100.[25] The document added to the normal *computus* discussions of celestial motions, accounts of planets' influences. Moving one step beyond Pliny, it also considered the variation of such influences depending on planetary relationships with the zodiac.

At this stage, then, sometime between 800 and 1000, between the reigns of Louis the Pious and Henry II, the use of horoscopes and the appreciation of astrology as an intellectual discipline re-entered the intellectual consciousness of the West. The evidence suggests that professional casters of horoscopes, who had largely disappeared in the West in the fifth century, seem to have made a reappearance, and philosophers began to seriously debate the limits of what astrology could actually achieve. However, we do need to consider the fortunes of Curry's 'low', or popular, astrology. What happened to the beliefs and practices of people, whether Roman, Celtic or Germanic, who fell outside the scholarly world, who had no interest in classical cosmology and little concern with theological worries about whether astrology was permissible or not? What did such people feel about the full moon? Did they celebrate the solstices? Did they employ charms which related to the sun? Did they tell stories about constellations or evoke the power of the stars? Were there variations between such ideas or practices on the Mediterranean basin, the north-west, especially Ireland which, of course, was never Romanized, and the many Germanic peoples who settled in the western empire? Of these three cultural spheres, we know enough about the use of astral magic in the Roman empire – the widespread use of talismans bearing astrological images, for example – but we have little evidence of the use of such magic between the fifth and eleventh centuries.[26] It is, though, frankly unlikely that such practices died out. As far as the Germanic peoples are concerned we also have little idea of their beliefs, beyond the idolatry angrily condemned by Christian evangelists. We have evidence to suggest, for example, that the constellation of the Bear was both important and featured in bear mythology and rituals across northern Europe.[27] It is also suggested that the Germans held their assemblies at the full moon although, in this sense, the moon may have functioned purely as a calendar marker. Whether this practice was widespread has never been investigated. We do have occasional references in the chronicles to the prevailing mentality in which, as across the ancient world, the entire natural environment was seen as a message board on which one's moral conduct and the future of society could be written. One example, which is especially apocalyptic in tone and deserves to be quoted in full, comes from Geoffrey of Tours' *History of the Franks*. Of the year 587, Geoffrey wrote:

> Many portents appeared at this time. In the homes of a number of people vessels were discovered inscribed with unknown characters which could not be erased or scraped off however hard they tried. This phenomenon began in the neighbourhood of Chartres, spread to Orleans and then reached the Bordeaux area, leaving out no township on the way. In the month of October new shoots were seen on the vines after the wine-harvest was over, and there were misshapen grapes. On other trees new fruits were seen, together with new leaves. Flashes of light appeared in the northern sky. Some said that they had seen snakes drop from the clouds. Others maintained that an entire village had been destroyed and had vanished into the air, taking the houses and the men who lived in them. Many other signs appeared of the kind which usually announced a king's death or the destruction of a whole region.[28]

The natural world formed a boundary, a liminal zone between the visible world of people, animals and plants, and the invisible realm of angels, demons and spirits. The whole was presided over by God and his unfathomable plan. As one looked up, one was gazing at the divine realm. As Geoffrey said, 'When our Lord had risen again . . . He was taken up on a cloud where He sits in glory on the right hand of the father.'[29] Christ was not just in the sky, though; he was omnipresent, everywhere. Within this context, signs in the sky formed just one zone of the world which was continuously sending messages. In the year 587, the celestial message was conveyed by flashes in the sky, perhaps a meteor shower or an unusual occurrence of the Northern Lights, and the conclusion was, in the words Shakespeare gave to Hamlet, 'the time is out of joint'.[30] Geoffrey provided a flavour of the times in his next paragraph, reporting on the dramatic appearance of an itinerant preacher called Desiderius who healed the sick, conveyed messages from the dead and drew huge crowds with his charismatic sermons. He gave another slant on the sixth-century astronomy of the Christian West when talking about three partial eclipses of the sun which took place sometime in the early 480s, during the reign of the Vandal king Huneric who died in 484. As an Arian Christian, Huneric had been especially savage in his treatment of Catholics, so here's what Geoffrey had to say about the cause of the eclipses: 'In my opinion this happened because of all the crimes which had been committed and all the blood which had been shed.'[31] The eclipses happened in response to Huneric's behaviour. Let's be quite clear about this: human action was the direct cause of astronomical events: the stars, as the Anglo-Saxon Homilies of Aelfric claimed, 'were created for man'.[32] The only question we have is the mechanism by which this happened. Did Geoffrey think that the murder of so many Christians produced a disturbance in the heavens through natural means, or did God arrange the eclipses as a sign of his distress? Both are equally possible within the thought of the time.

Questions of continuity between pagan and Christian cultures in Ireland suffer from a similar lack of evidence. Only at the most obvious level can we track the conversion of the eight festivals of the solar year into Christian festivals and saints' days.[33] Pagan time was to be contested and Christianized: between the fourth and tenth centuries, Samhain became All Saints (1 November), Imbolc was dedicated to St Brigit (1 February), Beltaine was linked to the Conception of Christ on 2 or 3 May, and Lughnasa either to St Justus (4 August) or St Oswald (5 August). Brigit's cult became particularly popular in Ireland and she seems to have been regarded, at least by some, as the Mother of God; Stephen McCluskey regards the gatherings that took place at her festival as an example of direct continuity with pagan calendar ceremonies, and therefore perhaps with Neolithic culture, back to the lost culture of Stonehenge and New Grange.[34] Traditions of sun and moon worship in Britain were remarkably persistent, and survived beyond the prohibitive laws of King Canute after 1013, and well into the seventeenth century, when the Protestant Reformation effectively stamped out all 'superstition'.[35]

It is relatively easy to track such simple matters as the conversion of pagan festivals into saints' days. Far more difficult is to identify the details of whatever form of astrology was practised in the oral traditions of northern Europe. That either popular astrological customs, or the practice of horoscope astrology, continued to be perceived as a problem is evident from another condemnation from the next century in the Homilies of Aelfric, compiled by the Abbot of Eynsham in the English kingdom of Wessex. Aelfric, who was born around 955 and died about 1010, had been a former student in the Dominican monastic school at Winchester, at a time when the study of new texts from elsewhere in Europe was being actively encouraged. It's not clear whether he had any direct experience of astrology, or encountered it in information coming from France. We read in Aelfric's work that:

> . . . we are also to know that there were some heretics who said that every man is born according to the position of the stars, and that by their course his destiny befalls him, and advised in support of their error, that a new star sprang up when the Lord was corporally born, and said that the new star was his destiny. Let this error depart from believing hearts . . . Man is not created for the stars, but the stars for man. [36]

This condemnation is an apparent reference to past errors but the declaration that 'No Christian man shall practise anything in the way of divination by the Moon' is a more explicit reference to practices which were probably contemporary. If Aelfric had no worries about the practice of astrology in England at the time then why did he make these statements? Were literary contacts the only ones that English scholars had with astrology? Theodore Wedel assumes that they were and that those who repeated Isidore's condemnation of astrology did so merely because this was the custom.[37] So much depends on our interpretation of the evidence. And so, at the beginning of the second millennium, when we read that Gilbert Naminot, bishop of Lisieux and chaplain and physician to William the Conqueror, would rather spend his nights watching the stars than sleeping[38] we do not know if he was gazing on the glory of God's handiwork, or searching for portents. No doubt, though, he observed the comet – again, Halley's comet – of 1066, which heralded the final collapse of the English Saxon monarchy and, recorded in the Bayeux tapestry, is the last great omen before the revival of judicial astrology in the Latin West.

3

The Twelfth Century: Renaissance and Revival

Others say that a man in his intelligence does things not caused by the
stars, and can, through [the power of] his mind, change the decree of the
stars . . . others say that God has created man with the power to change
his luck.

THE RABBIS OF THE SOUTH OF FRANCE[1]

A thousand years after Christian evangelists began their assault on astrology as a dark, demonic threat to humanity, scholars in the Latin West began seriously to question the concept that to practise what Isidore called 'superstitious' astrology was inherently immoral. Instead, they were seized by the idea that astrology was, potentially, a source of profound wisdom, not to mention political and personal advantage. Those fragments of classical wisdom which had survived the decline of secular learning in the fifth and sixth centuries had been sufficient to keep at least some curiosity regarding Greek and Latin concepts of the heavens for several hundred years. By the twelfth century the quest for such knowledge was to become one of the most powerful intellectual movements in European history, transforming the prevailing world-view and reconnecting the Catholic world with its roots in the philosophy of pre-Christian Greece. The Middle Ages, from around 1100 to 1400, were, for philosophers, a period of deep intellectual curiosity, not least about humanity's relationship with the cosmos. Old caricatures, though, as eloquently summarized by Jacob Burckhardt in 1860, still shape popular perceptions. 'In the Middle Ages,' Burckhardt claimed, 'both sides of human consciousness – that which was turned within as that which was turned without – lay dreaming or half awake beneath a common veil. The veil was woven of faith, illusion and childish prepossession, through which the world and history were clad in strange hues.'[2] This view of the past, at once both colourful and comforting, in which medieval scholarship was mired in primitive stagnation, prior to its eventual rebirth in the spiritual and intellectual awakening of the Renaissance of the fifteenth century, still shapes attitudes to the history of science and astronomy.[3] Yet, for historians of ideas, the theory of the dark Middle Ages was completely demolished in 1927 by the Harvard historian Charles Homer Haskins.[4] Haskins pointed out that, beginning around 1000, but reaching a peak in the late twelfth and early thirteenth centuries, there was a dramatic intellectual encounter between scholars in the Latin West – Spain, France, Italy and Germany – and the rich intellectual traditions of the Islamic world. Haskins deliberately challenged the notion of the fifteenth century as a unique rebirth of culture by naming his chosen period the 'Twelfth Century Renaissance'. In the process, he temporarily reinforced the idea of the preceding period as a 'Dark Age', but his point was well made. Haskins even encouraged the search for other 'Renaissances', such as the Carolingian Renaissance of the eighth and ninth centuries. Some historians now talk about the Renaissance of the thirteenth century, as if every culture in every period has its own phase of scholarly rebirth. One feature of the three Renaissances of the eighth–ninth, twelfth and fifteenth centuries, though, quite aside from developments in the arts and technology, was a significant expansion in the number of available cosmological texts, including astrological works. The twelfth and thirteenth centuries were marked by the translation of almost the entire collected works of the fourth century BCE Greek philosopher, Aristotle, prompting a revolution in Western thought.

The evidence suggests that the entire scholarly process in the twelfth century was partly driven by the need for astrological texts. This should not be surprising. After all, astrology was the most important application of astronomy for any prince or prelate who wished to gain advantage over his rivals, or for any scholar who believed, as the Old Testament told him, that the heavens revealed the glory of God, or that the End of Days and Christ's second coming, prophesied in the New Testament, would be presaged by celestial signs. We might point to Isaiah, who prophesied that 'For the stars of the Heavens/ and their constellations will not give their light;/ The Sun will be dark at its rising/ And the Moon will not shed its light,' or Luke, who warned, 'And there will be signs in sun and moon and stars, and upon the earth distress of nations in perplexity at the roaring of the sea and the waves.'[5] For the devout Christian, to watch the stars was an obligation, even if the word 'astrology' was shunned. And for the philosopher, astrology might demonstrate the wonders of God's creation and explain the workings of his divine plan through the heavens. As Notker Labeo (c.950–1022), a French monk well known for his translations of Boethius, Martianus Capella and some fragments of Aristotle, put it, the complexity of computing the date of Easter by the sun and the moon pointed to a mystery, the solution of which encouraged the devout to turn their minds to the splendour on high, and from earthly darkness and sin to the light of celestial piety.[6] This was good Christian Platonism. But, for the baron or cleric who was more concerned with worldly matters, astrology held out the promise of vital political foreknowledge. Astrology, once theological objections were put aside, offered the medieval world an overarching organizing principle of quite extraordinary power.

Of the other practical needs of the early scholars, improvements in medicine were probably the most pressing, but, even then, the available Arabic medical texts, strongly influenced by Hippocrates or Galen, frequently assumed that knowledge of the stars was critical in effective diagnosis and treatment. It was to be astrology's medical applications that made it an unavoidable part of medieval Western culture, regardless of the objections of conservative theologians. Even those who abhorred the demonic practice of horoscope-reading could not refuse to be bled in accord with the lunar cycle. After all, had not Augustine himself acknowledged the existence of celestial influences?

By the late tenth century, European scholars were visiting such scholarly centres as Toledo, one of the most important cities in Spain, the most accessible part of the Islamic world. The earliest formal contacts in Spain seem to have been facilitated through a delegation sent by the Holy Roman Emperor Otto I to the Caliph of Cordoba, Abd al-Rahman III, in 953, with the express aim of putting a stop to Islamic incursions into southern France.[7] During three years of lengthy and intermittent negotiations, the Caliph was represented by a Christian, Bishop Recemund of Elvira, and a Jew, Nasdei Ibn Shaprut, a court official, scholar, physician and leader of the Jewish community in Corboba. Otto's embassy, meanwhile, included John of Gorze, a monk who was both an expert in *computus* and an observational astronomer, as well as Bernacer, a deacon who was also known for his skill in *computus*. Stephen McCluskey has speculated that, even though we know of no manuscripts which changed hands during this long exchange, the conversation between the four men must have turned to the sky. He pointed to Recemund's authorship, along with another court official, of the Calendar of Cordoba, a daily almanac containing information on religious feast days, the sun's location, the length of day, the rising of stars and such information as found in the Carolingian anthologies of the eighth century including such gems as, for 15 March, 'the birth of horses begins now in the maritime regions and continues until the middle of April'.[8] There was one further practical consequence which we need to note regarding such contacts (if not of Otto's embassy itself), though, and that was the introduction of the astrolabe into Western Europe by about 1030.[9] Previously, astronomical observations had been 'qualitative' in Steve McCluskey's terms – noting such obvious visual phenomena as the changing phases of the moon, the appearance and disappearance of stars, or the position of planets in relation to the constellations.[10] The astrolabe was to allow a far more detailed level of quantitative timing and measurement of celestial motions, the consequence of which was that astrologers could, hopefully, have a much greater degree of confidence in their prognostications.

We may have no positive evidence of the consequences of Otto's embassy to Cordoba, but we do know that, immediately after it took place, Western scholars realized that the libraries of the cities of Islamic Spain might have much to offer. It was a Spanish scholar, Lupitus of Barcelona, who seems to have been first into the field. In 984 he received a letter from Gerbert d'Auvergne, who later went on to occupy the Vatican as Pope Sylvester II (999–1003), asking for a copy of a book on astrology which he, Lupitus, had apparently translated. Gerbert, we know, had crossed the Pyrenees in 967 to study mathematics with Hatto, the bishop of Vich, the result being a fascination with the potential, and so far, untapped knowledge contained in the libraries of Islamic Spain. Even though there was political competition between the Christian kings of the north and the Islamic rulers who still dominated most of the peninsula, there was also considerable mixing between the populations of their respective realms, especially through the Mozarabs. These were Arabic-speaking Christians who provided a cosmopolitan bridge between the two cultures. Gerbert would have found little difficulty in ascertaining the wide range of material available in the Arabic libraries and his letters reveal the extent to which he collected such texts. He wrote to one Mozarab, Joseph the Spaniard, asking for a book on numbers and, of course, to Lupitus requesting his astrological text.[11] After his death, Gerbert was to acquire a legendary reputation as a magician of mighty achievements. He was certainly the first to introduce the use of Hindu–Arabic numerals, including the all-important zero, to Latin Europe outside of Spain, and designed astronomical instruments on the grounds that it was vital to be able to make one's own observations rather than relying on tables; in 989 he sent an account of his observations of the sun to a monk named Adam, in which he reported that he was checking Martianus Capella's statements on the changing length of the day through the year.[12] Contrary to the increasingly old-fashioned view that the Middle Ages were intellectually stagnant, we could not have a clearer instance of a scientifically inquiring mind than in Gerbert. More significantly for astrology, Gerbert may also have been the author of the first home-grown European astrological text, the *Liber Planetis et Mundi Climatibus*, which seems to have been composed anonymously some time between 1010 and 1027.[13]

Aside from questions of its authorship, the *Liber's* contents point to the priorities of a typical tenth- or eleventh-century cleric whose attention is being drawn to the wealth of intellectual stimulation available in the Arabic world. The work began with a description of the 'sphere' – the cosmos (nobody with access to such knowledge ever believed the earth was flat) – and moved on to geography (an essential consideration for astronomical calculation was to know one's location) before tackling astrology. A promised section on detailed natal astrology is lacking, perhaps never completed, leaving a passage on the planets' general characteristics and natures. The influences of the sun (hot and dry) and moon (cold and wet) are taken for granted and are justified by the observation that more 'humour' (of the cold, wet lunar variety) collects in men's heads when they sleep out of doors, presumably resulting in a tendency to head colds. Although the planets' influences vary as they move through the 12 signs and 28 lunar mansions, each has an essential character. Crucially and, potentially heretically, one of the cited authors was Macrobius, whose commentary on the dream of Scipio was the core account of the ascent of the soul to the stars. In Saturn, the text relates, the soul busies itself with reasoning, intelligence, logic and theory. Of the other planets, Jupiter represents the power of practical action, Mars of animosity, Venus is desire and Mercury interpretation. The last three descriptions are fairly conventional and rooted in Hellenistic and Islamic tradition, although Saturn's description in particular smacks more of its role as the gateway to the stars than its strictly malefic astrological character. That the *Liber's* content was later to become standard European cosmology should not blind us to its revolutionary nature. The soul, the seat of human reason, that part of the individual which might achieve salvation and return to God, possessed a personality that was partly dependent on, or at least indicated by, the planets.

One's chance of both committing sin and achieving forgiveness was dependent on one's location in space and time, and influenced by forces embedded in the natural environment. A millennium of theological opposition to astrology was about to be systematically unpicked in a cosmological revolution to rival that which was to take place in the fifteenth and sixteenth centuries. The author of the *Liber Planetis* had demolished Isidore's carefully constructed, but ultimately untenable, distinction between natural and superstitious astrology.

The evidence of the *Liber Planetis* aside, we are not certain of the extent of textual access to horoscopic astrology in the late tenth century, although manuscripts of Manilius's first-century Latin work, the *Astronomica*, have survived from the eleventh century, and Julius Firmicus Maternus's *Mathesis* seems to have been available in the early twelfth century – which means they must have survived, even if ignored, in monastic libraries from the fifth century onwards.[14] There is a legend that Gerard, Archbishop of York under the English King Henry I (1100–35), died unexpectedly with a copy of the *Mathesis* under his pillow, a crime for which his bier suffered the indignity of being stoned by small boys on its route to the cathedral, and for which the canons initially refused to bury him: such was the conservative reaction to one found guilty of 'addiction to magical and forbidden arts'.[15] Ecclesiastical disapproval aside, discussion of the nature and function of the stars was, by 1100, an important part of theological debate at the highest level. There was nothing surprising in this, for Calcidius's commentary on the *Timaeus* was available.

One of the first theologians into the field was Peter Abelard, who was born in 1079 and had achieved considerable fame as a teacher by his death in 1142 (as well as for his celebrated love affair with Heloise). He was particularly interested in the philosophers', in other words, the Platonists', theory that the planets are animated and moved by spirits, or whether they hold their courses according to the will of God, as Boethius would have said.[16] The Platonic theory, he reasoned, could not be entirely ruled out, especially as even St Augustine himself was unsure whether to class the sun, moon and stars on the one hand with the angels on the other. And, if Augustine was uncertain on such a vital matter, who was Abelard to argue that the Platonic cosmos was un-Christian? Even when Augustine stepped back from the Platonic view that the world is an animal, that is, a rational, living being, it was only because he could prove it true neither by reason nor scripture. Abelard's problem was one of logic, not faith, and the dividing line between the two cosmologies, the Christian one in which the cosmos was controlled by God, and the Platonic in which, in a sense, the cosmos *was* God, was a difficult one for devout theologians to maintain, though not absolutely impossible. Abelard was therefore able to gradually relax Augustine's condemnation of astrology, taking his – Augustine's – own acceptance of natural celestial influences as his cue. He not only accepted the reality of planetary influences, as a species of natural cause but, like the author of the *Liber Planetis*, dipped a toe into the realm of horoscopic, judicial astrology with his concession that the force of the planets varied with their location in the 'houses', by which he meant zodiac signs. Even

Isidore's distinction between natural and superstitious astrology was, in practice, difficult to maintain, for the boundaries between the two were inevitably blurred. The philosophers and theologians were catching up with the popular astrology of the *Spheres* and *Lunaria*, which served up popular astrology refreshingly free of theological angst. However, here Abelard stopped. Having breached the technical distinction between natural and superstitious astrology by allowing the latter's use of horoscopes in the former, he had to define what kinds of information it was then possible for the horoscope to reveal. His solution was to draw a major distinction between the prediction of what were known as *contingentia* – contingent events (in which divine providence, chance or human free-will play a part) – and *naturalia* – natural events, such as the weather. There was no doubt that natural events could be predicted, the most obvious being seasonal changes, as well as agriculture and disease, both of which were dependent on the constant changes of wind, rain, heat and cold. *Contingentia*, though, took the cautious astrologer into much more dangerous territory. There was an undoubted theological difficulty to be dealt with here, and Abelard had to address the thorny problem of whether, if a person is going to commit a good act, and God, being all-knowing, knows that he is going to commit it, does the act then become predetermined and hence of no moral value? In other words, is it possible to be genuinely good? Does God's foreknowledge of the future suggest that astrologers can foresee individual actions? Abelard concluded that God's foreknowledge of our free acts makes them no less free, so it is therefore impossible for the stars to predict such acts. He produced a neat argument to demonstrate his point, which suggests that he might have had some exposure to practising astrologers. They will always, he told his reader, make precise forecasts for third parties, but never directly to the client, just in case the client then proves them wrong by taking a different course of action.

Abelard's argument points to the existence of professional astrologers, which, in turn, suggests a demand for their services, even one which was not yet extensive. We know that Alexander of Tralles's medical astrology manuscripts were available, that *Spheres* were in use, and that the comet of 1066 was retrospectively seen as an omen of the Norman conquest of England in 1066. Certainly, the need for astrological texts was apparent in a succession of major translations.[17] In 1126, Adelard of Bath, who may have provided astrological services to the future King Henry I, translated Al-Khwarizmi's Arabic astronomical tables, which enabled astrologers to perform their calculations, while his construction of an astrolabe plate for the latitude of southern England also enabled horoscopes to be cast easily and efficiently by English astrologers.[18] In 1136 Hugh of Santalla translated one of the most significant works of astrological philosophy, the tenth-century Arabic *Centiloquium*, which was given huge importance because it was mistakenly believed to have been written by Claudius Ptolemy. Plato of Tivoli translated Ptolemy's *Tetrabiblos* two years later, in 1138, Herman of Carinthia followed with Abu Ma'shar's *Maius Introductorum*, translated from the Arabic in 1140 and, in 1160, an anonymous version of Ptolemy's *Almagest* appeared, direct from the Greek.[19] Gerard of Cremona's authoritative Latin edition of the *Almagest* in 1175 or 1176 provided the last of a series of texts that provided the complete astronomical mechanism and rationale for the new European astrology. Much of the Hermetic corpus was also translated, and doctrines of the intimate relationship between the soul and the stars lent a religious force to the otherwise naturalistic writings of Aristotle.[20] The *Emerald Tablet*, one of the key philosophical texts of Hermetic astrology, probably first appeared in the West in editions of the pseudo-Aristotelian *Secretum Secretorum*. This was actually a translation of the *Kitab Sirr al-Asar*, which purported to be an account of the advice given by Aristotle to his young student Alexander the Great, and as such was considered essential reading for any young prince with even a modicum of ambition.[21] The *Secretum* was translated into Latin first by Johannes Hispalensis around 1140, and then by Philip of Tivoli in about 1243. Other translations of the *Tablet* itself may have been made during the same period by Plato of Tivoli and Hugh of Santalla, perhaps from different sources.

While the translation of Arabic texts into Latin was most influential, we shouldn't imagine that the process was simple. There were multiple lines of contact between Catholic Europe and its neighbouring cultures. Both Byzantine and Saracen influences remained very strong in tenth-century Italy, and it was these that the Holy Roman Emperor Otto II was attempting to control when Gerbert visited his court in November 980.[22] In the eleventh century Catholic scholars were translating Greek texts, partly with the active encouragement of enthusiasts such as the Emperor Manuel I, who actively promoted links between his court and those of the Western courts. Manuel personally sent a copy of Ptolemy's *Almagest* to the Holy Roman Emperor, Frederick Barbarossa, from which the first Latin translation was made.[23] Syriac and Hebrew texts were also translated into Latin, opening lines of communication between Catholic and Jewish thought. There were, though, many translation and copying errors when Arabic was rendered into Latin, which compounded those when Greek or Syriac were originally converted into Arabic. The technical minutiae of horoscope interpretation was therefore subject to change not just because innovations were made, but because so were mistakes. Over the next few hundred years there was an increasing awareness that technical astrology contained inaccuracies and, by the fifteenth century, the consequence was the major programme of astrological reform and astronomical discovery.

Long before such doubts set in, though, a parallel route for the transmission of astrology into Europe was provided by Judaism, whose most creative contribution to Western cosmology, one which was later to be increasingly attractive to Christian Platonists, was Kabbalah, the traditional or, more importantly, 'received' lore. And here we mean 'received' partly in the same sense that Gnostic truths were received from an experiential encounter with the divine, and partly in the sense that it was received from the accumulated body of Jewish tradition.[24] Kabbalah was, at least in part, an attempt to codify the spontaneous and ecstatic encounters with the celestial realms, such as were recorded in Jacob's dream of the ladder to heaven, or Elijah's ascent to heaven.[25] Just as Mithraism had structured Platonic notions of the soul's ascent with ritualized planetary initiations, so Kabbalah devised ten points of spiritual power and knowledge, known as sephirot, which were placed in ascending order on the three pillars of the tree of life – itself a likely reference to Jacob's ladder. The sephirot are the substance of all things, not unlike Platonic archetypes; they are the principles that mediate between God and his creation. Like the archetypes, they emanated, along with the entire material cosmos, out of God. The classic and profoundly enigmatic description of them is found in the *Sefer Yetzirah*, the core text of Kabbalah:

> Ten Sefirot of Nothingness:
> Their measure is ten
> Which have no end
> A depth of beginning
> A depth of end
> A depth of good
> A depth of evil
> A depth of above
> A depth of below
> A depth of east
> A depth of west
> A depth of north
> A depth of south
> The singular Master
> God faithful King
> dominates over them all from his holy dwelling
> until eternity of eternities.[26]

The *Sefer Yetzirah* is a remarkably short work which varies, in different versions, between 1300 and 2500 words. That the original source may have been only 240 words invites comparisons with the Hermetic *Emerald Tablet* as a pithy statement of spiritual truth. The essence of Kabbalistic teachings is their secrecy, which makes their origins inevitably difficult to trace. A reasonable supposition is that there may be roots in the close encounter between Jewish, Egyptian and Greek thought in Hellenistic Alexandria, as well as in the creative period which followed the end of the Babylonian captivity and the building of the second temple. The iconic imagery of the tree of life occurs in Assyrian reliefs, suggesting an earlier spiritual tradition as scholars whose concern was human dialogue with the divine struggled to find visual images in order to express their aspirations.[27] Tradition holds that the secrets of Kabbalah were revealed by Moses to Joshua, but the first direct transition to Europe was probably about the year 917, when the Babylonian scholar, Aaron bin Samuel, took the teachings from Mesopotamia to Germany. There may have been a separate transmission to Spain, where legend holds that the secret doctrines were revealed by the prophet Elijah to Jacob ha-Nazir in the 1000s, although the main exponent was one Isaac the Blind, who was teaching in the 1100s, and his probable student Azriel (1160–1238). The earliest manuscript of the *Sefer Yetzirah* itself probably dates from the tenth century, around the time that Kabbalah was making its way from Mesopotamia to Spain and Germany, suggesting that transmission required the conversion of a probably oral tradition into literary form. From Spain, Kabbalah spread into Provence. By the late fifteenth century it was to attract the serious attention of Renaissance scholars who saw it as an authentic counterpart to Platonic teachings on the ensouled, living cosmos, infused with divinity. The heart of Kabbalah was an attempt to come closer to God by living a life of spiritual purity and, and here the comparison with Platonic Islam and Christianity is clear, through using reason as well as faith; scripture was to be interpreted allegorically and metaphorically, drawing out the hidden meaning, and to believe in literal truth was to completely fail to grasp God's true message to humanity. Study, though, was to lead to practice and, as an experiential art, Kabbalah developed a participatory, magical approach to the cosmos. The essential forms of things, the archetypes, on which everything in the world is based, are represented by the 22 letters of the Hebrew alphabet. These hover on the boundary line between the physical and spiritual worlds, and the real existence of things can only be understood through language. But each letter also corresponds to a number, so divine and cosmic meaning may also be revealed through mathematics. There was, therefore, an extensive use of divine names, letter permutations and similar methods to reach higher states of consciousness in order to influence or alter the natural world. It was absolutely necessary to use such methods to read the signs God had sent precisely because his very first act was to engrave the constellations as signs on the heavenly vault.[28] The *Sefer Yetzirah* recorded that, as the creation proceeded, God:

> made the letter Heh king over speech
> and He bound a crown to it
> And He combined one with another
> And with them he formed
> Aries in the Universe
> Nissan in the Year
> And the right foot in the Soul
> male and female.[29]

So, by understanding the relationship between the time of the year and the constellations, the Kabbalistic initiate might comprehend scripture and the soul. By focusing on Kabbalah's hidden meanings, the initiate would be better able to understand time, the heavens and the soul. And, if the initiate knew that the letter Heh is a component of the name of God, Yahweh, and meant 'to embrace', he would be better able to locate the path to the divine. Even if the Kabbalistic path is a demanding one, there is a simple logic by which one's place in the structure of the cosmos is identified. By converting the letters of one's name into numbers and dividing the result by 12 one would establish one's ruling zodiac sign. Divide by 12 and one's dominant planet is established. There is a hint here of one of the prevailing paradigms of Babylonian astrology, in which the universe is analysed in terms of abstract, theoretical possibilities, rather than observed, empirical evidence.[30] It pays no heed to observation of the material cosmos and relies instead on total abstraction, by reference to the order which underlies the visible planets.

The Kabbalistic cosmos was structured along lines which bear comparison with the Gnostic system, in which a remote creator plays little or no part in the material world, which is presided over by a more immediate power.[31] Kabbalah, though, unlike Gnosticism, which generally assumed that the physical cosmos was inherently evil, tended to the Platonic view of the cosmos as essentially good and the lower power is definitely benign. God was too exalted for mortals, and even for angels, to comprehend, so, in order to be visible he created a 'majesty' or representative out of the divine fire, which itself is visible to the angels. This power is the anthropomorphic God of scriptural imagery, of whom Isaiah wrote 'Heaven is my throne and the earth is my footstool.'[32] There were in total four worlds in the Kabbalistic Cosmos, arranged in a vertical hierarchy: those of the glory (the visible God), the angels, the intellectual soul and the animal soul. It was up to the Kabbalist to control the animal soul and live through the intellectual soul and so attempt to contact the visible God.

The astrology that emerged from Kabbalah was partly derived from lunar time. There was considerable attention to the 28 times listed in Ecclesiastes – 'a time to be born, a time to plant', and so on.[33] Twenty-eight, of course, is approximately the number of days in the lunar month. These times corresponded to the 28 camps of the divine presence and the zodiacal constellations which, in turn, could refer back to the names of God.[34] A true Kabbalistic astrology was therefore, like its classical Hermetic and Mithraic cousins, concerned less with the use of horoscopes to analyse worldly affairs than with ritual intended to take the initiate on a path to the divine source and transcend the cosmos of celestial influences and planetary diktat. Such ideas found their full expression in the *Sefer HaZohar* (The Book of Splendour). Usually known simply as the *Zohar* (translated as 'splendour' or 'radiance'), this was a Kabbalistic commentary on the Torah which seems to have been written in Spain in the thirteenth century by Moses de Leon, even though he claimed it was based on a second-century original.[35] The *Zohar* argued that the act itself of studying the Torah provides divine protection from the heavenly laws of nature, including celestial influences. Before the Torah was given to the Jews all the people in the world were dependent on *mazal*, a word which may be understood as stars, or stellar influence, or destiny. But, after the Torah was given to Moses, the Jews were, potentially, released from the rule of the stars. This is only absolutely true, though, for one who studies the Torah. Study, though, needs to be combined with practice and there were seven stages of initiation on the ascending path, each of which might produce an ecstatic experience. This could be envisaged as taking place through an imaginal cosmos in which the soul travelled through inner space, rather than a literal journey through the seven material spheres. The individual who takes this path will be united with God and shares his existence above the world of celestial influence and natural law. The ignorant, on the other hand, are still subject to the stars, even if they are Jews.

Such overt Platonism and Hermeticism, with its emphasis on the cosmos as a mystery, was conceptually acceptable to the Catholic scholars of the twelfth century. For them the radical move was into the study of a natural world, away from total reliance on scripture and faith. By the late twelfth century the leading philosophers of Catholic Europe had access not just to the technical astrology of the Hellenistic and Arabic worlds, with their Babylonian and Indian legacies, but the passages in the *Emerald Tablet* and *Centiloquium* which spoke of the reciprocal and magical relationship between the heavens and earth. In short, in the course of a century or less, the spiritual, conscious, living cosmos of the classical pagans, together with its application in horoscopic astrology, which the Church Fathers had done so much to combat, was recreated at the highest levels of Catholic theology. The *Picatrix* itself, the great magical manual of the Islamic world, was translated into Latin under the patronage of Alfonso X of Castile in 1256, a century after the main texts of horoscope interpretation became available. The development and acceptance of astrology as an important feature of the medieval scholarly world is demonstrated by the appearance of the well-known 'zodiac-man' images, in which a human body is labelled with the signs of the zodiac, from Aries and the head down to Pisces and the feet. These depictions, which were clearly for the education of medical students, become common as the twelfth century progressed, but are almost unknown beforehand.[36] The introduction of the complete spectrum of classical and Islamic astrological theories, techniques and practices was complete by the mid-thirteenth century, when Guido Bonatti (d. c. 1296/1300), the most renowned professional astrologer of his day, produced the first major astrological text of medieval Europe, the *Liber Astronomiae*.

Among the Jews the Spanish Rabbi Abraham Ibn Ezra (1089–1164) published his basic textbook on astrology, *The Beginning of Wisdom*, in 1148.[37] Covering the zodiac signs, houses, planets and aspects, the book contained the elementary knowledge required for horoscope intepretation for a Hebrew reading audience in Western Europe. Ibn Ezra, though, was overshadowed by Moses Maimonides (1135–1204), one of the most famous of all Jewish philosophers. He was born in Cordoba but seems to have lived most of the latter part of his life in Cairo where he was head of the Jewish community and physician to the vizier of Saladin.[38] Maimonides's philosophical importance lies in his keen advocacy of Aristotelianism and his recognition of the need to reconcile Aristotle's cosmology with mainstream Judaism, a task in which he was both very successful and very influential on the next generation of Catholic Aristotelians, particularly Albertus Magnus and Thomas Aquinas. His teachings were spread throughout the Jewish world with great enthusiasm, in both Islamic and Christian countries. When the rabbis of northern France rejected his ideas, those of the south reported their colleagues to the Inquisition, who reportedly punished several of the accused by ripping their tongues out. Maimonides's position on astrology illustrated well the dilemma of the Aristotelian who held to a religious faith whether

Islamic, Christian or, as in his case, Jewish. He was a keen advocate of the broad cosmology in which all movement on earth began in the celestial spheres, and in which there was always a broad relationship between planetary movements and terrestrial events, but rejected any notion whatsoever that this might justify judicial astrology – the casting of horoscopes. In a famous letter to the rabbis of southern France, written in 1194, he set out his objections.

> And now, we, your servants who live in a far away land, have come to drink from your fountain of wisdom. It occurred to some of us to ask you about the saying of the old rabbis that 'Israel is not governed by the stars,' and the answer that was given by Rabbi Shrira and Rabbi Haii regarding this matter. Astrologers say that everything depends on the constellations, every movement of people, and even their thoughts. All worldly affairs are like images stamped in wax by the signs which are the stampers and nothing can be added or subtracted. Others say that a man in his intelligence does things not caused by the stars, and can, through [the power of] his mind, change the decree of the stars. Some say that the source of the soul and spirit of a person is above the stars and the constellations and can change what's caused by them, and through it so can man; others say that God has created man with the power to change his luck.[39]

The rabbis, for their part, were quite clearly as concerned about the spread of astrology and the extent to which Aristotle's *Philosophy* was providing acceptance for it, as were their Christian colleagues. This was the second letter they had written – the first had gone unanswered – and they were looking to Maimonides, who they described as a 'redeemer, a proclaimer of justice, righteous [and] learned' to fulfil the same service for them as Thomas Aquinas was to provide later for Catholic reconciliation of scripture with classical cosmology. The problem was similar and based around Abu Ma'shar's extension of planetary influence, following Ptolemy into the soul, and therefore morality. As an example, according to Guido Bonatti, the moon signified 'the reformation of the soul' and, if linked to Mars, it signified jealousy and malicious gossip but, if connected to Jupiter, it indicated honesty.[40] We have a philosophical question here: does the horoscope indicate psychological tendencies in which there is no direct causality, or is fate somehow astrologically ordained? In either case, astrology was providing a direct challenge to the soul's ability to gain forgiveness and salvation.

Maimonides conceded the reality of the Neoplatonic cosmos, which he had already strongly supported in his Arabic writings; the whole cosmos is alive, the stars have living souls and intelligences and, just as miracles are delivered through the angels, so creation is accomplished through the stars.[41] There is no ambiguity here. Maimonides took issue with the astrologers on two counts: philosophy and faith. He had quite clearly read the Greek sceptics and, although he didn't quote any by name, Plotinus was a likely influence. What Maimonides clearly objected to in matters of faith was the suggestion that God's power was in any way limited, and he raged against the astrologers' stupidity and lies and their 'thousands of books of nonsense', which he blamed for the destruction of the Jewish state and the diaspora.[42] He argued that, even though it was true that some Jewish scholars did indeed advocate astrology, the only acceptable science of the stars was that which dealt with the size and motion of the stars and planets, in other words, Ptolemy's first variety of astronomy. He brought forward no evidence against astrology, though. He ignored standard rationalist objections, such as the 'twins' problem (how do twins, who have the same horoscope, have different lives?), and avoided astronomical questions such as precession and the shift of the zodiac signs from the constellations.

It is clear from the Rabbi's questions, which went on to more detailed issues of medical, mundane and natal astrology, that there was no single orthodoxy among astrology's advocates. The debate, which hinged around levels of determinism, was polarized between those who inclined to the Stoic position and thought that stellar influences were absolute and unavoidable, on the one hand, or those who followed a Neoplatonic line and thought that they could be negotiated and the future changed, on the other. To simplify the ancient positions on the individual relationship with the universe, one could either accept a Platonic cosmos that emphasized one's submission to celestial order, or fall in with a primarily Babylonian perspective in which astrology required the daily negotiation of one's destiny. Platonic orderliness was always likely to appeal more to those whose primary allegiance was to the equally ordered cosmology of Genesis, Deuteronomy and Leviticus, but believers in cosmic order themselves fell into two camps: there were those for whom the soul was subject to astrological influences or patterns, and those for whom it wasn't.

Texts such as the *Liber Planetis* and *Beginning of Wisdom* provided a literary basis for the practice of astrology by the end of the twelfth century, but there were also technical requirements. It has been estimated that it could take five hours to calculate a horoscope. However, that assumes that one is working from scratch. This time could be reduced with the use of a device such as the equatorium, which was employed to calculate the positions of the planets. The first equatorium was supposedly made by the Toledan astronomer al-Zarqālī (1028–87).[43] Known in medieval Europe as Arzachel, al-Zarqālī's technical brilliance knew no bounds. He also constructed a 'universal' astrolabe which could be used at any latitude, and a water clock which not only told the time but showed the days of the lunar month. Al-Zarqālī's work was translated into Latin by Gerard of Cremona in the twelfth century, after which the production of equatoria began, and therefore more rapid astrological calculation became possible.

Tables of houses – which contained house positions – and ephemerides – which contained planetary positions, were produced, satisfying a demand fed by the need to cast horoscopes with a minimum of fuss. One major set, the Toledan Tables, were produced by a group of Islamic scholars in Toledo in the second half of the eleventh century. A second set, the Alfonsine Tables, were published in Toledo under the patronage of Alfonso X, appropriately known as 'the Wise', king of Castile, and dated to 1252.[44] That both tables were produced in Spain points to the creative encounter between Islamic, Christian and Jewish scholars that took place there. That the compilers were Jewish – Isaac ben Sid and Judah ben Moses ha-Cohen – is a warning against assuming that scholars worked in isolation, enclosed within the boundaries of their religious affiliations. The tables are also testimony to the extent to which the drive for astronomical accuracy was motivated largely by the needs of astrology. But, more importantly, the tables' diffusion throughout Europe provided the necessary technology for horoscope calculation. Armed with the *Liber* and the Toledan Tables, any aspiring astrologer could begin to predict the future or pronounce on the past.

4

The Thirteenth Century: The Aristotelian Revolution

*Of course, acts of choice and movements of the will are controlled
immediately by God. And human intellectual knowledge is ordered by
God through the mediation of the angels. Whereas matters pertinent
to bodily things, whether they are internal or external, when they come
through the use of man, are governed by God by means of the angels and
celestial bodies.*

THOMAS AQUINAS[1]

The revolutionary consequences of the translations of the twelfth century on European cosmology – and intellectual thought in general – cannot be underestimated. We can compare the wholesale introduction of Aristotelian thought to the impact of later intellectual upheavals such as the combined effect of Galileo's discoveries and Newton's theories in the seventeenth century, or of Marx and Darwin in the nineteenth, and even Freud and Einstein in the twentieth. In each period the scholarly consensus about humanity's relationship with the cosmos altered dramatically, with results that filtered through to the rest of society. We can make the comparison best if we summarize the cosmology of the medieval West from around 500 to 1100. The scriptural demand for faith in God combined with a Platonic belief that all truth was ultimately abstract had resulted in a prevailing scepticism concerning the value of evidence gleaned from the natural world. In this world-view, astrology suffered from the twin obstacles of Platonic scepticism about the value of knowledge based on physical observation of the stars, together with the Church Fathers' denunciation of astrology as demonic. This all changed in the twelfth and thirteenth centuries as new radical doctrines, largely derived from Aristotle, but including strong elements of Neoplatonism, focused scholarly attention on the material world and a cosmos which functioned through interlocking networks of psychic and physical 'sympathies', and in which astrology was to be a means of navigating a course through this sea of influences.

The importance of astrology in this process was profound. It has been convincingly shown that the first exposure to the Aristotelian revolution which was on its way from the Arab world was not though Aristotle's works themselves, but through the Herman of Carinthia's Latin translation of Abu Ma'shar's mighty work of astrological historiography, the *Maius Introductorum*.[2] The effect was compounded by Plato of Tivoli's translation of Ptolemy's masterpiece, the *Tetrabiblos*, with its naturalistic rationale for astrology, in 1138, and Gerard of Cremona's edition of the *Almagest* in 1176. There is a powerful argument, then, that the Aristotelian revolution arrived on the back of a demand for astrological texts. Astrology became part of the curriculum of the rapidly spreading network of cathedral schools and the universities which were emerging at such centres as Paris and, around 1167, Oxford. The character of the liberal arts curriculum was derived from the convenient relationship between two meanings of the Latin word *liber*, the root of such modern terms as library and liberate: to read was the attribute of the classical freeman, to the medieval mind to read was to set one's self free – the twelfth century was to be one of philosophical liberation.

This intellectual revolution in thought in Catholic Europe was fuelled by the rediscovery of the classical Greek texts, especially Aristotle. Curiously, a similar process was taking place in the Orthodox East, where both Plato and Aristotle, having been republished in the ninth century, were eagerly studied in the eleventh and twelfth.[3] The immediate consequence was a revival of interest in both alchemy and astrology and, in the Eastern Roman – Byzantine – emperor Alexius I (1081–1118), we find the first Christian monarch to be known as an enthusiastic user of astrology, an interest which was also pursued by his grandson, Manuel I (1143–80).[4]

In 1100, Aristotle's teachings in the West had been available almost entirely through the limited format of translations and commentaries by Boethius. However, it was Michael Scot's translations of Averroës's editions of and commentaries on Aristotle's *De Coelo* and *De Anima* that brought the works of the master himself into circulation. The result was a direct challenge to the Platonic universe which had been devised by the Church Fathers and which had served its purpose perfectly well since it was given its canonical form by Augustine in the fifth century. Plato's argument that true knowledge was gained from abstract reason rather than experiment complemented Christianity's emphasis on faith, and the latter's doctrine of the Fall found no quarrel with the former's view of humanity as occupying an imperfect world, separated from its perfect creator. Both, of course, were also monotheistic. The prime function of the early medieval cosmos had been to communicate divine meaning to humanity via celestial omens and to enable the organisation of the sacred, liturgical calendar.

In contrast to both Plato and scripture, Aristotle proposed a cosmos which could be understood as an interlocking, orderly network of natural influences, transferred though such means as motion and light. Speaking of the four elements, fire, earth, air and water, which were the building blocks of the cosmos, he wrote in one highly significant passage:

> The whole terrestrial region then is compounded of these four bodies and it is the conditions which affect them which, we have said, are the subject of our inquiry. This region must be continuous with the motions of the heavens, which therefore regulate its whole capacity for movement. For the celestial element as source of all motion, must be regarded as first cause.[5]

For the medieval mind, this was potentially a fairly shocking statement. God, as the first cause of all things, has been replaced by motion, a physical force. True,

Platonic readings of Aristotle conceived of the 'First Mover', the force which initiated all motion, as akin to the remote, conscious, good, supreme creator of Plato's cosmogony, and this was to be a means of making Aristotle acceptable in a Christian context. Even Aristotle conceded that his First Mover, which initiated all motion in the cosmos, was equivalent to the highest divinity of what he called 'the more popular philosophical works'.[6] But Aristotle's raw words speak for themselves: it's not God that rules humanity but the cosmos.

Aristotelian mechanics, with its planetary causes and influences, added a set of laws to the cosmos which, even when God was still nominally in charge as the First Mover, implied a set of processes which could threaten humanity's ability to make moral choices. The issue became a serious one as astrologers began devising rules for calculating whether an individual was likely to be saved. The rules for establishing whether a newborn infant would have faith, and if so, what kind, were set out by Guido Bonatti in the thirteenth century: if the moon, he wrote, was in the ninth house or Mercury was in Libra or Taurus and well-aspected by Venus, the chances of a devout religious practice, and hence of avoiding Hell, were slight.[7] One seventeenth-century text, based on endless repetition and copying since the twelfth century, made the problem plain: 'Shall the Native prove Religious?' – yes if Jupiter, Venus or the Dragon's head are in the ninth house, the individual will be Godly, Honest, Vertuous and Religious.'[8] So, could the poor, mean individual, born under unfortunate stars, ever have a chance of achieving salvation? Humanity's relationship with God therefore became correspondingly more complicated. For the Aristotelian, it was emphatically no longer enough for men and women to live through faith alone, and reason and logic were as important as paths to salvation as were prayer and meditation on the Holy Scriptures. Worse, at least as far as traditionalists were concerned, the revived notion of planetary influence once again brought the soul under the possible sway of the stars, threatening the individual's duty to make free moral decisions, to choose the law of God over the devil. Even if the soul could be excused from celestial influence, the planets' impact on the physical body might still stir up lust and other vices, threatening one's soul with eternal damnation. The question of astrology, apparently settled once and for all by Augustine, was once again central to the theological agenda.

The fatalistic, Stoic tone with which astrological rules were often composed, even when the notion of an astrologically precise fate was explicitly denied, presented an overt challenge to each individual's need to freely seek salvation in Christ. However, the position was far from clear. The seminal discussion on determinism was contained in the *Tetrabiblos* in a passage in which Ptolemy argued that, while the individual is subject to a precise mathematical order and myriad physical and planetary influences, the very fact that one can predict the future only makes sense in a context in which it can be changed.[9] This was especially so in Ptolemy's section on the qualities of the soul in which he documented the consequences if one's soul was ruled by, say, Saturn (austere and thoughtful but mean) or Jupiter (generous, God-fearing and affectionate).[10] Life was surely unfair if the jovial man stood a better chance of salvation than the saturnine on account of his divinely ordained fear of God. True, concepts of the elect, who were bound to be saved, were never far from theological discussion, and were eventually to surface strongly in Calvinism, but to consider an astrologically selected elect was to enter into dangerous territory, even if the planets were doing God's work. If this were not enough, though, the popularity of Macrobius's commentary on Cicero's 'Dream of Scipio' preserved the notion of the Platonic ascent of the soul as a commonplace. From one perspective this was perfectly logical. God ruled in Heaven, and Heaven was in the sky so it was obvious that, to get there, one had to travel through the planetary spheres. However, while Ptolemy and Macrobius might, perhaps, be theologically acceptable by themselves, taken together they represented an explosive mix, threatening the very basis of Church power – its ability to lay down universal moral laws which applied to everyone, regardless of individual disposition. In the astrological religions of the classical world one's character, read in the stars, could chart an appropriate path to salvation. The *Tetrabiblos* contained a mixed message for Christianity: one could negotiate the future, which was not fixed, but one's ability to do so was circumscribed by the condition of the cosmos at the time of one's birth.

A succession of major Aristotelian philosophers behaved as if there was no question of astrology's essential truth. Typical was Robert Grosseteste (c.1168–1253), bishop of Lincoln, one of the first chancellors of Oxford University and a Council Father at the First General Council of Lyons in 1245, who regarded astrology and astronomy as a single discipline, as the 'supreme science', necessary for the understanding of every natural process in the world.[11] His original contribution was to set out an ingenious theory to explain why comets are signs of looming disaster. What happens is this: a position of terrestrial fire is separated from its original location and carried up the celestial spheres, attracted by the virtue of one particular star or planet. The evidence for attraction was found in magnetism, so the theory did have some basis in observation. Now, as the star or planet which has attracted the cometary fire also rules people and objects on the earth, this is a sign of a more general release of spiritual nature and corruption of terrestrial objects. A breakdown in cosmic harmony will therefore be manifested in war, plague and famine in human society. Like Abelard, in fact like all cosmologists, Grosseteste had to reconcile the notion of external influences with the freedom to choose salvation through Christ. Humanity, he argued, was a microcosm, a model in miniature of the cosmos, but he followed Augustine in the *City of God* in proposing that the rational soul is more sublime than the stars and therefore that human beings are not necessarily subject to a celestially ordained fate. Humanity has the ability, as the *Centiloquium* insists, to rise above the stars.

The idea of reason as equivalent to faith, which was introduced largely through the work of the Islamic philosopher Averroes, attracted high-profile supporters, notably two Dominicans: Albertus Magnus (1193–1280) and Thomas Aquinas (c.1224/7–1274). The Dominicans appear to have been interested in astrology, so both men were in agreement with the general direction of thought in their order, if not in the Church as a whole. In 1267 a comet had caught the attention of John of Vercelli, the Order's Master General, and, in view of the various well-known scriptural prophecies of celestial signs and wonders, it was exceedingly important to understand exactly what it might mean.[12] Initially, various learned members of the order put questions directly to Thomas but, in the spring of 1271, John himself intervened and sent 43 questions concerning issues of astral influence to Albertus and Thomas, together with a third member of the order, Robert Kilwardby. Ptolemy, the three scholars knew, had discussed comets briefly but had made it clear that they had to be interpreted in terms of their shape, direction and accompanying planetary configurations,[13] although they were generally regarded as ominous; later Albertus himself was to discuss their significance for war and the death of kings.[14] For the Dominicans, there was no easy solution to a matter of such pressing theological concern. Europe had just experienced one unsettling wave of apocalyptic fervour, prompted by the Franciscan Joachim of Flores's prediction that the current world would come to an end, to be replaced by the spiritual Age of the Holy Ghost, in 1260.[15] The scholarly Dominicans were generally averse to such wild notions, but knew as well as anyone that Christ might return at any moment; to imagine otherwise was to deny God's power to act at will, whenever He chose.

Albertus's stature in the thirteenth century is indicated by the fact that he was given the appellation Magus while he was still alive; every scholar in the Latin West acknowledged his greatness. Born in Lauïngen, in Germany, he studied briefly at Padua, where he first encountered Arab Aristotelianism. He joined the Dominicans in 1223 and became a regent master at Paris from 1242 to 1248, where Aquinas was his most accomplished student. Albertus was deeply influenced by Avicenna, especially by his particularly articulate advocacy of the standard Platonic cosmology of emanation from the One down through levels of reality, including the planetary spheres, down to the earth; each stage was dependent on the one above it and superior to the one below. Aesthetically pleasing as this model was, it set up certain acute cosmological problems: if planetary influences were real, even if subordinate to higher levels of reality, including God, then to what extent did these translate into a workable astrology and, if so, how exact were the judgements that could be made and what were the implications for the human ability to make moral choices? The problem became critical when it extended to the issue of whether Christ himself, through his physical body, was also subject to fate and fortune.[16] Such questions were contained within the bigger and pressing problem of reconciling Aristotelian natural philosophy with Christian theology in order to deal with the schism between conservative and progressive theologians. Indeed, European thought did seem to be moving in two, not always compatible, directions.

As far as Albertus was concerned, there was little problem with the rediscovered classical learning, at least none that couldn't be explained. Neoplatonism, with its doctrine of a living cosmos, solved the problem of celestial movement in a perfectly Christian manner. Albertus's writing on astrology was almost entirely theoretical. Scot and Bonatti set out the details of horoscope interpretation but Albertus contented himself with setting out the general principles of the science, mainly in his major work on the subject, the *Speculum Astronomiae*.[17] Planets, like people, he argued, move because they are animated by soul, a theory which only reinforced his faith in a Christian cosmos.[18] His attitude to astrology was strongly favourable – he regarded it as demonstrably true – but he was loath to accept anything which might impinge on human freedom. Interrogations, with their tendency to seek definitive answers to questions about the future, were therefore suspect. 'The stars', he wrote, 'have the power to alter the elements, to change the complexion of men, to affect human mutations, and moreover, to provoke an inclination to action and even to determine the issue of battles'; to which he later added, 'the stars are never the causes of our actions, indeed we have been made free agents by the Creator and are the masters of our acts'.[19] The stars and planets could therefore have both psychological and physical effects, but none that can't be controlled by the wise and the faithful. In defence of Ptolemy and all Aristotelians he insisted that (in spite of Ptolemy's own words in the *Tetrabiblos*) they never placed the soul under the stars. He adopted the notion of influences as the principal means by which astrology worked, but insisted that the planets were only the deaf and dumb instruments of God's will, transmitting the influence of the First Mover, rather than powers in their own right.[20] The nature of a celestial influence, though, depends on the nature of the object receiving it. In a sense this is quite obvious: a cold object should react differently to a cold influence than would a hot object. No precise predictions are possible precisely because all contingent things, that is, objects and beings lower down the celestial hierarchy, are necessarily uncertain, the evidence for which he found in the *Centiloquium* which, of course, he believed had been written by Ptolemy. This was useful because, even though the *Tetrabiblos* discussed planetary factors on the length of life, Albertus could now argue that spiritual factors, and free will, had to be taken into account alongside the astrological data.[21] He argued that human beings contain a two-fold principle of action, nature and will, the former being ruled by the stars, the latter free from it unless, like children, we have not matured, or, as adults, we surrender to our instincts.

In the *Speculum Astronomiae* Albertus discussed planetary conjunctions and their impact, and how they cause a fluctuation in the four elements, resulting in major accidents and the appearance of prodigies, and how such general indications could be made specific when the influences acted through particular planets and zodiac signs: for example, a conjunction of Mars and Jupiter in Gemini would be responsible for pestilential winds and plague. He was also keen to find rational explanations for pagan superstitions, explaining how the idea that the god Jupiter hurled thunderbolts was a mistake which arose from the fact that the planet of the same name can cause thunderstorms by disturbing the atmosphere. Life is so lavish in equatorial zones, he argued, because the stars' rays fall perpendicularly and more directly, and are therefore more concentrated.

Astrology, though, was more than a matter of divination or study of the natural world: it was operational, a means of managing the world. Albertus spoke approvingly of elections, repeating the old story that the astrologer Nectanebus who, according to legend, was Alexander the Great's real father, chose a moment to impregnate Alexander's mother when the sun was entering Leo and Saturn was in Taurus.[22] And, if Alexander had conquered most of the known world, this was surely evidence of astrology's power. Albertus only held back from conceding that Christ, as a physical man, was influenced by the stars. Instead, he said, Christ possessed grace and knowledge which released him from the stars' power, while the star of Bethlehem was itself a sign, not a source of influence.

In a lesser work, *A Short Discourse on the Nature, and Qualities of the Seven Planets*,[23] Albertus set out the qualities of the planets, their herbs and stones, diseases, days and hours. The moon, for example, ruled Monday, a man's brain and right eye, a woman's left eye and sexual organs, and all cold, wet plants, places and people. The astrological cosmos, though, linked all things in the great chain of being. One could, for example, work with stones, and Albertus summarized the knowledge of the time on their multifarious uses. One can be rendered invisible, he reported, by wrapping a piece of Opthalmus in a laurel or bay leaf; Memphites mixed with water relieves pain while a crystal, held in front of the sun, can be used to start fire.[24] The last example reveals the rationale: a magnifying glass can set paper alight because it concentrates the fire which is found in the sun. There was a logic in such ideas which belies their modern description as magic, with all that word's pejorative connotations. The Aristotelian cosmos was above all rational – it was the product of reason. The significance of Albertus's argument, in terms of the ongoing dialogue between astrology and conservative theology, was that he extended Abelard's limited view of what was and was not astrologically acceptable. The single statement that permitted this to happen was Augustine's acceptance of celestial influences and first Abelard and then Albertus justified more of astrological practice according to natural influences rather than divination. Whereas, for Abelard, most astrology was still divination, for Albertus it was almost all a matter of influence, the star of Bethlehem being an exception to the rule. Judicial astrology as a whole could therefore be classified as non-demonic and its practice legitimised in a Christian context.

It was Albertus's student, the equally brilliant but more influential Thomas Aquinas, who took up his master's cosmology and converted it into the foundation of Catholic philosophy until the seventeenth-century. An aristocratic Italian, Aquinas was born in the castle of Roccasecca in the Kingdom of Naples, into the family of the counts of Aquino, although he was actually brought up in the famous Benedictine monastery at Monte Casino. At the age of 14 he enrolled at the university of Naples, a progressive institution and one of the few universities of the time where a full range of Aristotelian studies were on the curriculum. He joined the Dominicans as a friar, probably when he was 20. According to one account, he was apparently kidnapped and imprisoned by his brothers, who were in Frederick II's army and objected to their brother's religious vocation. Their plan backfired and, while in prison, Thomas studied Aristotle's *Metaphysics*, as well as the theological classic, Peter Lombard's *Sentences*, and emerged as an expert on all aspects of thirteenth-century cosmology. He studied in Paris, then in Cologne under Albertus Magnus, read the Jewish sages, including Maimonides, and returned to Paris in 1251/2. He also taught and debated the new Aristotelian physics in some of the greatest centres of European culture – Orvieto, Rome, Viterbo and Naples – and became the most important evangelist for the revolutionary new world-view. His work was condemned by the Augustinian dominated University of Paris in 1277, in a comprehensive attack on 219 individual items, but in the power-politics of the twelfth-century Church, Aquinas had the natural support of his own order even if others, such as the Franciscans, vehemently opposed him. In 1278, four years after his death, the Dominican General Chapter officially imposed his teachings upon the order. Eventually Aristotelianism, like all radical creeds, lost its revolutionary edge and in 1323 he was canonized. There was one slight problem – he had never performed any miracles. The Pope, John XXII, got around this small difficulty by arguing that every answer Aquinas gave to every theological problem was, in effect, a miracle.

Aquinas' opinions on astrology were expounded in both the *Summa Contra Gentiles* and the *Summa Theologiae*. His views were strongly influenced by Albertus's, and it is actually difficult to find any difference between them, but it was his monumental work rather than Albertus's that became the basis of Catholic thinking. His arguments were set out at great length – they had to be if he was to have any chance of persuading his more conservative colleagues that astrology was acceptable within a Christian context. His solution, simply, was that celestial influences affected the body, which was exactly what St Augustine had conceded, but not the soul, which was directly answerable to God.[25] The soul, though, could be influenced by the body, and so indirectly affected by the planets. The remedy for difficult planetary influences was prayer, virtue and devotion to Christ. Imagine an individual suffering under a difficult influence from Mars. His body may become overheated, the consequence on his mind might be anger and the result violence. In the case of a bad influence from Venus, the sexual organs might be stimulated, sexual desire encouraged and the result might be adultery. In each case the ability to choose is paramount and the faithful Christian will stay on the path of righteousness while the corrupt will stray into sin. Thomas quoted Aristotle, Avicenna and other authorities, but the key statement for astrology was his citation of the *Centiloquium* of Claudius Ptolemy – that 'the wise soul assists the work of the stars'.[26]

Thus, any form of astrology which dealt with the natural world and the consequences of natural disorder or physical passion was permissible as long as it was clearly understood that moral choice was paramount. Medical astrology was acceptable, as was the prediction of war and peace. Actually, of course, medical astrology was indispensable. As David Lindberg said, 'no reputable physician of the later Middle Ages would have imagined that medicine could be successfully practiced without it'.[27] The election of auspicious astronomical moments to inaugurate new enterprises was deemed unacceptable because it impinged on God's providential right to dictate the outcome of events, as was the use of interrogations, the casting of horoscopes to answer precise questions about the future. Natal astrology, which dealt with individual lives, was acceptable inasmuch as it dealt with physical existence but not if it denied moral choice. Stated in simple terms, the formula that Thomas – and Albertus – devised held that the stars (though on God's behalf) rule the body but not the soul, which remains directly answerable to God. And, therefore, astrology and Christ the redeemer were compatible.

In spite of Albertus's and Thomas's stature and monumental contributions to Catholic teaching, let alone the pro-astrology advocacy of men as respected as Robert Grosseteste and Roger Bacon, theological objections to astrology were deeply held and remain so down to the present day. The key to such objections is adherence to Augustine's denunciation of astrology and a resistance to the idea that it can be reclassified as a matter of influences rather than divination. Coordinated opposition to astrology was focused on the condemnations of Aristotelian teachings which were issued regularly in Paris, in 1210, 1215, 1231, 1245 and, most importantly, 1277.[28] The list of 219 items which were denounced in 1277 were mainly individual aspects of Aristotelian cosmology, but the core objection to astrology was that it denied God's unlimited authority. The conservative authors of the 1277 document also ignored the subtleties in the pro-astrology position and it is difficult to avoid the conclusion that the whole dispute was more a question of power politics and, to adapt Thomas Kuhn's term, paradigm shifts.[29] Albertus and Thomas articulated the new paradigm, in which humanity's relationship with God could only be understood in terms of natural, physical connections, and the authorities in Paris identified their own status with a strict adherence to Augustine's cosmology.

The dispute between the anti- and pro-astrology theologians was of direct concern to practitioners such as Guido Bonatti. He felt sufficiently strongly about what he considered to be clerical ignorance to address the matter in his *Liber astronomia*, attacking astrology's critics on the grounds that astrologers know far more about the stars than theologians do about God, 'of whom they none the less preach daily'.[30] Besides, he argued, Abraham had taught astrology to the Egyptians while Christ himself implied the truth of electional astrology when he asked 'are there not twelve hours in the day?', implying that he might seek a more fortunate time to act. Bonatti was stretching his textual interpretation a little too far, but the point is that arguments about astrology's veracity were based almost entirely on theology. The crucial questions concerned such matters as the soul's relationship with the stars or whether scripture condemned or supported the practice of astrology.

The problems of reconciling the contradictions between Aristotle and scripture may have been resolved in principle by Thomas, but too many untidy details remained. The result was a system of theoretical cosmology whose experts were often known as spherists, after the common understanding that both planet earth and the entire universe were, as Aristotle believed, spherical. The classic text was John of Sacrobosco's *Sphere*, whose title reinforces the point that no educated individual in the Middle Ages entertained the idea that the earth was flat.[31] There were various proofs that the world is spherical; the fact that the stars rise in the east earlier than in the west, that the latitude of certain stars increases as one travels from north to south and, most convincingly, the 'sailors proof', based on the simple observation that a mariner on top of a mast can see further than one on the deck.[32] The general style of teaching was the question and answer method, the *questiones*, first found in Alcuin's writings in the eighth century, developed significantly in the *Sentences* of the twelfth century Archbishop of Paris, Peter Lombard (1100–61) and the *Questions on De caolo*, by the German scholar Albert of Saxony (c. 1316–90). Eventually there were about 100 formulaic questions which might be posed by a student in order to elicit a suitable answer from the master.

Astrology's reintroduction into early medieval Europe was an example of a curious sequence of intellectual adaptation. Having been roundly condemned by the Church Fathers as satanic, astrology found a safe host in Aristotelianism which, in turn, was found to be compatible, at least by the progressive thinkers of the time, with Catholic Christianity. For Terry Eagleton, this adaptive skill is the mark of a successful ideology: 'Successful ideologies,' he writes, 'are often thought to render their beliefs natural and self-evident – to identify them with the "common sense" of a society so that nobody could imagine how they might ever be different.'[33] But judicial astrology in the extreme sense – the use of horoscopes to answer any question – never made a successful re-entry into Christian society to the extent that it was entirely unquestioned. It has never reclaimed the position it occupied in Mesopotamia or still holds in India. For the 'ultras', who believe that astrology can solve any problem, astrology as expressed in the use of horoscopes was an all-embracing ideology. But for European society as a whole, even though belief in celestial signs was scripturally sanctioned, and the concept of general planetary influences was universally accepted, judicial astrology has always had to struggle for its position, even at those moments at which it held sway at ecclesiastical and royal courts. The Babylonian astral priesthood survived in Christian culture, but was never institutionally legitimized or officially sanctioned. But, where it did exist, it did so in a direct lineage back to the royal courts of ancient Sumer and the temples of Old Kingdom Egypt.

5

The Thirteenth Century: Practice and Problems

*Judgment must be regulated by thyself, as well as by the science. They only
who are inspired by the deity can predict particulars.*
'CENTILOQUIUM' OF CLAUDIUS PTOLEMY[1]

Much of the flood of information that swept Europe in the twelfth and thirteenth
centuries, mainly from the Islamic world, was theoretical. New ways of seeing
the universe were encouraged, and this was all very exciting for the literate
classes. With no need for supporting evidence, scholars were free to pursue
logical lines of thought to their ultimate conclusion. The consequences sound
more like an account of twentieth-century cosmology than thirteenth. Marcia
Colish understood this perfectly. Her conclusion was that 'medieval logicians and
theologians had made widely thinkable the concept of possible worlds, different
from ours, and had made rigorous thinking about counterfactuals possible.'[2]
It was in this context that Roger Bacon, the brilliant Franciscan friar, began his
radical experiments with the natural world, exploring different ways of seeing the
cosmos.[3] In mechanics, theologians, keen to regulate the ecclesiastical routine, all
the better to harmonize earth with heaven, spent a huge amount of money on
clocks, of which the greatest surviving example was installed at Wells Cathedral,
in the west of England.[4]

There was one other practical consequence of this intellectual ferment: astrology. Philosophers understood that, in the new integrated cosmos preached by
Aristotle, astrology offered a practical means of managing humanity's relationship with the eternal. People at all levels of society saw its benefits. In many cases
it was the philosophers themselves, the scholars who translated the Arabic texts
into Latin, who were the foremost practitioners of astrology. Adelard of Bath,
for example, is the probable author of a set of horoscopes in the British Library
which appear to have been cast on behalf of the young Prince Henry – the future
King Henry II – in the long civil war between his mother, the rightful Queen
Matilda, and King Stephen in the 1130s and 40s.[5] We know that Adelard dedicated
a treatise on the astrolabe, written somewhere between 1142 and 1146, to the
future king, and translated Abu Ma'shar into Latin;[6] between them, the astrolabe
and the text would have provided Adelard with the technical and methodological
means to calculate and read horoscopes, providing advice for his royal patron.
The horoscopes, though, appear to be either cast for the time of important events
and intended to anticipate their outcome, or were interrogations, calculated to
determine the answer to specific questions; one is set for the swearing of allegiance

to King Stephen by the barons, suggesting a desire to know whether this would genuinely strengthen Stephen's position. Another horoscope was cast to answer the question whether a Norman army would come to England: the answer was no and, although an army did come in 1153, the question appears to have been asked two years earlier, in 1151, around the time that Henry was invested as Duke of Normandy by the French king, Louis VII. It would have been natural for an astrologer, perhaps prompted by a powerful political patron, to inquire at this point whether Henry was going to use his enhanced status to strike quickly.

By the early twelfth century four main branches of judicial astrology were recognized, all of which required the calculation of horoscopes. Nativities were cast for the time of birth, interrogations were calculated for the time at which specific questions were asked, and elections were horoscopes computed to establish the most auspicious moment to arrange future events. Revolutions, the fourth branch, were generally cast for the moment at which the sun entered Aries every year, usually on 21 March, and were concerned mainly with political and economic fortunes, the weather and public health for the coming year. One of the most high-profile practitioners of all branches was Michael Scot (c.1135–c.1232), whose subsequent reputation as a magician was enough for Dante to place him in Hell with all the other souls condemned to look backwards for ever as a punishment for prying into the future: 'That other one, whose thighs are scarcely fleshed, was Michael Scot, who most assuredly knew every trick of magic fraudulence.'[7] Scot translated Aristotle's De Coelo and De Anima, along with Averroës's commentary on them, and also worked as personal astrologer to the Holy Roman Emperor Frederick II.[8] Frederick's court in Sicily provided as convenient a physical connection between the Christian and Islamic worlds as Spain – Scot had previously studied at Toledo – and a direct route for radical ideas which were to prove profoundly disturbing to conservative Christian theology. Scot had adopted, most likely from Avicenna, Neoplatonic ideas of a living universe inhabited by celestial intelligences, including planetary spirits. This was not so far from the standard Christian cosmos, populated by angels and demons, except in the sense that, in the Platonic tradition, the entire natural and supernatural universe was itself ensouled and alive. It was this Platonic learning which provided the context for the fundamentals of magical practice outlined in the Picatrix. Even though this was not translated into Latin until 1256, the attitudes and practices it represented entered Catholic Europe in the 1100s. In particular, the magician, in order to manipulate celestial virtues, powers and sympathies, should 'have faith in his procedures, put himself unto an expectant and receptive mood, be diligent and solicitous' and, often, resist sexual temptation and practise chastity.[9] It was this tradition to which Scot belonged.

Scot's great work was his Liber introductorius, an introduction to the cosmos that begins with an account of the creation which is at once Aristotelian and scriptural. The world is created in six days but God is also the First Mover and First Cause, the ruler not just of the soul, but of the mechanics that keep the universe in motion. From this premise, it was self-evident to Scot, as it was to most of his fellow Aristotelians, that astrology was an effective way both of analysing the nature of celestial influences and of using them to maximum advantage. One might disagree on the detail, but of the principle there was no question. Scot was one of those who had no qualms about astrology's delicate theological position and followed every detail of its rules and regulations handed down via the Arabic texts. This is actually not as problematic as it seems: Christian denunciations repeatedly equated astrology with divination, so all one had to do was justify it according to Augustine's admission that celestial influences are real. At a stroke, astrology is no longer divinatory, it is natural philosophy and so no longer subject to prohibition.

Of particular interest was Scot's use of constellations, which offered an additional frame of references to the zodiac signs. The detail and the moral implications of one's birth fate were apparent. The baby born under the constellation of Draco, for example, is not to be envied: he or she will 'be an evil person, such as invidious, seducer, a litigant, quarrelsome, scornful . . . a vagabond and pauper'; under Cassiopeia, on the other hand, life will begin well, 'handsome, luxurious, rich, of comfortable life' but end badly – 'in an evil death'.[10] The medieval conception of time one encounters in the work of a man like Scot is one in which each moment has significance, but in a way that may differ sharply from the preceding hour, day or year. Such moments are also closely related to space in that it's the constantly changing relationships of the planets to one another as viewed from the earth that provide a guide to the incredibly complex, interlocking and constantly shifting qualities of time. As Plato said, the planets are the keepers of time.[11]

Scot condemned the use of magic, as one had to in order to avoid censure from conservative churchmen, but by this he meant ritual and demonic magic, not the sympathetic variety – the manipulation of the subtle sympathies which connected all things. It's partly due to his advocacy of such practices, combined with his role as adviser to the greatest European ruler of the time, that Scot became known as a powerful wizard. Stories were told about his command of the invisible world, as when he summoned guests to a banquet only to sit them down at an empty table. Once they were all seated, Scot, it was reported, summoned a series of demons, carrying marvellous dishes personally sent by the kings of France, Hungary and other European countries, overawing his guests with his power over supernatural forces.

It is difficult to estimate Scot's actual influence. The profile of his patron and client, Frederick, was greater than any other European monarch: he controlled much of Germany and Italy, and was crowned king of Jerusalem, the Holy City, in 1228. We have little surviving evidence concerning any political or military advice that Scot might have provided for Frederick, even though he wrote extensively on 'elections', so certainly had the skill required to arrange key events in the emperor's life. The problem for historians is that astrological advice was scarcely ever committed to writing. It was usually delivered verbally, leaving no direct testimony as to the extent of its use. We are told that Frederick refused to consummate his marriage with Isabella, wife of the English King Henry III, until his astrologer – we don't know if this was Scot – gave the word, but not whether he ever asked for advice on the actual timing of an audience or battle. Scot appears to have accompanied Frederick to the Holy Land in 1228–9, so we can assume he was advising Frederick on military matters as well as on his treaty with the Saracens, which was to bring the sixth crusade to a successful conclusion. Scot himself gives us a number of examples of rebellions on which he offered advice. In the first instance, Frederick was faced with a rebellious city and asked Scot to provide a prognosis.[12] Setting the horoscope for the time that Frederick asked Scot for his advice, the astrologer followed the rules of interrogations. The basic procedure was actually more simple than it sounds and, once the horoscope had been calculated, which would have been the laborious part of the exercise, Scot would have identified the relevant planets at a glance. Aries was rising, so Frederick was ruled by Mars, Aries' ruling planet, which was, in turn, in Cancer, along with Venus. He read this Mars–Venus conjunction as giving victory to Frederick on the grounds that Mars, being a warlike planet, would overwhelm peaceful Venus; the rebels, in short, would have no heart for a fight. The curious feature about this reading is that Mars, representing the imperial army, was actually weak in Cancer.[13] We have to assume that Scot either overlooked this at the time, or ignored it as an inconvenience when explaining the horoscope as a retrospective case study. Or perhaps he made a political decision, believing either that Frederick had to be encouraged to crush the rebellion, or calculated that the imperial forces were so strong that victory was assured. Perhaps he reinforced Frederick's position with a little sympathetic magic, which he chose not to describe.[14] Whatever the case, Mars's location in Cancer was so fundamental to the reading of the chart that we can only assume that Scot's account of his work was economical with the truth. Or, alternatively, we have a classic example of judicial astrology, in which the astrologer's judgement, based in the messages communicated by the planets, was more important than blind obedience to cosmic order.

Our knowledge of the astrological rules of war owes much to the writings of Guido Bonatti, another of the astrologers summoned by Frederick II.[15] Bonatti, who was born around 1210, was the best known astrologer of his time – indeed, one of the most famous astrologers in European history. He was sufficiently notorious in some circles to be placed by Dante alongside Scot in the fourth division of the eighth circle of the Inferno, with those spirits who were condemned to look backwards forever as a punishment for trying to pry into the future in life.[16] He seems to have been a professor at Bologna in his middle years, but his real significance lies in his reputation as the first high-profile astrological practitioner in Europe to have had no part in either translating Arabic texts or teaching, commenting on or propagating Aristotelian or Neoplatonic cosmology. He was a professional astrologer pure and simple. His enduring legacy was his comprehensive textbook, the *Liber introductorius ad iudicia stellarum*, also known as the *Liber astronomicus* or *Liber Astronomiae*,[17] which was still a classic 200 years later; Henry VII of England possessed a deluxe edition in the 1490s. A volume of his aphorisms – a facsimile of the 1886 edition of the 1676 translation – was republished in England in 1986, a sign, perhaps, of an enduring fascination with his work.[18] The work opens with a classic statement of medieval psychology and Aristotelian cosmology with Christian faith. The astrologer, Bonatti wrote, should consider the psychological condition which prompted the questioner to consult the astrologer, as well as their free will in doing so, and then 'with a devout spirit, pray unto the Lord' for guidance.[19] For Bonatti, as for Ptolemy, in a cosmos in which all things are interconnected it is obvious that the rules of astrology can only ever provide part of the answer, and must be interpreted within a context in which, as a Christian, the final solution always lies with God. Astrology is not, indeed cannot, be an absolute system and uncertainty can creep in from any level in the Chain of Being, from God's unlimited power to change the future, to human error. For example, no horoscope cast for an 'interrogation' will give a correct answer when the questioner 'is so silly that he knows not how to ask'; the situation is even worse when people go to an astrologer for amusement, or to test him, 'just as the Jews propounded questions to our Lord Jesus Christ, not so much to be resolved, as to tempt and ensnare him'.[20] Under such circumstances there could be no answer: if the question is not genuine then the astrological inquiry is doomed from the outset. Once again – and this is a point we need to emphasize – the rhetoric of astrology inclined very much to the Neoplatonic model in which the cosmos was subject to a predetermined order, but the soul was free to choose.

Bonatti's comparison of astrologers to Christ sounds somewhat arrogant, a flaw which, no doubt, encouraged Dante to consign him to Hell, but his obvious irritation at clients who had come to consult him for a joke lends a human touch to his otherwise dense technical work. He went on to elaborate the other complex astrological factors which might prevent an accurate answer: the astrologer may also err 'when the Lord of the Ascendant and the Lord of the Hour are not the same, nor of the same Triplicity, or not be of the same Complexion with the Ascendant'.[21] The precise technical meaning of this sentence is less important than the sense that, unless all the wheels of the great celestial machine were synchronized, the voice of God would not be clearly heard. These days we would know this as a feedback loop: the astrologer acts, the cosmos responds and the astrologer can then recommend a different course. Such complex rules, of which these are only a part, may have emerged as a result of the frequency with which the astrologers were wrong; each time they had to establish a reason for their error so that, next time, they would know whether an accurate reading was likely. A horoscope which fulfilled all the criteria and might be read by the astrologer was known as radical. Although the interpretative procedures had become far more complex, the principle is essentially the same as the Babylonian assumption that a celestial observation did not necessarily constitute an omen. From a pragmatic perspective, such rules might mean that there were whole sections of the day when astrology simply did not work, except – and here is where things become curious – it was astrology itself which revealed that it could not work.

The astrologer's job would also be made easier by the possibility that there would be periods of several hours, even of days, when the answer to most questions might either be a simple 'yes' or 'no'.

We know from contemporary chronicles that Bonatti was involved with Guido de Montefeltro, count of the northern city of Urbino from 1255 to 1286, in the defence of the town of Forli against Pope Martin IV in 1282. We also have his own accounts of three other incidents, including two concerning a struggle between Florence and Lucca. Montefeltro was prominent in the factional infighting that dominated relations between the Italian city states in the thirteenth century and Bonatti apparently advised him on strategy in line with rapidly moving astrological considerations. On one occasion, Montefeltro, 'captain of the people of Forli, together with lord Guido Bonatti, a citizen, philosopher and most eminent astrologer, having called the people in the public square',[22] set out a plan in which the local forces were to stage a mock retreat and then take the enemy unawares once they had entered the town, and were exhausted from drinking and feasting. The plan worked and Bonatti received most of the credit for his skill in forecasting and timing. Whether the use of astrologers by competing armies was more widespread than this, though, we cannot say. Astrological advice, being designed to gain a strategic advantage, would necessarily have been secret and rarely committed to writing, so there are, quite simply, no sources. The nearest modern equivalent is the lack of any detail of the advice provided to US President Ronald Reagan by his astrologer, Joan Quigley.[23]

The Church was never to have a single policy on astrology, which is hardly surprising for, beyond the need to find salvation through Christ, medieval Christianity was marked by its diversity as much as common themes. In this sense the debates of the early Church reappeared, along with the revival of classical philosophy, chiefly the works of Aristotle. These only added to the diversity that had marked the Church since the first century, in spite of all efforts to achieve uniformity since Constantine. Bonatti was attacked by clerics, to whom he responded contemptuously that he knew more about the stars than his accusers did about God, but also appears to have had ecclesiastical clients who consulted him on their chances of promotion. However, while astrology could be either supported or condemned by the scriptures, depending on which passages one turned to for support, the Aristotelian translations added an entire new complication, adding powerful support for its practice from a pagan whose monotheism made him difficult to dismiss. Aristotelian astrology was a matter of divinely originated natural causes and influences with no requirement for demons, ritual magic or any other practice which might lead to eternal damnation.

The Franciscan Friar Roger Bacon (1214–94) was one of Robert Grosseteste's great publicists but went on to achieve much greater fame, achieving a reputation, similar to Michael Scot, as a great magician, or, more recently, as a father of modern experimental science.[24] He was prepared to go further than Grosseteste in accepting the full implications of the Aristotelian cosmos. He strongly condemned magic, but advocated the power of words, one of the keys to a successful operational magic. Words, as much as anything, are part of the web of sympathies that connect the entire cosmos, and a word spoken by a man in touch with his rational soul will receive the virtues of the sky and have the power to affect and heal the world. Bacon pushed astrology into potentially dangerous realms by suggesting that it had a role in the unfolding religious history of humanity. He provided a theological justification, it is true, which is that God matched terrestrial events to their celestial equivalents in order to increase the sense of wonder at the heavens, and ultimately love for him. This is precisely what God was doing when he sent the star of Bethlehem. However, he went further than this, and argued that, as a physical man, Jesus himself was subject to the stars, and that Catholic faith should recognize this. From Abu Ma'shar and Masha'allah he adapted the notion that religions themselves rise and fall in line with the Jupiter–Saturn cycle, in which each of the other six planets formed significant conjunctions with Jupiter which then defined the nature of the corresponding religion.[25]

> Jupiter conjunct Saturn = Judaism
> Jupiter conjunct Mars = Chaldean Religion
> Jupiter conjunct Sun = Egyptian Religion
> Jupiter conjunct Venus = Islam
> Jupiter conjunct Mercury = Christianity
> Jupiter conjunct Moon = Antichrist

The sequence is listed according to the distance of planets from the earth, beginning with Saturn, the furthest, down to the moon, the closest, and does contain an internal logic: the Jewish Sabbath is on Saturday, the Islamic holy day on Friday (Venus's day) and the Egyptians' supreme deity was the sun. Bacon was pleased that Christianity was associated with Mercury, lord of wisdom, oracles and prophecies, and Hermes Trismegistus, 'Hermes Mercurius, the father of philosophers'.[26] The planet Mercury, he wrote, was ruler of Virgo, the constellation of the Virgin, while its unpredictable orbit reminded him of the way in which the mysteries of Christianity defy understanding. The theological difficulty with such a system, naturally, was its assumption that Christianity was both tied to astrological patterns and of limited duration. The strength was its demonstration that Islam was bound to come to an end in 1315, 693 years after the Hejira – a number suitably close to the number of the beast in Revelation 13.17–18, which Bacon stated wrongly was 663 rather than 666. However, for Bacon such speculation was just the beginning of the exercise. He proposed a full scale use of astrology in order to manage society from the individual level through to affairs of state. Astrological images which, just like a newborn baby, absorb the celestial influences at the moment they are made, should be combined with elections – the use of auspicious moments – to maximize human society's harmonious connections with the cosmos. Astrology, properly used for individual purposes, could shepherd the faithful through life from the cradle to the grave. On the global scale, Roger recommended that the papacy use astrologers to forecast the coming of the antichrist, which, at a time when the Mongols were threatening Eastern Europe, was a matter or urgency.

Our earliest surviving account of the Persian astrological theories of world history espoused by Roger Bacon had been written down by Masha'allah, a Jew who was born in Basra, in modern Iraq, around 740 and died in 815. In the course of his life, Masha'allah composed around 25 astrological texts, a number of which were to become standards in medieval Europe, where he was known as Messahala. At the age of 22 he worked on the astrological foundation of Baghdad and he also seems to have lived at Harran, home of the Sabians, surviving heirs to the planetary religion of Babylon. The theory of Jupiter–Saturn cycles and historical epochs was set out in his *On Conjunctions, Religions and Peoples*, in which he related the astronomical pattern to socio-political and religious shifts which occurred every 240 years, and the periodic conflagrations or catastrophes, such as Noah's flood, which were thought to take place every 960 years.[27]

The fundamental premise was that the nature of any Jupiter–Saturn conjunction, on which was based its use as a forecasting mechanism, was indicated by the horoscope cast for the preceding spring equinox, the date every year when the sun entered Aries. The apparent logic was that, at this moment, a new cycle of time began, within which all possibilities for that cycle were contained. Masha'allah included the horoscopes for the spring equinoxes preceding the Jupiter–Saturn conjunctions prior to the great deluge (it was believed that the rains which caused the flood began at midnight precisely, on 18 February 3101 BCE, with a conjunction of planets in Pisces, appropriately the last of the 'water' signs) and the births of both Christ and Mohammed. These were, naturally, fortunate horoscopes. They could hardly be anything else. However, both were Saturnine, and Saturn, Masha'allah reminds us, indicated 'general misery and violence'.[28] In Scorpio, the sign of the Arabs, this pointed to Mohammed's death in the East, but the chart was saved by an exalted, benevolent, Venus in Pisces, a counter-indication which revealed the Arabs' essential strength. Masha'allah's work was potentially heretical, suggesting that God's plan was subject in some way to mathematically regulated planetary cycles. His God, though Jewish, was also the supreme mind of the Neoplatonic philosophers, whose divinity was revealed in his devotion to a somewhat mathematical, bureaucratic, cosmic order. Political changes are permitted a quarter way through the cycle, around every 240 years, while great prophets appear when the cycle is complete: every 960 years a new prophet appears.[29] Of course, nothing could be so exact, and Mohammed and Christ were separated by only 600 years. All the same, the structure of planetary cycles acted as an ideal, fixed framework within which God could act. Yet the tension between two competing cosmologies is obvious: could God, or the gods, act spontaneously, as theology decreed, or were they bound by mathematical order? The solution worked out by devout Jews, Christians and Moslems was that the order itself was created by God and was subject to him. But, as soon as one drifts towards the Platonic cosmos, we enter heretical terrain on which moral choice, and so the prospect of individual salvation, is precisely ordered. For

Masha'allah, God might be free to send prophets whenever he wishes, but those wishes just happen to coincide with the multiples of the 20-year Saturn–Jupiter cycle. There is a further heresy evident in such thinking, and that is a kind of religious relativism which teaches that, while God's Truth may be absolute, the truths that any prophet, including Mohammed, teaches, are provisional, and likely to be superseded by his successor.

Masha'allah's work was repeated and developed by many imitators, of whom the most illustrious was Abu Ma'shar. His *Introduction to the Science of the Judgement of the Stars*, known in the Middle Ages as the *Maius Introductorum* (Greater Introduction) was translated into Latin by Herman of Carinthia in 1140. For those who were unable or unwilling to read the entire work, Abu Ma'shar thoughtfully composed an *Abbreviation* of the *Introduction*, which was translated into Latin by Adelard of Bath in the early twelfth century.[30] Every European scholar from the late twelfth to the sixteenth century would have known his name and considered his view of history to be more or less accurate. They may have disputed the detail, but the notion that God's plan unfolded in line with long-term planetary cycles was broadly accepted as a given.

Like the teachings on Jupiter–Saturn conjunctions, the philosophy of medieval astrology was also imported from the Islamic world, and was found in two texts in particular, the *Centiloquium of Claudius Ptolemy* and the *Emerald Tablet of Hermes Trismegistus*. The *Centiloquium*, which contained the pithiest and most telling statements of astrological philosophy, was actually composed in the mid-tenth century by the philosopher Ahmet Abu Ja'far, known in Latin Europe as Abugafarus, in his *Kitab al-Thamara* or *Book of the Fruit*.[31] The English translation of 1679 records the spirit of Abu Ja'far's cosmology with the following words: '*Sapiens*, a wise Man doth Co-operate with the Coelestial Operations, and doth assist Nature, as the Husbandman in the ploughing and preparing his Ground'.[32] The simpler formula is 'the wise man rules his stars, the fool obeys them' or, as one sixteenth-century English version had it, 'One skilful in this Science may evade many effects of the Stars, when he knows their Natures, and diligently prepares himself to receive their effects.'[33] Or, as the *Corpus Hermeticum* put it, 'Those men who are devoid of mind are merely led along in the train of Destiny.'[34] True, one had to understand the natural universe: 'None can know the Mixtures of the Stars, unless he first know their Natural differences and mixtures one with another,' the *Centiloquium* insisted.[35] But there was a complete understanding that the astrologer, like all people, stood within the system and that even the reading of a horoscope or election of auspicious times is conditioned by the astrologer's own emotional state, moral condition and relationship with the stars.[36] These views were consistently reinforced by other influential astrologers, by Guido Bonatti, for example, in the thirteenth century, and Jerome Cardan in the fifteenth.[37] There is absolutely no question that, in the hands of astrology's leading practitioners and theoreticians, it was not deterministic. Quite the opposite. Above all, it was participatory, a matter of the astrologer's active engagement with the cosmos. Bonatti's first two considerations made the point, establishing the following preconditions for a successful horoscope reading: the client's mental condition and motive should be considered separately to any question of celestial influence; the fact that they have free will should be acknowledged; and the astrologer should first pray and then approach the reading with the utmost sincerity.[38] A charlatan, like a magician with less than worthy motives, would be unsuccessful. We come back, then, to the commercial imperative: financial success required a devout relationship with God and a respectful attitude to the client.

The formula had been codified in the *Centiloquium*, from where it was to become the ideological basis of practical astrology in the Islamic world – and in the Christian West from the twelfth to the seventeenth centuries. In the sixteenth-century English version, the first paragraph insisted that 'it is impossible that the Artist should foresee the particular Idea of things; neither can Sense receive a particular, but a general notion of the sensible matter; wherefore he ought in these things to use Conjecture, for none but one inspired, can predict particulars'.[39] In other words, the appearance of precision in a work like *Liber Astronomiae* was a mirage: the astrologer's inability to speak the absolute truth, let alone reconcile the internal contradictions which would inevitably arise from such complex rules, required that personal judgement must overrule technical determinism. Astrology alone, without divine intervention, can only identify future trends, and point to possibilities which may or may not come to pass. The *Centiloquium* continued with two other pieces of classic Neoplatonism, one to be expected, the other radical in its implications. The first was that the horoscope always derives from a question in the astrologer's mind ('What is this child's fate?', 'What is the outcome of this enterprise?') which itself originates in a Platonic Idea.[40] That is, the astrologer is connected to the *Nous*, or God perceived as a supreme mind, the cosmos as consciousness. The second was that, if all things are connected by a web of sympathies then so are astrologers and both their clients and topic of inquiry.[41] If an astrologer was engaged in a historical inquiry, as was Mash'allah, then his own horoscope should contain some of the same patterns as he might expect to find in his historical examples and, if a client with a Saturnine problem visits an astrologer then, according to the theory, that astrologer should have similar configurations in his horoscope. The astrological inquiry itself is then embedded in a larger astrological process and the encounter between astrologer, question and client is always purposeful and redolent with meaning. Ultimately, the appearance of determinsm in the textbooks on astrological delineation was purely because astrology works in an inevitable sense only for those who are dominated by their emotional souls, and who have never developed their rational souls. This was the Aquinian formula as articulated by Jerome Cardan in the fifteenth century: 'Men may be said almost to be compelled by the Stars, even in voluntary actions, by means of their corrupt affections and ignorance.'[42] In other words, the accuracy of individual astrological forecasts can only be guaranteed for the venal, the uneducated and the stupid. Forecasts made for the self-aware and those close to the Divine would be inherently uncertain. The astrological texts therefore have to be read within this context as a genre of literature directed at a particular segment of the population – even if it constituted the vast majority.

The professional astrologers could offer their clients a wide range of subjects, commenting on almost any matter except, of course, questions of eternal salvation. Judicial astrology constituted what we would now call a meta-narrative, a complete package by which one could give order to one's life, arranging the present and planning the future. We have to remember, though, that there was no boundary between the inner and outer worlds; the mind–body split which has so profoundly shaped modern Western culture lay in the present. Thoughts, feelings and emotions were as real as physical events and sensations.

In a world in which few people knew their date of birth, and virtually nobody their time of birth, it was easiest for all concerned for the astrology to use interrogations, horoscopes cast for the moment that the client asked a question. It was also much easier to reach a definite judgement on any matter using interrogational charts, rather than from natal charts. The rules of interrogations allowed the astrologer to focus much more clearly on the fundamental issues, and there were many cases when the astrologer might reach a definite 'yes' or 'no' answer in a matter of minutes, as long as the question was phrased simply. Common questions included the outcome of any sort of enterprise, but could also include financial prospects including, in the days before banks, the location of hidden or buried money, and matters affecting personal relationships, including paternity matters (a husband, for example, might wish to establish whether he was the father of his wife's child). Such issues could often be resolved with a fairly simple reading of the horoscope. Each area of activity was linked to a particular house of the horoscope: money to the second, siblings and short journeys to the third, and so on. The planet ruling the zodiac sign on the cusp of the relevant house became the key to the answer. That planet's 'condition', its strength or weakness, could be established by examining its location by zodiac sign and house. The planet's aspects, or relationships with the other celestial bodies, might then elaborate on the prospects for success and offer a possible timing measure. For example, if a client was to ask a question about whether she should undertake a short journey, the astrologer would look to the third house. If the cusp of that house was in Taurus, ruled by benevolent Venus, a positive answer might be indicated. If Venus was in Libra, which it rules, and in a harmonious trine aspect with helpful Jupiter, the answer would almost certainly be 'yes'. There would, of course, be other factors to weigh up, but this gives an idea of the basic procedure. Depending on the complexity of the situation the astrologer might also give a qualified answer, advising the client to undertake certain actions to strengthen their position. It made sense to focus on questions at a time when few people had any idea of their date or time of birth. Besides the mathematical demands on the astrologer were far less; if the astrologer was seeing several clients an hour, he might have a notebook with blank horoscopes waiting to be filled in. Aside from the moon, the planetary positions would vary little, if at all, during the course of a day, while the ascendant and house positions could be updated with the aid of tables. In such cases it would take only a minute to update a horoscope. There might also be periods of several hours when the answer to any question might be 'yes', even if the answer was qualified, and other periods when the astrologer's response might be a definitive 'no'. For example, if the moon was about to make an opposition (was on the other side of the zodiac) to the 'malefic' planets Mars or Saturn (or worse, both), the result would almost certainly be negative. The only question which might elicit a positive answer in such circumstances would be 'Will my plan fail?' Equally, if the moon was approaching a positive aspect to the benevolent planets Venus and Jupiter, which it might do for several hours, the tendency would always be for a positive answer. It was even possible that the astrologer would be unable to read a chart, and that this information would be revealed in the horoscope. Some of the astrological rules pointing to an unreadable horoscope might be in place for under an hour. But one, which was active when the moon was in the so-called Via Combusta, between the middle of Libra and the middle of Scorpio, could prevent any horoscope being used to answer a question for between two and two and a half days.[43] Rules were set out for the question of whether a brother, sister or neighbour shall love each other or, at least, agree. It was the state of mind that mattered, not the physical event and the assumption was that the stars affect the psyche directly; professional astrologers were required to perform services for the clients and could not observe the conservative theologians' delicate claim that the planets influenced the body but not the soul. The theologians were paid by the Church or by their universities. Astrologers had to satisfy a market. This, at least, was the public face. Yet, in the texts they wrote for each other, it is clear that the astrologers regarded themselves as in a free negotiation with the divine as much as did any Babylonian astrologer.

Among those texts from the Islamic world that were to form the centrepiece of later astrological thought, the shortest, and perhaps most influential, was known in the West as the *Tabula Smaragdina*, or *Emerald Tablet*.[44] Originally, it was part of a longer text, the *Kitab Sirr al-Asar*, a respected book of advice to kings probably written about the year 800 and attributed to Aristotle, at least in its later, Latin version, the *Secreta Secretorum*.[45] Some authorities have thought it may have been written in the year 650, or even 400, and includes influences from as far east as China. Legend records that it was originally composed by Hermes himself and later discovered by Sara, wife of Abraham, the Hebrew patriarch. According to the story, when the tablet was found, it was clutched in the hands of the corpse of Hermes himself. The tablet's crucial lines 'That which is above is from that which is below, and that which is below is from that which is above, working the miracles of one, As all things were from one,' are cited to this day as a rationale for astrology in the simplified form 'as above, so below' – as in the sky so on earth. A popular series of astrology books in the 1970s were even marketed under this title.[46]

The *Emerald Tablet* provided the rationale for alchemy, one of astrology's most practical applications. The physical process involved in alchemical work was typically the attempt to transmute lead into gold, but the real goal was union with the divine, of which the gold was the material embodiment. Alchemy may, on occasion, have appealed to greed, but it was essentially a means of engineering the soul's union with the One, or the stars, if one prefers, and provided an alternative to other means, including ritual magic or scholarly enlightenment. In this sense, it is comparable to yoga, as what Mircea Eliade called a technique for the escape from time, or 'halting the temporal flux': by working with time and matter one eventually transcends it.[47] The first great Islamic exponent was the legendary Jabir ibn Hayyan (721–c.815), known to medieval Europeans, for whom he was the great master, as Geber.[48] Alchemy's cosmological context was provided by the relationship between metals and planets, so the chemical process could only take place in collaboration with the heavenly bodies.[49] The alchemist took the theory of correspondence, or sympathies, and set out to manipulate it for the common good, chiefly through medicine.

However, the true radical significance of the *Emerald Tablet*'s words is the first part of the phrase, 'That which is above is from that which is below'. In other words, events here on earth shape the heavens as much as those in heaven influence the earth. These words, almost completely forgotten by historians of ideas, hold the key to centuries of scientific and intellectual endeavour in the Islamic and, later, the Christian worlds. They are the philosophical foundation of the magical tradition and the assumption that human action, carried out in the right spirit, can affect the heavens in a physical sense and, in spiritual terms, can feed back to the One, to the Creator. Not only can humanity shape the cosmos but, if the attempt is successful, it becomes a path straight back to God. Indeed, the practice of magic could be seen as an absolute requirement of the true seeker after salvation. This was not new, of course. The *Emerald Tablet*'s sentiments echo those of the Babylonian *Diviners Manual*, which held that the 'signs on earth just as those in the sky give us signals. Sky and earth both produce portents though appearing separately, they are not separate [because] sky and earth are related.'[50] The phrase survived into the sixteenth century, when the astronomer Tycho Brahe adopted the motto 'By looking up I understand what is below,'[51] and the twentieth century: a recent introductory text defined astrology as 'the experience and interpretation of correspondence between the natural and human worlds below and the heavens above'.[52]

The astrologer was therefore very far from being a disinterested observer, a detached practitioner capable of giving neutral, objective advice, even if that was what his patrons required. He was, instead, an integral part of the cosmic process, capable, on account of his own relationship to that process, of discerning variations in the divine plan and offering helpful advice about possible future developments.[53] In spite of the astrologers' constant genuflection to Christian orthodoxy, there is a clear sense in which they constituted an alternative, clearly Gnostic, priesthood that offered practical advice based on direct knowledge of the heavens. Conservative theologians could insist that only God could know the future, an essentially useless proposition for people who need to know what course of action, precisely, they should take. Astrologers, on the other hand, could offer precisely this kind of practical service.

While it was prediction that aroused criticism of astrology from religious conservatives, forecasting the future was only a part of the astrological project. Astrology's most important function was to manage the present and change the future, a goal which could be achieved through magic, by which we mean the manipulation of the sympathies, rays and correspondences recognized by the Islamic Neoplatonists Al Kindi and Avicenna.[54] These theoretical models found their practical expression in a work known as the *Ghayat al-Hakim* (the Aim of the Wise), composed in Andalucia around the year 1000. Translated into Latin in 1256 by the Castilian monarch Alfonso the Wise, it was known in medieval Europe as the *Picatrix*, and was to be the key text of magical astrology until the seventeenth century. The *Picatrix* provided a direct line of transition for Islamic Hermeticism, and hence for Babylonian celestial deities, direct into the thirteenth-century Christian West. Once the required invocation of Allah had been completed, the text began with a standard formulation of Neoplatonic cosmology: all things derive from the One, the most important human attribute is wisdom, and wisdom itself lies in knowing the reasons for the existence of things which derive from the One. All things being derived from the One, exist in relation to each other, and those relations may be close or distant, sympathetic or hostile. Magic is defined simply as 'everything that absolutely fascinates minds and attracts souls by means of words and deeds.'[55] In other words, it's the attempt to change the world by actively engaging with the sympathies that link everything, including words, thoughts, objects, plants, animals, planets, angels – literally everything. These aims can be achieved through sound, through music and incantations, through words and images written down or inscribed. In Christian terms, a Gregorian chant becomes a magical incantation designed to keep the cosmos functioning, while the Mass is an overtly magical ritual in which the bread and wine are converted into the body and blood of Christ. The central tool of such magic was the talisman, a 'spirit within a body'.[56] The talisman was a physical object designed to possess the sympathy, or even the life-force, for want of a better term, of a larger slice of the Chain of Being. The astrological component enters the magical process through the manipulation of the qualities of time, as represented by the zodiac and planets. An effective talisman should take into account the planet most relevant to the sympathies or correspondences which need manipulating and be constructed when that planet is strong, at its hour, on its day and out of a substance it rules. A Venusian talisman, which might be made to enhance a love affair or soothe a fever, would have been be made out of copper, Venus's metal, on Friday (Venus's day), after dawn (the first hour on Friday was ruled by Venus), when Venus was in a sympathetic part of the zodiac, such as Taurus or Libra (the signs it ruled) and making good aspects to other planets. One talisman was made to ensure permanent love according to the following instructions:

make two talismans in an ascendant of good luck when the moon and Venus are in Taurus. In the first picture draw 220 numbers of thousands or zeros and draw in the second picture 284 numbers also of thousands or zeroes. Then make them embrace one another and bury them in the location of one of them and permanent love and strong affection will ensue.[57]

As there are only a few days in the year when both Venus and the moon are both in Taurus, patience was required. Talismans could be made to perform any function, to attract people or drive them away, to achieve prosperity or power, even to catch more fish. For this, make a picture of a fish in the moon's hour (the first hour after dawn on Monday, the second on Tuesday and so on), while the moon and Mercury are both rising in the first part of Pisces;[58] we are assured that this exercise was personally tested by the great philosopher al-Khwarizmi. On the largest scale the magical manipulation of cosmic harmonies was embodied in the sacred dimensions used to design and decorate mosques.[59] The range of actions in which the astrological rituals enshrined in the *Picatrix* could ensure success, encompassed pretty much everything of concern to a powerful individual in the medieval world, from attaining the woman of one's dreams, to obtaining an influential post, making money from trade, winning battles or improving or, alternatively, destroying a city. We see an early alternative form of marriage guidance ('a talisman for permanent love'), political management ('a talisman for the people to support a governor of a town whose population turned against him'), physical health ('a talisman for the treatment of a scorpion bite') and mental well-being ('a talisman to treat a certain person from depression until he recovers completely').[60]

If magic is the deliberate attempt to change the future then all astrology which moves beyond a simple prediction into any sort of action must be considered magical. And in this context astrological texts were more than a manual for astrological prediction, of use to those whose attitude to life was passive and fatalistic. Rather, they offered a code to be deciphered by those who were willing to begin the path of personal liberation from the chains of Necessity.

Obviously, the most abundant information comes from the kind of topics that astrologers could deal with, as outlined in the major instructional manuals. One could, for example, estimate good fortune and length of life, or find lost goods, and we should not underestimate the complexity of doing this; to estimate good fortune, for example:

> You should look at the lords of the triplicity of the luminary which is appropriate to the native, in a diurnal nativity [the lords of triplicity] of the Sun, and in a nocturnal nativity [the lords of the triplicity] of the Moon; if these are in angles and free from malefics, this indicates good fortune all of the days of his life.[61]

It is not necessary to understand the details of this passage in order to glean several important pieces of information. First, the cosmos can be reduced to a numerical code, as all the positions described above are defined mathematically, or geometrically. There is, undoubtedly, a sense of absolute determinism. However, there is a hint of the need for personal judgement in the phrase 'appropriate to the native': the astrologers must decide for themselves what constitutes 'appropriate'. But the real indeterminism is located in the sheer complexity of the factors which need to be taken into account. It is extremely rare that an unambiguous assessment can be made, and therefore judgement must, in the words of the *Centiloquium*, always be uncertain, unless God is invoked. And it's this indeterminism which permitted astrology's real project, not to predict the future but to manage the present. No doubt, though, some astrologers spoke in terms of certainty, for this is what clients need: if you want your lost property found or, more seriously, the parentage of a child established, you need to know the answer exactly. In this sense the astrologers' dialogue with the public may have been different from that which they held among themselves.

The evidence suggests astrologers existed at all levels of society, from the court and philosophical schools, to the street. Most clients were women, the fees that astrologers might charge varied from the exorbitant to the minimal, and, while some were full-time professionals, others combined their work with other professional activities, often medicine, or saw it primarily as a hobby. This is exactly the situation we might have found in ancient Rome, or modern Delhi or even Los Angeles. The existence of street astrologers does, though, raise difficult issues about astrology's status. No doubt some astrologers preferred to work on the street; in any pre-modern city this is how a large number of trades are carried out.

To consider astrology's general situation, we could turn to the southern Mediterranean, to the Tunisian scholar Ibn-Khaldun (1332–1406), who was critical of the practice. His opposition to astrology was not absolute, and it was the personal relationship between astrologer and client that aroused his righteous anger. With no mechanical or ideological rationale to sustain the doctrine of nativities, there was nothing left to explain its popularity except human gullibility. To be interested in the future, he conceded, was a perfectly natural human trait, but his description of the activities of the diviners in general (in addition to astrologers) and their clients was not exactly flattering:

> In the towns we find a group of people who try to make a living out of predicting the future, because they realise that the people are most eager to know it. Therefore, they set themselves up in the streets and in shops and offer themselves to those who [wish to] consult them. All day long, woman and children of the town and, indeed, many weak-minded men as well, come and ask them, how it will affect their business, their rank, their friendships, their enmities, and smiliar things. There are those who make their predictions by writing on sand [geomancy], those who cast pebbles and grains [of wheat], and those who look into mirrors and into water. These things are very common in cities, and their reprehensible character is established by the religious law.[62]

And as on the southern shores of the Mediterranean, so on the northern. Ibn-Khaldun was talking of Islamic society, but everything we know about Christian culture suggests that his description applied equally in Europe.

6

The High Middle Ages: The Uses of Astrology

The children of Mercurie and Venus
Been in hir wirkynge ful contraries;
Mercurie loveth wisdom and science
And Venus loveth ryot and dispence.

GEOFFREY CHAUCER[1]

On an April day in the late fourteenth century, perhaps in the 1380s or '90s, a group of fictitious English pilgrims set out from London to visit the great shrine of St Thomas à Becket at Canterbury. This motley crew was to feature in Geoffrey Chaucer's literary epic, *The Canterbury Tales*. Chaucer employed astrology at various points in his narrative in order to move the plot along. The Wife of Bath herself, he tells us, was born with Mercury and Venus both in weak locations, indicating a lecherous, lusty and ignorant character, driven mainly by instinct, rarely by intelligent thought. Chaucer gambled on his audience being sufficiently versed in the arts of the stars to understand this. His readers inhabited a world in which earth and heavens were intertwined and interrelated – a cosmic state.

In the mid-twelfth century, another writer, the English chronicler Geoffrey of Monmouth, had composed a life of the mysterious magician, Merlin. The opening section contained an account of the structure and mechanics of the cosmos which is interesting precisely because it was aimed at a lay readership rather than a philosophical one. The universe was created by God, is inhabited by angels (who live above the stars), demons (who inhabit the space above the moon), stars moving on their regular courses and planets which emit rays: when the rays of Venus pass through Pisces, heat and water merge to make shining gems with benevolent qualities.[2] This was the world inhabited by the average person in the twelfth century, one when modern distinctions between magic, science and religion, between natural and supernatural, or between morality and the fabric of the cosmos, did not make sense. It was in this cultural environment that astrology was to flourish. Whereas for Geoffrey, though, theological matters were of little significance, for others they were a mater of supreme importance. Nicole Oresme (c.1320–382), bishop of Lisieux, and a harsh critic of judicial astrology, penned an eloquent reconciliation of scriptural and classical cosmology. He argued that:

> Again, this lower world is governed by the heavenly bodies and their movement, as Aristotle says, for they are the instruments of God, by means of which he governs nature,

and which incline the hearts of men to various fortunes, without violence or necessity, and to know these bodies and these movements, astrology has been especially ordained, that great science which would be, as it were useless, unless by its aid we could know the things of the future. And of these the sun, moon and stars, are signs as our Lord said when he made them, according to the exposition of St. Augustine on Genesis.[3]

Medieval cosmology was a combination of the classical and the scriptural. Even though the conservative, thirteenth-century condemnations of Aristotelianism pointed to the presence of potentially irreconcilable differences between it and scripture, the obvious point of agreement was provided by the logical extension of scriptural teachings that, if God was truly omnipotent, he could do whatever he wanted. If he wanted to set up a universe in which nature was governed by Aristotelian celestial motion and influences, he could do so. And if, like a Babylonian deity, he wished to communicate with humans via celestial signs and wonders which disrupted the natural order, that was his right. As Bernard Savage argued, the 'sky and the stars are a book in which are written the fortunes of kings, and things to come in this world'.[4] We can therefore identify two fundamental cosmologies. One, the biblical universe, created in seven days, presided over by God and his supernatural legions of angels and saints, and often, especially in the Orthodox Church, administered by Christ cosmocrator – ruler of all – came with the force of scripture and the threat of Hell for the unbeliever. The other, the Aristotelian world, was justified by empirical evidence. It was, for example, a matter of undeniable truth that the sun sent heat and light, an observation of the reality of celestial influence which was extended into more subtle matters such as the coincidence of significant movements of Mars, say, with drought or outbreaks of war, or those of Saturn with cold conditions and the likely failure of new enterprises. The universe was still, in the great sociologist Max Weber's terms, enchanted, alive and brimming with meaning.[5] The modern radical theologian, Don Cupitt, has coined a different term, which is no less applicable, 'energetic Spinozism', after the seventeenth-century Dutch philosopher Benedict Spinoza, in which the world is seen as 'a continuously outpouring self-renewing stream of energies read-as-signs'.[6] William James, who was the first to intelligently discuss the nature of religious experience, had another term for it. He promoted the notion of 'cosmic consciousness', an awareness of the life and order of the universe that requires an extension of the mind beyond our normal intellectual faculties.[7] But such ideas, of course, though apparent discoveries of modern thinkers, were but truisms to Plato and Aristotle. For Aristotle the world was a single living organism in which stones and plants played their part along with people, while for the Catholic Church the cosmos was populated by hosts of invisible beings, angels and demons, and for the rural masses, the pagan world of natural spirits blended into the Christian framework that they learned about in church. The double rationale of astrology according to signs and influences became the standard defence of astrology, reinforced by pseudo-Aristotelian works such as *Of the Properties of the Elements*, which were composed by medieval writers to include the overt astrology which was absent from the genuine works.[8]

The careful astrologer could, though, distinguish events caused by influences to those indicated by signs. One who faced this problem was John of Legnano, in his discussion of the comet of 1368.[9] John progressed naturally from the argument that comets, by disturbing the upper atmosphere, in turn caused winds, made men choleric – or angry – and so caused wars. By examining a comet's location and colour, one might then move to more precise conclusions, such as whether the king is likely to be threatened by enemies from within or afar. This was the cosmos of cause and effect, of the changing qualities of time, or of seasons as Genesis would have it. Yet if, as John worried, the three comets which appeared under the reign of Nero had coincided with the spread of Christianity, could they really have caused people to turn from sin to Christ? Of course not. In this case the comets' connection to the coinciding events was one of supernatural divine virtue. The comets were signs that God's plan was being fulfilled. The further problem, of the determinism inherent in the whole concept of God's plan, was, wisely, left alone in the astrological texts themselves.

The speculative, logical arguments that dominated most works on the Sphere contained little of direct relevance to either technical astronomy or astrology. The commentary of Robertus Anglicus was typical in that it described the planetary rulership of signs and exaltations, but no more.[10] The need to work out exactly how the earth moved was related to the pressing question of establishing more accurate measurements of the planets and so more accurate astrological forecasts, let alone a better appreciation of the marvellous design of God's universe. However, such speculative discourse carried profound implications for astrology, particularly in relation to the question, fudged by both Aquinas and Oresme, of whether its mechanism should be seen primarily as natural – as a matter of celestial influences – or supernatural – of divinely inspired signs. The key text was the passage in Matthew 27.51 which was widely interpreted as pointing to a solar eclipse during Christ's crucifixion, which had featured in the Eastern Emperor Manuel's defence of astrology. 'Now from the sixth hour,' Mathew claimed, 'there was darkness all over the land until the ninth hour.' Luke (23.44–5) added that 'the sun's light failed'. The problem with the eclipse theory is that the crucifixion occurred at Passover, which is always set for a full moon, at which point a solar eclipse is an astronomical impossibility; an eclipse of the Sun can only occur at the new moon. Sacrobosco dealt with the problem by contrasting the universe of natural order with one of divine spontaneity. In a passage titled 'Eclipse during the Passion Miraculous', he wrote:

> From the aforesaid it is also evident that, when the sun was eclipsed during the Passion and the same Passion occurred at full moon, that eclipse was not natural – nay, it was miraculous and contrary to nature, since a solar eclipse ought to occur at new moon or thereabouts. On which account Dionysius the Areopagite is reported to have said during the same Passion, 'Either the God of nature suffers, or the mechanism of the universe [*machina mundi*] is dissolved.'[11]

The cosmic *machina mundi*, as Sacrobosco described it, was sufficient to justify an astrology in which the future could be reliably predicted as planetary orbits were projected into the future, but no prediction was as important as that of Christ's second coming, and that would most likely only be announced by God at the last moment: an astrology of signs could always trump one of planetary cycles and influences. For practical purposes, though, the most effective explanatory model for astrology remained the Great Chain of Being, the web of vertical and horizontal relationships which connected all things through their essential 'sympathies'.[12] It was these which justified magic, the active participation in cosmic forces, the means by which medieval philosophers might, like Marx, move beyond analysing the world to changing it. The medieval cosmos was far from being fatalistic and deterministic – space, time and morality were interdependent and the contextual literature of both scripture and astral magic, within which astrology operated, indicates the extent to which individuals were able to engage with the cosmos.

In most cosmologies based on either Aristotle or scripture, the moral fabric of the universe was located within the physical – heaven was up, beyond the stars, and hell was down. In the works of the Italian poet Dante Alighieri (1265–1321), especially his cosmological allegory *The Divine Comedy*, the moral structure was as important as the physical, if not more so. Dante's attitude to astrology was typical of that of the educated Platonist. And he embodied all the contradictions of that position and the Platonic paradox – that devout Platonists can be either the most cutting sceptical opponents of astrology, or its most devout evangelists. Dante was torn between the two attitudes, and, through his writings, the complexities of medieval cosmology are starkly revealed. Dante was dismissive of the practitioners of astrology, which is why poor Guido Bonatti was confined to Hell, but he treated natal astrology as a philosophical teaching with the utmost seriousness and saw the source of his own genius in his birth with the sun in Gemini. Referring to the 'Heaven of the Twain' (Gemini) he admitted 'to you I owe such genius as doth in me lie'.[13] Gemini was, of course, ruled by Mercury, the celestial messenger. In the *Convivio*, in which Dante outlined his view that the desire for knowledge is a means for humanity to grow closer to its natural condition, perfection, he drew attention to one's birth circumstances – if one was poor, disadvantaged or disabled – which might, along with the tendency to live a dissolute lifestyle, constitute an impediment to learning. The reference to astrology was no more direct than was Aristotle's discussion of better and worse births, but it's clear that Dante's position was derived from Plato and Aristotle. Like the former, he believed that wisdom was a path to God and, like the latter, he believed that all things are driven by a desire to return to their source which, in humanity's case, is the perfection of the soul.[14] Yet, it's part of the Platonic paradox that one's ability to choose is constrained by Necessity, by the fact of having been born into the natural world, with its unavoidable order. Dante realized that he should confine his choices to those offered him at birth. 'I restrain my talent,' he wrote, 'lest it run a course that virtue has not set; for if a lucky star or something better has given me this good, I must not misuse it.'[15] Dante's problem was that he believed in astrology in the looser sense that the cosmos contained meaning and significance, but not in the meticulous certainties that came with the art of horoscope interpretation. His problem with Bonatti was not that the astrologer predicted the future from the stars but that he did so with such precision. After all, Dante himself made a historic prophecy based on the stars: 'I clearly see those stars, already near,' he wrote, 'that will bring in a time . . . Its advent nothing can prevent.'

But Dante was more like an Old Testament prophet than a classical astrologer – he sees the stars and, inspired by their closeness to God, he speaks the truth. But in this case the future he sees is, like that of the most determinist astrologer, inevitable. Elsewhere Dante treated the problem through the question of the soul's origin in and return to the stars, though that he locates this theory in the *Timaeus* rather than the *Republic* suggests that he had not read the original. Reincarnation is quite clearly unpalatable so Dante finds a solution in Augustine and Aquinas. What Plato really meant, he suggested, was not that there is a psychic connection between human and star, but just a system of general planetary influences.[16]

The Divine Comedy is the greatest example of the celestial journey literature which originated with Plato's Myth of Er; Dante did not have access to Plato's text, but he was inspired by Cicero's 'Dream of Scipio' and Macrobius's commentary on it, and included references to them in his own work.[17] The *Comedy* begins on Good Friday 1300, the commemoration of Christ's descent to the underworld, when Dante embarked on a journey through Hell conducted by the Roman poet Virgil. The notion of Good Friday as a critical prophetic-cosmic date seems to have had some currency for, 200 years later, Hanz Holbein's famous painting, *The Ambassadors*, appears to have been a codified horoscope for Good Friday 1533.[18] Dante's Hell is structured as a mirror image of the celestial spheres, with nine concentric spheres of its own, exactly as the underworld, in the myth of the Mesopotamian goddess Inanna's descent, had contained seven gates, an implied parallel with the seven planets.[19] Dante was not aware of the Babylonian tale, but has clearly had the same insight into an essential symmetry between the structure of the under and heavenly worlds. But, in Dante's version, it's the notion of Hell as having its own centre which removes his work from the Aristotelian cosmos with its one centre. After his journey through Hell, Dante moves through Purgatory and then begins his ascent to Heaven via the planetary spheres. His concern, though, is not with astrological meanings, of which there are little trace, but with the stars as poetic images, as allegorical guides for the pilgrim and seeker for perfection, in a Platonic cosmos which is alive, intelligent and filled with God's love; the sun and stars are actually moved by God's love.[20] The stars are mainly treated as symbols of virtues, as guides to perfection or, in one passage, as an image of truth.[21] As Dante emerges from the underworld in Canto I of 'Purgatory', he sees four stars (which may represent the Southern Cross) and embody Prudence, Temperance, Justice, and Fortitude. In Canto 8 he spies three more stars which embody Faith, Hope and Charity. The stars, in this sense, are images whose purpose is to train Dante's spiritual insight so that, when he finally reaches the starry sphere itself, he can see the angels, heaven and God as they truly are. Education, of course, had a divine purpose, and Dante sought inspiration for his theories in Cicero and Boethius. He was influential, perhaps decisively so, in restoring the classical humanism that was to be such a potent feature of the Renaissance. For humanists the secret of humanity's return to God lay not in blind faith but in reason and education. So, for Dante, who dealt with these questions in his *Convivio*, the ascent to heaven could be read as a journey through the seven liberal arts: the student began with grammar (the moon) and progressed via dialectic (Mercury), rhetoric (Venus), music (the sun), arithmetic (Mars) and geometry (Jupiter) to astronomia (Saturn).[22] Astronomia, of course, included astrologia, but Dante's astrology featured the spiritual journey of Plato and Cicero and had no place for the rule-bound, detailed horoscopy of Ptolemy, Bonatti and Masha'allah. The stars, he believed, like the Roman emperor Marcus Aurelius, are best used as objects of contemplation than guides to the future.[23]

After he passed through the primum mobile, the outermost sphere which rotates the other, inner spheres, Dante finally saw the light of God himself and perceives the true moral structure of the cosmos in a section which suggests he had access either to the *Corpus Hermeticum*, or accounts of its theories. Like Hell, Heaven consists of a series of nine concentric spheres, each inhabited not by planets but by 'Dominations, Virtues and Powers', including the archangels and angels, each of which praises God and, like the human soul, strives to be closer to him. God, at the centre is like the sun. Dante described how 'One Point I saw, so radiantly bright. So searing to the eyes it strikes upon, they needs must close before such piercing light.'[24] He had earlier described the sun as 'the planet which leads men straight ahead on every road', a clear metaphor for God.[25] The idea of God as the sun, at the centre of the cosmos, is both profoundly Hermetic and a form of pre-Copernican spiritual Copernicanism. The spiritual cosmos, the ancient tradition to which Dante subscribed, was not geocentric – earth-centred – as it is in a physical sense, but theocentric.[26] In his pivotal position as one of the initiators of the Italian Renaissance of the fifteenth century, Dante himself stood as a poetic link between Hermetic myth and Copernican science.

Medieval astrology told stories about the individual's relationship with the cosmos. It had a clear narrative structure, which progressed, like a pilgrim's journey, from the initial thirst for knowledge, to the construction of the horoscope as a metaphorical device, and from the solution of the riddles it revealed, to the ultimate prize, a glimpse into the future. Chaucer, who was born around 1357 and died in 1400, was concerned with astrology as a literary device, a means to reveal the foibles of human nature. That he used it is a fact which itself indicates the extent to which the language of planets and zodiac signs was familiar. His chosen subjects were ordinary people, the embryonic bourgeoisie, such as the Wife of Bath, or a nameless merchant, and we know of no instance in which he advised the great and powerful, in spite of his high-level contacts. Richard II (1377–99), king of England in Chaucer's old-age, was himself a keen patron of astrology, perhaps because he also admired French fashions. Richard's contemporary on the throne of France was Charles V (1338–80), who was at once known as 'the Wise' and one of the most influential patrons of astrology in Europe; he should be seen as the successor to astrologically inclined emperors such as the Roman Hadrian, the representative of a tradition that can be traced back to the monarchs of ancient Mesopotamia. Like them, Charles combined various forms of divination and relied heavily on geomancy, a form of astrology which used symbols on stones which were thrown, and their patterns read.[27] He was in no doubt that his use of astrology had provided vital assistance in his dramatic reversal of English fortunes in France. As a young man, Charles had become regent after the English had virtually destroyed the French monarchy, first at the battle of Crecy in 1346 and, ten years later, under the Black Prince, the heir to the English throne, at Poitiers. The French king, John II, was an English prisoner and complete conquest by England seemed inevitable. As regent, Charles began to reorganize the government and resist the English advance, becoming king on the death of his father in 1364. By 1380 the English had been driven back to six coastal ports and their immediate hinterland. At the time this success was credited in part to the skills of Thomas de Pizan, Councillor of the Republic of Venice and former professor of at the University of Bologna, where his specialities included astrology.[28] As Charles's astrologer, alchemist and physician, Thomas was charged with the protection both of the monarch and his realm. There could be no more vital task. Aside from Charles's diplomatic and military skills, Thomas's skills were widely credited with driving the English back to the coast. In an exercise which illustrated the extent to which astrology was designed to manipulate the future, as a participatory rather than passive exercise, Thomas made five hollow human figures out of lead, corresponding to the malefic planet Saturn. He filled these with earth taken from the five regions of France, the centre and four quarters, and then labelled them with the names and key astrological features of the English king, Edward III, and his four chief commanders. Each figure then had its hands tied behind its back and, at the most auspicious astrological moment, was buried face down, one on the centre and one for each quarter, while the appropriate magic incantations were recited. Magic might be justified on a number of grounds, from the 'sympathetic' connections between terrestrial and celestial objects (by manipulating one it was possible to affect the other) or the belief that images were, like religious icons, 'alive', inhabited by spirits.[29]

The magicians of the fourteenth century were well aware of their place in an ancient tradition and their debt to the Babylonians, Egyptians and Jews, who were equally respected for their knowledge and skill. One well-used text, *The Book of Angels, Kings, Characters and Images of the Planets*, was clearly based partly on personal revelation derived from the ecstatic union with heaven to which all theurgists, alchemists and magicians aspired. 'Messayaac reported an amazing revelation of *experimenta*,' it began, before advising all magicians 'to make a ring of the Sun', impressing the power of the sun in a gold ring, inscribed with the sign and name of the Sun's angel.[30]

In spite of the magical texts' emphasis on upright and moral behaviour, this was potentially dangerous work, for charges of magic could lead to serious consequences. In 1358, following disturbances in Paris, the future Charles V accused his rival, Charles of Navarre, of attempting to overthrow him by employing an astrologer named Dominic, who was found in possession of 'rings, powders and other detestable paraphanalia of sorcery'.[31] Conservative theologians reinforced political unease over the overtly magical use of astrology and were constantly on the watch for such practices. In the 1320s Pope John XXII gave the inquisitors of Carcassone and Toulouse the power to act against those who practised witchcraft, sorcery and other demonic practices, and, in 1326 or 1327, he issued a bull, *Super illus specula*, which was a general condemnation of magic.[32] The arguments, though, were not purely theological, and the Church did examine the evidence. According to the inquisitor Eymeric, John XXII's bull against magic followed a conference in which critics and supporters of alchemy were called to debate whether the practice had any basis in nature. The alchemists were unable to prove their case, the critics won and the Pope, according to this account, followed the evidence as a modern scientist would. It is perfectly understandable that the alchemists failed to prove that they could transmute lead into gold, for this has only become possible with modern technology, but alchemy has an easy justification in nature. It's a perfectly logical consequence of the proposition that all substances are mixtures of elements and the conclusion that one can therefore change one into another by altering its balance of fire, earth, air or water. It seems that Eymeric was embellishing his case, but the enthusiasm of an inquisitor for natural evidence is indicative of an uneasy marriage of convenience between theology and empirical observation. Magical practices were dangerous and alchemy suspect, but no astrologer, though, was ever executed just for casting horoscopes.

The safest form of astrology, which could offend nobody, was weather prediction. Again, as in the Pope's investigation of alchemy, we see what we would now call a scientific mentality in the work of some practitioners. One was William Merle, or Merlee, a fellow of Merton College, Oxford, who flourished in the first part of the fourteenth century (he died in 1347). Merle was the first medieval astrologer to attempt anything like the empirical collection of data that the Babylonian astrologers had long ago compiled in the *Diaries*, from the eighth century BCE onwards.[33] Although he focused mainly on meteorological data, Merle did mention economic matters (such as the effect of Saturn's transit of Taurus on grain prices in Franconia in 1355) as well as other occurrences such as the small English earthquake of 28 March 1343.[34] Merle published a sample of his weather data in a manuscript titled 'The State of the Weather at Oxford for Seven Years' (from 1337 to 1344), and provided a supporting theoretical manual on astrological weather prognostication, probably composed in 1340, which adhered to the tradition evident in Hesiod's *Works and Days* in the eighth century BCE, and emphasized the observation of rising and setting stars (which can be used to indicate changing seasons) at the expense of horoscopes. Merle's principal sources were Aristotle and Ptolemy and, as a Ptolemaic astrologer, he paid attention to the inferior levels of the celestial hierarchy, focusing on signs in the immediate natural environment as much as the more distant planetary one. For example, he claimed, if flies bite more painfully, bells are heard at a greater distance or if salt liquefies, that is a sign of greater humidity.

From weather prediction, it was a short step to medical astrology, based on the principles established by the classical authorities Hippocrates and Galen combined with the astrological detail provided by Ptolemy. Individual diagnosis and treatment was, technically, a relatively simple matter: if the horoscope for the diagnosis indicated that Mars was the offending planet, the complaint – typically a hot fever if Mars was involved – might be soothed by administering cool Venusian herbs. However, a major preoccupation was with epidemics, particularly the Black Death, which wiped out between a third and two-thirds of the population of Europe (having previously devastated parts of Asia) in 1347 and 1351. One cause of epidemics, it was thought, might be comets. There were differences of opinion about what exactly these strange celestial bodies were.[35] One argument held that they were creations of the divine will sent as signs of future marvels. Others regarded them as disturbances stirred up in the material world caused by planetary movements. This was the stuff of cosmic drama, and comets could be harbingers of catastrophe. There were precise rules for determining their consequences, and a comet's significance could be judged by the part of the zodiac in which it first appeared together with the accompanying planetary patterns. A treatise on the comet of 1337 composed by Geoffrey of Meaux, who, as one of the physicians of Charles IV of France, occupied a position of great influence, illustrated the logic. The comet's appearance was immediately preceded by a solar eclipse (which lasted 3 hours, 29 minutes and 54 seconds precisely – a measurement which indicates the concern for precision with which such matters were treated) and coincided with an approaching, and highly threatening, conjunction between Mars and Saturn in Gemini. Apart from the astonishing concern with accuracy (according to Ptolemy the duration of an eclipse indicated the duration of its effect), these events were seen both as causes of the comet and indicators of its significance. Eclipses were inherently dangerous but this one was also linked to two dangerous planets: according to Geoffrey, Mars signified lies, robberies and violence, Saturn pointed to extortion, hatred, fear and death. Gemini, meanwhile, targeted magnates and the clergy. Really, it couldn't be worse, at least for aristocrats and priests. Geoffrey concluded that the comet would indicate diseased blood (Mars) with an excess of melancholic and choleric complaints. Melancholy might indicate sleeplessness and problems with the gall bladder, choler pointed to people who are easily angered and liable to suffer from difficulties focused on the spleen. This might sound trivial but at a time when the smallest complaint might escalate into a potentially fatal condition, the warning was of a possible epidemic and wholesale death.

It was the Black Death, though, which exercised Europe's best medical minds. If ever there was a catastrophe – a stellar induced crisis – which required rational explanation, this was it. The obvious culprit, it was concluded, was the lunar eclipse in Libra on 18 March 1345, which coincided with a triple conjunction between Mars, Jupiter and Saturn in Aquarius. Jupiter–Saturn conjunctions, according to the well-accepted Persian theory, pointed to major historical developments, while the combination of a destabilizing eclipse and malefic Mars was bound to lead to a serious epidemic.[36] A number of astrologers claimed to have predicted the plague in their annual almanacs for 1345, and undoubtedly many did predict serious epidemics for this would have been standard procedure, especially if Mars was involved. The problem is that the tone taken by such forecasts tended to be sweeping and disastrous and takes its cue from the apocalyptic language of the Book of Revelation. One set of predictions warned of 'corruption of the air, epidemics . . . violent winds and disease . . . changes of kingdoms, famine, wars [and] seditions'.[37] Another, by John de Murs, which it is thought relates to the 1345 conjunction, prophesied that 'the son reigning in the better part of the world will be moved against the seed of the lion and will stand in a field of thorns'. 'Then,' the text continued, 'the son of man will come bearing wild beasts in his arms and his kingdom is in the land of the moon,'[38] This went further than the prediction of melancholy diseases and comes perilously close to a forecast of the End of Days, the cataclysm which will precede Christ's second coming. The line between astrological prediction and apocalyptic prophecy was not a clear one and the prophetic tradition of the books of Daniel and Revelation appealed to Jean de Murs as much as to anyone who welcomed the prospect of an end to history.[39]

All the monarchs of the time employed astrologers.[40] Charles VI of France (1380–1422) continued the traditions of his father, while Richard II of England (1377–99), always keen on French fashions, made astrology a part of the decision-making apparatus of his court. In England there was a supply of astrologers, such as William Merlee from Oxford University, especially Merton College, although it seems that most were happier left alone with their scholarship than employed as political advisers. Edward III (1327–77) may have used the eminent scholar Thomas Bradwardine, although Bradwardine himself attacked astrology very publicly. In his victory sermon after the English victory over the French in 1346, he attacked the view that the stars were responsible. Only God, he claimed, could exert such absolute power. Another Merton scholar, John of Eschenden, or Ashendon, who wrote extensively on the impact of eclipses and Jupiter–Saturn conjunctions on politics, did his best to attract the king's attention but apparently without much success. Ashendon had predicted that the triple conjunction of Mars, Jupiter and Saturn in Aquarius in 1345, combined as it was with an eclipse of the moon, was to lead to war, death, poor harvests, violent storms and earthquakes, a forecast in which he claimed great success. However, this kind of combination of general disasters was predicted with monotonous regularity. One can only assume that the astrologers were fixated by the power of the malefic planets Mars and Saturn and gave little weight to their benevolent counterparts, Venus and Jupiter. Most such public predictions offered little that was more specific than the broad apocalyptic sweep of the Book of Revelation, with its warnings that nation shall rise up against nation. John I, king of Aragon

(1387–96) took offence when a certain master Francesch issued the apocalyptic prediction that the king of France would become universal emperor before the year 1400. This was an especially powerful prophecy, as the Last Emperor was to be the legendary monarch who, it was expected, would open the gates of Jerusalem, the sacred city, for the returning Jesus Christ. The astrologer, wisely, denied saying any such thing. The Holy Roman Emperor Wenceslaus (1378–1400), immortalized in the Christmas carol, was another user of astrology. It didn't save him, though, from being deposed and imprisoned by his rivals.

Royal astrologers were, unlike their Babylonian predecessors, not exclusive. They were independent operators who offered their services to the monarchs of Europe as need and the market dictated. We hear of one, a Spanish astrologer, called Loys – or Louis – de Langle, who was based at Lyons in the mid-fifteenth century.[41] De Langle had a thriving public consultancy but also made forecasts for Charles VII of France (1422–61), including, it was claimed, the Battle of Formigny in 1450, the poisoning of the young Prince of Piedmont and an epidemic at Lyons. De Langle was also mentioned in the scandalous trial of Jean, duke of Alençon in 1458. The astrologer had apparently provided a charm to the duke so that he might better enjoy the company of his duchess. The duchess proved resistant and the charm, we are told, did not work.

Pressure to gain the most up-to-date astrological predictions was intense and, in England, astrology took hold of high society under Henry V (1413–22) and his son, Henry VI (1422–61). Both kings were apparently too pious to consult astrologers themselves, even though a certain Master Welch is said to have chosen the time for Henry VI's coronation, but two trends are noticeable during their reigns. First, the amateurs, the scholars of Oxford, men like Ashendon, tended to be replaced by professionals whose primary purpose was to serve their patrons. Second, astrologers, sensing money to be made, crossed from France to serve the English nobility. Clearly astrology was spreading from Catholic Europe's most cosmopolitan cities to its less sophisticated capitals, not always with welcome consequences for its practitioners. In 1474 the first trial of astrologers began in England. Charged with treasonable behaviour, it was alleged that two Oxford graduates, John Stacy and Thomas Blake, had been employed by one Thomas Burdett, a friend of George, Duke of Clarence, the younger brother of the king, Edward IV. It was claimed that they had been asked 'to calculate the nativities of the King and of Edward, prince of Wales, his eldest son, and also to know when the King would die', a charge which was extended when it was alleged that 'in order to carry out their traitorous intention into effect, [they had] worked and calculated by art, magic necromancy and astronomy, the death and final destruction of the King and Prince'.[42] The astrologers may well have been caught up in what was in reality a plot to undermine Clarence; as in the Roman Empire, charges of magic proved a most effective means of destroying one's rivals.

While the use of magic could be dangerous, astrology as a means of time-management and decision-making seems to have been risk-free. Some astrologers, such as John of Legnano, who wrote an extensive discussion of the comet of 1368, included a ritual warning against astrology which seems to have been more of a safeguard in case the theological atmosphere should turn nasty. John concluded his treatise with a warning to good Catholics to avoid a list of astrological authors from Ptolemy and Abu-Ma'shar to Michael Scot, and to observe Augustine's prohibition of astrology, but only after extensive discussion of its uses. It is typical of many astrologers that they condemned the practice in order to forestall the unwelcome attention of the ecclesiastical authorities

Of all the uses of astrology, its medical applications were probably the most in demand.[43] The range of possible diagnoses and treatments was summarized in the fifteenth century's most influential textbook, Jean Gavinet's *Amicus medicorum*, or *Friend of Physicians*, published in 1431. At least five other editions were published between then and 1614, testifying to the book's popularity. Preventative treatments could be inferred from the natal chart. If the planets at birth revealed an imbalance in the humours then evasive action could be taken. A Saturnine person, liable to suffer from cold complaints, might be prescribed hot, Mars-ruled, remedies as a prophylactic; a diet containing astringent herbs and plants such as nettles, onions, garlic, mustard and ginger would certainly help. Interrogations might reveal the prospects for a recovery. Gavinet gave one account of a question asked by Henry Amicus of Brussels whether the dean of Vienne, who was then sick, would survive his illness. The horoscope for the moment that Amicus put his question was so profoundly unfortunate that Gavinet replied that the dean would not only die, but go mad first. And so it came to pass, we are told, within two days. If surgery was required, the moon's phases should be consulted to find the safest time; one should never operate on a fractured skull at the full moon, when the brain is at its largest and its pressure on the bone most dangerous. Such questions were partly a matter of tradition, but also of continual debate. In 1437 a controversy broke out at the University of Paris over what days were most favourable for blood-letting or the taking of laxatives, an important matter if one was to survive the year. Such practical discussions were the mundane counterpart of the great cosmological controversies on the size of the universe or the existence of multiple words.

Geoffrey Chaucer knew of such arguments, but didn't let them trouble him. He was born sometime between 1343 and 1345 and rose to a position of wealth and distinction by seeking employment with influential patrons. By 1357 he was in the service of the king's son, Prince Lionel, Duke of Clarence, and his wife, Elizabeth Countess of Ulster, and, by 1367, he was employed by the king himself, Edward III, who granted him a handsome pension of 20 marks per year for life. In 1368 he travelled to Italy, probably on the king's behalf, on a series of diplomatic and trade missions which extended over the next ten years. Sometime between 1366 and 1374 he married Philippa Roet, sister of Katherine Swynford, afterwards the third wife of John of Gaunt, son of Edward III. This may have been the same wife of John of Gaunt who consulted the astrologer John Somer.[44] Being related by marriage to the royal family, the number of posts open to him expanded, and he was trusted sufficiently to be used for diplomatic work, such as negotiating a marriage between Richard II and Isabella of France in 1396. Chaucer's most well-known overseas visit was in 1372–73, during which time he visited Florence and Genoa. Significantly for his grasp of literary cosmology, it seems Chaucer also became familiar with Dante's work and may have met the writers Petrarch and Boccaccio, two of the towering figures in Italian culture at the time.[45]

Chaucer's knowledge of natural philosophy was certainly extensive and was demonstrated through the *Canterbury Tales*. He inserted references to optical theory in 'The Squire's Tale'; had the learned clerk in the 'The Franklin's Tale' practice geomancy (literally earth-divination[46]), which included astrological correspondences, but relied on the patterns made by stones when thrown from the hand, rather like a sophisticated form of fortune-telling dice; and gave the wife of the cock Chauntecleer in the 'Nun's Priest's Tale' a knowledge of the psychology of dreams. Chaucer himself was also clearly something of an expert on astronomy and astrology, and the first use of the astronomical terms 'ascension' and 'declination' in English occur in the 'Franklin's Tale' and the 'Merchant's Tale'.[47] His influences included a series of classical astrologers, including Dorotheus, Firmicus, Rhetorius and Ptolemy, whom he calls 'the wise astrologien'.[48] He also read a number of astronomical works; to judge from the fact that he was the author of two technical treatises and that these were, like his poetry, written in English rather than Latin, confirms that he wished to reach the widest possible audience. Scholarly discourse held few attractions for him as compared to spreading knowledge about the heavens. The first work, which he wrote in 1393, was a treatise on the astrolabe, drawing on Masha'allah's work, which he had clearly read, and addressed to his ten-year-old son, Lewis. The second was a manual on the equatorium, a device which, in the absence of astronomical tables, was used to determine the positions of the sun, moon and planets.[49] Both instruments were essential for casting horoscopes, so we have to assume that this was Chaucer's intention. Many of Chaucer's works can be shown to relate to planetary positions at particular moments, unlike Dante, who relied only on the general structure of the moral cosmos.

In particular, Chaucer used astrology for plot development. One classic example is the 'Merchant's Tale', a poem whose story has a timeless quality. The leading character is May, a beautiful young woman who, for reasons which are not entirely clear, marries Januarie, an old and ugly man. Inevitably, May's sexual desires erupt and she takes a lover, Damyan. The ensuing crisis was resolved amicably, but not before the planets had their say. Chaucer launched his narrrative with a seasonal and astrological allegory: in May the sun is in Taurus, ruled by Venus, the maiden, but in January it is in Capricorn or Aquarius, both signs ruled by Saturn, the old man.[50] January is winter when the nature is dead, May is spring when new life shoots forth. Chaucer flattered his audience's scholarly awareness, letting us know that the cosmological background to the seven liberal arts was relevant by mentioning Martianus Capella and the *Marriage of Philology and Mercury*. Chaucer's reference to classical myth pointed to his own cosmopolitian influences, gleaned from his travels in Italy, particularly when he used Venus as a synonym for sexual desire and the youthful, handsome Damyan's lust for May. He evoked Ovid's tale of *Pyramus and Thisbe* and included Pluto, 'kyng of Fairye', and his wife Proserpina, in the cast of characters. But he also moved beyond myth and allegory into the sort of detailed astrological descriptions which only a technically sophisticated audience would have understood. He included two key passages in which he related the quality of time to the development of the plot in a manner entirely in keeping with the rules of astrology. The first instance takes place when, following her wedding, May remains in her chamber, as dictated by custom. Chaucer adds detail to the plot by telling us about the moon's motion. 'The moone,' he reported, 'that at noon was thilke day that Januarie hath wedded fresshe May, in two of Tawr, was into Cancer glyden: so long hath Mayus in hir chamber abyden.'[51] The code is impossible to crack with no knowledge of astrology, but simple with it. The key is in the next passage in which Chaucer then reported that May had spent exactly four days in her chamber – from noon on the first day until noon on the fourth. Chaucer's sophisticated courtly readership would have known that, for the moon to travel from two degrees of Taurus into Cancer, means that it must have moved at least 58 degrees, an average of 14 ½ degrees a day. Now, the moon's mean motion is in the region of 13 degrees per day. When May was in her chamber the moon was therefore moving faster then usual, always an auspicious indication.[52] Chaucer, having taken care to specify the moon's exact location, was making a definite point about the plot, namely that May was in a strong position. Besides, the moon in Cancer is in its own sign, so May could hardly put a foot wrong. But what is especially interesting, though, is that at a point in the story at which the crisis caused by May's near-adultery has not yet broken, Chaucer told his astrologically aware audience that the story has a happy ending. It's as if there are two levels of plot, the cosmic and the human, and, by examining the first, the outcome of the second was revealed. This is Ptolemaic astrology dramatized.

Anyway, May emerged from her chamber, met Damyan and was overwhelmed by lust. As the plot unfolded, Januarie was conveniently struck blind, allowing May to hatch her plans. She decided that it was safest to have sex with Damyan in a tree where Januarie would never accidentally blunder into them. Chaucer preceded the action with a second set of astrological information: the sun is in Gemini but is about to enter Cancer, the sign of Jupiter's exaltation.[53] 'Bright was the day,' Chaucer wrote, 'and blew the firmament, Phebus hath of gold his stremes doun ysent, to gladden every flour with his warmnesse. He was that time in Geminis, as I gesse, but litel fro his declynacion of Cancer, Jovis exaltacion.'[54] Simply, the sun, Phebus, was about to enter Cancer, the sign in which Jupiter, the most benevolent planet, was at its strongest. Again pre-empting the approaching crisis, Chaucer tells us that the future was bright. The threatened adultery is about to take place but, at the critical moment, Pluto, who is furious at May's deception, restores Januarie's sight. The old man is naturally outraged but May persuades him that all she was trying to do was work some magic to heal his eyes and that, in any case, no actual penetration took place. Januarie is mollified and takes May back. Her attempt to commit adultery was the cause of Pluto's restoration of Januarie's sight; her lies soothed his anger and all ended happily. Again, Chaucer has combined his seasonal allegory – the sun is in Cancer in the summer – with a more precise astrological one – under Jupiter's exaltation all things end well. And, in his reference back to Cancer's significance in the moon's movements after the marriage, Chaucer tells us that all loose ends have been tied up and celestial harmonies, briefly disrupted by the falling out of spring and winter, have been restored.

Another precise, graphic use of astrology occurred in the prologue to 'The Wife of Bath's Tale', in which Chaucer used the stars to paint a psychological portrait of the tale's key character, a lecherous, lusty woman who is incapable of restraining her desires. She is precisely the sort of foolish individual that the philosophers regarded as being ruled by their stars. Chaucer's description of the Wife's horoscope was simple enough to be clear to anyone with a simple level of astrological education and yet still assumed that such knowledge was widespread.

> The children of Mercurie and Venus
> Been in hir wirkynge ful contraries;
> Mercurie loveth wisdom and science
> And Venus loveth ryot and dispence.
> And, for hire diverse disposicioun
> Ech falleth in otheres exaltacioun.
> And thus, God woot, Mercurie is desolat
> In Pisces, wher Venus is exaltat;
> And Venus falleth ther Mercuie is reysed.[55]

The interpretation of this passage is relatively simple and rests in the system of exaltations which Chaucer would have known from the *Tetrabiblos*.[56] Both Mercury, ruling wisdom, and Venus, the lady of love, are in their weakest positions in the zodiac, and this simple code would have been understood by every educated person who read the passage. Mercury in Pisces, the sign of Venus's exaltation, is opposed to Virgo, which it rules and where it's strong. Therefore, the Wife of Bath, the stars tell us, is seriously lacking in wisdom. Venus, meanwhile, falls where 'Mercurie is reysed' – in either of the signs ruled by Mercury, either Gemini or Virgo, but where Venus itself is weak. This is not to be read literally, though, for Chaucer is dealing in allegory. In fact, the Wife of Bath's horoscope was astronomically impossible – Venus and Mercury can never be in opposite signs. Chaucer's purpose was metaphorical – to demonstrate that the Wife of Bath is at once selfish and stupid. She is a pawn, in other words, of her planetary fate, a salutary lesson to all those who fail to develop their Active Intellects. But the fate to which the Wife surrenders is not derived from the astronomical alignment at her birth, but a poetic representation of the heavens. Like a Babylonian astrologer, Chaucer has based his reading on a celestial pattern which has never occurred but might do one day in a cosmos in which all things are theoretically possible.[57]

Technological developments in the middle of the fifteenth century assisted in the wider public dissemination of astrological predictions. In 1455 Johann Gutenberg produced the first book to be printed in Europe (the Chinese had been using the same methods for several centuries) with moveable type – the so-called Gutenberg Bible. Once the sacred scriptures had been reproduced, there were two other boom areas in printing – pornography and astrology. Astrological almanacs spread rapidly. They were published in Italy in the mid-fifteenth century, spreading to Germany and France, and to England from the early sixteenth, while the first Scottish version seems to have been published in 1603. In some cases they were commissioned by town councils in order to release information for the year ahead. More often they were issued for commercial reasons by astrologers who saw the chance to boost their incomes at the same time as they got their message across to a vast audience. The almanacs might contain any general information and astrology itself might constitute most of the content or only a small part. Apocalyptic forecasts could be combined with forecasts for the year (based on the time that the sun entered Aries at the spring equinox), a calendar which included lunar phases, and advice on farming and medical matters, including anything from when to kill pigs or cut one's hair; a letter written in 1587 by the young Lady Arabella Stuart recounts how she observed the lunar phases in cutting her hair.[58] For the cognoscenti, who might understand such things, there could be an ephemeris – a listing of the planet's locations in the zodiac signs. For those who wanted something much simpler, some almanacs were sold with a handy wall chart which included symbols, together with a key, which told people what days were auspicious for any ordinary activity: travelling, doing business, visiting the doctor and so on. The almanacs provided a valuable interface between different astrological traditions, combining the astrology of the scholars and churchmen – such as d'Ailly – with the literary traditions of popular astrology, including lucky and unlucky days, and the folk astrology of rural life with its lunar lore. Almanacs functioned partly as educational devices – on how to make sundials or interpret horoscopes. They made possible the expansion of well-informed and self-taught practitioners who were able to both stimulate – through their advertising – and meet a rising demand for astrological services. By the time production peaked in France in the mid-seventeenth century, astrological thought seems to have been essentially moribund, the turning point being a vibrant debate on the eclipse of 1654, in which astrologers took political sides, many preaching warnings of revolutionary destruction of the old order.[59]

By the mid-fifteenth century, astrology had assumed a role as an almost unquestioned (except by a few theological doubters) part of both scholarly discourse and mass popular culture. The stage was set for the next phase of its crisis-ridden relationship with conservative Christian cosmology.

7

The Renaissance: The Pagan Revival

*What shall I say about light? For it is the action, or if you will,
the image, of the Intellect.*

MARSILIO FICINO[1]

In the year 1462 a thin, melancholic, scholarly, 29-year-old priest named Marsilio
Ficino was installed by his patron, the banker Cosimo de Medici, one of the
richest men in Europe, in a beautiful villa at Careggi, in the hills above the great
north-Italian town, Florence. There, Ficino embarked on a series of translations
of the mystical works of the classical and Hellenistic world, along with his own
commentaries. Pre-eminently, Ficino, who lived from 1433 to 1499, was the cosmic
ideologue of the Italian Renaissance.[2] He wrote the celestial script to a movement
that had begun with Dante and Petrarch long before he was born. And, as we shall
see, he was to have a significant, if indirect, influence on Nicholas Copernicus,
the genius who showed the world that the sun and not the earth was at the centre
of the universe. In their time, the revolutionary impact of Ficino's works was
as great as those of Aristotle had been in the twelfth and thirteenth centuries
and, arguably comparable to that of Newton's in the eighteenth century, Marx's
in the nineteenth, or Freud's in the twentieth. It was Ficino who propelled the
European scholarly mentality first towards the 'Enlightenment' of the seventeenth
to eighteenth centuries and then, shorn of much of its cosmological mystery, to
modernity. Charles Boer, one of his modern translators, described 'Ficino's genius
[as] acclaimed in his own lifetime as the inspiriting force behind some of the
greatest poets and painters, philosophers and statesmen of his era'.[3] Note Boer's
use of the word 'inspiriting'. Ficino didn't just inspire the Florentine artists, he
gave them a reason to create that was as much to do with the good of their souls
as the production of art for art's sake which, in any case, is a modern concept.

Ironically, by the fifteenth century, Aristotelian philosophy was no longer
radical. It had become the accepted way of studying and participating in the
cosmos, compatible, for most conservatives, with scripture. The cosmological
revolution that helped kick-start the Renaissance was in many ways a natural
successor to that of the twelfth and thirteenth centuries in that it was focused on
the rediscovery of classical texts. Yet, while the earlier period saw the triumph of
Aristotle over the residual Platonism of the early medieval period, the fifteenth
century witnessed a profound return towards Plato, reinforced by the translations of the Hermetic texts along with the writings of the classical Neoplatonists.

The consequence was a reordering of the relationship between the soul and the cosmos which took the Christian world, or at least a sympathetic part of it, back to before the Church Fathers' denunciation of astrology. The seminal figure in this revolution was the Florentine physician and priest Marsilio Ficino. A devout Christian at a time of widespread corruption in the Church, Ficino set out to replace Aristotle with Plato as the philosopher most akin to Christianity, formulating a Neoplatonic religion within a Catholic context. In this he was very much a successor to Aquinas. It is important to understand that the nature of Ficino's revolution was progressive in that he sought not to overthrow the existing Christian order, but to improve it. He was adding the missing pieces to the existing synthesis of Aristotle and scripture, restoring God to the entire cosmos, making soul central to cosmological inquiry. Aquinas had been the great compromiser, the man who steered a middle way between Aristotle and scripture. Ficino was sufficient of a politician to realize that he had to appeal to Aquinas's confirmation of the Aristotelian principle that celestial influences are imposed on infants at birth, as a seal into hot wax, and so confound astrology's conservative opponents.[4] But he was also an evangelist whose astrological texts gave a practical voice to Platonic cosmology just as Masha'allah's had done for Aristotle. His compromises were uneasy ones borne of very real political pressure from the Church and a sincere desire to reconcile competing cosmologies – pagan and Christian. The search for points of similarity rather than difference between the two was to raise tensions both between Ficino and his critics, and in his own conscience, as evident in his denunciations of astrology – which completely contradicted his own use of it. Together, Augustine, Aquinas and Ficino defined three differing Christian positions in relation to astrology, the soul and the stars. Augustine had accepted the reality of planetary influences but condemned all horoscopic astrology as satanic and a threat to the soul's eternal salvation; Aquinas incorporated Aristotle into Christianity, allowing the practice of horoscopic astrology as long as it dealt with the body and not the soul; Ficino welcomed a fully-fledged Platonism into a Christian context and advocated an astrology of the soul: although, in his great work, the *Platonic Theology*, Ficino repeated Aquinas's claim that the rational soul was above the stars, and therefore not subject to their influence, the facts of his astrological writings and practice suggest the opposite.[5] No longer was it taboo to consider that the stars might have significance for one's spiritual prospects.

Platonism had, of course, been known to the Catholic world through fragments of the *Timaeus* together with Platonic works such as Macrobius's *Dream of Scipio* and Platonic influences in Islamic and Arabic literature. But the medieval Latin world had seemed uninterested in reading further, even though all the Platonic writings had been studied in Constantinople since the 1200s. Plato's belated introduction to the Latin West was facilitated by the gathering crisis in the Greek world as the Ottoman Turks gradually surrounded Constantinople, occupying what was left of the Eastern Roman – Byzantine – Empire. In 1439 the Byzantine emperor, John VIII Palaeologus, desperate for Western military support, attended a Church council at Florence, his intention being to offer his submission to the Pope and resolve the almost thousand-year-old feud between Greek and Roman churches. The two churches had only formally split in 1054 but in effect had been bitter rivals since the Roman Empire collapsed in the West. The emperor was accompanied on his visit to Florence by Georgius Gemisthus, better known as Pletho, one of the greatest classical scholars of the empire.[6] Pletho was author of *De Differentiis*, a description of the differences between Plato and Aristotle's conceptions of God, as well as a comparative summary of the teachings of Zoroaster and Plato. We shouldn't imagine that Constantinople was necessarily a haven for Platonic scholars, though. Pletho himself was accused of heresy and exiled, and part of his work, including that on Zoroaster and Plato, was destroyed after his death. Yet, radical scholars had always managed to survive, in spite of the Church authorities' attempts to crush them. Pletho took the opportunity of his stay in Florence to set up a series of philosophical lectures, in which he denounced Aristotle, about whom he was much more knowledgeable than the Westerners, and proposed that Plato was a more suitable philosopher for any true Christian. Unlike their Eastern colleagues, those Catholic theologians who attended the Florence Council had only a passing acquaintance with Plato, and they were naturally suspicious and hostile, especially as the most prominent classical Neoplatonists, including Plotinus and Porphyry, had bitterly attacked Christianity. Even though Pletho was turning the clock back to before the Aristotelian revolution of the twelfth century, his impact, in the Italian context, was revolutionary.

The thought of restoring the wisdom of the ancient Greeks instantly enthused Cosimo de Medici, head of the banking clan whose fabulous wealth dominated Florentine politics. Cosimo himself presided over Florentine political life for three decades, from 1434 until his death in 1464, and saw his purpose as not just to maintain his family's position but to create a political and civic society in which humanity was in balance with heaven. The restoration of the direct connection between the soul and stars suited the rising tide of Humanism, which emphasized humanity's central and rightful place in the cosmic order. The notion of a universal harmony in which matter and reason were ultimately united in the Mind of the Creator matched the aspirations of a man such as Cosimo, a great patron of learning and the arts. Cosimo met Pletho and discussed the foundation of a new Platonic Academy, yet, for the time being, nothing came of the idea. In 1453, just 14 years after the Byzantine mission to Florence, Constantinople fell to the Turks, followed in 1461 by Trebizond, the last independent Greek outpost on the southern shore of the Black Sea. And, with that, Italian scholars who had an interest in rediscovering Greek learning became the only ones in the Christian world who could actually preserve it; in 1457 the Greek philosopher John Argiropolos arrived in Florence to lecture on Aristotle and, by popular demand, Plato. His arrival provoked such deep concern among conservative churchmen that the young Marsilio Ficino, eager to attend, was actually forbidden from doing so by his archbishop.

Ficino had begun his clerical training in 1451 and met Cosimo in 1452 – he was already well connected, and may have been a friend of Cosimo's son Piero through his father, who was one of Cosimo's physicians. In turn, he became tutor to Cosimo's grandson Lorenzo, who was nicknamed the Magnificent, at least partly on account of his lavish patronage of the arts. Our dates are uncertain, but it seems that from 1458/9 to1459/62 Ficino studied medicine at the Aristotelian-dominated University of Bologna, a significant fact in view of his emerging belief that the function of astrology was not so much to manage the present but to heal it. His philosophical essays, including the *Platonic Institutiones*, completed in 1456, attracted such attention that, in 1459, he was summoned by Cosimo who had decided on the young man as the head of his long-planned restoration of the ancient Athenian Platonic Academy, the home of wisdom and learning. The academy was established at Careggi in 1462, and Ficino's first translations were of the Orphic and Homeric *Hymns* and the *Sayings of Zoroaster*. In 1463 he completed his version of the *Corpus Hermeticum*, which was to be the seminal revolutionary manifesto of Renaissance cosmology, and he followed this with Plato's dialogues in 1468/9 (the complete translations were published in 1484), the Roman Neoplatonists Proclus, Porphyry and Iamblichus in 1489, and Plotinus in 1492. It was the publication of the Hermetic texts, though, that sent shock waves through the Catholic world.

Some Hermetic texts had been known for centuries, but these tended to be magical, and magic, although perfectly rational within an Aristotelian context, was forbidden by scripture.[7] Ficino changed that. After all, as he showed, the Hermetic God was One, good and supreme, exactly like the Christian one. In fact, as Ronald Hutton has convincingly demonstrated, all the pagan philosophers whose works Ficino introduced to the Christian West were good monotheists.[8] Ficino believed that Hermes was as great a teacher as the Hebrew patriarchs, and the fact that he was not a Christian could no more be held against him than against Abraham. He become ever more concerned with the discovery of the *prisca theologia*, the original pure religion, which underpinned the world religions of his day and which, he believed, had been devised in Persia by Zoroaster and in Greece by Hermes, revived and developed by Orpheus and Pythagoras, and perfected by Plato. Ficino reasoned, quite properly, that if there was a range of religious teachings which proposed the existence of one god who required not just submission but good behaviour, they may all have had one origin. If this original, pure, teaching could be found then the true religion would be revived and humanity, perhaps, restored to a state of grace. What all the ancient teachers had in common, of course, was that they were monotheists, and could, in Ficino's logic, be seen as proto-Christians. As Iamblichus had said, the language of Hermes had once been common to all priests.[9]

It was not enough for Ficino to translate and comment, though. The literary life was necessary but, in itself, inadequate. Philosophy for him, as for the classical Platonists, was a matter of action as much as thought. It was not enough to study the world; the philosopher's goal should be to change it. Neither was philosophy separate from religion. Both were manifestations of the spiritual life, and philosophy, by training the reason, could help religion defend itself against doubters. Ficino became immersed in the spirit of Hermeticism. He sang Orphic hymns on his lyre and performed every pagan ritual he could devise. He decorated the villa at Careggi with images of pagan deities and astrological motifs, which he thought should be contemplated daily for the elevation of the soul. There was a bust of Plato in front of which he set up a candle whose flame was never allowed to go out, and he inscribed around the walls a Latin Inscription, which directly anticipated the US Constitution, and which read 'All Things Are Directed To The Good By The Good, Be Happy In the Present, Don't Value reputation, Don't Seek Prestige, Flee Excess, Flee Trouble, Be Happy in the Present'.[10]

The truth was more complex, though, and happiness was a goal to be strived for, not a condition to relax into. In 1457/8 Ficino entered a two-year personal crisis brought on by the tensions of being at one and the same time a devout Christian and a practising pagan. His eventual solution was a decision to rededicate himself to Christianity, following Augustine, who had followed a similar path, converting from Manichaeanism to Christianity while preserving those teachings of Plato which he found compatible with the scriptures. As Ficino explained in his *De Christiane religione* (1474), he took Augustine's sympathy for Plato as his model, but he was far less restrained in his admiration for the pagan teacher. Essentially, Ficino's renewed Christian commitment enabled him to accept the entire structure of Hermetic and Neoplatonic astrology, complete with its horoscopes, image-magic, belief in the soul's ascent to the stars, and planetary deities. What he really objected to was conventional classical and Islamic astrology with its heavily codified mathematical determinism and what he saw as its mechanistic rationale in Aristotelian causality. His Christian commitment climaxed in his ordination as a Dominican priest in 1473, and Lorenzo de Medici, his new patron, rewarded him with a living in Florence. Yet, even though Neoplatonic astrology was a route to the divine, Ficino was aware of the fact that many of his colleagues in the Church could not resolve the contradictions between a thorough-going use of astrology and Christianity, and, shortly after his ordination, he wrote to the Archbishop of Florence in defensive mode:

> People will laugh at a priest who heeds astronomy. But I, relying on the authority of the Persians, Egyptians, and Chaldaeans, considered that while earthly matters were indeed the concern of others, heavenly matters in truth were the sole concern of the priest; so that while human affairs might be left to human counsel, matters for supreme authority should be referred to the ruler of heaven.[11]

Ficino continued to live and work at Careggi and, in 1489, completed his astro-logical masterwork, the *Liber de Vita*, or the *Book of Life*.[12] The spirit of *De Vita* was summed up by the title of the third book, largely inspired by Plotinus, *De Vita Coelitus Comparanda* – On Obtaining Life from the Heavens. Ficino's purpose was neither prediction of the future nor the answering of interrogations, nor the election of moments to begin new initiatives on the basis of personal advantage.

He was concerned with harmonizing one's personal physical and spiritual existence with the heavenly order so that one might live a long and healthy life; book 1
was titled *De Vita Sana* (On a Healthy Life) and book 2 *De Vita Longa* (On a Long
Life). In the context of ecclesiastical alarm at the new thought and the general
conservative assault on astrology that was taking place in the 1480s, *De Vita* was
brought to the attention of Pope Innocent VIII, and the work narrowly escaped
being banned. Yet the attack did prompt Ficino to compose an *apologia* which
was appended to the main text. In this he deliberately placed his astrology in the
classical tradition of Hippocrates and Galen and claimed his task as that of the
physician, in an attempt to place himself above criticism:

> The most outstanding duty without a doubt, most necessary and especially desired by all,
> is to see to it that men have a sound mind in a sound body. This we can accomplish only
> if we join medicine with the priesthood. But since medicine is quite useless and often
> harmful without the help of the heavens – a thing which both Hippocrates and Galen
> admit and I have experienced – astronomy certainly pertains to this priestly charity no
> less than does medicine.[13]

Unlike the typical Neoplatonic position, as outlined by Plotinus in the third
century, which was sympathetic to motions of heavenly signs but sceptical of
the concept of celestial causes and dismissive of the claims of most astrologers,
Ficino was content to read horoscopes in the standard manner, through a series
of prescribed and complex technical procedures, but with a major emphasis on
sympathetic magic – the harmonization of one's life with the cosmos through
ritual, meditation, the use of talismans, colour, music and herbs. So, in the face
of a problematic astrological alignment, one might defuse the threat and alter
the future by singing: 'But remember,' Ficino wrote, 'that song is a most powerful
imitator of all things. It imitates the intentions and passions of the soul as well
as words.'[14] All such ideas had been present in medieval astrology, but Ficino's
contribution was to substantially alter the emphasis. Not only did he legitimize
astral magic in a Christian context but he also elevated the planetary deities to
a more important function by emphasizing their role as aspects of the internal,
individual psyche with whom one can genuinely communicate – as opposed
to seeing the planets merely as external transmitters of primarily physical
influences.[15] Physical influences were real and were key to the functioning of astral
magic, but they were also, as was the entire cosmos, of divine origin. There is
well-established logic to Ficino's thought here: if human beings are a microcosm,
a cosmos in miniature, and the planets are divine, then not only must they
relate to the classical planetary deities, but these must have an internal presence.
Jupiter, then, is not just outside but inside every human being, as are the other
planetary gods and goddesses. The distinction with medieval cosmology is clear
and radical: whereas Aquinas had reinforced the dogma that celestial influences
were primarily on the material world, and that the soul was entirely independent
of them, Ficino emphasized the contrary position, that the psychic and physical
worlds were so intertwined that the planets were as alive in our minds and

souls as in our bodies. It's for this reason that Ficino has been identified as a precursor of late twentieth-century depth psychology, especially Jungianism and its offshoots, with its adaptations of Platonic archetypes and celestial deities as internal psychological functions.[16] It is, though, more accurate to see Jung and his disciples, in common with Ficino, as heirs of classical Platonism. Ficino's cosmos was psychological in the sense that psyche is soul, but his world was that of the Hermetic texts, the meeting of the Egyptian temple tradition, Babylonian astrology and Platonic philosophy. His religion echoed that point in the history of Christianity under Constantine in which it had blended with the cult of Sol Invictus. In fact, his view of the relationship between the sun and the divine was taken directly from the *Corpus Hermeticum's* reworking of Egyptian solar religion. As Frances Yates, who did so much to enhance our understanding of Renaissance paganism, put it, 'Ficino therefore seeks to cultivate the sun and his therapeutic astral cult is a revival of sun worship.'[17] In brief, God, the One, to which the soul has an irrepressible desire to return, shines through the sun. And as Ficino himself claimed in a passage whose revolutionary significance was to become clear in the next century, 'the astrological property of every one of us as individuals . . . is Solar'.[18] He believed, as Thorndike put it, that 'our spirit draws in the spirit of the universe through the rays of the sun'.[19]

At the heart of Ficino's psychology was the concept of melancholy, the natural condition arising from the Neoplatonic orthodoxy that the soul does not want to be in the body. There is, then, an existential problem in the human condition which can never be solved – although it can be managed. Ficino and all the philosophers in his circle regarded themselves as melancholics – for melancholia was particularly special to scholars. His account of his own horoscope was composed in traditional terms as the balance between different astrological factors:

> Saturn seems to have impressed the seal of melancholy on me from the beginning; set as he is, almost in the midst of my ascendant Aquarius, he is influenced by Mars, also in Aquarius, and the Moon in Capricorn. He is in square aspect to the Sun and Mercury in Scorpio, which occupy the ninth house. But Venus in Libra and Jupiter in Cancer have, perhaps, offered some resistance to this melancholy nature.[20]

The key to this passage is the ability of the generous, benevolent planets Venus and Jupiter, well placed in Libra and Cancer, to counter the effects of a strong malefic Saturn and a weakened moon.[21] Ficino's way of working was based in the operational potential of the Great Chain of Being, in which every single thing in the cosmos was linked into a set of horizontal and vertical correspondences. Having identified the disposition of any horoscope, the individual concerned might then manipulate their physical and spiritual condition by evoking the physical influence and/or divine nature of a star or planet in order to achieve a balance. This might be done by behavioural changes, wearing talismans, meditating on images, playing music or taking the relevant herbs, all at the appropriate times. In a passage directly relevant to his own horoscope, Ficino explained how to counter Saturn's life-shortening effects by enhancing the expansive qualities of one's life:

If someone were to accuse Saturn and Mars of being harmful by nature, I would not believe it, for they, too, are to be used sometimes, the way doctors must sometimes use poisons, as Ptolemy in his *Centiloquio* says. When the power of Saturn is cautiously taken, it is useful, just as the things doctors use are useful for binding up and holding together. After all, they even use things to stupefy, like opium and mandrake. The same goes for Mars, with euphorbia and hellebore. The Pythagorean maguses seem to have been extremely cautious in this matter, when they would become frightened that their constant philosophizing was the tyranny of Saturn, so they would dress up in white garments, and each day sing songs and make music with Jovial and Apollonian things, and in this way they lived a long time under Saturn.[22]

This simple passage is of the most profound significance for it contains a solution to the problem of evil which asserts human responsibility for the creation of good in a manner which no longer requires the two great supernatural powers, God and Satan. Ficino's bold statement of the Humanist position, buried deep in his astrological writings, deserves a focal place in Western secular culture.

To be clear, evil in the Platonic cosmos resulted from error, that people subject to 'worse births', presumably victims of poor choices made by their daemons, were incapable of developing their rational souls and instead lived through the animal souls. By contrast, the Hermetic cosmos was inhabited by daemons who were now evil. The Hermetic teachings, which Ficino brought back into European culture, existed in that schizophrenic space created by Plato in which the entire cosmos is good but human society, even though contained within, and containing, the good, is a place of misery from which the only escape is through the philosophical life and preparation for death – and the longed-for ascent through the stars;[23] the world is a miserable place, a prison. Evil was part of the cosmos. So awful is it that most people are incapable of receiving the 'Good' even when they want to.[24] The prisoner is the architect of his own imprisonment but the true philosopher practises dying, and death is to be welcomed because it leads naturally to rebirth. Poimandres, the narrator in the Corpus Hemeticum, presented Hermes with a set of instructions for salvation: look 'at what you yourself have in you;' he ordered, 'for in you too, the word is son, and the mind is father of the word ... Now fix your thought upon the Light ... and learn to know it'.[25] We are reminded of the Pharaoh's journey to the sun as the archetypal origin of literal 'enlightenment'. As Ficino asked rhetorically, 'What shall I say about light? For it is the action, or if you will, the image, of the Intellect.'[26] And, if the Good is light then 'He who has recognised himself,' that is, acknowledged the divinity within, then 'enters into the Good.'[27] If there is such a thing as the 'Enlightenment Project' in Western culture, with its emphasis on education as a means of transforming humanity, then this is it.

Such high-spirituality was not confined to some mystical arena of private contemplation: it had practical consequences in everyday life. Quite simply, if one is miserable, then one can do something about it: the best remedy may be a party, a symposium in Platonc terms, at which one might drink wine, play music and engage in philosophical debate. If one's complaint is Martian – perhaps a hot fever, or an excess of anger, then the best remedies are likely to be Venusian: surround oneself with soothing, cooling images and influences, including flowers such as lilies, and to ingest herbs such as vervain; eat fruit such as peaches; wear lapis lazuli, or talismans made of copper, Venus's metal. For maximum effect one should perform such tasks at a Venus hour of Venus's day (Friday) when Venus itself is well placed, in a favourable degree of the zodiac (such as in its own signs, Libra or Taurus) and a prominent sector of the sky (rising towards the eastern horizon, perhaps, or culminating overhead). In the medieval and Renaissance perspective, by acting in such a fashion we draw down the virtues of heaven, some aspect of the One, the Good. Ficino's use of magic was intended to prepare the imagination to receive the appropriate celestial influences; an image drawn from astral mythology might be imprinted inwardly on the mind with such force that the mind would become unified with the associated image from the higher world.[28]

Ficino also suggested, following the Hermetic text, the *Asclepius*, that the power of emotionally charged spoken (or sung) words may intensify the effect of an image, as the Arabs and Egyptians believed: 'they hold that certain words pronounced with a quite strong emotion have great force to aim the effect of images precisely where the emotions and words are directed'.[29] The Orphic Hymns, for example, sung with the right intent at the appropriate time, will enable the psyche to connect with the stars, whose healing power is required in order to solve psychic disturbances, as well as physical. He claimed that:

> a certain compound of plants and vapours made through both medical and astronomical science yields a common form [of a medicine], like a harmony endowed with gifts from the stars; so tones first chosen by the rule of the stars and then combined according to the congruity of these stars with each other make a sort of common form [presumably a melody or chord], and in it a celestial power arises. It is indeed very difficult to judge exactly what combinations of tones are suitable for what sorts of stars, what combinations of tones especially accord with what sorts of constellations and aspects. But we can attain this, partly through our own efforts, partly by some divine destiny.[30]

Magic's great idea was that the powers of heaven could be drawn down to earth and embodied in the icons, images, statues, paintings, talismans, herbs and medicines, both natural and artificial. Ficino's astrology was overtly and avowedly magical – it had neither meaning nor relevance without the active participation of the astrologer or his client. Indeed, magic's rationale was derived directly from the *Asclepius*, the focus of which was the soul's return to the One, a feat which could never be achieved without an immense personal effort. To predict the future or analyse the past with no personal involvement was therefore fundamentally pointless. To heal one's self and to live in harmony with the celestial order was everything. But Ficino was aware of the dangerous path he was treading and the need to rehabilitate the whole concept of magic. In his apologia to *De vita* he pointed out that the word shares the same root as Magus, and that the three Magi were the first to venerate Christ. Why, then, he asks, should one fear magic? Crucial, though, is the distinction between 'profane magic which depends on the worship of the daemons', which is prohibited, and 'natural magic, which, by natural things, seeks to obtain the services of the celestials for the prosperous health of our bodies'.[31] Above all, Ficino's astrology is a call to action: 'Whoever therefore wants to have the heavens propitious,' he wrote, 'let him undertake above all this work, this way of life; let him pursue it zealously, for the heavens favour his undertakings.'[32] All action, though, should be pursued in line with one's nature. One should harmonize with the heavens, never challenge them. And this takes us close to another distinction between two varieties of magic: one is instrumental, in which the magicians tends to stand outside the cosmos, manipulating it; and the other is concrete, in which the magician's identity merges with the cosmos in a perhaps ecstatic union. J.R.R. Tolkein described this state as 'enchanted'.[33] Ficino wrote that there are two sorts of people who are especially unfortunate: on the one hand those who act against their nature, contradicting the cosmos; and, on the other, those who do nothing at all, submitting to it. They will be subject to fate. Following the Neoplatonists Ficino argued that Providence radiated from the Divine Mind into the intellect first of angels and then of the rational souls of humans. Freedom lay in the attempt to contact the Divine Mind.

Ficino's revolutionary significance is undeniable. But, like many revolution-aries, his opposition to the status quo rested securely both in a desire to restore a distant past, and a continuity with more immediate currents of thought. In his theology Ficino challenged the Church more substantially than Copernicus or Galileo were to do: they were interested only in the physical structure of the cosmos, whereas Ficino's concern was the soul. But, in his practice, Ficino was very much the medieval magician and there was nothing that he advocated that had not been in the public domain for centuries. His influence on the wider world of astrological practice is also to be doubted, for the teaching of the subject in universities retained its Aristotelian character. Such issues run straight to our understanding of the Renaissance itself. Our concept of it as marking a complete dividing line between medieval ignorance and a dramatic restoration of reason is largely due to the nineteenth-century historian Jacob Burckhardt, who, as Paul Kristeller pointed out, sustained his argument by the simple tactic of ignoring philosophy.[34] Kristeller convincingly showed that the examination of Renaissance philosophy indicates more similarities than differences between Renaissance and medieval thought, and it was Ficino who provides the link between the two.

In terms of technical astrology, Ficino followed the medieval canon in his reading of birth charts and use of 'electional' charts to arrange his affairs. On one occasion, for example, he failed to call upon the archbishop of Florence because the stars were unfavourable. On another, he instructed Lorenzo to beware of the malefic planets Mars and Saturn on the following day, but added that he had delayed his warning until the last moment for fear that Lorenzo's fearful anticipation would make matters worse. This statement was crucial to an understanding of Ficino's astrology: in Ficino's Platonic, ensouled universe,

Lorenzo's state of mind was capable of enhancing or minimizing the effects of an astrological alignment. Aquinas would have struggled to acknowledge such a possibility, except in that the rational soul could inhibit lusts stirred up in the body by the planets, but Ficino was treading in potentially heretical territory, envisioning the mind, including its moral choices, as in a direct relationship with the stars. On one occasion Ficino argued that his friend Barbaro was astrologically suited to the priesthood, another claim which would have shocked Aquinas. He related that the death of the astrologer Guido Bonatti was caused when he was thrown from his horse, exactly as the stars foretold. On another occasion, Ficino predicted that, within two years, Italy was due to be ruled by pious men, thanks to benevolent Jupiter's imminent replacement of Mars as the dominant planet. He also wrote an apocalyptic warning to Sixtus IV, claiming that the war, pestilence, famine and false prophets of the coming year could only be averted if the Pope enacted a miracle. Ficino, the greatest intellect of the fifteenth-century Renaissance, was following the same well-trodden path as astrologers had for the previous three centuries.

There is one last conundrum to consider: Ficino's bitter criticism of astrology.[35] From the 1470s onwards, there are references to a book he composed attacking astrology. He wrote to his friend and student Poliziano that he was writing a 'Disputationes contra Astrologorum iudicia' which, in the event, was never published. However, we do know something of Ficino's arguments. His objections seem to have been theological and very traditional. When an astrologer friend told him that his (Ficino's) horoscope predicted a man who would revive the learning of antiquity, Ficino replied firmly that such things were the work of God's ministers and the striving of the mind to reach the eternal, not some destiny written in stone at birth. In 1494 Ficino wrote again to Poliziano claiming that he had always been an enemy of the astrologers and that, for Platonic philosophers, the signs of the zodiac were no more than convenient images. How can we reconcile such attacks with Ficino's very obvious devotion to mainstream astrology? One explanation may be a charge of Platonic elitism. Like Plotinus, who attacked astrologers but simultaneously defended the role of the stars as signs, Ficino believed in the Platonic notion of the philosopher king. Like Plato, he was suspicious, contemptuous even, of the common people. The tradition of the lone astrologer asserting that they and they alone have the truth and that all others are mistaken is a long and honourable one. Yet Ficino's particular genius was to compensate for Plotinus's simultaneous criticism of contemporary astrology and failure to offer an alternative interpretative framework. One thousand years after Plotinus, Ficino could also attack the astrologers of his time, but unlike Plotinus he offered something better in return – a practical astrology that could assist the soul's return to the One.

One immediate consequence of Ficino's work, which was of massive significance for Renaissance art, was a revival of respect for pagan learning which was now no longer seen as automatically un-Christian. True, Augustine had announced his respect for the Platonists, but a natural aversion to pagan teaching was reinforced

in medieval Europe by the fear of the damnation that would inevitably follow if
one surrendered one's soul to pagan practices. But, in the late fifteenth century,
it became possible to create images of pagan deities even if one didn't follow
Ficino in meditating on them.[36] The most enduring examples of such pagan art
are Botticelli's two paintings, the *Primavera* and the *Birth of Venus*. Both relate
in part to Ficino's belief that the soul returns to God through nine muses, or
possible combinations of planetary deities.[37] The *Primavera* portrays Venus and
Mercury, the central pair of Ficino's sequence. Venus was the representative of
universal love but also of beauty, the symbol of harmony and the reconciliation
of opposites. Mercury was at once the guide of souls to the beyond and, as
Hermes, the revealer of celestial mystery, calling the mind to higher things. Such
meanings may appear obscure, but would have been immediately apparent to any
educated viewer, as would the knowledge that the paintings could be concerted
into musical, mathematical or geometrical analogies, any one of which could
provide its own path to the One.

Ficino himself valued the company of artists, but he stood above the politics
of his day especially, perhaps as he was all too aware that his patrons, the Medicis,
faced an uneven and often bitter struggle with their rival banking families to assert
their control. Eventually they were rewarded with supreme power and assumed the
title of Duke of Tuscany. For the Medicis, it was astrology's political applications
that were most significant. If Ficino's philosophy was a self-conscious revival
of classical learning, the Medicis modelled their use of astrology on the Roman
emperors. Identifying himself with Augustus, Cosimo I (1537–74) turned astrology into a powerful propaganda tool, asserting his own imperial presentations
as a representative of heaven on earth.[38] Cosimo's destiny was spelt out when he
won a great victory against his enemies at the Battle of Montemurlo, fought on
1 August 1537, which he well knew was the anniversary of Octavian's (Augustus's)
defeat of Mark Antony and Cleopatra at Actium. As Octavian's rise to imperial
splendour as Augustus was confirmed at Actium, so Cosimo's was assured at
Montemurlo. And like Octavian, Cosimo finally laid a republic to rest, in this case
the Florentine Republic that had been briefly restored following the murder of
the first duke, Alessandro I de Medici. As Claudia Rousseau explained:

> The idea that Divine Providence had intended Cosimo to rule Florence was perhaps also
> underscored . . . astrologically by the fact that on the day of his victory at Montemurlo the
> Sun had been found in the same degree of the sign of Leo as propitious Mars had been
> in Cosimo's birth chart. Mars, the ruling planet of Florence because it was traditionally
> held to have been founded under Aries, was parallel to the star Regulus, the 'heart of the
> Lion'. Indeed, the placement of Mars with the Lion's Heart in Cosimo's nativity may itself
> have been seen as an omen of his future victory, suggestive as it is of Florence's 'ruler'
> with the legendary Florentine Lion symbol, the Marzocco.[39]

Following the battle, Cosimo moved to reinforce his relationship with Augustus.
Just as the Roman emperor had minted coins stamped with Capricorn, the zodiac
sign containing the moon at his birth, so Cosimo struck a victory medal bearing

the image of Capricorn, his ascendant – the zodiac sign rising over the eastern horizon at his birth. Capricorn was ruled by Saturn which everyone knew was, in strict astrological terms, an unfortunate planet. But, in Hesiod's familiar myth, dating back in its written form to at least the seventh century BCE, Saturn, as the Greek Cronos, was also the ruler of the lost golden age.[40] The symbolism was obvious. Cosimo, like Augustus, was to be the ruler of a new golden age; anyone who opposed him was guilty of obstructing the common good and denying the Florentines a better future – and standing in the path of history. That Cosimo used astrology for propaganda should not let us imagine that he was cynical and did not totally accept its world-view. His use of it was perfectly genuine and he really did believe in his own destiny as restorer of the golden age. We have one surviving astrological prognostication for Cosimo, composed by the astrologer Formiconi, which is set out for 1553–34. The following extract gives a flavour:

> The 35th year of your Excellency's most fortunate life began in 1553 on the 11th of June, at 7 hours, 14 minutes, and 33 seconds of the succeeding night, in the hour of Venus, and the lord of that year is Mars, who is found in the 5th house, retrograde, and received by Mercury, and in opposition to Saturn, which evil aspect means struggles and the enmity of the people, with the death of certain persons and much mental stress. There would also be a possibility of losing the State if Mercury were not found among these planets, in the house of the Moon, taking sextile rays from the aforesaid Mars, and sending them in trine aspect to Saturn, where they calm the anger of the inflamed Mars, and the bad influence of the iniquitous Saturn.[41]

We can see exactly the same kind of logical argument that characterized the astrological reports to the Assyrian emperors, over 2000 years earlier, even though the technical factors on which the interpretation was based are more complex. At the heart of the matter, though, was the danger caused by the position of violent Mars as 'lord of the year', ruler of the ascendant at the moment when the sun entered Aries at the spring equinox. This configuration was then compared to the horoscope not just for Cosimo's birthday, 11 June 1553, but for the exact moment on that day that the sun reached the precise position it occupied at his birth. The astrologer Formiconi found that Mars on 11 June was in an opposition to Saturn, the other unfortunate planet, which signified great danger to Cosimo; this was, after all, just 16 years since the victory at Montemurlo and the Medicis still faced a host of jealous enemies. Formiconi continued his analysis, judging that Mercury, which was powerful because it was the ruler of Gemini, the sign in which the sun and moon were placed, saved the situation because it was harmoniously aspected to both Mars and Saturn. In Platonic and Pythagorean terms, the planetary relationships were geometrical: Mercury was one sixth of the circle away from Mars and a third from Saturn. Performing a Ficinesque healing function, Mercury then calmed the dangerous influences of the malefic planets. Formiconi concluded, correctly, that the threats to Cosimo would come to nothing. And here we see just how much Renaissance political theory was tied to that of the ancient world. A report sent to the Assyrian emperor by the astrologer Balasi, over 2000 years previously, had recorded a threatened approach of Mars to Saturn with the words 'It did not come close. It did not reach it. I have nevertheless copied the relevant omen. What does it matter? Let the pertinent namburbi ritual be performed.'⁴² Formiconi did not recommend a similar ritual. After all, the medal struck after Montemurlo was a talisman for Cosimo's entire reign, impressed with the protective celestial virtue, like Augustus's coins, of Capricorn. Yet, mindful perhaps of Ficino's criticism of astrology, Formiconi concluded with a prayer to the almighty: 'May it please God,' he wrote, 'to effect that which my judgement has understood from the planets, ministers of his infinite Providence, and I submit myself to the much greater wisdom of his Divine Majesty, which I pray will be favourable to Your Excellency.'⁴³

The Renaissance: Radicalism and Reform

The most infectious of all frauds . . . it weakens religion, begets or strengthens superstition, encourages idolatry, destroys prudence, pollutes morality, defames heaven, and makes men unhappy.

PICO DELLA MIRANDOLA ON ASTROLOGY[1]

In 1494 Simon de Phares, the king of France's favourite astrologer, was condemned by the Faculty of Theology at Paris and imprisoned, for the crime of possessing books on divinatory astrology. He languished in his cell for the rest of the century, perhaps for the rest of his life. Few events could have better illustrated the crisis which was to afflict astrology for the next one and a half centuries, and which helped transform European thought. In a sense, the seed of astrology's eventual intellectual decline was contained within its complete restoration as a system of cosmic existence under Marsilio Ficino. Ficino's work for the Medicis represented a new high-point for judicial astrology's philosophical development and application in culture and politics. Yet Ficino's own attacks on astrologers point to the extent to which the practice was under attack from high-level critics. Ficino's immediate concern was with religious critics and, to attack the abuses of low-grade astrologers could be seen as a defensive device, designed to divert religious censure. But when the attack on astrology came it was launched by both conservative theologians who believed that it challenged God's overarching power, on the one hand, and Platonic sceptics on the other.

Condemnations of astrologers had actually been relatively rare. Perhaps surprisingly so, considering their dangerous propensity to subordinate the evolution of religion to the cycles of Jupiter and Saturn.[2] It appears that in 1482 Giorgio da Novara was condemned at Bologna for the crime of teaching precisely this version of history. Another astrologer, Loys de Langle, was charged with 'superstition' in the 1450s and summoned before the French king, Charles VII. De Langle had provided forecasts for the king, so was never under serious threat, and, in his defence, he provided copies of his work, which was purely astrological and therefore not superstitious; the king acquitted the astrologer, sent him back to Lyons to continue his work and added a pension as a token of his support.[3] In Cologne, the university's theological faculty examined an astrologer called Harting Gernod in 1488. Fearful of the consequences if he failed to cooperate, Gernod promised not to write any more books and the local populace was told to hand over any copies of his works that they owned for burning. Gernod was found to be an ignorant man, obviously low down in the astrological hierarchy, but the Cologne University theologians quite clearly had their eyes on the astrologers and, in 1492, they asked the Inquisitor to arrest the famous astrologer Johann Lichtenburger, accusing him not of using judicial astrology but of predicting 'killing' or 'hanging' from some unfortunate's birth chart. If true, and it may have been, this was precisely the kind of abuse which Ficino himself also condemned.

The most notorious case of the time, though, and one which alarmed Ficino, was brought against Simon de Phares who, in 1491, had been spoken of by no less a person than King Charles VIII of France as his own astrologer. By his own account, de Phares had an interesting and adventurous life. In his quest for learning he had travelled between Ireland and Egypt, and had spent four summers collecting medicinal herbs in the mountains of Savoy and Switzerland. He was astrologer to John, Duke of Bourbon but had resisted, for reasons that are not clear, employment by Charles VIII's father, Louis XI. Thorndike wondered whether de Phares knew that Louis was not to live much longer (he died in 1483) and was therefore reluctant to be involved.[4] On All Saints Day 1490, the young King Charles visited de Phares at his study in Lyons and observed his work on behalf of a continuous stream of clients, probably using interrogation charts, cast for the asking of questions or the moment of the consultation. It was later reported that he had given the answers to questions about thefts, hidden treasure and, revealing astrology's ability to yield psychological insights, 'men's secret thoughts'.[5] This was practical astrology, dealing with the realities of people's lives, their hopes, fears, aspirations and insecurities. It was also the kind of astrology which high-minded thinkers like Ficino rather looked down on, even though there was clearly a huge demand for it. We are not told whether Simon's clients knew that the king himself was present, or what their reaction would have been. It was his work for Charles in Lyons, and later in Paris, de Phares claimed, which prompted his persecution. He may well have been correct, for to attack the astrologer was a means of undermining the patron, especially as the king had referred to de Phares as his dear and well-loved astrologer. De Phares was first barred from practising in Lyons and, when he moved to Paris, his books were submitted by the law court to the university theologians. De Phares was drawn into a relentless and ruthless bureaucratic exercise in which he became a pawn of forces greater than himself. The king was in Italy until 1495 and, even when he was back in France, does not seem to have returned to Paris. De Phares, the favourite royal astrologer, was handed over first to the bishop of Paris and then to the Inquisition, in whose prisons he languished for a number of years. We are not sure whether de Phares was ever actually released from his incarceration. But, in 1498 he had his literary revenge on his persecutors by penning his major work, the *Recueil des plus celebres astrologues*, a defence and history of astrology from the Greek heroes and Hebrew patriarchs – de Phares had read the Talmud and was proud of his knowledge of Jewish texts – down to present day.

Before we leave the story of the sad end of Simon de Phares, we should refer to the precise condemnation of the books in his library: it was they and not his practice which was the technical excuse for the complaint against him. When the Parisian theologians delivered their verdict on 19 February 1494, they condemned divinatory astrology, which included the casting of birth charts and magical images, but allowed for 'true astronomy' which, as good students of Isidore of Seville, they defined in the following words. They wrote that it:

> Considers the magnitude of the heavenly bodies, their oppositions and motions, which predicts the conjunctions, oppositions and the conditions of the sun, moon, and other planets and which conjectures some of their natural effects in a probable and prudent manner (which we would honour as a liberal, noble and useful art).[6]

This was a wholesale attack on the Ficinian project and, for good measure, attempted to turn the clock back to before Aquinas. The persecution of de Phares came from traditional quarters, from conservative churchmen who feared and resented the judicial astrologers' freelance role in connecting individuals with their destiny. The astrologers represented a democratic alternative to the organized priesthood, which those who saw the Church as an institution as more important than its message would have like to have crushed, but were powerless to do so. All the representatives of Church power could do was keep up the pressure and pick off the occasional vulnerable character. However, a new and powerful front in the assault on judicial astrology was launched in 1495 and came from an entirely different quarter – from a devout Neoplatonist. Giovanni Pico della Mirandola's *Disputationes adversus astrologiam divinatricem* was at once a throwback to Platonic scepticism of the classical philosophers Carneades, Cicero and Plotinus, who regarded the stars as sources of general knowledge, but never detailed information, and a profound assertion of human freedom from stellar influence. It was this paradox, inherent in Neoplatonism, which allowed its followers to simultaneously advocate and condemn astrology, which was precisely what Ficino did. This is why Stephen Vanden Broecke has pointed out that the *Disputationes* can be read simultaneously as a condemnation of astrology and as an exhortation to reform it.[7] It has, though, been remembered by historians more for the former than the latter.

Pico was born in 1463, studied at the heavily Aristotelian University of Padua from 1480 to 1482 and met Ficino and Lorenzo de Medici apparently, although the coincidence is too neat to be entirely believable, on the very day in 1484 on which Ficino completed his translation of Plato into Latin. The two men, scholar and wealthy patron, recognized a like-minded soul in Pico and took the young man on as a protégé. Ficino's cosmology was constructed within the context of the Humanism which was largely formulated by the great Italian poet Petrarch (1304–74). Deeply influenced by Cicero, Petrarch argued that human thought and action was of value in itself, irrespective of divine intervention – that, in the well-known phrase, the proper study of man is man. The direct challenge was to the belief that only scripture can tell us about the nature of humanity. The Humanist movement was to receive its greatest manifesto in the *Oration on the Dignity of Man* opened by Ficino's student, Pico della Mirandola (1463–94).[8]

The Humanists believed the Neoplatonic dogma that human beings possessed a universal ability to envision and attain the highest good, to draw close to God, the One. Astrology, in the hands of Ficino, was to be a vehicle for obtaining the Humanist goal. To start with, the prevailing cosmology, as set out in the *Emerald Tablet*, established that humanity had an equal and reciprocal relationship with the cosmos. The concept of astrological healing, which was so dear to Ficino, depended on the belief that the universe was as much an interior phenomenon as an external one. Success depended on the physician's ability to locate the patient's inner planets and zodiac.

Pico's great and enduring work was the *Oratio de hominis dignitate – Oration on the Dignity of Man* – published in 1486 as the definitive statement of, as the title implied, the dignified location within the cosmos of human beings as creatures who can aspire to divinity. The *Oration* has a considerable reputation as a foundation for modern Western scientific scepticism, the only explanation for which is that those who believe that this is the case have not read it. Pico asserted the principle of Humanism through the old astrological notion of macrocosm–microcosm principle, familiar from the *Emerald Tablet*, that human beings contain the universe within them and the universe reflects humanity back at itself, acting as a celestial mirror. The *Oration* is actually a kabbalistic interpretation of the cosmos, containing a powerful defence of magic couched within a devoutly Christian framework. Pico was at pains to criticize demonic magic and the invocation of spirits, but he was an intense advocate of natural, or sympathetic, magic, the study of the natural world and the manipulation of the essential, psychic and material connections between all things. The word magus, he pointed out, means in Persian, 'interpreter' and 'worshipper of the divine'.[9] The magician does not tinker with the material world for profit, as imagined in the *Picatrix*, but is a seeker after divine wisdom.

Pico's *Oration* accompanied his *Conclusions philosophiae, calabisticae et theologicae*, better known as the *900 Theses*. As the title proclaims, the heart of Pico's philosophy was Jewish mysticism in the form of Kabbalah; in one passage, which was to attract the hostile attention of the papacy, he wrote, 'No science offers greater assurance of Christ's divinity than magic and the cabala.'[10] Pico was one of the first Western scholars to study Hebrew, and Jewish thought formed the basis of one of his subsequent works, the *Heptaplus*, which appeared in 1489.[11] And it's this work that offers the clue as to Pico's intent. Like Ficino, Pico was looking back to the past, to a purer time, before the present religious muddle alienated humanity from God.

For Pico, the advantage of Kabbalah, which Christian scholars now spelled as cabala, was that it offered a path to the Divine which was unimpeded by celestial influences. In this sense he was at one with the early Church Fathers. In the sense that he regarded Kabbalah as an equal partner with magic, he was at odds with them. Yet, being theologically cautious, Pico rejected any form of magic that required the assistance of daemons and, instead, followed the Ficinesque version. Magic, Pico asserted, was the 'the absolute consummation of natural philosophy'.[12] But, when he turned to astrology in the *Disputationes*, he was savage in his denunciation.[13] Having defined astrology narrowly as the 'reading of forecoming events by the stars', he went on to add that it was:

> A cheat of mercenary liars, prohibited by both civil and church law, preserved by human curiosity, mocked by philosophers, cultivated by itinerant hawkers, and suspect to the best and most prudent men ... the most infectious of all frauds ... it corrupts a philosophy, falsified medicine, weakens religion, begets or strengthens superstition, encourages idolatry, destroys prudence, pollutes morality, defames heaven, and makes men unhappy, troubled and uneasy; instead of free, servile, and quite unsuccessful in nearly all their undertakings.[14]

Astrology was philosophically and technically flawed, and denied by empirical evidence. Simply, astrology cannot and does not work; worse, it was the cause of all human suffering. Pico's rage was not just rational, but moral, his self-appointed goal being to save human beings from themselves. In this he was a true heir to both Plato and the Church Fathers as well. He was well-meaning but, in his conviction that he was absolutely right, deeply arrogant. He was, after all, an aristocrat – the Count of Mirandola. Yet his critique of astrology provides an acute analysis of its various philosophical rationales.[15] To Roger Bacon, who argued that astrology was useful to religion, Pico responded that biblical prophecies resulted from divine inspiration, not from the calculation of horoscopes. To those who believed that it was possible to 'cultivate' the heavens and elect auspicious moments to begin enterprises, he asked how one could genuinely do this when the astrologer himself was subject to celestial influences? Yet Pico was accused by his critics of being disingenuous. In this case he should have known that astrology contained injunctions to the astrologer to develop self-understanding, or to lead a pure life, precisely because the problem of the astrologer's own subjection to celestial influences had long been recognized by astrologers themselves through the opening paragraph of Ptolemy's *Centiloquium*. This inconvenient truth was one which Pico chose to ignore. Besides, he argued, there were other difficulties. For example, an astrology of signs, which allowed for negotiation with tutelary gods and goddesses, was equally capable of being employed to choose fortunate moments as an astrology of influences. And here Pico touched on a further theoretical basis for astrology, one which is too often overlooked: analogy, or what he called *parabola similitude* – the argument from similarity. The basic principle can be identified in the embryonic judicial astrology of fifth-century-BCE Mesopotamia. Venus is fertile, the theory runs, because it rules Taurus, which is represented by bulls, and bulls are fertile, while Gemini rules brothers because its brightest stars are the twins Castor and Pollux.[16] Pico's example runs as follows: fathers love sons; in his own horoscope a father is shown by the first house; the first house is connected to the fifth by one-third of the circle, a trine aspect, which is harmonious; the fifth house indicates that which the father loves; therefore a father loves his sons. For Pico, such a proposition, relying on arbitrary connections, word play and Pythagorean geometry, was patently absurd. Add to this that astrologers invariably disagreed with each other, suggesting that there was no single astrological truth, together with a denunciation of astrologers for profaning the heavens with a zodiac of animals, crude beasts, and astrology had no option but to reform or die. The key to Pico's assault on astrology, though, lay in his definition of it as prediction, its chief activity as the casting of birth charts, and its practitioners as itinerant hawkers. Like Ficino he was speaking as a member of the intellectual elite venting his revulsion at what he saw as the antics of commercial fortune-tellers, those who catered for the masses. Unlike Ficino, though, his critique of astrology was so wide-ranging as to leave nothing left, or so it seemed. In fact, his narrow definition of it as horoscopic prediction allowed for any sort of astrology that was intended to elevate the soul and ascend to heaven. His title was also significant. He was opposed to divinatory astrology, not the natural astrology of planetary influences. How could he oppose these, any more than any other Christian critic of astrology, in view of Augustine's concession that they existed? He objected to zodiacal images, but his fondness for numerology, of the notion of the cosmos as number, was an encouragement to later Renaissance magicians, such as Agrippa. But, whatever the nuances in Pico's position, it was read for what he intended, a bitter, brutal and decisive attempt to put an end to the demeaning practice of judicial astrology.

Self-consciously radical as he was by the standards of the 1480s, though, Pico was nevertheless, and naively, shocked by the Pope's condemnation of 13 of his theses in 1487, his admiration of Kabbalah attracting particular censure. He fled to France in 1488 but the long arm of the papacy caught up with him and he was thrown into prison at Vincennes. The French king, Charles VIII, interceded to have him released and arranged for him to live at Florence under Lorenzo's personal protection. All seemed well, but Pico had begun his scholarly life studying canon law in 1477 and he now seems to have experienced a personal crisis which drew him away from his Kabbalistic radicalism and back to a more conventional form of Christianity. On his release from incarceration and arrival in Florence, he adopted an ascetic lifestyle and a deepened interest in biblical studies by 1488, and, in 1490, he unwisely persuaded Lorenzo to invite his friend, the unprepossessing Dominican monk Girolamo Savonarola (1452–98), to live in Florence. Savonarola was a fanatical puritan whose constant preaching against the venality and corruption he found amidst the opulence of Florence's massive wealth began to attract capacity crowds.[17] Christian piety, he taught, was displayed by goodness and simplicity, not the displays of pomp characteristic of the Medici, or of the new Pope Alexander VI (1492–1503), the notorious Rodriguo Borgia. Savonarola assisted Pico in his preparation of the *Disputationes* and it is tempting to see the puritanical preacher's influence in Pico's statement that the zodiac signs defame the heavens, as if they demean the glory of God. Certainly, Pico's closing pages recall the University of Paris's traditional hostility to astrology. Pico died in 1494, the year in which Savonarola temporarily drove out the Medicis and instituted a brief-lived puritanical republic of God, a forerunner of the Calvinist republics of the following century.

The *Disputationes'* publication in July 1496, rational text though it was, became an integral part of Savonarola's plan to wipe out all learning except that of which he personally approved, and the argument that Pico's work was essentially religious is difficult to refute.[18] Savonarola's hatred of astrology was visceral. As Remo Catani put it, Savonarola saw astrology 'as an enemy of faith ... an impediment to Christian government and a violation of divine prophecy'.[19] Savonarola's rule climaxed in 1497 with the bonfire of the vanities, a destruction of literature, art and finery in which the citizens of Florence were persuaded to destroy all symbols of anti-Christian luxury and frivolity in a great public conflagration; in the ensuing hysteria even the greatest of artists, Sandro Botticelli, burnt his own paintings. At that point, though, the frenzy also burnt itself out. Savonarola was deposed, excommunicated and, in the following year, simultaneously hung and burned. Pico had moved a long way since the *Oration on the Dignity of Man* and, in retrospect, his work, taken up by Savonarola, served the cause of the suppression of knowledge which echoed the worst excess of the Inquisition and presaged the book burning of Nazi Germany. But his denunciation of astrology had been launched into the world of Catholic Europe and there was no turning back.

The astrologers, though, were not caught off guard. News of Pico's book had leaked out and at least two defences of astrology, published as pre-emptive strikes, appeared more than two years before the *Disputationes*.[20] One was composed by the Italian Humanist and poet Giovanni Gioviano Pontano (1426–1503), whose own astrological works included a commentary on Ptolemy's *Centiloquium*. Pontano, whose attitude to astrology was more conventional and naturalistic than Ficino's soul-oriented variety, noted that Pico was now persecuting astrology as he had once persecuted religion. Pontano knew how this barb would sting the newly devout Pico, but expunged it from the text of his *De rebus coelestibus* on hearing of Pico's death. Pontano, though, regarded the *Disputationes* as an outrage and led the response to it, publishing a series of refutations, beginning in 1501 with *De fortuna*, a book whose title betrays its content. The attacks on astrology continued with Pico's nephew, Gian Francesco Pico, who was particularly incensed at astrology's suggestion that Christianity was subject to the stars. We should make no mistake about the way in which the intellectual battle lines were drawn. The supporters of astrology were aligned with the Humanists and free thinkers, the opponents sheltered in the reactionary tentacles of the Catholic Church.

The astrologers, faced with this onslaught, were split. One group, the conservatives, of whom Pontano was a figurehead, insisted that astrology was fine as it was, and that Pico had either misunderstood what astrologers really do, or had deliberately misled his readers. Contrary to what Pico claimed, the conservatives responded that astrologers were not deterministic and didn't subordinate God's plan to the stars. Another group of conservatives, with whom I shall deal later, saw the solution in magic, rather than horoscopes. However, a third, and, from the point of Western history, far more important group, emerged. These were the reformers, who conceded that much of what Pico said was true; astrologers did indeed get their predictions wrong and there was a confusing profusion of techniques, not all of which could be right.[21] Some techniques, it was agreed, such as the lucky and unlucky 'Egyptian days' had no basis in astronomy and, worse, the entire astronomical model for astrology had been undermined as the constellations shifted in relation to the zodiac signs. This group began the search for a more accurate astrology, one based on what they saw as first principles. One solution was to establish an astrology which was more textually correct. Ptolemy's *Tetrabiblos* was seen as the potential literary basis for a reformed astrology and Arabic 'superstitions', as far as they could be identified, were blamed for the undignified condition into which astrology had descended. The question, though, was how far judicial astrology could be stripped of those parts of its interpretive structure which had no basis in either reason or observation. A text such as Bonatti's *Liber Astronomiae* contained Babylonian, Egyptian, Greek, Persian and Indian contributions, which were virtually impossible to distinguish, so their task, in the end, was a hopeless one. One interpretative technique which came in for the reformers' anger was the so-called 'Arabic' part. 'Parts', or 'Lots', had been devised by the Greeks and were usually calculated by adding together the celestial longitude of any two astrological factors and subtracting a third. The astrologers of the Islamic world added a huge number of potential parts, such as the 'parts of lentil' or 'fig', which could be used by farmers or merchants to predict the size of their crop or profit. The reformer Albert Pigghe denounced the use of parts in 1519, on the grounds that they had no basis in astronomy; far better, he said, for farmers to observe the weather.[22]

The reformers themselves divided into two, so we can identify a fourth reaction to Pico. This group, of whom the principal exponent was to be the great astronomer Johannes Kepler, wanted to go even further, abandoning astrology's entire technical structure, including zodiac signs, retaining only what could measured – chiefly planetary motions. Their goal was to keep records of events which coincided with astronomical cycles, observing the correlations in order to restore a truly accurate astrology which, once again, could be used to predict and manage the future for the common good. It was the reformers, who were all too aware of astrology's failures, who were to drive the astronomical discoveries of the next 200 years.

If Ficino had found a revolutionary follower in Pico, though, he was to have another, one far more famous, in Nicholas Copernicus (1473–1543), the man who demonstrated that the sun, not the earth, was the centre of the cosmos.[23] Born in Torun in Prussia (now Poland), Copernicus pursued the traditional medieval curriculum, including astrology, at Jagiellonian University, Cracow, from 1491. Although the standard astronomical education would have included only the *Tractatus de sphaera* of John of Sacrobosco and the *Theorica planetarum Geradi*, there was a separate school of mathematics and astronomy at which Copernicus could have studied. He would have been familiar with the Alfonsine tables and became aware of the pressure for astrological reform from the works of the 'father of observational astronomy', Georg von Peuerbach (1423–61) and the famous astrologer Johannes Müller von Königsberg (1436–76), better known as Regiomontanus, and John of Gogów, one of his teachers, had written on the effects of planetary conjunctions. In the autumn of 1496 Copernicus moved from Cracow to the University of Bologna, where he was registered to study canon law (later civil law) and became the assistant to the astrologer, Platonic philosopher and professor of astronomy Domenico Maria Novara (1454–1504). Novara was well known for his technical achievements, especially work he had published in 1489 showing that the latitudes of Italian cities were then 1° 10' to the north of those listed in Ptolemy's *Geography*, from which he inferred a slow modification of the direction of the earth's axis, over a period of 395,000 years. The conclusion, which was unremarked on at the time, but which might perhaps have influenced Copernicus, was that the earth was no longer the fixed point at the centre of the Aristotelian universe. Since 1404 the University of Bologna had required the professor of mathematics to issue annual astrological prognostications, an expectation which Novara conscientiously fulfilled, issuing an annual almanac which included general predictions for the year along with auspicious and ominous dates, the date of Easter, phases of the moon, weather forecasts and times of other occasional phenomena, such as eclipses. Copernicus assisted Novara in the preparation of these almanacs, and his subsequent studies of medicine at Padua in 1501–3 would have further exposed him to the practice of horoscopic astrology. Our evidence of his use of judicial astrology, though, is frustratingly slight and the few surviving horoscopes which he cast have never been published and are still awaiting scholarly analysis.

Copernicus had arrived in Italy just months after the publication of Pico's *Disputationes*, and the air was thick with the argument over whether judicial astrology was firstly possible and, secondly, legitimate. At one end of the spectrum lay Ficino's controversial, sympathetic astrological magic, at the other the belief in physical celestial influences and nothing more. Copernicus was to take two approaches to the problem of astrological reform. The first was to attempt more accurate astronomical measurements. We know that he was making astronomical observations by 1497; at around 11 p.m. on 9 March of that year he observed an occultation of Aldaberan, the brightest star in Taurus, by the moon. We also know that, while in Rome to celebrate the jubilee year of 1500, he observed the partial eclipse of the moon on 6 November. However, the astronomy of the time was still primarily theoretical rather than observational and, like all his contemporaries, Copernicus's inspiration came from classical philosophy. It is well known that Copernicus set out to reform astronomical computaton, by returning to first principles and reconceptualizing the universe on the basis of Platonic geometry. Nowhere did he discuss astrology but, given the context within which he was working, astrology, calendar problems and navigation were the three problems to which astronomy was directed. But only the first of the three required the sort of work which Copernicus undertook.

In 1503 Copernicus was finally proclaimed a doctor of canon law at the University of Ferrara, after which he returned to Poland and became secretary to his uncle, the bishop of Varmia, or Warmia. His astronomical research remained more important than his administrative duties, though, and he realized that the core problem lay in the 2000-year-old question of how Plato's doctrine of motion in perfect circles could be true if the planets self-evidently pursue erratic paths through the sky. By 1510 he had worked out that the only realistic answer must be to remove the earth from the centre of the universe and replace it with the sun. For reasons which are still disputed, but which, some suggest, may have something to do with its inherent danger and a profound reluctance to shake the basis of Catholic faith, this work, the *Commentariolus*, which was completed by 1514, was never published, at least not until the nineteenth century.[24] It is quite possible, though, that Copernicus delayed publication merely because he wanted his ideas to be presented in a properly finished state before he went into print. This is plausible, especially as it is difficult to see exactly what was inherently controversial in his ideas, especially in the context of medieval cosmology. Nowhere in the Genesis creation myth was it claimed that the earth was the centre of the cosmos and orbited by the sun; this was a Greek idea and the notion that it was necessarily shocking has more to do with the modern myth of science confronting, and overcoming, medieval superstition than the intellectual climate of Catholic Europe in the 1500s.

Copernicus's major arguments were contained in the *De revolutionibus orbium coelestium libri sex*, a book he also kept suppressed until the year of his death, 1543. He was finally persuaded to publish by his sole disciple, the distinguished astrologer Georg Joachim von Lauchen, better known as Rheticus (1514–74).[25] That the bishop of Chelmo, Copernicus's closest friend, encouraged him, and that he showed a preface to Pope Paul III without causing undue alarm, is a warning against facile assumptions that the Catholic Church was standing in the way of scientific progress. If this were not enough to make the point, in 1533, Johann Albrecht Widmannstetter delivered a series of lectures in Rome, outlining Copernicus's theory. He was heard with considerable interest by several Catholic cardinals as well as the Pope, Clement VII. Three years later, the archbishop of Capua, Nikolaus Cardinal von Schönberg, wrote to Copernicus, pleading with him to publish; Copernicus was to include the letter in *De revolutionibus* as a demonstration of the moral support he had received from prominent churchmen. In the event, Copernicus succeeded in his aim by making Plato's theory that the planets orbit in perfect circles even more convincing than it had been before. He abandoned epicycles, moved the sun to the centre of the universe and had the planets, including the earth, orbiting in a manner of which even Plato would have thoroughly approved. In point of fact, the centre of Copernicus's cosmos was not the sun but the centre of the earth's orbit; it is not until the next century and Kepler's later work, the *Astronomia nova*, that the physical sun was settled on as the centre of the universe. That, though, is a detail. Copernicus's masterstroke in simplifying the geometrical Platonic cosmos, saving it from Aristotelian complexities, matched perfectly the prevailing notion of celestial harmony as a metaphor for political and social harmony.

The significance of Copernicus's sun-centred cosmos was to be revolutionary but his purpose, like that of a number of the other great astronomical reformers, including Tycho Brahe, Johannes Kepler and Isaac Newton, was essentially conservative, to improve human understanding of the existing cosmos, not to change it. The destruction of the old models of the cosmos was not intentional, but a classic example of that awkward feature of existence, the law of unintended consequences. His argument opened with the statement that the world was named *Mundus* (Greek cosmos), the root of our word mundane, because it means purity and elegance.[26] The sky meanwhile is the *caelum* because the word's root is *caelo*, 'I carve';[27] the constellations were still living images engraved on the celestial orb, exactly as they had been in classical Greece – and for Isidore of Seville. The universe was beautiful and alive, and this was the reason for gaining a more accurate understanding of its motions. He continued by setting out his political purpose, again absolutely and unambiguously rooted in the ideal of the harmonious, managed in line with cosmic principles. As long, he argued, that the moments of civic and religious rituals were properly timed, so the state would remain 'alive and watchful'. The problem, Copernicus claimed, was that astronomical measurements were inaccurate. His particular genius was to realise that it wasn't the measuring tools or methods which were the problem, but the underlying mathematical and geometric models. Get the model right, his logic ran, and the rest would fall into place: planetary positions would be accurately measured, rituals would be properly timed and the state would prosper. This was exactly what Plato had said.[28] Copernicus's astronomy was subservient to astrology and astrology served political priorities.

The entire milieu in which Copernicus moved was astrological. His sole disciple was the brilliant astrologer Georg Joachim Rheticus, who had begun his career by travelling to visit different scholars, beginning with Johannes Schöner (1477–1547), the distinguished astronomer, cartographer, globe-maker and author of the *Three Books on the Judgment of Nativities*, a complete compendium of medieval natal astrology.[29] When not casting horoscopes, Rheticus was a physician as well as a maker of maps and navigational instruments. And when he was dealing with astrology, Rheticus was firmly in the reformers' camp and was eager to reformulate astrology as the practical mathematical science he believed it had been in Egyptian antiquity. Copernicus's new mathematical description of the cosmos provided an extraordinary opportunity for Rheticus to reclaim those ancient truths. This was to be the fulfilment of Copernicus's great work, and the confusing, misleading, astrology inherited from the previous century, epitomized by Schöner, would be safely laid to rest.[30] So keen was Rheticus to bring Copernicus to public attention that he published his own summary of his teacher's theories, the *Narratio Prima*, in 1539, and was instrumental in securing the eventual publication of the *De revolutionibus*. Others agreed. In 1541, Reiner Gemma Frisius (1508–55) wrote how the *De revolutionibus* of which he, like many others, had received advance reports, was eagerly awaited, the hope being that it would end the astronomical errors and uncertainties that afflicted astrology.

If any other evidence were needed concerning Copernicus's ideological context, it is provided by his immediate influences. He mentioned the sixth-century-BCE Pythagorean philosopher Philolaus as an authority for the theory that the earth moved in space, although it is doubtful whether he had access to his work. It is more likely that he had some knowledge of the Greek astronomer Aristarchus of Samos (c.312–c.230 BCE), who had long ago worked out that the earth orbits the sun, and perhaps of the statement by Martinus Capella that Mercury and Venus orbit the sun.[31] It is equally plausible that he had access to thirteenth- and fourteenth-century Persian astronomy, although just how is not clear. He was also aware that the vigorous theoretical cosmological debates of the late Middle Ages had included the possibility that the sun might be the centre of the universe; the idea was rejected, but considered nonetheless.[32] But his insistence that the sun was the centre of the universe was lifted directly from Ficino's translations of Hermes and Orpheus and, as John Christianson argued, from Ficino's concept of *amor* – best translated, perhaps, as Platonic love – which placed humanity at the centre of the nexus of cosmic spiritual hierarchies.[33]

That Hermeticism exerted a profound influence on Copernicus is clear from the tone of *De Revolutionibus*. Copernicus was convinced by the Hermetic notion that a 'spiritual' sun was the heart of the cosmos, irrespective of the location of the physical sun, and concluded that it made sense for the latter to occupy the same space as the former.

> In the midst of all assuredly dwells the Sun. For, in this most beautiful temple, who would place this luminary in any other or better position from which he can illuminate the whole at once? Indeed, some rightly call Him the Light of the World, others, the Mind or the Ruler of the Universe: Hermes Trismegistus names him the visible God. Sophocles Electra calls him the all-seeing. So indeed the Sun remains, as if in his kingly dominion, governing the family of Heavenly bodies which circles around him.[34]

Compare this to Ficino, who wrote in his 1487 work, *The Book of the Sun*:

> For these reasons Orpheus called Apollo the vivifying eye of heaven, and what I am about to say is taken straight from the Hymns of Orpheus: 'The Sun is the eternal eye seeing all things, the pre-eminent celestial light, moderating heavenly and worldly things, leading or drawing the harmonious course of the world, the Lord of the world, immortal Jupiter, the eye of the world circling round everywhere, possessing the original imprint in whose image all worldly forms are made. The Moon is pregnant with the stars, the Moon is queen of the stars.' These things Orpheus says. In Egypt, on the temples of Minerva, this golden inscription could be read: 'I am all those things which are, which will be and which have been. No one has ever turned back my veil. The fruit I have borne is the Sun.' Whence it appears that this Sun born of Minerva – that is, of divine intelligence – is both flower and fruit.[35]

The sun was universally recognized in medieval thought as the living, celestial symbol of kingship.[36] Equally impressive is the manner in which Copernicus's discussion of the ordering of the planets in Book I, Chapter X, of *De revolutionibus* draws on two earlier passages, Ficino's account of the movements of Mercury and Venus in Chapter 4 of *The Book of the Sun*, and Pico's in Book X, Chapter 4, of the *Disputationes*. Copernicus was *the* key member of the astrological reform programme that followed Ficino and Pico. Copernicus's aim was to 'save the appearances', a term derived from Simplicius's sixth-century commentary on Aristotle, meaning that astronomers were engaged in a constant mission to develop a theory to explain the apparently disorderly movements of the planets.[37] The phrase was a familiar one and used by Galileo when writing about Copernicus in 1615.[38] Copernicus came not to bury the old cosmos but to save it, and the victory of heliocentrism, placing the physical sun at the centre of the cosmos to match the spiritual sun actually marked the consolidation of the Hermetic tradition.[39] Yet, Copernicus's work came to be seen as marking a decisive break with the superstitious, medieval cosmos, ushering in the modern universe of reason and experiment. The 'Copernican Revolution' has even become the paradigm for the whole notion of scientific revolution.[40]

One of the most frequently repeated clichés about Copernicus holds that he deposed man from his privileged position at the heart of the cosmos, beginning the long process of alienation that has led now to the earth's position as a tiny speck on the edge of a small galaxy in a small corner of a universe which may itself be one of an infinite number of universes. But there is little evidence to support this case, especially as, from the pessimistic point of view, humanity was hardly the centre of the universe, but the miserable, sinful creature mired in sin, envisioned by St Augustine. In any case, in Dante's cosmology, Satan, not humanity, stood at the dark heart of the cosmos. The more convincing point of view, especially in view of subsequent history, suggests that Copernicus's new sun-centred universe, far from diminishing humanity's security, reinforced it. The location of the Hermetic sun, the symbol and instrument of God, at the centre of the universe, reduced the power of Satan; humanity was no longer midway between the two, pulled up by the one and down by the other, in their perpetual struggle for supremacy. Ernst Cassirer dealt with this problem at some length and his conclusion was that the 'glorification of man' was one of the favourite themes of early Renaissance literature.[41] Freed from the constant attack of demons, the Renaissance intellectual was taken further along the Humanist path, towards the confidence of the eighteenth-century Enlightenment – and the triumph of the light of reason over the darkness of superstition. There were, though, competing Copernican narratives, and that God's divine reason now shone at the centre of everything could be construed as authoritarian rather than liberating. Even for William Harvey (1578–1657), who discovered the circulation of the blood, sun, king and heart were to be equals at the centre of their respective systems, heavenly, political and physiological.[42] Meanwhile, the supporters of absolute monarchy seized on the sun's new location at the centre of the celestial universe and claimed that the king, the sun's astrological equivalent, occupied a cosmically sanctioned position at the heart of society.[43] To challenge the king was to challenge the entire cosmic order. The monarch who took this theory to its logical conclusion was, of course, Louis XIV of France (1643–1715), the sun-king. Louis was, incidentally, also the last dauphin to have had an astrologer present at his birth. But, in the ideological iconography which accompanied Louis' absolutist aspirations, we see the ultimate triumph of political Copernicanism, one of the most vivid products of the crisis of the 1490s.

9

The Sixteenth Century: Reformers and Magicians

I consider the rational basis of his celestial art as right, while the art itself is uncertain. That is, the signs in heaven and on earth do not fail. They are the work of God and the angels.

MARTIN LUTHER[1]

On 31 October 1517, according to the German astrologer Philip Melanchthon, the priest and theology teacher Martin Luther nailed his 95 theses, objecting to corrupt Church practice, to the door of the Castle Church in Wittenberg. This seminal event, later chosen by Melanchthon as the 'birthday' of the Protestant Reformation, initiated a process which was to fracture the Church and divide Europe between Catholics and reformers. There is a direct comparison to be made in the way in which European thinkers were simultaneously questioning their relationship to the stars and God. The debate on the cosmological reform certainly bears comparison with the religious reformation. There is an obvious coincidence in time: Copernicus completed the *Commentariolus* between 1510 and 1514, just a few years before Luther triggered the Reformation in 1517. Luther did not approve of judicial astrology.[2] Neither did Calvin, Luther's more extreme rival, who criticized it in his posthumous *Traité or Avertissement contre l'astrologie* in 1549.[3] Like Savonarola, whose sermons against astrology he seems to have read, Calvin was addressing the masses rather than engaging in scholarly debate, but he did show the difficulty of effectively condemning astrology. He attacked judicial and divinatory astrology but had to allow for astrological agriculture and medicine: physicians, he wrote, use the heavens wisely when they elect auspicious moments for bleeding and administering medicine.

Luther and Calvin, though, were not representative of the mass of Protestants, who reflected as many shades of opinion as did Catholics. The most eminent of the Reformation astrologers was Philip Melanchthon (1497–1560), the organizational genius of Lutheranism, who was the movement's effective leader while Luther was in hiding in Wartbug Castle from 1521 to 1522. He was also a considerable scholar, was professor of Greek at Wittenberg and had a distinguished Humanist pedigree; he was the grandson of Johann Reuchlin's sister and the two were extremely close until the Reformation pushed them apart. Melanchthon believed that the reform of religious knowledge, faith and ritual should be accompanied by a parallel reform in the whole of knowledge. God, he reasoned, had created nature, so nature itself must be studied and, significantly for astrology, that included nature's effect on humans.[4] Melanchthon had studied astrology at Thubingen from 1512 to 1518 under Johannes Stoeffler and, from then on, he considered knowledge of astrology to be an essential part of Humanism. He was a keen friend and supporter of Rheticus, securing him a post teaching astrology, astronomy and mathematics at Wittenberg, and the two men were at one on the need to reform astrology. Melanchthon argued that, as people are, in their physical selves, creatures of nature, so they must receive influences from the stars. This is a simple logical truth. He also, though, found evidence for astrology in the strange fact that healthy parents may have one fit child and one sick one. The only cause of such differences, he concluded, had to be the stars, which were, then, the rulers of chance.[5] Normally the inference drawn from such arguments was that astrology indicated the existence of natural law, a sort of fundamental uniformity. For Melanchthon, astrology explained the diversity which challenged natural law, a proposition whose radical significance he never developed. Neither, he thought, did astrological influences affect everyone equally; true to Luther's reverence for political authority, he declared that princes were closer to God and less subject to the stars. God, himself, though, was a democrat; he cared for everyone and could always intervene to moderate a celestial influence. And this leads straight into Melanchthon's absolute belief in divinatory astrology, an astrology of signs based on planetary conjunctions, comets, eclipses and the whole panoply of related practices and events, from dreams to monstrous births.[6] This was all, of course, Babylonian and condemned in the Old Testament, but for Melanchthon, whose reading of the texts was different, it was completely justified by scripture.[7] Melanchthon was a reformer, but his inspiration came from the word of God as much as from Ptolemy. It is a fascinating thought that the man who systematized and organized the Lutheran Reformation was an enthusiastic user of astrology, but the willingness of evangelical Protestants to look to the sky for signs of the coming apocalypse was sustained into the twentieth century.

Luther's own regard for prophecy was reinforced by the belief that he was the subject of a forecast made when the religious reformer Jan Hus was burnt at the stake in 1415. It was believed that a new reformer, perhaps even the Messiah, would be born a hundred years later and, although Luther was born in 1483 or 1484, he identified himself with the prophecy. It became part of the standard apocalyptic fare of the late fifteenth century when it was included in the *Prognosticatio*, a set of prophecies issued by Johannes Lichtenberger in 1488.[8] Lichtenberger also included a previous apocalyptic prophecy associating the day of judgement with the conjunction of Jupiter with the malefic planets Saturn and Mars in November 1484. Given that this dire event failed to take place, astrology's critics were encouraged, and the events leading to de Phares's imprisonment and Pico's *Disptuationes* were set in train. By the 1530s, though, there was eager discussion as to whether Luther was born in 1483 or 1484. If the latter, then he might be the anti-Christ of Lichtenberger's prophecy, if the former, he was safe. The debates were ecumenical and Melanchthon engaged in a correspondence with Lucus Gauricus (1476–1558), a leading Catholic astrologer, on this very topic, as well as with another influential practitioner, Johannes Schoener (1477–1547).[9] The astrologers engaged in micro-calculations in the attempt to solve the problem. Gauricus's preferred birth time for Luther was 1.10 a.m., while Philo Pfeil argued for 3.22 a.m., both for 22 October 1484. Melanchthon himself eventually settled on 1483, the previous year. Luther, though, ignored such details. He was more interested in his own role in fulfilling his prophetic mission. He was well aware, as was everyone else in Europe at the time, of the coming conjunction of Jupiter and Saturn in Pisces in 1524. Pisces being a water sign, it was widely – and logically – expected that this mighty celestial event was to preside over a catastrophic repeat of the biblical deluge.[10] When Luther triggered the Reformation by nailing his theses to the door of the Castle Church in Wittenberg in 1517, he knew what the heavens were planning, even more so when, in 1524, he arranged for a new publication of Lichtenberger's *Prognosticatio*. Luther's conclusion was that, while astrology, the celestial art, is infallible, being based on signs and wonders sent by God (he seems to have ignored the question of celestial influence), astrologers themselves are fallible. Besides, the devout should have no need of astrology when they can look direct to God:

> What are we then saying about Lichtenberger and his like? This is what I say. Firstly I consider the rational basis of his celestial art as right, while the art itself is uncertain. That is, the signs in heaven and on earth do not fail. They are the work of God and the angels, sent to warn us, and it is nothing to make an art out of it and to attribute such connections to the stars. Secondly, next to this it nevertheless might be that God or his angels have moved him [Lichtenberger] to make many forecasts which have come true but, to let him understand that the art is uncertain, God has let him fail many times. And this is our conclusion: Christians should not ask for such a prophecy because they have devoted themselves to God and therefore don't need such readings and predictions. But because Lichtenberger indicates the signs of the sky, godless people become afraid of all such prophecies.[11]

Luther and Melanchthon could agree that astrology's assumptions were reasonable, but differed on its effectiveness. Luther held to the formula that astrology may be a source of truth but astrologers themselves, being mere mortals, were all too fallible and liable to error. Those of Luther's followers who advocated cosmological reform could go in one of two directions. They might, like their spiritual leader, look primarily to God or, like Rheticus, they could follow Copernicus. While the reform movement was generally devoted to stripping astrology back to its essentials, there was another significant consequence of Ficino's translations – the encouragement of a new breed of magician. Some of these men were themselves ardent reformers in the sense that they wished to build a new system of learning.[12] One of the foremost, the Englishman John Dee, was himself a committed Copernican. In a wider sense this phenomenon occurred because of the extraordinarily tolerant spirit of Humanism of which Ficino was himself a part, in particular a respect for Judaism which ran entirely counter to the conventional scapegoating of Jews as Christ killers. This did not mean, before we imagine that the Humanists were modern liberals, that they were tolerant of Jews, but, in their pursuit of the original true religion, they were prepared to use whatever texts and teachings were quite obviously survivals of it. What most impressed Catholic scholars was Kabbalah, which, rather than simply asserting that reason was a possible route to the One, provided a practical programme of study, meditation and ritual by which this great goal might be achieved. The first Christian scholar known to have been aware of Kabbalah was Raymond Lull, who used it as a unifying principle for all knowledge, but he appears to have been unusual for his time. Kabbalistic teachings were effectively introduced into the Catholic world by Pico, following which they became the core feature of Western esotericism to the present day.[13]

Pico was himself an influence on the German Humanist Johann Reuchlin (1455–1522) who, in turn, did much to restore the dignity of Jewish teachings in a generally hostile Christian world. Reuchlin was, like so many leading scholars, extremely well connected. He held a post in the household of Charles I, Margrave of Baden, in which capacity he was asked to accompany Frederick, the Margrave's third son, to Paris, where he was to train for an ecclesiastical career. While in Paris he became associated with the leader of the Paris Realists, Jean Heynlin, who he then accompanied to Basel in 1474.[14] Travelling in Italy in 1482, he visited Ficino's Platonic Academy and made contacts for the Medicis. In 1492 he took part in an embassy to the Holy Roman Emperor Frederick III where he began to read Hebrew with the imperial physician, Jakob ben Jehiel Loans, who was himself Jewish. Enthused by the belief that reading the scriptures in Hebrew could lead to a better understanding of God's word, Reuchlin published a number of works including a grammar and lexicon, *De Rudimentis Hebraicis,* and wrote his own exposition of Kabbalistic cosmology in two works, *De Verbo Mirifico* and, in 1517, *De Arte Cabbalistica.* In 1510 he also successfully defended, in front of the Emperor Maximilian, the right of the Jews to possess religious works in Hebrew which were the subject of a hostile campaign, partly led by the Dominicans; it was thought that, if their own sacred texts were banned, Jews would be more likely to become Christians. As a Kabbalist, though, Reuchlin's private position was that divine, cosmic truths unavailable in Latin or Greek versions were only accessible in the Hebrew. The advocates of Kabbalah and magic, it had to be understood, were the radicals and freethinkers of the time. They were, in the sense that Bohemia was later to become a centre of such ideas, the first Bohemians.

The paradox inherent in this turning back to Plato and Kabbalah has to be understood. By looking back to pre-Arabic, even pre-Greek, philosophies in an attempt to discover the pristine theology, Pico and those who followed him were setting up a challenge to the existing cosmological consensus which was to first overthrow it and then take Western scholarship forward. The radical ideas of the extravagantly named Swiss scholar and physician Aureolus Philippus Theophrastus Bombast (1493–1541), better known as Paracelsus, illustrate the process.[15] There was no reason for Paracelsus to question the overall cosmology of his day, or of an astrology which consisted equally of celestial influences and signs, especially as one deeply influenced by Kabbalah. His philosophy in this sense was standard:

> Know that there are two kinds of stars – the heavenly and the earthly, the stars of folly and the stars of wisdom. And just as there are two worlds, a Little World [the Microcosm, man] and a Great World [the Macrocosm, the Universe] and just as the little one rules over the great one, so the stars of the microcosm rule over and govern the Stars of heaven.[16]

There is in each person, Paracelsus thought, as well as every animal, bird and plant, a star which mirrors, matches or is in some sense the same as, a star in the heavens. God, though, was absolutely supreme and all disease came from him, even if via the spirit. The radical component in Paracelsus's medical philosophy was a logical extension of Ptolemy's cosmology in the sense that Ptolemy argued that human beings were subject to a hierarchy of influences from celestial to climatic, geographical and cultural. The good physician could follow Ptolemy and yet completely ignore his astrological rules for diagnosis and treatment of disease. Paracelsus argued that, while the astrological correspondences between planets and body organs (sun to the heart, moon to the brain, and so on) were to be assumed, at the moment of birth the infant becomes an autonomous physical unit with an independent – and predetermined – lifespan.[17] The physician should therefore examine the patient's physical processes on their own terms and make the evidence of what is happening in the body the primary focus for treatment and cure, rather than using an arbitrary astrological model which is imposed on every ailment. In Paracelsus's hands Kabbalah, by inducing reverence for God's creation, encouraged the empirical study of the natural world. It wasn't just theology, though, which drove Paracelsus, but the observation that astrology's successes were erratic. 'Christ and His apostles prophesy the seasons of the nations,' he wrote, 'but the astronomer prophesies the seasons of Nature ... For what God prophesies happens and nothing can prevent it.'[18] But what the astronomer predicts either may or may not happen depending on factors which cannot be forecast. Thus, prophecy springs from one source, astronomy from another. The true knowledge of man's essence, Paracelsus wrote, can be attained only on the basis of his life; 'it cannot be understood by any other sign'.[19] Paracelsus's emphasis on the functional separation of nature and spirit, even if they were theoretically intertwined in the Kabbalistic cosmos, presages the mind–body split written into Western thought by Rene Descartes in the next century, and enabled him to propose natural cures for mental disease and combat superstition, which he realized could make people ill; fear that the sight of a black crow might cause death might become self-fulfilling. This was exactly the problem which Formiconi had faced in his decision whether to warn Cosimo de Medici of a dire planetary pattern, and so risk making the consequences worse. Paracelsus's route into this way of thinking was itself taken from medieval magic, and his statement that the stars of the microcosm – that is, human beings – can exert an influence on the cosmos is framed within the doctrines of the *Emerald Tablet*. His humanism, like Pico's, operates within the realm of the rational soul, that extended part of the intellect which links humanity to heaven. If it is possible, he argued, to ward off a Martian complaint by the creation of a Mars talisman then the planetary correspondences are being manipulated, but the process is also working on a psychic, or mental, level.[20] And if this is possible, then the physician should also be able to cure disease of a mental origin and this, as with physical ailments, can be done by working from empirical observation rather than preconceived models. Now, Paracelsus, no less than any modern scientist, had a preconceived theoretical framework, but he was shifting the balance towards the collection of data and, as a good Humanist, he favoured a focus on the patient rather than the stars. Magic, in Paracelsus's work, was a stepping stone to modern medicine.

The first of the new wave of magicians, inspired by the work of Ficino, Pico and Reuchlin, was the German Johannes Trithemius (1462–1516), an intellectual prodigy who became abbot of the Benedictine Abbey of Sponheim at the age of 21 after being unexpectedly stranded there in a snow storm in the previous year.[21] Trithemius set out to transform the Abbey from the state of undisciplined decay in which he found it, to a centre of learning. Learning, for Trithemius, should have no limits and he expanded the Abbey library from around 50 to 2000 volumes. His growing reputation as a magician attracted considerable attention and, in 1506, he was forced to move and became abbot of the Schottenkloster, or 'Scottish monastery' in Würzburg, under the patronage of the Lord Bishop of Würzburg, Lorenz von Bibra. Among his own writings was his 1508 astrological work the *De septum secundeis*, or *The Seven Secondary Intelligences*, a work whose ideological foundation is evident in its title: each planet possesses a living consciousness, personality and character. Trithemius's most famous work was the *Steganographia*, which appears to have been written around 1499. Even though it was not published until over a hundred years later (and placed on the Index, the Catholic Church's list of prohibited reading, in 1609), the *Steganographia* circulated in manuscript form and had an immense impact on European occultists. At first sight, the *Steganographia* is a work about necromancy – about using spirits to communicate over long distances. An alternative view is that it is a work of cryptography setting out cyphers for secret messages.[22] This may well be true but, if so, does not suggest that Trithemius's concern with magic was anything other than genuine or the existence of spirits was universally taken for granted. Trithemius's problem, as far as the Church was concerned, was that he was a free thinker, prepared, like so many medieval magicians before him, to talk to spirits outside of the tightly controlled rituals of the Church in which, after all, prayer to dead saints was a central part of Catholic practice.

Among Trithemius's pupils was a man with one of the most resonant names in magical history, Henry Cornelius Agrippa of Nettesheim (1486–1535), a counsellor to the Holy Roman Emperor Charles V, the most powerful monarch in Europe, and a Judge of the Prerogative Court.[23] These honours were proudly carried on the title page of the 1651 English language edition of his compendious work, *De occulta philosophia*, a book which, more than any other, gave the word 'occultism' its modern definition as the practice of hidden arts and the pursuit of secret knowledge.[24] Agrippa was a child when the polemics on astrology were at their height and in the fallout he clearly took the conservative line – that the traditional art was absolutely fine and needed no criticism. He was perfectly happy to quote the 'Arabians', and saw no reason to expunge oriental superstition from the noble art. He followed the well-trodden esoteric path of syncretism, using all previous available work from Pliny to Pico, whose *Oration on the Dignity of Man* he admired, taking in Ptolemy, the *Picatrix*, Albertus Magnus, Thomas Aquinas and Ficino, especially the latter's translation of the *Corpus Hermeticum* and Neoplatonic works. The *Three Books of Occult Philosophy*, as his work was known in English, was written in 1509–10, when he was a precocious 23 year old, suggesting that it was the product of intense reading rather than personal experience. After circulating in manuscript form for about 20 years, it was published and became the core text of magic to which most subsequent works referred. It was immediately condemned by the Dominican Inquisitor Conrad Köllin of Ulm and Agrippa subsequently wrote that there is no certainty in anything other than the word of God. Such a statement could, of course, be perfectly compatible with continued allegiance to a world within which magic depended on God's creation for its operation. After all, the heart of Platonic cosmology was the uncertainty principle – that all knowledge gleaned from the material world is likely to be false, and only God, or *Nous*, can be the course of wisdom. Magic, Agrippa announced, was a 'faculty of wonderfull vertue, full of most high mysteries, containing the profound contemplation of secret things'.[25] He then went on to describe its ability to reveal the workings of the natural world in a style which clearly indicates the continuity between medieval magic and modern science. Where the two differ, though, is in the importance magic gives to the merging of the consciousness of the individual, whether philosopher, alchemist, astrologer or magician, with the mind of the star, angel or any other superior intelligence which was being invoked. Having accomplished this union of minds, the magician might then appropriate the superior being, the planetary intelligence, in the attempt to influence the lower world, to imprint his will on it all the more effectively. This was Agrippa's dangerous idea. It was an idea which Ficino had approached but shrunk from – that man could play God. This was exactly what destroyed Christopher Marlowe's Faust. The key to the exercise of this power, though, was not some sort of coercive force, but self-knowledge. 'Every one therefore that is willing to work in Magic,' Agrippa wrote, 'must know the vertue, measure, order and degree of his own soul, in the power of the universe.'[26] Magic, in other words, could not be conducted for any reason other than good. Black magic was not just the fantasy of the fearful, conservative theologian; it was a theoretical impossibility.

Agrippa's magic depended, like the medieval art, on the manipulation of the Great Chain of Being. He was a keen systematizer and produced different versions based on the division of the cosmos by series of numbers from one to twelve. In the medieval Realist cosmos, each number had to be more than just a description of quantity; it possessed power, or 'virtue'. Agrippa gave the example of the five-leaved herb cinquefoil, which resisted poisons and drove away devils according to the power of the number five. Each of the 12 significant numbers had its own set of correspondences, an extraordinary notion that suggests, in effect, a series of parallel universes, though ones which are interlocked instead of, as in the modern version, completely separate.[27] If one magically engages with the realm of a particular number, the correspondences of the Chain are entirely different to those in the preceding and following number. Agrippa began with the number one which, he explained, was associated with the Hebrew letter Iod, the 'One Divine essence, the fountain of all vertues, and power, whose name is expressed with one most simple Letter'.[28] As the *Sefer Yetzirah* had claimed, 'He made the letter Yud king over action and he bound a crown to it.'[29] From Iod one moves down the sequence through the World Soul, the sun, the 'One King of Stars, fountain of life' to the Philosophers' Stone, 'the instrument of al virtues, naturall and supernaturall', the heart, the source of life and finally Lucifer, the 'one Prince of Rebellion, of Angels and darkness'. From the one the sequence progressed to the 12, in which the Hebrew names of God descended via the 12 'orders of blessed spirits', angels, Hebrew tribes and prophets, apostles, zodiac signs, months, plants, stones, parts of the body and devils. Agrippa's systematizing tendencies had simplified the extensive lists of animals, plants and other objects and phenomena available in other texts. But the system still had practical as well as psychic power. If, for example, one suffered from a throat problem the cure might be found in the vertical column of correspondences containing the neck. The cure might involve an appeal to the apostle Simon or the angel Ambriel, or the consumption of a tea made from vervain or the wearing of a talisman containing topaz.

A much fuller list of correspondences was contained in William Lilly's encyclopaedic English volume, *Christian Astrology*, published in 1647. Summarizing the medieval lists, Lilly argued that Jupiter, to take one important example, was related to the zodiac signs Sagittarius and Pisces, modesty, sobriety and justice, polite and prudent behaviour, an upright stature, a clear complexion if it is visible at dawn, a short stature and flaxen hair if it was seen at dusk, judges and bishops, students, clothiers, inflammation of the lungs, sweet smells, purple objects, cloves, mace and nutmeg, cherry, fig and pear trees, sheep, deer, elephants and unicorns, pheasants, peacocks and hens, dolphins, whales and serpents, amethysts, sapphires and emeralds, middle-aged men, the north wind, Babylon, Hungary and Spain, the number three, the angel Zadkiel and Thursdays.[30] This is just an extract from Lilly's list, of which there was one for every planet. Lilly's particular interest was in making political forecasts but his main business was in offering advice on the basis of interrogations – horoscopes cast for the moment that questions were asked. But the system of correspondences was perfectly designed for magical manipulation, which is as it was used by John Dee, arguably Lilly's predecessor as best-known English astrologer.

John Dee (1527–1608) is regarded unfairly by most scholars variously as an eccentric, a charlatan or a genius flawed by what was, in his detractors' opinion, his addiction to the occult. The typical, and now discredited, position was pushed forcefully by Wayne Shumaker who thought Dee was 'a remarkable oddity' and completely out of step with Renaissance thought.[31] The truth, which more recent scholars have established, is the opposite, and Dee is now seen as one of the leading figures in the English Renaissance. More balanced is Deborah Harkness's perceptive suggestion that Dee's clairvoyant work should be seen within the context of Elizabethan theatrical techniques, which provided the imaginative boundaries to the mediumistic conversations with angels for which he is famous.[32] He was certainly one of the most brilliant mathematicians in Europe, a keen supporter of Copernicus's sun-centred universe, and a Renaissance man, a polymath whose self-appointed goal was universal knowledge. As a historical figure, Dee's interest for us lies more in the details of his life than in his contribution to the history of ideas.[33] His work was highly derivative and based largely on Agrippa who he introduced to an English audience almost a century before Agrippa's own writing appeared in English. But his life was certainly colourful, at least in retrospect, which is why he may have attracted more scholarly interest and biographies than any of his fellow astrologers. He was a well-known figure at the time, notorious to many because of his reputation as a magician; it is said that he was the model for Prospero, the magician in Shakespeare's *Tempest*. Prospero's boast that, through his magical powers, 'I have bedimmed the noontide sun', was certainly in line with the powers commonly ascribed to Dee.[34] Dee achieved some degree of power as Elizabeth I's astrologer. He elected the most auspicious time for the queen's coronation (although the horoscope is lost) in 1558, arranging pairs of planets so that they were separated by harmonious distances of either 60 or 120 degrees, and provided her with regular astrological advice, including his insights into her various suitors. Dee's scholarship was considerable, and driven by the Pythagorean theory, which was common to all Renaissance Hermeticists, that the creation of the cosmos was a numbering process. It followed that mathematics was a path to divine knowledge. His 'Mathematical Preface' to Euclid's *Elements*, published in 1570, was based on the democratic principle that the study of mathematics should be available to everyone. From his mathematical interests Dee became an expert on cartography and navigation, becoming a close friend of the great map maker Gerardus Mercator (who followed the reformers in criticizing astrologers but supporting the principle of astrology[35]) and an important adviser in the English voyages of exploration. In 1556 he proposed the formation of a national library; it was turned down by an unimaginative government so Dee turned his own library into one of the finest in Europe. He provided espionage reports for Elizabeth during his European travels and used a Kabbalistic symbol which the thriller writer Ian Fleming was to convert into James Bond's number, 007. He was also a pious Christian who criticized the emperor Rudolf II and the king of Poland for their ungodly ways. In 1582 Dee began a series of conversations with angels, conducted through the aid of the medium Edward Kelly. These were conducted in a devout atmosphere, following acts of purification and fasting. Dee, being well versed in magic, knew that the magician had to have a pure heart and Godly purpose. For daring to talk to angels, though, historians have completely distorted Dee's work, presenting him as a fool, a charlatan and a quack. His conversations with angels were in fact a thoroughly normal part of the sixteenth-century ideological landscape. In a world in which witchcraft had been made illegal – in 1542 in England – the existence of supernatural beings was given legal as well as theological force. And, if angels played a prominent part in Milton's *Paradise Lost*, the greatest seventeenth-century exposition of the spiritual journey of Reformation man, it was natural for Dee to engage with them. His crime was to do so as a natural philosopher, almost as a scientist, without the sanction of the Church. His mission was to obtain knowledge about the world rather than guidance on matters of faith. For this he has been damned as a charlatan rather than as one of the most brilliant men of his age. Yet, at a time when communication with the dead, in the form of saints, along with prayer to angels, was still an essential part of Catholic religion, if not most Protestants, to call Dee a charlatan because he was conducting séances is a gross failure of historical imagination. His real crime was to communicate with them as an equal, as a Humanist, and attempt to gain knowledge from them, rather than come to them as a helpless supplicant seeking protection. Dee was actually engaged in the noblest of Humanistic enterprises, the attempt to solve the problems of human strife and misery in sixteenth-century Europe.[36] From the beginning of the Reformation in 1517 the Christian world in the West had split into Catholic and Protestant regions, the latter then dividing between varieties of Lutheran and Calvinist who often had no more in common with each other than they did with Catholics. The result was war, rebellion and the constant fear of subversion. In Dee's opinion the accumulated wisdom of European scholarship, including astrology, had proved singularly ineffective in resisting what he saw as the tide of chaos. He therefore set out on a programme of investigation designed to establish the true condition of the world and, ultimately, to provide a programme which might resolve the afflictions of the sixteenth-century world. The final chapter in Dee's research was the conversation with angels. The reasoning was plain. If angels were close to God then they, of all intelligences in the cosmos, must have the greatest insight into his Mind, but also the best view, from their heavenly perspective, of events on the earth. Dee failed. But that his attempt was unsuccessful was to lead to a turning point in the development of modern science.

The spirit of reform pervaded the astrological world-view in the sixteenth century, at least at the elite level, amongst the 'high' astrologers. That the magicians took a generally liberal view on religious matters, one which had social consequences, is illustrated by the work of Johann Weyer (1515/16–1588), a Dutch physician and one of Agrippa's prominent students. Weyer was a demonologist, an expert on the categories and hierarchies of demons, and the author of a number of major works on the subject: the *De Praestigiis Daemonum et Incantationibus ac Venificiis* (*On the Illusions of the Demons and on Spells and Poisons*), published in 1563; the *De Lamiis Liber* (*Book on Witches*) and the

Pseudomonarchia Daemonum (*The False Kingdom of the Demons*), both published in 1577. The witchcraft question is a particularly interesting one in relation to the Renaissance, mainly because of the close parallels in time. The *Malleus Maleficarum*, the most elaborate and notorious of the anti-witch tracts, was published in 1487, just two years before Ficino's *De vita*. The legitimization of educated men contacting spirits, at least in some circles, seems to have coincided with the wave of fear that (mainly) uneducated women were doing the same. The boundary between the spirit-raising of astral magicians and the allegations of demonic association against supposed witches were by no means well defined. A high proportion of those accused of witchcraft were men while the elite magicians always ran the risk of accusations of sorcery. The difference between an alleged male witch and an astral magician seem to reside mainly in the level of education and magical technology required by the latter.

Weyer was one of the first to argue against the then widespread persecution of witches, so much so that, even in the late seventeenth century, he could still be regarded as 'the most notorious of the small band of witchcraft sceptics'.[37] Weyer's problem was not with the existence of demons, which he took for granted – it would be astonishing if he didn't – but with the web of beliefs which identified women (although a high proportion of accused witches were men) as sexual partners of the Devil and sources of all misfortune. The astrological magicians might have denied the reality of witchcraft but the astrological reformer Jean Bodin (1529/30–1596), was quite convinced they were a real threat and, in 1580, published his *De la Démonomanies Sorciers*, in which he argued strenuously that even children should be tortured in witchcraft investigations.

It is difficult to generalize, but the evidence suggests that those who followed the Humanist tradition, such as Agrippa, even when they believed that they themselves could invoke spirits, might be more liberal on the witchcraft issue than were the more traditional astrologers. Yet, the situation is not a simple one. If Weyer believed that Kabballists could enter the world of angels and celestial intelligences, why did he doubt the ability of witches to do the same?

Other astrologers, though, the conservatives, regarded reform as entirely unnecessary, and believed that astrology was fundamentally fine as it was. Their reading of horoscopes was conducted in the style developed by the Hellenistic astrologers; to which they added the healing arts, often with magical aids, as a matter of course. Some were singularly unsuccessful, in which case the Italian William Parron is notable.[39] Parron arrived in England soon after 1487, shortly after Henry VII (1485–1509), one of the most brilliant administrators to sit on the throne, began his reign. It seems that Parron presented the king with a special treatise, the *Liber de optima fata Henrici Eboraci ducis et optimorum ipsus parentum*, devoted to the future of the young Henry, Duke of York, the future Henry VIIII, and his parents, the king and his queen, Elizabeth of York. Unfortunately Parron predicted that the queen would live to be 80, shortly before she died at the age of just 37 in 1503. Parron should have known better than to make such a forecast and, coming so soon after the publication of the

Disputations, it was precisely the sort of embarrassment that exposed astrology to ridicule. Sir Thomas More, England's leading Humanist, took the same line as Pico on judicial astrology and bitterly mocked Parron's efforts. The astrologer's claim to have predicted heavy rains in 1499 did not save him and he was never heard of again. Parron was, though, an entrepreneur and produced the first English almanac in 1498, around half a century after they had become commonplace in Italy, France and Germany. Parron's predictive blunder was repeated by Jerome Cardan (1501–76), one of the most brilliant mathematicians in Europe; his books on chance (he was an enthusiastic gambler) represent the first attempt to work out a theory of probability.[40] Cardan was a skilled and erudite astrologer but forecast a long life for the king, Edward VI (1547–53). Edward died young not long after. Cardan also should have known better; he had himself advised astrologers to 'always deliver judgements from the Stars in general terms'.[41] Cardan also predicted his own possible death for the age of around 40 or 45, partly on the basis of the location of the malefic planet Saturn. In the event, after a period of ill fortune exacerbated by his fear of death, in 1539, at the age of 38, Cardan became the most popular physician in Italy. Another Italian astrologer who resisted the reformers was Lucus Gauricus (1476–1558), who had some of the most powerful people in Italy for clients and succeeded Ficino as a protégé of the Medicis.[42] He is reputed to have predicted that Giovanni de Medici, Lorenzo's son, would become Pope, which he did as Leo X (1513–21) and also worked for Lorenzo's nephew, Giulio, who became Pope under the name Clement VII (1523–34). He would have provided the full range of astrological services for both men, from advising them on their rivals' horoscopes to timing political initiatives and electing auspicious moments for anything from audiences to laying the foundation stones for buildings. After Clement died, Gauricus was employed by his successor, Alessandro Farnese, who reigned as Paul III. Paul was an enthusiastic user of astrology but singled Gauricus out for favour after the astrologer had apparently predicted his election as Pope, exactly as he had done for Leo. He is also said to have predicted Paul's death, an act which did not prevent the Pope appointing him bishop of Giffoni. Gauricus's most famous successful prediction came about as a result of his work for another Medici, Catherine, Lorenzo's great-granddaughter and wife of King Henry II of France. According to the account which has come down to us, Gauricus told Catherine that the king ran the risk of death or blindness from a head wound in a duel, a prediction he published in 1552. The prediction was quite plausible on the basis of unfortunate Saturn's transit of the king's birth chart.[43] On 1 July 1559, around the time of maximum threat, a joust was held to celebrate the Peace of Cateau-Cambrésis, which brought to an end the war with the Hapsburgs and their English allies. During the final bout, the king's eye was pierced by a splinter from his opponent's lance, which penetrated his eye and entered his brain. The king died about ten days later. The episode was lent added interest by the supposed relevance of one of Nostradamus' quatrains, published in 1555. Nostradamus' text was suggestive:

Le lion jeune le vieux surmontera,
En champ bellique par singulier:
Dans caige d'or les yieux lui crevera
Deux classes une, puis mourir, mort cruelle.[44]

In English this passage translates as 'The young lion will overcome the older one, in a field of combat in single fight: he will pierce his eyes in their golden cage; two wounds in one, then he dies a cruel death.' Michele de Nostradame (1503–66) is, under his Latinized name, Nostradamus, perhaps the most famous astrologer of all time. As a successful physician he came to the attention of Julius Scaliger (1484–1558), a leading Humanist, Aristotelian and student of Gauricus. But, aside from this, Nostradamus played no part in the scholarly debates that involved many of the other prominent astrologers. Instead, in 1550, he began publishing annual almanacs. He then began his major project, the composition of *Les Propheties*, a book of 1000 quatrains, the enigmatic four-line prophecies which are his most famous legacy. Most of these remain incomprehensible, in spite of retrospective attempts to analyse them, and the apparent reference to Henry II is perhaps the only one which is at all plausible. Nostradamus's publishing enterprises attracted a series of aristocratic clients, notably Catherine de Medici herself. Legends about Nostradamus started to circulate during his lifetime, and one apocryphal tale, which still occurs in the popular literature, has an ironic twist. Apparently Nostradamus encountered a group of young monks in Italy and spontaneously knelt down before one of them, an ex-swineherd, and addressed him as 'Your Holiness'. The young monk, Felix Peretti, went on to become Pope Sixtus V in 1585, 21 years after Nostradamus's death. Ironically it was Sixtus who, after one year on the papal throne, issued the first Papal Bull forbidding the practice of judicial astrology. The coincidence of the Gauricus and Noastradamus Pope-prediction stories rather suggests that they were the sort of miraculous prophecies attached to the hagiographies of famous astrologers. Except, of course, that in Gauricus's case, the imposition of a Medici on the papal throne was a reasonable possibility. In spite of his enduring fame, Nostradamus was a practitioner who contributed nothing to either the theory or technique of astrology, even though his life makes for a fascinating story.

Neither was the Catholic Church immune to the use of magic, and the use of judicial astrology at the highest levels was prevalent, even as more devout and conservative theologians condemned it. Eventually those who had imprisoned de Phares found an apparent ally in the Vatican in Pope Sixtus V (1585–1590). Like the Church Fathers, Sixtus attacked astrology on the theological and the empirical levels; astrology was at once both demonic and did not work. One of his first actions was to prepare a Bull condemning astrology, which was issued in 1586 under the title *Coeli et Terrae*, or *Heaven and Earth*. The astrologers, the Bull declared, 'err and bring others into error . . . they employ an idle, false knowledge of the planets and stars, and with the utmost audacity busy themselves now with anticipating a revelation of God's arrangement of things'.[45] The Bull, which was

confirmed in 1631 by Urban VIII, does seem to have seriously inhibited astrological publishing in Italy; in 1557 the Pope began placing prohibited works on
the so-called Index, and Sixtus's Bull encouraged the censors in their task. Yet, as
the utopian Tommaso Campanella was to point out in his angry retort to Urban's
Bull, neither edition had denied the existence of celestial influences.[46] Besides,
Campanella himself was called in by Urban to perform a magical ritual to ward
off alarming astrological predictions of the Pope's death. Campanella performed
a ritual which had evolved in a seamless tradition since the Babylonian *namburbi*.
Campanella described the scene:

> First they sealed the room against the outside air, sprinkled it with rose-vinegar and
> other aromatic substances, and burnt laurel, myrtle, rosemary and cypress. They hung
> the room with white silken cloths and decorated it with branches. Then two candles
> and five torches were lit, representing the seven planets; since the heavens, owing to the
> eclipse, were defective ... The other persons present had horoscopes immune to the
> evil eclipse. There was Jovial and Venereal music, which was to disperse the pernicious
> qualities of the eclipse-infected air and, by symbolising good planets, to expel the
> influences of bad ones. For the same reason they used stones, plants colours and odours
> belonging to good planets (that is, Jupiter and Venus). They drank astrologically distilled
> liquors.[47]

As a picture of the survival of ritual magic in the early seventeenth century,
especially as its use as a defence against astrological influences, Campanella's
description is unrivalled, and as an account of life behind the scenes in the papacy
it is astonishing. The Pope's position was hypocritical on a grand scale, though no
more than that of the Roman emperors who had always believed that astrology
was too dangerous to be practised by the common people. Campanella himself,
of course, was an astrologer, a utopian who believed that human society should
be modelled on celestial principles, and a close friend of Galileo, risking his own
liberty in his public defence of Galileo's theories.[48]

   That there was also a popular astrology, not dependent on the literary arts of
the 'middling' astrologers or the philosophical speculations of the 'high', has to
be assumed. The ethnographic literature from around the world emphasizes the
significance that pre-modern people attached to the sky, and often their personal
relationship with it.[49] There is strong evidence of such beliefs in sixteenth- and
seventeenth-century England and evidence that they continued into the early
twentieth century. Owen Davies has made the point that, in the days before
medicine was both efficient at saving lives and available to all, which in Britain
(his area of expertise) means sometime between 1900 and 1945, the treatment
and diagnosis of disease depended on folk remedies, often with magical associations.[50] In the seventeenth century, diseased people, plants and animals were often
said to be 'planets struck' or 'moon struck', or suffered from 'moon disease', in
recognition of the power that came from the sky.[51] It was up to the rural 'cunning
folk', the village healers, to deal with such problems. In 1619 a woman from the
English Midlands was accused of witchcraft; she expounded on the nature of the

planets, claiming that they came in four colours; blue, green, yellow and black, of which the last signified death. Keith Thomas's comment that the term planet seems to have been conflated with 'familiar spirit' or fairy is not improbable, given the Hermeticists' opinion that planets were divine intelligences or moved by angels. We have one account of a spirit instructing a certain Susan Snapper to visit a cunning woman and obtain some 'planet water' in order to treat the Mayor of the English town of Rye. The combination of spirits, folk healers and some sort of simple astrology is indicative of the real state of play away from the dogmatic theological arguments of those who insisted that such-and-such a form of behaviour was or was not permitted by scripture. There would have been parishes where the local vicar denounced demonic practices from the pulpit, but sick people needed treatment and had to be pragmatic about where they found it. But one of the most interesting lessons of these anecdotal accounts is that, at the popular level, within rural communities, most astrologers were probably women. They may not have been casting horoscopes or citing Ptolemy and Masha'allah but they were using astrology. And that they may have been combining it with various forms of magic and spirit communication only brings them into a similar intellectual world to that occupied by the astral magicians from the *Picatrix* to Agrippa and Dee.

We can also turn to textual evidence for insights in Renaissance astrology, which made occasional appearances in the literature of the period, enough to tell us more about attitudes towards it, as well as its uses and philosophy.[52] Rabelais mocked it in his spoof almanac, *Pantagruéline Prognostication pour l'an 1533, 1533–1535*. Cervantes' famous tale, *Don Quixote*, published between 1605 and 1615, contains the story of a young student of astrology from the University of Salamanca, whose family and friends grew extremely rich on the basis of his astrological advice.[53] It permeates the work of the great English poet and playwright Edmund Spenser (1552/3–1599) His famous *Shepheardes Calendar* rested firmly in a highly literate understanding of classical astrology while the *Faerie Queen* embodied Pythagorean numerology.[54] The greatest literary accounts of Renaissance astrology, though, were those of William Shakespeare. His account of the Platonic cosmos of balance, harmony and purpose is more convincing than anything Ficino wrote, and very much simpler:

> The heavens themselves, the planets and this centre
> Observe degree, priority and place
> Insisture, course, proportion, season, form
> Office and custom, in all line of order:
> And therefore is the glorious planet Sol
> In noble eminence enthroned and sphered
> Amidst the other; whose medicinable eye
> Corrects the ill aspects of planets evil
> And posts like the commandment of a king
> Sans check, to good and bad . . .[55]

Shakespeare used astrology as a literary device, enabling the characters to convey information in an indirect, symbolic manner. A vivid example occurs in *King Lear*, one of Shakespeare's three great tragedies and, it is clear, one of the great discussions of sixteenth-century political thought.[56] The key scene, 1.2, takes place between Gloucester, one of Lear's courtiers, and his two sons. One son, Edmund, is evil, the other, Edgar, noble. Shakespeare eloquently combines the ambiguities of natal astrology with the current unsettling mundane transits. The plot, actually a subplot in the main tragedy of *Lear*, is based in a non-astrological fact of Edmund's nativity: his illegitimacy, which bars him from any proper inheritance. At his birth the stars were badly aligned, but now, under an opportunity presented by the current eclipse, he sees the chance to change the preordained order and become his father's heir. He has ingratiated himself into his father's favour by turning him against his brother, Edgar.

The scene begins with Gloucester, a devout believer in astrology, setting out the current malefic transits, which have already disturbed Lear's mind and set the kingdom on an inexorable slide towards chaos. The audience would have understood implicitly that Lear, the king, was an earthly counterpart of the sun, the symbolic centre of the society of humans corresponding to the symbolic centre of the community of stars. They might also have implicitly equated Lear's three daughters with the three Moirae, the fates responsible for spinning human destiny. Gloucester's specific comments would therefore have been taken in the context of a set of broader political-cosmological assumptions. Gloucester begins:

> These late eclipses in the sun and moon portend no good to us: though the wisdom of nature can reason it thus and thus, yet nature finds itself scourged by the sequent effects. Love cools, friendship falls off, brothers divide: in cities, mutinies; in countries, discord; in palaces, treason; and the bond cracked twixt son and father: the king falls from bias of nature; there's father against child. We have seen the best of our time: machinations, hollowness, treachery, and all ruinous disorders, follow us disquietly to our graves! Find out this villain, Edmund; it shall lose thee nothing; do it carefully. And the noble and true hearted Kent banished! his offence, honesty! T'is strange indeed.

Gloucester's speech reads much like a section from a standard text on eclipses composed just over forty years later by William Lilly:

> Nay, this very Eclipse doth designe out some such thing, viz, severall designs in agitation at present in forraigne parts against the Common wealth by the Agents of the Scottish King, and I doe fear some secret plots are now acting in forraign parts, yea in England and Scotland, with intention to make Ireland the feat of some the seat of some further unlucky War.[57]

We are not told whether Gloucester's eclipse was solar or lunar, but the use of the plural implies both. Thus, as the sun was eclipsed by the moon so Lear, in abdicating, has been eclipsed by his daughters, at least by the evil two, Regan and Goneril. Shakespeare then introduces a delicious irony by making Edmund, the victim of his birth, a sceptic who mocks Gloucester's belief in the power of the stars to reveal upheavals in the body-politic. Once Gloucester has left the stage Edmund breaks in:

> This is the excellent foppery of the world, that when we are sick in fortune, (often the surfeit of our own behaviour) we make guilty of our disasters the sun, the moon, and the stars: as if we were villains by necessity; fools by heavenly compulsion; knaves, thieves, and treachers, by special predominance; drunkards, liars, adulterers, by an enforced obedience of planetary influence; and all that we are evil in, by a divine thrusting on. An admirable evasion on the charge of a star! My father compounded with my mother under the dragons tail; and my nativity was under Ursa major; that that it follows I am rough and lecherous. Tut, I should have been that I am, had the maidenliest star in the firmamant twinkled on my bastardising. Edgar – and pat he comes, like the catastrophe of the old comedy: my cue is villainous melancholy, with a sigh like Tom o'Bedlam.

What a rich passage this is. Edmund discounts astrology, yet tells the audience of his poor conception, conceived under the South Node. He argues that even had he been born with the best placed Venus ('the maidenliest star'), he would still have been villainous. Perhaps he would, for Shakespeare gives another clue as to who Edmund is and what he represents: he was born under Ursa Major. Yet Ursa Major is one of the polar constellations, which never sets: all born at the latitude of England are born under the Great Bear. Who, then, is Edmund? He is everyman, the average sinner, or fallen human, and Shakespeare uses celestial symbolism to tell us this. There is, though, another possible double meaning in this simple phrase: not only is Edmund universal man in a moral sense, the fallen sinner, but as an ordinary citizen he is ineligible for the high destiny saved for those close to the king. No doubt the mob in the pit at the Globe theatre would have missed the reference, but John Dee, Philip Sidney or Walter Raleigh, comfortable in their cushioned seats, would have chuckled elegantly at the playwright's educated reference. Edgar, the good but wronged brother, then enters and Edmund changes his tack. Pretending to believe in astrology in order to manipulate his brother, he continues, ironically imitating a mad person ('Tom o'Bedlam').

> O, these eclipses do portend these divisions! fa, sol, la, mi.

The scene then continues with a brief dialogue between the two brothers:

> Edgar: How now, brother Edmund! what serious contemplation are you in?
> Edmund: I am thinking brother, of a prediction I read this other day, what should follow these eclipses.
> Edgar: Do you busy yourself with that?
> Edmund: I promise you, the effects he writes of succeed unhappily; as of unnaturalness between the child and the parent; death, dearth, dissolutions of ancient amities; divisions in state, menaces and maledictions against king and nobles, needless diffidences, banishment of friends, dissipation of cohorts, nuptial breaches, and I know not what.

Edgar, who cannot believe his ears, is moved to ask his cynical brother in astonishment:

How long have you been a sectary astronomical?

The scene then continues with Edmund warning Edgar that Gloucester has been alerted to his (Edgar's) alleged treachery (which Edmund himself fabricated) and warns his brother to flee. Edmund is thus using astrology to manipulate Edgar, playing on what at this point in the narrative looks like his gullibility. At this stage in the proceedings, Edgar, the believer in astrology, is presented as a gullible fool, prey to the malicious schemes of Edmund, the charlatan.

However, we must wait for the key to Edmund's dramatic function, indeed the key to the entire celestial play-within-a-play in Shakespeare's political drama, until his closing private thoughts: 'Let me if not by birth, have lands by wit.' Here is the crux: Edmund, who contemptuously dismisses the astrological reading of his nativity, is determined to overturn the social-political-biological fact of his birth, his illegitimacy. In the language of the sixteenth century he is a Humanist, asserting his individual freedom, anticipating the egalitarianism and republicanism of the Age of Reason, the Enlightenment and the French Revolution, even the social attitudes of the 1980s and '90s – that there is no stigma in illegitimacy. Edmund, in short, is modern man. He is man against the elements; man against nature. He is a meritocrat, asserting wit over birth. And, here is the rub. After many travails, he loses. The play ends with good triumphant, with Edmund dead and Edgar installed as the new duke of Gloucester. Nature, Necessity and the Stars have won.

But, what is Shakespeare really saying? Remember that the astrological plot parallels the social plot – Edmund is trapped by his circumstances. Is Shakespeare attacking society's treatment of illegitimate children? Or, given Edmund's malicious character, is he reinforcing the stigma? Or is he perhaps implying that Edmund's character is the product not of some inherent moral weakness in the illegitimate personality, but of his unfair treatment by society? The debate is quite clearly open ended, with Shakespeare suggesting questions rather than supplying answers, and running the threads of his sociological arguments together seamlessly with his astrological imagery.

Shakespeare followed the clear and unambiguous cosmology of the time, in which humanity was inextricably a part of the celestial as well as the terrestrial environment.[58] Repeatedly his plays, especially the great political tragedies, *Lear*, *Hamlet* and *Macbeth*, pursue a familiar theme in which his lead characters are caught in a cosmos which reverberates between order and disorder. The initial state, as Hamlet reported, is that the 'the time is out of joint'.[59] The problem then becomes the restoration of harmony, as in Greek science, in which the elements repeatedly moved into a harmonious mixture, indicating political balance, and then separated out, indicating political chaos. Planetary movements are then seen not as causes or determinants but as symptoms of larger celestial motions, and in this sense they are parallel to the movement of social trends. In the Kabbalistic cosmology of the time there would have been two spheres in heaven beyond the stars, and these would have been the realms of the angelic intelligences responsible for moving the planets themselves. Thus the planets, while being higher up the cosmic hierarchy than human beings, held no independent role in human life. They were just the most direct indication of the ebb and flow of celestial motions at a still higher level. The 'late eclipses' Gloucester mentions when the astrological theme is introduced are therefore descriptions of the social calamity following Lear's abdication.

The question then becomes not did Shakespeare believe in astrology, but did he regard astrology as an effective metaphor for the social and political scene, of the inexorable rise and fall of kings, of the ebb and flow of seasons in human affairs? Quite clearly he did, for as order is restored in the closing scene, and as the elements return to a state of balance, Edmund is dead and Edgar is duke. Birth had won, and wit had failed. If Shakespeare did not take this view, he would have been out of step with the entire intellectual consensus of his time. The literature on Shakespeare's attitude to astrology is surprisingly sparse in view of its importance as metaphor in his plays. We do know that Shakespeare's landlady, no less, had the famous astrologer Simon Forman cast her horoscope.[60] Charles Nicholl provides an analysis of *King Lear* as an alchemical journey, but touches only lightly on astrology.[61] However, F.E. Halliday proposed a provocative historical connection. According to Halliday, Shakespeare was writing *Lear* in the autumn of 1605. It was on 5 November 1605 that Guy Fawkes was arrested in the Gunpowder Plot, and accused of conspiring to blow up Parliament and the king – the entire British government. Halliday writes that 'The Moon, indeed, portended no good. There was an eclipse on the 27th, and only a fortnight before there had been a total eclipse of the sun.'[62] In the resulting governmental reaction new oppressive laws were introduced, Fawkes was savagely tortured and executed and Roman Catholics forbidden to proselytize, on pain of death. These were savage times. Halliday convincingly draws a direct connection between Gloucester's gloomy description of the effects of the eclipse in the play, and Shakespeare's own observations of the aftermath of the November eclipses. In his thesis, the fictitious astrology in *Lear* is therefore very much more than mere dramatic imagery. Shakespeare's most famous astrological statement, though, remains profoundly enigmatic. In *Julius Caesar* he places the following words into the mouth of Cassius: 'The fault, dear Brutus, is not in our stars, but in ourselves, that we are underlings . . .?'[63] Cassius's words can be read as a classic statement of Aquinian astrology: we may be influenced by the stars but we are responsible for our own moral actions. Yet the same passage is frequently read as support for modern anti-astrology scepticism. Shakespeare was the dramatist, reflecting the different positions of his time. In that Cassius was asserting familiar Humanist principles he was a creature of the sixteenth century, but if he was truly attacking astrology, he was a prophet of the seventeenth.

The debates about astrology in the sixteenth century concerned only the extent to which astrologers could make detailed or general pronouncements, and whether the magical use of talismans or prediction of life-events were permitted. The general principle on which it rested was no more doubted than is gravity today. No amount of mock theological rage or empirical observation could suppress it. Its intellectual demise would only come later, with a fundamental shift in the cosmological model, which was to deny the personal cosmos, in which each individual was tied to the stars. The process that culminated in the demolition of the theory of influences began in the wake of Pico's *Disputationes* at the beginning of the century, but its effect had hardly been noticed when Shakespeare was writing at the end.

10

The Seventeenth Century: Horoscopes and Telescopes

Philosophy and thus also astrology are a testimony of God's work and . . . sacred.
JOHANNES KEPLER[1]

On the evening of 11 November 1572, the Danish royal astrologer, Tycho Brahe (1546–1601), was returning for supper after working late in his alchemical laboratory.[2] An acute observer of the heavens, his attention was caught by a most surprising sight, a brilliant star in the constellation Cassiopeia. This was a nova, literally a new star. We now know what it was – an exploding star. In theory, to sight an unexpected object in the sky was not an unusual incident. New stars were rare, but comets were less so and meteors common, and all were assumed to occur in the imperfect, corruptible space between the earth and the moon. In Tycho's own words, though, the star was a miracle, a word he could not have used without some reference to the star of Bethlehem. His motto, after all, appears to have been adapted from the *Emerald Tablet*: 'By looking up I understand what is below.'[3] Tycho observed the star over the following months until, at the end of November, it began to fade and change colour. From bright white it gradually dimmed to yellow, orange and a faint red, eventually fading away from visibility in March 1574. Aristotelian cosmology dictated that, as the regions of the cosmos beyond the moon were essentially perfect, it was impossible for new stars to appear further away from the moon, for the simple reason that any sort of change indicated imperfection. Comets and shooting stars, along with thunder and lightning, could be viewed as part of meteorological phenomena and existed in the imperfect space between the moon and the earth, where change was permitted. They were literally elemental in that they represented disturbances in the balance of the four elements, especially air and, of course, fire. Tycho, though, calculated that this new star had appeared beyond the moon in the region which Aristotelian cosmology defined as unchanging and perfect. This was profoundly and utterly shocking and, for many people, completely impossible. It is difficult to overestimate the critical nature of this single fact and its implications were to be as great as Einstein's theory of relativity was for the twentieth century. An old certainty had been destroyed and the world would never be the same again. Tycho's publication of his findings in the following year in *De Nova et Nullius Aevi Memoria Prius Visa Stella* (*On the New and Never Previously Seen Star*) is one of those publishing moments, along with Darwin's *Origin of Species*, from which there was no way back. But, like many other revolutionary works, the implications were slow to sink in, even after Tycho demonstrated that the comet which appeared in 1577 was also beyond the moon, further evidence that the heavens were no longer perfect. Perhaps the radical significance of Tycho's discovery was underplayed because he personally saw no reason to question the Aristotelian cosmos permeated by celestial influences and based on a fundamental unity. That the heavens were no longer perfect need not undermine the doctrine of celestial influence. Plus, like all medieval cosmologies, Tycho's was largely theoretical. Even though he was watching the night sky, Tycho's claims were accompanied only by mathematical evidence. They lacked direct observational confirmation in the sense that he could not prove beyond any doubt that the nova and the comet were both beyond the moon. Like Copernicus's sun-centred universe, initially one could either take it or leave it, accept the evidence or reject it. And, even Tycho seemed not to understand the significance of his 'miracle'.

Tycho's primary concern was not with astronomical reform, but with making his astrology more accurate. Even though he was obliged to use the tools on offer in his work for the Danish king, Frederick II (1559–88), which meant the standard rules of horoscopic astrology, Tycho was firmly in the reformist camp. But, like Copernicus, by whom he was deeply influenced (as he was by Luther, Melanchthon and Paracelsus), he set as his task not the cleansing of astrological techniques but the pursuit of astronomical accuracy. Already, when observing the Jupiter–Saturn conjunction of 1563, he noticed that the existing astronomical tables were wildly inaccurate; the Alfonsine Tables were out by one month and the Prutenic Tables, which were based on the latest information from Copernicus, by a few days.[4] Such errors were vital for, as Tycho argued in 1574, the conjunction had caused a major outbreak of plague. His work took him down a different path to, say the French philosopher Jean Bodin (1529/30–1596), who had proposed empirical research into astrology itself. Bodin's concern was with astrology's truth-claims, Tycho's with accuracy. Tycho realized that no such work would be possible unless one actually knew where the planets were with any precision and began to equip himself with the most accurate, which meant the biggest, measuring equipment. To give an idea of the scale in which Tycho was working, in 1569 he devised a wooden quadrant 19 feet in diameter for Paul and Johann Hainzel, the astronomers of Augsburg. In this case, big can be better: the larger the instrument the more precise the measurement.

Tycho's most interesting opinion piece on astrology, a never-published tract entitled 'Against Astrologers for Astrology', has unfortunately been lost. But what we know of it suggests that Tycho was following Ficino in blaming astrologers for astrology's failings even though, in his surviving work, he defends astrology staunchly aganst its critics. He appears to have been deeply influenced by Ficino's Neoplatonism and to have accepted the notion of a divine, living comsos, popu- lated by angelic entities, a position which tends often to have led to disapproval of the mundane concerns of ordinary, jobbing astrologers.[5] But, whereas for Ficino, astrology was to be improved by better engagement between the soul and the cosmos, for Tycho, the key lay in improved accuracy of calculation and a proposed new method of dividing the heavens into astrological houses points to his desire to make the casting of horoscopes more accurate. Tycho did make his views known on other occasions, though. When the king, who was personally interested in the subject, asked Tycho to compose an explanation of how astrology affected the seasons, the great astrologer was now too busy and delegated the task to his protégé, Peter Jacobsen Flemløse. The result was the *Astrologia* of 1591, a work of astrological weather forecasting, reflecting the evident royal interest in the variations in nature.[6] Weather forecasting, of course, was a matter of state because the well-being of one's subjects, not to mention the stability of the throne, might depend on abundant harvest. We get a clearer insight into Tycho's astrology from his predictions on the 1572 star. He predicted 'great and unusual effects' as one would expect from such an unexpected event, originating in Russia and Scandinavia and then spreading throughout the rest of Europe, followed by 'a new condition in kingdoms, different from the earlier, and likewise a different order of religion, conditions and laws'.[7] The tone is evidence that Tycho followed the conventional rules for interpreting such phenomena as eclipses and comets, which always led to general tumult.

The 1572 star made Tycho's reputation as one of Europe's great astronomers. He was invited to lecture on astrology at Copenhagen University, where he spread the word about Copernicus and explained the working of astrology according to divinely ordained natural influences. 'If,' he argued, 'the celestial bodies are placed by God in such a way as they stand in their signs, they must of necessity have a meaning, especially for mankind, on behalf of whom they chiefly have been created ... our spirit is part of heaven itself.'[8] The king, who valued the prestige Tycho brought their association – not to mention his skills as a political astrologer – provided him with the small island of Hven near Copenhagen as both a home and a source of revenue. In 1576 Tycho began the contruction of Uraniborg, the observatory which served as his court over the following years; he regularly received princes and scholars who came to pay homage to the great man of knowledge. And, while not enjoying his fame, Tycho set out on a 20-year programme of precise astronomical measurement, assisted by a team of disciples and assistants. Setting out to make his mark on history, he had his eye on the big picture and devised an idiosyncratic variant on the Copernicial scheme. He agreed with Copernicus that all the planets orbit the sun, but believed that the sun, Mercury and Venus also constituted a mini-solar system that orbited the earth. He regarded this system as the most significant achievement of his career, although nobody else agreed with him and its publication in 1588 as the *De mundo aetheri recentioribus phaenomenis – Concerning the more recent phenomena of the ethereal world* – failed to attract the attention he thought it deserved. Tycho's legacy lay elsewhere.

Tycho's patron, Frederick II, died in 1588, leaving the astrologer exposed to the resentment of the many powerful people he had offended with his haughty manner, not to mention the many tenants he had overtaxed in order to fund his exploration of the night sky at Uraniborg. He finally left Denmark in 1597 and, in 1599, settled at the court of the emperor Rudolf II in Prague where he took on the official role of Imperial Mathematician. Tycho's duties were both astrological and astronomical. He had the usual predictive duties to undertake for his new patron but devoted most of his time to continuing his observations, particularly – and this was vital for the future of astronomy – of the planet Mars. He died in 1601, but not before he had taken on as his assistant a young astrologer by the name of Johannes Kepler.

Johannes Kepler (1571–1630) was born to an impoverished Lutheran family in Weil der Stadt in southern Germany.[9] With the support of a scholarship from the Duke of Wurttemberg he attended the University of Tubingen where he had the good fortune to study astronomy and mathematics under the brilliant Michael Maestlin (1550–1631) who was not only familiar with Copernicus's writings but became an enthusiastic early proponent of the new sun-centred universe. Kepler's ambition, though, was to become a Lutheran minister, an aspiration which was aborted when he reluctantly, for financial reasons, accepted a position as a mathematics teacher in a school at Graz. Unsatisfying as his work may have been, it allowed him to devote a great deal of attention to cosmological questions, to which he brought his profound Christian belief: he was in absolutely no doubt that the visible cosmos, including the stars and planets, was made in the image of God. It was, as Gibbons wrote, a 'hymn of praise to its creator'.[10] To explain its operation was therefore to understand God's working in the world. This is what Kepler believed that he himself had achieved. To believe Kepler's own account, he actually discovered the truth of the universe's geometrical structure. He was, he claimed, drawing a figure on the blackboard for his class when he experienced a moment of profound cosmic truth; that the universe was composed of a series of geometrical figures, the triangle, square, pentagon and so on. It is difficult to imagine that Kepler really believed that this, in itself, was his original idea. What he had stumbled upon, of course, was a commonplace of Platonic thought, well known from the *Timaeus*.[11] However, his brilliant insight lay in a realization that the geometrical forms progressed through time. This is how it works. Every time Jupiter and Saturn come together, forming a conjunction, they do so one-third of the zodiac further on from the previous conjunction. Three conjunctions therefore form a triangle – though not quite. There is a constant slippage of conjunctions so that, for example, each time a conjunction falls in Aries it is a few degrees further on from the previous conjunction, until eventually the sequence moves into Taurus. The result is that the triangle rotates. If this is represented visually, which is precisely what Kepler was doing when he had his revelation, the outer limits form a circle and there is also a space in the middle where there are no lines, and another circle enclosing a blank space. Kepler, who knew well enough the Platonic dictum that the circle is the most perfect shape, felt he had stumbled upon the secret of creation. The next year, at the precocious age of 25, he published his monumental work on geometrical cosmology, the *Mysterium Cosmographicum*.[12] At a time when scholarship still relied heavily on the refining of existing theories, Kepler's first step on his revolutionary path was a treatise that summed up and perfected all that was known about the Pythagorean and

Platonic geometrical cosmos. Working, like almost every other scholar at the time, in the wake of Ficino's translations, Kepler accepted the standard model of the creation – or emanation – of the cosmos out of the One. What bothered him, though, was the coincidence that, together with the sphere, there were six Platonic solids and six planets. There must be, he concluded, some significant relationship between the two numbers. This thought, of course, was possible only after Copernicus. Before *De revolutionibus* there had been seven planetary spheres, plus another two for the stars and the Prime Mover. Copernicus had deducted two – the sun and moon – from the seven, and added one, the earth. The cosmos, by 1600, was still Platonic in its essence (alive, infused with meaning and divinity) – that was not questioned – but the central point had shifted and the notion of crystalline spheres was beginning to look anachronistic.

The *Mysterium Cosmographicum* fortuitously brought the 25-year-old prodigy to the attention of Tycho, who was so impressed that he dispatched an invitation to Kepler to join his staff, an offer Kepler accepted in 1600 after the school at Graz had closed and Tycho had settled in Prague. Kepler then used his time at Prague to develop his cosmological theories, publishing two highly original treatises on optics and, in 1606, *De Stella Nova*, a study of the new star of 1604 – another supernova. However, in a decision which was to have far-reaching consequences, Tycho set Kepler to work on the theory of Mars's motion, a choice of critical significance for the development of Kepler's theories, for only this planet has an orbit whose deviation from circularity has a significant effect on its observed motion. It therefore presented a particular problem for the Platonists. Even Copernicus had set out to maintain perfectly circular planetary motions, so there was no disagreement on this score. In 1601 Tycho died and Kepler succeeded him as Imperial Mathematician, in which role his principal task was to perform astrological services for the Holy Roman Emperor. But, while he was worrying away on the problem of circular motion and trying to make Tycho's Mars data fit the Copernican model, Kepler had a revelation that far outstripped the significance of the 1595 discovery, even if the first had set him on the path to the second. He realized that the planets don't need to move in circles. The Mars data pointed in a radical direction, one which, happily, was supported by his geometrical model. In 1605 he formulated the first two of his three laws of planetary motion. The first, and from the point of view of Western cosmology, easily the most important, proposed that the planets move in ellipses. Published in his *Astronomia nova* in 1609, Kepler's theory drove a further stake through the heart of the old cosmology. The earth-centred cosmos had gone. Now circular motion was abandoned as well.

After a series of disasters, including the death of his wife and favourite son in 1611 and the abdication of his patron, Rudolph II, in 1612, Kepler moved to Linz in Upper Austria, where the governor had created a special post for him. While there he completed the *Harmonices Mundi* – the *Harmony of the World* – a work whose title reveals its Pythagorean and Platonic inspiration and which contained the third of his planetary laws. Its publication in 1619 coincided approximately with the appearance of his essential textbook on Copernicanism, the *Epitome of Copernican Astronomy*, published at Linz and Frankfurt in 1618 and 1621.[13] The publication of the *Tabulae Rudolphinae* in 1627, planetary tables based on Tycho's data and Kepler's theories, both confirmed in their accuracy the superiority of his work over all previous explanations for planetary motion and confirmed the ultimate practical goal of his work – to enable astrologers to produce more accurate predictions. Politics intervened once more when, in 1628, war and rebellion in Linz forced Kepler to move again, and he settled in Sagan in Silesia. There he was under the patronage of Albrecht von Wallenstein, the imperial general and the most famous of his astrological patrons. Two years later Kepler fell ill while in Regensburg attempting to reclaim debts owed to him by the Imperial treasury, and died. Before his death, though, Kepler had become, briefly – and reluctantly – the last of Europe's great military astrologers. Wallenstein was commander of the imperial armies for much of the Thirty Years War, between 1618 and 1634, and such was his success that, in 1622, the Emperor Ferdinand II elevated him to the highest honour possible, conferring on him the title of Prince of the Holy Roman Empire. Kepler's relationship with Wallenstein has been systematically misrepresented. In Caspar's strangely dismissive judgement, Wallenstein's willingness to consult 'the stars regarding all his political and martial decisions and transactions' was evidence that he was 'caught in astrological delusion', as if this was a kind of psychological sickness rather than standard behaviour for the time.[14] The two men made contact in 1608 when an intermediary obtained from Kepler a lengthy written analysis (possibly anonymous) of Wallenstein's birth chart. Wallenstein was then just 25, and the imperial astrologer did not spare his feelings. After describing the future commander's stronger points – his industrious, alert, innovatory nature – Kepler dealt with the moon: 'and because the moon stands in abject position, its nature would cause considerable disadvantage and contempt among those with whom he has dealings so that he would be considered a solitary brute'.[15] He then returned to more positive themes, to indications that Jupiter suggested success in old age and Mercury might point to future leadership. The text certainly indicates his familiarity with traditional astrological wisdom. For the opposition between Mercury and Jupiter (the two planets were in opposite zodiac signs), Kepler wrote, 'it almost looks as if he might yield to wild schemes and by means of these attract a great many people to him, or perhaps at some time be raised by a malcontent mob to a leader or ringleader'.[16] This looks remarkably like a combination of Julius Firmicus Maternus's readings in the fourth century for Mercury and Jupiter in opposition ('they stir up fearful popular riots') and conjunction ('powerful, outstanding in counsel and oratory . . . the object[s] of general admiration').[17] So, Kepler was well-versed in classical astrology. This we know. He heard no more from Wallenstein until 1624 when the now imperial commander was at the height of his powers. The general, it turned out, had annotated Kepler's text and kept it with him through the intervening years. This time Kepler was asked to update the horoscope with predictions for the coming years, including detailed questions about Wallenstein's health (would he have a stroke?) and military prospects. The astrologer responded with a grudging letter in which he declared that conventional astrology was no more than a form of entertainment which dishonoured the true, sacred astrology which was an extension of God's work. Yet, he took the commission and did the work and, as a testimony to his skill in the work he despised, stopped his prediction in 1634, for which year he forecast 'horrible disorder' for the month of March; Wallenstein was murdered on 24 February. The two men finally met in 1628 and, after Wallenstein settled a large retainer on his new astrologer, Kepler's attitude softened considerably; he referred to his generous patron gushingly as a 'second Hercules'. He remained, though, deeply resistant to the practice of conventional judicial astrology. Wallenstein, accepting this, apparently allowed Kepler to take a back seat and perform the calculations for his other astrologers, who would then provide him with astrological advice.

Of the astronomers responsible for the astronomical revolution, Kepler's astrology is the most well known, though it is largely ignored by scholars of his work.[18] There is a fair amount of confusion about his attitude to the subject. It is widely thought that he was a believer early, but gradually came to see its fraudulent nature and only continued to work for Wallenstein and his other patrons for the money. The truth is, Kepler was a committed astrological reformer. He was familiar with all the main arguments for and against judicial astrology, including Pico's *Disputationes*, which he studied closely. It is quite clear that he sympathized with Pico yet insisted that astrology's theoretical rationale in both Platonic geometry and Aristotelian influences was fundamentally sound.[19] But he was determined to discard medieval stupidity, which, following the reformers, he called 'superstitious, prophetic and a supplement to Arabic fortune telling', and return to classical purity.[20] In March 1598 he wrote to his teacher, Maestlin, 'I am a Lutheran astrologer, I throw away the nonsense and keep the hard kernel.'[21] He was profoundly dissatisfied with medieval astrology, in spite of his success with it, and his astronomy was designed to create a new, more accurate astrology, based on planetary aspects (the distances between pairs of planets) rather than sign and house position. He preserved aspects because they were based on the measurable positions of the planets whereas zodiac signs and houses were notional divisions of the sky. Relying on Pythagorean principles, he reasoned that all numbers can be significant and that the five 'Ptolemaic aspects', which underpinned interpretation of the distances between planets, were therefore only a part of the picture.[22] He therefore added further divisions of the circle such as the quintile, a division of 360° by five, and the decile, a division by ten. Planets separated by 72° and 36° were therefore, he argued, significantly linked in a position which, once its correlations with terrestrial affairs were understood, could be used to understand the future. Kepler also devised a still-used system of prediction known as secondary progression, in which planetary positions a certain number of days after birth could be used to forecast events in the individual's life an equivalent number of years after birth; events 30 years after birth, for example, could be predicted by the planetary positions 30 days after birth. Kepler's rationale was a variation on the old system of sympathies, in which all complete periods of time were linked. In this version of the theory, Kepler believed the complete cycle of the sun through one day was equivalent to its complete passage through one year. Though a reformer in terms of astrological technique, Kepler's philosophical attitude, like those of Copernicus and Tycho, remained intensely conservative and loyal to medieval Aristotelianism, as is clear from this extract from the *Tertius Interveniens*, his major work on astrology, published in 1610.

> **Thesis 64**. All powers coming down from above are ruled according to Aristotle's teaching: namely, that inside this lower world or earthly sphere there is a spiritual nature, capable of expression through geometry. This nature is enlivened by geometrical and harmonic connections with the celestial lights, out of an inner drive of the Creator, not guided by reason, and itself is stimulated and driven for the use of their powers. Whether all plants and animals, as well as the Earth's sphere, possess this faculty, I cannot say. It is not an unbelievable thing, for they have various faculties of this kind: in that the form in every plant knows how to put forth its adornment, gives the flower its colour, not materially, but formally, and also has a certain number of petals; nor [is it unbelievable] that the womb, and the seed that falls into it, has such a marvellous power to prepare all the body parts in appropriate form . . . The human being, however, with his soul and its lower powers has such an affinity with the heavens, as does the surface of the Earth, and this has been tested and proven in many ways, of which each is a noble pearl of astrology, and is not to be rejected along with [all of] astrology, but to be diligently preserved and interpreted.[23]

Kepler loved astrology. It was, for him, part of the divinely ordered cosmos, a means of understanding God's plan and marvelling at his works. Yet he was an angry man; like Plotinus and Ficino, angry at what he regarded as the abuses of the ordinary astrologers who belittled God's marvellous work with their vulgar advice on lost property and adulterous wives. In his first manifesto of astrology, published in 1601, he began with a rant against the astrologers whose annual almanacs 'are in greater part inadequate, for the most part imaginary, foolish and false, and finally altogether worthless'.[24] When such fools make correct predictions, he wrote, it is due to luck rather than some higher reason. Yet, Kepler himself also produced annual prognostications. His forecasts for the year 1602 are typical. They read much like an extended version of the Babylonian *Diaries*, though written for the future rather than the past; the purpose was the same, though – to build up a body of empirically-based, reliable astrological rules. Unlike the almanacs he despised, Kepler discussed probabilities for the coming year's weather, harvests and political developments, steering away from precise forecasts. Where he did make a definite statement, he was quick to qualify it. For January 1602 he considered, on the basis of a prolonged sextile (60° separation) between Mars and Saturn, that 'there will be a vehement commotion and a very definite excess in atmospheric conditions. But,' he added, 'it is not easy to say how the excess will be manifested.'[25] His most brilliant prediction was in his diary for 1618 in which, building his astrological judgement carefully upon previous examples, he wrote:

> My fundamental argument is this: that a Conjunction of Mars and the Sun takes place next March in Aries, under the influence of which Germany stands; while numerous Conjunctions take place in May in Taurus near the Pleiades; and that we have precedents to show us the effects of such aspects in definite instances, as in the Peasants' War in 1525, in the Revolt in the Netherlands in 1565, and in 1604 in Hungary.[26]

On 23 May 1618, as the moon was in Taurus, between Mars and Saturn, fulfilling Kepler's prophecy, the Protestant assembly, meeting in the castle of Prague, threw two imperial governors out of the windows of the Chancellery onto a pile of manure, an amusing incident, at least for the spectators, which unfortunately launched the Thirty Years War. This disastrous conflict was, in effect, the first Europe-wide war, and was responsible for massive devastation in Germany. The making of predictions required Kepler to take a position in relation to the thorny problem of determinism, whether the fulfilment of a forecast meant that it was predetermined, and he was quite clear that the Taurean alignments did not indicate that war was inevitable. Instead, adopting Ficino's model of the astrologer as healer, he described himself as a *medicus*, whose task was to diagnose, warn and offer remedies; whereas Ficino believed in sympathetic magic, Kepler advocated a mixture of social reform and tough government to ward off revolution, and strong generalship to win wars. Kepler's central use for astrology can only be understood in the context of the instability of Europe at the time. Like John Dee in England, his goal was to establish an astrology which could help the government effectively avoid conflict. But, like Jean Bodin, the leading French philosopher of the late sixteenth century, Kepler wanted to achieve this by a stripped down, simplified astrology.

Bodin's works on political and legal theory mark him out as the founder of modern jurisprudence and political thought, but his programme for a reformed government enclosed within a proposal for cosmological reform.[27] Bodin observed the chaos induced by the Reformation, including the savage religious wars which wracked France, and he realized that astrology had singularly failed to contribute in any way to the cause of a more peaceful and tolerant world. He went much further than the reformers of the 1500s and recommended that the entire structure of astrology should be abandoned with the sole exception of the planets. Houses, zodiac signs and planetary aspects were to be dropped, along with all predictive techniques. Only the planets, whose real positions could be accurately measured, were to be saved. The government, Bodin suggested, should institute a programme of research (similar to the Assyrian *Diaries*, if he had but known it) in which planetary movements were to be correlated with political events. When the results were in then the government, through its teams of astrologers, would be able to anticipate conflict and take steps to maintain the peace.

The young Kepler devoted an entire chapter of the *Harmonices Mundi* to a critique of Bodin's harmonic philosophy of history. Bodin's work had clearly made quite an impact on Kepler, for he was quick to respond: although Bodin's *Republic* was published in 1576, a Latin edition did not appear until 1586, while the edition cited by Kepler appeared in 1591. The *Harmonices Mundi* itself was planned in 1599, three years after Bodin's death, although not published until 1619. Aiton, Duncan and Field conclude that Bodin's theories 'fascinated Kepler, in spite of crucial differences'.[28] Kepler himself wrote supportively of Bodin's demonstration that 'God the creator has embellished this work of his by joining the ratios of equal and of similar in one concerted harmony,' concluding that 'I agree with his purpose' and adding a final compliment: 'In this passage Bodin touches my heart by referring to the themes of my *Secret of the Universe*, though in ignorance.'[29]

In the *Harmonices Mundi* Kepler confined himself to a discussion of Bodin's political theory, not his astrological ideas, particularly addressing the three forms of the state, the popular, aristocratic and royal, which he compared to arithmetic, geometry and musical harmonies respectively. Bodin's overall approach appealed to Kepler, even if Bodin's specific arguments were often flawed. It was Kepler who moved Bodin's political cosmology from theory to practice. And, as he wrote, in his usual cautious style, 'astrology clearly has some say in political and military matters'.[30] Kepler made cautious predictions, warning of the possibility of defeat should there be war with Poland at the time of the Mars–Saturn conjunction in August and September 1601. Once such problems had been foreseen, they could be guarded against by military leadership: 'a great safeguard for the army lies in their loyalty to and high regard for their commander; for every victory depends on a driving force of the spirit'.[31] Such leadership might be combined with sensible political management. His advice was typical: 'it is preferable for peace and quiet to prevail, and sedition is feared, let meetings not be held in August and September, or let them be broken up, or better yet, let the causes exasperating people's dispositions be taken quickly away, or by the introduction of some new deterrent, let their minds be changed'.[32] Following Bodin's pragmatism, Kepler's cosmic state would manage dissent by social and political reform where possible, but propaganda and repression if necessary. We can, perhaps, see him helping to prepare the groundwork for twentieth-century social democracy. It was a form of political Platonism which, unlike Ficino's, was preparing to enter the modern world.

Kepler's astrological programme, though, was heading down a blind alley. Even in the seventeenth century he had just a handful of imitators. One was the English merchant Samuel Jeake (1652–99), who made his personal affairs the object of empirical observation. Jeake kept a diary which survives, incomplete, from 1652 to 1699, in which he compared events in his own life with planetary transits for the day. Anything from buying hops to having sex was noted. For 7 November 1687 he recorded 'Moon. About 6 h p.m. A Chapman came to buy wooll: sold him 14 packs at £8 5s per pack' and, referring to his nocturnal activities, for the 17th, 'Jupiter. About this night but once c[arnal?] c[opulation?]'.[33] Then there was the English meterologist John Goad (1616–89), who attempted to find a Keplerian method of predicting the weather, but nobody took up Kepler's goal of a politically effective, empirically-based predictive astrology any more than they had Jean Bodin's. Only his new aspects, ironically, were adopted by conventional astrologers, notably the distinctly anti-reform English astrologer William Lilly, who combined them with everything that Kepler despised as Arabic superstition.

Ironically it was Kepler himself, who had set out to save astrology, who contributed to the destruction of its credibility, at least among educated people, by destroying the theory of circular motion and showing convincingly how the planets moved free from angels or celestial intelligences. This in itself was no bar to astrological practice, as witnessed by its survival in the twenty-first century, but eventually, by the end of the seventeenth century, astrology had lost its rationale in the medieval theory of natural influence. Kepler's first two laws of planetary motion were published in 1609. This was the year that the Italian astronomer Galileo Galilei (1564–1642) made his first telescopic observations. Galileo neither invented the telescope nor was the first to use one, but he did make more detailed observations than anyone else, realized their significance and rushed into print.[34] He published the results in 1610, sending shock waves through European culture. So profound was the combination of Kepler and Galileo's work for the future of Western cosmology, and the way that Europeans came to see themselves, that the years 1609 to 1610 should be considered as the start of the modern age. They certainly have as good a claim as any subsequent date. It is difficult, if not impossible, to imagine, any more revolutionary moment in European thought. As an added blow to the old order, in 1614 a brilliant philologist by the name of Isaac Casaubon proved through linguistic analysis that the *Corpus Hermeticum* was Greek and was no longer contemporary with Moses or Abraham. This made no difference to those who believed in its essential truths, but indicated to those who were sceptical that their authenticity could no longer be rooted in an imagined antiquity. It was in this context that Galileo, the 'father of modern physics', emerged in the early seventeenth century. Of all the astrological reformers, he was less concerned than any with the Ficinesque return to an imagined, pristine past.

Galileo was born at or near Pisa on 15 February 1564. In 1581, at the age of 17, he enrolled at the University of Pisa to study medicine but was diverted by a fascination for mathematics, a discipline he pursued with such success that he was appointed to the university's chair of mathematics in 1589. In 1592 he moved to Padua, where he taught until 1610, spending most of this time dealing with problems of motion, a problem which was to lead to his famous, and perhaps apocryphal, ball-dropping experiment. He was also the principal teacher of astrology at the university. Galileo's earliest instincts were conservative and he was not initially a Copernican. His earliest surviving composition, the *De universo*, probably written in 1584, explicitly rejected Copernicanism for both philosophical and astronomical reasons; he regarded the notion that the sun was at the centre of the universe as inherently unlikely. It does, after all, defy empirical observation; everyday experience demonstrates that the earth stands still and the sun moves. In 1590, though, he appeared to be changing his views, and in his lost commentary on Ptolemy's *Almagest*, he appeared to support a mixed system, not unlike Brahe's. Finally he came out as a Copernican and, in 1597, he told Kepler that he was sympathetic to the sun-centred universe, a conclusion he reached on philosophical grounds; we should remember that there was still no incontrovertible evidence to support the theory. Apart from that conversion, Galileo showed little concern with astronomy, his main concern being the explanation of motion. However, during the appearance of the supernova of 1604 he gave public lectures attacking the, by now, distinctly shaky Aristotelian doctrine of the immutability of the heavens.

Galileo's interest in astronomy was sparked in 1609 when, hearing about the newly invented device called a telescope, he constructed his own crude instrument and began to examine the heavens. Galileo was not the first to use a telescope. In England, the astronomer Thomas Harriot (c.1560–1621) had been using one to observe and sketch the moon in July 1609, several months before Galileo turned his improved version toward the skies late in the year.[35] He quickly discovered that the moon was covered with mountains and pitted with craters, rather than being the perfect sphere envisaged by Aristotle. If the moon was like the earth, covered with hills and valleys, that was shocking enough, but there's an extra conclusion: the earth is like the moon; in other words, like the heavens, suggesting that, perhaps, Copernicus was right. Far more sensational, though, were the four satellites Galileo discovered orbiting Jupiter. If anyone still hung onto the Aristotelian cosmology after the new stars of 1572 and 1604 then the discovery of Jupiter's first four moons must have finally convinced them that the entire universe was filled with the potential for change. Galileo lost no time in announcing his discovery in the *Siderius Nuncius* – *Starry Messenger* – of 1610. He named the new moons the Medicean stars in honour of the Medici family, an overt appeal for patronage that appealed to Cosimo II's belief that the banking clan's glorious destiny was uniquely represented in the heavens. Galileo was rewarded later in the year when Cosimo appointed him court mathematician and astrologer. Galileo's identification of Jupiter's moons was followed by three other remarkable discoveries – the sun's rotation, sunspots and the phases of Venus – all of which added further nails to the coffin of Aristotelianism. Venus, he found, had phases, just like the moon, moving from new to full and back again, a phenomenon which can only be explained if Venus orbits the sun, providing convincing observational evidence for Copernicanism, which he finally publicly defended in 1613 in his *Letters on Sunspots*.

Whereas Copernicus had been extraordinarily cautious in the promotion of his heliocentric theory, Galileo was an evangelist. In 1613 he began arguing that scripture and heliocentricity were compatible as long as one realized that the Bible was primarily metaphorical, a perfectly reasonable line to take. The Church authorities began to take notice and, in 1616, a commission under Cardinal Roberto Bellarmine forbade only two things; attempts to reconcile Copernicanism with the Bible (an effort that the Church clearly thought was its responsibility) and the assertion of literal truth for heliocentric theory. Copernicus's *De revolutionibus* was suspended pending the removal of selected passages, one on biblical exegesis and others in which the earth was called a 'star', implying it moved like a planet. The Catholic Church's attitude seemed to be more concerned with its own authority to speak on biblical matters than with heliocentricity as such, and Copernicans were not suppressed. Instead, it tended to treat Copernicanism as merely one hypothesis rather than, as Galileo's observations had demonstrated, the truth.

In 1623 Maffeo Barberini, an admirer of Galileo, was elected Pope under the name Urban VIII. The following year the astronomer, who had justifiable hopes that the 1616 edict might be eased, visited Rome and was granted no less than six audiences with the new pontiff. Optimistically, he began working on a new work to be titled *Dialogue on the Tides*, in which he hoped to demonstrate that a valid reason for discussing the motion of the earth was its possible causal relationship with the tides. The manuscript was shown to the censors, who removed anything that might violate the 1616 edict, and to the Pope, who ordered the removal of the word 'tides' from the title, lest it be thought that the Church was endorsing that particular theory. The book appeared in 1632 under the simple title *Dialogue* (since 1744 it has been known as the *Dialogue Concerning the Two Chief World Systems*). Constructed in the form of a Platonic dialogue between different characters, the *Dialogue's* three participants discussed the merits and problems involved in both the geocentric and heliocentric systems. In spite of the fact that the book was published with the Church's permission, that was not enough to protect Galileo and an anonymous charge of heresy resulted in his famous investigation by the Inquisition. Even though Galileo had the weight of legal evidence on his side, seven of the ten cardinals who sat in judgement on him condemned him; he agreed to recant his views and submitted to lifelong house arrest. Even hypothetical discussion of Copernicanism became evidence of heresy and the Catholic Church backed itself into a corner in which its chosen earth-centred cosmology was increasingly regarded as manifestly absurd. There is considerable uncertainty over the exact nature of the Church's argument with Galileo. It has been suggested that his real crime was to publicly challenge the authority of a Catholic hierarchy that, paradoxically, in fact included many who were sympathizers or supporters, or even that the heliocentric issue was less of a problem than his atomic theories, which undermined the doctrine of transubstantiation (the conversion of the bread and wine into the body and spirit of Christ in the Mass). The truth is rather more complex than the simple fantasy of the persecution of a brave scientist by ignorant churchmen. Galileo had sent his manuscript of the *Dialogue* to his friend, the Dominican Nicolo Riccardi, who was Master of the Apostolic Palace and the official responsible for authorizing the publication of books.[36] Riccardi passed the manuscript on for an opinion to his fellow Dominican, Raffaelo Visconti, who was sympathetic to the new astronomy as well as a practising astrologer and, perhaps, magician. Visconti was, in turn, a close friend of Orazio Morandi, the astrologer, Hermeticist and abbot of S. Prassede in Rome. On 24 May 1630, on his arrival in Rome, Galileo accepted an invitation to dine with Visconti, Morandi and another friend, Lodovico Corbusio, consultor to the Holy Office. Morandi's papers were later found to have a copy of Galileo's horoscope, so perhaps this was a topic of conversation at the dinner. We need to absorb the significance of this encounter: Galileo was welcomed to the circle of occultists, astrologers and Hermeticists at the very senior reaches of the Catholic Church, who were sympathetic to his work and included the Pope himself. Galileo's troubles started because, probably unknown to him, Morandi had recently published an astrological tract predicting the Pope's death. Even before the dinner with Morandi, a scurrilous journalist called Antonio Badelli had circulated notices spreading the rumour that Galileo had personally forecast the Pope's death, and was in Rome to attack the Jesuits. The rumours were widely believed, although not by Galileo's friends in the Catholic hierarchy, and contributed to the atmosphere which led to his trial. Morandi, meanwhile, was tried and imprisoned, and his unfortunate prediction was the direct cause of Urban's Bull Against Astrologers, of 1 April 1631. Seen in the wider context, the attack on Galileo and rejection of Copernicansim was part of a sequence of events which included the imprisonment of Morandi and an assault on astrology.

Undaunted, Galileo developed his ideas further in the *Discourse on the Two New Sciences* in 1638, a text which is credited with laying the foundation of modern physics. Whereas the astronomies of Copernicus, Brahe and Kepler were designed to conform to Aristotelian and Platonic cosmology (even if they failed to do so), Galileo applied a new physics based on his studies of motion. This was to be profoundly significant for astrology's future credibility. Gailileo's work was much more dramatic than Copernicus's and had an immediate effect on European thought. It really did demolish the old Aristotelian structure of the solar system with remarkable speed. The impact on educated European thought was immediate. One of the first public reactions was published by the English poet John Donne.[37] In his *Anatomy of the World*, written in 1611, the year after Galileo's first observations, he wrote:

> And new philosophy calls all in doubt
> The element of fire is quite put out
> The sun is lost, and th' earth, and no man's wit
> Can well direct him where to look for it.
> And freely men confess that this world's spent
> When in the planets, and the firmament
> They seek so many new . . .
> 'Tis all in pieces, all coherence gone . . .

Following Galileo's publication of the *Starry Messenger*, the English ambassador to Venice (and friend of the same Isaac Casaubon who had challenged the ancient origin of the *Corpus Hermeticum*), Henry Wotton, wrote a letter to King James I of England concerning the impact of the new physics, which pretty well sums up the mood of the times. He informed the king of the invention of the telescope and the resulting discovery by the 'Mathematical Professor at Padua' of the moons of Jupiter. In what may be the first official comment concerning the impact of the new astronomy on astrology he wrote:

So as upon the whole subject he hath first overthrown all former astronomy – for we must have a new sphere to save the appearances – and next all astrology. For the virtue of these new planets must needs vary the judicial part, and why may there not yet be more?[38]

As an astrologer, Galileo is actually something of an enigma. Copernicus, Tycho and Kepler were all devoted to the Platonic–Aristotelian vision of a perfectly ordered cosmos, united by the world soul and filled with influence and sympathy. As astrological reformers their astronomical work, with varying degrees, was intended, at least in part, to make astrology more accurate and, as Galileo said of Copernicus, reflecting Wotton's letter to James I, to 'save appearances'.[39] What he meant was that physical observation of the planets' erratic movements conflicted with the theory of circular motion which itself had to be saved. Plato had said it was so, and Aristotle had concurred, so it had to be so. The theory of cycles and epicycles, crystalline spheres and Copernican heliocentricity were all designed to reconcile physical observation with theory in order to explain celestial motions. And here lies the radical significance of Galileo's experiments with motion. It is fascinating to watch his own shift away from Aristotelian cosmology. In 1605 he observed the new star, like every other astrologer in Europe. Eventually, Galileo provided experimental proof of the way that objects move and his telescopic observations demonstrated to all who could see that the crystalline spheres, cycles and epicycles of the traditional model were not part of the equation. Yet, Galileo was himself an enthusiastic astrologer, exactly as were Tycho and Kepler.

The chief source for our knowledge of Galileo's practical astrology is his *Astrologica Nonulla*, which exists only in manuscript form in Florence. This consists of about 50 pages containing horoscopes cast by him, some with scribbled notes, which are our only indication of how he actually worked.[40] Galileo's patron and employer was Cosimo II de Medici, Grand Duke of Florence, for whom he provided professional services; he appears to have adjusted Cosimo's birth time, a perfectly legitimate practice known as rectification, in order to move Jupiter, the most benevolent planet, to the highest – and, naturally, most powerful – part of the chart. He also cast horoscopes for his own personal interest, and we have surviving copies of his own birth chart, together with those of his daughters Virginia and Livia, and his friends Sagredo (later ambassador to Venice) and Cesare Galli. His analysis clearly shows his use of Claudius Ptolemy's astrological model of the soul – *psyche* – which was divided into two, arranged in a hierarchy with a 'higher', rational soul, closer to God and the stars than the lower, emotional, or 'sensitive' soul. Of Virginia, who was born on 12 August 1600, he wrote 'Mercury and the Moon are in separate places, sharing no aspect but having a certain discord, and this denotes a jarring between the rational and sensitive powers of the soul.'[41]

The evidence also suggests that, like Kepler, Galileo was well versed in conventional astrological rules and, unlike Kepler, was, initially, at least, very happy to use them. In 1609, during the final illness of Grand Duke Ferdinand I, he was called in by the Grand Duchess to establish her husband's prospects for recovery.

He repeated the mistake made by a number of previous highly distinguished astrologers of their distinguished clients and predicted that the Duke would recover, only to see him die 22 days later.[42] Galileo's error was not as bad as it seems; he had set out his reasoning and invoked the help of God, so failure could be attributed to one or the other. But this kind of incident drove him into the reformers' camp. He adapted certain rules, such as those for establishing the 'lord of the geniture', or most powerful planet, in the chart, but no more so than any other astrologer might have done. However, by 1611, following the discovery of the Medicean stars, his position does seem to have shifted to reform. In a letter to his friend Piero Dini, dated 21 May 1611, he argued that Jupiter's moons must exert an influence which astrologers should take into account. (This was in contrast to Kepler, who believed that they existed only for the benefit of the inhabitants of Jupiter.) But how could one establish how their influence was felt? Galileo proposed a research programme which was different to Kepler's, though complementary. He suggested that, using case histories it should be possible to establish how the changes in the configuration of the four moons corresponded to terrestrial events.[43] As with Bodin, though, there is no evidence that Galileo ever pursued a programme of empirical research. By the 1630s, he was making distinctly sceptical noises. In the *Dialogue Concerning the Two Chief World Systems* he had Salviati ridicule astrologers who are wise after the event; 'who after the outcome see it so clearly in the chart, or that is to say in the celestial figure'.[44] This, though, was reminiscent of the standard criticism of the ordinary professional astrologer by the elite, from Plotinus to Kepler. It was a matter of the high-brow criticizing the middle-brow. But, more revealing, though, was Galileo's equivocal response, in 1633, to the work of the French royal astrologer, Morin de Villefranche. Morin had been present at the birth of the future Louis XIV (he had become close to Louis XIII after predicting the king's recovery from illness and worked for the Queen, Marie de Medici, and Cardinal Mazarin, the chief minister), though hidden behind a curtain, apparently, and was now the Sun King's astrologer.[45] Morin fancied himself as an astrological reformer, though his position was less extreme than Kepler. Whereas Kepler advocated root-and-branch rejection of medieval, and even Hellenistic, astrology, Morin believed that astrology's classical foundations were fine and merely needed perfecting, rejecting techniques which didn't work and developing new ones that did.[46] Galileo had received Morin's book, along with one by another astrologer called Fromondo, six months after the *Dialogues* were published. He was sorry for this, he said, because otherwise he would have had a chance to praise them both, in spite of Fromondo's naïve use of scripture to ridicule Copernicus. On Morin he wrote:

> I am amazed by the very great esteem he has for judicial astrology, and that he expects to establish with his conjectures (which seem to me quite uncertain, if not to say very uncertain) the certainty of astrology. It would be a really admirable thing if, by his shrewdness, Astrology were placed in the higher seat of human science, as he promises. I shall wait with great curiosity to see this marvellous novelty.[47]

Was Galileo's apparent irony genuine, or are we missing something here in the translation of seventeenth-century Italian to twenty-first-century English? At any rate, his praise of Morin does seem to be tinged with biting sarcasm and his position in 1633 would appear to be much like Kepler's – or Ficino's. Favaro's cautious comment was that 'These words are not to be taken in the sense of complete criticism, that some have been pleased to recognise.'[48] Galileo had immense respect for what Kepler had called 'true astrology', but was frankly doubtful whether astrologers were capable of recognizing exactly what it was, still less of doing justice to it. Morin himself was using astrological arguments to oppose Copernicanism and support the earth-centred cosmos, and we cannot really imagine Galileo approving such a position in the 1630s, no matter what he thought of Morin's attempts to reform astrology.

The story of Tycho, Kepler and Galileo, the trio of astronomical geniuses and astrological reformers, runs to the heart of the mythology of Western science. The mythic version, which remains central to the history of science, holds that science emerged as a reaction to superstition, that the darkness of medieval ignorance was vanquished by the brilliance of the Enlightenment. It's a view which received its full dramatic treatment in Bertolt Brecht's play *Galileo*.[49] Astronomers tend to get very excitable about this version of history. One, Colin Ronan, came out with a particularly triumphalist opinion: 'We come now to a period in which modern science was finally launched and set out on its unprecedented voyage of conquest.'[50] The alternative, and increasingly accepted view, is that science emerged seamlessly out of magic as the latter's attempts at problem-solving eventually proved inadequate. The concept of a revolutionary break in human thought then seems increasingly less convincing. 'The so-called "astronomical revolution" – an historiographically somewhat dodgy concept,' grumbled Kusukawa and Maclean in a recent review.[51] Charles Webster, who has done much to challenge the orthodox astronomers' position, made his feelings clear: 'One of the chief effects of the history of science as the subject has developed in the present century has been to drive a wedge between the cultures of Paracelsus and Newton.'[52] The radical conclusion, which few have dared propose, is that modern science is similar, at least in some respects, to medieval magic. Mary Midgley is one philosopher who has flirted with this model of history, suggesting that the link is the shared principle that 'the laws of thought turn out to be the laws of things'.[53] There was no scientific revolution in the sense of a new world order, pioneered by a few brave men who pursued a titanic struggle to overthrow the old world. There was instead a complex interplay of ideas as competing cosmological narratives vied with each other, and the principal protagonists remained deeply engaged with ancient and medieval concepts of the world. Galileo's life illustrates this well. His encounters with the Inquisition in 1616 and 1633 arising from his enthusiasm for Copernican theories are well known. Less familiar is an earlier trial, which took place in 1605, in which he was charged by the Paduan Inquisition with astral fatalism, or making astrological predictions.[54] The Church authorities' problem was not with science, but with any form of thought, activity or debate which it did not control.

Galileo's indirect influence extended beyond astronomy and physics to the organization of society as a whole. Unlike Kepler, he did not dwell on the theory of astrology's application to society's well-being, so the English political philosopher Thomas Hobbes (1588–1679) made the connection on his behalf. Hobbes met Galileo on his third continental trip, and was profoundly impressed by the experience. As normal for anyone educated in the classics, he had already considered the possibilities of applying geometry to political theory. Fuelled by enthusiasm after his encounter with Galileo, he resolved to apply the new laws of planetary motion to society, with a view to succeeding where Bodin had failed, and discover the rules for the preservation of political stability.[55] Galileo's argument that all bodies were in motion unless physically restrained made a great deal of sense to Hobbes, disturbed as he was by the chaos of the English Civil War. Like Plato, he believed that all human behaviour could be analysed according to elementary motions of body and mind, from which the scientists could then deduce general laws for the stable ordering of society. The problem was essentially one of mechanics: 'The skill of making, and retaining Common-wealths, consisteth in certain Rules, as doth Arithmatique and Geometry.'[56] He set as his personal goal the discovery of the correct form of authority necessary to restrain a nation's citizens. Human beings were, he concluded, like the planets, in a continual state of motion, and the state's primary function was to restrain them. His view of people as essentially disorderly was directly comparable to the Hebrew prophets' dislike of the planets on the same grounds, and Galileo's astronomy, with its demonstration of a new planetary order, pointed the way to an effective authoritarian system: the orderly laws of astronomy could be used to inhibit the disorderly tendencies of human society. It was Hobbes who first spoke of the solar system as a clock, an analogy which has since been associated with Newton: 'For as in a watch, or some such small engine, the matter, figure and motion of the wheels cannot be known, except it be taken in sunder, and viewed in parts; so to make a more curious search into the rights of states, and duties of subjects, it is necessary . . . they be so considered, as if they were dissolved.'[57]

Hobbes had a typically ambivalent view of astrology, which recognized it as a branch of learning while, in his epic on political philosophy, *Leviathan*, published in 1651, he condemned the superstitious awe with which the ignorant greeted every eclipse.[58] Like so many critics of astrology from Plotinus onwards, Hobbes saw a core of truth in the doctrine of human connections with the cosmos, but despised popular judicial astrology as a superstitious cul-de-sac. He, like Bodin, was appalled by religious conflict, and believed that the stability of the state counted for far more than the correct ideology. He may be counted among those whom Curry identifies as political opponents of astrology, writing as he was during the radical astrological fever of the English republic. He was certainly a member of that coalition of astronomers and philosophers who were rendering the medieval cosmos untenable.

11

The Seventeenth Century: Practitioners and Politics

Queen and huntress, chaste and fair
Now the Sun is laid to sleep.

BEN JOHNSON[1]

When Thomas Hobbes poured scorn on the astrologers, he would have had his sights on English practitioners such as William Lilly (1602–81). England in the middle decades of the seventeenth century provides us with one of the best case-studies of astrology in action, partly because the breakdown of censorship in the period of the Civil War and republic, the 1640s and 1650s, allowed the development of a flourishing community of practitioners and a thriving culture of almanacs.[2] In the rest of Europe the position was less certain. In Italy, by comparison, the publication of astrology appears to have suffered from the Papal Bull of 1631. The best-known English astrologer of his day, Lilly's reputation in Europe was considerable.[3] His good fortune was due in part to a series of shrewd marriages which guaranteed his financial position; his first wife left him an income of £20 a year and his second, an elderly widow, left him the handsome sum of £1000. In his professional life Lilly was an entirely unreconstructed practising astrologer and paid no attention whatsoever to the reform programme. As far as he was concerned the accumulated wisdom of Greek, Arabic and medieval astrology was perfectly fine for the job it was supposed to do, which was to answer virtually any question human beings could pose of it. Lilly appreciated Kepler's work, but only inasmuch as he could incorporate it in his own. So, to his soup of astrological rules and guidelines culled from every known source, some acknowledged, some not, he added Kepler's new aspects – rules for ascertaining the significance of planets based on their apparent distance from each other. It didn't matter to him that Kepler had intended his aspects to replace the old ones. In Lilly's world astrology was a morass of techniques and methods, many contradictory. But it was precisely this complexity which enabled him, and astrologers like him, to navigate their way through the rules with a fair level of subjective choice, and reach a satisfactory judgement.

Lilly's enduring reputation is based on his publication of *Christian Astrology*, the first textbook of astrology to appear in the English language.[4] It's an uncontroversial book, little different in tone or assumptions to so many previous works. Its appeal for his contemporaries was the sheer number of examples of horoscope interpretation, which made it ideal for students. Its importance for historians rests in its encyclopaedic approach, even though electional and mundane astrology are largely ignored. The use of the word 'Christian' in the title has nothing whatsoever to do with the content and was a clear defensive posture designed to forestall clerical censure. The book contained all the rules for reading horoscopes with extensive case-histories, mainly interrogations – horoscopes cast for the asking of questions, with birth charts as an after-thought. Guido Bonatti had set out in the thirteenth century the rules used by Lilly and had warned that a horoscope reading would fail when the client visited the astrologer out of idle curiosity or asked a silly question, while Jerome Cardan added that astrologers with 'too great a conceit' of themselves would also fail.[5] According to the rationale behind the so-called 'Considerations before Judgement', the cosmos, being intelligent, would be observing such psychic problems and would send warning signs. This was magical Neoplatonic cosmology in action, operating on a level in which no detail was too small. But the medium through which it operated was mathematical; it was number which determined, measured and described the positions of the planets and zodiac. Astrology may have been endlessly complex in theory, and to work out predictions from a birth chart could be extraordinarily laborious, involving a high degree of subjective choice as to which techniques should be prioritized, and then considerable uncertainty over their final meaning, but, in everyday practice, the astrologer's lot could be an easy one. This much is clear from Lilly's collection of his own case-studies in *Christian Astrology*. His answers are frequently arrived at after considering just a few planets in very simple terms, but he would add further description for the reader just to show how the horoscope also described the context within which the question was asked. There was virtually no question beyond the scope of astrologers like Lilly. Advice could be given on one's entire professional and personal life, health, family, marital prospects, whether one's cow was sick or neighbour a witch; his casebooks contain over 50 such cases, of which 23 occurred in two years between 1654 and 1656. Keith Thomas, whose ideas in this area are influential, believed that witchcraft and astrology functioned as rival systems of explanation on the grounds that to attribute a celestial origin was to deny that one's neighbour could be the cause of distress; he describes a client of the astrologer Richard Napier in 1635 who 'feared he was bewitched *or* blasted by an ill planet', as if the two possible causes are mutually exclusive.[6] Are the two, astrology and witchcraft, mutually exclusive explanations? Not exactly, for witches might engage with the sky when they 'called down the moon', while astrologers were quite clear that the origins of any event might lie in human activities as much as the celestial sphere. What we really have in astrological rules on the identification of witches is a specific example of the implementation of a logical procedure which claimed to be able to analyse any form of human behaviour, not just witchcraft. Among the questions posed to Lilly by his clients were one from a woman asking whether her sailor husband was still alive, another on what kind of death the archbishop of Canterbury would suffer, and one from an aspiring alchemist on whether he would discover the philosopher's stone (the answer was 'no', followed by the friendly advice that the questioner should look after his health).[7] Other rules allowed the astrologer to function as marriage guidance counsellor, assessing whether a marriage would actually happen; if so, how long it would last; and what the likely causes of strife might be.[8] The very techniques that Lilly was using to resolve such dilemmas were those denounced by Pigghe and the reformers a century earlier.

Astrologers also gave advice to employers about runaway servants, adapting the rules in classical writers such as Dorotheus on the location of escaped slaves. In 1528 the Warden of New College, Oxford, and the Bishop's staff, employed an astrologer to establish the location of the Lutheran heretic Thomas Garrett. On another occasion, Thomas Pitches, the underkeeper at Ludgate gaol in London, asked for advice on the whereabouts of a prisoner who had been in his charge.[9] The reading of horoscopes existed, though, within a wider milieu of folk beliefs in which, as in Babylon, any random or unexplained event could be considered an omen, a warning of some future event. In the countryside, to be born with a birthmark might be the equivalent, for the illiterate, of a particular planetary configuration in the birth chart of a wealthy infant.[10] And it might not be Neoplatonic intelligences who were involved behind the scenes, but fairies. These two worlds, of sympathetic magic and educated astrology on the one hand, and age-old folk-customs on the other, were not discrete. In an environment in which most of the rich and powerful grew up in the same natural environment as the poor and ignorant, there could be no precise boundary between the two. Lilly himself was also called on to comment on the apparent activities of fairies. The antiquarian John Aubrey recorded the following anecdote: 'Anno 1670, not far from Cyrencester, was an Apparition: Being demanded, whether a good Spirit, or a bad? returned no answer, but disappeared with a curious Perfume and most melodious Twang. Mr W. Lilley believes it was a Fairie.'[11] Aubrey's story points to the connections between literary astrology and the lost world of rural folk beliefs, but such a view was quite in keeping with the mood of the times and Lilly's own work. His original, brief seven- or eight-week apprenticeship had been with a hard-drinking, wise – or cunning – man in London called John Evans. While he was learning the rudiments of judicial astrology Lilly also received a short training in ceremonial magic and the conjuring of spirits; John Dee's work had not died when he did.

The outbreak of the English Civil War in 1642 offered all astrologers scope for expanding their work, partly because censorship relaxed but also on account of the public thirst for predictions. Lilly made his first parliamentary contact in 1643 when he treated, and was credited with curing, the MP Sir Bulstrode Whitelocke. Grateful to Lilly for saving his life, Whitelocke became the astrologer's ally and protector. In the following year, Lilly published his first annual almanac, tapping into traditions of popular prophecy by naming it after King Arthur's magician: *Merlinus Anglicus Junior*. He sold out within a week, evidence, if any were needed, of the demand for such work. The parliamentary licenser (and fellow astrologer) had used his position to censor Lilly's work, but Lilly, never one to accept a slight, complained and was allowed to issue a second edition in the following year, 1645, under the title *Anglicus, Peace or no Peace*. The Civil War had entered its third year and the outcome was still wide open. Lilly's reputation was made when he noticed that, in June, Mars was due to make a dangerous aspect to the king's ascendant. Realizing that this was profoundly damaging for the royal cause, Lilly, who supported the rebels, wrote 'if we now fight, a Victory stealeth upon us'.[12] When the parliamentary army decisively defeated the king at the Battle of Naseby, changing the course of the war, Lilly was credited with foreknowledge of the victory, with excellent commercial consequences: sales of *Merlinus* rose relentlessly from 13,500 copies in 1646 to 30,000 in 1649, and the 1650s saw Dutch, German, Swedish and Danish translations. Lilly was politically allied with the Independents, who were well represented in the army and were Protestants but rivals of the highly authoritarian Calvinist Presbyterians who dominated the House of Commons, and he was consulted on the fortunes, and hoped-for decline, of the latter. In 1649, during the final days of the Civil War, Lilly and his colleague John Booker (1602–67) were both invited to join the parliamentary army at Colchester, which was being held by 4000 troops in a protracted siege. Their commission was to raise the troops' morale by persuading them that victory was imminent; there can rarely have been such an explicit example of a self-fulfilling prophecy. Lilly, never one to deny his own influence, was proud of his relationship with the Roundhead soldiers. 'All the soldiery [were] my friends, for when [Cromwell] was in Scotland, the day of one of their fights, a soldier stood with *Anglicus* in his hand, and as the several troops passed by him "Lo, hear what Lilly saith; you are in this month promised victory, fight it out, brave boys;" and then read that month's prediction.'[13] But Lilly was also a professional astrologer and not inclined to turn down business. He was also employed by members of the Royalist cause, notably Lady Jane Whorewood, who consulted him three times in 1647 and 1648 when she was secretly plotting King Charles's escape from imprisonment. On the first occasion, Charles was locked up at Hampton Court. Lilly advised that he should flee to Essex but Charles settled on the Isle of Wight where he was captured again and imprisoned in Carisbrooke Castle. The next time that Lilly sent Lady Whorewood to see the king, his astrological advice was accompanied by a metal saw, all the better to cut through prison bars with. Once again the king ignored the astrological advice. In fact, he was inclined to ignore all reasonable advice, as he had done all his life, and was duly executed in 1649.

One other incident in Lilly's career merits examination because it provides a direct link between astrology and other prophetic traditions. In 1652 he had published a mysterious work called *Monarchy or no Monarchy* which consisted of a brief introduction followed by a series of woodcuts showing various future events. What these were to be, though, was no easier to gauge than it was from Nostradamus's verses. One image, though, featured a pair of inverted children, which would have been widely read as representing the twins, and so Gemini, London's traditional ruling zodiac sign, suspended over a roaring fire. The picture remained in the public mind and, in 1666, Lilly was summoned before the panel investigating that year's Great Fire of London; he was exonerated of any suspicion that he had started the fire to fulfil his own prophecy. However, far more interesting than the thought of the astrologer being suspected of arson is the plausible argument that the figures surrounding the twins and the fire are a visual representation of the horoscope for the outbreak of the fire itself.[14] If true, and the evidence is convincing, Lilly had performed one of the most amazing prophetic feats in history.

Lilly paid little attention to the philosophical framework within which he was operating, although he must have been aware of the battering the old physical cosmology had received from the three famous continental astrologers, Tycho, Kepler and Galileo, even if Kepler and Tycho, at least, adhered to the old metaphysics. Ann Geneva has described Lilly's astrology (and that of his seventeenth-century colleagues) as 'a symbolic language system functioning within a diminished though not yet discredited neo-Platonic framework'.[15] It's not quite clear why the Neoplatonism of the 1640s, at least that of the judicial astrologers, should be in any way 'diminished'. What seems to have happened in the course of the century was that, while Platonism was stripped down by the emerging founders of the scientific revolution to the notion of an underlying world order, the magical riches of Neoplatonism went underground, or at least moved to a place that modern historians have done their best to ignore – with notable recent exceptions – nestling in the emerging 'western esoteric tradition'.[16] Lilly gave one visual clue to his philosophy and ideological alignment. He had his portrait painted with his hand on a blank horoscope bearing the words 'non cogunt' – meaning the stars do not compel. So, in this respect he was in the mainstream, conforming to the middle way established by Thomas Aquinas. The problem is, though, that his sample case histories are composed in the fatalistic tones of the Stoic for whom the future is predetermined and written in the stars. Lilly's analysis of his client's questions leads inexorably to the conclusion that he may well have offered advice – as he did to the unfortunate alchemist with looming health problems – but the answer to the client's query was always contained within the universe's mathematical structure, the *machina mundi*. And this is a problem which afflicts astrology as a whole, and had done so throughout the Middle Ages. The texts from which the student was expected to learn and the readings given by the professionals all tended to assume that the outcome was already set. One can open *Christian Astrology* at any page and, bearing in mind one is looking at the accumulated lore of horoscopic astrology back to the fifth century BCE, one finds little room for doubt. To take an example of a frequent problem the astrologers encountered, let us consider marriage break-up.[17] In rules which can be traced back to classical astrology, and certainly to the Islamic period, if the husband consults the astrologer, he will be signified by the planet ruling the zodiac sign in which the ascendant (the zodiac sign rising over the eastern horizon) is placed: if the ascendant is in Mercury, for example, the husband in the horoscope will be represented by Mercury, Gemini's ruler. There are other factors as well, but none of them open to dispute. The wife, if she consults the astrologer, will be represented chiefly by the planet ruling the zodiac sign on the cusp of the seventh house. There are then a series of rules for interpreting the outcome: if the planet which represents the source of difficulty is in the seventh house the problem will be a friend, if in the eighth, death, and so on. There is no doubt. This *will* be the problem. The state of the world is set, fixed, unchangeable. But then in comes the paradox; once the problem has been identified it can be prevented. And this is the dance that medieval astrology inherited from the Greeks; its cosmos is neither totally determinist nor completely free, but both. The Christian context required deference to the principle of free moral choice, reinforced by Neoplatonic notions of a higher soul, free from celestial influence. But, if the moment at which a question was asked resulted in a valid horoscope, there was clearly a connection between the individual's reason and the stars which suggests that, in the practical astrology of the mid-seventeenth century, the soul–star connection was still assumed. Lilly's declaration, 'non-cogunt', should then definitely be read as the prudent astrologer's deference to Thomas Aquinas.

Judicial astrologers in Christian Europe were forced to navigate a confusion of classical philosophies, some more or less fatalistic, others more or less natural-istic, and still leave the required room for the soul to choose salvation. But the high-profile commercial astrologer faced different pressures to the courtly philosopher. Lilly was neither without enemies nor above public ridicule. Samuel Pepys, the famous diarist, repeated a comment by John Booker to the effect that Lilly was paid to distort his predictions. Pepys actually spent an entertaining evening at Lilly's house in October 1660, but later described how he and his friends 'laughed at Lilly's prophecies this month in his Almanak this year'.[18] But Lilly was also highly respected, venerated, almost, by many of his peers and contemporaries. He had an extensive and influential clientele and was consulted by his colleagues when astrological questions needed resolving. Ann Geneva concluded that he was a genius at his art – judicial astrology. This is certainly how he was regarded by many people at the time. The problem here is that his published case histories are all retrospective and designed to display his skills, whereas his surviving political predictions, the Naseby success aside, are all of the standard, vague format characteristic of such work for the previous 500 years. His chance to seriously influence the flow of events came three years after the rebels' victory in the Civil War.

The year 1652 was an apocalyptic one which attracted typical forecasts. There were to be two lunar eclipses and one solar, all harbingers of doom. The solar eclipse, which took place on 29 March, attracted feverish speculation in a Europe which was recovering from the Thirty Years War, and an England still shocked by the execution in 1649 of its king. Lilly's verdict on 'Black Munday' was eagerly awaited, but one can read in vain through his almanac, the *Dark Year*, for any sign of anything other than a rehash of the standard work. He opened with a Hermetic passage in praise of the sun, which would have pleased Copernicus: 'The Sun is infused in all things, intimate in all things, by him so many glorious Lamps of Heaven do shine, by him the Elements stand, the Winds blow, the plants flourish, living Creatures have sense; and what us wonderfull, at the same moment of time he produces the Day here and the Night there.'[19] He then went on to quote Plotinus, Avicenna and Ficino, taking care to make frequent references to God and Divine providence. Finally, after a lengthy preamble, he arrives at his prediction. He began:

> The Conjunction of the two Luminaries in Aries, occasions strange Alienations of friendship and Death. *viz* break of Leagues, Amities and friendships: from thence Warre and controversy, after which follows quarrels, and then Death and Destruction; many times a Famine and scarcity of provisions ... Nor are men or Cattle onely concerned in this our great Eclips: without doubt whole Kingdomes, Nations, People, Cities and Common-wealths.[20]

This is pretty much the same interpretation for every eclipse, in every sign of the zodiac, with slight variations, since the twelfth century. It was the kind of astrology which Ficino and Pico had rejected and which Kepler had attempted to reform, seeing how it had failed to avert war and bring stability. It was certainly the kind of thing that was familiar to Gloucester in *King Lear*. There are signs that in the following pages Lilly will become more specific. We are told that Zealand and Holland, ruled by Cancer, which happened to be the rising sign in the horoscope for the moment of the eclipse, would be subject to storms, loss of shipping and rebellion; but then so would all other Cancerian locations, including Scotland, Algiers, Venice and Constantinople. Lilly did concede uncertainty: 'how far the influence of this Eclipse', he wrote, 'shall operate upon the common Lawes of our Nation, I cannot very well tell'.[21] In spite of the vagueness and failure to reach either any sort of conclusion or offer advice, such was Lilly's reputation that people listened. In 1699 the diarist John Evelyn recalled that many people were so terrified of the eclipse that they stayed indoors, presumably believing that if they could not see it – or it could not see them – they would be spared its dire consequences. One anonymous tract complained that more people believed in Lilly than in God. The comparison with Kepler, though, is stark. Lilly may have been skilled in the rules of horoscope interpretation but there is a complete failure to engage with the fact that such predictions were either too vague or plain wrong, and none of Kepler's desire to improve his art for the good of society. Ultimately, though, it was Kepler's reformed almanacs which died out (until revived by a few enthusiasts in the late twentieth century) and those in the style of Lilly which survived in an unbroken tradition into the twenty-first century.

Lilly stood at the centre of an astrological world which, by virtue of the breakdown of censorship, gives us a colourful picture of a society in which astrology was practised with very little restraint, beyond the normal precautions against being seen as heretical (such as inserting the word Christian in one's book title). Lilly had his acolytes, like Henry Coley (1633–1704) whose astrological textbook the *Clavis Astrologiae* or *A Key to the Whole Art of Astrology* included extensive sections on mundane astrology, which Lilly had ignored; Lilly, proud of his student, regarded the *Clavis* as an excellent complement to his own work. But its attitude to the reformers is telling. Like Lilly, Coley knew of Kepler's work and included it as a gesture to reform. The book was very well received and the much expanded 1676 edition included 750 pages of text of which a further 100 pages of astronomical data were drawn from Kepler and the French reformer and royal astrologer Jean-Baptiste Morin de Villefranche. So, while Kepler wanted to abandon the superstition of Arabic and even most Greek astrology, it was the fate of his work to be absorbed into the very traditional astrology which he despised. There was just very little call for Keplerian astrology, especially among professional astrologers who required a full range of tools to provide a proper service for their clients.

The public wanted to know if they would recover their lost property, if their lovers were faithful and if their neighbours were lying to them, and Kepler's astrology couldn't help them. For example, astrologers were frequently consulted by clients who believed they had been bewitched, and they were obliged to create tests to ascertain this, for which we have accounts from the sixteenth century. The English astrologers Richard Saunders and Joseph Blagrave went so far as to assert that astrology offered the only certain means of discovering witchcraft, an argument which would certainly have got them into trouble with the more aggressive religious witch-finders, had they noticed. William Lilly's surviving casebooks contain well over 50 cases of suspected witchcraft, 23 of which date from 1654 to 1656, the high point of Cromwellian rule in England. From Lilly we learn that an astrologer testing for witchcraft would most likely cast an 'inter-rogation', a horoscope set for the moment of the asking of a question such as 'Is the subject bewitched?' If the subject was sick and witchcraft was the suspected cause, an alternative would be to cast a 'decumbiture' (literally 'lying down'), a horoscope set for the moment that the diseased individual took to their bed. Lilly set out the rules for establishing whether witchcraft was a cause of illness or distress, advising on treatment and assessing whether it might be overcome.[22] In the horoscope, witches were indicated by the 'twelfth house,' the sector of sky immediately above the eastern horizon, and by the planet ruling the sign of the zodiac in which the house cusp (its beginning, in this case its uppermost point) was placed. For example, if the uppermost point of the twelfth house was in Leo, the ruling planet would be the sun, Leo's 'ruling planet'. Lilly defines six rules for the positions of house rulers in which he had 'found more certain [the] suspicion of Witchcraft'. For example, if the planet ruling the sign of the zodiac on the cusp of the twelfth house ruler was in the sixth house (that is, immediately below the western horizon), witchcraft, Lilly claimed, was likely. Saturn and Mars were likely both to reveal the presence of witchcraft and indicate the subject's vulnerability to it, while Venus and Jupiter might suggest the opposite. Only five of the horoscopes in Lilly's casebooks include a judgment, and all of those are negative. He was clearly inclined to find that the accused were innocent. Whether this suggests a level of scepticism is not clear, but is certainly possible. While the rules of interpretation are clearly set out, and while some horoscopes would give an unambiguous answer, in many cases the horoscope contained sufficient internal contradictions for the astrologers' judgement to be vital. Yet Lilly's own comments point to a belief in the reality of witchcraft, claiming that 'people are troubled with witches . . . in many places of this Kingdome'.[23] Other astrologers are known to have diagnosed witchcraft. For example, in 1654 Christopher Hall, the Norfolk astrologer, declared that the cause of a client's disease was one of three witches in her home village. The very existence of such astrological work confirmed the existence of witchcraft at a time when its reality was openly challenged. The same applied to astrological palliatives: if witchcraft wasn't real then there could be no reason for such remedies. These treatments, which could be adapted for cattle, were not explicitly astrological but worked according to the principles of sympathetic magic. For example, according to Lilly, if the horoscope established the presence of witchcraft then it might be overcome if a tile from the witch's house is heated in a fire, then has the urine of the bewitched person poured on it, and is finally returned to the fire until 'extremely hot'.

The presiding patriarch of English astrology throughout this period was the alchemist Elias Ashmole (1617–82). Ashmole fought for the Royalist army in the civil war, loyalty which saw him richly rewarded by Charles II when the monarchy was restored in 1660. From this position Ashmole was able to protect other astrologers, particularly those, like Lilly, who had backed the losing side. Ashmole was a keen student of Dee's magical and angelic work and compiled a still-valuable alchemical source-book, the *Theatrum Chemicum Britannicum*. Ashmole's speciality was electional astrology, important, of course, if he was to time his alchemical experiments.[24] He elected the most auspicious moment for his own wedding in 1649, for which he ensured that the benefic planets Venus and Jupiter were well aspected and that Saturn, the malefic, was in a position to ensure security and longevity. We have a record of him electing auspicious moments for making talismans, or sigils, in 1681. His text for 7 April 1681 records that at 6.45 a.m. exactly he started making a sigil of Jupiter and Venus, clearly to assist with good fortune. His own words record the incident:

> I began to cast the 5 Gemini ascending/ but the metal spluttered and burnt my fingers and the sigil came not/ Mars behold[s] the ascendant with square/ Those cast about 6H.45' were for a continued health and favour with great and good men and women/ Those cast about 7: were to strengthen and enlarge memory, fancy and tongue, and wit/ to assist and encourage a search into mysteries and learning.[25]

For an insight into the practical life of an alchemist, this account is unrivalled, even down to the square (a difficult aspect) of Mars (heat and accidents) which pointed to the spluttering of the metal and his burnt fingers. And, as an indication of the importance of accurate timing, the talisman cast at 6.45 had a very different power to the one cast 15 minutes later. Ashmole's work for Charles II took place in the context of the unresolved struggle between king and Parliament for supremacy and constant fears that the horror of the Civil War might return. In 1672, Charles attempted to extend religious toleration via the Declaration of

Indulgence, which his enemies thought was intended to assist the succession of his heir, the Catholic Duke of York, the future James II. Parliament responded with the Test Act, requiring all holders of public office to take the sacrament of the Church of England – which a Catholic like the Duke of York could never do. In the midst of this crisis Lord Clifford, the Lord High Treasurer, asked Ashmole (at 8.15 p.m. precisely on 15 January 1673, Ashmole noted) whether Parliament was likely to cut Charles's revenue as revenge for the Declaration. At the end of October the king himself consulted Ashmole on the crisis. Ashmole in turn consulted Lilly for a second opinion. The two astrologers compared the horoscopes for the times at which Clifford and the King put their questions, with the king's birth chart and solar revolution (the exact minute at which the sun returned to its place at his birth) and suggested auspicious times for the king to act. On 23 October Lilly wrote to Ashmole about the king's proposed speech to Parliament four days later:

> The Caball of Presbitery begins I see early; its now in Yorks power to ingratiate himself forever, but what God hath decreed must stand – The Tayle of the Comet in 1664 begins, so Saturn in Aries. And the last comet of 167 – *Cunctando restituet Rem* – so now, Carolus, *Cunctando* may effect *idem*. – Moon next promiseth well – provided Moon ad conjunction of Jupiter at 2H P.M. that aspect bee not elapsed before his Majesty make his speech.[26]

Lilly had his dates wrong. The auspicious conjunction between the moon and benevolent Jupiter was at 2 p.m. on 28 October. Charles gave his speech at 1.50 a.m. on the 27th, as planned, with the moon approaching a decidedly more risky conjunction with Mars. Charles asserted himself and promptly prorogued Parliament, avoiding any more trouble.

At the opposite end of the political spectrum to Ashmole was Nicholas Culpeper, the herbalist, physician and republican. He specialized, among other practices, in decumbiture charts, horoscopes cast for the decumbiture or 'lying down' of the patient. The horoscope would be calculated for the moment that the individual fell ill or, if that was not known, the moment that the physician received news of the illness, hopefully accompanied with some material evidence such as a urine sample. The techniques of diagnosis and treatment were fundamentally those worked out by the Greek astrologers of between 1500 and 2000 years earlier; Mars was a hot planet, indicated fevers and could be calmed by watery lunar treatments, including herbs and talismans, while bleeding was never to be undertaken at the full moon.[27] The humours were balanced and the patient, hopefully, recovered. Culpeper was ostracized by the medical establishment for the crime of translating Latin medical texts into English, breaking what he believed was a conspiracy to deny the ordinary people the right to heal themselves. Culpeper lost no chance to proclaim the end of monarchy and the dawn of freedom. Writing on the conjunction between Mars and Saturn which followed the eclipse of 1652 he declared 'kings and magistrates cannot agree with one another, but only in one thing, and that is in oppressing the people', adding a nationalist spin for good measure: 'let the Hollander beware how he meddles with us'.[28] Culpeper's mood was shared by other astrologers. John Booker, who had so irritated Lilly, also shared his opinions on the 1652 eclipse and interpreted the moon moving in front of the sun as a warning that 'the common men of equality will usurp the great and mighty'.[29] He added that all tyrants were threatened, not just kings.

Culpeper was a republican and populist, for whom astrology was a means of creating a better world by offering medical aid to the poor and overthrowing tyrants. The overtly Neoplatonic trend in English astrology, meanwhile, was represented by Robert Fludd (1574–1637).[30] Fludd's major work, the *Utriusque Cosmi, Maioris scilicet et Minoris, metaphysica, physica, atque technica Historia* (*The metaphysical, physical, and technical history of the two worlds, namely the greater and the lesser*) contained a series of elaborate woodcuts of geometrical and angelic imagery, portraying an imaginal comsos which is at once alive and mathematical. Fludd's vision of the relationshp between earth and heavens has a distinctly dramatic quality which has prompted speculation that Shakespare's Globe Theatre was inspired by it; the Globe then itself becomes a model of the cosmos, an appropriate setting for the universal themes which underpin Shakespeare's plays.[31] Fludd's philosophy overlapped with that of Lilly and the traditionalists, but their astrology was very different. For Fludd there was no point in pandering to human ignorance by dealing with such trivia as lost property or marital disputes. The professional astrologers engaged with the cosmos on behalf of their clients but their astrology was essentially earth-bound. Fludd was concerned with the soul's passage to the stars, the inner relationship between soul and heaven. Work this out, he reasoned, not unlike Ficino, and one's personal problems either disappear or are put into a proper perspective. Neither did Fludd have any time for the reformers who were busy taking the mystery out of astrology. The publication of the *Utriusque Cosmi* in Germany between 1617 and 1621 attracted Kepler's attention who, rightly, regarded it as an affront to his own philosophy. Kepler the Platonist and Fludd the Neoplatonist engaged in a celebrated public argument, competing for the right to represent classical philosophy in the modern world. Thorndike summarized their respective positions in a way which does simplify their positions but still draws a telling contrast between an old cosmology and an emerging one:

> 'Fludd drew from old authorities; Kepler, from the nature of things by observation and experience. Fludd's affinities were with alchemists, Hermetics and Paracelsians; Kepler's, with astronomers, and mathematicians. Fludd interpreted harmony in terms of light and darkness; Kepler, in terms of motion. Fludd was mystical and obscure; Kepler, geometrical and natural. Fludd dealt in enigmas, symbols and analogies; Kepler, in demonstrated measurements. For Fludd the primary reality was visual, for Kepler it was numerical'.[32]

Fludd's Neoplatonic cosmology lost favour with the astronomers and with the scholars who increasingly defined what was and was not acceptable thought. In Fludd we see a link between medieval cosmology and the esoteric tradition which flourished underground, influenced Freemasonic cosmology, and carried Hermeticism into New Age thought via nineteenth-century theosophy. H.P. Blavatksy, the founder of the Theosophical Society, considered that Fludd, whom she greatly admired, was the chief of the 'philosophers of fire'.[33]

Fludd's continental equivalent was the German Jesuit Kabbalist Athanasius Kircher (1602–80).[34] Kircher was a noted mathematician and physicist – he was appointed as Imperial Mathematician in 1630 in succession to Kepler. His historical significance lies in his rare position on the boundary of alchemy and chemistry. As a Kabbalist, Kircher believed that one could know God directly, but as a natural philosopher he believed that God's creation should be investigated as seriously as possible. This, one could say, was one's obligation to the Creator. Kircher was one of the first people to observe microbes through a microscope and developed theories of magnetism to explain the operation of the universe; magnetic attraction was absolute proof, if any were needed, of occult, or hidden, relationships between separate material objects. Kircher's mix of Kabbalah and science was a mixture of old and new which strained credibility and was eclipsed by Descartes, Leibnitz and Newton, all of whom rejected the living Neoplatonic cosmos. Like Fludd, though, Kircher's influence has fed through the nineteenth-century theosophist Helena Blavatsky, who had a high regard for his magnetic theories (the chief magnet, she wrote, was the central spiritual sun of the Hermeticists[35]), into New Age culture. It was under Fludd, Kircher and their colleagues that a series of what are still core texts of the modern esoteric magical tradition were composed.[36] Of these the most important is the *Chymical Wedding of Christian Rosencreutz*, almost certainly written in 1616 by Johann Valentin Andreae (1586–1654), a member of a distinguished Lutheran dynasty in Swabia. The *Chymical Wedding* relates the initiatory journey of the hero, Christian Rosencreutz, told through alchemical metaphors intended to describe the mystical marriage of God with the Creation and Christ with his Church. The novel's significance for the development of astrology lies not in any attention to the interpretation of horoscopes but the inspirational framework it provided for the lasting notion of a meaningful cosmos pervaded by the divine as soul, symbol, metaphor and mathematics.

Another Kabbalist to catch Blavatsky's eye was the German Lutheran Jacob Boehme (1575–1624). She referred to him as 'the inspired but ignorant shoe-maker', drawing attention to his unschooled mysticism in, what was for her, a most complimentary manner.[37] Inspired by a vision of the universe in 1600, Boehme discovered in Kabbalah a means of participation in the cosmic mysteries which conventional Lutheran faith denied him. His God was at once the personal judge of Christianity and the Platonic, Kabbalistic divine intelligence, and his concern was to compensate for the disasters of the Fall and Lucifer's rebellion by struggling to return to the divine source. But the return can be accomplished inwardly rather than by a literal journey of the soul through the planetary spheres. Just as love and light emanate from the heavens, he wrote, so one can achieve divine unity by contacting these things within one's self. The seven planets each represent, in their different ways, a different part of the soul's hunger to return to God.[38] Boehme's writings read very much like early Gnostic texts, a testament to Kabbalah's roots in the mysticism of the classical world. The seven planetary spheres are described as rays, planes or states of existence or eternal nature and spirits of God, comparable to all other seven-fold systems including colours, tunes and chemical substances.[39] Boehme was persecuted as a heretic but he acquired a band of followers and his use of the term theosophy – divine wisdom – opened the way to Blavatsky.

The medieval cosmological world, which had always included competing ideological narratives, some deeply hostile or contemptuous of each other, had nevertheless been characterized by continuity. There was a continuum between devoted Gnostics or advocates of necromancy at one end of the spectrum, and pious, conservative, theologians at the other. Most thinkers adopted a position in the middle, prepared to countenance the practice of judicial astrology to some extent. But, in the seventeenth century, gradual shades of opinion were becoming intellectual fault lines. By the early eighteenth century conventional astronomy had severed its ties with Christian Kabbalah but the Kabbalists never disappeared. Instead, they flourished as a subculture which has survived to the present day.

The English astrological reformers were represented by a group of astrologers whose inspiration was John Dee's slightly younger contemporary Francis Bacon (1561–1626), one of the most distinguished politicians of his day (he was Lord Chancellor from 1618 to 1621), but may as well have been Kepler. All were inspired by Bacon's call for a sane astrology – an *astrologia sana* – which was purged of its superstition.[40] Bacon's ideas were formally proposed in his epic survey of knowledge, the *Novum Organum*, which was published in 1620. Bacon accepted the physical influences of the planets though he had little interest in the rest of astrology, which he regarded as an act of the imagination, if a useful one.[41] His plan, like Nicole Oresme's, three centuries earlier, was to remove the psychic, the soul, from the field of natural inquiry. In the process he was also to dispose of magic, which required the existence of psychic relationships between the scholar – or magician – and the natural world, and set the world on a path to modern materialistic science. By the late seventeenth century, magical practices, at least as far as some of the educated elite were concerned, had been driven underground. Both Dee and Bacon were Ficinian Utopians who set out to restore the prelapserian state of grace and control over nature that Adam had enjoyed before the Fall – the expulsion from Eden.[42] Both men were reformers: Dee wished to reform society; Bacon, knowledge. Dee wished to do so by embracing astrology, magic and the spiritual arts, while Bacon rejected them. Yet the break between magic and science was not a clean one and magical and scriptural notions of the Book of Nature, engraved by God with his holy message, which could be read by the perceptive, effortlessly began to slip into scientific notions of nature as the home of scientific truth. The attempt to control nature through mental power and alchemy was to become the desire to control it through intellectual inquiry and chemistry.[43]

Another reforming English astrologer, Joshua Childrey (1625–70), took as his goal the creation of a Copernican astrology by revising his calculations to put the sun at the centre of the system, to create an astrology based on the way things are rather than the way they seem. He appealed for support from Henry Oldenburg, the secretary of the newly formed Royal Society, the home of the emerging spirit of scientific inquiry. But he received no more support from that quarter than from astrologers who could not see why the sun should be the centre of the astrological system, even if it was the centre of the astronomical system, when nobody lived on it. John Gadbury (1628–1704), a former radical, Leveller and member of the 'Family of Love' which flourished in the heady atmosphere of the 1650s, took a long path to being a Royalist and finally notorious Jacobite and crypto-Catholic. His parallel voyage through astrology took him from enthusiastic writer of books and almanacs to disillusionment as he realized that the astrological phenomenon disappeared when subject to the consistent observation that Bacon advocated. Another reformer was John Goad, headmaster of the Merchant Taylors School in London and a lifelong Catholic at a time when practising the Roman faith was as dangerous as practising magic. Goad's self-appointed task, summarized in his 1686 work *Astro-Meteorologica*, was the creation of a scientifically based astrological system of weather prediction. He kept voluminous records, noting the time of the major planetary aspects and the associated conditions – rain, lightning, wind and so on. But the endless variations in meteorological data, combined with the lack of any statistical method, meant that his efforts came to nothing. Still, he did win support from John Flamsteed (1646–1719), the first Astronomer Royal. In 1678 Flamsteed wrote:

> To conclude my letter I cause my man to transcribe you the remainder of an Ephemeris of the weather for this moneth composed by Dr. Goad whose conjectures I find come much nearer truth than any I have hitherto met with, they are derived from the aspects and positions of the planets . . . You know I put no Confidence in Astrology, yet dare I not wholly deny the influences of the stars since they are too sensibly impressed on.[44]

Flamsteed himself had a somewhat ambivalent attitude to astrology. He was initially a keen student and taught himself from Gadbury's *Doctrine of Nativities*, aided by the *Collectio Genitarum*, Gadbury's collection of birth charts compiled as a study-aid for those testing out the rules of judicial astrology.[45] In 1665 he studied the subject in depth but by 1666 had already concluded that horoscopes could yield only 'strong conjectural hints, not perfect declarations'.[46] Even though a substantial number of astrologers would agree with this statement, and it was certainly central to Platonic, Aristotelian, Aquinian and Ficinian philosophy – in other words, the philosophical-astrological mainstream – to announce oneself in favour of conjecture was to become an ally of Kepler and Bacon. In 1669 Flamsteed made his first approach to the Royal Society by sending in papers on impending celestial phenomena to the astrologer John Stansby. In 1678, three years after he became Astronomer Royal, Flamsteed praised Goad and through the 1690s he provided astronomical data to two astrologers, John Wing and

George Parker. He clearly maintained a belief that astrology, at least in terms of natural influences, was theoretically valuable, but he appears to have lost interest in judicial astrology. He did collect his own notes of birth times, including that of Edmund Halley, the discoverer of the comet, and the Danzig astronomer Johann Helvelius, famous for his engravings of the constellations, suggesting that he cast their horoscopes. One horoscope he did calculate was for the founding of the Greenwich Royal Observatory at Greenwich at 14 seconds and 3 minutes past 10 on 10 August 1675. The chart contains the marking in pencil by Flamsteed, 'Risum tenatis, amici', or 'can you keep from laughing my friend'. This enigmatic comment has been taken as suggesting that the Astronomer Royal found judicial astrology risible. The problem with this assumption is that the horoscope is actually a good one, certainly if a contemporary text such as William Ramesey's *Astrological Restaurata* is concerned. Published in 1653, Ramesey's work included a complete section on the rules for electing propitious astrological moments and Flamsteed appears to have followed the rules very closely. The strongest planets were Jupiter, ruler of the ascendant, Sagittarius, and Mercury, which was associated as Hermes and so with all magical wisdom. The sun and Venus were also strong, while the dangerous planets Mars and Saturn were very weak. The moon, though strong, was 'translating the light', moving from a harmonious aspect to Jupiter to one to the sun. This was a most auspicious indication, carrying Jupiter's benevolent power to the Lord of the Universe. On the other hand, in 1674, the year before the Observatory was founded, Flamsteed had composed an angry, and unpublished polemic against astrology called *Hecker*, in which he denounced the 'superstitious', 'vulgar', 'pretended' and 'false' art.[47] It is clear, though, that what Flamsteed couldn't stand was not astrology, which he considered was theoretically possible and valuable in the right hands, but the sheer ignorance and incompetence of its practitioners. Gadbury came in for particular opprobrium for pretending to be a reformer while being quite as awful as the traditional astrologers, such as Lilly. The Observatory foundation horoscope might have been written off as an aberration had Flamsteed not elected another auspicious moment 20 years later, this time for the founding of the Royal Naval Hospital at Greenwich, a grand institution designed by Sir Christopher Wren and Nicholas Hawksmoor and Sir John Vanbrugh, all of whom donated their services to the cause of helping England's seamen. The foundation stone was laid at 5 p.m. exactly on 30 June 1694. The diarist John Evelyn, who laid the stone, recorded the moment. Wren was present, as was Flamsteed himself; 'Precisely at five o'clock in the evening, after we had dined together; Mr. Flamsteed observing the punctual time by instruments'.[48] The problem this time is that, unlike in 1675, the horoscope is not especially fortunate. True, in a similar pattern to the one we find in the Observatory horoscope, Jupiter was in a harmonious aspect to the ascendant in Sagittarius, Jupiter's sign, and the moon was moving towards a harmonious aspect to the sun, both important features. But the rest of the chart hardly justifies the effort Flamsteed put in with his instruments unless he was following some unknown system or his own innovation.

Although Flamsteed quickly moved away from his youthful enthusiasm for all things astrological, he clearly believed that it was astrologers who were at fault and that some sort of natural astrology was possible. If the Greenwich Observatory chart was genuine on his part, he may also have believed that judicial astrology might be effective if practised by competent astronomers. But he never pursued any work himself which might have led to a reformed astrology. Neither did Robert Boyle (1627–91), the chemist whose experiments with air pressure led to the discovery of the vacuum, a startling discovery in a world previously fully occupied by matter. Boyle accepted the principle of occult and planetary influences and the election of auspicious moments for divining, but his work took him in other directions, more directly concerned with the investigation of natural phenomena.[49] Instead, with Gadbury's death in 1704, the line of English reformers came to an end. There was then a 200-year hiatus until the twentieth century.

The astrological reformers in other countries, too, went their own way, gradually separating from astronomers, just as they did from traditional judicial astrologers. In France, where Bodin had put forward such strong arguments for reform, the music theorist Marin Mersenne (1588–1648) and the royal astrologer Morin de Villefranche were both in the reform camp, but neither the traditional astrologers nor the astronomers paid any attention. In Germany, Placidus de Titis, the Benedictine monk and astrologer to Leopold-Wilhelm von Hapsburg, Grand Master of the Teutonic Knights, continued the modernizing programme. Placidus's textbook, the *Primum Mobile*, published in 1657, was the most significant attempt to elaborate a Keplerian astrology, discarding zodiac signs for the most part, and abandoning the labrynthine house of cards that medieval judicial astrology had become. Placidus realized that celestial influences must be communciated to earth somehow and, as Aristotle's fifth element, the ether, was being abandoned, he suggested light.[50] Actually, Aristotle himself had suggested that the movement of the stars and planets transmitted light to the earth, the quality of the light changing as the celestial bodies moved.

Although the progressive collapse of the old cosmology undoubtedly shook faith in judicial astrology, at least in some quarters, the reformers welcomed the opportunity that the astronomical revolution gave them to develop a reconstructed scientific means of reading horoscopes. The speed with which the new theories of the French philosopher René Descartes (1596–1650) were adapted is instructive. Descartes denied the existence of Platonic archetypes and Aristotelian final causes, removing from the astrological cosmos the sense both of an underlying order and of a future purpose. He asserted the absolute freedom of action within God's creation and set out to explain the nature of occult influence, as evident in magnetism, arriving at a physical theory which rejected the four elements. We know of two astrologers who set out to explain astrology acording to Cartesian principles.[51] One was John Placentinus, astrologer to the Elector of Brandenburg in the 1640s, who argued that the way human beings move was explained by Descartes' theory of celestial matter. He cited a certain

Jean de Raey who had sought a mechanism to explain the birth chart, arguing that when a baby takes its first breath, it fills its lungs with minute particles of celestial matter. Placentinus was followed by Claude Gadroys, whose *Discourse on the Influence of the Stars according to the Principles of Descartes* used Descartes' theory of celestial matter, out of which the whole celestial region was made, as a universal explanation for astrology, even touching on talismans and astrological images. This was natural enough. After all, if there were such things as celestial influences, they must affect everything on earth, even if the model is an entirely new one. Descartes himself, though, was somewhat unkind about astrology!

> And, in fine, of false sciences I thought I knew the worth sufficiently to escape being deceived by the professions of an alchemist, the predictions of an astrologer, the impostures of a magician, or by the artifices and boasting of any of those who profess to know things of which they are ignorant.[52]

The astrological reformers completely failed to capture the popular imagination. Their work had none of the elaborate appeal of Kabbalistic astronomy, with its legions of Neoplatonic intelligences and the promise of access to God. It lacked the commercial advantages of traditional astrology because, with its limited range of techniques and devotion to probabilities rather than prediction, it had no means of answering questions about personal wealth or marital infidelty or whether one's neighbour was a witch. Neither did it have much practical use: for example, there were no rules for making talismans. That's in spite of the reformer Israel Hiebner's attempt to promote more effective talismans cast on the basis of more accurate astronomical measurement. Hiebner was a professor of astronomy and mathematics at Erfurt, and the translation of his tract *Mysteries Sigillorum* (1651) into English in 1698 caused considerable excitement.[53] Yet, it was too late, and astrology's appeal to the emerging scientific mentality failed because the inexorable mood of the times, at least as far as the educated elite was concerned, was away from judicial astrology altogether.

The almanac writers, and their readers, remained for the most part completely unconcerned by the debates of the astronomers and philosophers. With sales that averaged a third of a million copies a year in England alone, almanacs were the popular press of their day. Yet, while their appeal grew stronger as social status declined, the almanacs less a vehicle for the dissemination of popular ideas, than of elite intellectual theories among the middle and lower orders.[54] Folklore beliefs were often mentioned only to be condemned and the natural causes of eclipses and other astronomical phenomena were explained. Not, of course that rustic superstitions were always that far removed from scholarly opinion. When Robert Hooke informed the Royal Society that he knew of a man whose brain grew 'turgid at a full moon, and flacid at a new', the society promptly commisioned a detailed investigation.[55] The almanacs' political tone was often apocalyptic, an inevitability if they were to catch public attention. Then, as now, lurid headlines sell copy. But the mood of the times was genuinely millennial, for there was no reason to doubt Christ's promise that he would return. The only question was when, and that, it was thought, might be revealed in the stars. In 1637 John Booker issued a reasonably relaxed prophecy, anticpating that the stars would 'alterations cause i' the microcosm, as likewise wonders in the macrocosm'; Henry Hill's millenarian forecast for 1684 was more doom-laden and combined popular Platonism with the Book of Revelation in a vivid dealcation of the horrors to come: 'there were to be storms in the Archetype, between Jesus Christ and Belial: in the Intelligible world, between good and bad angels; storms in the Elementary world: unheard of winds and floods; in the Microcosm, the heart and brains being at odds; and in the habitable world, between good and bad men'.[56] Lilly, the master of technical astrology, likewise discussed Aristotle and Ovid in his set of predictions up to the year 1666, *The World's Catastrophe*, and drew on Geoffrey of Monmouth's version of *A prophecie of Ambrose Merlin ... aenigmatically delivering the Fate, and Period of the English Monarchy.* He also translated a work by Trithemius on *The heavenly Intelligences, governing the Orbes under God*, detailing the angelic rulers of both planetary spheres and periods of history. In this we read, for example, that 'The first Angell or Spirit of Saturn is called Orisiel, to whom God comitted the government of the World from the beginning of its Creation; who began his government the 15 day of the month of March, in the first year of the World, and it endured 354 years and 4 months'.[57] Quite aside from their content, there was another distinctive feature of the English almanacs: their writers were personalities, unlike France where most almanacs were, with the notable exception of Nostradamus's, anonymous. Bernard Capp has put forward the plausible case that in France the ambitious political astrologer aspired to work for the king, from whom all patronage derived (Morin owed his chair at the Univerity of Paris to the Queen, Marie de Medici) whereas in England he was a pamphleteer, eager to engage in the cut and thrust of public debate.[58]

The success of the almanacs takes us to the heart of the problem of the decline of astrology in the last half of the seventeenth century. In 1700, almanacs were still selling in huge numbers, as they continued to do through the following two centuries, but the horoscope business had virtually disappeared and no leading European intellectual was to express more than a passing interest in astrology until Carl Gustav Jung in the twentieth century; most were overtly hostile or contemptuous. In 1680 the French philosopher Pierre Bayle rejoiced that the French court was no longer home to astrologers; it was 'cured of that disease', he observed.[59] There is no adequate explanation for what, following the philosopher of science Thomas Kuhn, is one of the major paradigm shifts in European history.[60] There was no necessary reason why the Copernican revolution should have destroyed astrology. After all, the heliocenric cosmos was promoted by astrologers, and astrology thrives today, 300 years after the old cosmology finally disappeared. Neither was astrology ever disproved. Simply, there was no mechanism for doing so. Patrick Curry has made a convincing case that astrology in England suffered from its association with radicals in the Civil War and republic.[61] In the increasingly conformist air after the restoration of the monarchy in 1660, all forms of what was designated as 'enthusiasm' were regarded as dangerous, a category which included republicans and puritanical preachers along with astrologers. It might be thought that astrology's ability to get its predictions wrong was a problem. Yet economists get their predictions wrong and their position in the twentieth century was as exalted as that of astrologers in the sixteenth.[62] Neither did medical advances threaten astrological healing, for the latter declined before there were any significant advances in the former. The same applies to insurance which, it has been argued, then provided the security which was once astrology's job. But insurance can only make up for a few of the problems astrologers answered, questions such as 'Will my ship arrive safely?' One of the most familiar problems astrologers dealt with was the problem of missing ships. The owners of lost ships – and relatives of the passengers and crew – sought information, and those about to embark on a long voyage came for reassurance.[63] But then security is not the only function astrology provided. It also offered a range of information from the paternity of one's children to the condition of one's soul. Besides, religion provides security and it didn't appear to have suffered from the rise of the insurance business. A rise in social aspirations has also been cited. The argument assumes that, as the spirit of Humanism pervaded all aspects of European culture, at least in the Protestant north, a new spirit of self-help led to a rejection of stellar determinism. The flaw in this theory is obvious: in practice, astrology was rarely deterministic. For individuals it functioned more as a means of self-empowerment. Armed with predictions, talismans and advice, the seventeenth-century citizen, one could argue, was more fitted to take control of their lives than those who never used astrology, especially those among the faithful who could never take a decision without some recourse to God. Magic itself was not an issue, for many judicial astrologers used it. The assumption that the power of heaven could be diverted was not seriously questioned, only its legitimacy on theological grounds. All this, as the astrological reformers would say, is conjecture. Religious opposition to astrology was maintained and the old arguments that astrologers worshipped the creation rather than the creator, and denied God's power, were recycled by Puritan divines in northern Europe and Catholic priests in the south.

The extent to which religious censure inhibited astrology in Catholic countries is open to question. There are some signs that the volume of astrological publishing in Italy fell after the papal Bulls but, whether this inhibited the practice of judicial astrology, or interest in it, is an as yet unanswered question. One French royal astrologer, Smelles, was sentenced to the galleys in France in 1631, but that was for the reckless act of predicting the death of the king, Louis XIII.[64] Astrology was taught at Bologna well into the seventeenth century and there was a chair of astrology at Salamanca University in Spain that was occupied intermittently until 1770.[65] This is astonishingly late and rather suggests that Catholicism might have provided a defence of astrology against Enlightenment scepticism as much as threaten it with inquisitorial fervour. There is evidence that the Inquisition was unwilling to clog up its courts with investigations of occult practice purely because there would have been so many of them. It took a persistent and high-profile offender to run into trouble, and even then, he had highly placed ecclesiastical friends and the punishment was minimal.

The truth is that popular, or 'vulgar', attitudes to astrology remained the same, while educated opinion shifted perhaps as a result of the combination of astrology's repeated high-profile predictive blunders and the monotonous regularity with which each eclipse or inauspicious conjunction was used to forecast a comprehensive range of disasters, together with the shift in cosmological model. The effect was to make astrology seem both unreliable and implausible. There is some evidence of this shift in fictional treatments of astrology. John Webster's masterpiece, *The Duchess of Malfi*, first performed about 1614 and published in 1623, uses astrology as a metaphorical device to advance the plot, letting the audience know the unfortunate details of one of the key protagonist's horoscopes, exactly as Shakespeare had done for Edmund in *Macbeth* and his 'star-crossed' lovers, *Romeo and Juliet*.[66] But, by 1668, John Dryden was using astrology for comic effect. In his play *An Evening's Love: or the Mock Astrologer*, Wildblood confesses to Jacinta words which contain a lewd subtext, 'I am afraid/ your Spanish Planet, and my English one have been acquainted,/ and have found out some by-room or other in the twelve houses: I /wish they had been honourable'.[67] With even stronger sexual innuendo William Congreve had the following suggestive exchange in his 1695 comedy, *Love for Love*:

> Foresight: . . . there's but one Virgin among the twelve signs, spitfire but one Virgin.
> Angelica: Nor had there not been that one, if she had had to do with anything but astrologers, uncle. That makes my aunt go abroad.[68]

Ben Johnson (1573–1637) preferred pagan inspiration in his 'Hymn to Diana', goddess of the moon:

> Queen and huntress, chaste and fair
> Now the Sun is laid to sleep;
> Seated in thy silver chair
> State in wonted manner keep:
> Hesperus entreats thy light
> Goddess excellently bright.[69]

Just when most educated people had given up on judicial astrology, abandoning the ancient notion that the cosmos revealed a complex code which could reveal the lives of every single person in extraordinary detail, and could be manipulated to their advantage, Jonathan Swift, the greatest satirist in the English language, decided to launch a contemptuous assault on it. Swift's target was the almanac writer John Partridge. This was not the first satire to mock the almanac's style, which was at once deliberately vague and supremely portentous. Swift was not entirely original. He had several earlier models in attacks on Partridge by the pamphleteer Tom Brown. Swift's work was also reminiscent of Rabelais's spoof almanac, *Pantagruel's Prognostication*.[70] With Rabelais for inspiration and Partridge already set up as a target, Swift was on top form. He posed as a fictitious astrologer, Isaac Bickerstaff, Esquire. Swift was obviously aware of the reformers for he had Bickerstaff begin with a bitter denunciation of the condition of astrology in England: 'I have considered the gross abuse of astrology in this kingdom, and upon debating the matter with myself, I could not possibly lay the fault upon the art, but upon those gross imposters who pretend to be artists.'[71] The target is a wide one, including all those astrologers from Plotinus to Kepler, who claimed to support astrology while despising its practitioners. Bickerstaff then announced, in true pompous style that, in due course, he intended to publish a full defence of the art. He adhered to the standard philosophical line – that the stars only incline and do not compel – and quoted his past successes, such as the failed naval assault on Toulon in 1707. In a mockery of the astrologers who believed that, with just a little more research, they could make their predictions more accurate, he considered his failure to forecast the exact date of the wreck of the English fleet on 22 October 1707: 'I was mistaken as to the day,' he conceded, 'placing that article about thirty-six hours sooner than it happened; but upon reviewing my schemes, I quickly found the cause of that error.'[72] And then, having reviewed his past record, Bickerstaff embarked on his predictions for 1708. For April,

'on the 9th a mareschal of France will break his leg by a fall from his horse. I have not been able to discover whether he will then die or not ... On the 15th, news will arrive of a very surprising event, that which, nothing can be more unexpected. On the 19th, three noble ladies of this kingdom will, against all expectations, prove with child, to the great joy of their husbands.'[73]

With the move to June, political affairs assumed a greater importance:

'On the 10th, a great battle will be fought, which will begin at four of the clock in the afternoon, and last till nine at night, with great obstinacy, but no decisive event. I shall not name the place for the reasons aforesaid; but the commanders on each left wing be killed. I see bonfires and hear the noise of guns for a victory.'[74]

The mock uncertainty, typical of the reformers' love of conjecture rather than prediction, as well as the fudge of the almanac makers, matched with the belief in accuracy, which was the aim of astrologers such as Placidus, managed to satirize the two reforming schools at the same time: those like Kepler who believed that astrology should be constructed on the basis of empirical observation and those such as Morin who believed that adding further techniques would lead to the accuracy they craved. Swift's target, though, was Partridge himself, whose imminent demise he predicted:

My first prediction is but a trifle, yet I will mention it, to show how ignorant those sottish pretenders to astrology are in their own concerns: it relates to Partridge the almanack-maker. I have consulted the star of his nativity by my own rules, and find he will infallibly die upon the 29th of March next, about eleven at night, of a raging fever: therefore I advise him to consider of it, and settle his affairs in time.[75]

Partridge wisely ignored Swift's jibe. Ironically, Swift, whose sense of humour could be subtle, was widely misunderstood and Bickerstaff was translated and republished on the European mainland, where it was regarded as a serious prophetic tract and attracted at least one serious public refutation. Swift, though, continued the joke. He penned a response from a 'person of quality' who advised Partridge to take note of Bickerstaff's warning and concluded with the prophecy that Bickerstaff himself had died but had reappeared in spirit form for four hours, nine days ago, and might do so again: Swift was satirizing himself. It was then up to the third of Swift's alter egos to report that Partridge had, in fact, died, exactly as forecast. Swift even posed as Partridge, claiming that he was still alive, prompting a further retort from Bickerstaff that Partridge was, in fact, mistaken: he had, as predicted, died. To this he appended, under the name of T.N. Philomath, posing as a defender of Partridge, a spurious 1000-year-old prophecy of Merlin, the 'British Wizard'. Philomath analysed the prophecy, demonstrating its relevance to the year 1709, exactly in the style of other prophetic texts, such as Nostradamus's *Centuries*, or Lilly's *Prophecy of the White King*.

Swift's mockery of Partridge was well known all over Europe and caused much amusement among the intelligentsia, for whom astrology was now an object of ridicule. The old consensus of the educated critics of judicial astrology – that planetary influences or signs were possible but that the detailed claims of horoscope readers were implausible – was giving way to the idea that neither influences nor signs exist, with the exception of lunar gravity and the heat and light of the sun. But the impact on sales of Partridge's almanac was negligible. The almanac was republished in 1713 after a brief hiatus and was issued every year from then until the 1790s, though obviously compiled by anonymous writers. Popular culture was impervious to the concerns of the elite.

Swift's joke appealed to other satirists, though. His friend John Arbuthnot followed with a spurious tract on the *Annus Mirabilis or The wonderful Effects of the approaching Conjunction of the Planets, Jupiter, Mars and Saturn* (which fell in Sagittarius in 1723). After appealing to Plato on the coming transformation of the world, Arbuthnot predicted that some men had such broad hips that, with only a little physical change, they might become buxom wenches. In America, Benjamin Franklin, one of the towering figures of the American Enlightenment, published his own version of Bickerstaff under the byline Richard Saunders, a genuine and prominent seventeenth-century almanac writer. *Poor Richard*, as it was known, hit the right note and Franklin repeated the exercise annually after his first edition in 1733. Franklin's Partridge was Titan Leeds who, Poor Richard calculated, was to die at 11 a.m. on 26 October 1733, close to that month's eclipse. Franklin, alias Richard, was concerned about more than Leeds's death, though: 'There are so many invisible eclipses, this year,' he wrote, 'that I fear, not unjustly, our pockets will suffer full inanition, be full empty, and our felling at a loss. During the first visible eclipse Saturn is retrograde: for which reason the crabs will go sidelong, and the ropemakers backwards.'[76] He also had a dig, which smacks of the English gentleman, at the New Yorkers and what seems to have been the characteristic Bronx accent, as well as New Englanders: 'Mercury will have his share in these affairs and to confound the speech of the people . . . When a New Yorker thinks to say this, he shall say diss, and the people in New England and Cape May will not be able to say cow for their lives, but will be forced to say keow by a certain involuntary twist in the root of their tongues.'[77]

That astrology had become, for many, little more than a joke is illustrated by the *Memoires* of the self-declared legendary lover Casanova (1725–98). In what he clearly intended to be an amusing anecdote he declared how 'A curious fancy increased my delight, namely, the thought of becoming a famous astrologer in an age when reason and science had so justly demolished astrology. I enjoyed the thought of seeing myself sought out by crowned heads, which are always the more accessible to superstitious notions.'[78] Having half-heartedly attempted to deceive his victims, Casanova abandoned his ploy. His effort had simply failed to produce sufficient amusement.

The satirizing of astrologers had no impact whatsoever on the sales of almanacs but does seem to have had a serious and deleterious effect on the profession of horoscope casters, whose lack of any professional or institutional structures – apart from a society that met for annual dinners in London from the 1650s to 1680s – meant that there could be no collective defence.[79] It is, in any case, doubtful whether there could have been any sort of corporate identity in a profession in which so many practitioners regarded each other as frauds. The astrological world was as schismatic as the religious, only much smaller. And in its devotion to the earth-centred cosmos as an interpretative model, astrology was being recast as a study of the universe as it seems, rather than as it is.

12

The Eighteenth Century: Newton's Children

This most beautiful system of the Sun, planets, and comets could only proceed from the counsel and dominion of an intelligent and powerful Being.

ISAAC NEWTON[1]

In 1663, the young Isaac Newton, then an undergraduate at Cambridge University, found himself at a fair in the English village of Stourbridge. And, while at the fair, Newton browsed at a bookstall where he picked up and purchased a work on the calculation and interpretation of horoscopes. This serendipitous event was, according to John Conduitt, who married Newton's niece, Catherine Barton, to trigger one of the greatest turning points in the intellectual history of humanity. In Conduitt's account, we are told that, perhaps after a brief examination, Newton developed a profound contempt for 'the vanity and emptiness of the pretended science of Judicial astrology', but a fascination for mathematics which was to lead directly to his greatest work.[2] It would be surprising indeed if this was seriously Newton's first encounter with mathematics, but sometimes small events do change the way we think, and there is no reason to doubt that the 20-year-old Newton's determination to comprehend celestial mechanics was fired-up by what he saw as the absurd and clumsy reduction of the grandeur of the cosmos to the kind of trivia that was the substance of much of the astrology of his day.

Newton was born in 1642, the year of Galileo's death, just as English astrology was entering its brief 'golden age' in the Civil War and republic, and died in 1727, when the casting of horoscopes had pretty much died out.[3] He is recognized, with justification, as the towering genius of Western cosmology, only equalled, later, by Einstein. Newton, of course, stood on the shoulders of giants, in particular Copernicus, Galileo and Kepler, but, in the sense that he drew their work to a conclusion, his historical impact was greater. And that is why we tend to speak of the entire world-view of the West in his wake, as Newtonian. His reputation is not just a matter of retrospective historical judgement and his revolutionary impact was widely recognized by his contemporaries. As the poet Alexander Pope wrote, 'Nature and Nature's Laws lay hid in Night; God said "Let Newton be!" and All was Light.'[4]

Newton's extraordinary accomplishments included the creation of calculus, the invention of the reflecting telescope, the development of the corpuscular theory of light, terrestrial and celestial motion and, most famously, the development of the theory of gravity. It was Newton who explained the planets' elliptical orbits, discovered by Kepler, in his own three laws of motion. Together Kepler and Newton provided the formulae which have enabled us to measure planetary motions so precisely that planetary probes can be despatched with total confidence. It was left to Einstein to clear up certain minor anomalies in, for instance, the measurements of Mercury's orbit in 1915 in his General Theory of Relativity. So sweeping was Newton's work that we should speak of a Newtonian world-view which permeated economics, politics, social theory and religion. So convincing was his demonstration of universal laws in physics and astronomy that people began to look for them in every aspect of human endeavour and life on earth.

Astronomy in the early seventeenth century had been faced with a huge problem: how do the planets move?[5] Newton's alternative solution was the theory of universal gravity, published in his *Philosophia Naturalis Principia Mathematica*, normally known simply as the *Principia*, in July 1687. Mathematical law, not matter, Newton argued, kept the planets in position and, finally abandoning ether, Aristotle's fifth element, Newton invented empty space. Space, he claimed, adapting Robert Boyle's recent discovery, was a vacuum. In this context, the theory of gravity had a number of simple advantages. Couched in mathematical terms, it kept the planets from falling to earth while the absence of matter in space meant that there was nothing left to slow the planets down. The whole system was beautifully elegant. In fact, hanging onto Greek concepts of the perfect cosmos, this was exactly how Newton described it: 'this most beautiful system of the Sun, planets, and comets' he wrote, 'could only proceed from the counsel and dominion of an intelligent and powerful Being'.[6] Newton's disagreement with Descartes was largely theological, for he regarded Cartesian materialism as a short-cut to atheism. He was far closer to Jacob Boehme, whose notion of a universe filled with mysterious forces of attraction and repulsion was far more compatible with Newton's devotion to a divinely created cosmos.[7]

So great was Newton's contribution to eighteenth-century ideas of the working of the universe that his ideas, it was thought, could be applied to every single area of human life. As the poet James Thomson proclaimed in 1744:

> Let Newton, Pure Intelligence, whom God
> To mortals lent to trace His boundless works
> From laws sublimely simple, speak thy fame
> In all philosophy.[8]

If 1609 and 1610 were the revolutionary years when Galileo and Kepler took European intellectual life into the modern world, in 1687 modernity received its ideological underpinning in a universe which was to be entirely explicable by mechanical forces, with no need for deity, divinity, demons or angels. This, it must be said, was not exactly how Newton himself saw it. For him, the universe was filled with divine purpose. But, during the course of the eighteenth century, he became the icon of the anti-religious materialists who gradually came to dominate the ideology of modern science and Newtonianism, as the doctrine of the lifeless, purposeless, mechanical cosmos emerged. To paraphrase Jacquetta

Hawkes, every generation gets the Newton it deserves.[9] If we are discussing Newton's cultural impact then it makes more sense to talk about Newtonianism as a form of world-view distinct from Newton's own.[10] As we shall see, even Newtonianism comes in different forms which probably share no more than the belief that it is possible to know and understand the universe, with no doubt, and without God. Newtonianism's impact on culture through the eighteenth century was twofold. So sharply opposed were the two consequences that we should talk about the Newtonian paradox. On the one hand there was the reinforcement of classical notions of the deterministic cosmos, underpinned for the first time by observational astronomy and impressive mathematical proof. On the other hand, by locating absolute determinism in the stars and planets, it was removed from the human sphere leaving political philosophers to argue that this very stellar determinism was the basis of individual freedom in human society.

Newton's own attitude to astrology is fairly simple to sum up. We can trust Conduitt's claim that he had no interest whatsoever in judicial astrology. However, he did believe that comets were messages from God, that history unfolded in line with the movement of the constellations, and that he practised alchemy.[11] His impact on astrology, though, was huge. First of all, as far as many educated people were concerned, he finally disposed of the sense that the planets and zodiac signs might have personalities, a theory which had been one of the foundations of astrology for two millennia. But, second, his proof that the universe operates according to a single set of laws implied that people and planets were part of a single system. This, in turn led to the creation of new forms of astrology, some of which acknowledged that name, while others rejected it.

There is no question that, after half a millennium of (almost) unquestioned popularity, the practice of casting horoscopes went into such a rapid decline between 1650 and 1700 that, from being a familiar feature of social, financial and political life, as well as an aide to salvation and enlightenment, it almost died out. This seismic intellectual earthquake was a Europe-wide phenomenon, which makes its causes all the more difficult to pin down. There has been much discussion of the causes for astrology's sudden loss of intellectual respectability, none of them entirely satisfactory, perhaps because changes in ideology are even more resistant than other historical trends to a cause-and-effect analysis.[12] Some historians imagine that astrology died out altogether. Typical is the conclusion to Jim Tester's *History of Western Astrology*. 'We have brought the story of Western Astrology down to its second death, at the end of the seventeenth century,' Tester wrote, continuing, 'Only the servant-girl's laughter rings through the eighteenth.'[13] Astrology, in this view, was henceforth fit only for the poor, no doubt illiterate and gullible, young women. Tester, though, lacked the advantage of recent scholarship, and the evidence now points to a picture which is rather more complex.

One argument we can reject with ease is that astrology was scientifically proven to be false. There were no scientific tests and besides, the early members of the Royal Society who, in any case, would have called themselves philosophers rather than scientists, were frequently perfectly amenable to astrological ideas.[14]

Patrick Curry's persuasive argument that astrology in England declined after the restoration of the monarchy in 1660 because its unfortunate associations with religious and political radicalism. But that doesn't explain the Europe-wide decline of astrology.[15] In Italy, we know that the Papal Bull of 1631 contributed to the closing down of astrological publication, and there may have been local factors in other countries. For the larger picture, we should consider less definable changes in the *zeitgeist*. Perhaps disgodding, or disenchantment, in terms of the removal of the divine, or soul, from nature was a most significant factor. The expulsion of spirit from the cosmos probably did more than scepticism to erode astrology's power among the educated elite and their middle-class imitators, for the effect was to remove the personalities and numinous intelligences from the planets and zodiac signs. A universe devoid of soul, or reason, was somewhat antipathetic to an astrology that relied on psychic communication between astrologers and stars. While it is theoretically possible to be an astrologer and an atheist, the evidence of modern times indicates that it is difficult.[16] There seems to be something in the nature of judicial astrology which requires the interaction of the divine and the human, consciousness and matter, soul and body. But this was not all. Newton's theory of inertia dictated that, if a body was at rest, it would remain so until an external force acted upon it. The astrological world-view had been embedded in a cosmos in which all matter was in a constant state of motion as a result of its inherent nature, fire struggling to rise to heaven, earth to fall downwards, and so on, without having a discernible force exerted on it. By the end of the eighteenth century, the industrial revolution was well underway – in Britain, at least – and the new-found ability to physically manipulate matter by harnessing the forces of fire, water and pressure, seemed to provide evidence that Newtonian cosmology was correct.[17] However, the disenchantment thesis is also suspect, resting as it does on the myth of the late seventeenth and eighteenth centuries as characterized, uniquely, by the rise of reason and science and the end of superstition. The evidence for such a proposition is, at best, weak, and, increasingly, is impossible to sustain. The Protestant world banished much of the dramatic ritual of Catholicism, but the universe was still full of angels and demons, come to save and tempt us. And were illiterate peasants aware that Descartes and Newton had banished nature spirits? It's unlikely.

From the early eighteenth century onwards, religious and anti-religious critics supported each other in their anti-astrology views. By the early nineteenth century intellectual contempt for astrology was a given for most educated men. In his *Philosophy of Mind*, based on lectures given in 1817 and 1820, the Idealist philosopher Hegel (1770–1831), who was deeply influenced by Plato and who, in his turn, exerted a profound effect on Karl Marx, made his feelings plain:

> The Church itself has therefore rightly rejected as superstitious and unethical the belief in a power exerted over the human spirit by these terrestrial and cosmic relationships. Man should regard himself as free from such relationships of Nature; but in that superstition he regards himself as a creature of Nature.[18]

Hegel's position was an interesting one. He had no sympathy for traditional Christian views, but saw Christianity's rejection of astrology as perfectly correct. His statement makes more sense when we consider that it was essentially Platonic in that his objection to astrology was moral, on the grounds that it regarded humanity as subject to Nature, with a capital 'N', and therefore unable to transcend it and develop the true Reason, with a capital 'R', which is humanity's salvation.

In spite of later arguments, there is nothing intrinsic in Newtonian thought itself which is necessarily hostile to astrology in all its forms. For one thing, there were those among his followers who saw no contradiction between the new cosmology and the art of making predictions from horoscopes. William Stukeley (1687–1765), Newton's young friend and biographer, certainly took this view: 'There is something in it so agreeable to nature, to the chequerwork of life, that ... it strikes a considering mind with great pleasure: and tempts us at least to wish it were agreeable to truth and fact.'[19] Neither was there any inherent theoretical problem. Far from it. Although Newton rejected the Platonic theory of archetypes, which had provided such an easy rationale for astrology, in the opening page of the *Principia*, his demonstration of action-at-a-distance could in theory have led to an entirely new physical explanation for astrological effects.[20] This, at least, was the first response of the philosopher George Berkeley (1685–1753), who initially argued that celestial movements in a completely material universe exerted a direct influence on the mind.[21] Berkeley later swung to the other extreme and denied the existence of matter altogether, reverting to the Idealist, Platonic, notion that primary reality lies in human consciousness, not in the physical world. This, ironically, was precisely the view that had sustained astrology for so long. But the point is made, that, if any reforming, Keplerian, astrologer were to require a model for astrology to replace the old cosmology, Newton could provide it.

Then there's the accuracy issue: from the eighth century BCE onwards, astrologers had periodically returned to the pressing need to make their prediction of planetary positions more accurate in order to improve their prediction of events, and Newton's laws now suggested that, if the initial position and state of an object is known, then all future events can be predicted until the end of time. Immanuel Kant put it in suitably theological terms:

> This infinity in the future succession of time, by which eternity is unexhausted, will entirely animate the whole range of space to which God is present, and will gradually put it into that regular order which is conformable to the excellence of His plan.[22]

Yet Kant had nothing but contempt for astrology. Here was to be no room for it in his Newtonian utopia.

The history of European astrology after 1700 is best understood through the class model adopted by Patrick Curry.[23] Adapting the simple scheme of upper, middle and lower class, Curry devised a system of high, middling and low astrology. The philosophers and thinkers were 'high' and would have included Kepler, or Frances Bacon. Middling astrology was centred on the professional casting of horoscopes, a profession along the lines of medicine or law. Low astrology found its voice in the almanacs and folk beliefs. Individual astrologers could move between the three, naturally; Kepler cast horoscopes and Lilly, the horoscope maker, published best-selling almanacs. Low and high might be connected where rustic beliefs about the effect of the full moon might not be so different to those of members of the Royal Society.

High astrology suffered most from the consequences of the astronomical revolution. Humanism, which, under Pico, had asserted humanity's primacy within a living Neoplatonic cosmos, in which magic, in the sense of psychic manipulation of the universe, was still possible, had, by 1700, arrived at a point at which the world was essentially seen as material, and God was retreating to some distant region, beyond even the power of prayer. The telescope and microscope between them had allowed natural philosophers to explore both the old Hermetic macrocosm and microcosm respectively, and see that both seemed to work perfectly adequately without the aid of invisible intelligences. The theoretical assault on the Aristotelian cosmos was completed by the Scottish philosopher David Hume (1711–76), whose development of the notion of probability did much to erode any idea that one could have certain knowledge of anything, as well as mocking the traditional notion that matter emerged from the divine.[24] One of the key items of Aristotelian dogma to be abandoned was the 'Final Cause', the belief that the cause of an event could lie in the future, suggesting a purposeful element to human activities. Doubts about the existence of Aristotle's 'Formal Causes', according to which objects were thought to be the way they were because of their underlying 'archetype', had been expressed centuries earlier by William of Ockham (c.1288–c.1348), the thirteenth-century Franciscan friar and scholastic philosopher.[25] By the seventeenth century, all the Aristotelian causes had been disposed of except, perhaps, the 'Efficient Cause', which was an object's maker. Hume, though, undermined even this link in the causal chain, arguing that we can never argue that action A causes effect B. All we can do is look for the correlations which enable us to work out the probability of two events coinciding. Certainly, Aristotle's world did not die out entirely. His categories for living things survived in the system set out by Linnaeus (1707–78), the Swedish botanist and zoologist who laid the foundation for the modern classification of plants and animals, even though he defined his own criteria. But Hume made it very difficult to assert that a planet might cause an effect on earth, undermining even the kind of empirical research project pursued by Kepler: however good the data Kepler might have assembled, this could never have decisively proved a connection between planetary pattern and political event. The best that could be achieved is a correlation, a pattern of coincidences, which could never be used to prove a definite connection. When statistical theory was developed in the nineteenth century, the means were developed to construct statistical proofs, but never definite causal relationships. Hume himself made his position clear, claiming that astrology should be rejected by 'a strong presumption against all supernatural and miraculous relations' and that it flourishes 'amongst ignorant and barbarous nations'.[26] The Enlightenment philosophers needn't have worried. Astrology was intellectually exhausted. Bernard Capp has said that it was in search of its own Newton, but nobody came forward.[27]

What was taking place as the modern world emerged, blinking from the medieval, was a progressive dislocation between the culture of the educated elite, for whom astrology became unbelievable, and the mass of the people, for whom it remained largely credible. The consequences therefore differed, depending on the social context. If we take Curry's threefold division, 'high' astrology apparently disappeared, 'middling' astrology almost died out, but 'low' astrology', which took no notice of changes among the world's philosophers, continued happily on its way. The process was a gradual and uneven one: in 1710 one critic complained that the gentry were as besotted with astrology as the common people ever were, while in 1725 members of St John's College, Cambridge, founded a Zodiac Club, based on astrological rules. The question is only partly one of class and it is doubtful whether society ladies were any more averse to using astrologers in 1700 – or 1750 – than they are today. The use of astrology as an occasional plot-moving device by the novelist Laurence Sterne in his *Tristram Shandy*, published between 1759 and 1769, suggests some familiarity with the practice. At one point Shandy reports:

> Confusion! cried my father (getting up upon his legs a second time) – not one single thing has gone right this day! Had I faith in astrology, brother (which, by the by, my father had), I would have sworn some retrograde planet was hanging over this unfortunate house of mine, and turning every individual thing out if its place.[28]

Sterne tells us two things. First, faith in astrology had declined but, second, there was sufficient awareness of its language for him to include in the story. It is unlikely that the broad appeal of 'superstitious practices' altered substantially from the seventeenth to twentieth centuries except among middle-class males who seem to have imitated the beliefs of their perceived superiors, as represented in the metropolitan intellectual elite. This process, though, does not seem to have been pronounced until the nineteenth century.[29] It is clear that astrology ceased to be a universal explanatory model of use at all levels of society, from court to commoners and from high theology to political decision-making, business, marriage and medicine. While the evidence for its survival in the eighteenth century is largely anecdotal, it does add up to a picture in which it remained as an integral part of popular fortune-telling, while the casting of horoscopes might be available to those who knew where to look.

There is also the difficult and, as yet, unresolved question of the Church in all its various forms, which was at once dismissive of popular superstition yet deeply possessive of its own range of occult beliefs. While Curry's model is useful in terms of describing astrology's output – philosophical debates, horoscopes or almanacs – it doesn't deal with motive, such as the need to predict the second coming. We know that apocalyptic ideas continued unabated through the century, sustaining, on good scriptural grounds, the link between astrological signs and the expected upheavals. Millenarianism and Old Testament scripture allowed the language of astrology and the concept of celestial signs to survive even in the British colonies in North America – the future USA – where the political power of Puritan divines brought continual pressure to restrict occult and astrological practices, suggesting that these were, in fact, quite popular – even necessary as medical aids.[30] One strange indication of the way in which Puritan millenarian thought occurred is the *Magnalia Christi Americana* (1702), a triumphalist work published by the influential American preacher Cotton Mather (1663–1728). Mather, who set the tone for much of the discussion of the 13 colonies and, later, the USA, as the New Jerusalem, was determined to show that the colonies in general, and New England in particular, were the promised land. Along with most other Puritans he denounced judicial astrology as satanic, but (as well as stirring up the hysteria that was responsible for some of the most cruel episodes in the witch hunts) he included in one section of the *Magnalia* a form of spiritualized horoscope. In his biography of Jonathan Mitchel, a recently deceased Puritan divine, Mather became excited by the coincidence that Mitchel was born in the same town as Sacrobosco, the great medieval cosmologist. Converting the meaning of the houses of the horoscope into biblical form (just as others had Christianized the constellations), Mather wrote:

> The precise *day* of his birth is lost, nor is it worth while for us to enquire, by an *astrological calculation*. What aspect the *stars* had upon his birth, since the *event* has proved, that God the Father was in the *horoscope*, Christ in the *mid-heaven*, the Spirit in the *sixth house*, repentance, faith and love in the *eighth*: and in the *twelfth*, and eternal happiness, where no Saturn can dart any rays.[31]

This kind of Christianized astrology first occurred in the late Roman period and appears to have flourished among those radical seventeenth-century Christians, like Boehme, who found Hermeticism a perfect complement to their faith. This strand of thought reached one conclusion in the occultism of the early Mormons, which owed as much to Cornelius Agrippa as to scripture. Joseph Smith, the movement's founder, actually owned a Jupiter talisman, a magical guarantor of good fortune.[32] There is no question that an astrology of celestial signs survived among millenarian Christians, but its main evidence is found in the almanac's continuing apocalyptic preoccupations. In 1702, Partridge wrote that the millennium was due to dawn in the following year and reach perfection in 1778, and, in the 1750s, *Moore's* almanac announced that the great Lisbon earthquake signified the beginning of the fall of the Antichrist: the city had been inhabited by bigoted papists who had richly deserved their punishment.[33] Over the course of the century the almanacs lost some of their political rhetoric and religious fervour, with notable exceptions, although they tended to remain staunchly traditional in the religious sphere, denouncing the Enlightenment radicals' dalliance with a deism which could look dangerously atheistic.[34] Even so, in eighteenth-century England the almanacs maintained their seventeenth-century role of educating and informing the masses while presenting them with the dramatic forecasts, calendars and other information and features on general living (such as etiquette and good manners), which guaranteed sales. There was one attempt to produce an almanac which did more than recycle seventeenth-century material, Henry Season's *Speculum Anni*, which was published annually from 1733 to his death in 1775 and managed modest sales of around 3000 a year. Season, a largely self-taught assistant funeral undertaker, had studied Paracelsus, whose three alchemical elements (salt, mercury and sulphur) he compared to the Trinity, while giving himself a political platform to denounce papists, atheists, Jews, moral degeneracy and pubic drunkenness, those enemies of the Protestant faith and life.[35] Season had strong links with the radical Whigs and saw his vocation as much to defend liberty as to predict the future, a mission which placed him in the lineage of Culpeper and Booker. Season's circulation, though, was dwarfed by the *Vox Stellarum* – the voice of the stars; it clearly satisfied a public demand and its circulation spiralled from 107,000 in 1768 to a peak of 560,000 in 1839, making a profit of almost £3000 in 1802. This handsome sum, it was remarked, was more than many a German principality could expect.[36] Under its dynamic editor, *Vox Stellarum* offered the latest astronomical information, including accounts of the newly discovered planet Uranus. Like Season, Andrews, *Vox Stellarum*'s editor, was a radical Whig, rejoicing in the rebel victory in the War of American Independence which, he hoped, would pave the way for freedom elsewhere, and welcoming the outbreak of the French Revolution in 1789; the French monarchy, he wrote, was one of the beasts of the Book of Revelation. Even after the outbreak of war with France in 1793 required a sensibly patriotic tone, Andrews' sensibilities continued to lie with the revolutionaries. The magazine's success seems to have been due to its mixture of astrology and biblical prophecy with a blunt political message, standing up for the farmers and labourers who were being dispossessed by the enclosure of common land, and driven into penury or into the cities.

'Low astrology', the popular of Curry's three categories, can be further divided into two forms. One was the published version, the almanacs, in which ideas were fed to the masses, often in an overtly propagandistic manner, by men who considered themselves their superiors and believed they had a duty to educate and inform. Separate to the literary tradition was the world of popular fortune-telling and medicine, which flourished in a milieu in which cunning men and women might well possess some educated knowledge, which could be transmitted orally, but were essentially advice givers and carriers of popular knowledge.[37] However, here, as so often in the history of astrology, we run into historiographical problems and questions of interpretation. E.P. Thompson was one who considered the problem of popular superstition and argued that it was precisely its class base that gave it the coherence which he thought it otherwise lacked.[38] Thompson was a Marxist, for whom so-called superstitious practices were evidence of a 'false ideology'. Any belief in a non-material reality therefore presents the sociologist or political scientist with a problem to be explained. Thompson made several errors, assuming that superstition did not exist among the upper classes, and that it was lacking a rationale. His arguments, though, reflect those which pervade the historical literature. We need look no further for coherence than to the ancient model in which the world is endowed with meaning and inhabited by a host of invisible forces and beings. That such ideas were prevalent among the poor and illiterate in the eighteenth century, makes them no less coherent.

In that the almanacs were written by literate astrologers and required a literate public, they overlapped with the world of middling astrology And that two books of predictions were published in 1722 about that year's triple conjunction of Mars, Jupiter and Saturn points to an educated market, even if one which was substantially reduced from the boom years of just 60 years earlier.[39] Yet, while almanacs flourished, astrological publishing in general all but died out. Between 1700 and 1790 just six books teaching judicial astrology were published, of which two were reissues of seventeenth-century texts and one was an edition of the classic second-century work, the *Tetrabiblos*.

The practice of astrology, though, may have been sustained by particular local considerations, such as maritime areas. There seems to have been some association of astrology with those involved in the sea, a natural consequence, perhaps, of the obvious effect of the moon on the tides and the use of the stars for navigation. In the middle of the eighteenth century in North America it was, it seems, common for horoscopes to be cast to determine sailing dates.[40] In England, Ebenezer Sibly, a member of a seafaring Freemasons' Lodge in Bristol, reported that a group of naval officers consulted him in 1779 on the likely success of Admiral Rodney's expedition to the West Indies. England was at war with Spain and France, as well as with the American rebels, so they had good reason to be concerned.[41] There appears to have been some continuity in the British colonies in North America; in his almanac for 1746 the astrologer Jacob Taylor claimed that he learned his art, as well as other occult practices, which he didn't specify but which he had come to detest, from certain 'Sons of Art' in Pennsylvania in the 1690s and 1700s.[42] Regional variations may also have played a part. One network of horoscope-casting astrologers, based in the English counties of Lincolnshire and Leicestershire, included the noted antiquarian William Stukeley (1687–1765), who found his vocation when he gave up medicine in order to become an Anglican minister in 1729. He was a keen astronomer who as a young man was a friend of Isaac Newton, and his memoir of the great astronomer, published in 1752, is the major source for most subsequent accounts of Newton's life. In terms of eighteenth-century astrology, Stukeley's interest for historians lies in the fact that he existed in a world in which judicial astrologers were so rare.[43] But his impact on twentieth-century popular culture is immense. In 1740, five years after he discovered astrology through having his horoscope cast, Stukeley published his great survey of Stonehenge.[44] With this work, megalithic culture makes its grand reappearance in the modern age, even though the book's impact was to gradually unfold over the following two and a half centuries. It was Stukeley who first identified the orientation of Stonehenge with the summer solstice sunrise, so he has a claim to be the remote founder of the modern discipline of archaeoastronomy, as well as modern druidry.

Judicial astrology's intellectual vigour had definitely departed, but the practice did not disappear entirely. But what creative energy remained was diverted into attempts to apply Newtonian cosmology to a reformed discipline. While Stukeley himself does not appear to have applied Newton's cosmology either for or against the traditional practices of horoscope reading, we can perceive consistent attempts to develop a Newtonian astrology. Some of these used Newtonian ideas to support astrology, while others rejected both the label astrology and its entire technical and philosophical apparatus in order to establish mechanical connections between the planets and human affairs. Some of Newton's colleagues followed his minimalist view and gave astrological power only to comets. Prominent among these was the evangelical theologian William Whiston (1667–1752), Newton's deputy and successor, in 1703, as Lucasian Professor of Mathematics at Cambridge. Borrowing an idea from Edmund Halley, Whiston believed that a comet must have been responsible for the biblical deluge.[45] In a series of works published between then and 1717, Whiston argued that the discovery of Newtonian cometography itself marked the beginning of the final apocalyptic act: the comet's final collision with the earth, followed by its fiery destruction and restoration to its state before the Fall and the expulsion from Eden.[46] Whiston's work attracted attention among precisely the same people who had previously followed the almanacs and such was his impact on apocalyptic fervour that, on 13 October 1736, a huge crowd gathered on the hills to the north of London to watch the city's promised destruction and the inauguration of the End Times. It was the archbishop of Canterbury himself who reassured the public that Whiston's prophecy was false, a fact of some significance which completely demolishes the notion of courageous, rational Newtonians leading the world to a brave new, secular, world. In this case it was the Newtonian who stirred up popular superstition, and the senior churchman who was summoned to make the rational case. This is sufficient warning, if any were needed, against the temptation to simplify the complex currents of eighteenth-century thought into crude notions of the struggle between science and religion. Whiston's astrology was Copernican – on the day in question, if one had stood on the sun, the earth, the moon and the comet would all have been in conjunction (of course, for an observer on the sun, the earth and the moon are *always* in conjunction). But, in considering the error of traditional judicial astrology, he began to develop an explanation of how, given that it was, in his view, palpably false, it could have developed and flourished among otherwise rational people. Whiston considered that, when a major planetary conjunction coincided with some disaster, such as the deluge, it was quite understandable for ancient people to have linked the two, in view of the limited state of their knowledge. However, he still believed these early astrologers were guilty of a fundamental error, for, of course, there was no direct relationship between celestial cause and terrestrial effect. The mistake, though, was Whiston's, as the original Babylonian astrologers had assumed that the planets functioned either as divine signs or, as some evidence suggests, as indicators of the unfolding of a universal order, not as direct causes of terrestrial events.

Newton's ideas were also adopted by astrologers who had a less religious, more practical mission than Whiston, and who fit better into the tradition of astrological reformers running back through Kepler and Bodin. In France, in 1711, Henri de Boullainvilliers published a work tracing the relationship between human history, the sun's apogee (its furthest distance from the earth) and precession of the equinoxes, the slippage of the constellations in relation to the zodiac signs.[47] Boulainvilliers was most likely unaware of Newton's own work in this area, which was unpublished at the time, but he was inspired by what he knew of Newton's accurate determination of the rate of precession. More influential, though, was the adaptation of Newton's ideas to a medical model by Richard Mead (1673–1754), who served as the Vice President of the Royal Society in 1717 and, for half a century, was one of the most eminent physicians in London; his patients included Newton himself, and Stukeley was among his students.[48] Mead's text on solar and lunar influences, *De Imperio Solis ac Lunae in Corpora Humana, et Morbis inde Oriundis*, appeared in 1704 and was republished in 1710 and 1746; English translations were issued in 1708, 1712 and 1748, testimony to the popularity and influence of his ideas. Citing Goad's work on meteorology, Mead explained a range of periodic physiological conditions, including menstruation and epilepsy, according to the gravitational affects of the sun, moon, planets and comets on the atmosphere. So influential was Mead that in 1771 the *Encyclopaedia Britannica* used him as an authority for the claim that epileptic fits tend to happen when the moon is new, full or at its quarter phases. Such ideas were so persistent that it even remained possible for astrological physicians to obtain licenses to practise throughout the eighteenth century, which is somewhat surprising considering the general contempt within which astrology was held by the emerging medical consensus. Ideas of lunar influence proved enduring perhaps because the moon's impact on the oceans is so dramatic that the idea that it influences emotional moods as well has a certain compulsive logic. In 1817 and 1820, Hegel delivered a series of lectures in Heidelberg in which he argued that, although the moon has only a 'limited influence on the physical nature of man', its influence on lunatics is apparent because they are subject to nature and incapable of exercising their reason.[49]

Today Mead himself is forgotten, but he is remembered through the work of his most famous follower, the Austrian physician Franz Mesmer (1734–1815), who cited him in his own MD dissertation, *De planetarum influxu in corpus humanum* (*Concerning the Influence of the Planets*), published in Vienna in 1766.[50] Mesmer is best known as the founder of hypnotism, although that word seems to have been first used by James Braid, who roundly rejected ideas of planetary influence, in around 1842. Mesmer's theory depended on the effect of the planets on humans via a substance he knew as animal magnetism.

After graduating, Mesmer (like William Lilly) made a fortunate marriage to a rich, upper-class widow who subsidized his medical experiments and opened the door to the best social circles in Vienna. Among Mesmer's supporters was Wolfgang Amadeus Mozart; Mesmer was an amateur musician and a close friend of Mozart's father, Leopold (both were Freemasons), as well as an acquaintance of Glück and Haydn. It is said, though not proven, that the first performance of Mozart's first opera, *Bastien et Bastienne*, was commissioned by Mesmer and took place in his garden. Certainly, in *Cosi Fan Tutte*, Mozart poked gentle and affectionate fun at Mesmer by having two fake suicides apparently 'magnetized' back to life. Mesmer built up a thriving practice with clients in the upper echelons of society, but was forced to move to Paris in 1778, following a scandal provoked by an unsuccessful attempt to cure an 18-year-old musician, Maria Theresa von Paradis, of blindness. Once settled in his new home, Mesmer's clinic in the elegant Place Vendôme became a centre of fashion and he acquired a number of high-profile collaborators, notably Charles d'Eslon, who encouraged him to publish his ideas. This he did in 1779 as the *Mémoire sur la découverte du magnétisme animal*.[51]

Mesmer's astrology (although he would never have used the word), was based on an exclusively natural version of planetary influence. He was a devout child of the Enlightenment in his thoroughgoing rejection of any divine power, along with anything that might connect his work with traditional judicial astrology. Yet he was also an enemy of Enlightenment elitism, of the notion that only philosophers should be the arbiters of truth. Anyone, he argued, could develop healing powers and everyone had a right to a form of treatment which was effective, such as his, even if the Academicians decided otherwise. In his essential democracy and opposition to what he saw as the vested interests of a closed medical establishment, Mesmer was the heir to the radical physician Nicholas Culpeper. If there was a difference, it was that Culpeper excluded himself from the establishment, whereas Mesmer was an unwilling reject. Even though he never used the word 'astrology', which he knew was entirely unacceptable, Mesmer is best understood as a member of the lineage of astrological reformers. This much he made clear in enigmatic language: 'Philosophy has occasionally made efforts to free itself of errors and prejudices, but by overturning those edifices with too much vigour it has covered the ruins with disdain, without fixing the attention on the precious things contained there.'[52] Don't, he was pleading to astrology's Enlightenment critics, throw out the grain of empirically observed evidence with the chaff of vague and frivolous speculation. This had been Kepler's view. Like Kepler, Mesmer ignored the zodiac and had no interest in the planets' astrological personalities. Nor did he allow any role for the divine. In theory his cosmology was completely acceptable to any radical, atheist materialist. Only one cosmological error was unpardonable. His invisible fluid violated the Newtonian dogma that space was 'empty'.

Mesmer drew the quite correct conclusion from Newton that, due to the familiar principles of universal attraction, as he put it, or the law of gravity, all material objects can exert an effect on each other. His appeal to Newton could not have been more explicit. 'The great Newton,' he wrote, 'clarified to the highest degree the reciprocal attraction of all things', by which he included both planets and people.[53] Maria Tatar, recognizing Mesmer's eclectic mix of Newtonian action-at-a-distance with traditional occult sympathies, has called his model a 'nebulously conceived admixture of astrological theories and Newtonian principles'.[54] Her assessment is essentially correct. However, Mesmer departed from Newtonianism (and agreed with a number of English almanac makers) in rejecting the notion of a vacuum in space. He could not comprehend how action-at-a-distance could work unless it was through some sort of material substance, so he postulated a kind of Aristotelian ether, which permeated the earth as well as the entire universe. It is this substance that he called animal magnetism, as a form of magnetism which, he believed, affected living bodies. This was not, he was most insistent, the same as ordinary mineral magnetism, even though magnets could be used to assist the operation of animal magnetism.

Like Mead, Mesmer saw evidence for the effects of planetary movements in the periodicity of certain medical conditions, especially nervous or chronic complaints, which would go through periods of crisis and remission. Like the tides, he believed, all diseases ebb and flow. Disease results from the blockages of the channels through which animal magnetism flows and the physician's task was to release these obstacles. If the bodily rhythms could then be synchronized with celestial ones, the flow of animal magnetism from planets to humans would be harmonized, and a cure for individual ailments affected. At the heart of Mesmer's method for capturing celestial influences was the bacquet, a large vat, about a foot and a half high, filled with water and magnetic material, such as iron filings, which stored animal magnetism. In group sessions, up to 20 patients sat around the bacquet, holding both each other's hands and the iron rods which projected out from the bacquet at different heights, depending on the part of the body to be healed. Mirrors, which intensified light, and sound were used to enhance the available levels of animal magnetism and the strongest effects when Mesmer drew close, focusing the animal magnetism by moving his hands and eyes. In individual sessions he would fix the patient with his eyes and pass his hands over the areas which were in need of healing, sometimes holding them for hours.

Not surprisingly, Mesmer and d'Eslon aroused the hostility of the entire Parisian medical faculty. When the faculty threatened to remove d'Eslon's name from its register of practitioners, Mesmer abandoned his extraordinarily lucrative practice and stormed out of the city, in spite of the efforts of no less a person than the queen, his fellow Austrian Marie Antoinette, to entice him to stay. D'Eslon continued to practise and, in Mesmer's absence and confident of his success rate, asked the faculty for a formal committee of investigation. Mesmer was furious that d'Eslon, a mere student (though an experienced physician), should pose as an expert and ask for an investigation of his own work. On 12 March 1784 Louis XVI convened a commission which included the distinguished astronomer Jean-Sylvain Bailly (1736–793), the newly appointed United States ambassador, Benjamin Franklin, and Dr Jospeh-Ignace Guillotine, inventor of the coming

Revolution's favourite means of dispatching its enemies. Mesmer made several personal appeals, including one to Franklin, but the commission pressed ahead with its investigation of Mesmerism on the basis of d'Eslon's practice. The inquiry pursued a clear strategy which can only be understood within the context of the manipulation of scientific theory to discredit awkward mavericks. Positive testimonials from patients were not accepted as evidence, while the absence of a mechanism by which Mesmer's techniques could work, regardless of their results, was considered fatal to his claims. The commission duly concluded that 'the imagination does everything, the magnetism nothing', adding for good measure that touch and 'imitation' were an essential part of the therapeutic process.[55] In the inevitable crisis that followed, 17 of d'Eslon's 21 assistants renounced the power of magnetism rather than lose the title of doctor. D'Eslon, though, persevered, gathering around him a group of wealthy and influential supporters, some of whom had benefited from his cures. Mesmer himself never established a settled clinic again. In 1811 he declined an invitation from Professor Reil, head of the Prussian Faculty of Medicine, to demonstrate his methods in Berlin, but in 1814 he did publish a complete account of his work in German, the *System der Wechselwirkungen*. The following year he died.

Mesmer's methods were undoubtedly effective in many cases – the Paris faculty's challenge had been to his theoretical mechanism, not his results – and were increasingly practised, spreading through the German states. The condemnation of Mesmerism pinpoints one feature of Enlightenment rationalism, an anti-scientific current which could deny the evidence because its explanatory model was considered impossible: there were no planetary influences, it was concluded, and therefore the empirical evidence pointing to the benefits of Mesmer's treatment should be overlooked and denied to those who might have benefited from them. It was not until the 1880s that the great neurologist Jean-Martin Charcot (1825–93) managed to convince the physicians of Paris that Mesmerism, stripped of its planetary theory, and reborn under its new name, hypnotism, worked.

Mesmer's condemnation by the Paris medical faculty meant little either to those who benefited from Mesmer's cures or found his theories sympathetic to their own, such as the English astrologer Ebenezer Sibly (1751–c.1799), who included prints illustrating a Mesmerist at work in his *A New and Complete Illustration of the Celestial Science of Astrology*, published in four parts between 1784 and 1788. Aside from ending the long drought in astrological publishing by issuing the first major astrology text in English for over a century, Sibly was a physician, a radical, a supporter of American independence, a Freemason, a supporter of the Swedish visionary Emmanuel Swedenborg (1668–1772) and a fellow of the Harmonic Philosophical Society, founded in Paris to promote Mesmer's work. Sibly, in other words, was exactly the sort of person to disregard the orthodox medical profession's dislike of Mesmerism. We can see, as the world of science gradually defines itself, a divergence between science's ideal view of a universe founded on replicable evidence and the alternative, based in personal experience. The progressive separation between the emerging scientific paradigm on the one hand, and popular belief and practice on the other, was now evident and, in the case of Mesmer, each side had its failings. The medical faculty rejected Mesmerism's benefits because it was opposed, on *a priori* grounds, to his model. His supporters, conversely encouraged by his success, assumed the reality of a theory of celestial influence which was neither demonstrable nor necessary to the cure – unless, that is, we look at the activities that went on around the bacquet as a sort of shamanistic healing ritual, in which success depended on belief in Mesmer's cosmological principles.

Although Mesmer's model of planetary influence has been abandoned, through his development of hypnotism as a means of curing nervous ailments, he has had a huge influence in spiritualism and forms of spiritual healing, including Christian Science, and has a claim to be, in Gilbert Frankau's words, 'the father of modern psychotherapy'.[56] For Maria Tatar, Mesmer was a 'transitional figure in the development of therapeutic procedures for functional disorders' and a bridge between a form of revived shamanistic exorcism and psychoanalysis.[57] As the occultist poet Alphonse Esquiros wrote in 1841, 'God alone knows my torments and my anxieties, the mysterious aim of my youthful studies. As a young man I sought, following Mesmer, to plumb the deep sea of sleep.'[58]

Mesmer's theories were certainly rejected, but other models for celestial influence were proposed. In 1799, Humphry Davy, future President of the Royal Society and inventor of the miner's safety lamp, argued, like Placidus, that light was the medium by which celestial influences reached the earth. Light was embodied, he believed, in the blood, in the form of an ethereal fluid which maintains consciousness in the brain. In a passage which strongly suggests some familiarity with Hermetic texts, and certainly echoed Copernicus and Newton, Davy wrote that 'We may consider the Sun and the fixed stars, the suns of other worlds, as immense reservoirs of light destined by the great ORGANIZER to diffuse over the universe organisation and animation.'[59] But so great was conventional Newtonianism's opposition to any effect of action-at-a-distance other than on the motion of objects, that any suggestion, no matter who made it nor how good their evidence, was henceforth to evoke only ridicule and hostility. The most notable attempt to restore a natural astrology, although he didn't use the term, was made in 1801 by William Herschel, the discoverer of Uranus, and renowned as one of the greatest astronomers of his age. Relying on data originally published in 1776 in Adam Smith's *Wealth of Nations*, Herschel published two papers that launched the field of solar influences and lunar tides on the earth's weather. In the first, he discussed an inverse correlation between the price of wheat and the number of sunspots – dark, cold spots which appear on the sun's surface in regular cycles.[60] By using a mixture of his own observation and records dating back to around 1650, Herschel found that the price of a bushel of wheat was higher during periods of prolonged sunspot scarcity, which was the opposite of what he expected. His explanation was that, when there were fewer sunspots, solar radiation was abnormal and resulted in poorer growing conditions, bad harvests, scarcity and, consequently, higher prices. The response of Herschel's fellow astronomers was far from polite. As Stuart Clark put it, 'his words fell on entirely deaf ears. Those who did listen decided not just to criticise him but also to ridicule.'[61]

The word astrology, though, could not be used in connection with such naturalistic theories; even though the strict Aristotelian astrology of the twelfth and thirteenth centuries could be seen to have a naturalistic rationale, by the seventeenth century, much of judicial astrology had been completely submerged beneath a mass of angels, spirits, intelligences and biblical prophecies and was, in all intents and purposes, magical in a manner which the eighteenth-century philosophers increasingly found unacceptable. For such people, astrology had, early in the century, assumed the bizarre and ridiculous connotations which it still carries. As Pierre Bayle had said in his *Dictionnaire Historique et Critique*, published in 1697, astrology was a disease. In 1704 it was dismissed in one sentence in the *Lexicon Technicum* of John Harris, another Royal Society member. It was, he wrote, a ridiculous piece of 'Foolery' which deserved to be entirely omitted.[62] Harris did include respectful mention of Robert Boyle's theories of planetary influence and his own that planetary light might contain some virtue. But these ideas that had formerly stood at the centre of natural astrology and provided a rationale for judicial astrology were now to be redefined and reclassified as astronomy. And this is where they, or their modern equivalents, remain. Isidore of Seville's strict distinction between superstitious and natural astrology was now so blurred that all astrology was considered superstitious, and the word was so tainted that it could not be used to describe physical effects. Discussion of astrology was now increasingly effectively prohibited in elite educated society. Even to describe its claims or contents in an impartial manner was considered, by those who followed Harris, to be wrong. And so judicial astrology began to attain its present status as forbidden knowledge. However, the history of ideas is never simple. It is messy, and complex and sometimes contradictory, and the rejection of traditional astrology did not mean the rejection of astrology as a whole. The astrology of planetary influences advocated, in their very different ways, by Mesmer and Herschel was, in effect, astrology-in-disguise, an attempt to maintain a universe that was influential or significant, but that was finally free of that curse of sixteenth-century thought, Arabic superstition.

13

The Eighteenth Century: Magicians and Poets

The Sun is God.

JOSEPH TURNER[1]

On 7 April 1778, the 81-year-old François-Marie Voltaire, one of the greatest of all Enlightenment philosophers, was initiated into a Parisian Masonic Lodge, Les Neufs Soeurs, accompanied, apparently, by Benjamin Franklin, one of the most distinguished scientists of the day, and a signatory of the American Declaration of Independence. Also present at this momentous event was Antoine Court de Gébelin, one of the seminal figures in the history of modern occultism. A Protestant pastor from Switzerland, de Gébelin settled in Paris where, in 1771, he was initiated into the Masonic Lodge Les Amis Réunis, later joining Les Neufs Soeurs where, in 1778, he assisted in the initiation of Voltaire. In 1783 de Gébelin was treated by Mesmer, becoming an enthusiastic propagandist for animal magnetism. Unfortunately he had a relapse and died during a treatment at the bacquet in 1784.

Newtonianism was nothing if not a broad church and, while some of its adherents used their master as a weapon to beat esoteric ideas, others found his theories to be a positive boon. One of these was de Gébelin, who set himself the Ficinian, Newtonian, task of discovering not just the *prisca theologia*, the pure, primeval religion, but the entire nature of the original universal civilization. He set out to publish his findings in a series of works under the title *Monde primitif, analyse, et compare avec le monde moderne*, a comparative study of the ancient and modern worlds. Although most of de Gébelin's ideas were speculative and now discredited, his studies of language, for example, later influenced the attempt to establish the nature of the presumed early Indo-European tongue and the origin of all its successor languages. The *Monde primitif* was an instant success and attracted a thousand subscribers. The royal family alone ordered 100 copies. Nine volumes were published between 1773 and 1784, and only death prevented the series' completion. For the future of occultism, though, the work's significance was its inclusion in 1781 of the first-known published essays on the Tarot, one by de Gébelin himself and one by an aristocratic cavalry officer, the Comte de Mellet. De Gébelin was gushingly enthusiastic about the Tarot. He believed that it was Egyptian in origin and, far from being a mere fortune-telling device, was an allegory which revealed the complex linkages made by Egyptian priests between all things in the universe.[2] The Tarot is probably the most commonly used system of divination in the modern West, largely because of its simplicity. When nineteenth-century occultists matched its symbolism with that of astrology, astrological imagery was to begin to resemble its magical medieval past.

The coincidence and contradictions that brought de Gébelin, whose cosmo-logical medicine was based on faith as much as evidence, together with Voltaire, the arch-sceptic, in the same lodge, ran through eighteenth-century Masonry. Some lodges invoked what has been described as a fashionable mysticism, heavily indebted to Boehme, Fludd and Christian Kabbalah, such as the 'seventh-degree of the Rose-Croix', while others provided safe havens for aristocrats, radicals or philosophers.[3] In the 1770s, a Masonic order called 'The Golden Rosy Cross', inspired by Valentin Andreae, was formed in Germany and was joined by Frederick William II of Prussia.

The *Corpus Hermeticum* had been translated into German in 1706, just as its practical application, judicial astrology, was disappearing into intellectual oblivion.[4] It seems that Plato's psychic cosmos, characterized by its living, spir-itual qualities and expressed through Hermeticism and Behmenism, was not threatened by the end of the physical Platonic cosmos, with its geocentric, crystal spheres, in the same way as horoscopic astrology, magic and initiatory societies apparently flourished in an environment which had come to find the casting of horoscopes as ridiculous. One of the most interesting groups was the Illuminés d'Avignon, founded in the 1740s by the Benedictine monk Antoine-Joseph Pernety (1716–96). Pernety was swept up by the fashionable interest in alchemy and Hermeticism, and was enthused by the popular survey of hermetic teachings, the Abbé Langlet-Duffresnoy's *L'Histoire de la philosophie hermétique*, which appeared in 1742. Influenced by the Ficinesque notions of the *prisca theologia* and the perennial wisdom, Pernety expounded the theory that all ancient myths were hermetic allegories, which he set out in two widely read books, *Les Fables égyptiennes at grecques*, published in 1758, and the later *Dictionaire mytho-hermétique*. Pernety joined the Masons in Avignon and set up his own *rite hermétique* based heavily in alchemical symbolism. The three core symbols of the flaming star, sun and moon, for example, represented the alchemical processes of putrefaction, purification and completion. He later founded a second order, the Chevalier du Soleil, in which members received instruction in hermeticism and Gnosticism. After a period collaborating with occultists in Berlin, Pernety returned to Avignon where he set up a new fraternity, the Illuminés d'Avignon, which included a hundred members, most of them Freemasons. Such orders were at risk from two quarters; first the papacy, which issued an anti-Masonic Bull in 1738, and later by the revolution which persecuted illuminist orders in the early 1790s. In spite of such harrassment, there were an estimated 30,000 Masons in Europe in 1790, all of whom would have been active participants in, or had some contact with, the occultists who joined the various lodges in large numbers. The Grand Orient, the umbrella body for French Masons, consisted of 104 lodges a year after its formation in 1779, and 629, ten years later, when the revolution broke out. Christopher McIntosh has observed that the members divided themselves into three groups, political, religious and 'quasi-mystical', the last group being influenced by Cagliostro, Mesmer, Swedenborg and Saint-Martin.[5] The quasi-mystics, or 'occultists', favoured designation as 'illuminés' provides a provocative contrast with the Enlightenment and is evidence that the latter's claim that rationalism was necessarily linked to a materialist rejection of magic and the supernatural is misleading. Alongside, and perhaps intertwined with, the conventional Enlightenment of the philosophers there seems to have been a parallel 'occult' Enlightenment, Joscelyn Godwin's 'theosophical enlightenment', with tentacles which permeated both aristocratic and bourgeois society.[6] Isaiah Berlin argued rather that the magical, esoteric world constituted a 'counter-enlightenment', a reaction against the sceptical, rational current of the times.[7] For E.P. Thompson, such currents of thought as flowed from Boehme, Fludd, Neoplatonism and esoteric Christianity, should also be seen as a counter-Enlightenment, a reaction to the spirit of rationalism represented by Locke and Voltaire.[8] But it was natural for Thompson, like any other believer in progress, to identify forward-moving trends in thought as taking humanity into the future, while apparently incompatible ideas have to be identified as reactionary, positioned somehow in opposition to the rational flow of events. The truth is invariably more complex and such a view relies on the extraction of such 'occult' beliefs from the totality of Enlightenment thought, which is then reduced to an impoverished, narrow, materialist atheism, ignoring such complexities as the role of Masonry as a mediating influence between esoteric and atheist thinkers. I am aware, when making this argument, that we need to be conscious of Roy Porter's warnings against 'complex revisionisms', debunking the concept of the Enlightenment as the 'Age of Reason' because it fails to chime with modern political sensibilities, horrified by other features of the eighteenth century, such as its love affair with slavery.[9] My point, though, is that esoteric and occult mentalities, being derived from Plato, may be considered perfectly rational. The most public symbol of Enlightenment political thought was the reverse image on the Great Seal of the USA, adopted in 1782, with its famous pyramid capped by an all-seeing eye of Horus. This is not to say that those American revolutionary leaders, such as Thomas Jefferson, who were Masons were occultists, for this would be to misrepresent and overdramatize their situation. However, they did owe allegiance to a cosmology that owed due deference to the ancient mysteries. It is only to be suspected that, in a culture in which every gentleman received a classical education, and Plato stood at the pinnacle of the classical canon, that Platonism should remain an influential force. The view of the Enlightenment as dominated by a handful of determinedly anti-religious and, in their own account, ultra-rational philosophers needs to be abandoned as a misleading caricature.[10] The Enlightenment actually consisted of complex strands of thought, some of which were actively concerned with establishing a new religious settlement, stabilizing orthodox belief by making it consistent with reason. Within this movement the esotericists, with their discrete and invariably non-horoscopic astrology, played an important part. And, in the United States' Great Seal, the visual counterpart of the Declaration of Independence, the Enlightenment's most famous political document, Hermeticism was absolutely central. This was not an accident. It was a deliberate attempt to tie the new republic into the ancient, pre-Newtonian, cosmological mysteries.

France's reputation as a home to the esoteric tradition was deepened by Martines de Pasqually (1727–74), who founded a theurgical order known as the 'Elect Cohens' and practised a ritual magic derived partly from the Catholic Mass and partly from Cornelius Agrippa.[11] De Pasqually's magic was not unlike a ritual form of Mesmerism, one in which, true to theurgical tradition, magic was actively performed on one's own behalf rather than passively received from the power of the magician. His cosmology, like Mesmer's, emphasized the material. The bodies of the universe, he believed, were all vital organs of eternal life. The sun was particularly powerful as the source of light, and the moon because of its proximity to the earth. The equinoxes, when the sun and day are of equal length and light and dark are in perfect balance, and the appearance of the new crescent moon, were the most auspicious moments for collective rituals and magical invocations, and the most important of de Pasqually's rituals were performed over three consecutive days, beginning with the crescent moon. The invocations began with the reading of the office of the Holy Spirit and ended with a plea to God for a sincere and humble heart. Adepts were also expected to lead a pure lifestyle, avoid fornication, and refuse to eat the blood, fat or kidneys of any animal, or the flesh of domestic pigeons. De Pasqually attracted various disciples, including Louis Claude de Saint-Martin (1743–1803), a former army officer, strict Catholic and follower of Jacob Boehme, who set out to teach the occult principles behind all knowledge and believed that the world should be governed by a 'natural and spiritual theocracy', 'divine commissioners' chosen by God himself.[12] Saint-Martin died in 1803, leaving a body of writing which proved influential throughout the nineteenth century. De Pasqually departed for the Caribbean in 1772, leaving the Elect Cohens in the hands of two disciples, Bacon and Willermoz, who unfortunately lacked their master's charisma and organizational skills. In the absence of its charismatic founder, the Elect Cohens floundered, but that there were alternatives is a testimony to the survival of an occult culture in the heart of the Enlightenment. Willermoz joined another Masonic order, the Rite of Strict Observance, which had been founded in 1754, while Bacon went over to the Grand Orient. It was another of Pasqually's followers, though, Saint-Martin, who assumed his master's role as charismatic leader.[13] Saint-Martin translated the writings of Jacob Boehme into French and was influenced by both Emanuel Swedenborg and Franz Mesmer. Saint-Martin's followers, the Martinists, were to flourish in the nineteenth century and provide a direct link between eighteenth- and twentieth-century magical groups; Martinism influenced the teachings of the Hermetic Order of the Golden Dawn, founded in London in 1887, and, through that society and its most notorious member, Aleister Crowley (1875–1947), the magical and pagan subcultures of the modern West.

Just as Newton's theology and alchemy was an integral part of his thought, not an aberration, so Joseph Priestly (1733–1804), the famous chemist and discoverer of oxygen, was equally concerned in the 1770s and 1780s to square the new science with the Gospels. In this, like Newton, he was distinctly unorthodox and was condemned by the revivalist preacher John Wesley.[14] Materialist he may have been, but Priestly's devotion to the Swedish thinker Emmanuel Swedenborg (1688–1772) put him well outside the narrow view of the Enlightenment as rational and sceptical in the sense understood by late twentieth-century science. For many, and this was a line of thought which continued through the nineteenth century and twentieth centuries, the new scientific discoveries didn't disenchant and demystify the universe. Instead, the discovery of gravity and the better understanding of magnetism and electricity provided a rationale for what was previously mysterious. This line of thought was later to be expressed through two major initiatives in the late nineteenth century. In 1875 Henry Olcott and Helena Blavatsky founded the Theosophical Society, a reforming religious movement which couched esoteric ideas in terms of contemporary scientific knowledge. Seven years later a group of Cambridge dons founded the Society for Psychical Research with the express intention of launching scientific investigations of paranormal claims, especially the evidence for life after death. The link between the seemingly incompatible currents of Enlightenment rationalism and esoteric thought is, of course, reason. If the eighteenth century is so closely identified with rationalism, then so were Renaissance Neoplatonism and Kabbalah, both of which argued that the higher mind, or active soul, however it was described, was the path to illumination. For Christian Kabbalists, like Boehme, the soul's 'Luminous Mirror' accessed divine and prophetic wisdom while its 'Non-Luminous Mirror' coped with ordinary knowledge.[15] The boundary between 'illuminism' in its Hermetic sense, and the 'Enlightenment' in its rational, sceptical sense, was fluid and porous.

From its Hermetic roots, Masonry adopted mystical language about the sun which, from the 1740s onwards, led to the self-conscious use of the word 'enlightenment' to describe the current philosophical mood. Its use could clearly be metaphorical – a French almanac of 1787 claimed that 'we have given ourselves the title of children of the light', and revolutionary Freemasons in Philadelphia in the late 1770s, as the British colonies were fighting for independence, spoke of being 'enlightened and enlivened by a Ray from Thee', in language adapted from the *Corpus Hermeticum*.[16] The sun, at the centre of the Copernican universe, bound men together in the divine principles of Friendship, Affection and Knowledge, the key features of the new Enlightenment state, the new 'Heavenly City'. The Enlightenment thinkers liked to think of themselves as anti-Christian or even irreligious, but the case can be made that, behind their assertion of knowledge as the true path to truth, they locked themselves into a system of faith as profound as that of medieval theology.[17] The sun that was invoked, though, was the Newtonian sun, the servant of the intelligent Being of the 'Scholia' to the *Principia*.

Newton was the father of competing strands of Enlightenment philosophies which often had little in common. Emmanuel Swedenborg, for example, is usually described as a mystic but may be best thought of as a creature of the Enlightenment.[18] After a successful career as an engineer, anatomist and scientific writer, Swedenborg entered into a series of encounters with angels and demons and traveled to other planets, which he found to be inhabited. He also announced that the Kingdom of God had begun in 1757, although it existed in spiritual form and hence was invisible to people who did not follow the correct spiritual path. This announcement was to be attractive to radicals such as Ebenezer Sibly and Joseph Priestly. Swedenborg's followers, including Priestly, went on to found the New Church, a form of radical Christianity which was deeply influential among believers in the USA as the New Jerusalem, and is one of the influential ancestors of modern New Age culture.[19] Swedenborg's Newtonianism lay in his materialism; he really did, in his own account, travel to the planets and meet their inhabitants, in contrast to the psychic, or metaphorical journeys which predominate in the magical and Neoplatonic traditions from Plato's *Republic* onwards. Yet, to a rival Newtonian, the more sceptical Immanuel Kant (1724–1804), Swedenborg cut a ridiculous figure. In his *Dreams of a Spirit Seer*, Kant described Swedenborg's belief in the medieval doctrine of sympathies and a spiritual influx from the 'invisible world', the 'foolishness of which,' he wrote, 'is too great for me to quote even one of them'.[20] Kant stood in the tradition of Platonic sceptics, although he doubted the possibility that reason alone could lead to truth, unless supported by empirical observation – in which he departed from Plato and allied himself with Hume. Even Kant's position was not a simple one; he was familiar enough with the classical tradition to acknowledge Plato's statement that the study of the stars takes one closer to the gods: 'two things fill the mind with ever new and increasing admiration and awe,' he wrote, 'the oftener and the more steadily we reflect on them: *the starry heavens above and the moral law within*'.[21] But in Kant's vision there was no space for anything approaching astrology, for which he had complete contempt, especially as it is clear from his mockery of Swedenborg that he despised those who prophesied the future and then, yielding to 'vice and corruption', he wrote, could think of nothing to do aside from cowardly 'means cunningly to escape the threatening consequences of the future'.[22]

While the notion of the counter-Enlightenment as a dark shadow of the Enlightenment may be a modern anachronism, opposition to what was seen as the sterile rationality of the leading Enlightenment thinkers was overt and was led by the Romantics, beginning with their inspiration, Jean Jacques Rousseau (1712–78), in the 1740s. It was Rousseau who pioneered the notion of a return to the natural innocence of nature, as a rejection of the urban, artificial sophistication of the French 'Philosophes'. For Rousseau, true religion arose from natural law, and was rooted in the harmonious relationship between people and their environment, which he saw as essentially benevolent.[23] The *prisca theologia* was to be found in the simple life. Whereas the Enlightenment philosophers admired the artificial as a means of civilizing barbaric humans, the Romantics saw the natural as a way of liberating humans, who were naturally good, from the tyranny of the artificial. The Romantics' cosmology was best described by

Isaiah Berlin. Speaking specifically of what he called 'the most extravagant of the German romantics', he argued that they 'looked on the universe not as a structure that can be studied or described by whatever methods are most appropriate, but as a perpetual activity of the spirit and of nature'.[24] Whereas, for the Newtonians, the outer world was all that mattered, the Romantic alternative was, as Alex Owen put it, an intensification of the ancient Platonic doctrine of the transcendental 'I', the self conceived as an extended consciousness, which could touch the divine and, though an act of will, connect with the cosmos, the planets and stars.[25] Such ideas were to profoundly influence the artistic movements of the later nineteenth century and a large part of the depth psychology of the twentieth, in particular Jungian analytical psychology. It was Anita Brookner who truly penetrated the Romantics' sense of mission, speaking of their passion, 'their infinite longing ... a longing for what is missing and an attempt to supply it'.[26] The Romantics were driven by nostalgia for a lost paradise in which humanity and cosmos were one. The main vehicle by which the anguish of loss might be assuaged, and the truth of the spirit in nature and the universe revealed was the man of genius, the artist or poet. Yet we shouldn't imagine that the Romantics necessarily stood in a state of opposition to everything the Enlightenment thinkers believed in. They reacted against Newtonianism, but only in its materialist, mechanical form. Convinced that the universe defied scientific explanation, the Romantics instead sought to restore spirit and soul to it, to re-enchant it, as Weber would have said. Newton himself, ironically, might not have objected. As the English radical and Romantic Samuel Coleridge wrote in heroic style:

> There, Priest of Nature! Dost thou shine
> NEWTON! A king amongst the Kings divine.[27]

William Wordsworth, whose Romanticism was thoroughly Platonic, was of a similar mind:

> Newton with his prism and silent face
> ... a mind for ever
> Voyaging through strange seas of thought alone.[28]

Wordsworth's concern was with what Alan Bewell called 'Enlightenment anthropology' – the attempt to trace human evolution from the state of nature to culture, examining the origins of social institutions in the human imagination, passions, the fear of death and ideas of the supernatural.[29] Primitive people, it was believed, including not just natives in faraway places, but wild children, disabled people and criminals, were thought to provide insights into the unshaped, natural condition of ancient people. In an intriguing sense the Romantics' attitude to nature paralleled that of the scientific world-view, which was emerging out of the new discoveries about nature, and how the human body worked. Both Romantics and scientists were in revolt against the disgust for nature which followed on from strict Christian doctrines of the Fall and original sin. Both denied that the cosmos and the human body were fundamentally wicked, and both found salvation and redemption in nature. More than that, they both identified, behind the beauty of nature, an underlying cosmic truth. For Wordsworth the natural world extended to the sky, and his concern was very far from astrological significance, but with the elevation of his soul. On 25 February 1841 he described the new crescent moon which was close to Venus in the westerly sky, shortly after dusk:

> The Crescent-moon, the Star of Love
> Glories of evening, as ye there are seen
> With but a span of sky between
> Speak one of you, my doubts remove
> Which is the attendant Page and which the Queen?[30]

Platonic respect for the world of ideas, which had once been so linked to astrology, found an expression in the Romantic Idealism of a succession of German thinkers from Herder (1741–1804) to Schelling (1775–1854) and Hegel (1770–1831).[31] It was Hegel who, in a move which was to influence Karl Marx, adapted the Platonic theory of history into a version in which the World Spirit, working through the three-phase dialectical process, became manifest in four great cultural epochs.[32] Like the medieval thinker Hugh of St Victor, he believed that the four historical phases corresponded to a cultural progression from east to west, following the sun's diurnal motion. In the first phase of history, corresponding to sunrise, the despotic East was dominant. As the world then progressed to sunset, human civilization moved progressively through the Greek and Roman phases, becoming ever more free as it did so. The final phase, which was imminent, was to see the triumph of the Germanic peoples, a future golden age when all people would be free, by which Hegel meant living under monarchy, the natural form of government.

One of the rare figures in the eighteenth century to actually speak approvingly of astrology was Johann Wolfgang von Goethe (1749–1832), perhaps the greatest of the German Romantics. For Goethe, it was part of the natural world which he so revered. Environmental influences extended beyond the earth – this much was obvious to him, and, in this sense, he was pursuing a Ptolemaic agenda, echoing the naturalistic rationale of classical astrology. Goethe's autobiography, which is regarded as a shift forward in the nature of such personal stories in view of his emphasis on the historical context for individual experience, began with a listing of his planetary positions at birth. His horoscope was auspicious, he wrote, and supported this claim with an anecdote to illustrate its benefits not just for him but all future infants in the same town.

> On the 28th of August, 1749, at mid-day, as the clock struck twelve, I came into the world, at Frankfort-on-the-Main. My horoscope was propitious: the sun stood in the sign of the Virgin, and had culminated for the day; Jupiter and Venus looked on him with a friendly eye, and Mercury not adversely; while Saturn and Mars kept themselves indifferent; the moon alone, just full, exerted the power of her reflection all the more, as she had then reached her planetary hour. She opposed herself, therefore, to my birth, which could not be accomplished until this hour was passed.

These good aspects, which the astrologers managed subsequently to reckon very auspicious for me, may have been the causes of my preservation; for, through the unskilfulness of the midwife, I came into the world as dead; and only after various efforts was I enabled to see the light. This event, which had put our household into sore straits, turned to the advantage of my fellow-citizens, inasmuch as my grandfather, the Schultheiss [Magistrate], John Wolfgang Textor, took occasion from it to have an *accoucheur* appointed, and to introduce, or revive, the tuition of midwives, which may have done some good to those who were born after me.[33]

Goethe's reference to astrologers tells us that the practice of horoscope-casting may have survived in Germany, as well as in Britain and North America. His rationale for astrology was set out in a letter to his close friend, the famous poet and dramatist Johann Christoph Friedrich von Schiller (1759–1805), in 1798. Goethe's ideas provided a context for Mesmerism, suggesting that there might have been a little more support for theories of planetary influence than Mesmer's condemnation by the scientific community suggests. After all, Goethe, though best known as a Romantic writer, also held the post of chief minister in the German state of Weimar for ten years, a fact which testifies to his practical abilities. Schiller himself had been working on Wallenstein, Kepler's astrological client, for his *History of the Thirty Years War* and a subsequent play. He turned to Goethe for advice on how to handle Wallenstein's use of astrology, a delicate topic in the context of Enlightenment mockery. Goethe began his reply with an appeal to the by now commonly accepted sense of a primeval religion and then segued neatly into Aristotelian naturalism:

The superstition of astrology has its origins in our dim sense of some vast cosmic unity. Experience tells us that the heavenly bodies which are nearest us have a decisive influence on weather, on plant life and so forth. We need only move higher, stage by stage, and who can say where this influence ceases? The astronomer constantly observes that the heavenly bodies are subject to mutual disturbances; the philosopher is inclined, nay rather forced, to assume that action can take place even at the greatest distance; this man, in his presentment, needs only to go a stage further, and he will extend such influence to the mortal life, to happiness and misfortune. Such fanciful ideas, and others of the same kind, I cannot even call superstition; they come naturally to us and are as tolerable and as questionable as any other faith.[34]

Goethe was clearly taking a cautious line, but that astrology may have been 'fanciful', does not mean that it was not true. Rather, it was natural. Both Enlightenment devotees and Romantics were impressed by the translation of Persian sacred texts late in the century, which added force to the idea that the tenets of Christianity were shared by other religions, and so shared an ancient, common origin. The new respect for paganism which flowed from the Persian translations was far from universal. There was no shortage of militant Christian apologists while many radicals, such as Shelley, remained convinced atheists, as dismissive of pagan religion as of Christianity. However, it would be misleading to divide eighteenth-century thinkers into hermetically sealed bubbles of Christians, pagans and atheists, for many individuals crossed the boundaries between the three. In the visual arts the most notable was the painter J.M.W. Turner (1775–1851), famous for his revolutionary experiments with the portrayal of light. From 1798, Turner began to use poetry to amplify the message of his paintings: his *Morning amongst the Coniston Fells* was accompanied by a passage from Book V of Milton's *Paradise Lost*:

> Ye mists and exhalations that now rise
> From hill or screaming lake, dusky of gray
> Till the sun paints your fleecy skirts with gold
> In honour to the world's great Author, rise.[35]

Turner was also well versed in classical mythology and had studied Hinduism. The sun was not only God's messenger, as in Milton. It could represent the power of Apollo, it might be a lingam or phallus, or might be related to the Indian god Brahma, who had created the world by means of a 'spirit of the colour of flame', ideas which he may have picked up from Alexander Dow's 1768 *History of Hindostan* or Payne Knight's essay in comparative religion, the sensational *Account of the remains of the Worship of Priapus lately existing in Isernia*, published in 1786. Knight, for whom Turner worked in 1808, was deeply anti-religious but the orientalist William Jones, who greatly influenced Turner, was at once a devout Christian and very respectful of Hinduism. Jones, whose work on oriental languages, which spanned the years 1770 to 1794, believed that there must be a relationship between the Hindu and classical Greek Pantheons, and that both were fundamentally expressions of the sun. He concluded that, 'It seems a well-founded opinion that the whole crowd of gods and goddesses in ancient Rome and modern Varanes [Varanasi], mean only the powers of nature, and principally those of the SUN, expressed in a variety of ways, and by a multitude of fanciful names.'[36] According to John Ruskin, the famous nineteenth-century critic and Turner's biographer:

> In Turner's distinctive work, colour is scarcely acknowledged unless under the influence of sunshine. The sunshine is his treasure; his lividest gloom contains it; his grayest twilight regrets it, and remembers. Blue is always a blue shadow; brown or gold, always light; – nothing is cheerful but sunshine; wherever the sun is not, there is always melancholy or evil. Apollo is God; and all forms of death in sorrow exist in opposition to him.[37]

For Turner the sun was a natural power, yet that power itself had long been recognized as the source of divinity. In his 1816 painting *The Temple of Jupiter, Panallenius, Restored*, he included a painted frieze of a chariot race to the left of the picture. He added a Greek inscription which appears to identify the victor as *Anikētos*, Unconquered, a gesture of respect to Mithraism and the Roman state religion, Sol Invictus, the unconquered sun. In Ruskin's opinion, 'Turner meant it [sun worship] as Zoroaster meant it, and was a sun-worshipper of the old breed' – a genuine sun worshipper, not a dilettante artist.[38] Again, according to Ruskin, just a few weeks before Turner died, he had made the simple declaration that 'the Sun is God'.[39] Was Turner merely uttering a poetic metaphor? Ruskin, who knew Turner as well as anyone, thought not. Turner's deathbed profession of celestial faith marks the survival and regeneration of the notion that the universe is a mystery, a belief which had been battered by Enlightenment radicals and was to be so in the future by positivist science. But, in the early nineteenth century it was precisely this attitude that provided a safe home for the resuscitation of judicial astrology.

14

The Nineteenth Century: Enlightenment Entrepreneurs

*If the doors of perception were cleansed, everything would appear as it is:
infinite.*

WILLIAM BLAKE[1]

On 21 June 1792, midsummer evening, when the sun was at its northernmost
latitude and the days were longest, the itinerant poet and scholar Iolo Morganwg
(1747–1826) met at the top of Primrose Hill in London with a group of other
Welsh poets and held the first Gorsedd – Druidic gathering – since Christianity
overwhelmed Celtic culture in the fifth and sixth centuries. Iolo was a Welsh
patriot, a friend of the radical writer and ideologue Tom Paine, who inspired the
American revolutionaries, and he is said to have influenced the visionary artist
William Blake.[2] And so, with a self-conscious nod in the direction of the lost
culture of Stonehenge, inspired by William Stukeley, a new twist was added to
eighteenth-century cosmology, one which simultaneously looked back wistfully
to a lost golden age and set out on a defiant path to the counter-culture of the
1960s. And, within this romantic context, it seems that the neglected art of
horoscope interpretation made its first, tentative reappearance, at least as a form
of literary occultism.

The astrological view of history, as set out by Plato and elaborated at great length
by the Islamic historians and accepted as a commonplace in the Renaissance, is
that decline is followed by an inevitable restoration as the cosmos turns in its
cyclical journey. From the view of a late-eighteenth-century astrologer it was
inevitable that, just as judicial astrology had all but died out, some enthusiast
somewhere would start practising it again. Its revival coincided almost exactly
with the final death knell of the old order, for it was only in the 1770s, around
the time that the publication of serious astrological texts began, that the chair
of Astrology finally fell vacant in Salamanca.[3] In France, *Le Zodiaque Mystérieux*
by Alliet le Jeune (1731–91) appeared in 1772, and combined astrology with
the Tarot, prior even to Court de Gébelin's influential promotion of the cards.
In Germany, the evidence suggests that developments were a little later, and
the first astrology book of the new wave appears to have been Wilhelm Pfaff's
(1734–1835) *Astrologie*, which was published in 1816, to be followed by a set of
pocket books on astrology in 1822–3 and then *Der Mensch und die Stern*. The
end of the publishing drought in England took place 40 years earlier and was
signified by the appearance of the compendious *A New and Complete Illustration
of the Celestial Science of Astrology*, issued in four parts between 1784 and 1788 by
the Freemason Ebenezer Sibly (1751–99/1800). And it was in England, following

Sibly, that the revival in astrology in the Western world was launched. Or, perhaps, to be clear, we should say 'middling' astrology for it had never ceased to be a part of the culture of almanac readers and the clients of fortune-tellers. The *Illustration's* significance lay in its extensive and detailed account of astrology, as set out by Claudius Ptolemy in the second century BCE. As the foundation of the revival in the fortunes of horoscopic astrology in the English-speaking world, its publication marked the long-overdue triumph of one group of sixteenth-century reformers, those for whom the salvation of astrology lay in its rejection of 'Arabic superstition' and a return to the purer astrology of the Greeks. Actually, such a goal was never possible, for no one had sufficient grasp of the textual sources to distinguish the astrology of 2000 years ago from its later Islamic and medieval accretions. This small problem did not dent Sibly's enthusiasm. His aim was encyclopaedic and he included examples from all the major branches of astrology – natal, mundane, horary and electional – and his reconciliation of ancient knowledge with the emerging styles of modernism was evident. The *Illustration* met a demand among semi-erudite, self-taught, middle-class urban readers and there were 12 editions by 1812, some appearing under the amended title *A New and Complete Illustration of the Occult Sciences*; the last known edition appeared in 1826. Sibly, encouraged by his success, followed in 1789 with a new edition of Nicholas Culpeper's classic of astrological medicine, the *English Herbal*. This went through 14 editions by 1813, evidence, again, that there was sufficient demand to make such ventures a commercial proposition. Meanwhile, Sibly's younger brother, the well-known Swedenborgian preacher Manoah (1757–1840), translated astrological works by Placidus and reprinted Ptolemy's *Tetrabiblos*, now the essential source text. The other Hellenistic astrologers, such as Valens, were ignored, as were Abu Ma'shar and Masah'allah, the giants of Arabic astrology. Ebenezer's last major work, *A Key to Physic and the Occult Sciences*, was published in 1794 and reached five editions by 1814. Sibly had some public success which contributed to his reputation, although not to nearly the same extent as it would have done a century and a half earlier, when astrologers had huge and attentive audiences. In an essay first published in 1787, analysing the sun's ingress (entry) into Aries on 19 March 1789, he concluded that:

> here is every prospect ... that some very important event will happen in the politics of France, such as may dethrone, or very nearly touch the life of, the king, and make victims of many great and illustrious men in church and state, preparatory to a revolution ... which will at once astonish and surprise the surrounding nations.[4]

This is, by any account, a provocative prediction which removes at least one supposed problem from the history of astrology; that its appeal is inexplicable in view of the invariable failure of its predictions. It may frequently have been wrong but it was also capable of being remarkably prescient and members of the public who were not impressed by the dominant Enlightenment view that astrology was inherently ridiculous could judge for themselves. The middle classes were beginning to grow in power and complexity and were showing patchy signs of intellectual independence from the patrician hegemony, which taught that one should automatically respect one's intellectual betters. The Sibly brothers were part of the self-taught artisan culture of the time and, denied a university education by their social class, they became autodidacts, teaching themselves from whatever sources they could find. They were, in Theodor Adorno's phrase, 'semi-erudite'.[5] Such people were fundamentally dislocated from the various establishments which controlled – or attempted to control – intellectual thought in their differing ways. Owen Chadwick also located a social context in which we might place them. Comparing free-thinkers in the 1740s and 1840s, he suggested that the latter were 'lower in the social scale and ... associated their cause with a social cause'.[6] The Siblys were political radicals in the populist tradition of Nicholas Culpeper (Ebenezer enthusiastically supported the rebels in the American War of Independence), and were keen to disseminate knowledge among the masses. They were also religious nonconformists with little respect for the established Anglican Church (witness Manoah's membership of the Swedenborgian New Church). Similarly, the news that astrology was now considered unacceptable by the educated elite as a matter of principle, completely failed to impress them. It probably failed even to reach them. Mesmer may have distanced himself from astrology but for Ebenezer there was no doubt about the matter: animal magnetism was an astrological mechanism.

Ebenezer's overarching philosophy was stated in terms which were at once Platonic, democratic and tied to the Enlightenment. 'Wisdom,' he proclaimed, 'is the light of Reason and the bond of Peace. It assimilates Man to God, and elevates his mind above unworthy pursuits. Ignorance and superstition may be considered the curse of God ... The soul of man is free, independent and immortal.'[7] Sibly's eclectic mix of reformist astrology, Neoplatonic angelogy, Hermetic sympathies and modernist materialism was summarized in the title page of a *Key to Physic*. His goal, he proclaimed, was to describe:

the SYSTEM and ORDER of the Interior and Exterior HEAVENS; the ANALOGY betwixt ANGELS, and SPIRITS of MEN; AND THE SYMPATHY between CELESTIAL AND TERRESTRIAL BODIES ... An obvious Discrimination of Future Events, IN THE Motions and Positions of the Luminaries, Planets, and Stars; the universal Spirit and Economy of Nature ...; the Principles of etherial, and atmospherical Influx ... the Foundation and Necessity of that invisible Agitation of Matter which stimulates and impels every living Creature to the Act of begetting its like; the Properties of Vegetable, Mineral, and ANIMAL MAGNETISM: the fundamental Causes and Qualities, visible or occult, of all DISEASES, both of Mind and Body, and the simple Modes prescribed by NATURE FOR THEIR Prevention and Cure.[8]

If we examine this statement closely then the reasons for the appeal of Sibly's work become clearer. The reference to angels is acceptable to the vast Christian majority, whether Anglican or nonconformist, and the emphasis on matter acknowledges the emerging scientific paradigm. The incorporation of animal magnetism brings in a form of healing which, regardless of the reality of planetary influences, was known to produce pronounced effects, and the appropriation of nature relies on an appreciation of the natural, as opposed to the artificial, which remains a potent marketing tool to the present day. The concept of celestial order and the existence of a close and meaningful relationship between humanity and heaven is an enduring source of astrology's appeal, but it was the emphasis on healing which was crucial. Orthodox medicine was brutal, bloody, frequently ineffective, more backward than that practised under the Romans and had no concept of hygiene or nutrition.[9] Most people, both in town and country, still had access to traditional cunning men and women. In the countryside the rural poor would have had no other form of medical treatment. In such areas the belief in witchcraft was also persistent, even if the witch-hunts had died out. As Owen Davies has convincingly demonstrated, nineteenth-century farmers and labourers had no interest in discrete categories of supernatural knowledge, or the difference between 'science' and 'superstition'.[10]

The Sibly brothers' combination of the worlds of ancient magic and modern science, together with their alienation from conservative politics and conventional Anglican religion, marks them both as heirs of the seventeenth-century radicals and prophets of the modern New Age movement. It was the Swedenborgians who, inspired by the teaching of the New Jerusalem, were the first to use the term 'New Age'. They represent the shift to what Wouter Hanegraaff has defined as 'esoteric secularism', the significant feature, in his opinion, of modern New Age culture.[11] The Siblys were esotericists in their adherence to a tradition which elevated the inner and spirit worlds in a manner that the emerging materialist paradigm was to find incomprehensible, yet secular in their emphasis, through Mesmer, on materialism and, in spite of their emphasis on angels, their alienation from both pagan deities and the mainstream Church.

Others followed in the Siblys' wake and there seems to have been a market or, at least, the promise of a market, for students eager to connect with this new version of ancient wisdom. Francis Barrett's 1801 book *The Magus, or Celestial Intelligencer* contained an advertisement to prospective students promising that they 'will be initiated into the choicest operations of Natural Philosophy, Natural Magic, the Cabala, Chemistry, the Talismanic Art, Hermetic Philosophy, Astrology, Physiognomy, &c.&c. Likewise they will acquire the knowledge of the *Rites, Mysteries, Ceremonies,* and *Principles* of the ancient Philosophers, Magi, Cabalists, Adepts, &c.'[12] Yet the legal situation had not eased and astrologers were still liable to harassment. On 14 October 1807, William Blake, the visionary artist and dedicated enemy of the Enlightenment, wrote of 'a circumstance which has again raised my Indignation':

> I read in the Oracle and True Briton of 13 Octr 1807, that a Mr Blair, a Surgeon, has with the very cold fury of Robespierre, caused the police to seize upon the person and Goods or Property of an Astrologer and to commit him to Prison. The Man who can read the Stars often is opposed by their Influence, no less than the Newtonian who reads Not and cannot Read is oppressed by his own Reasonings and Experiments. We are all subject to Error; who shall say, except the Natural Religionist, that we are not all subject to Crime.[13]

Blake concluded his outburst with a measure of his anger: he expected the Sheriff, to whom the letter was addressed, to pay for the postage. Astrologers may or may not be in error, he raged, but that is no reason to prosecute them at public expense. Some years later, in 1824, Blake, by then 67 years old, became the centre of attention of a group of eccentric, radical and Romantic young artists, including Samuel Palmer, Edward Calvert and George Richmond, who specialized in sensitive, idealized images of the English countryside and, in Palmer's case, of the moon.[14] Joscelyn Godwin continues the story: 'The group was known by the locals as the "Extollagers," because it had got around that they were doing astrology. Under Blake's spell they talked of animal magnetism, ghosts, and clairvoyance, and doubtless much else.'[15]

The mini-publishing boom continued, unaffected by such unfortunate incidents as the prosecution of Blake's poor astrologer. The Sibly brothers had a notable contemporary in John Worsdale (1766–c.1828), a member of the flourishing community of astrologers and astronomers, who had survived in the English counties of Lincolnshire, Leicestershire, and Rutland in an unbroken lineage back to the seventeenth century and therefore connected tenuously to Stukeley.[16] Worsdale wrote several books defending and explaining astrology, including *Genethliacal Astrology*, a study of birth horoscopes issued in 1796 (and republished in 1798) and *A Collection of Remarkable Nativities*, produced in 1799 as a reference for students, enabling them to examine the birth charts of famous people and reflect on the significance of planetary motions for events in their lives. He satisfied the public hunger for information on the international situation in 1805 in *The Nativity of Napoleon Bonaparte*, written before the British victory at Trafalgar removed the serious threat of French invasion, while his last two works, *Astronomy and Elementary Philosophy* (1819) *and Celestial Philosophy* (1828), suggest an aspiration to reach a broader audience and, perhaps, achieve a wider respect. Like Sibly, Worsdale was a radical and supporter of the American rebels, and predicted, optimistically, that America would 'establish FREEDOM and LIBERTY in every part of the habitable Globe'.[17] Worsdale's God was a purely mechanical version of the Aristotelian first cause, whose only role was to keep the universe in motion, and his righteous religious anger seems to have been reserved equally for 'Infidels, Deists, and Atheists' as well as 'deceitful Popish priests', though his view that comets might be instruments of divine vengeance was perfectly Newtonian.[18] Like Sibly, Worsdale was also influenced by the stalled astrological reform programme. Both men found authority and vindication in seventeenth-century precedents. Worsdale was rigorous, purist and technical and, if Lilly was the best seventeenth-century authority for Sibly, Worsdale looked to Partridge. For Worsdale, astrology's salvation lay in the implementation of strict Ptolemaic principles in line with a framework of Aristotelian influences and Newtonian mathematical rigour. He was equally hostile both to any attempts to develop an empirically based astrology in the style of Kepler, which would have meant abandoning tradition, and to the 'wretched compilations of borrowed and stolen trash' he saw in Sibly's works.[19] Yet he did believe that the testing of horoscopes in relation to events in individuals' lives could indicate which techniques worked and which didn't. 'I have tried all the rules,' he wrote, 'both ancient and modern, in an impartial manner, that have been published.'[20] Worsdale's main achievement, by his own account, was the development of a new system of rectification, by which, it was believed, a more accurate time of birth could be calculated by retrospectively matching events in a person's life with their horoscope, and his overriding interest was in the prediction of death. And death itself, he knew well enough, might result from any one of a series of possible accidents, providing him with a wealth of fascinating material. In one delineation, he observed that 'at the age of twenty-seven year the life of the Native was in imminent danger from a lingering illness, which continued upwards of sixth months. She also suffered much injury by a fall from a Horse. The ascendant was then directly opposite of Saturn.'[21] There is no indication here of the inner life; it is almost as if Ficino had never lived. There is nothing remotely artistic about this astrology, nor even anything occult. It is concerned with the infolding of the clockwork universe, with the matching of precisely measurable events with observable planetary motions. This does, of course, evoke the spirit of Kepler, but really positions Worsdale as a child of Enlightenment secularism. Romanticism was to be the dominant vehicle for a return to the magic of the universe, but Enlightenment values were to have a profound effect on a certain sort of astrological thought, particularly the notion that astrology, or at least parts of it, could be 'proved'. We can also see traces of pessimistic classical stoicism in Worsdale's language. His language was pervaded with an almost Calvinist sense of despair at humanity's condition. In one judgement he concluded that:

> These positions and violent motions of the Stars, combined with the evil stations of the Satellites of the Luminaries, will . . . always produce sorrows, and many difficulties, with various calamities during the whole period of the Native's Life; and I shall further observe, that in all Genitures . . . where such hostile positions, and configurations as the above are discovered, those persons will be subject to contempt, and reproach; innumerable troubles, and losses, with dangers to Life will surround them, and in the end they will always descend below the sphere of Life in which they were Born.[22]

Worsdale did indeed appear to have had misanthropic tendencies. He was obliged to earn a living casting horoscopes, and most of his clients would have been highly parochial – the rural middle class of Lincolnshire. Yet, he raged against such people as vulgar, illiterate and completely incapable of understanding the celestial mysteries. His punishment was to enter local folklore as 'the Lincolnshire wiseman or astronomer', forever accompanied, like a witch, by a familiar spirit such as a blackbird or black cat.

Even though evangelists such as Sibly and Worsdale were keen to restore what they saw as the true teachings of the past, they tended to welcome astronomical innovation. Both men, each in their own way, had to adjust to the most substantial additions to the heavens since Galileo spotted Jupiter's moons in 1609. In 1781 the astronomer – and professional musician – William Herschel discovered

Uranus, the first body to be added to the list of known planets since historical records began. This was an inspirational moment in astronomy which showed for the first time that the solar system was considerably larger than previously thought. Twenty years later, on 1 January 1801, Guiseppe Piazzi, working in Palemero, discovered Ceres. The latter, together with a series of other small bodies which were spotted over the succeeding years, were later reclassified as 'asteroids' but, in the 1800s, their existence destroyed the ancient symmetry, part of the very foundation of astrology's interpretative structure, in which the sun and moon ruled one zodiac sign each, and the other five planets each took charge of two. It was now not just the physical and metaphysical models that underpinned classical astrology which had been challenged but the traditional rationale for the technical procedures according to which horoscopes were analysed which were undermined. Modernism was confronting practices which dated back to the last centuries BCE. Faced with this challenge, Worsdale took the scientific point of view, concerned with the evidence. 'There has been much contention among many who pretend to calculate Nativities,' he wrote, 'concerning the power of the Georgian Planet [Uranus] and the other four, which have been recently discovered, I have omitted them in all my computations, being convinced that we have not had any Examples sufficient to prove the existence of their power.'[23]

Ceres and the asteroids were dropped from astrological practice by the middle of the nineteenth century, making a reappearance only in the 1980s, but Uranus became established as a regular feature of horoscopic work, initially as an evil influence. One story of its early use concerns a shocking incident in the life of John Varley (1778–1842), the noted water-colourist and close friend and confidant of William Blake.[24] It was in Varley's house that Blake drew his famous visionary heads, related to the types of the zodiac signs. Some of these were less than traditional; Blake's Geminian icon was a chained flea with a human head. Varley himself wrote about the origins of the zodiac and the shifts in religious forms as the stars and zodiac signs moved over the spring equinox.[25] The stars as well as the sun changed their religious forms as the process developed. Spica, for example, became Io (a mythical Greek priestess of Hera who was seduced by Zeus) when in the sign Gemini; Levi, the father of the Jewish priesthood, when in Cancer; Apollo when in Leo; and so on. Returning to the new planet, on the day in question, 21 June 1825, Varley had worked out that at a few minutes before noon precisely, Uranus would make a particularly risky aspect to his own birth chart. At 11 a.m., Varley called his son, Albert, to his studio in London, and asked him to take his pocket watch to the watchmakers to have it set for exact Greenwich time, all the better to observe the planet's significance. When Albert returned from his errand, Varley shared his concerns. The Uranian alignment was approaching, but its effects, while thought to be dangerous, were not yet properly understood, and Varley could not tell whether its impact would be on him personally, or on his property. He had taken precautions, cancelling his morning appointments and staying indoors, but was still concerned. As the scheduled time approached, Varley began to think he may have been mistaken.

But, as he sat down at his desk to reconsider his calculations he heard a cry of 'fire' from outside. Varley and his son ran outside to find that it was their own house which was on fire and, to his delight, his home and most of his property – which was uninsured – was destroyed. As an insight into the astrological mentality or, at least, Varley's version of it, this anecdote is unparalleled. Everything on the earth, including one's life and material possessions, is tied to the stars with an absolutely mathematical precision. This was good, traditional Stoicism, filtered through eighteenth-century Newtonianism. But the subtleties by which classical, medieval and Renaissance thinkers had preserved free will within a deterministic cosmos were being lost, but not completely. After all, Varley assumed that the event signified by the progress of Uranus through his birth chart was determined to the nearest minute but he still had the ability to calculate and predict the future, and to respond to it when it happened. Whereas once freedom lay in the active soul's capacity to contact the divine, astrology was entering a period in which the engagement between individual and planets went no further than the adage that the stars incline but do not compel. In the absence of Neoplatonic concepts of the higher and lower soul, one above the stars, the other below them, there was no longer any credible idea either of how the stars incline or, if they did, how people can respond to such inclinations. The first wave of astrological publishing in the early part of the century was concerned with technical education devoid of any real philosophical context.

Whatever the philosophical problems astrology encountered, the publishing record does indicate an ongoing demand for astrological texts. In England, James Wilson's *Complete Dictionary of Astrology* appeared in 1819, followed in 1820 by a volume of tables for horoscope calculation and, in 1822, by J.M Ashmand's translation of Proclus's fifth-century *Paraphrase of Ptolemy's Tetrabiblos*. Varley himself published his *Treatise on Zodiacal Physiognomy* in 1828, combining astrology with his interest in phrenology, the theory that the shape of the skull was a clue to character. By the 1820s there was clearly a circle of educated men interested in reviving the practice of astrology in all the technical sophistication it had possessed a century and a half earlier. There was a problem, of course. If the revivalists ever thought that they were rediscovering a singly body of knowledge, they were to be disappointed. It could hardly be otherwise, for seventeenth-century astrology had no single philosophy or set of rules. From Fludd's Rosicrucianism to Lilly's combination of medieval technique with self-promotion, and Kepler's pared-down, reformed, planetology, there was no united voice. The pioneers of the 1780s to 1820s had to revive a discipline that came in different forms, all of them now without an accepted coherent astronomical or philosophical rationale. Plato was still the great classical philosopher, but his divine, living universe had no more relevance to the new world of the astronomers than did Aristotle's system of celestial causes and influences, or the Hermetic world of sympathies and correspondences.

Into this world strode two English astrologers of remarkable energy and enthusiasm who, between them, succeeded in establishing a new public presence for astrology beyond the almanacs. Both assumed angelic pseudonyms, one Raphael (1795–1832), the other Zadkiel.[26] Raphael was born Robert Cross Smith in March 1794, to respectable parents in Abbots Leigh, a village near Bristol. In 1824, after moving to London and finding work as a journalist, he became the editor of *The Straggling Astrologer*, a weekly periodical that included astrology with articles on magic, dream interpretation and clairvoyance very much in the style of a modern news-stand magazine such as the English *Prediction*. When *The Straggling Astrologer* folded after 22 issues, Smith combined them in a single volume, *The Astrologer of the Nineteenth Century*, with the elaborate subtitle, 'The Master Key to Futurity, and Guide to Ancient Mysteries, being a complete system of occult philosophy', for the first time using his angelic pseudonym, Raphael. In keeping with the Gothic revivalism of the times, and in order to project a greater degree of gravitas, Smith adopted the portentous Arthurian title Merlinus Anglicus Jun – England's Junior Merlin. *The Astrologer of the Nineteenth Century* contained a good deal of astrology along with other snippets of 'occult philosophy', from descriptions of such famous horoscopes as those of Napoleon Bonaparte and Lord Byron to predictions regarding the effects of Saturn's transit of Gemini. The didactic principles of the seventeenth-century almanac makers were continued and over 30 pages were devoted later in the book to teaching any aspiring student of astrology the rudiments of the art.

However, commercial failure undermined Raphael's next venture, another magazine launched in 1825 under the title *Urania, or The Astrologer's Chronicle, and Mystical Magazine*. Undaunted, he found a successful formula the next year when he launched a third magazine, *The Prophetic Messenger*. This time he abandoned his attempt to secure a mass readership by including topics which he thought might have a wider interest than astrology and, instead, hit upon a way of giving astrology itself a mass appeal. He included forecasts for every day of the coming year, in the style of medieval *lunaria*, giving astrology a personal appeal which it had previously lacked. The idea was not new – since the sixteenth-century, almanacs had highlighted good and bad days for particular activities, from travelling to getting married or having one's hair cut. However, Raphael presented the system in a new format providing a simple paragraph for every day. He satisfied what Curry has called the search for 'stronger meat' among those of the burgeoning middle classes who hungered for complex ways in which to understand or enrich their lives, but who were not so learned that they subscribed passively to religious and scientific dogma that esoteric truths were, in fact, false.[27] The formula proved a marketing masterstroke and ended Raphael's run of bad luck; *The Prophetic Messenger* survives today as *Raphael's Almanac* and its derivatives flourish as the horoscope columns in newspapers and women's magazines.

Buoyed up by this success, Raphael published his enduring contribution to astrology, a textbook titled, simply, *A Manual of Astrology*, in 1828. This was notable for the story of two remarkable time-twins, King George III and a certain Mr Samuel Hemmings. According to Raphael, Hemmings and George III were both born on the same day, Hemmings went into business in October 1760, the month when George succeeded to the throne. Both men then married on 8 September 1761 and died on 29 January 1829. For Raphael, this was anecdotal evidence of the traditional view that the heavens indicated tendencies that are then expressed through individual circumstances; as a timing measure, he believed, planetary cycles can be exact to the day but their manifestation varies with circumstances. When Smith died, both his name and *The Prophetic Messenger* were assumed by a series of men who continued the almanac in its original spirit. The last well-known Raphael, Robert T. Cross (1850–1923), brought circulation to around 100,000 copies – evidence both of enduring and substantial popular interest in astrology and the success of Smith's original formula.

Raphael's colleague Zadkiel was also born in 1795. Both men came of age once Sibly and Worsdale had attracted attention to the old astrology but Zadkiel survived longer – he died in 1874 – and so his attempts to popularize astrology were more successful. Born Richard James Morrison to a genteel north London family, Zadkiel had entered the navy at the age of 11. After he retired he retained his rank (he was always known as Commander Morrison) and began to study astrology. Inspired by Raphael and brimming with evangelical fervour, he launched *The Herald of Astrology*, a cheaper rival to *The Prophetic Messenger*, which was better known under its later name, *Zadkiel's Almanac.* He published a number of astrological textbooks in the ensuing years as well as developing a private practice. He attempted to establish several different societies that obliquely or overtly intended to study astrology, but all of them folded through lack of support. Astrologers were continuing to be prosecuted under the Vagrancy Act, but Zadkiel remained convinced of astrology's validity and soon the Act's repeal became an equally passionate pursuit. He boldly attempted to secure sponsorship from Members of Parliament for a bill to revise the Act, and attempted, through the contacts he made, to form the 'Wellington Telescope Company' with the support of two other peers. All of these efforts were unsuccessful, perhaps to some degree because of Zadkiel's blunt nature, but also because society's objections to astrology were firmly entrenched. Zadkiel's view was that astrology was a science waiting to be proved and, once the evidence had been presented, he was certain that it would receive acceptance not just from the masses who bought and read almanacs but among the educated elite. One of his vehicles was the Astro-Meteorologial Society, which he hoped would provide such proof, but never really functioned; Zadkiel had little idea of how to conduct the required research and had few supporters. After the society folded, his protégé, Christopher Cooke, described its hopeful purpose:

> The permanent establishment of the Astro-Meteorologial Society would have been the means of introducing and of popularizing astrological facts, by means of deductive reasoning, in a clear, positive, and satisfactory manner; because it would have been proved that the planets affected the earth according to their angular positions; and then their influences upon its inhabitants might have been shown in a similar manner, giving a tangible reason for the 'horoscope'. Astrology would cease to be treated as a superstition, for it would be proved to be 'a scientific art', namely experience reasoned upon and

then brought under general principles, and distinguished from merely accumulated experience, which is simply *empiricism*.[28]

Zadkiel's programme was a political one, intended to re-educate intelligent people who had, he believed, abandoned a way of looking at the universe which was self-evidently true. His greatest chance for notoriety and the public attention he craved, however, arrived in a fashion even he could not have foreseen. In his almanac for the year 1861, he posted a prediction for the full moon of March. He wrote:

> The stationary position of Saturn in the third degree of Virgo in May, following upon this lunation, will be very evil for all persons born on or near the 26th of August; among the sufferers I regret to see the worthy Prince Consort of these realms. Let such persons pay scrupulous attention to health.[29]

Albert, the Prince Consort and Queen Victoria's beloved husband, died suddenly in December 1861. At first, few people noticed the coincidence of Zadkiel's prediction. However, a certain Alderman Humpherey commented upon the prediction in court, and the result was a huge fuss in the press. All of London's regular newspapers attacked Zadkiel as if his prediction had actually caused the prince's death, and generally condemned astrology as outrageous. Calls were made for Zadkiel's identity to be revealed so that he could be prosecuted under the Vagrancy Act. A few months later a letter was published in the *Daily Telegraph* giving details of Zadkiel's naval career, relating an incident in which he had used a crystal ball and accusing him of outright fraud and financial impropriety.

Zadkiel was furious. After establishing that the author of the letter was a certain Rear Admiral Sir Edward Belcher, he took him to court for libel. As the trial proceeded, astrology became less of an issue than allegations of impropriety during Zadkiel's crystal-gazing sessions. The case centred on the facts of the crystal-gazing, but included a fair amount of mockery of astrology. The judge attacked belief in astrology – and all occult arts – in his summing up. The very fact that Zadkiel believed in astrology was taken as damning evidence, implying that he was essentially fraudulent. While the jury eventually found in his favour, the award was a derisory 20 shillings, reflecting the court's overall contempt for Zadkiel and his injured dignity. The resilient astrologer never abandoned his attempts to prevent further prosecutions by reforming the Vagrancy Act, although he increasingly shunned public appearances and concentrated his energies on the ever more successful *Almanac* until his death in 1874.

Like the most prominent of the seventeenth-century almanac makers, Raphael and Zadkiel combined high aspirations, including a didactic need to educate and inform the bourgeois and artisan classes about the true, meaningful nature of the cosmos and truth of ancient wisdom with the commercial reality that, unless their work sold, they would be out of work. Like Lilly and his colleagues, they crossed the boundary between middling and low astrology. The latter continued to flourish throughout the nineteenth century, appealing to very much the same constituency as modern sun-sign columns, the mass of people who had no vested interest in the orthodoxies of Enlightenment secularism. Some almanacs declined in sales, others rose, but the overall picture was healthy. *Old Moore's Almanac*, the largest selling publication of its kind, sold 362,449 copies in 1801, a figure which dwindled to 50,000 in 1895 and 16,000 in the 1920s. This decline was more than offset by the launch of a cheaper version, *Old Moore's Penny Almanak*, which had been founded in 1842 and of which over a million were printed in 1898. *Raphael's Almanac* and *Zadkiel's Almanac*, which contained more detailed general astrological forecasts than *Old Moore's*, sold around 300,000 in 1898, suggesting continuing high demand.[30] Amongst rural communities, which have been little studied, traditions of lunar influence on illness and misfortune, combined with magical remedies, continued unchallenged, but for the aspiring judicial astrologer a move to the town was a commercial necessity. The astrologer Philip Wood, who died in 1855, moved from the small English village of Painswick to the slightly larger town of Stroud, where he blitzed the population with leaflets, advertised in the local papers and set up a sign with 'Philip Wood astrologer' on one side, surrounded by the sun and moon, and seven stars on the other.[31] We are not told whether his efforts were successful: even in the twenty-first century it is difficult, if not impossible, to make a living as an astrologer in the average small English town. In 1894 the *Spectator* magazine commented that 'it seems strange that the astrologers should live in towns like Bristol, and not on the "blasted heaths" on top of Mendip, but such is the fact'.[32] Away from the world of rural folk-beliefs, cunning folk and fortune-tellers, astrology remained a pursuit for the erudite – or semi-erudite – of the towns. Its complexity appealed, apparently, to those in the more complicated social and economic environment of urban life.

The revival of astrological practice in the nineteenth century was gradual but unmistakable, but there was no one single narrative, so consensus on where astrology should be positioned in the West's intellectual life as a whole, beyond, perhaps, the hubristic conviction that it should be central to all science and religion. Ancient teachings were filtered through modern eyes, and Romantic sensibilities, in which there was a desire to reconnect with the cosmos, competed with Enlightenment mentalities that required an objective distance from the evidence and, hopefully, convincing proof of astrology's efficacy. We may identify four types of astrologer, depending on ideological inclination: the first yearned to be accepted as a scientist; a second had a more religious approach, believing that astrology revealed the perfect cosmos of the 'Creator'; the third was most interested in establishing occult knowledge of the world of spirits or the future; and the fourth were the cunning folk for whom such items of traditional know-ledge as moon-lore were a part of traditional herbal practice.[33] To these four, we will add, at the end of the century, those for whom astrology was to be a matter of self-understanding and spiritual growth.

15

The Nineteenth Century: Magicians and Sociologists

*Behind the veil of all the hieratic and mystical allegories of ancient
doctrines . . . are found indications of a doctrine which is everywhere the
same and everywhere carefully concealed.*

ELIPHAS LÉVI[1]

The astrology of the nineteenth-century English pioneers was essentially concerned with practice rather than theoretical speculation – high astrology had not re-appeared along with its middling cousin – and the philosophical world was following its own trajectory. The situation was similar in the USA, where Luke Broughton (1828–98) provided very much the same function as did Zadkiel in the UK, including providing a running astrological commentary on the American Civil War. It was to France, following from the 'illuminism' and esoteric Masonry of the eighteenth century, that we must look for a concern with magical and philosophical applications of cosmology, as well as the most successful application of the Newtonians' belief in the absolute sway of universal forces. These speculative developments in France took two forms, one which emphasized a heightened form of magical practice and which was to link with the arts, the other which regarded itself as scientific and attempted to fulfil the Newtonian programme, in which all human life would be explained by reference to celestial laws.

Among the Newtonians, political Platonism, in which the state was to be made more efficient by being closely tied to a mathematically ordered cosmos, assumed a radical new form in the work of the French radical Auguste Comte (1798–1857), the founder of sociology and one of the most significant influences on modern socialism.[2] Comte was the former secretary of Claude Henry de Rouvroy, Comte de Saint-Simon (1760–1825), the 'father' of French socialism. Saint-Simon himself was an economic determinist whose views were to be influential on Marx, and who believed in government by a meritocratic, administrative elite, and in a unified Europe. His political theory was in part a critique of the revolution of 1789, whose failure, he was convinced, was found in its excessive individualism.[3] For Saint-Simon, a successful revolution should have a corporate, collective ideology reinforced by a set of institutions which was to replace the moral and institutional theocracy that had so successfully managed the medieval state. Saint-Simonism fractured into different tendencies, one of which became a religion with its own pope. Comte took on himself the task of explaining in detail how the

Saint-Simonist state should be run by adapting the Newtonian cosmos.

The result of the Newtonization of astrology was a number of forms of dis-guised astrology which maintained the principle that the heavens form a model of life of on earth, but have no use for horoscopes. Chief among these, as Keith Thomas provocatively observed, is sociology, the study of social relationships, which has, to a large extent, replaced medieval political astrology as the principal means of understanding collective patterns and trends.[4] As such, there should be comparisons between the astrological and sociological world-views – as, indeed, there are. While it was true that Comte, no more than Mesmer, would have accepted the term astrology, his work was undoubtedly a disguised, secularized astrology in that it projected celestial law onto human life. It was, far more than a man like Boulainvilliers could have dreamt, the culmination of previously unsuccessful attempts to create a Newtonian astrology.

The foundation of sociology was laid in Comte's massive *System of Positive Polity*, first published in Paris in 1851–4, revealing it to be rooted in a deeply authoritarian version of Platonic social engineering. Comte's fundamental hypothesis was that the trinity of Kepler, Galileo and Newton had engineered a revolution in human understanding of the cosmos, but that humanity's political condition remained mired in the institutionalized superstitions of the Middle Ages, by which he meant monarchy.[5] The revolution of 1789, he argued, following Saint-Simon, had fatally wounded the old order but had failed to completely destroy it, followed as it was first by Napoleon's empire and then the restoration of the Bourbon kings. Comte believed devoutly that, through the traumas and crises of the French Revolution, the world was gradually becoming a better place and that, following the revolution of 1848, the law of progress was in its final stages. He termed the destructive revolution of 1789 the negative revolution; the coming revolution which was to institute the new era was the positive revolution. His fundamental proposition was that, if Kepler and Newton had discovered the laws of celestial motion and, if these were universal, then they must apply to all things on earth, including human behaviour and relationships. These laws, as Newton had demonstrated, were mathematical and therefore, logic dictated, the rules which governed human behaviour must be exactly the same as those which governed the heavens. People, Comte reasoned, moved in the same relation to each other as did planets. In theory, it should therefore be possible to investigate human behaviour mathematically with sufficient precision to identify the manner in which they conformed to Newtonian law. Comte's cue for this reasoning was contained within Newton's preface to the *Principia*, in which he had written, 'I wish we could derive the rest of the phaenomena of nature by the same kind of reasoning from mechanical principles,' but concluded that this was not possible within the current state of knowledge.[6] Pierre Laplace shared Newton's aspiration to describe the entire universe with one set of laws in what J.T. Merz called the 'astronomical view of nature'.[7] This was the context within which Comte was working when he set out to complete Newton's plan, to explain, if not all of nature, at least human behaviour, according to celestial mechanics.

Comte called his science sociology, and its central law, the mathematical science by which the coming era should be governed, was positivism. As adapted by Comte's successors, positivism then came to mean the belief that only science, however defined, has the ability or right to answer any question about human life: all other forms of inquiry are illegitimate. Comte, who was, in effect, founding a Newtonian religion, would have agreed absolutely. In practice, everything in Comte's positivist sociology was subordinated to the quasi-religious prophecy that society, governed by the law of development through three phases, was about to enter a communist new age characterized by industrialization in the economy, a form of limited democracy in politics and justice and morality in human behaviour. In practice he advocated rule by experts, in other words, by sociologists, who would interpret and determine the common good. This was, in short, a secular version of Saint-Martin's theocracy of divine commissioners. Any ideas that conflicted with the march of progress, including, ironically, astrology, were regarded as outmoded, old-fashioned and replaced by the march of progress to the Comtean multicultural new age. Comte's religious inclinations, inherited from Saint-Simon and revealed in the subtitle to the *System of Positive Polity*, is responsible for some of the contradictions with which sociologists have grappled ever since, especially the tension between the avowed reverence for the facts on the one hand, and a devotion to theory on the other. Comte's own position was clear; like Plato, he was under no doubt that theory came first, and fact second: when the evidence was found it would support the proposition that people were subject to the same law as planets and merely indicate how human law could be changed to reflect celestial principles.

Comte was also deeply influenced by Stoicism, his purpose being to discover how to live in harmony with Necessity, instead of being dominated by it. He believed that his generation, living in the aftermath of the events of 1789, was the first to approach an understanding of this great deterministic force. He was convinced that for the first time in history human beings were in a position to affect the future. Yet the irreconcilable paradox between human liberty and economic survival, or between Freedom and Necessity in the Platonic jargon, remained, for the simple reason that economic development could only be altered once its laws had been studied and, paradoxically, in view of his emphasis on liberty, obeyed.[8] Ironically Comte failed to recognize the similarity between his theories and their Stoic, Platonic, Hermetic and Babylonian antecedents. This was precisely because he believed that such belief systems were now thoroughly discredited and subject not to historical investigation but caricature. In the *System of Positive Polity* he wrote confidently that 'those who look into the future of society will feel that the conception of man becoming, without fear, or boast, the arbiter, within certain limits, of his own destiny, has in it something far more satisfying than the old belief in Providence, which implied our remaining passive'.[9] The truth was that, from the namburbi rituals of the ancient Sumerians down to the natural astral magic of Marsilio Ficino, the ancient belief in a cosmically ordered necessity had required active human participation. This was not an optional add-on to astrological forecasting but an essential feature of astrological engagement with the cosmos in medieval and Renaissance Europe. By devaluing the past, Comte was unable to accept that his ideas owed any genuine debt to ancient beliefs. And, with his unshakeable belief in progress he was bound to argue that he and his theories were automatically superior to all earlier ideas; everything modern was better than all that was old.

Comte's apocalyptic belief in the coming revolution and resulting utopia places him firmly in the European millenarian tradition which, seeking inspiration in the New Testament Book of Revelation, had long anticipated an imminent release from worldly oppression. Economic determinism conferred a modern gloss on Comte's millenarianism and in keeping with many other early-nineteenth-century progress theorists, he believed that successive modes of economic production provided a focus for political development, which progressed inexorably towards its culmination in communism. His world-view was fundamentally materialistic, for he held that action preceded thought, and his goal was material prosperity for all. He believed absolutely that the astronomical laws devised by Kepler, Galileo and Newton should be applied to social development, and that the universe was to be studied not for its own sake but in the service of humanity. Physical relationships between the planets should be a suitable model for the relationships between people. His determinism, in this sense, was qualified by his belief that only the solar system and cosmos are absolutely unchangeable. Social trends, while broadly predetermined, are therefore open to human intervention.[10]

The methodological problems involved in correlating human behaviour with celestial phenomena are considerable, so the link has been assumed more often than actually demonstrated. After making the initial comparison between social and astronomical laws, sociologists have therefore generally confined themselves to the more immediate comparisons between human behaviour and biological laws, returning to Plato's argument in the *Republic* that the state could be explained by human gestation and growth. The German sociologist Max Weber expressed a common view when he wrote that 'Human mortality, indeed the organic life cycle from the helplessness of infancy to that of old age, is naturally of the very greatest importance through the various ways in which human action has oriented to these facts.'[11] The universal implications, though, were never far away. The great English sociologist Herbert Spencer (1820–1903), whose *Social Statistics*, published in 1851, inaugurated a new attempt to establish the laws of social evolution, believed that, by collecting sufficient information about human beings and subjecting it to mathematical analysis, the truth about their relationships would be revealed: the quality of an individual life might then be understood by reference to the mathematical patterns relating to the whole.[12] The raw data, though, is nothing without human selection and interpretation, which makes for exact comparisons with the manipulation of astronomical data in judicial astrology. According to Emile Durkheim (1858–1917), who was, along with Weber, one of the twentieth century's most influential sociologists, Spencer demonstrated that 'a single law dominates the social and the physical world' while his achievement was to link 'societies more directly with the universe'.[13] And, for Max Weber, the purpose of sociology itself was to seek 'the interpretative understanding of social action in order thereby to arrive at a causal explanation of its course and effects'.[14] Spencer himself was an ardent supporter of laissez faire liberal economics, and a millenarian believer in the inevitable domination of the world by Western society. In Bowler's words, he 'shared the almost teleological view of those historians who saw modernism as the product of an inexorable social trend'.[15] Through Comte and Spencer, Modernism emerged as an ideology of those who believed that history had come to an end, through Newton's discovery of the final laws of the universe, and that they were the guardians of a new order whose duty was to express these laws. They were not esoteric secularists, in Hanegraaff's phrase, but militant, materialist secularists. Yet, in their own way, they shared the modern New Agers' naïve faith in the future.

After Comte, sociologists abandoned all mention of astronomy as the justification for their study, but Comte had set out the Newtonian philosophy which they were obliged to follow, whether they knew it or not. Yet, as it developed, the language of sociology continued to draw on Newtonian principles. For example, according to Wilbert Moore, writing in the 1970s:

> Human acts, groups, rules of conduct and goods or values are interrelated, not isolated and autonomous variables. The interrelationships constitute the major data for meaningful description or analysis of social systems. They underlie so-called functional analysis, which asks the systematic consequences of given patterns of action. By their predictability, their persistence, they constitute a major source of order, of reliability in social affairs, that makes life tolerable if not wholly without risk and uncertainty. The establishment of the relationships among social phenomena, the attempt to achieve precision in concepts for elements and processes and to achieve precision in measuring the degree of predictability from one set of variables to another . . . [are among] the major concerns of contemporary sociology.[16]

The direct debt owed to the Keplerian–Galilean–Newtonian cosmic state by the new politics of the left is clear: somewhere out there, there is a great universal law by which individual human insecurities, uncertainties and inequalities may be resolved. People, for Durkheim, as for Hobbes, were like the planets of the new astronomy and, stripped of their mystery and deprived of their souls, their relationships could be reduced to mathematical formulae. A serious, and dangerous problem arises, though, when human belief or behaviour fails to conform to the Comtean expectation. As Max Weber wrote, in a passage which would almost have slipped unnoticed into Plato's *Republic*, 'For the purposes of typological analysis, it is convenient to treat all irrational, effectively determined elements of behaviour as factors of deviation from a conceptually pure type of rational action.'[17] Behaviour disapproved of in the Comtean cosmos is considered predetermined (subject to Fate or Necessity in Hermetic language), and deviant.

The intellectual milieu established by Newtonianism, in which astronomy provided an overall framework for the understanding of human relationships, allowed the continuing study of natural astrology, even if that word was not used, in the limited form of the investigation of seasonal and diurnal effects on human behaviour, questioning whether human character alters depending on the earth's orientation to the sun. The Belgian sociologist and astronomer Adolphe Quetelet (1796–1874), who founded the Royal Observatory of Belgium, produced one of the pioneering studies, *Sur l'homme et le développement de ses facultés, ou Essai de physique sociale*, in 1835.[18] Quetelet moved from the mere collection of facts to the formulation of a social science based on laws, and cautiously concluded that there are seasonal influences on human character. In studying the frequency of births he found a peak before midnight and midday, implying a solar effect on the combined physiology of mother and baby. Quetelet's concern was with the average man who conformed, he believed, to the mathematical mean in his behaviour. Criminals (criminology was another of Quetelet's interests) are therefore people who deviate from the cosmically sanctioned order.

Comte's achievement was to take political Platonism in a new direction by allying it with materialist Newtonianism. Comtean astrology, like Mesmerism, was disguised. It sought to regulate human life by reference to celestial law, but rejected any use of the term astrology, which was linked to the supposedly superstitious and discredited practice of reading horoscopes. Astrological it undoubtedly was, though. To make the point, here is the first part of the definition of astrology proposed around 1900 by Alan Leo, the most influential astrologer in the English-speaking world in the early twentieth century: 'The science which defines the action of celestial bodies upon human character, and its expression in the physical world.'[19]

Leo went on to define astrology in esoteric terms as the 'soul' of astronomy, which would have made perfect sense to the second group of thinkers, those who, inheriting the mantle of eighteenth-century Illuminism, had begun to formulate a philosophical context for modern astrology as magic. Auguste Comte's sociology represented the application of the mechanical strand of Newtonian thought to the problem, which Bodin and Kepler had tackled, of the efficient ordering of society. A parallel manifestation of astrological thinking was overtly magical and was heir to the tradition of Cornelius Agrippa, John Dee and Robert Fludd. And, again, the philosophical focus was in France, where the mantle of Pernety and Pasqually was inherited by Eliphas Lévi (1810–75).[20] Lévi, whose real name was Alphonse Louis Constant, was the son of a shoemaker, sharing the artisan background of so many self-taught esotericists, and had been training to enter the Catholic priesthood when he fell in love, left his seminary and found a more satisfying way of expressing his religious instincts. He wrote a number of minor works, including *Des Moeurs et des Doctrines du Rationalisme en France* (*Of the Moral Customs and Doctrines of Rationalism in France*), which appeared in 1839, and, in 1844, *La Mère de Dieu*. Two radical tracts, *L'Evangile du Peuple* (*The Gospel of the People*) and *Le Testament de la Liberté* (*The Testament of Liberty*), followed, the first in 1840 and the second in 1848, the year of revolution, earning him a brief prison sentence. Lévi's radicalism is indicative of an emerging role which esotericism was to fulfil. It was to provide an alternative for those who rejected both the religious and political status quo but were socially or temperamentally unsuited to the emerging world of revolutionary socialism. It was in 1848, the year that Lévi went to prison, that the bourgeois revolutions failed and the young Karl Marx published *The Communist Manifesto*, the new revolutionary call to arms. In 1854 Lévi visited England where he met the distinguished novelist and minor aristocratic politician Edward Bulwer-Lytton. Aside from his literary and political involvements (four years later he was appointed Secretary of State for the Colonies in the Conservative government, alongside his friend Benjamin Disraeli), Bulwer-Lytton had a deep interest in the occult. He and Lévi discussed the writing of a new treatise on magic for the modern age, which they both felt was necessary. This appeared in 1855 under the title *Dogme at Rituel de la Haute Magic*, although an English translation had to wait until 1896. The beginning of organized and popular interest in spiritualism, which had until then been a rather refined affair confined to Swedenborgians and other religious groups, provided a receptive atmosphere for Lévi's books. After all, if Lévi was drawing back the veil – an increasingly common metaphor – on the world beyond then that world undoubtedly contained the souls of the dead as much as angels and planetary powers.

> Behind the veil of all the hieratic and mystical allegories of ancient doctrines, behind the darkness and strange ordeals of all initiations, under the seal of all sacred writings, in the ruins of Nineveh or Thebes, on the crumbling stones of old temples and on the blackened visage of the Assyrian or Egyptian sphinx, in the monstrous or marvellous paintings which interpret to the faithful of India the inspired pages of the Vedas, in the cryptic emblems of our old books on alchemy, in the ceremonies practised at reception by all secret societies, there are found indications of a doctrine which is everywhere the same and everywhere carefully concealed.[21]

Lévi's sentiments were seductive. He offered to reveal, as esotericists had since Ficino, the original true religion, which everyone shares. He promised an end to schisms, dogma and the lies and rivalries of orthodox religion. To make a comparison with political developments, his vision of a single truth was profound for his followers as was that of Marx for his disciples. It was to find echoes in the writings of the Romantic poet Gerard de Nerval (1808–55). 'They shall return,' he wrote, 'these Gods whom you mourn! Time will bring back the order of ancient days; the earth has quivered with a prophetic gust.'[22] We might imagine that Lévi's invocation of the distant past was somehow at odds with the soon-to-emerge world of Modernism, a sort of last gasp of anti-modernity, were it not for the importance of notions of lost and hidden truths to the whole Modernist project. Lévi's astrology was embedded, even more than Ebenezer Sibly's, in the medieval system of magical relationships by which nature's secrets could be penetrated and manipulated. Lévi, following in the tradition of the esoteric Masons and illuminists of eighteenth-century France, advocated practical magic in the style of Agrippa and the Picatrix, while Sibly was content with the sympathetic variety, gently manipulating the cosmos through Culpeper's herbal medicine. The difference between the two opened a fault line which has continued to the present day, between small, secretive magical groups and a wider public world of organized astrological schools and societies. While some individuals move between the two, on the collective level, they regard each other with bemusement or superstition. Those engaged in magic tend to regard the casting and reading of horoscopes for character analysis or prediction as a passive, and therefore inferior, practice. Typical was the opinion expressed by the Marquis Stanislas de Guaita, a leading member of the Paris-based 'Cabalistic Order of the Rosy Cross', in the 1880s. 'I do not believe in astrology,' he wrote, 'though I do believe completely in the possible virtue of talismans,' he continued, ignoring the fact that the rules for constructing talismans are astrological.[23] This was essentially the position Pico della Mirandola had taken almost 400 years earlier.

In 1861 Lévi followed the *Dogme at Rituel de la Haute Magic* with *La Clef des Grands Mystères*. Other books with similar themes followed, all designed to satisfy a public hunger. *Fables et Symbols* was published in 1862, *La Science des Esprits* in 1865 and *Le Grand Arcane, ou l'Occultisme Dévoilé* – occultism unveiled – was written in 1868 but published posthumously 30 years later.

The magical, alchemical and Kabbalistic theories which Lévi advocated so enthusiastically were promoted by other astrologers such as Jean-Baptiste Pitois, who adopted the pseudonym Paul Christian. Christian was a Jacobin by inclination, involved in left-wing politics as editor of the *Moniteur Parisien*, when he met Levi in 1852. Christian published his first text, a work on 'onomantic, cabbalistic' astrology, titled the *Carmen Sybillum*, in 1854.[24] Two years later a prediction he made in the book was interpreted as a forecast of the birth of a son and heir to Napoleon III and his wife, Eugenie. And he began his life as a high-society astrologer, cabbalist and tarot reader.

The theories also pervaded the literature of the time. A new French translation of Swedenborg's works had already appeared in 1820 and an exposition of his theories of spiritual ascent to the heavens was included in Balzac's 1835 novel *Séraphita*. The Séraphita of the title is an other-worldly character whose function is to teach the virtues of heavenly as opposed to earthly love, and who eventually ascended to heaven – to become a seraph. At this point the single spiritual unity of the cosmos is revealed to the story's leading characters. 'Your invisible moral universe and your visible physical universe are one and the same matter,' he wrote.[25] This is not to say that Balzac had any interest in astrology. What's important is the reinforcement of a culture, through popular literature, in which the assumption of such possibilities as spiritual contact with other planets is assumed. It does not even matter whether such ideas are intended as mere literary devices. It is precisely through such means that mythic truths are propagated. The novelist Victor Hugo (1802–65) went further than Balzac and apparently believed himself to be endowed with occult powers, at least for a time.[26] He became actively involved in spiritualism, holding regular séances for many years, often using his son Charles as a medium. Having made contact with his daughter, who had died in 1843, he then, on the auspicious date of Friday, 13 January 1854, made contact with Shakespeare with whom he developed a close relationship. Shakespeare, Hugo believed began dictating verses to him, as did the spirits of Aeschylus and Molière. The poet Arthur Rimbaud (1854–91) delved further into the mysteries than even Hugo. Driven by his reading of magical, alchemical and Kabbalistic works, Rimbaud reasoned that it was not enough just to communicate with spirits. It was necessary for the poet to go through the initiatory process of the true magician, achieving oneness with the absolute through self-annihilation and becoming an illuminé. In the alchemical heart of self-transformation, the initiate would contact the Gnostic source within: 'I lived,' he wrote 'a golden spark in the light of nature,'[27] Like a medieval Realist, he believed that words should have the quality of the things they expressed, and for this a new poetic, alchemical language must be forged. But this could only come from the state of deranged madness, achieved partly by large quantities of absinthe and hashish, which would blur the boundaries between the real and unreal. 'The Poet,' Rimbaud wrote, 'makes himself a seer by a long and gigantic derangement of all the senses. All forms of love, suffering and madness.'[28] Rimbaud took the Romantic image of the artist as a sensitive, suffering soul, perfected by Shelley, Byron and Coleridge, and converted it into the mad hysteria which, through a lineage that stretched from the surrealist painters to the beat poets of the 1950s, entered mass culture in the psychedelic rock music of the 1960s. And this was a moment when astrology and all forms of mystical cosmology achieved a new audience. The early music of Pink Floyd in the late 1960s, pieces such as 'Astronomy Domine' and 'Set the Controls for the Heart of the Sun', set the motif of the celestial journey in terms of the madness of the inner quest at the precise moment in history when, as Michael York put it, astrology became the 'lingua franca' of the New Age movement.[29]

Again, as with Balzac, it's not the presence or absence of astrology in Hugo's or Rimbaud's worlds which matters, as much as the culture which, by ignoring Enlightenment strictures against superstition, preserved a safe environment within which judicial astrology might be nurtured. As Christopher McIntosh has noticed, though, there was a problem with literary applications of the occult.[30] Alchemy, astrology, Kabbalah and spiritualism might all open the doors to the inner world but, once intellectual interest turns to direct involvement, personal experience becomes much more personal and difficult to communicate. That is why the next wave of artistic experimenters in the occult were to be painters.

In 1874, as Rimbaud's life in France was at its decadent height, and Zadkiel's in England was coming to a close, a new twist was added to the story of nineteenth-century astrology. The Reverend Archibald Henry Sayce (1846–1933), the pioneer Assyriologist and linguist, published the first translations of Babylonian astrological texts.[31] These were followed the next year by the first accounts of the *Enuma Elish*, the creation myth, followed by other tales, such as the Gilgamesh flood story and Inanna's descent to the underworld. These discoveries excited almost no interest among astrologers, even though the respect for Chaldeans as founders of the art was universal in the field. The effect on the arts, though, was immediate. Ishtar became a fascinating subject for painters, even more so after 1896 when Oscar Wilde, inspired by the French occultist and anti-realist novelist J.K. Huysmans, premiered his play *Salome*, converting Inanna's descent to the underworld through seven gates into Salome's dance of the seven veils.[32] By performing salaciously for her uncle, King Herod, Salome obtained the head of John the Baptist. From there to Mata Hari, the spy, and Theda Bara, who starred in the 1918 film of *Salome*, Inanna as the irresistible lover and destroyer of Dumuzzi was reborn as one of the most potent images of modern cinema. As Wendy Buonaventura has written, 'in the space of a few years, she [Salome] became the most popular temptress of a period obsessed by the *femme fatale*. Amateur and professional dancers, actresses, even society hostesses, all had a stab at portraying her.'[33] The astrologers may have, inexplicably, ignored the Babylonian translations, but those who followed in the wake of the Inanna myth were precisely the women who filled the consulting rooms of astrologers, fortune-tellers and spiritualists in the fin de siècle. In Britain, women even took a leading role in this process in an explicit statement of equality between the sexes, and rejection of the social status quo.[34]

The newly translated cuneiform texts' religious consequences were also profound – and a welcome surprise for Christians who were beleagured by Darwin and the atheists. The discovery of ruins mentioned in the Old Testament, and the discovery of apparently independent verification for the biblical flood myth, created an intense interest in the possibility that archaeology might verify scriptural history. The past was coming alive, verified by evidence rather than faith. Sayce himself, along with his colleagues, took this historicity along a slightly different line to the biblical scholars and adapted the belief that there was an original, single civilization into a sort of cuneiform triumphalism. At the same time the German orientalist Max Müller was recovering and translating the entire body of Indian sacred texts. Among the conclusions reached by Müller was that all early religion was sun-worship, and that all deities, whether Christ, Buddha or Krishna, were solar in nature.[35] For evidence, one can, for example, point to Christ's birthday at the winter solstice, when the sun is at its lowest, and his death at the spring equinox, when it is halfway through its journey to the longest day. Müller's theory had long been commonplace in esoteric circles but he, with the massive weight of his scholarship, gave it intellectual credibility. Müller and Sayce were not quite in agreement, even though for occultists they were providing the source material on which theories of universal ancient knowledge could be based. Without denying the antiquity of Indian culture championed by Müller, Sayce argued that Babylonian cosmology had reached its final, complete form by 4000 BCE, at which time it provided the basis for the original version of all Near Eastern religion. It was in effect the original universal religion sought by so many since Ficino. Panbabylonism, as the theory was called, was discredited by the early years of the twentieth century but, from the 1870s to 1890s, while it was still credible, the notion of an original universal religion, whether Muller's Aryan cult or Sayce's Babylonian version, was endowed with ample scholarly support. The impact on the occultists was immediate – unsurprisingly, for here was vindication of their belief in a universal ancient knowledge. And so it was that Joséphin Péladan, the ex-bank clerk who became one of the most colourful characters in Parisian occultism, renamed himself Sar Mérodack Péladan. Sar was the Assyrian word for king, and Mérodack was Marduk, the Akkadian Jupiter, the presiding deity of the Babylonian state.[36] Péladan was deliberately identifying himself with Merodach-baladan, the king of Babylon mentioned by Isaiah.[37] And with Péladan and his esoteric compatriots we enter the world of the late-nineteenth-century occult underground.

16

The Nineteenth Century:
The Theosophical Enlightenment

In the shoreless ocean of space radiates, the central, spiritual and
Invisible sun

HELENA PETROVNA BLAVATSKY[1]

On the evening of 17 November 1875, in New York, the city of migrants and seekers, a group of spiritualists, esotericists and free-thinkers gathered with a radical plan. This motley group of occultish revolutionaries had a plan – to form a revolutionary vanguard whose task was to take the entire world into its next great historical phase, a time of promised enlightenment, equality, peace and justice. These people, theosophists all, rejected the notion of violent political revolution – this was just four years after the dramatic upheavals of the Paris Commune – and argued that the way to the future was through personal spiritual enlightenment. The society's prime mover was a remarkable charismatic Russian émigré by the name of Helena Petrovna Blavatsky (1831–91).[2] Theosophy, with a small 't', meaning divine wisdom, may have been a familiar term among hermetic thinkers, who aspired to union with the cosmos since the seventeenth century, but the Theosophical Society, with a capital 'T', became one of the defining cultural movements of the late nineteenth century. Theosophy with a small 't' was, and remains, hugely influential but, as a creative force, the Theosophical Society itself came and went in the space of a little over 50 years. It still exists, but as a shell of its former self. Yet the society's revolutionary impact is central to any real understanding of the fin de siècle, the gestation of Modernism, the ideology of the counter-culture of the 1960s and the late-twentieth-century flowering of New Age and alternative spiritualities. Joscelyn Godwin has rightly, and provocatively, talked of the consequences of this gathering of all the esoteric, mystical and occult tendencies in European culture in one body of people as the 'Theosophical Enlightenment'.[3]

Blavatsky's historical purpose was in the tradition of Marsilio Ficino, and so many thinkers since – to demonstrate that all religions had a single origin and contained the same core of truth. In *Isis Unveiled* she declared her purpose: 'What we desire to prove is, that underlying every ancient popular religion was the same ancient wisdom-doctrine, one and identical, professed and practiced by the initiates of every country, who alone were aware of its existence and importance.'[4] Her colleague and collaborator, the society's President, Henry Olcott, meanwhile, set out the society's cosmological task as to reveal the true, hidden, nature of the universe and refute materialist science.[5] We need to examine this statement closely for its explicit appeal to science, secularism and 'Enlightenment values'. This is the language of Modernism. The society's political goal – to form a universal brotherhood devoted to the pursuit of truth – threw down the gauntlet to conventional society. At a time when slavery had only recently been abolished but the racist theories which justified the oppression of blacks in the deep south, the genocide of the Native Americans in the west, together with the rapidly expanding European empires, were gaining wide currency, the Theosophical Society preached a gospel of equality. There was no room for the oppression of the working class or the denial of rights to women, and the society was heir to the tradition of spiritualism as a form of radical feminist spirituality.[6] And, in her combination of egalitarian pluralism and cosmological determinism, Blavatsky was exactly in tune with the Enlightenment's confused mix of democracy and autocracy.[7] It is important to be clear about the Theosophical Society's political context precisely because it provides the foundation for understanding the place in Western culture occupied by twentieth-century 'alternative' cosmologies – and the various forms that modern astrology has taken.

Blavatsky herself was very close to one prominent British astrologer, Walter Gorn Old (1864–1929), known better under his angelic pseudonym, Sepharial, but had very little to say about astrology herself.[8] However, one passage in *Isis Unveiled* was to be as influential on the changes that were to occur in modern astrology as Plato's statement in the *Timaeus* that astrology was fine in principle but in practice was in dire need of a proper theoretical model. She claimed that:

> Astrology is a science *as infallible* as astronomy itself, with the condition, however, that its interpreters must be equally infallible; and it is this condition, *sine qua non*, so very difficult of realisation, that has always proved a stumbling block to both. Astrology is to exact astronomy what psychology is to exact physiology. In astrology and psychology one has to step beyond the visible world of matter, and enter the Platonic and Aristotelian schools, and it is not in our century of Sadducean scepticism that the former will prevail over the latter.[9]

Buried deep in Blavatsky's works, this is the key statement of New Age astrology, indeed, of most modern astrology. The influence of the Newtonian Enlightenment is apparent in the claim that science can be infallible. Astrology, as a science, is infallible but astrologers are merely human. They may aspire to infallibility but the task is a difficult one. The solution is to leave the material world behind and enter the realm of spirit. And so the foundation was laid for an astrology which downplays prediction, ignores the trivia of life and focuses instead on self-awareness and spiritual growth. That astrologers may rarely have succeeded in the second two goals does not deny the aspiration to do so. Most important, if we consider the entire historical sweep of Western astrology in Blavatsky's last sentence: theosophical astrology and its modern offshoots are, in the essence, Platonic, concerned with locating the apparently random and meaningless chaos of individual life within the orderly and purposeful unfolding of a spiritual cosmos. Blavatsky's cosmology is simple to grasp, in spite of the two hefty books and hundreds of articles she wrote about it.[10] The universe is essentially spiritual in character and the material world is essentially an illusion concealing spiritual reality. Evolution is cyclical and begins with the cosmos in a state of pure spirit. Spirit gradually condenses into matter and, as it does so, physical beings appear, including humanity. Eventually the process begins to reverse and physical forms begin to return to spirit until the entire cycle is complete. She believed that the whole universe is currently at its most corrupt, crudely physical condition and that the beginning of the return to spirit was imminent. The whole relates to one passage through the zodiac, which is why her followers labelled the coming phase, the Age of Aquarius.[11]

We can demonstrate the influence of Blavatsky's work in modern astrology, by anthropological work among astrologers. One concept which became very popular with theosophical astrologer members, and was promoted heavily by Blavatsky, was that of reincarnation, and with it, the Hindu idea of karma, which she explained grimly as 'a law of retribution'.[12] She believed that the physical body was the material vessel for a soul which had lived many times before and was struggling to evolve into a higher state of being, ultimately to reunite with the cosmos itself. As an example of the penetration of Blavatsky's ideas into modern astrology we can point to the figures for belief in reincarnation among astrologers, which vary from 64 per cent to 82 per cent in different surveys.[13]

If Blavatsky was the prophet of New Age astrology, the man who put her dreams into effect, who rejected what he condemned as the 'exoteric' or outer astrology of event prediction and created a reformed astrology of spiritual evolution, was Alan Leo (1860–1917).[14] Born William Frederick Allan, Leo, as he called himself on account of his belief that he was born with that sign rising, grew up as a member of the evangelical Plymouth Brethren. But his experience of his own poor upbringing, combined with a revulsion of the poverty he saw in the sprawling slums of England's industrial cities, was to decisively influence his metaphysics. He regarded it as fundamentally unjust that one child should be born to riches and another to gross deprivation and, after encountering theosophy, he decided, after a visionary experience at the age of 22, that karma was the only reasonable explanation.[15] Those who suffered, he concluded, must be punished for their past actions. Yet he had immense compassion for the poor precisely because it was incumbent on him, as one who had seen the truth, to work for the welfare of all. This was a task he believed he could best accomplish through promoting, reforming and teaching astrology. He made his motives clear when he wrote:

Souls come forth into manifestation to gain experience, to grow in wisdom, in love, and in power; and they can only do this by coming into practical touch with the world around them by experimenting and then learning from the results. Power is gained by the exercise of practical ability, by going out into the world and living the life of action, by doing all manner of works, some wise, many unwise, and by registering within the soul the consequences that follow from each.[16]

Leo's encounter with astrology began before he met Blavatsky. He was deeply engaged in the study of natal astrology by the age of 28, honing his skills in the spare time he found while working as chief salesman for a confectionery company. He was an evangelist who believed astrology could be the salvation of humanity and he set out to succeed where Zadkiel had failed and create an infrastructure of astrological societies and periodicals which could facilitate communication, raise standards and help humanity prepare for the coming of the Age of Aquarius. Leo had a fine commercial sense as well as a spiritual vocation. He devised the 'shilling' horoscopes, so-called because they cost a shilling. Members of the public would send in their money, along with their birth data, and Leo's staff would produce readings of their birth charts, handwritten and running to about 20 pages. It's with Leo that we enter the world of mass-produced individual horoscope readings. His purpose, though, was only partly profit. He was more concerned to draw a wider circle of individuals into the network of the faithful preparing for the Age of Aquarius, which he believed was to begin on 21 March 1928 with the appearance of the new World Teacher.[17] It was incumbent on every individual to prepare spiritually for his arrival, and the essential tool by which this noble goal might be accomplished was astrology. His societies were the astrological versions of the Blavatskyan theosophical revolutionary vanguards, which would play their part in the preparation for the coming world transformation, or so he hoped. 'I am actuated,' Leo wrote, 'by the primary motive of expressing what I believe to be the true Astrology, for the new Era that is now dawning upon the world.'[18]

Here we come to Leo's other great contribution to popular culture – his role in developing the concept of the 'sun-sign', a feature of modern life also known as the 'birth-sign' or, in downmarket media, the 'star-sign'. Leo had been particularly impressed by Blavatsky's teachings on the 'Central Spiritual Sun'. This was the old Hermetic doctrine that the cosmos has two centres; a physical earth at the centre of the physical universe and a spiritual sun at the heart of a spiritual universe. 'In the shoreless ocean of space,' Blavatsky wrote, 'radiates, the central, spiritual and *Invisible* sun,' the origin and end of the incorruptible and eternal spirit.[19] In the latter part of the nineteenth century, immediately before Leo's introduction to astrology, there was an emerging naturalistic tradition of 'solar biology', relying on the sun's location at birth to analyse individual character. Leo, though, took his evangelical commitment to the coming spiritual era to this developing form of astrology. It was in a passage in his book *The Art of Synthesis*, first published in 1904, that he set out the foundations for a technical revolution in twentieth-century astrology. He began by paraphrasing Blavatsky and then moved straight to the direct statement that the sun is the most important single feature in astrological interpretation, nothing less than the 'Solar Logos' divine reason.[20]

This single passage marked a profound shift in the technical procedures of astrological interpretation, perhaps as great a change as any since the development of the horoscope in the Hellenistic world. Given that the language of birth signs is now so familiar, we need to establish just how recent it is. Until the late nineteenth century there had been virtually no change to Claudius Ptolemy's descriptions of the zodiac signs, set out in the second century, and which had served the medieval world so well. Ptolemy had been primarily concerned with the systematic attribution of particular qualities to the signs in order to allow their use either in the analysis of individual horoscopes, or in the prediction of specific events. Aries was, for example, hot, dry, diurnal and masculine, attributes which might be applied to description of character, the diagnosis and treatment of disease or the prediction of general events for the year, but is not exactly useful to the environment of the modern counselling session.[21] Ptolemy's list of qualities was adapted and added to over the next 1400 years and appeared in English for the first time in William Lilly's 1647 *Christian Astrology*. The space given by Lilly to the signs of the zodiac was minimal compared to the attention given in many modern astrology books. In just half a page of an 832-page book Lilly outlined all that it was necessary for the astrologer to know about Aries in order to apply its qualities to matters as diverse as the diagnosis and judgement of the sick, the finding of lost objects, the outcome of battles and success in marriage. Of this section only three adjectives, 'luxurious, intemperate and violent' might apply to individual personality, although they could as easily refer to the weather, the entire nature of the times or any other matter of interest to the astrologer.[22] More important to Lilly than the nature of Arien people was the sign's rulership of 'sand and hilly grounds, a place of refuge for Theeves', associations of vital importance if one was tracing stolen property.[23] The same accounts were repeated time and again in subsequent literature. One typical nineteenth-century description of Aries was Zadkiel's in his 1849 *Grammar of Astrology*. His account of the sign was brief, but what he did include was almost entirely physical (the use of which would have been to recognize characters described in horary charts), and contained only seven words of psychological delineation. 'This sign,' he wrote, 'produces a dry, lean body, middle stature, strong limbs, large bones, long and meagre face, sharp sight, neck rather long and scraggy, dark eyebrows, swarthy complexion, hair reddish and wiry, thick shoulders; disposition, angry and violent as the ram.'[24]

In Leo's opinion, such descriptions were of no use at all if people were to prepare for the New Age, so he set out to create a zodiacal astrology which would fulfil this purpose by encouraging people to reflect on their inner character, rather than measure the extent to which they conformed to a set of externally imposed criteria. He embarked on a programme of deliberate invention without which modern astrology would be simply unrecognizable. Leo's description of Aries was typical. At almost four times the length of Zadkiel's version, Leo's completely ignored physical characteristics and set the tone for all future descriptions of the sign. Aries, he wrote, in 1903:

Represents undifferentiated consciousness. It is a chaotic and unorganised sign, in which impulse, spontaneity, and instinctiveness are marked features. Its vibrations are the keenest and most rapid, but without what may be called definite purpose, except towards impulsiveness and disruption. It signifies explosiveness, extravagance and all kinds of excess. Its influence is more directly connected with the animal kingdom, in which life is full and without the directive power of fully awakened self-consciousness.[25]

Leo had no wider cultural contacts outside of the narrow worlds of astrology, theosophy and Freemasonry within which he moved. But the unbridled optimism of his vision dovetails exactly with the utopianism which pervaded late Victorian society. It made little difference whether one was an imperialist or a social reformer, celebrating the triumph of science and technology or hoping for revolution, there was cause to look forward to the future.[26] Even though, in his own lifetime, Leo's esoteric astrology was opposed by most of his peers, it was in line with the metaphysical direction of middle-class society as a whole. Bram Dijkstra, eloquently summed up the atmosphere within which Leo was operating:[27]

> In response to the dizzying contradictions of the commonplace, intellectual mysticism became the order of the day throughout Europe. Theosophy, Rosicrucianism, millenarian philosophies, and even elaborate theories, inspired by Poe, concerning the immortality of the soul as a material entity attracted the devoted attention of the educated middle classes and artists everywhere. Man's ambition was to rise to levels of divinity never dreamt of before, and many thought these levels might be achieved by their own generation.[28]

Leo's astrology was disseminated by the Theosophical Society, which developed flourishing branches in most Western countries and published the series of textbooks in which he set out his astrological vision. Similar developments took place in other major centres, especially Germany and France, where theosophy galvanized the tradition of initiatory and magical practices inspired by Eliphas Lévi. The 1880s saw a spreading fascination for the occult, Hermeticism, Kabbalah and astrology, in what has to be seen as partly a nostalgia for a lost world when technology and the factual knowledge of science was balanced by wisdom, intuition and spiritual insight. Just when the claims of conventional science to answer all questions were becoming more insistent, there was an equal and opposite sense that it was failing to do precisely this, and that occult inquiry remained as important as ever. The novelist Jules Lermina, a convert from hardcore materialism, encapsulated the mood in his book *La Science occulte*, published in 1890: 'For some time now,' he wrote, 'there has been widespread discussion of subjects that, it must be admitted, had for a long while been relegated to a position among the most deplorable fantasies of the human mind, subjects never mentioned except as fit objects of mistrust, if not contempt, on the part of sensible people.'[29] Various establishments sprang up to satisfy the hunger for lost wisdom. Lévi had encouraged the belief that there was a genuine lineage of teachers and ideas which stretched back to ancient Egypt, Chaldea and, beyond them, the original universal religion. The 'Librairie générale des Sciences occultes' was founded in 1884, the 'Groupe independent d'Etudes ésotériques' was set up after 1890, and the 'Librairie de l'Art indépendant' soon after. The latter was founded by Edmond Bailley who began by publishing theosophical works and symbolist poetry, which may not have achieved any recognition without his sponsorship. Artists, such as the symbolist painter Gustave Moreau (1826–98), whose *Salome*, painted in 1871, inspired Oscar Wilde's play of the same name, took this esoteric-artistic subculture in imaginative directions.[30] From publishing, Bailley established a salon which attracted many of the most distinguished writers of the time, including Mallarmé, Huysmans and, later, André Gide. The network extended to other European countries; the Russian composer Alexander Scriabin (1871/2–1915) was a member of Salon d'Art Idealiste, founded by the Belgian symbolist painter, writer, and occultist, Jean Delville (1867–1953).[31] At the centre of this extraordinary world of esotericists and artists stood the astrologer Gerard Encausse (1865–1916), who played a very similar role in France to Leo in Britain, and is better known under his nom de plume, Papus. His astrology was not to have the revolutionary impact or global reach of Leo's, partly because it was neither translated nor disseminated by the Theosophical Society. Yet, it displays the Kabbalistic concern with the different levels of existence which also marked Leo's work. We read of the planet Mars that, symbolically, it represented divine honours, Kabbalistically it indicated the 'power of taste in the human constitution', esoterically it became the angel Samael, astrologically it was the 'spirit of cruelty', intellectually it symbolized enterprise and courage, physically it equated to those involved in the production of iron and steel, and physiologically it signified individuals with strong bodies and ruddy complexions.[32] For Papus the sun was, as for Leo, the central spiritual sun of Hermeticism, the great 'I Am', Osiris, Krishna, Beklus of Chaldea and Ormazd of Persia, the indicator in the birth chart of the life-force and vitality.[33] This was the astrology which circulated through the literary, artistic and esoteric circles of fin de siècle Paris. But Papus, like Leo, also had a political mission, expressed through his literary vehicle, the magazine *L'Initiation*, which was published from 1888 to 1912 with the express purpose of demonstrating to all theosophists, Kabbalists and Hermeticists that they were following a common tradition. Papus, the great unifier, aimed to bring all these people together under one banner.

Papus's concern, and his dislike of schism, was prompted partly by the tensions within the Theosophical Society between two ideological tendencies, the Eastern theosophists and their Western rivals.[34] The Easterners followed Blavatsky, whose profound distaste for institutionalized Christianity and her admiration of Indian teachings led to a devaluation of the Christian contribution to esoteric thought. The Theosophical Society, though, had attracted a large number of esoteric Christians, who emerged from a tradition which combined Boehme with Swedenborg and for whom it was the spiritual Christ rather than the historical Jesus who showed the way to salvation. The sense that there was an authentically Western esoteric tradition which had no need of Eastern teachings paralleled the difficult debate which Leo encountered in the astrological circles over theosophy. It attracted others whose concern was more with Kabbalah than Christ, and whose sense was that esotericists should follow the teachings of their own land and culture. In 1887 a group of British 'Westerners', all theosophists or Freemasons, decided that the moment had come to set up a group which could safely ignore Hindu and Buddhist teachings and focus on the tradition of Western magic and Kabbalah in the style of Eliphas Levi. And so the Hermetic Order of the Golden Dawn was founded by William Wynn Westcott (1848–1925), Samuel Liddle MacGregor Mathers (1854–1918) and William Woodman (1828–91).[35] Woodman had already had a long career in esoteric Masonry but died relatively early in the Order's history. It is Westcott and Mathers who are most associated with the Order's development, from its foundation on the basis of a supposed magical cipher attributed to the Renaissance Christian-Kabbalist Johannes Trithemius, to the establishment of the 'inner' order in 1892, whose function was to move from the study of magic into its practice. The visual evidence left in the historical record by Westcott and Mathers makes a pompous impression with their imaginative Egyptian robes (though no more so than the conventional churchmen they were imitating), but they shared the radicalism which appears to have been a consistent feature of the esoteric underground. They set up the Golden Dawn in part precisely because they wanted to give women the equal and respected role which they were denied in Masonry, and this when the overwhelming majority of men regarded the looming prospect of the female franchise as a ridiculous, if not horrifying, prospect. The Golden Dawn's teachings had little to say about judicial astrology even though some of its individual members, such as the poet William Butler Yeats (1865–1939), were enthusiastic astrologers, and one, A.E. Waite (1857–1942), produced an essential guide to calculating and interpreting horoscopes which was still commonly used in the 1980s.[36] Instead, the Order incorporated astrological symbolism in its initiatory rituals in the style of Cornelius Agrippa, involving the wearing of special robes, the recitation of Hebrew letters and numerological codes, the lighting of candles and so on. It was theurgic, in the tradition of Iamblichus, concerned with the 'God-work' which was to take the initiate through the planetary spheres, conceived metaphorically, past Saturn, the 'prince of spiritual initiation through suffering and of strife against evil', to the spiritual liberation beyond.[37] There is little or nothing about the reading of horoscopes in Golden Dawn literature, but a great deal about using sacred cosmology to facilitate ritual union with the Divine. In his notes on the '6=5' ritual, Patrick Zalewski remarks how at one stage, the 'Third Adept' points to the 'Venus Wall' and, as the Divine Force is petitioned to receive the initiate's astral body, 36 bells are rung, one for each of the Egyptian decans (divisions of zodiac signs into three); and, lest we should imagine this behaviour can be simply described as 'pagan', the assembled congregation faces East and offers the following prayer:

El, Lord of Light, bestow on us The Grace that we in unity with Thee may impart these Mysteries, a Father may only bestow upon a son Initiate; that he, becoming thus the

Eagle, may soar to Heaven and contemplate Thy Face ... Grant we beseech Thee most Merciful, that he may be Holy even as Thou art Holy, that being made one with Thee, he may draw all men unto Thee. Amen.[38]

To be explicit, this passage represents an attempt to provide an alternative to orthodox Christianity, just as the Theosophical Society presented an alternative to conventional revolutionary movements. The tradition of practice it embodies connects back via the Roman Neoplatonic philosophers to Egyptian temple-magic, and underpins the esoteric Christianity of twentieth-century New Age culture.[39] And, as ritual magic, it aims to make the initiate Christ-like, as son of God, and immortal.

The Golden Dawn itself may have been small – it had about a hundred members at most in the 1890s – but its interest lies in the model it set for magical groups ever since, especially with its perpetual schisms and chronic secrecy. Westcott himself left in 1897 after he suspected Mathers of planting papers which were sufficiently incriminating to threaten his respectable life as a coroner; ritual magic may have been acceptable within artistic circles in Paris but was still a risky pursuit in the politer echelons of Victorian society. But the behaviour of some leading members seems to have been less than holy. It's in the Golden Dawn's ideas that it's influence lies: we can trace a direct line of descent via the notorious magician and astrologer Aleister Crowley (1875–1947), who joined the Order in 1898, to Gerald Gardner (1884–1964), the founder of Wicca, the ideological and institutional heart of modern witchcraft and feminist–pagan spirituality. If we track the hugely commercial teen-witch phenomenon of the late 1990s to its origin, one line leads to the Golden Dawn. So, small and chaotic the Golden Dawn might have been, but it performed a vital role in transferring medieval magic to an environment in which teenage girls are told to perform love spells on Friday, the day, if they knew it, which is sacred to Venus.[40]

The attempt to establish whether what James Webb called the 'Occult Underground' ran counter to Modernism or was part and parcel of it is clearly impossible, for the lines which separate one cultural fashion from another are blurred, constantly shifting and often misleading. Clearly Blavatsky, Leo and Papus all believed that the present world had fulfilled its usefulness and should be swept away by the future. Astrologers such as Zadkiel had a fascination with modern science and scientists such as the founders of the Society for Psychical Research set out to find evidence for life after death. Yet the nostalgic search for a lost wisdom in astrology, Kabbalah and Hermeticism can only be read as a result of a profound distaste for materialism. The truth is that modernity, in the sense of a historical period characterized by materialist science and mass industrialization, has to be seen as distinct from Modernism, the belief that a new and better future must replace a corrupt and oppressive present. Modernism is a millenarian ideology, rooted in a profound Utopian belief that we can create a better future, and which preaches liberation from modernity, the historical period marked by drab industrialization and faceless urban sprawl. The Modernist future is fantastical, full of cities in the air and machines which think. But it can also have a high regard for the pre-modern. And here we may point to the arts for examples, to Wassily Kandinsky (1866–1944), the theosophist and founder of abstraction, and André Breton (1896–1966), the astrologer and originator of surrealism, and Antonin Gaudi, the Catalan architect and creator of fantastical buildings, who combined devout Catholicism with a fascination for alchemical symbolism. In 1908 the influential art critic Wilhelm Worringer (1881–1965) had spoken of the 'spiritual dread of space' felt by primitive people 'in relation to the extended, disconnected, bewildering world of phenomena'.[41] Aware of the illusory nature of material reality, the art primitive people created, he believed, was perfect, abstract and uniquely capable of inducing tranquillity and happiness. They lived in what Tolkein, writing in 1938, called a world of *Faërie*, or enchantment. *Faërie*, Tolkein said, is magic, but not the magic of the instrumental magician or scientist, setting out with a box of tricks to control the world. It is the magic that is of a state of mind in which the individual is completely at one with a world which is glowing and alive. '*Faërie* contans many things,' Tolkein wrote, 'besides elves and fays, and besides dwarfs, witches, trolls, giants, or dragons: it holds the seas, the sun, the moon, the sky; and the earth, and all things that are in it: tree and bird, water and stone, wine and bread, and ourselves, mortal men, when we are enchanted.'[42] This is the Romantic condition to which even perhaps Enlightenment astrologers might aspire. When we have put aside the mechanical cosmos of Worsdale and Comte, astrology becomes less a matter of prediction or even of knowledge, than of personal union with the One. It was, to be sure, a reaction to the disenchantment induced by the dead universe of materialist science and the grim, unrelenting horrors of industrial society, a rejection of modernity which was itself the very basis of Modernism.[43] This was not, as some have claimed, escapism, or a flight from reality.[44] Quite the reverse, it was a desire to overcome the alienation from nature, to return to Eden, to attain a state of enchantment and meet reality, that is, spiritual reality, head-on.

17

The Twentieth Century: New Age and Ancient Teachings

We are completing in this age a work begun in the Renaissance. We are re-uniting the mind and soul and body of man to the living world outside us.

W.B. YEATS[1]

On 20 May 1908, William Butler Yeats, the Irish nationalist, one of the greatest writers of his day and initiate of the Golden Dawn, was contemplating the significance for his life of a Mars–Uranus alignment, a classic indicator of conflict within the rules of nineteenth-century astrology.[2] On the following day Yeats received an angry, hostile letter denouncing the Abbey Theatre in Dublin, of which he was a founder member. In answering the letter, Yeats experienced an epiphany: he realized that he was completing a great work begun in the Renaissance, the reunification of the mind, soul and body of man, as he put it. For Yeats, the notion of an imminent global, spiritual transformation, driven by the stars, was an accepted fact. And it was very much part of the artistic milieu within which he lived. Yeats was one of the most high-profile public representatives of the new movement of theosophical astrologers, men and women for whom the cosmos was essentially a spiritual entity. In Britain, the creative powerhouse of this new way of thinking was Alan Leo.

Leo did not act alone, though. He was part of a wider movement, who are best defined as esoteric modernists on account of the weight they gave to the spiritual aspects of Modernism, as against the technological. All Modernists were utopians, but the esotericists were concerned less with cities in the sky or the ways in which the latest inventions could make for a better life, than with the ascent of the soul and the creation of communities based around shared spiritual values. The most significant of these esoteric modernists were the two most influential theosophists after Blavatsky, Rudolf Steiner (1861–1925) and Alice Bailey (1880–1949), and their fellow travellers, the Armenian mystic G.I. Gurdjieff (1866–1949) and his disciple, the Russian Pyōtr Ouspensky (1878–1947).[3] Gurdjieff turned up in Paris in 1922 together with a group of his followers, all refugees from the increasingly despotic communist regime in Russia. Once ensconced, Gurdjieff founded the Institute for the Harmonious Development of Man, teaching a cosmology which was not unlike Blavatsky's, in that its emphasis was self-awareness, although with a greater emphasis on science. This was, after all, a period when the implications of the radical new theories of relativity and quantum mechanics, with their interdependence of time and space, and matter and energy, were being absorbed in esoteric circles, a matter of some concern to Sigmund Freud who feared that the new science would lend a spurious rationale to ancient occultism.[4] It was Rudolf Steiner, though, who, of all the early-twentieth-century gurus, placed the greatest emphasis on interaction with the world, rather than just the self.[5] For the other teachers, an emphasis on transforming the self was an essential prerequisite for preparing the world for the coming age. For Steiner, transformation of the self and the world went hand in hand. His own astrology was deeply practical and is applied to both his farming and educational methods, but is also a radical and idiosyncratic departure from mainstream astrology in its use of the constellations rather than zodiac signs.[6] This astrology is largely hidden from public gaze but is part of the guiding philosophy which underpins his millenarian programme. The network of Waldorf Schools, Camphill Trusts (which care for and teach the mentally disabled) and Biodynamic farms, which rely heavily on the moon's location in relation to the constellations as part of a system of organic cultivation, testify to an extraordinary attempt to implement Steiner's version of the New Age, which he knew as the Age of Michael. Influenced by Eliphas Lévi, Steiner thought that the Age had begun in 1879, that the more highly evolved souls who were to dominate the age were already being incarnated, and that the result was to be a dramatic rise in 'Christ consciousness'.[7] Steiner was general secretary of the German Theosophical Society when the young Krishnamurti was discovered by theosophists at their headquarters at Adhyar, in India, and hailed as the avatar of the New Age, opening a fault line in the movement as a whole between the Easterners and the Westerners. As an esoteric Christian, Steiner was firmly in the Western camp and he left the Theosophical Society, as much in sorrow as in anger, in 1912. He had acquired a reputation as a charismatic teacher and took a large part of the German membership with him into his new organization, which he labelled Anthroposophy – 'human wisdom' or, more correctly, 'wisdom about humanity'. He believed that human souls lived on other planets, and followed Immanuel Swedenborg in arguing that Christ's second coming was a purely spiritual affair. He therefore believed that, as applied to individual lives, astrology's main function was to identify the nature and purpose of one's current incarnation. Each person had a cosmic purpose, which was identifiable through the birth chart, but the conventional prediction of life's daily events was of no interest whatsoever.

Like Blavatsky and Leo, Steiner was driven by his belief that individual self-knowledge was vital if people were to prepare for the coming global trans-formation. Steiner's view on the nature of the current times was traditional, mainstream, evangelical Christian, with just a hint of Plato's notion that different periods might produce 'better' or 'worse' births:

> There is much talk about periods of transition. We are indeed living just at the time when the Dark Age has run its course and a new epoch is just beginning, in which human beings will slowly and gradually develop new faculties and in which human souls will gradually undergo a change ... What is beginning at this time will slowly prepare

humanity for new soul faculties ... Faculties that now are quite unusual for human beings will then manifest themselves as natural abilities. At this time great changes will take place, and biblical prophecies will be fulfilled.[8]

Alice Bailey, the former Sunday-school teacher turned enthusiastic theosophist, shared many of Steiner's concerns.[9] Also an esoteric Christian, she moved from Scotland to the USA and rose to prominence in the Theosophist Society but aroused antagonism partly because she claimed to be communicating with the Ascended Masters, the mysterious beings who had revealed the hidden teachings to Blavatsky. Bailey's own favourite spiritual teacher, the so-called 'Tibetan', dictated most of her writings, including her astrological musings, but lifelong theosophists who had studied Blavatsky for years and never had so much as a whisper from her teachers, found it impossible to stomach Bailey's claims. Bailey made a graceful and gradual exit from the society, setting up her own school, the Arcane School, whose distinguished students included Robert Assagioli (1888–1974), the Italian psychiatrist and founder of psychosynthesis, and Dane Rudhyar (1895–1985), who was to be the most influential American astrologer of the century. Bailey's astrology was, in its own way, as idiosyncratic as Steiner's. It holds that the moon, being 'dead', has no relevance; it postulates the existence of hypothetical planets such as the non-existent 'Vulcan'; and it employs 'rays' which represents levels of spiritual existence.[10] More important than her astrology, though, which in its strict form has few adherents, is Bailey's impact on the astrological world as a whole through her repeated articulation of the nature and imminence of the Aquarian Age – and the New Age.

Bailey was as deeply committed to the apocalyptic astrological vision of the imminent global crisis as Steiner and is largely responsible for popularizing the term New Age as a synonym for the Age of Aquarius. The two concepts were in her eyes one and the same. She believed devoutly that, when the sun rises in the stars of Aquarius at the spring equinox, which she thought would happen late in the twentieth century, then the New Age will begin and the world's return to pure spirit will commence. 'Humanity itself,' Bailey wrote, in her typically obscurantist tone, 'is rapidly arriving at the point where its *united will* will be the determining factor in world affairs and this will be due to the unfoldment of the mind through the success of the evolutionary process.'[11] Fleshing out the idea of the age, she added:

> The functioning of the Law of Loving Understanding will be greatly facilitated and speeded during the Aquarian Age which we are considering; it will eventuate later in the development of a world-wide international spirit, in the recognition of one universal faith in God and in humanity also as the major expression of divinity upon the planet and in the transfer of the human consciousness from the world of material things to that of the more purely psychic.[12]

Or, as the Irish astrologer and friend of W.B. Yeats, Cyril Fagan, said, 'During this Age the whole world will be just one big happy family, speaking the same language and freely mingling and intermarrying one another.'[13] Building on Blavatsky, Bailey's extensive writings systematized its key features: its Gnostic emphasis on the inner divine, demand for personal transformation and use of astrology. If each individual contains a spark of the divine then it follows, as Hermeticists had always claimed, that the path to the divine is a personal one. The New Age ethic is, then, the 'self-ethic', its spirituality, 'self-spirituality'.[14] Astrology then shifts decisively towards a form of narcissism, the love of one's reflection. True, for the theosophical vanguard, individual growth serves the purpose of cosmic evolution, but for the New Age foot soldiers, personal growth becomes the beginning and end of the process. Bailey's vision of the future may have been apolitical in the sense that it shunned ordinary political engagement, but its prophecy of a world in which all existing national states and economic systems were to be swept away is communist, even if of a very different kind to the brutal, materialist, Marxist version. Bailey set up a public organization, the Lucis Trust, and a revolutionary vanguard, the Servers of the New World Order, whose support for the United Nations has been at least partially responsible for the hostility to that organization of the Christian right in the USA. Various of the American ultra-evangelicals really do believe that Bailey and her followers represent a satanic conspiracy to take over the world, and that astrology is one of the tools they employ.[15]

New Age culture, as it developed in the twentieth century, is essentially a continuation of the classical Platonic, Gnostic and Hermetic strands in Western thought.[16] Its cosmology is rooted in the idea of the cosmos as essentially a spiritual entity in which human beings contain the divine within themselves. However, whereas the goal was once to open one's higher, 'rational', soul to the Divine, New Age language depends on the concept of personal transformation or fulfilment, with opening up to the higher powers of the cosmos as a more distant aspiration. In each case, though, astrology can provide a vital tool in the process. In the classical world, astrology was vital, for the soul had to navigate the planetary spheres if it was to find salvation. In New Age culture, astrology is optional, but at some level, especially a near-universal knowledge of one's birth sign, it has become what Michael York called the lingua franca of New Age culture.[17]

The theosophical enlightenment pervaded middle-class culture. Blavatsky's influence extended beyond the small groups who gathered in theosophical lodges, particularly through artists, many of whom saw her proclamation of a new era in history as compatible with their own aspirations to build a new world. The Symbolist movement, expressed so well in the fantastic paintings of Gustave Moreau, drew heavily on theosophy's mystical cosmology. Modernism, in its esoteric form, concerned with the coming cosmological transformation from an old, dead world to a new one brimming with spiritual life, was a profound motivating force for radical artists. Many of the leading lights in the Modernist movement were also steeped in theosophy. Schoenberg, Scriabin, Klee, Mondrian, Gropius and Zemlinsky all carried theosophical principles into music, the visual arts and architecture.[18] In the visual arts the revolutionary pioneer of visual theosophy was Wassily Kandinsky (1866–1944), the Russian-born founder of abstract painting. Kandinsky began his artistic career as a figurative artist but his revelatory encounter with theosophy prompted a crisis in which he realized that his goal should be to capture the pure essence of the cosmos, the undiluted spirit from which the material had emerged and to which, some time in the distant future, it was to return. Being non-material, colour was close to spirit, and his experiments with it were prompted partly by the theosophists' claims to be able see the colours of the human aura.[19] Kandinsky's admiration for theosophy was based partly in its social and political radicalism, and its rejection of the racism and cultural elitism which was endemic in materialistic science and academia.[20] At a time when orthodox thought took it for granted that non-white races were inherently inferior, and ancient societies were somehow childish and their beliefs superstitious, all theories which provided a vital function in supporting imperialism, Blavatsky's determination to ignore gender and racial distinctions attracted radicals who were offended by the authoritarian and materialist strands within contemporary socialism. Kandinsky's manifesto, *Concerning the Sprirritual in Art*, written in 1911, reasserted the value of the spiritual and praised Blavatsky for acting as a bridge between modern Westerners and those 'savage' societies which they had been brought up to despise. He believed literally in the apocalyptic vision of the imminent arrival of what he called 'The Epoch of the Great Spirituality' and saw the world's entanglement in matter as the great obstacle standing in the way of this noble goal. Kandinsky needed a means, a form of Popperian activism, by which he could promote the reintegration of humanity with the spiritual cosmos, and he found it, naturally in view of his profession, in painting. But how could eternal truths be expressed in visual form? Not through the conventional portrayal of the very material forms that were the problem. And so Kandinsky set out on a journey, which took him through the 1910s and 20s, to the creation of abstract art.[21] Kandinsky's contemporary, Piet Mondrian (1872–1944), discovered theosophy in 1909, around the same time as Kandinsky, and experienced a religious revelation of similar force – that true reality was spiritual, that spiritual truths could only be represented in abstract form and that history would provide the proof of this simple truth when the New Age arrived.[22] Mondrian's solution, his way of preaching the spiritual cosmos, was to pioneer the painting of single blocks of colour, an attempt to portray pure colour as a representation of pure spirit. The levels of reality which Leo had indicated by geometrical relationships, usually triangles or six-pointed stars, Mondrian represented by his rectilinear forms. The notion of geometrical shapes, of course, was an indication of the intrusion of Platonism into the visual arts via theosophy. Later, after he moved to the Modernist paradise of New York, Mondrian decided that the city's street grid was an ideal pattern whose significance, in his imagination, fused with his love of jazz music and dance. This in itself is enough to provoke questions about Modernism's relationship to the present. Rather than an attempt to create the new, it aims to establish eternal truths which, by their very nature, are timeless, and beyond questions of past, present or future. The direct theosophical impact on modern art waned as the Theosophical Society experienced various schismatic problems, climaxing in Krishnamurti's resignation in 1929. But, indirectly, its influence remained profound. Jackson Pollock, who in the late 1940s pioneered the concept of apparently random, spontaneous painting, created by dropping paint onto a canvas laid flat on the floor (a process analogous to Blavatsky and Bailey's automatic writing), is said to have frequently perused his copy of Kandinsky's *Concerning the Spriritual in Art*.[23]

Kandinsky and Mondrian were devotees of the theosophical cosmology within which the new spiritual judicial astrology flourished, but never made the next step into the study and use of horoscopes. One painter who did was André Breton (1896–1966), the founder of surrealism. Breton, who was also a leading exponent of Dadaism, drafted the three surrealist manifestos of 1924, 1930 and 1942. Breton had studied medicine and worked in psychiatric wards in World War 1, so it was natural that he should study Freud.[24] The artistic territory claimed by surrealism, with its explicit reference to dreams as a manifestation of unconscious truths, was also claimed by the Freudians. The Freudians' problem as far as spiritually inclined individuals, though, was their denial of eternal spiritual truths. The theosophical belief that what the Freudians called the unconscious could reveal genuine timeless wisdom, as opposed to some pathetic failure to cope with reality, as Freud thought, was undoubtedly attractive to many artists. Some were adherents of both Blavatsky and Freud, ignoring the incompatible elements in their thought and, if there is a visual representation of the encounter between Blavatsky and Freud, it's the bizarre imagery produced by Breton and his fellow surrealists, Max Ernst and Pablo Picasso. Breton began studying astrology in 1927 and was introduced to the works of Robert Fludd and Jerome Cardan, absorbing Hermetic teachings on the true nature of creation – the belief that artists don't create and can only draw out what is already inherent in the cosmos. In his opinion, astrology's value lay in its unification of two discrete areas of knowledge, the self and the world. He summed up his views in an interview he gave in 1954:

> I see astrology as a lady, statuesque, utterly beautiful, and from such a distant realm that she cannot fail to enthral me. In purely physical terms, her attire alone is incomparable. But beyond the realm of the visible, astrology seems to me to contain one of the highest secrets in the world . . . a brilliant formulation of relationships between man and the universe . . . I consider its capacity for stretching and exercising the mind to be second to none. To unravel a destiny, beginning with the planetary placements, their aspects, their signs and houses, depending on the position of the Ascendant and Midheaven – this requires more than enough mental dexterity to silence any attempts at ridicule and, compared with this sophistication, conventional logical reasoning comes out looking like child's play.[25]

Breton was disappointed that, in spite of the value he saw in astrology, too many of his fellow surrealists ignored it. His devotion was, though, matched in music by the composer Gustav Holst (1874–1934), who was also aware of astrology from his theosophical background. His interest in it deepened around 1910 and in 1914 he began work on *The Planets*, a composition which was inspired by meditations on his own horoscope, inspired by Alan Leo. Holst himself said that *The Planets* dealt with what he referred to as the 'seven influences of destiny and constituents of our spirit'.[26] Holst owned a number of astrology books in addition to Leo's, including one by Raphael, which dealt with the planets' role in world affairs. But it was from Leo that he developed the grand vision of the planets which made *The Planets* such an enduring success, perhaps the greatest astrological art work of the modern age.

William Butler Yeats, theosophy's literary giant, appears to have begun his study of astrology even before he joined the Golden Dawn in 1890.[27] He may well have been inspired by some family tradition of astrology, for the Yeats family was related by marriage to John Varley, William Blake's astrological companion. Yeats's horoscope was first cast by his uncle, George Pollexfen and the surviving notes show that Yeats was born with the moon in Aquarius, well-aspected to Saturn in Libra, and to a Sun–Uranus conjunction in Gemini which, for Pollexfen, accounted for Yeats's profound imagination and his interest in astrology. If he had read Alan Leo on this alignment, Pollexfen would have found that it described people who were 'headstrong, socialistic, revolutionaries', possessed of a magnetic personality and an original and fertile mind.[28] Yeats's own earliest surviving astrological manuscripts date to 1888 or 1889, when he was in his early 20s, probably when he was studying with the Theosophical Society. His astrological notebooks survive from 1908 and indicate that from then on he was using astrology for most aspects of his life, including his management of Dublin's Abbey Theatre. Around 1934 the novelist Virginia Woolf recorded in her diary, 'He believes entirely in horoscopes. Will never do business with anyone without having their horoscopes.'[29] Yeats used conventional astrology extensively but also developed his own lunar-based system. Soon after he married in 1917, his wife, Georgie Hyde-Lees, also a member of the Golden Dawn, discovered that she was a medium and began taking dictation from the spirit world through automatic writing. The spirits taught the Yeats an entirely new system of moon-centred, visionary astrological interpretation and eventually, in 1937, he published his apocalyptic version of world history based on the lunar phases, *A Vision*, a work he dedicated to all his friends in the Golden Dawn.[30] Apparently intended for publication in this work, but never included, was a manuscript titled 'Astrology and the Nature of Reality', published posthumously as 'Seven Propositions'. The 'reality' within which he placed astrology was described in the following, deeply Blavatskyan terms:

> Reality is a timeless and spaceless community of Spirits which perceive each other. Each Spirit is determined by and determines those it perceives, and each Spirit is unique ... Human life is either the struggle of a destiny against all other destinies, or a transformation of the character defined in the horoscope into timeless and spaceless existence. The whole passage from birth to birth should be an epitome of the whole passage of the universe through time and back into its timeless and spaceless condition'.[31]

The direct expression by artists of the theosophical cosmos faded during the century as the Theosophical Society itself fractured and declined, but a handful of writers continued to make clear their deeper commitment to the astrological world-view, one of the most notable being Henry Miller, who peppered his books with astrological references. In 1942, for example, he devoted a paragraph in *The Colossus of Maroussi* to discussion of the attributes of Saturn:

> Saturn is a living symbol of gloom, morbidity, disaster, fatality. Its milk-white hue arouses associations with tripe, loathsome diseases, test-tubes, laboratory specimens, melancholy shades, morbid phenomena, sterility, indecisions, defeatism, red tape, working class conditions, sweat shops, Y.M.C.A.s, Christian Endeavour meetings, spiritist séances, poets like T.S. Eliot, statesmen like Chamberlain, trivial fatalities like slipping on a banana peel, drowning in one's own bath tub, dying of hiccoughs and so on ad infinitum.[32]

Struck by this 'revelatory passage', the celebrity astrologer Sydney Omarr collected all Miller's astrological references together under the title *Henry Miller: His World of Urania*. Miller responded with a flattering tribute to Omarr, writing that he 'is more than an astrologer, of course. He is possessed not only of a sixth sense but of a seventh and possibly an eighth ... He lives with the stars and not by them.'[33] In 1967, prompted by Omarr's recordings on the zodiac signs, Miller also summarized his thoughts on the nature of astrology as a means of transcending immediate petty concerns in order to perceive greater truths about the cosmos and one's self:

> We see what we want to see, we hear what we want to hear, whether it concerns the world, ourselves, our friends or our loved ones. The great opportunity which astrology offers is to permit us to see the whole ... The purpose of astrology is not to teach one how to thwart destiny but how to live up to it, in accordance with it. In other words, to become aware.[34]

Miller was also a huge fan of the theosophist and astrological reformer Dane Rudhyar (1895–1985). To the back cover of Rudhyar's 1970 celebration of the new cosmology Miller added the following words: 'Your almost incredible comprehensive grasp floors me sometimes. It's always an inspiration to read you, to see how you push away the walls.'[35]

The Irish poet Louis MacNeice (1907–63) went further and wrote an astrological textbook, mainly a historical survey, although the suggestion that he wrote it purely for the money is misleading. Writers take on professional commissions, but his knowledge of its finer points and his familiarity with the leading figures in contemporary astrology are the marks of the enthusiast, and his obvious support for the subject are the sign of a man who believed it had obvious value: 'To put it colloquially,' MacNeice wrote, 'the stars are part of our set up.'[36] He also cited extensively Miller's astrological manifesto. In any case, although he accepted the commission in early 1961, the book was not published until 1964, the year after his death. We don't know when MacNeice's interest in astrology began, although we do know that he met W.B. Yeats in 1934 when he was taken for tea to Yeats's house in Rathfarnham, near Dublin. MacNeice found the encounter seriously disappointing and complained afterwards that the elderly poet was less interested in discussing his verse than talking about the phases of the moon and the spirits which were then supposedly guiding his wife's automatic writing.[37]

Yeats's interest in astrology is well known, if little studied. Yet when, in 1998, the British Poet Laureate, Ted Hughes, who followed in the same tradition, published his last great volume of poems, *The Birthday Letters*, and a number of them revealed his deep interest in astrology, the critics either studiously ignored it or condemned him.[38] The critic Al Alvarez, a friend of Hughes, for example, denounced the poet's 'belief in mysteries, the under-life ... black magic ... mumbo-jumbo ... astrology, hypnosis, Ouija boards [and] the dottier forms of Jungian magical thinking' as partly responsible for the tragic suicide of his wife, the poet Sylvia Plath.[39] Hughes couldn't help it, Alvarez thought. As a country boy fallen among intellectuals he was out of his depth and liable to succumb to weird beliefs, but Plath's interest, as the daughter of middle-class American intellectuals, was incomprehensible to him: how could she be taken in by such obvious rubbish? Alvarez believed that although 'the baleful influence of the stars' didn't come naturally to Plath, 'she went along willingly when [she and Hughes] played spooky games with the Ouija board and read each other's horoscopes'.[40] Alvarez's pleading on Plath's behalf is slightly disingenuous and in his efforts to portray her as a dupe of Hughes's, to him, strange and dangerous beliefs, he undervalues her own independence and experience as a writer. It's without doubt, though, that Hughes's interest in astrology was a major source of inspiration to him, not in isolation but as part of the same fascination with the Western esoteric tradition that had influenced W.B. Yeats, Robert Graves and C.G. Jung. Like Yeats, Hughes was concerned with the magical transformation that arcane knowledge could bring and like Jung he saw esotericism as a path to self-understanding. Hughes was already deeply interested in astrology when he first encountered Plath at a Cambridge literary party on 25 February 1956. In 'St. Botolph's' (the party was called to launch the *St Botolph's Review*), Hughes describes the horoscope for the moment of their meeting. 'Our Chaucer,' he concluded 'would have sighed. He would have assured us, shaking his sorrowful head. That day the solar system married us'/Whether we knew it or not.'[41]

For the most part the poem is a precise description of the planetary transits over his and Plath's horoscopes, referenced to tie his own work into a venerable tradition, and indicating a moment of fate which neither could avoid: the marriage was to be followed by sorrow. Most of Hughes's details are correct: Jupiter and the full moon were conjunct, Jupiter was in Leo conjunct Plath's natal Mars (representing Hughes?), which ruled her Scorpionic sun, and transiting Venus (representing Plath?), was elevated on his midheaven.[42] Only Jupiter's opposition to Venus appears to be poetic licence designed as an omen of doom, unless he is using some obscure horoscopic technique.

While Alvarez minimized Plath's interest in astrology, portraying it as emblematic of her pathetic surrender to Hughes's inner demons, she was quite clearly able to think for herself. Hughes described her studies of astrology in 'Horoscope': 'You wanted to study/Your stars – the guards/Of your prison yard, their zodiac. The planets/Muttered their Babylonish power-sprach –/Like a witchdoctors bones.'[43]

Hughes's astrological allegiance was pre-Hellenistic, rooted in the religions of Babylonia, his 'Babylonish power-sprach' an obvious allusion to Nietchze's *Thus Sprach Zarathustra*. His description of the stars as prison bars is plucked straight from the pessimistic Hermetic belief that the soul is held captive by the material world. For her part, though, Plath hoped that she and Hughes might become 'a team better than Mr and Mrs Yeats, he being a competent astrologer, reading horoscopes, and me being a Tarot pack reader'.[44]

It is tempting to think of a transmission of astrological ideas from Blake and Varley to Yeats via the Pollexfens, and from Yeats to MacNeice to Hughes. It's better to think of them all inhabiting a milieu in which the cosmos is always meaningful for the poetic mind, that the universe speaks to humanity in enchanted, wonderful ways. Actually, somewhere around 90 per cent of modern astrologers also think that the universe speaks in metaphors, agreeing with the definition of astrology as a language; this figure is just slightly less that the birth chart represents a map of our potential, which it is up to each individual to develop as best they can.[45] Such attitudes, combining Blavatsky's literalism with the artistic mentality of some of her most culturally influential followers, was well expressed in the work of Miller's friend – and Alice Bailey's protégé – Dane Rudhyar. Rudhyar begin his writing career in the 1930s when European works on depth psychology were making their presence felt in the USA, and he combined their theories, especially those of the great Swiss psychologist, C.G. Jung. Rudhyar concluded that there were two types of astrology.[46] One which, as any medieval astrologer would have understood, was directed at people who were completely lacking in self-awareness, was capable of making exact forecasts for individual lives. People who had no spiritual life, he reasoned, would be creatures of fate. The second, esoteric, variety was, like Leo's, aimed at the soul. But unlike Leo, he realized that this astrology was entirely relative and had no objective, external reality. Spiritual truths, he believed, were absolute, but esoteric astrological rules were entirely a matter of convenience, changing from one culture to another as social requirements evolved. Astrological claims can therefore never be tested or proved. That is not the point. The issue is not their truth, but their usefulness in helping more people prepare for the New Age. Rudhyar was an evangelist with a message to spread. In 1938 he opened his second book, a detailed account of the planets and horoscope houses in terms of their potential for spiritual development, with a proclamation of the change of the ages:

> Today is a new birthday for the ancient gods. New men call for new symbols. Their cry rises, beyond their logical intellects ashamed of mystical longings, for new gods to worship and to use in order to integrate their harrowing mental confusion and to stabilize

their uprooted souls. Young gods, fresh and radiant with the sunshine of a new dawn, glorified with the 'golden light' of a new Sun of Power, ecstatic with virgin potentialities after the banishment of ancient nightmares.[47]

New Age ideology and practice has changed as it has entered the wider culture. There is no single entity as New Age astrology. Rather there are two types, one that emphasizes spiritual evolution and another that concentrates on personal development. We could characterize the former as derived from Alan Leo, the latter as Jungian. There's another significant distinction, though, devised by Wouter Hanegraaff, between a strict, sensu stricto New Age culture, which is devoted to the coming of the New Age as an imminent, real, literal event, and the wider sensu lato culture in which there is little interest in the coming historical shift, but a general adherence to the beliefs and practices which the strict culture has spawned, in spirituality, astrology, feng shui and complementary medicine.[48] In the New Age sensu lato, the image of the coming millennium is primarily an 'emblem' which provides symbolic evidence that history is on one's side. So, the astrologer who believes in using the horoscope for self-transformation is embedded in the New Age sensu stricto, but the newspaper or magazine horoscope column, thanks to Rudhyar's influence, has one foot in the New Age sensu lato. There remains a small, and over the last 20 years increasingly vigorous, group of astrologers who reject notions of astrology as concerned either with personal growth or spiritual development of the entry into the New Age, but they remain a minority. The belief that astrology itself, thanks to the next significant planetary alignment, or to the shift in Aquarius, is about to be recognized for the world-saving technique that so many astrologers believe, sustains them through what they experience as marginalization and, sometimes, victimization or ridicule.

In this new world the core task of the Aquarian Age astrologer is to listen carefully to the client and facilitate the healing process without any requirement even to interpret, change or, worst of all, predict.[49] This at least is the theory. In practice, few astrologers can resist the chance to impose their views on their clients. After all, astrologers are only human. Yet the relativist rhetoric is dominant in the literature: as American astrologer Donna Cunningham put it, 'The true usefulness of a chart, as I see it, is to get a better perspective on yourself, to appreciate your own individuality and potential, and to work toward your most positive expression of self. Your chart is only an instrument panel where you take readings on the course of your life. YOU ARE THE PILOT.'[50] Echoing down the centuries, we see a hint of Pico's humanism, fulfilled in an astrology which has done its best to abandon any trace of determinism.

18

The Twentieth Century: Psychology and the Popular Press

Astrology represents the sum of all the psychological knowledge of antiquity.

C.G. JUNG[1]

On 24 August 1930 the British newspaper the *Sunday Express* carried a small feature on the birth chart, personality and life-prospects of the newest member of the royal family, the infant Princess Margaret. The formula – royalty and the stars – may seem obvious as an attempt to attract readers, but only in retrospect. At the time, the *Express*'s move was an act of journalistic genius, a small but significant event, the consequences of which were to see astrology's triumphant re-entry to the public sphere. At the same time, in Switzerland, the psychologist Carl Gustav Jung (1875–1961) was developing sophisticated theories concerning astrology and the individual's psychic interaction with the universe. These apparently entirely distinct developments were to have a common link, as we shall see, in their shared reliance on Hermetic teachings.

Jung was the seminal figure in the development of twentieth-century astrological thought, probably even more so than Alan Leo. He gave astrology an intelligent modern voice, allowing it to appeal to a much wider educated constituency than had previously been the case.[2] Jungian theories exist on the margins of modern psychology, and one has to search high and low before finding mention of his work in university psychology courses, but their influence outside academia is immense, and pervade the worlds of therapists and counsellors. Jungians broadly divide into two camps: those aspiring positivists for whom Jung's esotericism is an embarrassment and who are in denial about his use of astrology; and those for whom his Hermeticism and Neoplatonism is the creative source of everything that is valuable in his work. Jung provided astrology itself with an appeal to the esoterically inclined, educated middle class which transcended that achieved by Sibly, Zadkiel or Papus mainly because, through his analytical psychology (so-called to distinguish it from Freud's psychoanalysis) he gave it a practical application which (in spite of his own metaphysics) had no necessary appeal to the supernatural. Instead of discussing the levels of the soul, as Leo would have done, a Jungian astrologer can discuss psychological complexes in a manner which dovetails neatly with more legitimate forms of modern discourse about the mind. Jung's esotericism feels as if it is of this world rather than the next – or the other. His healing methods were explicitly humanistic in that the patient's – or analysand's – thoughts, dreams and experiences were the centre of the therapeutic process, the means of diagnosis and the source of treatment. Jung also thoroughly disapproved of contemporary theosophists, who he thought were playing around with psychic forces that they completely failed to understand. His father had been a minister for the Calvinist Swiss Reformed Church and Jung himself always remained a self-declared Christian, retaining a respect for the traditional father God which was completely at odds both with Blavatsky's fervent contempt for mainstream Christianity and very different in tone to the esoteric Christianity of Steiner and Bailey. Yet, in spite of his dislike of the leading theosophists, Jung was heir to a similar Neoplatonic lineage. His religious ideology was formed by the same mix of Hermeticism and Christianity to that which permeated the ideas of Ficino and Boehme, and he was a firm adherent of the idea that there was an original religious truth, a *prisca theologia*. He didn't use the term 'perennial wisdom' but he assumed that there was such a thing and that the great teachers of the past, such as Paracelsus, who he held in particular esteem, understood and expressed it through their practice of spiritual alchemy and astrology. Jung believed that his philosophical education had begun in his seventeenth year when, not unlike the young Alan Leo, he began to see intuitively that the narrow Christianity into which he was born represented only a fraction of the spiritual reality of the cosmos. Even when he began his medical studies at the University of Basel, Jung's primary interest remained philosophical, and, as he read the classical philosophers, Pythagoras, Heracleitus, Empedocles, and Plato, he began to build a structure for his belief that the true nature of the universe was psychic – ensouled and alive.[3] Dreams, for example, were not mere night-time fantasies but real pointers to a deeper existence. He set out to challenge the nineteenth-century orthodoxy in which 'psyche' had lost its associations with soul, and psychology had been reduced to the study of the brain. But Jung was far more than a psychologist. He was a great religious reformer in the tradition of Plato.[4] He was a theurgist in the style of Iamblichus, the difference being that his form of magic, the analytical session, while alive to the numinous power of symbols, eschewed the other paraphernalia of ritual magic and preferred the gradual, rational ascent to the divine favoured by orthodox Platonism. Within this context, his dislike of Blavatsky and all she stood for takes him close to Plotinus: he considered himself a scholar, craved acceptance as a scientist, and looked down on those whom he saw as debasing divine knowledge. In crude terms, Blavatsky and Jung can be considered together as the most influential Neoplatonists of the late nineteenth and early twentieth centuries. Blavatsky, though, was concerned only to recover the knowledge of the past on behalf of a new audience. She saw herself as a medium, transmitting information which, being true, had no need of revision. Jung, though, recast Plato's ideas in a twentieth-century context, describing them in his poetic style as 'mythological motifs', 'categories of the imagination' or 'primordial thoughts'.[5] It's truer to say, though, that the recurrence of such motifs as ideas (such as the concept of the 'dying God' as a universal religious motif) or visual images (such as the mandala, a circular design focusing on a central point) throughout human civilization provide evidence of the existence of the Platonic archetypes. While Plato himself had conceived of the archetypes as fundamentally geometrical, Jung, while agreeing they can never be fully known, anthropomorphized them, arguing that they can be described through their manifestations in the human psyche and endowing them with personality. Through studying the dreams, conversations and paintings of his patients, Jung concluded that fundamental symbols were repeated across cultures, from east to west, first world to thirds, and through time, from the ancient world to the modern.[6] His conclusion was that there are universal themes and constant patterns in human psychology. Jungian astrology was to emerge as a means of identifying such themes and patterns.

Jung deliberately related all his theories to classical examples. He compared his theory of synchronicity to Aristotle's 'formal causation', and looked to Plato for his theory of archetypes, which he introduced in his usual enigmatic style. 'Archetypes,' he wrote, 'are like river beds which run dry when the water deserts them, but which it can find again at any time. An archetype is like an old water course along which the water of life has flowed for centuries, digging a deep channel for itself.'[7] The astrological adaptation of Jung's ideas operated by taking statements like this and argue, with good justification in Jung's own writings, that the archetypes then came to life – filled with water – when the planets formed significant alignments.

Over the course of his half-century of creative work, Jung changed his mind, clarified his thoughts and even contradicted himself, so there is no single body of Jungian dogma. But we can generalize. Broadly, he owed a debt to Freud in the concept of the personal unconscious as a repository for repressed and painful complexes, but added the notion of a collective unconscious, which contains racial, cultural, inherited and archetypal material. The dynamic is dialectical, the meeting of two forces producing a third, the resolution, but also conforms to the pattern of prehistoric cosmology as either shamanistic or geomantic. The former corresponds to the individualistic tendencies of the personal unconscious, the latter to the ordered, regular patterns of the collective unconscious. Applying the Newtonian mechanics adopted by Freud, the contents of the collective unconscious were thought to press up and erupt into the personal unconscious which is itself subject to downward pressures, the result being either personal or collective (as in the case of Nazism) psychosis. This model became one of the core interpretative schemes of late-twentieth-century astrology, assisted by Jung's tendency to endow the archetypes with anthropomorphic personalities, such as the *senex*, the wise old man, or the *puer*, the boy who, like Peter Pan, never grows up. It was precisely Jung's own use of the esoteric tradition that made it so simple to transfer his ideas to technical astrology. Astrologers who are influenced by Jung's ideas talk about the planets either as archetypes themselves or as representing an archetype. Discussion of astrology and its significance pervades Jung's work, but he left almost no indication of how he actually read a horoscope. It was up to astrologers themselves, some of whom had trained as analysts, to convert his broad picture into the details of astrological interpretation. The first task was to relate the archetypes to planets. Saturn, whose astrological character has long been pictured as Father Time – an old man carrying a sickle – is a natural fit for the *senex*. The *anima*, the archetypal feminine, is a natural fit for the planet Venus, who is known as the goddess of love, while the *animus*, the archetypal masculine, is linked with Mars, the god of war.[8] Equipped with this new lexicon, the astrologer is able to analyse and discuss the client's psychological complexes, desires and needs in a way that contrasts with all previous astrology, no matter how deeply it was concerned with the psyche, which could only describe emotional and intellectual tendencies. The difference was that in Hermetic thought before Jung, the psyche, as soul, had been largely fixed, a static entity which had descended from the stars. Jung saw the psyche itself, in terms of emerging psychological theories, as subject to internal developmental processes. Once these are linked to the planets then astrology was provided with an entirely new language. Leo's dislike of prediction and insistence that astrology be used for self-understanding was at last provided with a set of tools. Along the way Jung also provided a radical theory of astrology which undercuts any tendency to believe in it as a manifestation of universal order. If the collective unconscious, he reasoned, consists of mythological motifs or primordial images, then mythology becomes a 'projection' of the collective unconscious. And astrology itself, of course, is a form of celestial myth. 'We can see this most clearly,' he wrote, 'if we look at the heavenly constellations, whose originally chaotic forms were organized through the projection of images. This explains the influence of the stars as asserted by astrologers.'[9] The concept of the archetype then becomes itself a kind of explanatory model, in which the zodiac signs and planets have a role in human life precisely because they are 'archetypal'. That this is a kind of circular argument only reinforces its appeal, and among modern astrologers – or Jungians – to talk of an event as 'archetypal' means that it is meaningful, purposeful and significant, rather than just another of life's random coincidences.

Jung began studying astrology in 1910, spending, as he wrote to Freud, every day investigating it. In the next year he again wrote to Freud in tones which reveal an almost evangelical excitement: 'I make horoscopic calculations in order to find a clue to the core of psychological truth ... Some remarkable things have turned up which will certainly appear incredible to you ... For instance it appears that the signs of the zodiac are character pictures, in other words libido symbols which depict the typical qualities of the libido at a given moment.'[10] His initial enthusiasm never waned, and he always used horoscopes for people he thought might have a latent psychosis, using the women in his circle, including Lilliana Frei, together with his daughter, Gret Baumann Jung, and his lover, Toni Wolfe, to cast the horoscopes which he then used in his analytical sessions.[11]

Jung believed that astrology's value for psychologists lay in at least 2000 years' worth of accumulated insight into the human condition. As he said, succinctly, 'Astrology represents the sum of all the psychological knowledge of antiquity.'[12] As an aid to the therapeutic process, he considered it, together with alchemy, as a symbol of transformation, to be a vital component in the process he described as individuation, through which the unaware person becomes a self-aware individual.[13] Jung's enthusiasm for astrology never waned and in 1947 he set out his ideas in some detail in a letter to the Indian astrologer B.V. Raman:

> As I am a psychologist, I am chiefly interested in the particular light the horoscope sheds on certain complications in the character. In cases of difficult psychological diagnosis, I usually get a horoscope in order to have a further point of view from an entirely different angle. I must say that I often found that the astrological data elucidated certain points which I otherwise would have been unable to understand. From such experiences I formed the opinion that astrology is of particular interest to the psychologist, since it contains a sort of psychological experience which we call 'projected' – this means that we find the psychological facts as it were in the constellations. This originally gave rise to the idea that these factors derive from the stars, whereas they are merely in a relation of synchronicity with them. I admit that this is a very curious fact which throws a peculiar light on the structure of the human mind.[14]

The essence of Jung's argument is that the astrologer is psychically a part of the process of astrological interpretation rather than an outside observer, a view which connects him to the pre-Newtonian magical cosmos found in the opening paragraphs of Guido Bonatti and Jerome Cardan's collection of aphorisms. However, he was not entirely happy in a pre-modern world and added one qualification at the end of the letter, which was that he considered that statistical methods should be used to establish the fundamental scientific facts of astrology. He was deeply attracted to ancient wisdom, but still could not surrender himself to it wholeheartedly, and he kept one foot firmly planted in the Newtonians' camp, along with Comte and Quetelet. In spite of his instincts to the contrary he also long maintained the idea that astrological effects might result from celestial causes, could be justified by the latest astrophysics and was on the way to becoming a proper science.[15]

Jung's target for astrological experimentation and statistical proof was his own theory of synchronicity, first formulated in the 1920s, partly on the basis of his experience of the Chinese oracular system, the I Ching, and partly because he wanted to construct a psychic counterpart to Einstein's theory of relativity.[16] It is difficult to imagine a grander ambition than to set himself as an equal to Einstein, already recognized as the most famous scientists in the world. Just as Relativity, Jung thought, had explained the physical cosmos, so there must be a corresponding theory for the psychic universe. His logic was not dissimilar to that of John Locke and Auguste Comte, who believed that there must be a political or social law to match Newton's celestial law. If there is a universal law, Jung argued in common with most modern astrophysicists, then its application to everything must be susceptible to scientific proof. Jung's fascination with astrophysics dated back to around 1909 or 1911 when Einstein visited Jung's house in Zurich on a number of occasions. This was during the period when Jung was deeply engaged in studying astrology, although neither he nor Einstein mentions that they ever talked about the subject; Einstein himself appears to have forgotten all about the visits. But they made a huge impression on Jung and, in Einstein's absence, as he developed his theories Jung was assisted by Wolfgang Pauli (1900–58), who was not only one of the founders of quantum theory but also, conveniently for Jung, one of his patients.

Jung's original definition of synchronicity was set out in two stages. The first part has become the prevailing rationale for modern astrology, quoted in standard texts and recited by countless students. 'Whatever is born or done at this particular moment of time,' he wrote, 'has the quality of this moment of time.'[17] It seemed from this as if there was a direct correlation between events on earth and in heaven, exactly as would be expected in an ordered Platonic cosmos. This was a safe restatement of an astrological commonplace. But then Jung completely undermined his own apparent statement of objectivity by introducing a paradox, if not a downright contradiction of the earlier statement. 'If there are any astrological diagnoses,' he continued, '[they are] due . . . to our own hypothetical time qualities.'[18] The apparent regularity of the heavenly motions is undercut by a kind of shamanistic subjectivity in which the individual's participation with the cosmos really does matter. This time Jung, having deferred to Modernism, kept one foot firmly in the pre-modern magical tradition. In plain language Jung meant that coincidences, including the correlations which seem to be the basis of astrology, could be meaningful only if the astrologer declared them to be so; he believed that the therapist or astrologer, the client and the cosmos were all bound together in a kind of psychic conspiracy. The radical inference is that there could be no astrology without the astrologer. The horoscope is, then, not a map of objective truth, but a means of inquiry, an aid to what Edward de Bono called 'lateral thought' – forging subjective associations between feelings, ideas and events which are otherwise unconnected.[19] The logical conclusion is that there is no astrology 'out there' independent of the astrologer's readiness to relate a particular mood or event to this or that planet.

Two astrologers who were on a similar path to Jung were, ironically, theo-sophists – Dane Rudhyar, the patriarch of American astrology in the 1970s–1980s, and his protégé, Alexander Ruperti (1913–98), both members of Alice Bailey's Arcane School. We need to take a brief digression into their work because they both explored the implications of what Jung called 'hypothetical time qualities'. Ruperti took the exploration further than anyone else. In the early 1990s he argued provocatively that, 'the idea that an astrology with a capital A which exists somewhere, has always existed, and which we should all submit ourselves or be faithful to is merely the result of our imagination'.[20] There is, he implied, no such thing as an astrology that has any independent existence; there are only astrologers: people trying to interpret their relationship with the universe through astrological symbols. According to this view, the technical procedures of astrology are no more than a construct and spiritual truths are absolute, but astrology is entirely a culturally-dependent means of seeing the world, even if a particularly effective one. Meaning only emerges from the ritual construction and interpretation of the horoscope and each astrologer has his or her own astrological system, dependent on time and cultural context. Such astrology, New Age by virtue of its emphasis on self-knowledge, inner transformation and preparation for the Age of Aquarius, is an example of what the sociologist Brian Wilson defined as 'privatization', the phenomenon by which the collapse of established religion in the industrialized West allows individuals to construct their own spirituality from different traditions.[21] Sociology aside, we need to pause for a moment to reflect on the radical, sceptical nature of Ruperti's statement that astrology may be pragmatically useful but contains no objective, testable, truth claims. Rudhyar himself, who had inspired Ruperti, walked a delicate tightrope, introducing *The Astrology of Personality* with the twin and apparently contradictory statements that astrology both developed over time in line with changing cultural needs and that there is still an astrology which is capable of scientific investigation and therefore, logically, must be an objective quality of the natural world.[22] The latter was astrology as applied to individuals who are foolish, unenlightened and driven by instinct and who are therefore subject to fate. This, of course, was exactly what Aquinas had argued – that people who live by their animal natures have no control over their lives and are controlled by astrological influences. And here the theosophists' development of 'esoteric' astrology assumes its theological significance. Whereas Aquinas had argued that astrology had nothing to say about the soul, here was an astrology explicitly constructed to serve the soul. To return to Ruperti's statement, we are led straight to the common question – whether astrology is 'true' or 'made up'. Was Ruperti's astrology 'made up'? The problem is solved in the context of a Hermetic cosmos, in which mind and matter are inseparable. This much was recognized by André Breton, whose response was that astrology cannot be 'made up' because this would mean that it was a human creation and people do not create. Instead, they reveal what is hidden, and astrology, like painting, is an effective means of accomplishing this.[23]

It is difficult to believe from Ruperti's own work that he genuinely followed the somewhat anarchic point of view that astrology was purely cultural, for there seems to have been a gulf between his rhetoric and practice, and his own work depended on the assumption of a universal order.[24] It would also be misleading to move from here to any conclusion that the astrological is somehow 'unreal'. For Jung, the psychic world which could be read and revealed through astrology is as absolutely real as the material. While he called synchronistic connections 'acausal', meaning that the link between two events was that they happened at the same time, and that there was no need for a physical cause and effect relationship, he didn't doubt their fundamental location in the cosmos. It was just that they existed in the psychic world, not necessarily the material. Jung was ambivalent on astrology's nature. He was confused by his experience that it worked, but could never escape his belief that the manner in which it did so seemed to be dependent on the states of mind of astrologer and client. In the ultimately unresolved discussion on synchronicity we see him cross between the two views of the cosmos which Jude Currivan identified in prehistoric society: geomantic (fixed, stable) and shamanistic (spontaneous, ecstatic).[25] He shared Plotinus's opinion that the soul's connection with the cosmos was usually ordered and beautifully regular, but could be unpredictably spontaneous or ecstatic. His uncertainty is borne out of his struggle, as a positivist – witness his desperation to be recognized as a scientist – to enter into a fully medieval world-view in which there is no separation between the psychic and the physical worlds.

For Jung, following the principles of medieval magic, the outer world of events was inextricably linked to the inner psychic world and each of us becomes a participant, a co-creator in a vast cosmic drama. Astrology, he concluded, was not amenable to scientific investigation in the conventional sense because statistical methods aimed at establishing regular phenomena, and so concealed the rare events which, as he had found in his use of the *I Ching*, constellated astrological meaning at unique events in the consulting room. Yet he continued to follow a dual path, simultaneously rejecting and advocating the need for scientific evidence. Eventually, following his letter to B.V. Raman, Jung conducted his own astrological experiment, at last testing his theory of synchronicity. The task he set himself was to compare the positions of the sun and moon in the horoscopes of married couples.[26] His hypothesis was a simple one: that the sun in the husband's chart should be in a conjunction in the wife's, following what he saw as the universal alchemical principle of the sacred marriage between male (solar) and female (lunar) parts of the cosmos. His results were initially positive, holding out the prospect that he could indeed be mentioned in the same breath as Einstein. Yet, on reviewing his results, he found that they had been distorted by his own bias – his desire to see synchronicity scientifically validated. This, he concluded, was a clear example of the power of psychic projection to distort scientific experiments and he swung firmly to the view that astrology is a 'mantic art', and the horoscope a form of mandala which reveals the Self, that indefinable psychic essence at the centre of the individual human existence.[27] Although he never acknowledged his sources, Jung had also clearly read and absorbed those nineteenth-century religious theorists, such as Max Müller, for whom all religion originated in sun worship. He developed what has been called a 'Cult of the Interior Sun' in which Christ became psychologized as a symbol of the Self, rather than the sun as he was for Müller.[28] As the Jungian analyst Liz Greene put it, Jungian theory presents the horoscope-as-mandala as 'the symbolic expression of the potential wholeness of life and the human psyche . . . both [are] symbols of Self and symbols of God'.[29]

Jung's ideas were driven by exactly the same historical imperative which so powerfully motivated Leo, Steiner and Bailey. He was as convinced as any theosophist that the Age of Aquarius was coming.[30] Jungian analyst Ean Begg, speaking at the Astrological Association conference on 9 August 1999, reported a discussion with Gret Baumann Jung, Jung's daughter and herself an astrologer, after the BBC's centenary documentary on Jung in 1975. Begg asked her what she thought her father's major contribution was. According to Begg, she responded,

'I don't like to talk about it, but I think that he was one of the people sent to prepare for the Age of Aquarius.'[31]

Jung may not have lived to see the Age of Aquarius dawn, but he did leave a large circle of esoterically inclined psychologists who have continued to use and develop his theories. Prominent among these is James Hillman, whose debt to Jung (and Plato) is evident in the name he has given to his own adaptation of Jung's work, 'Archetypal Psychology'. Like Jung, he uses astrology in his therapeutic work but has written nothing practical on the subject. Hillman's younger colleague Thomas Moore, who has relied heavily on Marsilio Ficino, representing him as a precursor of modern psychotherapy, as well as Jung, is more overt in his use of astrology.[32] The cultural zone occupied by psychologists such as Hillman and Moore places the therapeutic process first and, while respecting astrology as a means of self-understanding, avoids direct discussion of astrological technique or horoscopic examples. Other models derived from Jung make no mention of astrology at all. The Myers-Briggs type indicator, for example, which was developed in the Second World War and has become one of the most widely used psychological tests, was derived from Jung's four psychological types which were, in turn, based on the four elements of classical cosmology.[33] Myers-Briggs testing is, like Comte's sociology or Mesmer's therapeutic use of animal magnetism, a fascinating example of 'disguised astrology', masquerading as science in order to claim respectability.

While Jung was formulating his theory of synchronicity and making the first serious contribution to 'high' astrology since the seventeenth century, 'low' astrology was also about to take a new direction. The link between the two, between Jung and the emergence of the horoscope column, was to be the pivotal New Age astrologer Dane Rudhyar. The 'oracles to the vulgar', as the almanacs had been dismissively labelled, were about to take on a new form as the modern sun-sign column.[34] These 12-paragraph columns, or horoscopes, carry interpretations for each of the sun-signs, or as the mass media calls them, 'birth-signs' or 'star-signs'. Without them the classic 1960s 'chat-up' line, 'What's your sign?', would never have been heard.[35]

The first regular newspaper astrology column was published in the British newspaper the *Sunday Express* on 24 August 1930, opening a new chapter in esoteric popular culture. The newspaper had asked the flamboyant society astrology and hand-reader Cheiro to provide an analysis of the horoscope of the infant Princess Margaret, daughter of the future George VI: a royal birth required a suitable editorial response and to settle on astrology as the vehicle for this was to prove a journalistic masterstroke. Cheiro was an obvious first choice. His client list had included the actress Sarah Bernhardt and King Edward VII, who, he claimed, had taken his advice on his coronation.[36] Cheiro was unavailable, though, so the feature was actually written by his assistant, R.H. Naylor, who had built up a reputation lecturing in London theatres. His speeches, titled 'What the Stars Foretell', appealed to the public concern with the world situation in the context of the Great Depression, the rise of the dictators and the continuing threat of communism. Naylor produced an astrologically orthodox interpretation of Margaret's chart, identifying her as an independent-minded 'woman of the New Age' and adding that 'events of tremendous importance to the Royal Family will come about near her seventh year [1937], and these events will indirectly affect her own fortunes'.[37] The year 1936 saw the abdication of Edward VIII, as shattering an event as the British monarchy had known since the removal of James II in 1689; the following year saw Margaret's father's coronation as George VI and her own elevation to second-in-line to the throne. Naylor's forecast, as simple as it was effective, was based on the movement of the progressed sun (using a method devised by Johannes Kepler) to a 90-degree aspect to Saturn, planet of responsibility and status: the aspect had actually happened on the seventh day of the Princess's life but, using Kepler's dictum that all cycles of time are qualitatively equivalent to all others, Naylor predicted that the appropriate event would take place in her seventh year. Naylor also adopted Raphael's successful editorial formula by adding (along with general political predictions) about 50 words per day of birthday predictions for each day of the coming week. Such birthday readings had been a familiar feature of mass astrology since the 1850s but, with Naylor, the format entered the popular press. His successful forecast for Margaret was forgotten by 1937 but a few weeks later, on 5 October, Naylor made a prediction based on the imminent, difficult opposition between the full moon and Uranus, a planet considered to represent sudden shocks. His exact words deserve repetition because they point to the logical manner in which Naylor constructed his forecasts in terms of probabilities rather than certainties. If anything, he was a follower of Hume. 'Earthquakes will occur,' he wrote, 'mostly near deep-sea level, and affecting peninsulas, in the autumn quarter of 1930. They may not actually occur in October – though from the 8th to the 15th is a real danger point – but they will be exceedingly likely in November or December. British aircraft will be in danger about the same date.'[38] On the same day, 5 October, the great British airship R101, one of the marvels of modern technology, crashed in a storm near Paris. There were 46 dead and just 8 survivors. Newspapers showed pictures of terrible wreckage and, to the readers of the *Sunday Express*, Naylor's immense skills as a forecaster were demonstrated beyond all doubt. The next week he revealed the simple astrological technique which underpinned his, by now, unassailable reputation as the leading media astrologer: 'My prediction last week was based on a very simple observation. It can be proved that, whenever the new moon or full moon falls at a certain angle to the planet Uranus, aircraft accidents, electrical storms, and sometimes earthquakes follow. Now ... the configuration referred to [full moon opposition Uranus] occurred on October 7; the destruction of the R101, therefore, prematurely fulfilled the indication.'[39]

The newspaper was already clearly delighted with the response to Naylor's column. An editorial note introducing his second feature reported proudly that 'enormous interest was aroused' in Naylor's predictions and treatment of the Princess's birth chart.[40] The potential increase in circulation clearly guaranteed support from the paper's editor and owner. Arthur Christiansen, the entertainment editor of the *Express* who hired Naylor, later wrote that, 'Naylor and his horoscopes became a power in the land. If he said that Monday was a bad day for buying, then the buyers of more than one West End store waited for the stars to become more propitious.'[41] Christiansen's testimony is an important part of the historical evidence suggesting that Naylor and the *Express* didn't create the demand for astrology but rather satisfied a thirst which was already present.

The spread of the new astrological language was remarkably quick, even if we must rely on anecdotal influence, such as Theodor Adorno's observation in 1953 that lonely hearts columns in German newspapers included frequent mention to the sun-signs of the advertisers.[42] This new media phenomenon was also sufficiently prominent to be featured in a Mass-Observation exercise in 1941, followed by a complaint to the British government that astrological forecasts were in danger of destabilizing the war effort. Mass-Observation's description of Naylor suggests that he occupied an established position within the tradition of radical, individualist, middle-class esotericists. Naylor, his observer concluded, was 'well educated, left-wing in an unusual way . . . is strongly anti-bureaucratic, anti-Conservative and anti-communist, but with an approach to what is going on in the world which is to a considerable extent Marxist'.[43]

Naylor was emphatically not a theosophist. He was representative of a substantial group of astrologers who remained outside the New Age big tent, and resented the notion that astrology required any sort of spiritual metaphysics in order to function perfectly well. His astrology was down to earth and direct, required nothing in the way of psychological insight and was designed to predict the future. If anything, Naylor was a Newtonian, interpreting a rule-bound cosmos, not interacting with it. But his contribution to media astrology was only to establish the commercial value of the astrological feature, not the 12-paragraph horoscope column itself; it was only in 1936, when he joined the newly launched *Prediction* magazine, that Naylor began writing sun-sign columns in the modern sense, rather than birthday forecasts. It's clear that, in 1930, he was unaware of this format. The first such columns appear to have been published in the USA, although the date is uncertain. A weekly feature of the type written by Naylor may have appeared in the *Boston Record* in 1931.[44] However, it seems that the first regular 12-paragraph horoscope columns appeared in the Detroit-based magazine *Modern Astrology*, edited by Paul Clancy, from around 1930. We do know definitely that they were published in *American Astrology*, Clancy's next venture, from the very first issue in March 1933. This was the seminal moment. This was the point at which the now ubiquitous language of birth-signs began to seep into the mass consciousness of the Western world. Within a few years every newspaper with an eye on a mass readership was carrying horoscopes. The conceptual trigger for the invention of the 12-paragraph sun-sign format lies with Dane Rudhyar, who it is thought, suggested it to Clancy, for reasons suggested by Alexander Ruperti: Rudhyar saw the mass magazine market as a tool for spreading his message, just as Blavatsky had used spiritualism to promoter hers.[45] The sequence of events through which the column was created moves from Blavatsky's fascination for the

Hermetic central spiritual sun, to Leo's identification of it as the most important factor in astrological interpretation and Rudhyar's apparent marriage of Leo's solar astrology with the conventional birthday-forecast format.

Rudhyar himself wrote some of the *American Astrology* columns. The style was similar to Naylor's but with a slightly greater emphasis on an open-ended, optimistic life brimming with potential for change, rather than a predetermined future to be passively experienced. In the very first issue, Ariens were told to anticipate 'happy change offering unusual opportunities and opening up a new avenue for personal progress'.[46] This sort of secularized New-Age Hermeticism continues to dominate a segment of the horoscope industry, with its constant reference to what readers can do for themselves, rather than what will happen to them. The link from the *Corpus Hermeticum* to the sun-sign column may be a surprising one but it is a simple one, from Blavatsky to Rudhyar to the popular press. Naylor's style is still evident, but the Rudhyar-esque horoscope column is Hermetic philosophy brought down to earth, applied to daily affairs, sometimes enigmatically, at others in terms of 'love, luck and loot'. The grand cosmologies of Blavatsky, Jung and Gurdjieff address personal concerns, the reader's immediate state of mind, within a metaphysical framework, which provides meaning and purpose.[47]

There's a wider context which also needs to be considered: the 1920s had been a decade of revolution in astronomy as great as that of 1609. Edwin Hubble's discovery that our galaxy was just one of many in an incomparably large and expanding universe, combined with the strangeness of Einsteinian relativity, became a powerful literary metaphor, in the hands of novelists such as Virginia Woolf, for the political and economic crises of the 1930s.[48] News of the vast, unfriendly universe was spread via Sir James Jeans's articles in the popular press, which had as great an appeal as Naylor's, and it is tempting to see the latter as an answer to the former. In 1940 Sir Arthur Eddington began his popular summary of the newly discovered expanding universe with the statement that 'I deal with the view now tentatively held that the whole material universe of stars and galaxies of stars is dispersing, the galaxies scattering apart.'[49] Naylor moved in the opposite direction, domesticating the cosmos, giving it boundaries, restoring its meaning, its personal link with his readers, and re-establishing its role as an immediate solution for human problems rather than a remote metaphor for them. It's as if he, along with most subsequent horoscope-column writers, was giving voice to Emile Durkheim's theory that it's in the nature of the religious mentality to convert cosmic relationships to social ones.[50]

The advent of the horoscope column opened a rift among professional astrologers, some of whom accused the leading columnists of being responsible for astrology's poor public image, an unconvincing argument considering it had been subject to serious ridicule since the Bickerstaff Papers. André Breton spoke for many when, in 1957, he denounced popular astrology as 'a prostitute who sits on the throne' once occupied by serious astrology.[51] Yet Rudhyar, the great proponent of astrology-as-self-knowledge, himself regarded sun-sign readings as 'oracular', by which he meant they could convey what he called 'general value judgments' on the appropriate responses that members of each birth sign may make to the circumstances they encounter from day to day.[52] It was then up to the reader to impart the astrologers' words with specific significance, exactly as a supplicant at an ancient oracle would have done. In 2003 Carl Weschke, president of the prominent American New Age publishing company Llewellyn, identified sun-sign astrology's mass appeal as 'all part of the adventure of self-knowledge. That is what was really new in the 20th century. Never before,' he added, 'had there been any system that could be applied on a mass market basis that "revealed" self to oneself.'[53]

19

The Twentieth Century: Sceptics and Scientists

We believe that the time has come to challenge directly and forcefully, the pretentious claims of astrological charlatans
BART BOK, LAWRENCE JEROME AND PAUL KURTZ[1]

By 1900, Enlightenment criticism of astrology had almost disappeared. After all, astrology itself seemed to have disappeared. Christian criticism was also muted. Why condemn something which impinged so little on the public consciousness? It was Sigmund Freud who stepped into this critical vacuum and restarted the war on astrology. In 1910 he made three requests of his student and protégé Carl Jung; the first was to hold to the 'sexual theory', the second was to go to church on Sundays, and the third was to join him in forming a bulwark against the 'black tide of mud ... of occultism'.[2] Jung had met Freud in 1907, two years after he became instructor of psychiatry in the Psychiatric Clinic, University of Zurich, but by 1910, he thought the request was bizarre for he was already an enthusiastic student of astrology. He had come to see that what Freud saw as dangerous occultism could instead be profoundly useful in the diagnosis and treatment of psychological neuroses. Freud himself made only one study of astrology, an account of a visit to an astrologer by one of his patients, which was written in August 1921 and included in a wider study of prophetic phenomena, written in the context of recent attacks on him by Jung.[3] He thought astrology was so dangerous that even to talk about it critically could encourage belief in it and lead to the destabilization of society which, so soon after the First World War, was already in a chaotic state. The report was presented only to a meeting of his closest followers and was not published for a further 20 years.

As Freud told the story, one of his well-known patients had visited a prominent Munich astrologer, an adviser, he added, to the Bavarian princes. The astrologer's exact prophecy was remarkably specific: the patient's brother-in-law, the astrologer predicted, was to die in the following July or August, a victim of either crayfish or oyster poisoning. Freud considered a forecast of such precision as impossible on the grounds that it exceeded astrology's technical capacity. However, his patient described the forecast as 'wonderful' because the event in question had, in fact, already occurred – in the previous August. Freud's response was as follows:

> You will no doubt agree with me in offering the most obstinate resistance to the possibility that so detailed an event as falling ill of crayfish poisoning could be inferred

from the date of the subject's birth by help of any tables of formulae whatever. Do not forget how many people are born on the same day. Is it credible that the similarity of the futures of people born on the same day can be carried down to such details as this? I therefore venture to exclude the astrological calculations entirely from the discussion; I believe the fortune teller might have adopted some other procedure without affecting the outcome of the interrogation ... Accordingly, we can also so it seems to me, leave the fortune teller (or, as we may say straight out, the 'medium') quite out of account as a possible source of deception.[4]

Freud's conclusion was that, as astrology was as a matter of principle incapable of making such exact statements, there must have been a simple, rational explanation, which was this: in the intensity of the consulting room, astrologer and client had been locked into a telepathic thought-transference in which the story of the crayfish incident had passed from one mind to another. Freud was happy in his ignorance. Rightly or wrongly, astrology was technically quite capable of making precise statements, and John Dee or Cornelius Agrippa would have been more than content with the use of telepathy as part of an astrological consultation. Indeed, psychic collaboration between astrology and cosmos was essential to the smooth functioning of medieval and Renaissance astrology. But for Freud, telepathy and astrological causation were incompatible, and any explanation was more palatable than that astrology could work.

In the struggle between the heirs of Jung and Freud, Jungians, especially those who follow their master's esoteric inclinations, remain broadly sympathetic to astrology. But academic psychologists who, even if sceptical of Freud, are part of the same positivist tradition, tend to be hostile to it. Like Freud, they see astrology as a substitute religion, a faith for people who are unable to cope with the modern world. Astrology's higher public profile in the wake of the invention of the sun-sign column required an answer and around 1941, when horoscope columns had spread through the popular press in the USA, the American Society for the Study of Social Issues grew alarmed and issued an official press release stating its concerns. 'Psychologists,' the statement began, 'find no evidence that astrology is of any value whatsoever.'[5] Astrology, the psychologists continued, appealed to people who were incapable of dealing with the problems of modern life and so turned to superstition as an easy way out. Astrology was not just of no value – it was positively harmful and, by offering meaningless statements with which anyone could agree, it encouraged the gullible to take the wrong decisions for the wrong reasons.[6] The results, as one 1990s study agued, could be bad for the American economy and bad for democracy.[7] Simply, astrology was un-American.

The sceptical belief that astrology appeals to the gullible is justified by various examples, such as the myth that Hitler used it. It is perfectly true that Hitler subscribed to a folk-mysticism in which he featured as saviour of the Aryan people, and saw the value in exploiting occult imagery, such as the Hindu sun-symbol the swastika. It is also true that, among the ideological strains which found expression in National Socialism, was a peculiar form of occultish nationalism.[8]

However, Hitler appears to have been a complete cynic who believed in nothing other than his own destiny. In fact, his position was somewhat closer to that of the American Society for the Study of Social Issues. 'Superstition,' Hitler said in 1942, 'is a factor one must take into consideration when assessing human conduct, even though one may rise superior to it and laugh at it.'[9] He reminisced that once he had advised Mussolini not to begin a 'certain action' on the 13th of the month, not because he or Mussolini regarded this as unlucky, but because the ignorant masses would.[10] Hitler was a fan of science and he despised astrology.

Attacks on astrology by secularists and scientists often have a decidedly religious tone, and Freud's view, speaking as a self-proclaimed scientist, that Jung should attend church in order to better resist the lure of the occult made the rhetorical alliance between the two explicit. Officially stated Christian views on astrology, which may have little to do with the opinions of actual church goers, vary from the mildly disapproving to the ferociously hostile. The 'official' Anglican view is not that astrology is wrong but that astrology is misleading because it takes no account of Christ.[11] More evangelical groups, though, stick to the strict line that it is satanic.[12] This opinion was recently reinforced by the latest version of the Roman Catholic catechism, which is essentially a paraphrase of St Augustine's views on the matter:

> All forms of divination are to be rejected: recourse to Satan or demons, conjuring up the dead or other practices falsely supposed to 'unveil' the future. Consulting horoscopes, astrology, palm reading, interpretation of omens and lots, the phenomena of clairvoyance, and recourse to mediums all conceal a desire for power over time, history, and, in the last analysis, other human beings, as well as a wish to conciliate hidden powers. They contradict the honour, respect, and loving fear that we owe to God alone.[13]

That Christian hostility to astrology can be pathological, by which I mean out of all proportion to the threat that astrology, under any circumstances, could pose to Christians, is indicated by the *Catholic Encyclopaedia*'s view on the matter, which indulges its antisemitism to an astonishing degree. In a passage which takes the historical and turns it on its head, as late as 2005, the *Encyclopaedia* made the following statement: 'The lower the Jewish nation sank in the scale of religion and civilization the greater was the power gained by the erratic doctrines of astrology and the accompanying belief in demonology.'[14] The passage was removed by 2008, but the fear and hatred of astrology as demonic is still evident. It is as if Aquinas's compromise, in which astrological influences impacted on the physical body, and left human beings free to make their own moral choices, had never existed. Yet, as at least one pro-astrology Catholic priest pointed out in response to the catechism, if astrology is defined as science rather than divination, there can be no objection to it.[15]

The most extravagant assault on astrology was launched by the Freudian–Marxist Theodor Adorno (1903–69) as a savage critique of the Los Angeles horoscope column from 1952–3, and shared completely the tone of those Christians who see astrology as satanic.[16] Adorno was one of a number of

Marxists, centred on the so-called Frankfurt School, who set out to explain why the Marxist prophecy of the worker's revolution had failed in advanced industrialized countries and, worse, why Germany, which Marxist theory proposed was the most likely candidate for such a revolution, had experienced quite the reverse – a reactionary take-over of the most appalling kind, culminating in the Holocaust. Adorno and his colleagues found the answer in Freud. Not until every individual, or at least a sufficient number, had experienced psychoanalysis, they believed, would the oppressed masses become truly aware of their position and a genuine revolution be possible. In order to explain fascism they developed the theory of the 'authoritarian personality', which they thought was characterized by an inability to exercise self-responsibility. Individuals who were subject to the authoritarian personality were supposedly willing to surrender control over their lives to greater forces, while bullying those who were, in their turn, weaker then them. Adorno thought that, just as those who supported the Nazis had surrendered control over their lives to Hitler, so the readers of horoscope columns surrendered theirs' to the stars. Astrology, he thought, was 'an ideology of dependence' which was marked by 'obvious similarities with paranoid systems of thinking'.[17] Readership of such columns was therefore, Adorno concluded, an indicator of potential fascist tendencies. Stamp out astrology, he thought, and a revival of Nazism would be less likely. This, of course, is essentially a fantasy position. Adorno provided no evidence for his assertions but he didn't need any: truth was already provided in the prophetic teachings of Karl Marx and Sigmund Freud. The theory of the authoritarian personality has long since been discredited, but Adorno's theory that astrology is akin to a pathological disorder lives on.[18] Robert Park, a physicist and prominent sceptical polemicist, referred to astrology in 2000 as one of 'the darkest superstitions that beset our species' and argues that belief in it arises from a breakdown in brain chemistry.[19]

The point about Adorno's work, when compared to that of the wildest Christians, is that criticism of astrology is so extreme in its rhetoric and uninformed in its comments: Freud had never heard of horoscopes, the *Catholic Encyclopaedia*'s is filtered through its righteous rage and Adorno thought that newspaper columns and their readers were representative of astrology as a whole. His simple view, that 'astrology is the metaphysic of dunces' is so far removed from the considered positions now taken within the history of ideas that we must apply Adorno's own comment on the astrologers to many critiques of astrology: they are 'semi-erudite'.[20] We might see sense in Adorno's comment that astrology is a closed system, within which all questions, including criticism of itself, are answered by the system itself.[21] But many systems of thought share this quality, including Adorno's two chosen ideologies, Marxism and Freudianism. In this sense, it's unclear how his criticisms are particular to astrology.

Adorno's damning – and deeply angry – critique of astrology is often taken as a given in the modern discipline of cultural studies which, amid its concern with 'popular' culture, completely ignores the phenomenon of mass horoscopes. For those rare cultural theorists who consider it, astrology is generally thought to be part of the culture industry's production of illusions, the, in Marxist terms, false ideologies which prevent human beings from encountering their true natures.[22] Elsewhere, academics use astrology as a synonym for stupidity and insecurity. In his searing denunciation of post-modernity, the British sociologist Kieran Flanagan complained that, when modern values have been abandoned, 'all that is left . . . is a belief in anything ranging from astrology to other fringe arts'.[23] Deprived of any sense of self-value by capitalism and consumerism, human beings, in their deluded ignorance, then fall prey to superstition, essentially counterfeit beliefs which are feeble substitutes for traditional theology. The flaw in such an analysis, apart from its obvious derivation from Christian polemic, is that it is ahistorical – it lacks any sense of the past and so can contribute little to the present.

Adorno's work can also be put into context through the Italian Marxist Antonio Gramsci's theory of hegemony, which is one of the foundations of much modern cultural theory.[24] In an attempt to find out why the prophecy of the workers' revolution had failed, Gramsci developed the notion that the repressive forces of the state are complemented by a 'superstructure', including the media, which exerts control over the flow of knowledge. Some forms of public discourse are effectively forbidden. For Adorno, astrology itself was part of the superstructure, an escapist tool supplied to the masses via daily newspapers in order to prevent them realizing the true cause of their oppressed condition. But, seen from another perspective, astrology is subject to public ridicule and condemnation precisely because its world-view challenges the scientific and religious orthodoxy that attempt to stamp out other world-views. Whereas science tends to regard the universe as devoid of meaning and conventional religion focuses meaning on God, astrology maintains the ancient idea that the universe is in itself meaningful, that meaning and purpose are woven into its fabric. In this sense astrology is not just an epistemological crime but an ideological one.

In spite of Freud, Adorno and the efforts of the American psychologists, astrology continued to spread, causing alarm to the protectors of scientific and psychological orthodoxy. Horoscope columns were an essential part of the popular appeal of newspapers and magazines from the 1950s onwards. Linda Goodman's 1970 book, *Sun Signs*, sold, it is claimed, over a million copies and the 1960s counter-culture produced a wave of interest in esoteric literature which was conducive to an interest in astrology. For many, LSD, blurring as it did the boundaries between mind and matter, was a fast track to a fascination with magic. Gerald Hawkins and Alexander Thom's astronomical studies of Stonehenge and megalithic culture was reproduced into alternative culture via 'underground' newspapers like the *International Times*.[25] Astrologers themselves pressed ahead with attempts to organize themselves, in spite of setbacks. In 1936, representatives of the various groups of British astrologers, including Naylor, set up a 'General Council', followed the next year by the Federation of British Astrologers, whose avowed aim of representing all professional astrologers was never fulfilled; the profession was still too small and individualistic. In 1948 the Astrological Lodge of the Theosophical Society set up the first successful astrological school to offer an organized vocational instruction, the Faculty of Astrological Studies. Ten years later a group of Lodge members who thought that the theosophical connection was a hindrance to astrology's search for respectability and scientific validation broke away to form the British Astrological Association. Similar developments took place in most Western countries.

In 1975, seriously alarmed by these developments, Bart Bok, the American astronomer who had published the 1941 attack on astrology, coordinated a statement signed by 186 individuals, listed as 'leading scientists', denouncing astrology as a magical system, lacking in scientific evidence and appealing, as Freud had argued, to people who were unwilling or unable to take responsibility for their lives.[26] Critics have identified a moral anger in the statement, driven by an unsupported assumption that astrologers cannot genuinely believe in something they know to be false and are therefore charlatans, defrauding a public which is in need of protection. The scientists themselves were accused of making statements which were anti-scientific in the sense that they lacked supporting evidence. The radical philosopher of science, Paul Feyerabend, condemned scientists and astrologers equally: 'it is interesting to see,' he wrote, 'how closely both parties approach each other in ignorance, conceit and their wish for easy power over minds'.[27] Bok and the coordinators of the anti-astrology Statement, though, went on to found their own organization, the Committee for the Scientific Investigation of Claims of the Paranormal, or CSICOP. The society became the centre of an international network of sceptical groups whose aim was to combat all of what, following Karl Popper, they call pseudo-science, including astrology. One of CSICOP's fundamental principles is the belief that the civilized world is suffering from a tidal wave of superstition, which needs to be resisted by any means; Richard Dawkins, a CSICOP fellow and Professor of the Public Understanding of Science at Oxford University, advocates the prosecution of astrologers for fraud.[28] Critics within the scientific world argue, though, that CSICOP is itself a quasi-religious organization, determined to close down debate on any theory which fails to fit its atheist, materialist and positivist paradigm.[29] It's difficult to place what we might call irrational scientific hostility into context. (I use the word irrational here to refer to literature which is primarily polemical rather than evidence-based.) There appears to be a sense that Enlightenment values are somehow under attack, and astrologers are represented as an anti-scientific, anti-modern danger, not unlike communists in 1950s America, or Muslims after September 2001, rather than as the amorphous, varied group they are, lacking any clear sense of the single direction which their enemies ascribe to them. In their fear of the imagined enemy the scientist Richard Dawkins and the Christian evangelical Constance Cumbey find themselves sharing a common rhetoric.[30] Such sceptics as Dawkins are not representative of the entire sceptical area, and should really be identified as fundamentalists in that they have established a certain unshakeable dogma about the way the world works, which can never be challenged. I make this observation in the knowledge that every area, including astrology, attracts its own fundamentalists.[31]

There is a substantial body of opinion that claims that astrology is, in its very nature, untestable, and that its claims can never be subject to scrutiny under controlled conditions. Some say that astrology depends on the unique time, date and place for which a horoscope is cast and, as this combination of data never repeats, so there can be no replicable experiments. A shrewd comment was made by Edward James who pointed out that astrology cannot be tested, or falsified in Popper's terminology, because it is not a specific theory or law, but a discipline or area of study.[32] It consists of many practices and truth claims, many of which may have little in common with each other. The methodological problems, though, run deeper than this. How do we investigate a discipline which regards its practitioners and clients as an integral part of the process being studied? Many astrologers argue that there can be no controlled conditions in situations which are necessarily unique – the exact same disposition of planets and zodiac never repeats. Guido Bonatti himself had written that any attempt to work out whether an astrologer is telling the truth, and whether astrology 'works', must fail because the question is not a genuine one, but a trick.[33] The cosmos will only respond to sincerity, never mere curiosity. Therefore, according to Bonatti, if a test fails it may well demonstrate the truth of astrology. The problem here for scientific research is obvious: if scientific method requires causal mechanisms and universally testable, replicable results, then any astrology which depends on the astrologer and cosmos engaging in a conscious, psychic relationship must fail. In this sense the philosophical problems associated with demonstrating the objective truth of astrological claims are the same as those for the existence of God.

Astrologers who claim that astrology is untestable are contradicted by those who believe that individual claims can stand up to scrutiny, often because of a desire to establish which techniques genuinely work and abandon those which don't, an attitude still rooted in the polemics of the 1490s. The story of scientific investigation of astrology is a complex one, largely due to methodological problems, and the results are mixed.[34] The tests, broadly, can be divided into two types. The first set of inquiries searches for statistical validation for the relevance of individual astrological alignments or patterns, usually in isolation from the rest of the horoscope. The second examine the actual reading by astrologers of birth charts, testing, for example, their ability to match occupation to horoscope in blind trials. These, the so-called Vernon Clarke tests, initially achieved positive results, later replaced by negative ones.[35] Current levels of research are negligible: there has, to my knowledge, been just one PhD investigating astrological claims so far in the twenty-first century, and that was favourable to astrology.[36]

The single most important figure in the twentieth century attempting to prove astrology within contemporary scientific method – using isolated factors and large samples to establish statistical significance – was the French statistician Michel Gauquelin (1928–91).[37] Gauquelin was a complex man. His charming and humble manner concealed a huge belief in his own importance and a tenacious ability to fight his case. He was deeply critical of most astrology yet found willing friends among astrologers when many of the sceptics who should have been his allies rejected him. Gauquelin collaborated with his wife Françoise on many of his most important projects although, as so often happens, his books appeared under his name alone. His interest in astrology began as a youthful fascination but, like so many reformers back to Plotinus and beyond, he was severely critical of the practical, mainly commercial, astrology of his time. He cited approvingly the surrealist poet André Breton's opinion that astrology is 'a very great lady, most beautiful, and coming from such a great distance that she cannot fail to hold me under her spell . . . What a shame that nowadays – at least for the common herd – a prostitute reigns in her place.'[38]

Gauquelin's work was a postscript to the reform programme that began in the 1490s. He was very much in sympathy with Kepler's project – to strip away astrology's unnecessary and, in his view, in all probability, false teachings and replace them with verifiable, hard evidence. Like Kepler and the earlier reformers, Gauquelin had a profound respect for astrology's past. With explicit reference to 50 centuries of tradition dating back to the Chaldeans, he announced his intention of 'seeking another astrology, a more venerable one that must be treated with more consideration'.[39] Unlike Kepler, he had no concern with its philosophical basis and was concerned solely with demonstrating the existence, or non-existence, of the correlation between celestial patterns and terrestrial events. Gauquelin's starting point was no longer the Platonic or Pythagorean doctrines of the divinity of the cosmos or harmony of the spheres, but the physical reality of solar and lunar effects, sunspots, tides and body-clocks. Like Ptolemy he reasoned that if such influences are real, and nobody can possibly deny them, then it is perfectly reasonable to suspect that planetary influences might exist as well. The objection, posed by so many astronomers, that planetary effects might be either inherently unlikely or too small to measure, wasn't really a serious issue for Gauquelin. To him such problems were theoretical and had no validity compared to experimental data. Besides, he reasoned, absence of evidence is not evidence of absence. By the time of his death in 1991 he had conducted a huge amount of research, had published a series of books and launched a scientific controversy which is still raging, albeit in a very small corner of the scientific world. His view of his own importance, reinforced by notable supporters such as the eminent and controversial psychiatrist Hans Eysenck of London University's Institute of Psychiatry, was reflected in the title of his last work: *Neo-Astrology: A Copernican Revolution*. Gauquelin believed that whereas the first Copernican revolution in astronomy had severed the ancient link between astronomy and astrology, his second Copernican revolution was destined, he hoped, to bring them back together.

Gauquelin set himself a simple question: 'is it possible to observe common positions in heavenly bodies for the births of individuals who have manifested common tendencies throughout their lives?' Commencing what was to be his life's work in 1949, he began by systematically collating the birth data of 7000 French people. He then made a simple comparison between planetary position in the diurnal cycle – in other words, during the course of the day – and professional success as measured by criteria such as inclusion in *Who's Who*: unexpectedly, his positive results worked only for individuals who had achieved outstanding success – the so-called 'eminence effect'. His first positive finding, based on a study of 576 members of the Académie de Médecine, established that his subjects were likely to be born when Saturn was either rising over the eastern horizon or culminating – at its highest point of the day. Smaller peaks were discovered for the opposite points – the planet's setting and lower culmination. Repeating the process with other professionals and planets he established a similar relationship between the moon and the births of successful writers; Jupiter and actors and politicians; and Saturn and scientists. The results were not exclusive though: Jupiter and the moon shared a connection with writers and politicians.[40] Once they'd established the professional connections with planetary position at birth, the Gauquelins moved on to the second phase, hereditary studies, discovering that if a parent was born with a particular planet rising or setting then the child would be statistically likely to share the same pattern. They also found that the effect disappeared with surgical intervention. The third phase took them into the investigation of psychology, attempting to demonstrate the 'character trait hypothesis', matching lists of descriptive trait words taken from biographical encyclopaedias with planetary positions.[41] Their hereditary results have been challenged while the character trait investigations have been seriously undermined by allegations that the selection was too open to subjective bias. The apparent connections between professional eminence and the positions of the moon, Jupiter and Saturn at birth, meanwhile, have effectively sunk without trace, the victims of scientific indifference.

However, one of the Gauquelins' findings has become a major cause célèbre in the battle between astrology and scientific scepticism. This is the famous 'Mars effect' – the statistically significant link between Mars' position at birth and sporting success. As soon he had published his results in *L'Influence des Astres* in 1955, Gauquelin began looking for independent verification of his results. Gauquelin's first approach, to the Belgian Comité Para in 1956, met with a simple rebuff justified by the statement that 'professional astronomers have studied the question a priori' and hence there was no need to proceed any further.[42] After 11 years of stalling, the Comité finally agreed to replicate Gauquelin's work in 1967 and, in 1968, it verified the Mars effect's existence, much to some of its members' alarm. There followed an unedifying internal squabble in which some members insisted that scientific rectitude dictated that the results be published while others tried to find objections. Publication was delayed until 1976 and, when the report did appear, it was a heavily partial account of the experiments and results, relying retrospectively on the argument that the positive results might have been due to demographic factors.

By then the American sceptic group, the Committee for the Scientific Investigation of Claims of the Paranormal, had taken up the case. Three of the committee's leading members, the philosopher Paul Kurtz, the astronomer

George Abell and the statistician Marvin Zelen, oversaw a test, designed by Zelen, which was intended to definitively demonstrate whether or not the Gauquelins had made a mistake. To their alarm Kurtz, Abell and Zelen discovered that, like the Comité Para, they had verified the existence of the Mars effect. Their subsequent attempts to re-evaluate their test's significance and deny its support for the Mars effect produced serious internal arguments within CSICOP, stirred up by the astronomer Dennis Rawlins, who was outraged by what he saw as an abdication of scientific standards by the very people who were supposed to be upholding them. It was, in fact, one of the most notorious scientific cover-ups of the twentieth century: only once did CSICOP literature ever acknowledge the Zelen test's support for the Mars effect, in a footnote to a heavily edited article by Rawlins in 1982.[43] Although the sceptical literature never refers to this incident, among other research groups, such as the Society for Scientific Discovery, it has become emblematic of CSICOP's identity as a 'debunking' rather than a genuinely sceptical organization while, among astrologers and others who are on the receiving end of CSICOP's propaganda, it has virtually discredited the entire sceptical project. Rawlins' description of CSICOP as a 'group of would-be debunkers who bungled their major investigation, falsified the results, covered up their errors and gave the boot to a colleague who threatened to tell the truth' was, for many scientists and astrologers, its epitaph as a credible organizsation.[44] Even though it remains, through its campaigning zeal, the organizational core of what is now a global sceptical movement, thanks to the Mars effect cover-up sceptics are widely seen by those they criticize as automatically biased and as having no more credibility then astrology's religious enemies. So, just as sceptics attack astrologers, astrologers react defensively to sceptics and there is almost nothing in the way of real dialogue between the two.

Since Gauquelin's death the tiny band of academics who are continuing to support the Mars effect have been led by Suitbert Ertel, Emeritus Professor of Psychology at Georg-August University in Goettingen. Ertel was himself instrumental in demolishing the trait word hypothesis but has consistently demonstrated the Mars effect's existence. Much of his energy, though, is spent continuing Gauquelin's guerrilla war with the sceptics, in which allegations of data manipulation and dishonesty continue to fly. By 1996, when Ertel summarized his work in *The Tenacious Mars Effect*, Hans Eysenck was so bemused by the sceptics' continued resistance to what he regarded as the facts that he regarded scientific scepticism itself as a suitable subject of psychological investigation – and argued that the Mars effect should be included in textbooks along with Freud's theories, which he regarded as somewhat less credible than Gauquelin's.[45] Since the failure to establish a consensus on the Mars effect there has been other studies that review the essential data, but only one further major contribution to the debate on its significance. This is from Geoffrey Dean, who accepts the validity of Gauquelin's statistics but argues that they are an artefact, produced by the deliberate manipulation of French birth records.[46] The theory claims that parents in the nineteenth century registered their children's births at times when

Mars was in one of the auspicious positions identified by Gauquelin in the 1950s. Critics respond that there was no knowledge of the Mars effect before Gauquelin, no parents would have wanted to saddle their children with unfortunate Mars in damaging places, and the scale of the unspoken conspiracy is so great that there should be at least some reliable corroborating evidence. The theory has the support of fundamentalist sceptics mainly because, like Freud, they prefer any explanation to the possibility that there might be any truth in astrology's claims. Ertel has pointed out, though, that by hitching their wagon to an untenable theory which itself confirms Gauquelin's statistics, if the parental tampering hypothesis fails, Gauquelin is vindicated.[47]

We can place these arguments, both religious and scientific, in their historical context by reference to those which took place in the Roman world, from Cicero's distinction between 'artificial' divination (such as the casting of horoscopes) which he rejected and natural divination (such as weather forecasting) which he accepted, to Augustine's claim that the former was satanic.[48] The Greek world was never entirely happy with the introduction of Babylonian astrology in the second century BCE, and that discomfort, and the resulting rhetorical positions, are with us still.

20

The Twenty-first Century: Epilogue

A good cosmology . . . is good for its adherents.
FREYA MATHEWS[1]

Astrology has survived into the twenty-first century. On that we can all agree. The challenge is to assess its cultural function, the appeal of its claims, practices and world-view. It is unfortunate that what little academic writing there is on modern astrology tends to be driven by the misplaced belief that its survival is an anachronism which automatically conflicts with the benefits of modernity. Having started from this a priori assumption, the mission is then too often to explain astrology as a species of superstition, or 'magical-thinking', which satisfies the needs of those psychologically flawed or sociologically marginal individuals who are unable to cope with the modern world. The difficulty with such studies is typically that the data is made to fit the conclusion, and this then becomes a problem for the historian who requires less value-laden sources.

The attacks on astrology by evangelical Christians and fundamentalist sceptics have a minimal effect on popular opinion, but do have an impact in higher education. The hostility is often surprising in its intensity. The astronomers Philip Ianna and Roger Culver remarked how a colleague physically attacked them in anger that they were considering even writing a book attacking astrology, mirroring Freud's belief that astrology is so dangerous that one shouldn't even mention it.[2] The anecdotal evidence I have collected contains many instances of academics who are sympathetic to astrology being afraid to admit their interest, or of students being warned that academic careers will suffer if they admit to belief in it. This hidden harassment has an effect on the world of organized astrologers in which there is sometimes a certain sense of victimization. As American astrologer Steven Forrest admitted, he lives with 'a primal fear', that a stranger is about to ask him 'that simple, ubiquitous social question – "By the way, Steve, what do you do?"; 'I'm embarrassed,' he continued, 'to say what I do. I'm embarrassed to say I'm an astrologer.'[3] Such nervousness, which might drive the faint-hearted away from astrology, is countered by heroic proclamations of astrology's destiny such as that by John Addey, President of the British Astrological Association, in 1971. 'Astrology,' Addey announced at the association's annual conference, 'is evidently about to undergo a rebirth and a period of new growth. It will be no ordinary rebirth and no ordinary period of growth. From being an outcast from the fraternity of sciences, it seems destined to assume an almost central role in scientific thought.'[4] The two views, victimhood and triumphalism, tend to exist in a dialectic relationship with each other, in which the latter offers a prophecy that the former is soon to be overcome.

But where does all this leave astrology today? Outside India, the numbers of professional astrologers are tiny. Those who make an adequate living from it in the UK may be just a few dozen, in the USA a few hundred.[5] In 2002, the leading organizations in the USA, the National Council for Geocosmic Research and the International Association for Astrological Research, numbered their memberships at something above a thousand, as did the British Astrological Association. The numbers are small and all are challenged by the growth of web-based cyber-communities: print journals are threatened by blogs, and horoscopes which were downloadable are now free. It's a feature of globalization that old institutions suffer as new networks evolve, and astrologers with a saleable product have access to a global market. Those who, as is common in the USA, give consultations by telephone, find that the technology has become both more efficient and free.

Just how prevalent astrology is in society as a whole depends on how the question is asked. Many people, anywhere between 40 per cent and 60 per cent, agree that their birth sign description is accurate, while the number who think that astrology can make accurate forecasts varies from less than 30 per cent to 20 per cent.[6] But when we inquire about behaviour, rather than attitudes, the figures tend to be higher, indicating a deeper penetration of astrology into Western society. For example, about 50 per cent–70 per cent of young people admit to reading about the sun-signs of a new girl- or boyfriend, and about the same percentage of adults in the UK value the advice they are given in horoscope columns. Readership of horoscope columns themselves varies from 25 per cent to 75 per cent of the adult population, with variations in frequency: a small number may read a column every day, a large number once a month.[7] A very few people are deeply engrossed in astrology but, for most, the awareness of its personal meaning is akin to what Harold Isaacs called a 'scratch on the mind', something of which we are usually only vaguely aware but can't forget, like an old song.[8] The figures, though, vary enormously, partly because investigation of belief is notoriously unreliable – many people are embarrassed to admit to any interest in astrology for fear of ridicule. This much was pointed out by David Hufford who argued that Modernism privileges disbelief and ridicules belief.[9] When a subject is couched in terms of belief, as astrology usually is, interest in it is often concealed. Its penetration into Western culture through the language of sun-signs is probably much wider than the sceptics fear.

Astrology certainly exists in popular culture.[10] In the eyes of literary critics it's acceptable for writers to use astrology as a literary device. The British thriller writer Ruth Rendell did just this in novels such as *The Killing Doll*, in which the main character's descent into murder is mirrored by his sister's use of a cocktail of occult practices, or *Lake of Darkness*, in which the plot unfolds as a generous, conservative Taurean is led into a web of deceit, and ultimately tragedy, by a devious, secretive Scorpio.[11] It is expected that the reader will understand such references, exactly as Chaucer's audience would have understood celestial allusions in *The Canterbury Tales*. Elsewhere Rendell summed up astrology's modern cultural context, at least one version of it, when describing the concerns of one of her characters as 'clothes, cosmetics, aids to beauty, homeopathy, work-outs, massage, cosmetics, sparkling water, lettuce, vitamin supplements, alternative medicine, astrology and having her fortune told'.[12]

Astrology's position in the modern West is somewhat ambiguous. It is clearly a major feature of popular culture in its familiar horoscope-column form, precisely in that it is set in opposition to high culture, in a state of tension with what claims to be the dominant culture.[13] And, for opponents of popular culture, such as Theodore Adorno, astrology is part of a matrix of ideas expressed through the 'culture industry' and designed to create 'a dependent, passive, and servile consuming public', which would accept its powerlessness and poor economic fortunes.[14] At this point, we should, of course, question the notion of 'dominant' culture. Reverse the argument and astrology, by virtue of its popularity, is the dominant culture. Astrology is also clearly subcultural to the extent that it thrives among modern pagans, has particular forms of expression in the Alice Bailey and Rudolf Steiner movements, and is marginal in the sense that astrological schools and societies are so small as to be insignificant.[15] Yet, horoscope columns are ubiquitous and astrology is taken for granted among large swathes of the population. There are clearly social and gender issues and women are more likely to be interested in astrology than men. Ninety per cent of the students at the average astrology class are female and, while glossy magazines aimed at women all contain astrology columns, none aimed at men carry them. Those newspapers which include horoscopes do so specifically because they wish to attract female readers. Sceptics respond by accusing women of being gullible, but supporters of astrology argue that women have found a voice which has been denied to them by patriarchal society, and that their ease in discussing feelings suits them particularly to astrology, or at least to its modern, New Age, version.[16] Even when men do study astrology, it is sometimes said that they have a greater tendency to favour 'hard', 'old-age' event-prediction and scientific approaches, rather than 'soft', counselling varieties, although there are many exceptions to this generalized rule.[17] Regarding astrology's wider appeal, attempts to show that it thrives among the socially or educationally marginal have floundered both on conflicting data and the unfortunate fact that the 'marginal', in at least one American study, included the poor, uneducated, Latinos and women.[18]

The problem is simple. Many historians, until recently at any rate, thought that astrology had died out in the seventeenth century, a belief which appears to have been due to the prevailing influence of the nineteenth-century anthropologists and cultural evolutionists, who argued that astrology was characteristic of primitive societies, and who were less concerned with whether astrology had died out than with the dogma that it *should* have died out.[19] In Herbert Spencer's influential view, the kind of mentality which saw significance in the stars was 'child-like', and modern – nineteenth century – examples of it were supplied by the 'savages' of Africa and Polynesia.[20] The few sociologists and psychologists who turned their attention to astrology from the 1960s onwards followed Spencer and thought that it *ought* to have died out and therefore treated it as some sort of anachronistic survival, a freakish relic of a superstitious past which contradicted the prevailing secular myth of inevitable progress towards scientific enlighten-ment.[21] These academics bought into a less extreme form of CSICOP's faith history. They may not have thought that they were on a moral crusade to defeat astrology, but they certainly believed that right-thinking educated Westerners should have no truck with it. The result was a complete failure to comprehend astrology's extent, role or appeal. As Terry Eagleton put it, in another context, such 'empathetic errors' meant that Western culture 'shows a lamentable failure to imagine other cultures. Nowhere is this more obvious than in the phenomenon of aliens.'[22] For aliens read astrologers, or any other group deemed odd by the guardians of intellectual orthodoxy. Astrologers are heterodox. In fact, they are often regarded as heretics, their very existence an affront to many representatives of mainstream science and religion. How in these circumstances, do we penetrate the world of the astrologers? How do we even find out how many there are?

Astrologers, as far as their critics are concerned, are epistemological criminals. They commit a crime of knowledge, approaching the world from the wrong direction. Yet the issues of verifying the truth of astrology, whether judged by scientific tests, anecdote or personal experience, are so great that there are clearly other issues, including the politics of knowledge. And here, a couple of case studies are illustrative.

The most famous political user of astrology in the twentieth century was US president Ronald Reagan. Reagan had used astrologers long before he moved into politics, hardly surprising for a Hollywood film star. He had been using a well-known astrologer called Ralph Kraum between at least 1937 and 1966 and Kraum's hand-drawn chart for Reagan was published in the early 1980s; given that Reagan didn't know his time of birth the chart was 'rectified' – the time of birth as calculated retroactively by matching events in Reagan's life with planetary transits. Ronald and his second wife, Nancy were also clients, and possibly even students, of Carol Richter, a celebrity astrologer based in Beverley Hills. Richter proudly displayed Nancy and Ronald's photographs on his desk along with Grace Kelly's. They also for a time in the 1980s used a certain James Harvey, who was a follower of the theosophist Alice Bailey.

In 1967 the press, as well as Democrat politicians, remarked on the curious moment chosen (probably by Richter) for Reagan's inauguration as governor of California – 16 minutes past midnight on 1 January 1967. As inaugurations normally take place at noon, it was widely assumed that Reagan's astrologer had chosen the time, prompting a Republican spokesman to reassure the electorate that 'this will be no star-gazing administration'.[23] When Reagan's use of astrology finally came to public attention in 1988, thanks to the revelations of his embittered former chief of staff, Donald Regan, the White House tried to deflect the damage to the President's reputation by claiming that Nancy had been the astrology fan and Ronald merely the innocent dupe. Even Regan was taken in by this fiction.[24] Regan referred to a mysterious 'friend' who was feeding astrological advice to the President via his wife, Nancy. When Regan's book was published with a massive wave of publicity, the White House spin machine moved to protect the President and claimed that Nancy alone believed in astrology. Yet Reagan's use of astrology over many decades suggests he was a keen enthusiast.

The mysterious 'friend' turned out to be an upper-class San Franciscan Republican, Joan Quigley. Quigley's astrology was clear, practical, and predictive, designed to manage the President's schedule, and not at all concerned with psychological or spiritual growth. She advised the President on his associates, often updating their horoscopes every week, and selected the most auspicious moments for his major engagements. Nancy, the President's wife, would send Quigley a note of the people and events about which she needed information and, on the few occasions on which Quigley was late with her calculations, the machinery of the White House might grind to a halt. During the Iran–Contra crisis, there were fears that, unless Reagan publicly addressed allegations that his government had sold arms to Iran to raise funds the Contra rebels in Nicaragua, he would be caught up in the scandal. Yet Quigley drove the White House staff to distraction by instructing the President to do and say nothing for a period of about four months. She was clearly following in the style of the seventh-century BCE Assyrian astrologers Balasi, who advised his emperor 'not to go out doors', and Munnabitu, who cautioned the emperor to stay in his palace for a month.[25] Quigley's work may have been ridiculed in the press but it provides evidence of a (now) underground tradition of political advice which extends in an unbroken line back to the emperors of Babylon. The connection is tenuous, but real.

The contempt which was poured on Reagan for his use of astrology, compared to the neutral manner in which accounts of its use by Asian governments are couched, is evidence of what we might call the racism of lowered expectations. That Indian politicians use astrology or that Chinese businesses incorporate it into their buildings in the form of Feng Shui is beyond criticism; in the minds of Western journalists, nothing better can be expected from non-white cultures. Similarly, the case of Princess Diana is evidence of the sexism of lowered expectations. High-profile women can use astrology without damage to their reputations whereas for men the same admission would spell professional suicide. This is why it is a woman, Judith Levy, the chief executive of the British retail chain High and Mighty, who is the only leading British executive to have spoken in public about her use of astrology in order to take commercial decisions.[26] Princess Diana herself used three astrologers in the 1980s and 1990s, of whom Penny Thornton is the best known. Thornton's work with Diana is a casebook example of the theosophical astrology pioneered by Dane Rudhyar, in which the purpose is to maximize the client's potential rather than predict the future.[27]

As a psychologically trained astrologer, Thornton was not content merely to describe Diana's character or predict possible events. She was also concerned to help Diana find a way out of her predicament. She suggested that Diana's psychological inclinations would make it virtually impossible for her to accept the British monarchy's restrictive conventions, and advised that tensions with her husband and in-laws would prove self-destructive. Diana could help herself, she concluded, by redirecting her energy into constructive projects, and she advised the princess to throw herself into positive activities. This advice steered Diana into her work with AIDS patients, visits to hostels for the homeless and involvement in the campaign to ban landmines. Diana would not be able to change the chart or her character, but she could decide how to reconcile her conflicting impulses.

Reagan was roundly mocked for his use of astrology, and Diana less so, but in both cases the use of astrology was regarded as a measure of inadequacy. The study of astrology as a cultural phenomenon therefore seems to find a safer home with religious studies, than among sociologists or psychologists. Within the literature on the sociology of religion, astrology is often characterized as a New Religious Movement or, perhaps, a form of 'new religion', or 'non-traditional religious belief'.[28] It is also widely argued that, if not a religion, astrology may be a substitute religion, or what Hill considered a 'God of the Gaps', one of many popular responses to the 'disenchantment', or loss of sacred character, of the modern world.[29] It is not clear why astrology should be regarded negatively as a pale imitation of something else, though, whether as a pseudo-science or a substitute religion. To stay within a religious context, it may equally well be described positively as a vernacular religion, the popular belief of the people, unsanctioned by the scientific or religious authorities.[30] It is unlikely, though, that any definition of astrology can be based on its essential nature, as even astrologers are sharply divided over what this is. It may be safer to ignore such problematic areas and define astrologers according to how they organize themselves, as a 'metaphysical community'. It is a community which, like any other, can be both flexible and intolerant. Anyone can be accepted into the community of astrologers who accepts the basic proposition that there is a relationship between celestial patterns and terrestrial events. Yet one former astrologer who decided that astrology did not work, complained to me that, among what he called the community of believers, to deny one is an astrologer is to be an apostate, adopting the same position as one who rejects any other religious or political ideology: how, he asked rhetorically, can one reject revealed knowledge? This, though, was the view of one individual and we really cannot separate the notion of revelation in astrology from the reality of the experience which sustains its practice. Astrology has its heresies and schisms, exactly like any other philosophy or practice. All astrologers share the experience that it 'works' but the 'community', such as it is, contains some who deny that other astrologers are real astrologers at all. The gulf between those who think that it can be proved statistically and those who imagine they are medieval diviners is deep. The rhetorical positions combine with rival allegiances, exactly as in any other field. Astrology exists in a variety of cultural milieux. There are those few Jungian analysts who use astrology, along with a small number of homeopaths and herbalists. There are the organized astrologers of the mainstream societies, such as the American National Council for Geoscosmic Research or the British Astrological Association, and the distinct circles of Baileyite and anthroposophical astrologers. Then there are the pagans, concerned as much with the sacred calendar as with horoscopes, and the Wiccans, who are as likely to be found 'pulling down the moon' as reading their birth charts.[31] The users are also diverse and, aside from the clear evidence that the majority are female, they range from bankers to New Age devotees, and there are no reliable studies (though there are unreliable ones) which enable us to identify patterns of, say, income, educational status or psychological profile.

Some astrologers regard each other as cultish, opening a whole new line of inquiry for sociologists. The sociologists Stark and Bainbridge regard astrology as a 'client cult'. Astrologers, they claim, deal in 'in serious magic'; for example, they 'do not offer access to heaven, but they do claim to be able to give us valuable advice by reading the heavens'.[32] The problem here is symptomatic of so much sociological literature in the field. A client cult is defined as a 'service and therapy occupation', and est, Scientology, Rolfing and psychoanalysis are given as examples. The self-evident weakness of Stark and Bainbridge's typology is that it enables anything to be defined as a cult; if a visit to a therapist is a cult activity, then so must be a visit to a doctor for reassurance. Is the British National Health Service, then, a cult organization? In other words, Stark and Bainbridge's typology can be applied to almost any public activity and, if every form of public behaviour can be cultic, then the argument about what is or is not a cult breaks down: either everything is a cult or nothing is. Essentially, certain sociologists of religion have fallen into the positivist trap. They assume that questions of truth are easy to establish and that, on the truth–falsity scale, astrology emerges as false, and therefore, in their terms, as religious. This in turn leads to a widespread but spurious notion that astrology is a rival to mainstream religion, and that, as regular church attendance in the West declines, at least outside the USA, so astrology rushes in to fill the vacuum, as if the decline in church-going and the rise in astrology exist in a kind of causal relationship.[33] There is actually no evidence for this proposition any more for the widespread idea that belief in astrology is increasing: we just don't have good data.

A more convincing view is that Western society's progressive secularization has led not to a decline of religious feeling but to its fragmentation, and to a process known to sociologists as privatization.[34] In this view, beginning in the early twentieth century, an increasing variety of forms of religious belief and practice became available to Westerners, some imported from the Orient or, latterly, from the Americas, while others were indigenous New Age creations. Siberian shamanism, Feng Shui, Australian Aboriginal rituals and MesoAmerican cosmology are all appropriated, modified and commodified for a Western audience. Rather than give in to what Adorno called 'disoriented agnosticism', astrologers have been enthusiastic consumers of these novel teachings and many new rituals, fleeing from any lingering affiliation to mainstream religion and becoming adherents of a perspective best labelled as 'non-aligned spirituality'.[35] And, in this respect, the language used by some astrologers takes on a religious hue. Many talk of the astrological consultation as a ritual, and somewhere between 65 per cent and 81 per cent of British and American practitioners use 'intuition', some vague extrasensory gift, in their horoscope readings, as if they are accessing a higher faculty.[36] For those who shun the concept of intuition, the horoscope can still assume a dynamic existence, as if the cosmos responds knowingly to the astrologer's thoughts.

Astrology quite clearly has an enduring appeal as a means of framing human experience, of locating patterns, purpose and meaning in otherwise random events. This much is evident from its survival. As Freya Mathews has said, 'Cosmologies are not of course pulled out of the air to suit the convenience of the communities to which they are attached. They are conditioned by many and various historical, environmental, technological, psychological and social factors . . . A good cosmology, in other words, is good for its adherents.'[37] But, in the sense that it is part of a recognizable social trend and is an important feature of popular culture we have to question the view that, along with all the other occult, weird and superstitious beliefs with which it is commonly linked are opposed to the mainstream. Simply, as Marion Bowman and Steven Sutcliffe put it, the alternative is now mainstream.[38] The paranormal is normal and the people who have supernatural experiences are, as Rodney Stark put it, no longer 'kooks . . . deviants [and] social misfits', but may actually 'be more emotionally healthy than those who do not have such experiences'.[39] As I argued earlier, the use of the concept of deviance by sociologists is an application of Newtonianism in which people, like planets, diverge from their orbits at their peril. According to this critique, science has become a form of authoritarian modernism, in which what have been called the 'imperial attitudes' of some modern scientists – their belief that they can explain absolutely everything – are designed less to understand the phenomena under discussion than to silence its adherents.[40] Yet, the proposition that belief in astrology needs to be explained is, ironically, itself the product of what sceptics would define as a systematic error of human judgement.[41]

The argument that astrology is a superstition left behind by history, that it is socially marginal or psychologically deviant has led to one further dubious conclusion – that it represents a 'flight from modernity'.[42] In this sense modernity is characterized by the grand narratives of Modernism, the notion that the whole world is moving in one direction, marked by urbanization, industrialization and secularization in the sense of the decline of religious feeling. Astrologers, as people who cannot cope with the modern world, must, the argument runs, be searching for an escape route from the modern world, preferably to the past. When sociologists discuss either New Age culture in general, or astrology in particular, they automatically assume that it is, for this very reason, post-modern, an aspect of 'modernity in crisis'.[43] It helps, though, to actually look at what astrologers do, something which most sociologists who have commented on it have avoided. So, for example, Alan Leo's dramatic simplification of the procedures of medieval astrology in the 1890s and 1900s was clearly a symptom of a Modernist desire to build a new world and nothing to do with post-modernism. The old rules were not to be rediscovered by Western astrologers until post-modernism struck in the 1980s and prompted a search for an authenticity rooted in a long-lost past, a half-forgotten golden age when astrology was vital and respected.[44]

The situation is rather more complicated than simple assumptions that astrology is automatically post-modern suggest. First of all, nobody is quite sure whether post-modern is a chronological phase, a period following the modern, or whether it is a form of culture which exists within the modern and, if the latter, whether it can apply to some activities but not others.[45] Patrick Curry has attempted to reverse the rhetorical argument, suggesting that post-modernity is positive by virtue of its rejection of the authoritarian Modernist assumption that there is only one truth in favour of multiple perspectives.[46] There is some support for this proposition. After all, as Anthony Aveni observed, a visit to the occult section of any bookstore reveals that 'today's occult movement is very personal, highly noninstitutional and democratic in the extreme'.[47] Yet each of the books on offer provides an absolute, revelatory and non-negotiable view of the truth, a single Modernist grand narrative. The problem is one of confusion amongst the main theoreticians, and we can restore some clarity by recognizing that modernity, defined as a single description of the modern world, its arts, science and ideologies, is not the same as the ideology of Modernism in the sense of a deliberate attempt to create a new and better world. Among the twentieth-century's leading astrologers, Alan Leo was clearly a Modernist, as were Carl Jung and Dane Rudhyar. All had a single view of the truth and wanted to put the world to rights. The argument that astrology is a science that can be proved, or the New Age proposition that its widespread acceptance will change the world for the better, both ideas which appealed to Jung, are both clearly aspects of Modernism.[48] As Patrick Curry wrote of the late-nineteenth-century astrologers, 'Far from being an irrational aberration, the new occult astrology was perfectly suited to the capitalism and individualism of the age.'[49] In practice, astrology crosses the boundaries between Modernism and post-modernism precisely because it has no single identity and astrologers disagree on its fundamental nature. It speaks with radically different voices, and the astrologer plotting correlations between planetary cycles and commodity prices has no need of an astrology of the soul.

To comprehend the world in which most astrologers live, whatever the competing rhetorical poses they adopt, it helps to return to Plato. Useful in this respect is the term 'imaginal', which was devised by the Jungian scholar Henry Corbin in order to distinguish products or characteristics of consciousness which are 'real', as opposed to the word 'imaginative', in which qualities of the mind have no reality.[50] The word also has other nuances which take us back to ancient teachings, associations with the 'image' as icon, or embodiment of numinous reality, or of the world as an 'image' of heaven. The 'imaginal' world is Plato's archetypal world of Ideas and Forms and, to extend Corbin's metaphor, if the Creator imagined the Cosmos into existence, then the route back to him can be found partly through the imagination. From the idea that humanity is in a reciprocal relationship with the cosmos, functioning as a co-creator in a process in which astrological rules are constructed and the cosmos then somehow conspires to make them 'work' (which is the conclusion of Alexander Ruperti's ideas), we slip back to post-modernism. Astrology leads by creating theoretical frameworks with which the cosmos then cooperates, an idea which takes us back to the Babylonian concept I explored in *Volume I* as the 'Enuma Anu Enlil' paradigm. In this respect the idea of the simulacrum, promoted by Jean Baudrillard and Umberto Eco, is helpful.[51] The simulacrum is a copy of an object which somehow becomes more real than the original, one of Eco's best-known examples being Disneyworld, the model of the USA which becomes a template for the real thing. The horoscope then becomes a hieroglyphic model of an ancient cosmos, using symbols which require the astrologer's active participation in the interpretative process, and which takes on a life that transcends the universe of modern science. Corbin, Eco and Baudrillard may provide models for one version of the astrological cosmos, one which takes us back to the *Emerald Tablet*, magical procedures and Lévi-Bruhl's *participation-mystique*. But, if we read most modern astrological journals the impression is overwhelmingly that the dominant narrative is Newtonian in the sense that it is taken for granted that astrological patterns possess a real, literal power or significance, independent of human consciousness, which the astrologer can read as if a set of immutable laws are at work. If the resulting interpretations are then vague it is, the theory runs, only because the manifestation of celestial law in terrestrial affairs is necessarily difficult to identify. This was the theory advocated by H. P. Blavatsky, amongst others, and is reminiscent of the other model of Babylonian astrology, the more 'scientific' 'Prediction of Celestial Phenomena' paradigm. Astrology actually exists in the tension created between one world of order and another of chaos. For the Babylonians, the cycles of the sun and moon could be measured accurately and formed the basis of the sacred calendar, but their endless variety (one could predict the moon's location but not whether it would be surrounded by a halo) allowed the negotiation of destiny through a process of prediction and ritual. The nature in which destiny is negotiated has evolved – for Ptolemy it was through management of the natural world, for Jung through analysis – but the principle remains.

For its practitioners, astrology clearly provides an aesthetically satisfying explanation for the past, a purpose for the present and, for some, a means of predicting the future. In spite of its managerial aspirations – and Leo, Jung and Rudhyar did their best to redesign astrology in order to actively manipulate the future – Western astrology remains primarily descriptive. It is in the very act of giving an account of one's feelings and circumstances that it accomplishes its goal. Somehow, in the cosmos in which it is assumed that the future is already real, the therapeutic act is accomplished by giving an account of origins, through the archaic symbols of the horoscope.[52] Those who go to astrologers certainly experience satisfaction. In one interview I conducted as part of my research, one client described a consultation by the London-based astrologer Howard Sasportas in the 1980s as like a 'psychic massage'. And the majority of those who read horoscope columns value the advice they find in them. Astrology's essential appeal is that it establishes an intimate connection between the heavens and earth. People who visit astrologers often say that they do so in order to find out about the future, but there seems to be a deeper desire to connect with something bigger, a sense of cosmic purpose and personal meaning, of enchantment. This has absolutely nothing to do with science; even if astrology was purely a matter of prediction and even if most predictions were wrong, this would make little difference. After all, economic forecasting thrives in spite of its own inability to predict the future.[53] Astrology's appeal depends on the value it provides, and this is not quantifiable. Jung, discussing the role of therapists in modern life, provided one answer to the question of why people visit astrologers. Some doctors, he said, deal with people as if they were mere machines, devoid of any need for meaning. Even though meaning is what most educated people are looking for, they would never think of consulting a priest.[54] The alternative, in Jung's opinion, was a visit to a therapist, or equivalent, including a suitably trained astrologer.

It is, ultimately, difficult to assess astrology's status in the contemporary West. It may still function as a 'sacred canopy', except that the visible sky no longer plays a part.[55] Astrological calculations are performed on computers in the time it takes to feed in the data, and most people in the West – and now a majority in the world as a whole – are shielded from the sky by light pollution. That we are in the middle of the electronic revolution, with its new narratives of cyber-communities, creates an appearance of profound change.[56] The Hubble space telescope has provided visual evidence of galaxies billions of light years away but, to all intents and purposes, the experiential world has shrunk. Twenty-first-century urban dwellers rarely see a starry sky and often fail to notice a brilliant full moon or sunrise and it is not far-fetched to argue that their world is actually smaller than the ancient cosmos, enclosed by a back dome with holes in it for stars. But astrology's function still seems to be similar. It is an organizing system, a scheme for identifying order in chaos, and meaning in otherwise random events. In its theosophical and New Age forms, it deals with the supernatural, the world which exists beyond, above or alongside the visible, material realm of nature. Does that mean that it is a religion? Not in the sense that it has a single set of dogma, or any necessity for divine beings, let alone worship, and no institutions beyond public societies, schools and study groups. But, in the sense that its goal is to reunite human life with the cosmos, it is indeed religious. Yet, it has an essential humanist core. Even the Mesopotamian astrologers, whose position in relation to their divine rulers was essentially powerless, were at least able to assert their humanity and engage in a dialogue with their gods and goddesses.

Astrology in the West survives in a context in which religion and spirituality are not dying out but diversifying. Its survival in the twenty-first century is therefore not an anomaly to be explained but an aspect of the modern world to be examined on its own terms. It is, as Bruno Latour pointed out, part of the 'anthropological matrix', the complex of pattern of belief and practice which connects modern Westerners to their prehistoric ancestors, a continuity which is not affected by the superficial gloss of technological change.

Notes

Notes to Introduction: Origins and Background

1 Immanuel Kant, *Critique of Practical Reason* in *Great Books of the Western World 42* (London: Encyclopaedia Britannica, 1952), p. 360; 'Zei Dinge erfüllen das Gemüt mit immer neuer und zunehmender Bewundering und Ehrfurcht, je oefter und anhaltender sich das Nachdenken damit beschaeftigt: der besternte Himmel über mir und das moralische Gestez in mir.'

2 Patrick Curry, 'Astrology', in Kelly Boyd (ed.), *The Encyclopaedia of Historians and Historical Writing* (2 Vols; London: Fitzroy Dearborn, 1999), Vol. 1, p. 55.

3 I follow David Juste in including calendars as astrological. See David Juste, 'The Catalogus Codicum Astrologorum Latinorum and the Bibliotheca Astrologica Numerica', Paper delivered at the Ancient Astrology Workshop, Warburg Institute, London, 16–17 February 2007.

4 Ernst Cassirer, *The Philosophy of Symbolic Forms, Vol. 2: Mythical Thought* (London: Yale University Press, 1971), p. 90.

5 Nicholas Campion, *The Great Year: Astrology, Millenarianism and History in the Western Tradition* (London: Penguin, 1994), ch. 9, and *What do Astrologers Believe?* (Oxford: Granta, 2006), p. 32.

6 Max Weber, *From Max Weber: Essays in Sociology*, ed. H.H. Garth and C. Mills Wright (London: Kegan Paul, Trench, Trubner & Co., 1947), pp. 274, 358–9.

7 See Henri Corbin, *Mundus Imaginalis, or the Imaginary and the Imaginal*, 1964, http://www. hermetic.com/bey/mundus_imaginalis.htm.

8 Ann Geneva, *Astrology and the Seventeenth Century Mind: William Lilly and the Language of the Stars* (Manchester and New York: Manchester University Press, 1995), p. xiv.

9 Terry Eagleton, *The Idea of Culture* (Oxford: Blackwell, 2000), p. 1.

10 Clifford Geertz, 'Religion as a Cultural System', in Michael P. Banton (ed.), *Anthropological Approaches to the Study of Religion* (London: Tavistock and New York: Frederick A. Praeger Press, 1966), p. 3; http://www.iwp.uni-linz.ac.at/lxe/sektktf/gg/GeertzTexts/Religion_System. htm (accessed 4 October 2007).

11 Patrick Curry, *Prophecy and Power: Astrology in Early Modern England* (Oxford: Polity Press, 1989).

12 J.R.R. Tolkein, *Tree and Leaf* (London: Unwin, 1964).

13 See Joscelyn Godwin, *The Theosophical Enlightenment* (New York: State University of New York Press, 1994), p. xii.

14 See Joshua Gunn, *Modern Occult Rhetoric: Mass Media and the Drama of Secrecy in the Twentieth Century* (Tuscaloosa: University of Alabama Press, 2003), esp. ch. 1.

15 See Antoine Faivre, *Theosophy, Imagination, Tradition: Studies in Western Esotericism* (Albany: State University of New York Press, 2000), esp. the Preface.

16 Lucien Lévi-Bruhl, *How Natives Think* (Princeton: Princeton University Press, 1985), esp. pp. 76–104.

17 D.A. Kidd, *Collins Latin-English English-Latin Dictionary* (London and Glasgow, 1957); Guido Bonatti, *Liber Astronomiae* (2 Vols; trans. Benjamin Dykes; Golden Valley, MN: The Cazimi Press, 2007).

18 Aristotle, *Metaphysics*, 1026a.27 (trans. Hugh Tredennick; Cambridge, MA and London: Harvard University Press, 1933).

19 Roger Beck, *The Religion of the Mithras Cult in the Roman Empire: Mysteries of the Unconquered Sun* (Oxford: Oxford University Press, 2006), esp. ch. 8; Edgar Laird, 'Christine de Pizan and Controversy Concerning Star Study in the Court of Charles V', *Culture and Cosmos 1*(2) (Winter/Autumn 1997): 35–48.

20 Claudius Ptolemy, *Tetrabiblos* (trans. F.E. Robbins; Cambridge, MA and London: Harvard University Press, 1940), I.1.

21 Arthur O. Lovejoy, *The Great Chain of Being* (Cambridge, MA and London: Harvard University Press, 1936).

22 Cicero, *De Divinatione*, I.vi12, xviii.34, xix.37, lv.124, lvi.127, II.iii.9, II.xi.25; Plato, *Phaedrus* (trans. H.N. Fowler; Cambridge, MA and London: Harvard University Press, 1914), p. 244.

23 Stephen McCluskey, 'Astronomies and Cosmologies in the Latin West', *Proceedings of the SEAC Conference*, Granada, 8–12 September 2008, forthcoming, Astronomical Society of the Pacific, 2009.

24 For general information on much of what follows, see the article on Islamic cosmology in Norris D. Hetherington, *The Encyclopaedia of Cosmology: Historical, Philosophical and Scientific Foundations of Modern Cosmology* (New York, 1993), pp. 322–9, and John M. Steele, *A Brief Introduction to Astronomy in the Middle East* (London: Saqi Books, 2008).

   For Islamic philosophy in general, see Majid Fakhry, *A History of Islamic Philosophy* (New York: Columbia University Press, 1983). For Islamic cosmology in general and Neoplatonism in particular, see Seyyed Hossein Nasr, *An Introduction to Islamic Cosmological Doctrines* (New York: State University of New York Press, 1993). For biographical details of the astrologers of the Islamic world, see Boris A. Rosenfeld, Ekmeleddin Ihsanoglu, *Mathematicians, Astronomers, and other Scholars of Islamic Civilisation and their works* (7th–19th C.) (Istanbul: Research Centre for Islamic History, Art and Culture, 2003).

25 Nicholas Campion, *Astrology and Cosmology in the World's Religions* (New York: New York University Press, forthcoming, 2011).

26 See the discussion in David Pingree, *From Astral Omens to Astrology. From Babylon to Bikaner* (Rome: Istitutio Italiano Per L'Africa E L'Oriente, 1997), pp. 9–10, and Muzaffar Iqbal, Islam and Science (Aldershot: Ashgate, 2002), p. 10.

27 Al Kindi, *On the Stellar Rays* (trans. Robert Zoller; Berkeley, CA: Project Hindsight, The Golden Hind Press, 1993).

28 Abu Ma'shar, *The Abbreviation of the Introduction to Astrology, Together with the Medieval Latin Translation of Adelard of Bath* (ed. and trans. Charles Burnett, Keiji Yamamoto and Michio Yano; Leiden, New York and Koln: E.J. Brill, 1994), 4.15, p. 55.

29 See the discussion in Majid Fakhry, *A History of Islamic Philosophy* (New York: Columbia University Press, 1983), pp. 298–301.

30 Barry S. Kogan, *Averroës and the Metaphysics of Causation* (Albany: SUNY Press, 1985); Olivier Leaman, *Averroës and his Philosophy* (London: Routledge, 1997).

Notes to Chapter 1: The Latin West: Decline and Disappearance

1 Boethius, *The Consolation of Philosophy* (trans. V.E. Watts; Harmondsworth, Middlesex: Penguin, 1969), II.VI, p. 90.

2 For the best account of the transition from classical to medieval cosmology, see Stephen C. McCluskey, *Astronomies and Cultures in Early Medieval Europe* (Cambridge: Cambridge University Press, 1998).

3 Rev. 21.23; see Rom. 6.8–11 for salvation through Christ alone, and Nicholas Campion, *The Dawn of Astrology: A Cultural History of Western Astrology, Vol. I*, (London: Continuum, 2008), ch. 17, for a wider discussion.

4 Augustine, *City of God* (trans. Henry Bettenson; Harmondsworth, Middlesex: Penguin, 1972), VIII.6–12; see also II.7.

5 See McCluskey, *Astronomies and Cultures in Early Medieval Europe*, pp. 33, 35.

6   See the discussion in Marcia L. Colish, *Medieval Foundations of the Western Intellectual Tradition* (New Haven and London: Yale University Press, 1998), p. 29.

7   See Polymnia Athanassiadi-Fowden and Michael Frede, *Pagan Monotheism in Late Antiquity* (Oxford: Oxford University Press, 2001).

8   Geoffrey of Tours, *The History of the Franks* (trans. Lewis Thorpe; London: Penguin, 1974), II.29, p. 141.

9   McCluskey, *Astronomies and Cultures in Early Medieval Europe*, pp. 40–1.

10 Geoffrey of Tours, *The History of the Franks*, p. 83.

11 Bruce S. Eastwood, *The Revival of Planetary Astronomy in Carolingian and Post-Carolingian Europe* (Aldershot: Ashgate, 2002), I.235.

12 For Calcidius, also spelt Calcidus, see Eastwood, *The Revival of Planetary Astronomy*, X171–209, and McCluskey, *Astronomies and Cultures in Early Medieval Europe*, pp. 119–20.

13 See William Harris Stahl, Richard Johnson and E.L. Bruce, *Martianus Capella and the Seven Liberal Arts* (New York: Columbia University Press, 1971), Vol. 1.

14 See Eastwood, *The Revival of Planetary Astronomy*, I.247, VII, VIII.

15 See Stahl, Johnson, and Bruce, *Martianus Capella*. See also McCluskey, *Astronomies and Cultures in Early Medieval Europe*, pp. 117–19.

16 Plato, *Republic*, (2 Vols; trans. Paul Shorey; Cambridge, MA and London: Harvard University Press, 1937), Book X, Cicero; Book VI. xiii.

17 Macrobius, *Commentary on the Dream of Scipio* (trans. W.H. Stahl; New York: Columbia University Press, 1990), VI.34. See also II.13–14.

18 Henry Chadwick, *Boethius: the Consolations of Music, Logic, Theology and Philosophy* (Oxford: Clarendon Press, 1981), pp. 78–107.

19 *Ibid.*, p. 107.

20 Boethius, *The Consolation of Philosophy*, p. 116.

21 *Ibid.*, III.IX, pp. 97–8. See also I.V, pp. 46–8, I.VI, pp. 49–50, IV.I, pp. 117–18.

22 *Ibid.*, III.VIII, pp. 91, 92.

23 *Ibid.*, IV.VI, p. 135.

24 *Ibid.*, IV.VI, p. 136.

25 *Ibid.*, IV.VI, p. 136. Conventionally the spheres were in order, from outermost to innermost, Saturn, Jupiter, Mars, the sun, Venus, Mercury and the moon. Actually, Boethius here seems to play with the flexibility in a cosmos based on metaphysical models to reverse the normal physical order, placing God, perfection and Providence at the centre, with increasing levels of Fate as one moves to the outermost circle, whose orbit is widest, fastest and therefore represents the greatest degree of change.

26 Julius Firmicus Maternus, *Mathesis* (translated as *Ancient Astrology: Theory and Practice*, Jean Rhys Bram, Park Ridge, NJ: Noyes Press, 1975), I.IV.4–5, VII.14–22.

27 Lynn Thorndike, *History of Magic and Experimental Science* (8 Vols, New York: Columbia University Press, 1923–58), Vol. I, p. 621.

28 See James J. O'Donnell, *Cassiodorus* (Berkeley: University of California Press, 1979). Online at http://ccat.sas.upenn.edu/jod/texts/cassbook/toc.html.

29 Cassiodorus, *Institutions of Divine and Secular Learning, On the Soul* (Liverpool: Liverpool University Press, 2004), p. 229.

30 Cicero, *De Divinatione* (trans. W.A. Falconer; Cambridge, MA, London: Harvard University Press, 1929); Campion, *The Dawn of Astrology*, ch. 12.

31 Thorndike, *Magic*, Vol. I, p. 575.

32 *Ibid.*, pp. 575–84.

33 'Sterile', or 'barren' signs were Gemini, Leo and Virgo. See William Lilly, *Christian Astrology* (London, 1647, facsimile edition, London: Regulus Publishing, 1985), pp. 86–90 for the best summary of the categorization of zodiac signs in medieval astrology.

34 A zodiac sign is a mathematical construct, a constellation a visual one. A planet is either in a zodiac sign or not: it cannot be 'under it'. However, visually, a planet can appear, in northerly climes, to be south of, and hence, 'under' a constellation.

35 Augustine, *City of God*, Book V, 6.
36 Cited in Eastwood, *The Revival of Planetary Astronomy*, III p. 142. See Eastwood in general for a wide-ranging discussion of early medieval astronomy in the Latin West.
37 For calculation of Easter, see McCluskey, *Astronomies and Cultures in Early Medieval Europe*, pp. 77–96.
38 To clarify the title of the emperors in Constantinople: they regarded themselves as emperors of the Romans, and the designation 'Byzantine' is a later, Western, term.
39 See the discussion in Eastwood, *The Revival of Planetary Astronomy*, III.142.
40 Isidore of Seville, *The Etymologies* (trans. Stephen A. Barney, W.J. Lewis, J.A. Beach and Oliver Berghof; Cambridge: Cambridge University Press, 2007), III.xxvii, p. 99.
41 *Ibid.*, VIII.ix, pp. 181–3.
42 See, for example, on Saturn as a cold planet, Pliny, *Natural History*, Book II (trans H. Rackham; Cambridge, MA and London: Harvard University Press, 1929), II.vi.34, Vol. 1. For a summary of Isidore's arguments, see Thorndike, *Magic*, Vol. I, esp. pp. 626–33.
43 As an example of a core of truth buried in romanticized history, Geoffrey claimed that Stonehenge was a healing sanctuary, a theory that was ignored in modern archaeology until the excavations at the site in 2008. See Geoffrey of Monmouth, *History of the Kings of Britain* (trans. Lewis Thorpe; Harmondsworth, Middlesex: Penguin, 1965), p. 196. While standing at the Giant's Ring on Mount Killarus in Ireland, the stones had been used for healing the sick. Merlin related the whole story: 'Many years ago, the Giants transported (the stones) from the remotest confines of Africa and set them up. Their plan was that, whenever they felt ill, baths should be prepared for them at the foot of the stones; for they used to pour water over them and to run this water into baths in which their sick were cured ... There is not a single stone among them which hasn't some medicinal value'. See the press report of the 2008 excavation in Maev Kennedy, 'The Lourdes of Ancient Britain? Dig Aims to Reveal Stonehenge's Purpose', *The Guardian*, 1 April 2008, http://arts.guardian.co.uk/art/heritage/story/0,2269815,00.html (accessed 21 June 2008).
44 Geoffrey of Monmouth, *History of the Kings of Britain*, XII.4, pp. 270–1.
45 Lynn Thorndike, *Michael Scot* (London: Thomas Nelson and Sons Ltd., 1965), p. 126.
46 R.N. Swanson, *The Twelfth-century Renaissance* (Manchester and New York: Manchester University Press, 1999), p. 61.
47 Nennius, *History of the Britons* (London: Dodo Press, 2007).
48 Marina Smyth, *Understanding the Universe in Seventh-Century Ireland* (Woodbridge: Boydell Press, 1996), pp. 18. 172, 305.
49 P.W. Joyce, *A Social History of Ancient Ireland* (2 Vols; London: Longmans, Green & Co, 1903), Vol. I, pp. 229, 230, 233, 435.
50 See T. Sharper Knowlson, *The Origins of Popular Superstitions* (London: T. Werner Laurie Ltd., 1930), p. 48. But see Ronald Hutton, *The Stations of the Sun: A History of the Ritual Year in Britain* (Oxford and New York: Oxford University Press, 1996) for the whole question of the antiquity of solar festivals.
51 Eastwood, *The Revival of Planetary Astronomy*, V.121.
52 See the discussion in Eastwood, *The Revival of Planetary Astronomy*, II.11 and 200–1.
53 See Charles W. Jones, 'Manuscripts of Bede's *De Natura Rerum*', *Isis* 27(3) (November 1937): 430–40.
54 Clement of Alexandria, *The Recognition*, in Alexander Roberts and James Donaldson (eds), *The Ante-Nicene Christian Library* (Edinburgh: Y and T Clark, 1847); Bruce S. Eastwood, *Ordering the Heavens: Roman Astronomy and Cosmology in the Carolingian Renaissance* (Leiden: Brill, 2007), p. 155.
55 Thorndike, *Magic*, Vol. I, pp. 635–6.
56 See David Pingree, 'Legacies in Astronomy and Celestial Omens' in Stephanie Dalley (ed.), *The Legacy of Mesopotamia* (Oxford: Clarendon Press, 1998), p. 113.
57 Bede, *The Reckoning of Time* (trans. Faith Wallis; Liverpool: Liverpool University Press, 2004), ch. 8 ('The Week'), p. 33. Bede was using Jerome's version: 'The spirit goes gyring in a gyre, and returns in its circle.'

58   Bede, *Ecclesiastical History of the English People* (trans. D.H. Farmer; London: Penguin, 1990), V.21, p. 315.
59   See Eastwood, *The Revival of Planetary Astronomy*, I.250.
60   Bede, *Ecclesiastical History of the English People*, V.23, p. 330.
61   Bede, *A History of the English Church and People* (Harmondsworth, Middlesex: Penguin, 1968), IV.13, p. 226, V.24, p. 334.

Notes to Chapter 2: The Carolingian World: Survival and Recovery

1   'Homilies', Vol. 1, p. 111 cited in Wilfred Bonser, *The Medical Background to Anglo-Saxon England* (London: Wellcome Historical Medical Library, 1963), p. 156.
2   Al-Biruni, *The Chronology of Ancient Nations*, trans. C.E. Sachau from the Arabic text 'Athar al-Baqiyah', or 'Vestiges of the Past' (London: W.H. Allen, 1879), p. 339. For Baghdad as a cosmic city, see Ibrahim Allawi, 'Some Evolutionary and Cosmological Aspects to Early Islamic Town Planning' in Margaret Bentley Sevcenko (ed.), *Theories and Principles of Design in the Architecture of Islamic Societies* (Cambridge, MA: Aga Khan Program for Islamic Architecture, 1988), pp. 57–72.
3   See A.P. Kazhdan and Ann Wharton Epstein, *Change in Byzantine Culture in the Eleventh and Twelfth Centuries* (Berkeley: University of California Press, 1985), and the discussion on esp. pp. 11 and 136–8.
4   David Pingree, *From Astral Omens to Astrology, from Babylon to Bikaner* (Rome: Istituto Italiano Per L'Africa e L'Oriente, 1997), p. 64.
5   Einhard, 'Life of Charlemagne', Book 2, ch. 25, p. 79; Notker the Stammerer, 'Charlemagne', Book 1, ch. 2, pp. 94–5. See also Stephen Allott, *Alcuin of York, c. A.D. 732 to 804: His Life and Letters* (York: William Sessions, 1974); Charles Gaskoin, *Alcuin: His Life and his Work* (London: C.J. Clay & Sons, 1904).
6   Ranee Katzenstein and Emilie Savage-Smith, *The Leiden Aratea: Ancient Constellations in a Medieval Manuscript* (Los Angeles: Getty Publications, 1988).
7   See the discussion in Mary Alberi, 'Alcuin and the New Athens', *History Today*, Sept. 1989: 35–6.
8   See Bruce S. Eastwood, *The Revival of Planetary Astronomy in Carolingian and Post-Carolingian Europe* (Aldershot: Ashgate, 2002), I.250.
9   Eastwood, *Revival*: V; Stephen McCluskey, *Astronomies and Cultures in Early Medieval Europe* (Cambridge: Cambridge University Press, 1998), pp. 133–4.
10 Notker the Stammerer, 'Charlemagne', Book 2, ch. 8, p. 143.
11 Eastwood, *Revival*: I.243.
12 *Ibid.* I.254, III.143.
13 Stephen McCluskey, 'Astronomies and Cosmologies in the Latin West', *Proceedings of the SEAC Conference*, Granada, 8–12 September 2008, forthcoming, Astronomical Society of the Pacific, 2009.
14 McCluskey, *Astronomies*, p. 149; see also pp. 163–4.
15 Lynn Thorndike, *History of Magic and Experimental Science* (8 Vols; New York: Columbia University Press, 1923–58), Vol. I, p. 673.
16 *Ibid.*, p. 680.
17 For the Coligny calendar, see Garrett Olmsted, *The Gaulish Calendar* (Bonn: Dr Rudolf Habelt GmBh, 1992).
18 Thorndike, *Magic*, Vol. I, pp. 683–4; McCluskey, *Astronomies*, p. 149.
19 Thorndike, *Magic*, Vol. I, pp. 678–9.
20 McCluskey, *Astronomies*, p. 147.
21 Thorndike, *Magic*, Vol. I, p. 672.
22 See McCluskey, *Astronomies*, pp. 140–5.
23 Bruce S. Eastwood, *Ordering the Heavens: Roman Astronomy and Cosmology in the Carolingian Renaissance* (Leiden: Brill, 2007), p. 151.

24 McCluskey, *Astronomies*, p. 144.

25 *Ibid.*, p. 162.

26 See, for example, the discussion of astrological talismans in the Roman Empire in Tamsyn Barton, *Ancient Astrology* (London: Routledge, 1994).

27 See R.M. Frank, 'Hunting the European Sky Bears: When Bears Ruled the Earth and Guarded the Gate of Heaven' in Vesselina Koleva and Dmiter Kolev (eds), *Astronomical Traditions in Past Cultures, Proceedings of the First Annual General Meeting of the European Society for Astronomy in Culture*, Smolyan, Bulgaria, 31 August–2 September 1992 (Sofia: Institute of Astronomy, Bulgarian Academy of Sciences and National Astronomical Observatory, Tozhen), pp. 116–42, and 'Hunting the European Sky Bears: Hercules Meets Harzkume', César Esteban and Juan Antonio Belmonte (eds), *Astronomy and Cultural Diversity, Proceedings of the 1999 Oxford VI Conference on Archaeoastronomy and Astronomy in Culture* (Tenerife: 2000), pp. 169–75. For a brief look at northern constellation stories, see also Prudence Jones Prudence, *A 'House' System from Viking Europe* (Cambridge: Fenris-Wolf, 1991) and *Northern Myths of the Constellations* (Cambridge: Fenris-Wolf, 1991).

28 Geoffrey of Tours, *The History of the Franks* (trans. Lewis Thorpe; London: Penguin, 1974), IX.5, p. 483.

29 *Ibid.*, I.24, p. 83.

30 William Shakespeare, *Hamlet*, I.V.943.

31 Geoffrey of Tours, *History*, II.3, p. 113.

32 'Homilies', Vol. 1, p. 111 cited in Wilfred Bonser Wilfred, *The Medical Background to Anglo-Saxon England* (London: Wellcome Historical Medical Library, 1963), p. 156.

33 McCluskey, *Astronomies* p. 63.

34 *Ibid.*, p. 71.

35 T. Wedel, *The Medieval Attitude to Astrology, Especially in England* (New Haven: Yale University Press, 1920), p. 42; K. Thomas, *Religion and the Decline of Magic* (London: Weidenfeld and Nicolson, 1971), p. 458.

36 'Homilies', Vol. 1, p. 111, cited in Bonser, p. 156.

37 Wedel, *The Medieval Attitude*, p. 30.

38 Thorndike, *Magic*, Vol. I, p. 673.

Notes to Chapter 3: The Twelfth Century: Renaissance and Revival

1 'The Letters of the Rabbis of the South of France' in Meira B. Epstein, *The Correspondence between the Rabbis of Southern France and Maimonides about Astrology* (Reston, VA: ARHAT Publications, 1998), para. 2, p. 6.

2 Jacob Burckhardt, *The Civilisation of the Renaissance in Italy* (trans. S.G.C. Middlemore; London: Penguin, 1990 [1860]), p. 98.

3 See, for example, Lloyd Motz and Hane Weaver Jefferson, *The Story of Astronomy* (New York and London: Plenum Press, 1995), pp. 52–7.

4 Charles Haskins, *The Renaissance of the Twelfth Century* (Cambridge, MA.: Harvard University Press, 1927). For more recent discussion, see R.N. Swanson, *The Twelfth-century Renaissance* (Manchester and New York: Manchester University Press, 1999).

5 Isa. 13.10, Lk. 21.25.

6 See Lynn Thorndike, *History of Magic and Experimental Science* (8 Vols; New York: Columbia University Press, 1923–58), Vol. I, p. 677.

7 Stephen C. McCluskey, *Astronomies and Cultures in Early Medieval Europe* (Cambridge: Cambridge University Press, 1998), pp. 166–71.

8 *Ibid.*, p. 167.

9 For a good recent account of the astrolabe and its uses, see James Morrison, *The Astrolabe* (Rehoboth Beach, DE: Janus, 2007). See also Otto Neugebauer, 'The Early History of the Astrolabe', *Isis* 40(3) (Aug. 1949): 240–56.

10 McCluskey, *Astronomies*, p. 171.
11 For Gerbert's letters to Joseph the Spaniard, see Harriet Pratt Lattin, *The Letters of Gerbert with his Papal Privileges as Sylvester II* (New York: Columbia University Press, 1961), letters 25, 33, pp. 63–4, 70.
12 Harriett Pratt Lattin, *The Letters of Gerbert with his Papal Privileges as Sylvester II* (New York: Columbia University Press, 1961), pp. 6, 18. See also letter 161, p. 189.
13 See the discussion in Thorndike, *Magic*, Vol. I, ch. XXX, esp. pp. 706–7.
14 For Marcus Manilius, see the *Astronomica* (trans. G.P. Goold: Cambridge, MA and London: Harvard University Press, 1977), p. cvi.
15 Thorndike, *Magic*, Vol. I, ch. XXIX. For wider discussion, see Valerie Flint, *The Growth of Magic in Early Medieval Europe* (Oxford: Clarendon Press, 1992); Richard Kieckhefer, *Magic in the Middle Ages* (Cambridge: Cambridge University Press, 1989).
16 For this and the following discussion, see John Marenbon, *The Philosophy of Peter Abelard* (Cambridge: Cambridge University Press, 1999), and the summary in Thorndike, *Magic*, Vol. II, pp. 5–6.
17 For details, see Francis J. Carmody, *Arabic Astronomical and Astrological Sciences in Latin Translation: A Critical Bibliography* (Berkeley and Los Angeles: University of California Press, 1956).
18 Charles Burnett, *Adelard of Bath: an English scientist and Arabist of the Early Twelfth Century* (London: Warburg Institute, 1987).
19 See Thorndike, *Magic*, Vol. II, pp. 66–93.
20 *Ibid.*, pp. 214–18.
21 Aristotle, *Secreta Secretorum* (New York: Da Capo, 1970). See the online version at http://www.granta.demon.co.uk/arsm/jg/index.html.
22 See the discussion in Harriett Pratt Lattin, *The Letters of Gerbert with his Papal Privileges as Sylvester II* (New York: Columbia University Press, 1961), p. 6.
23 Demetra George, 'Manuel I Komnenos and Michael Glycas: A Twelfth-Century Defence and Refutation of Astrology', part 1, *Culture and Cosmos*, Spring/Summer 5(1) (2001): 31.
24 For Kabbalah, see J.H. Laenes, *Jewish Mysticism: An Introduction* (London: Westminster John Knox Press, 2001); Gershom Scholem, *Origins of the Kabbalah* (trans. Allan Arkush; Princeton: Princeton University Press, 1987); Alan Unterman, *The Jews: Their Religious Beliefs and Practices* (Brighton: Sussex Academic Press, 1999), esp. ch. 6; Perle Epstein, *Kabbalah: The Way of the Jewish Mystic* (London: Shambhala, 2001).
25 Gen. 28.11–19, 2 Kings 2.12.
26 Aryeh Kaplan, *Sefer Yetzirah: the Book of Creation in Theory and Practice* (York Beach, ME: Weiser Books, 1997), 1:5, p. 44.
27 Simo Parpola, 'The Assyrian Tree of Life: Tracing the Origins of Jewish Monotheism and Greek Philosophy', *Journal of Near Eastern Studies* 52(3) (Jul. 1993): 161–208.
28 Gershom Scholem (ed.), *Zohar: The Book of Splendor* (New York: Schocken Books, 1963), p. 27.
29 Kaplan, *Sefer Yetzirah*, 5:7, p. 215.
30 The so-called 'Enuma Anu-Enlil' paradigm, for which see David Brown, *Mesopotamian Planetary Astronomy-Astrology* (Groningen: Styx Publications, 2000), chs 3, 5, esp. pp. 105–12, 285.
31 Hans Jonas, *The Gnostic Religion: The Message of the Alien God and the Beginnings of Christianity*, 2nd edn. (Boston: Beacon Press, 1963); Dawn Campion, ch. 17.
32 Isa. 66.1.
33 Eccl. 3.2–8.
34 Kaplan, *Sefer Yetzirah* pp. 221–6.
35 Harry Sperling and Maurice Simon (eds), *The Zohar*, (5 Vols; London: Soncino Press, 1949). For extracts, see Isaiah Tishby (ed.), *The Wisdom of the Zohar: An Anthology of Texts* (trans. David Goldstein, 3 Vols; Oxford: Oxford University Press, 1989); Daniel C. Matt, *Zohar: Annotated and Explained* (Woodstock, VT.: SkyLights Paths Publishing Co., 2002); Gershom Scholem (ed.), *Zohar: The Book of Splendor* (New York: Schocken Books, 1963).
36 Thorndike, *Magic*, Vol. I, p. 674.

37   Abraham Ibn-Ezra, *The Beginning of Wisdom* (trans. Meira B. Epstein, Reston, VA: ARHAT Publications, 1998).
38   For background to Maimonides, see Thorndike, *Magic*, Vol. II, pp. 205–213, esp. pp. 211–12 on astrology.
39   Meira B. Epstein, *The Correspondence between the Rabbis of Southern France and Maimonides about Astrology* (Reston, VA: ARHAT Publications, 1998), para. 2, p. 6.
40   Guido Bonatti, *Liber Astronomiae*, Part III (trans. Robert Hand and Robert Zoller, ed. Robert Hand and Robert Schmidt; Berkeley Springs: Golden Hind Press, 1994–6), ch. VII, pp. 36–7.
41   Epstein *Correspondence*, para. 17, pp. 15–16.
42   *Ibid.*, para. 6–7 pp. 13–14.
43   E.S. Kennedy, 'A Survey of Islamic Astronomical Tables', *Transactions of the American Philosophical Society*, New Series, Vol. 46, No 2, Philadelphia, 1956.
44   J. Chabás and B.R. Goldstein, *The Alfonsine Tables of Toledo* (Dordrecht: Kluwer Academic Publishers, 2003).

Notes to Chapter 4: The Thirteenth Century: The Aristotelian Revolution

1   Thomas Aquinas, *Summa Contra Gentiles*, 3.91.2, in *Summa Contra Gentiles* (4 Vols, trans. Vernon J. Bourke; Notre Dame: University of Notre Dame Press, 1975), Book, III, part 2, p. 40.
2   The argument that knowledge of Aristotle arrived initially via astrology is made in Richard LeMay, *Abu Ma'shar and Latin Aristotelianism* (Beirut: American University of Beirut, Oriental Series, No. 38, 1962). See also Charles Burnett's argument in support of LeMay in Herman of Carinthia, *De esentiis* (ed. and trans. Charles Burnettt; Leiden: Brill, 1982).
3   See David Pingree, *From Astral Omens to Astrology, from Babylon to Bikaner* (Rome: Istituto Italiano Per L'Africa E L'Oriente, 1997), pp. 66–8.
4   A.P. Kazhdan and Ann Wharton Epstein, *Change in Byzantine Culture in the Eleventh and Twelfth Centuries* (Berkeley: University of California Press, 1985), p. 152. For astrology, and especially the following discussion in Manuel and Michael Glykas, see Demetra George 'Manuel I Komnenos and Michael Glycas: A Twelfth-Century Defence and Refutation of Astrology', *Culture and Cosmos*, Spring/Summer 5(1) (2001): 3–48, Autumn/Winter 5(2) (2001): 23–51, Spring/Summer 6(1) (2002): 23–43, and Andrew Vladimirou, 'Byzantine Astrology in the Eleventh and Twelfth Centuries', PhD thesis, University of Birmingham, 2006.
5   Aristotle, *Meterologica*, (trans. H.D.P. Lee, Cambridge, MA and London: Harvard University Press, 1937), 339a19–24.
6   Aristotle, *On the Heavens* (trans. W.K.C. Guthrie, Cambridge, MA and London: Harvard University Press, 1921), 279.a–279.b.
7   Guido Bonatti, *Liber Astronomiae* (trans. Benjamin Dykes, 2 Vols; Golden Valley, MN: The Cazimi Press, 2007), treatise 9, chs. 1–2, pp. 1320–3.
8   John Gadbury, *Doctrine of Nativities* (London, 1653), Book 1, p. 153.
9   Ptolemy, *Tetrabiblos* I.3, esp. 11–12, trans. Robbins, pp. 23–5.
10 *Ibid.*, III.13, 158, 161, pp. 341, 447.
11 Lynn Thorndike, *History of Magic and Experimental Science* (8 Vols; New York: Columbia University Press, 1923–58), Vol. II, pp. 444–7. For Grosseteste's thought, see also James McEvoy, *Robert Grosseteste* (Oxford: Oxford University Press, 2000).
12 See the discussion in Paola Zambelli, *The Speculum Astronomiae and its Enigma* (Dordrecht: Kluwer Academic Publishers, 1992), p. 53.
13 Ptolemy, *Tetrabiblos*, II.9, pp. 191–5.
14 See Thorndike, *Magic*, Vol. II, p. 483.
15 Campion, *The Great Year*, pp. 372–9.
16 See the discussion in Paola Zambelli, *The Speculum Astronomiae and its Enigma* (Dordrecht: Kluwer Academic Publishers, 1992), p. 31.

17   See Thorndike, *Magic*, Vol. II, pp. 577–92 for discussion and the text in Zambelli, *The Speculum Astronomiae and its Enigma*.

18   Zambelli, *The Speculum Astronomiae*, p. 9.

19   *Ibid.*, p. 67.

20   *Ibid.*, p. 62.

21   Following Ptolemy, *Tetrabiblos* I.3.

22   Richard Stoneman (ed. and trans.), *The Greek Alexander Romance* (London: Penguin, 1991), I.12, p. 43.

23   Magnus Albertus, *The Book of Secrets of Albertus Magnus* (ed. Michael R. Best and Frank H. Brightman; Oxford: Clarendon Press, 1973), pp. 62–73.

24   *Ibid.*, pp. 3, 9, 19, 26, 30, 35.

25   Aquinas, *Summa Contra Gentiles*, III. esp. 84–7, 91–2.

26   *Ibid.*, esp. 85.22.

27   David C. Lindberg, *The Beginnings of Western Science: The European Scientific Tradition in Philosophical, Religious, and Institutional Context, 600 BC–AD 1450* (Chicago and London: University of Chicago Press, 1992), p. 275.

28   See Zambelli, *The Speculum Astronomiae*, pp. 11–23, for a summary of the arguments against astrology.

29   The theory outlined by Thomas Kuhn in *The Structure of Scientific Revolutions* (Chicago: University of Chicago Press, 1970) that scientific consensus changes not when old theories are disproved but when the old generation of scientists who believed those theories dies.

30   Thorndike, *Magic*, Vol. II, p. 831.

31   Lynn Thorndike, *The Sphere of Sacrobosco and its Commentators* (Chicago: University of Chicago Press, 1949). The encyclopaedic work on medieval cosmology is Pierre Duhem's monumental *Le Système du monde: Histoire des doctrines cosmologiques de Platon à Copernic*, 10 Vols, published from 1913 to the 1980s. For more accessible works on medieval cosmology, see Edward Grant, *Planets, Stars and Orbs: The Medieval Cosmos 1200–1687* (Cambridge: Cambridge University Press, 1966) and the relevant sections in Norris D. Hetherington, *The Encyclopaedia of Cosmology: Historical, Philosophical and Scientific Foundations of Modern Cosmology* (New York: Garland Publishing, 1993).

32   Thorndike, *Sphere*, pp. 120–1.

33   Terry Eagleton, *Ideology: An introduction* (London: Verso, 1991), p. 58.

Notes to Chapter 5: The Thirteenth Century: Practice and Problems

1   Claudius Ptolemy, 'Centiloquium', para 1, in John Partridge, *Mikropanastron, or an Astrological Vade Mecum, briefly Teaching the whole Art of Astrology – viz., Questions, Nativities, with all its parts, and the whole Doctrine of Elections never so comprised nor compiled before, &c.* (London: William Bromwich, 1679).

2   Marcia L. Colish., *Medieval Foundations of the Western Intellectual Tradition* (New Haven and London: Yale University Press, 1998), p. 324.

3   For Bacon, see Stewart C. Easton, *Roger Bacon and his Search for a Universal Science* (New York: Columbia University Press, 1952).

4   John North, *God's Clockmaker: Richard of Wallingford and the Invention of Time* (London: London and Hambledon, 2005); Gerhard Dohrn-Van Rossum, *History of the Hour: Clocks and the Modern Temporal Orders*, (trans. Thomas Dunlap; Chicago: University of Chicago Press, 1992), esp. chs 3–4.

5   J.D. North, *Horoscopes and History, Warburg Institute Surveys and Texts, XIII*, (London: The Warburg Institute, 1986), pp. 96–105. For Adelard, see also Charles Burnett, *Adelard of Bath: An English scientist and Arabist of the Early Twelfth Century* (London: Warburg Institute, 1987).

6   Lynn Thorndike, *History of Magic and Experimental Science* (8 Vols; New York: Columbia University Press, 1923–58), Vol. II, pp. 21–2.

7   Dante, *The Divine Comedy*, (3 Vols; trans. Mark Musa; Harmondsworth, Middlesex: Penguin, 1971), XX.115–17, p. 254; see also XX.13–15, p. 251.
8   Lynn Thorndike, *Michael Scot* (London: Thomas Nelson and Sons Ltd., 1965). See also Thorndike, *Magic*, Vol. II, pp. 305–37.
9   Thorndike, *Magic*, Vol. II., p. 817.
10 Thorndike, *Scot*, p. 97.
11 Plato, *Timaeus*, 38C.
12 The astrological details are given in Thorndike, *Scot*, p. 104.
13 Ptolemy, *Tetrabiblos*, I.19.
14 Ptolemy's 'Centiloquium' clearly permits such intervention: 'One skilful in this Science may evade many effects of the Stars, when he knows their Natures, and diligently prepares himself to receive their effects.' Claudius Ptolemy, 'Centiloquium', para 5, in John Partridge, *Mikropanastron, or an Astrological Vade Mecum, briefly Teaching the whole Art of Astrology – viz., Questions, Nativities, with all its parts, and the whole Doctrine of Elections never so comprised nor compiled before, &c.* (London: William Bromwich).
15 For a full account of Bonatti's work, see Thorndike, *Magic*, Vol. II, ch. LXVII. For his rules on war, see Zoller, 'The Astrologer as Military Advisor in the Middle Ages and Renaissance', *Astrology Quarterly* 62(3) (Summer 1992): 33–8; 63(1) (Winter 1992): 15–26; 63(2) (Spring 1994): 35–45; 63(3) (Summer 1993): 16–22.
16 Dante, *The Divine Comedy* (3 Vols; trans. Mark Musa; Harmondsworth, Middlesex: Penguin, 1971), XX.13–15, 118, pp. 251, 255.
17 Also known as the *Liber introductorius ad iudicia stellarum, or Liber astronomicus*.
18 Guido Bonatti, *The Astrologer's Guide* (London: Regulus Publishing Co., 1986).
19 *Ibid.*, para 1–2, p. 1.
20 *Ibid.*, para 7, p. 6.
21 *Ibid.*, para 7, p. 7.
22 See Thorndike, *Magic*, Vol. II, p. 828.
23 Joan Quigley *'What Does Joan Say?' My Seven Years as White House Astrologer to Nancy and Ronald Reagan* (New York: Birch Lane Press, 1990).
24 For Bacon, see Thorndike, *Magic*, Vol. II, pp. 616–91.
25 Roger Bacon, *Opus Maius* (trans. Robert Burke; 2 Vols; Philadelphia: University of Pennsylvania Press, 1928), Vol. 1, pp. 208–9; Thorndike, *Magic*, Vol. II, pp. 672–3.
26 Thorndike, *Magic*, Vol. II, p. 219.
27 This work has not survived intact, but part of it is included in a work written in the early/mid-tenth century by an Arabic Christian astrologer known as Ibn Hibintā (translated in E.S. Kennedy); David Pingree, *The Astrological History of Masha'Allah* (Cambridge, MA: Harvard University Press, 1971).
28 E.S. Kennedy; David Pingree, *The Astrological History of Masha'Allah* (Cambridge, MA: Harvard University Press, 1971), pp. 51–2; see also p. 45; David Pingree, 'Masha'allah's Zoroastrian Historical Astrology' in Günther Oestmann, H. K. von Stuckrad, G. Oestmann and D. Rutkin (eds), *Horoscopes and History* (Berlin and New York: Walter de Gruyter, 2005), pp. 95–100.
29 Jupiter–Saturn conjunctions take place every 20 years. For periods of around 240 years they take place in the same element, that is the Fire, Earth, Air or Water signs. The entire cycle is complete after 960 years.
30 There are two recent English editions: Abu Ma'shar, *The Abbreviation of the Introduction to Astrology, Together with the Medieval Latin Translation of Adelard of Bath*, edited and translated by Charles Burnett, Keiji Yamamoto and Michio Yano (Leiden, New York and Koln: E.J. Brill, 1994); and Abu Ma'shar, *The Abbreviation of the Introduction to Astrology*, translated by C. Burnett with historical and technical annotations by C. Burnett, G. Tobyn, G. Cornelius and V. Wells (Reston, VA: ARHAT publications, 1997).
31 For discussion, see Richard Lemay, 'Origin & success of the Kitab Thamara of Abu Ja'far Ahmad ibn Yusuf (ibn Ibrahim)' in *Proceedings of the first International Symposium for the History of Arabic Science*, University of Aleppo (1976), Aleppo, 1978. On account of its supposed

authorship by Ptolemy, the 'Centiloquium' was an authoritative text in European cosmology until the seventeenth century.

32   Ptolemy 'Centiloquium', para 8, in John Partridge, *Mikropanastron*.

33   *Ibid.*, para 5.

34   Walter Scott (trans.), *Hermetica: The Ancient Greek and Latin Writings which contain Religious or Philosophic Teachings ascribed to Hermes Trismegistus* (4 Vols; Boulder: Shambal, 1982), Fragment 19, p. 539.

35   Ptolemy, 'Centiloquium', para 7, in John Partridge, *Mikropanastron*.

36   *Ibid.*, paras 3 ('He that is desirous to study any Art, hath in his Nativity without doubt some Star of the same Nature very well fortified.') and 6 ('An Election of days or hours is then effectual, when it agrees with the Nativity; for otherwise, the Election although well made, will not profit.')

37   Guido Bonatti, 'The One Hundred and Forty-Six Considerations of the Famous Astrologer Guido Bonatus', trans. Henry Coley, in *The Astrologer's Guide* (London: Regulus Publishing Co., 1986 [1886]), pp. 1–72; Jerome Cardan, 'Choice Aphorisms from the Seven Segments of Cardan', ed. William Lilly, in *The Astrologers Guide* (London: Regulus Publishing Co., 1986 [1886]), pp. 73–104.

38   Bonatti, *Astrologer's Guide*, para. 7, p. 6.

39   Ptolemy, 'Centiloquium', para 1, in John Partridge, *Mikropanastron*. The date and authorship of the Centiloquium is disputed. It has been attributed to Abu Ja'far but the first authenticated reference is the commentary on it by Ahmed ibn Yusuf al-Misri (835–912).

40   *Ibid.*, para 2: 'When he that asketh a Question, shall better consider it, he shall find that there is but little difference between the thing sought, and the Idea thereof in the Mind.'

41   *Ibid.*, para 3: 'He that is desirous to study any Art, hath in his Nativity without doubt some Star of the same Nature very well fortified.'

42   Jerome Cardan, 'Choice Aphorisms from the Seven Segments of Cardan', ed. William Lilly, in *The Astrologers Guide* (London: Regulus Publishing Co., 1986 [1886]), para. 13, p. 75.

43   William Lilly, *Christian Astrology* (London, 1647, facsimile edition, London: Regulus Publishing, 1985), pp. 121–2.

44   E.J. Holmyard, *Alchemy* (Harmondsworth: Penguin Books, 1957).

45   Aristotle, *Secreta Secretorum* (New York: Da Capo, 1970).

46   Alan Oken, *As Above, So Below: A Primary Guide to Astrological Awareness* (New York: Bantam Books, 1973).

47   Mircea Eliade, 'Time and Eternity in Indian Thought' in Hari Shankar Prasad, *Time in Indian Philosophy* (Delhi: Sri Satguru Publications, 1992), p. 195.

48   See Holmyard, *Alchemy*, pp. 131–8.

49   The correspondences were: the sun–gold, the moon–silver, Mercury–mercury, Venus–copper, Mars–iron, Jupiter–tin and Saturn–lead.

50   Oppenheim, 1974: 204.

51   Owen Gingerich, 'Reflections on the Role of Archaeoastronomy in the History of Astronomy' in A.F. Aveni (ed.), *World Archaeoaastronomy*, (Cambridge: Cambridge University Press, 1989), pp. 4–44.

52   Geoffrey Cornelius, Maggie Hyde and Chris Webster, *Astrology for Beginners* (Cambridge: Icon Books, 1995), p. 3.

53   Ptolemy, 'Centiloquium', para 4, in John Partridge, *Mikropanastron*: 'The Mind naturally inclined to any Science, he attains to more perfection therein, than one that shall take hard pains and labour in study to attain it.'

54   See the studies in Charles Burnett, *Magic and Divination in the Middle Ages: Texts and Techniques in the Islamic and Christian Worlds* (Aldershot: Variorum, 1996), and Burnett and W.F. Ryan (eds), *Magic and the Classical Tradition* (London and Turin: The Warburg Institute and Nino Aragno Editore, 2006). For context, see Eugenio Garin, *Astrology in the Renaissance: The Zodiac of Life* (London and Boston: Routledge, 1976), ch. 2.

55   Anon., *Ghayat Al-Hakim. Picatrix: the Goal of the Wise* (trans. Hashem Atallah; Seattle:

Ouroboros Press, 2002), I.2, p. 7. This version is an English translation of only the first half of the whole work.

56   *Ibid.*, I.2, p. 11.
57   *Ibid.*, I.5, p. 39.
58   *Ibid.*, I.5, p. 41.
59   See Keith Critchlow, *Islamic Patterns: An Analytical and Cosmological Approach* (London: Thames and Hudson, 1983).
60   Anon., *Ghayat Al-Hakim*, I.5, pp. 36, 39, 40, 42.
61   Masha'allah, 'On the Fortune and Infortune of the Native', *Book of Nativities* (trans. Robert Hand; Berkeley Springs: Golden Hind Press, 1994), p. 19. For finding lost property, see Masha'allah, *On Reception* (trans. Robert Hand; Reston, VA: ARHAT, 1998), ch. VI.
62   Ibn-Khaldun, *The Muqaddimah: An Introduction to History* (trans. Franz Rosenthal, London: Routledge and Kegan Paul, 1987), 3.52, p. 259.

Notes to Chapter 6: The High Middle Ages: The Uses of Astrology

1   Geoffrey Chaucer, 'Wife of Bath's Tale' in F.N. Robinson (ed.), *The Works of Geoffrey Chaucer* (London: Oxford Univesity Press, 1966), lines 697–700.
2   Geoffrey of Monmouth, *The Vita Merlini* (trans. John Jay Parry; Bibliobazaar, 2008), p. 245.
3   Nicole Oresme, 'Livre de Divinacions', ch. 6, in G.W. Coopland, *Nicole Oresme and the Astrologers: A Study of his De Divinacions* (Liverpool: Liverpool University Press, 1952), p. 67.
4   Cited by Oresme, 'Livre de Divinacions', ch. 6.
5   Weber contrasted a pre-scientific enchanted world from a disenchanted scientific one: 'The increasing intellectualization and rationalisation do *not*, therefore, indicate an increased and general knowledge of the conditions under which one lives. It means something else, namely, the knowledge or belief that if one but wished one could learn it any time. Hence, it means that principally there are no mysterious incalculable forces that come into play, but rather that one can, in principle, master all things by calculation. This means that the world is disenchanted. One need no longer have recourse to magical means in order to master the spirits, as did the savage, for whom such mysterious powers existed. Technical means and calculations perform the service. This above all is what intellectualization means.' Max Weber, *From Max Weber: Essays in Sociology*, ed. H.H. Garth and C. Mills Wright (London: Kegan Paul, Trench, Trubner & Co., 1947), p. 139.
6   Don Cuppitt, *Solar Ethics* (London: SCM Press, 1995), p. 36.
7   William James, *The Varieties of Religious Experience* (London: Penguin, 1985 [1902]), p. 398; Richard Bucke, *Cosmic Consciousness* (London: Penguin, 1991 [1901]).
8   See for example the arguments of Geoffrey of Meaux in 1325 in Lynn Thorndike, *History of Magic and Experimental Science* (8 Vols; New York: Columbia University Press, 1923–58), Vol. III, pp. 287–8.
9   Thorndike, *Magic*, Vol III, pp. 595–6.
10   Lynn Thorndike, *The Sphere of Sacrobosco and its Commentators* (Chicago: University of Chicago Press, 1949), p. 221.
11   Thorndike, *Sphere*, p. 142; see also p. 117.
12   Arthur O. Lovejoy, *The Great Chain of Being* (Cambridge, MA and London: Harvard University Press, 1936).
13   Dante, *The Divine Comedy* (3 Vols; trans. Mark Musa; Harmondsworth, Middlesex: Penguin, 1971), Vol. 3 ('Paradise'), XXII: 109–114. For Dante's cosmology, see also Alison Cornish, *Reading Dante's Stars* (New Haven and London: Yale University Press, 2000), M. A. Orr, *Dante and the Early Astronomers* (Port Washington: Kennikat Press, 1913), Richard Kay, *Dante's Christian Astrology* (Philadelphia: University of Pennsylvania Press, 1994), and Richard L. Poss, 'Stars and Spirituality in the Cosmology of Dante's *Commedia*', *Culture and Cosmos* 5(1) (Spring/Summer 2001): 49–56.

14   Dante, *The Convivio*, trans. Richard Lansing, 1998, http://dante.ilt.columbia.edu/books/convivi/index.html.

15   Dante, *Divine Comedy*, Vol. I ('Inferno'), XXVI: 21–4.

16   *Ibid.*, IV: 22–63.

17   Campion, *Dawn*, ch. 10; Plato, *Republic*, Book X.

18   John North, *The Ambassadors' Secret: Holbein and the World of the Renaissance* (London and New York: Hambledon and London, 2002).

19   Campion, *Dawn*, pp. 52–3; 'From the Great Above the Great Below' in Samuel Noah Kramer and Diane Wolkstein, *Inanna, Queen of Heaven and Earth: Her Stories and Hymns from Sumer* (New York: Harper and Rowe, 1983), p. 52. The nine celestial spheres were accounted for by seven for the planets plus one each for the stars and the prime-mover.

20   Dante, *Divine Comedy*, Vol. 3 ('Paradise'), XXXIII:145.

21   *Ibid.*, XXVIII:87.

22   Dante Alighieri, *The Convivio*, trans. Richard Lansing, 1998 http://dante.ilt.columbia.edu/books/convivi/index.html (accessed 20 August 2008).

23   'Survey the circling as though yourself were in mid-course with them. Often picture the changing and re-changing dance of the elements. Visions of this kind purge away the dross of our earth-bound life.' Marcus Aurelius, *Meditations*, trans. Maxwell Staniforth (Harmondsworth, Middlesex: Penguin, 1964), V.47, p. 112; see also IX.29, p. 144. See also Plato, *Republic*, (2 Vols; trans. Paul Shorey; Cambridge, MA and London: Harvard University Press, 1937), 516B.

24   Dante, *Divine Comedy*, Vol. 3 ('Paradise'), XXVIII:16–18.

25   *Ibid.*, Vol. I ('Inferno'), I.17–18.

26   Richard L. Poss, 'Stars and Spirituality in the Cosmology of Dante's *Commedia*', *Culture and Cosmos* 5(1) (Spring/Summer 2001): 59.

27   Stephen Skinner, *Terrestrial Astrology: Divination by Geomancy* (London: Routledge and Kegan Paul, 1980).

28   See Thorndike, *Magic*, Vol II, p. 802.

29   As summarized in a manuscript owned by the Holy Roman Emperor Wenceslaus (1378–1400). See Thorndike, *Magic*, Vol III, p. 591.

30   Claire Fanger, *Conjuring Spirits: Texts and Traditions of Medieval Ritual Magic* (Stroud: Sutton Publishing, 1998), p. 47.

31   Thorndike, *Magic*, Vol. III, p. 588.

32   *Ibid.*, pp. 27, 30.

33   For the *Diaries*, see Campion, *Dawn*, ch. 5, and A.J. Sachs, *Astronomical Diaries and Related Texts from Babylonia*, Vol. 1, *Diaries from 652 BC. to 262 BC.* (completed and edited by Herman Hunger; Vienna: Verlag der Osterreichischen Akademie der Wissenschaften, 1988).

34   Thorndike, *Magic*, Vol. III, ch. VIII.

35   See, for example, the discussion in Thorndike, *Magic*, Vol. III, pp. 285–7.

36   See the discussion in Thorndike, *Magic*, Vol. III, chs 19–21; Abu Ma'shar, *On Historical Astrology: The Book of Religions and Dynasties (On the Great Conjunctions)*, ed. and trans. Keiji Yamamoto and Charles Burnett (2 Vols; Leiden: Brill, 2000).

37   Thorndike, *Magic*, Vol. III, pp. 306–7.

38   *Ibid.*, p. 305.

39   For full discussion, see Campion, *The Great Year*, esp. ch. 12.

40   For astrology at European courts in the thirteenth and fourteenth centuries, see the summary in Thorndike, *Magic*, Vol. III, ch. 34. For astrology in England, see Hilary Carey, *Courting Disaster: Astrology at the English Court and University in the Later Middle Ages* (London: MacMillan, 1992).

41   See Thorndike, *Magic*, Vol. IV, p. 554.

42   Cited in Carey, *Courting Disaster*, p. 298.

43   See Nancy G. Sirasi, *Medieval and Early Renaissance Medicine* (Chicago: University of Chicago Press, 1990), and the discussion in Thorndike, *Magic*, Vol. IV, ch. 44.

44   Carey, *Courting Disaster*, pp. 132–3.

45   John North, *Chaucer's Cosmology* in Norris Hetherington (ed.), *Encyclopaedia of Cosmology* (New York and London: Garland Publishing, 1993), pp. 58–62. For a longer account, see John North, *Chaucer's Universe* (Oxford: Clarendon Press, 1988). For Chaucer and astrology, see also Ann W. Astell, *Chaucer and the Universe of Learning* (Ithaca and London: Cornell University Press, 1988), and J.C. Eade, *The Forgotten Sky: A Guide to Astrology in English Literature* (Oxford: Clarendon Press, 1984).

46   Geomancy depends on the scattering of pieces of earth or stones, the same principle as the throwing of yarrow stalks or coins in the Chinese I-Ching, and had acquired astrological symbolism by the Middle Ages. It was clearly a much faster way of obtaining an astrological reading than casting a horoscope. See Stephen Skinner, *Terestrial Astrology: Divination by Geomancy* (London: Routledge and Kegan Paul, 1980), and Wim van Binsbergen, 'The Astrological Origins of Astrological Geomancy', paper read at The SSIPS/SAGP 1996, 15th Annual Conference: 'Global and Multicultural Dimensions of Ancient and Medieval Philosophy and Social Thought: Africana, Christian, Greek, Islamic, Jewish, Indigenous and Asian Traditions', Binghamton University, Department of Philosophy/Center for Medieval and Renaissance studies (CEMERS), October 1996. http://www.shikanda.net/ancient_models/BINGHAMTON%201996.pdf

47   Jacqueline de Weever, *Chaucer Name dictionary: A Guide to Astrological, Biblical, Historical, Literary, and Mythological Names in the Works of Geoffrey Chaucer* (New York: Garland Pub., 1996 [1987]).

48   Chaucer, 'The Wife of Bath's Prologue' 324, in Robinson, *Works*, p. 79.

49   For the 'Treatise on the Astrolabe', see F.N. Robinson (ed.), *The Works of Geoffrey Chaucer* (London: Oxford University Press, 1966) pp. 545–63. The editor, Robinson, excluded the 'Equatorie of the Planets', disputing Chaucer's authorship. North assumes it is genuine: see North, *Chaucer's Cosmology* in Norris Hetherington (ed.), *Encyclopaedia of Cosmology* (New York and London: Garland Publishing 1993), p. 59. The 'Treatise on the Astrolabe' is online at http://www.fordham.edu/halsall/source/chaucer-astro.html.

50   'Saturn … is a signifier of … grandfathers'; 'Venus … signifies woman and wives … and younger sisters': Guido Bonatti, *Liber Astronomiae* (trans. Benjamin Dykes; 2 Vols.; Golden Valley, MN: The Cazimi Press, 2007), 3.1.1, 3.1.5, pp. 149–50, 168.

51   Chaucer, 'The Merchant's Tale', 1885–8, in Robinson, *Works*, p. 121.

52   William Lilly, *Christian Astrology*, (London 1647, facsimile edition, London: Regulus Publishing, 1985), p. 115.

53   Ptolemy, *Tetrabiblos*, I.19, pp. 89–91.

54   Chaucer, 'The Merchant's Tale', 2219–24, in Robinson, *Works*, p. 125.

55   Chaucer, 'The Wife of Bath's Prologue', 697–705, in Robinson, *Works*, pp. 82–3.

56   Ptolemy, *Tetrabiblos* I.19, pp. 89–91.

57   Campion, *Dawn*, p. 48.

58   Bernard Capp, *Astrology and the Popular Press: English Almanacs 1500–1800* (London and Boston: Faber and Faber, 1979), p. 289.

59   *Ibid.*

Notes to Chapter 7: The Renaissance: The Pagan Revival

1   Marsilio Ficino, *Three Books on Life*, ed. Carole C. Kaske, and John R. Clark, *Ficino, Three Books on Life*, Center for Medieval and Early Renaissance Studies (Binghamton: State University of New York at Binghamton, 1989), III.17, p. 331.

2   For summaries of Ficino's thought, see Angela Voss, *Marsilio Ficino* (London: Random House, 2007); Ernst Cassirer and Paul Kristeller, *The Renaissance Philosophy of Man* (Chicago: University of Chicago Press, 1956), pp. 185–211; Thorndike, *Magic*, Vol. IV, ch. 63. See also the two papers by Angela Voss, 'The Music of the Spheres: Marsilio Ficino and Renaissance Harmonia', *Culture and Cosmos* 2(2) (Autumn/Winter 1998): 16–38, and 'The Astrology of Marsilio Ficino: Divination or Science?', *Culture and Cosmos* 4(2) (Autumn, Autumn/Winter

2000): 29–45. For context, see Eugenio Garin, *Astrology in the Renaissance: The Zodiac of Life* (London and Boston: Routledge, 1976), ch. 3.

3   Charles Boer, 'Introduction in Ficino', in Marsilio Ficino, *The Book of Life* (trans. Charles Boer; Irving, Texas: Spring Publications, 1980), p. iii.

4   Ficino, *Three Books*, III.8, p. 281.

5   See the discussion of Ficino's view of fate in Don Cameron Allen, *The Star-Crossed Renaissance: The Quarrel About Astrology And Its Influence in England* (Durham, NC: Duke University Press, 1941), esp. pp. 7–8.

6   C.M. Woodhouse, *Gemisthos Plethon: The Last of the Hellenes* (Oxford: Oxford University Press, 1986).

7   Deut. 18.10–11.

8   Ronald Hutton, *Witches, Druids and King Arthur: Studies in Paganism, Myth and Magic* (London: Hambledon Books, 2003), ch. 4.

9   Iamblichus, *On the Mysteries*, I.1.

10   Charles Boer, 'Translator's Introduction', in Ficino, *The Book of Life*, p. viii. For the pursuit of happiness in the US Constitution, see The US Constitution Online: The Declaration of Independence at http://www.usconstitution.net/declar.html: 'We hold these truths to be self-evident, that all men are created equal, that they are endowed by their Creator with certain unalienable Rights, that among these are Life, Liberty and the pursuit of Happiness.'

11   Marsilio Ficino, *The Letters of Marsilio Ficino* (trans. members of the Language Dept. of the School of Economic Science, London; 5 Vols; London and New York: Fellowship of the School of Economic Science, London, 1975–85), p. 16.

12   Ficino, *Book of Life*; Ficino, *Three Books on Life*, ed. Carole C. Kaske and John Clark., Renaissance Texts Series, Vol. II (Binghamton: The Renaissance Society of America, 1989).

13   'An Apologia Dealing with Medicine, Astrology, the Life of the World, and the Magi, Who Greeted the Christ Child at His Birth', 33–40, in *Three Books on Life*, Kaske and Clark, p. 397.

14   Ficino, *Three Books on Life*, Kaske and Clark; *Ficino, Three Books on Life*, Center for Medieval and Early Renaissance Studies (Binghamton: State University of New York at Binghamton, 1989), III.21, p. 359.

15   For the best account of Ficino's psychological cosmology, see the Introduction to Voss, *Marsilio Ficino* (London: Random House, 2007).

16   See James Hillman, 'Plotino, Ficino and Vico as Precursors of Archetypal Psychology', in *Loose Ends: Primary Papers in Archetypal Psychology* (Zurich: Spring Publications, 1975), and Thomas Moore, *The Planets Within: The Astrological Psychology of Marsilio Ficino* (Great Barrington, MA: Lindisfarne Press, 1990).

17   Frances Yates, *The Art of Memory* (London: Peregrine, 1978), p. 155.

18   Ficino, *Three Books on Life*, Kaske and Clark, book 3, ch. II, l. 13–15, pp. 250–1.

19   Lynn Thorndike, *History of Magic and Experimental Science* (8 Vols; New York: Columbia University Press, 1923–58), Vol. IV, p. 565.

20   See Kaske and Clarke, *Three Books on Life*, p. 20.

21   Malefic Saturn is strong in Aquarius, which it rules; the moon is debilitated in Capricorn, which opposes its own sign, Cancer; benefic Venus is strong in Libra, which it rules; and benefic Jupiter is strong in Cancer, in which it is 'dignified'. See Ptolemy, Claudius, *Tetrabiblos*, trans. F.E. Robbins (Cambridge MA and London: Harvard University Press, 1940), book I.

22   Ficino, *The Book of Life*, trans. Boer, p. 93. See also Aquinas Summa contra Gentiles, III, 89–14.

23   Plato, *Republic*, (2 Vols; trans. Paul Shorey; Cambridge, MA and London: Harvard University Press, 1937), X, 611D-612 A, p. 483; Plato, *Phaedo* (trans H.N. Fowler; Cambridge, MA and London: Harvard University Press, 1914), 68C, 67E, 77D, 82C-83A, 247B-C; Plato, *Phaedrus* (trans H.N. Fowler; Cambridge, MA and London: Harvard University Press, 1914), 247 B-C.

24   Excerpt IIA, Hermes to Tat, 9, in Walter Scott *Hermetica* (4 Vols; Boulder: Shambala, 1982), Vol. 1, p. 385.

25   Libellus I. 6, in Scott, *Hermetica*, Vol. 1, p. 117.

26 Ficino, *Three Books on Life*, ed. Kaske and Clark; *Ficino, Three Books on Life*, III.17, p. 331.
27 Libellus I.18, in Scott, *Hermetica*, Vol. 1, p. 125.
28 See the discussion in Yates, *The Art of Memory*, pp. 154–5.
29 Ficino, *Three Books on Life*, ed. Kaske and Clark, book 3, ch. XXI, 1–5, p. 355.
30 *Ibid.*, 39–47, p. 357. See also the discussion in Voss, 'The Music of the Spheres', pp. 16–35.
31 Ficino, 'Apologia', 60–5, in *Three Books on Life*, ed. Kaske and Clark, p. 397.
32 Ficino, *Three Books on Life*, ed. Kaske and Clark, book 3, ch. XXIII, 2–5, p. 371.
33 J.R.R. Tolkein, *Tree and Leaf* (London: Unwin, 1964), pp. 15–16.
34 Jacob Burckhardt, *The Civilisation of the Renaissance in Italy* (trans. S.G.C. Middlemore; London: Penguin 1990 [1860]); Paul O. Kristeller, *The Philosophy of Marsilio Ficino* (Gloucester, MA: Peter Smith, 1964 [1943]), pp. 10–11.
35 For what follows, see the discussion in Allen, *The Star-Crossed Renaissance*, pp. 12–19.
36 See Joscelyn Godwin, *The Pagan Dream of the Renaissance* (York Beach, ME: Weiser, 2002); Jean Seznec, *The Survival of the Pagan Gods: The Mythological Tradition and its Place in Renaissance Humanism and Art* (Princeton: Princeton University Press, 1953); Edgar Wind, *Pagan Mysteries in the Renaissance* (Oxford: Oxford University Press, 1980); and the useful collection of essays in Ingrid Merkel and Allen G. Debus (eds) *Hermeticism and the Renaissance: Intellectual History and the Occult in Early Modern History* (London: Associated University Presses, 1988).
37 Ficino, *Three Books on Life*, ed. Kaske and Clark; *Ficino, Three Books on Life*, I.1, p. 109.
38 See Claudia Rousseau, 'Cosimo de Medici and Astrology: The Symbolism of Prophecy', PhD thesis, Columbia University, 1983; and the summary in Claudia Rousseau, 'An Astrological Prognostication to Duke Cosimo I de Medici of Florence', *Culture and Cosmos* 3(2) (Autumn/Winter 1999): 31–59.
39 Rousseau, 'An Astrological Prognostication', p. 33.
40 Hesiod, 'Works and Days', 12–28, in Hesiod, *The Homeric Hymns and Homerica, including 'Works and Days' and 'Theogonis'* (trans. Hugh G. Evelyn-White; Cambridge, MA: Harvard University Press, 1917).
41 Rousseau, 'An Astrological Prognostication', p. 48.
42 Hermann Hunger, *Astrological Reports to Assyrian Kings* (Helsinki: Helsinki University Press, 1992), para 82, p. 49.
43 Rousseau, 'An Astrological Prognostication', p. 50.

Notes to Chapter 8: The Renaissance: Radicalism and Reform

1 Cited in Wayne Shumaker, *The Occult Sciences in the Renaissance: A Study in Intellectual Patterns* (Berkely, Los Angeles and London: University of California Press, 1972), pp. 18–19.
2 For this and the following discussion, see Lynn Thorndike, *History of Magic and Experimental Science* (8 Vols; New York: Columbia University Press, 1923–58), Vol. IV, ch. LXII.
3 *Ibid.*, Vol. IV, pp. 554–5.
4 *Ibid.*, p. 546.
5 *Ibid.*, p. 549.
6 Cited in Stephen Vanden Broecke, *The Limits of Influence: Pico, Louvain and the Crisis of Renaissance Astrology* (Leiden: Brill, 2003), p. 11.
7 *Ibid.*, p. 65.
8 Giovanni Pico Della Mirandola, *Oration on the Dignity of Man* (trans. Robert A. Caponigri; Chicago: Gateway, 1959).
9 *Ibid.*, p. 55; see also pp. 35, 53–4.
10 Cited in Shumaker, *The Occult Sciences*, p. 16.
11 Chaim Wirszubski, *Pico della Mirandola's Encounter with Jewish Mysticism* (Cambridge, MA: Harvard University Press, 1989).
12 Cited in Shumaker, *The Occult Sciences*, p. 17.
13 For a summary of the *Disputationes*, see Don Cameron Allen, *The Star-Crossed Renaissance:*

The Quarrel About Astrology And Its Influence in England (Durham, NC: Duke University Press, 1941), pp. 22–35

14 Cited in Shumaker, *The Occult Sciences*, pp. 18–19.

15 For the following, see Shumaker, *The Occult Sciences*, pp. 19–27, and Allen, *The Star-Crossed Renaissance*, pp. 19–35.

16 A.J. Sachs, 'Babylonian Horoscopes', *Journal of Cuneiform Studies* 6 (1952): 40–75.

17 See Roberto Ridolfi, *The Life of Girolamo Savonarola* (New York: Knopf, 1959).

18 See the discussion in Eugenio Garin, *Astrology in the Renaissance: The Zodiac of Life* (London and Boston: Routledge, 1976), pp. 76–82.

19 Remo Catani, 'The Polemics on Astrology 1489–1524', *Culture and Cosmos* 3(2) (Autumn/Winter 1999): 20.

20 *Ibid.*, 16–31; the general discussion in Allen *The Star-Crossed Renaissance;*, and Garin, *Astrology in the Renaissance*, ch. 4.

21 See the various papers in Paola Zambelli (ed.), *'Astrologi hallucinati': Stars and the End of the World in Luther's Time*, (Berlin and New York: Walter de Gruyter, 1986).

22 See Broecke, *The Limits of Influence*, p. 199.

23 For good introductions to Copernicus's work, see J.L.E. Dreyer, *A History of the Planetary Systems from Thales to Kepler* (New York: Dover 1953 [1906]), ch. 13; and John North, *The Fontana History of Astronomy and Cosmology* (London: Fontana, 1994), ch. 11.

24 For a full discussion of the circumstances surrounding the publication of Copernicus's work and its reception, see Owen Gingerich, *The Book Nobody Read: the Quest for the Revolutions of Nicholas Copernicus* (London: Arrow, 2004).

25 See Dennis Richard Danielson, *The First Copernican: Georg Joachim Rheticus and the Rise of the Copernican Revolution* (New York: Walker and Company, 2006).

26 The reference was to Pliny, *De Natura Rerum*, Book 2, III, 8: 'The Greeks have designated the world by a word that means "ornament", and we have given it the name of mundus, because of its perfect finish and grace.'

27 Nicolaus Copernicus, *On the Revolutions of the Heavenly Spheres* (trans. Charles Glenn Wallis; Amherst, NY: Prometheus Books, 1995), I.1, p. 8.

28 Plato, *Timaeus*, 40.C-D; Campion, *Dawn*, ch. 10.

29 Johannes Schöner, *Three Books on the Judgment of Nativities* (trans. Robert Hand; Reston, VA: ARHAT, 2001).

30 See Jesse Kraai, 'Rheticus' Heliocentric Providence', PhD thesis, University of Heidelberg, 2001. Rheticus's poem satirizing medieval astrology is analysed in Kraai, 'Rheticus' Poem Concerning the Beer of Breslau and the Twelve Signs of the Zodiac', *Culture and Cosmos* 6(2), (Autumn/Winter 2002): 3–16. For the wider context, see Claudia Brosseder, 'The Writing in the Wittenberg Sky: Astrology in Sixteenth-Century Germany', *Journal of the History of Ideas* 66(4) (October 2005): 557–76.

31 For Aristarchus, see J.L.E. Dreyer, *A History of the Planetary Systems from Thales to Kepler* (New York: Dover, 1953 [1906]), ch. 6. See also William Harris Stahl, Richard Johnson and E.L. Bruce, *Martianus Capella and the Seven Liberal Arts*, Vol. 1 (New York: Columbia University Press, 1971), book 8; Copernicus, *On the Revolutions of the Heavenly Spheres* (trans. Charles Glenn Wallis: Amherst, NY: Prometheus Books, 1995), 1.5, p. 13. See also the discussion in Bernard R. Goldstein, 'The Origin of Copernicus's System', *Journal for the History of Astronomy* 33(part 3) (August 2002): 219–36.

32 Michael Hoskin, *The Cambridge Concise History of Astronomy* (Cambridge: Cambridge University Press, 1999), p. 88.

33 John Robert Christianson, *On Tycho's Island: Tycho Brahe and His Assistants, 1570–1601* (Cambridge: Cambridge University Press, 2000), pp. 48–50.

34 Copernicus, *On the Revolutions of the Heavenly Spheres*, I.10, pp. 24–5.

35 Marsilio Ficino, 'The Book of the Sun [De Sole]' (trans. Cornelius Geoffrey, Darby Costello, Graeme Tobyn, Angela Voss and Vernon Wells) in *Sphinx: A Journal for Archetypal Psychology and the Arts* 6 (1994), ch. 6: 132. See also http://www.users.globalnet.co.uk/~alfar2/ficino.

htm. See also Henry Cornelius Agrippa, *Three Books of Occult Philosophy*, facsimile of the 1651 translation, (London: Chthonius Books, 1986), book II, ch. XXXII, p. 284.

36 For splendid images of the sun as king in alchemy, see Salomon Trismosin, *Splendor Solis* (trans. Joscelyn Godwin; Grand Rapids, MI: Phanes Press, 1991).

37 Alan C. Bowen, 'Simplicius and the Early History of Greek Planetary Theory', *Perspectives on Science* 10(2) (Summer 2002): 155–67. See the discussion of what was to be saved in Bernard R. Goldstein, 'Saving the Phenomena: The Background to Ptolemy's Planetary Theory', *Journal for the History of Astronomy* 28(1), (February 1997): 1–12.

38 'Galileo to Monsignor Pieor Dini, Florence, 23 March 1615', trans. Julianne Evans, in Nicholas Campion and Nick Kollerstrom, *Galileo's Astrology* (Bristol: Cinnabar Books, 2004)/*Culture and Cosmos* 7(1) (Spring/Summer 2003): 80.

39 See G.J. Gibbons, *Spirituality and the Occult from the Renaissance to the Modern Age* (London: Routledge, 2001), p. 45.

40 Thomas S.Kuhn, *The Copernican Revolution: Planetary Astronomy in the Development of Western Thought* (Cambridge, MA and London: Harvard University Press, 1957).

41 Ernst Cassirer and Paul Kristeller, *The Renaissance Philosophy of Man* (Chicago: University of Chicago Press, 1956), p. 19.

42 William Harvey, *The Circulation of the Blood and other Writings* (trans. Kenneth Franklin; North Clarendon: Everyman's Library, 1993), p. 3. See also the discussion in Gibbons, *Spirituality and the Occult*, ch. 3.

43 Keith Hutchison, 'Towards a Political Iconology of the Copernican Revolution' in Patrick Curry (ed.), *Astrology, Science and Society* (Woodbridge, Suffolk: Boydell Press, 1987), pp. 95–142.

Notes to Chapter 9: The Sixteenth Century: Reformers and Magicians

1 Martin Luther, cited in Aby Warburg, *Heidnisch-antike Weissagungen in Wort und Bild zu Luthers Zeiten* (Ancient pagan prophecies in words and pictures in the times of Luther; Hamburg, 1919), p. 85, cited and translated by Hoppman in 'The Lichtenberger Prophecy and Melanchthon's Horoscope for Luther', *Culture and Cosmos* (Autumn/Winter 1997): 50–1.

2 Ingetraut Ludolphy, 'Luther und die Astrologie' in Paola Zambelli, *'Astrologi hallucinati': Stars and the End of the World in Luther's Time,* (Berlin and New York: Walter de Gruyter, 1986), pp. 101–7.

3 See Wayne Shumaker, *The Occult Sciences in the Renaissance: A Study in Intellectual Patterns* (Berkeley, Los Angeles and London: University of California Press, 1972), pp. 44–6.

4 Sachiko Kusukawa, *The Transformation of Natural Philosophy: The Case of Philip Melanchthon* (Cambridge: Cambridge University Press, 1995). See also Lynn Thorndike, *History of Magic and Experimental Science* (8 Vols; New York: Columbia University Press, 1923–58), Vol. V, ch. 17.

5 Philip Melanchthon, 'Initia doctrinae physicae', book 2, in P.G. Maxwell-Stuart (ed.), *The Occult in Early Modern Europe: a Documentary History* (Basingstoke: Macmillan Press Ltd, 1999), pp. 93–4.

6 Stefano Caroti, 'Melanchthon's Astrology' in Paola Zambelli, *'Astrologi hallucinati': Stars and the End of the World in Luther's Time,* (Berlin and New York, Walter de Gruyter, 1986), pp. 109–21.

7 Deut.18.10–11 condemned all forms of divination and sorcery, but see Mk 13.24–32 for warnings of Christ's second coming.

8 Jurgen G.H. Hoppmann, 'The Lichtenberger Prophecy and Melanchthon's Horoscope for Luther', *Culture and Cosmos* (Autumn/Winter 1997): 49–59; Dietrich Kurze, 'Popular Astrology and Prophecy in the fifteenth and sixteenth centuries' in Zambelli, *'Astrologi hallucinati'*, pp. 173–93.

9 For Schoener's astrology, see Johannes Schoener, *Opusculum Astrologicum* (trans. Robert Hand; Project Hindsight Latin Track Vol. IV; Berkeley Springs: Golden Hind Press, 1994), and *Three Books on the Judgment of Nativities* (trans. Robert Hand; Reston, VA: ARHAT, 2001).

10   Thorndike, *Magic*, Vol. V, ch. 11.

11   Aby Warburg, *Heidnisch-antike Weissagungen in Wort und Bild zu Luthers Zeiten* (Ancient Pagan Prophecies in Words and Pictures in the Times of Luther; Hamburg, 1919), p. 85, cited and translated by Hoppman in 'The Lichtenberger Prophecy', pp. 50–1.

12   See D.P. Walker, *Spiritual and Demonic Magic from Ficino to Campanella* (London: University of Notre Dame Press, 1975), and the various papers in Brian P. Levack, *Renaissance Magic* (New York and London: Garland Publishing, 1992).

13   The most influential Christian Kabbalists of the next 200 years were Henry Cornelius Agrippa (1487–1535), Theophrastus Paracelsus (1493–1541), Jerome Cardan (1501–76), Johann Baptist von Helmont (1577–1644), Robert Fludd (1574–1637), Valentin Weigel (1533–88), Jacob Boehme (1575–1624), Joseph de Voisin (1610–85) and Athanasius Kircher (1602–84).

14   The Realists argued that there were 'universals' in the universe, that is, truths which transcend material reality, which is essentially a Platonic position. See Bertrand Russell, 'The World of Universals' in *The Problems of Philosophy* (Oxford: Oxford University Press, 1967).

15   For Paracelsus's writing, see Nicholas Goodricke-Clarke (ed.), *Paracelsus: Essential Readings* (Berkeley: North Atlantic Books, 1999); Jolande Jacobi, *Paracelsus: Selected Writings* (Princeton: Princeton University Press, 1988); Paracelsus, *The Hermetic and Alchemical Writings of Aureolus Philippus Theophrastus Bombast*, ed. A.E. Waite (2 Vols; Largs, Scotland: Banton Press, 1990). For a study of his influence, see Allen G. Debus, *The English Paracelsians* (New York: Franklin Watts Inc., 1966).

16   Jacobi, *Paracelsus: Selected Writings*, p. 152.

17   Paracelsus, 'Volumen Medicinae Paramirum', 2.12–13, in Goodricke-Clarke, *Paracelsus: Essential Readings*, pp. 52–3.

18   Paracelsus, 'Astronomia Magna', 9.5, in Goodricke-Clarke, p. 112.

19   *Ibid.*

20   Paracelsus, 'A Book Concerning Long Life' in *The Hermetic and Alchemical Writings of Aureolus Philippus Theophrastus Bombast*, ed. A.E. Waite (2 Vols; Largs, Scotland: Banton Press, 1990), pp. 120–1.

21   For the standard account of Trithemius's life, see Noel L. Brann, *The Abbot Trithemius (1462–1516): The Renaissance of Monastic Humanism* (Leiden: E.J. Brill, 1981).

22   Jim Reeds, 'Solved: The Ciphers in Book III of Trithemius' *Steganographia*', http:www.dtc.umn.edu/~reedsj/trit.pdf.

23   For Agrippa's life and thought, see Christopher I. Lehrich, *The Language of Demons and Angels* (Leiden: E.J Brill, 2003), and Charles G. Nauert, *Agrippa and the Crisis of Renaissance Thought* (Urbana: University of Illinois Press, 1965). See also the discussion in Frances Yates, *Giordano Bruno and the Hermetic Tradition* (London: Routledge and Kegan Paul, 1964), and Paola Zambelli, 'Magic and Radical Reformation in Agrippa of Nettesheim', *Journal of the Warburg and Courtauld Institutes* 39(69–103) (1976).

24   For recent editions, see V. Perrone Compagni, *Cornelius Agrippa: De occulta philosophia Libri tres* (Leiden: E.J. Brill, 1992), and Henry Cornelius Agrippa, *Three Books of Occult Philosophy*, facsimile of the 1651 translation (London: Chthonius Books, 1986). In 1801 Agrippa's text, in a slightly abridged form, was shamelessly plagiarized and published as his own work by Frances Barrett in *The magus, or Celestial intelligencer* (London, 1801). This work can still be found in print. Barrett's work was then plagiarized by L.W. de Laurence in *The Great Book of Magical Art, Hindoo Magic & Indian Occultism* (Chicago, 1915), which substituted apparently Sanskit terms for Hebrew ones.

25   Henry Cornelius Agrippa, *Three Books of Occult Philosophy*, facsimile of the 1651 translation (London: Chthonius Books, 1986), book I, ch. 2.

26   *Ibid.*, ch. 67.

27   *Ibid.*, book II, chs 3–13.

28   *Ibid.*, Book II, chap. 4, p. 176.

29   Aryeh Kaplan, *Sefer Yetzirah: the Book of Creation in Theory and Practice* (York Beach, ME: Weiser Books, 1997), 5:8, p. 216.

30   William Lilly, *Christian Astrology* (London, 1647, facsimile edition; London: Regulus Publishing, 1985), pp. 61–5.

31   Wayne Shumaker, 'Renaissance Curiosa: Jon Dee's Conversations with Angels, Girolamo's Horoscope of Christ, Johness Trithemius and Cryptograpy, George Dalgarno's Universal Language', *Italica* 62(4) (Winter 1985): 329–0.

32   Deborah E. Harkness, 'Shows in the Showstone: A Theater of Alchemy and Apocalypse in the Angel Conversations of John Dee (1527–1608/9)', *Renaissance Quarterly* 49(4) (Winter 1996): 722.

33   For Dee's life and work, see Nicholas H. Clulee, *John Dee's Natural Philosophy: Between Science and Religion* (London: Routledge, 1989); Richard Deacon, *John Dee: Scientist, Geographer, Astrologer and Secret Agent to Elizabeth I* (London: Frederick Muller, 1978); Peter J. French, *John Dee: The World of an Elizabethan Magus* (London: Routledge and Kegan Paul, 1972); Deborah E. Harkness, *John Dee's Conversations with Angels: Cabala, Alchemy and the End of Nature* (Cambridge: Cambridge University Press, 1999); William H. Sherman, *John Dee: The Politics of Reading and Writing in the English Renaissance* (Amherst: University of Massachusetts Press, 1995); Gerald Suster, *John Dee* (Berkeley: North Atlantic Books, 2003); and Benjamin Woolley, *The Queen's Conjuror: The Science and Magic of Dr Dee* (London: HarperCollins, 2001). For examples of Dee's work in print, see Dee, *The Mathematicall Praeface to the Elements of Geometrie of Euclid of Megara* (New York: Science History Publications, 1975); John Dee, *The Rosie Crucian Secrets: Their Excellent Method of making Medicines of Metals also their Lawes and Mysteries* (Wellingborough: Aquarian Press, 1985); Edward Fenton, *The Diaries of John Dee* (Charlbury, Oxfordshire: Day Books, 1998); and Wayne Shumaker (trans.), *John Dee on Astronomy: Propaedemata Aphoristica (1558 & 1568)* (Berkeley and Los Angeles: University of California Press, 1978).

34   William Shakespeare, *The Tempest*, V.i.41–2.

35   Thorndike, *Magic*, Vol. VI, ch. 35.

36   For this argument, see Harkness, *John Dee's Conversations with Angels*.

37   Christina Larner, *Enemies of God* (Edinburgh: John Donald, 2000), p. 190.

38   Keith Thomas, *Religion and the Decline of Magic* (Harmondsworth, Middlesex: Peregrine Books, 1971), p. 757.

39   John Armstrong, *An Italian Astrologer at the Court of Henry VII* (London: Faber and Faber, 1960).

40   Anthony Grafton, *Cardano's Cosmos: The Worlds and Works of a Renaissance Astrologer* (Cambridge and London: Harvard University Press, 1999). For Cardan's own account of his life, see Jerome Cardan, *The Book of My Life (De Vita Propria Liber)* (trans. Jean Stoner; London and Toronto: E.P. Dutton, 1931).

41   Jerome Cardan, 'Choice Aphorisms from the Seven Segments of Cardan' in *The Astrologers Guide* (London: George Redway, 1886), no 15, p. 75.

42   Germana Ernst, 'Many ends for the world. Luca Gaurico Instigator of the Debate in Italy and Germany'; Paola Zambelli, *'Astrologi hallucinati': Stars and the End of the World in Luther's Time*, (Berlin and New York: Walter de Gruyter, 1986), pp. 239–63.

43   See the discussion in Liz Greene, *The Astrology of Fate* (London: Mandala, 1985), pp. 143–50.

44   Erica Cheetham (trans. and ed.), *The Prophecies of Nostradamus* (London: Corgi, 1981), 1.35, pp. 40–1.

45   Pope Sixtus V, *Coeli et Terrae* (1586) in P.G. Maxwell Stuart (ed.), *The Occult in Early Modern Europe* (London: MacMillan Press, 1999), pp. 111–12.

46   Tommaso Campanella, *Disputatio contra murmurantes citra et ultra montes, in Bullas SS. Pontificum Sixti V et Urbani VIII adversus iudiciarios editas* (1636) in Maxwell Stuart, *The Occult in Early Modern Europe*, pp. 113–14.

47   Tommaso Campanella, 'De Fato Siderali Vitando' in *Astrologicorum Libri VI*, 1629, cited in Stephen Skinner, *Terrestrial Astrology: Divination by Geomancy* (London: Routledge and Kegan Paul, 1980), p. 127.

48   Thomas Campanella, *The City of the Sun* (Frankfurt, 1623), trans. A. M.Elliot and R. Millner,

intro. A.L. Morton (London, 1981); Germana Ernst, 'The Sky in a Room: Campanella's *Apologeticus* in defence of the pamphlet *De siderali fato vitando*', *Culture and Cosmos* 6(1) (Spring/Summer 2002): 3–10; and 'Astrology and Prophecy in Campanella and Galileo' in Nicholas Campion and Nick Kollerstrom, *Galileo's Astrology* (Bristol: Cinnabar Books, 2004/ *Culture and Cosmos* 7(1) (Spring/Summer 2003): 21–36; John M. Headley, *Tommaso Campanella and the Transformation of the World* (Princeton: Princeton University Press, 1997).

49   There is little work in this area, but for a summary of some ancient sources, see Elizabeth Chesley Baity, 'Archaeoastronomy and Ethnoastronomy So Far', *Current Anthropology* 14(4) (Oct 1973): 389–449.

50   Owen Davies, *Witchcraft, Magic and Culture, 1736–1951* (Manchester: Manchester University Press, 1999).

51   See the discussion in Thomas, *Religion and the Decline of Magic*, pp. 757–8.

52   See Don Cameron Allen, *The Star-Crossed Renaissance: The Quarrel About Astrology And Its Influence in England*, (Durham, NC: Duke University Press, 1941), ch. 4; and J.C. Eade, *The Forgotten Sky: A Guide to Astrology in English Literature* (Oxford: Clarendon Press, 1984).

53   Bernard Capp, *Astrology and the Popular Press: English Almanacs 1500–1800* (London and Boston: Faber and Faber, 1979), p. 270.

54   See Alastair Fowler, *Spenser and the Numbers of Time* (London: Routledge and Kegan Paul, 1964); and J. Michael Richardson, *Astrological Symbolism in Spenser's The Shepheardes Calendar: The Cultural Background of a Literary Text* (Lampeter: The Edwin Mellen Press, 1989).

55   *Troilus and Cressida*. 1.iii.

56   See Harry Rusche, 'Edmund's Conception and Nativity in King Lear', *Shakespeare Quarterly* 20(2) (Spring 1965): 161–4; and, for the wider context, Moriz Sondheim, 'Shakespeare and the Astrology of his Time', *Journal of the Warburg Institute* 2(3) (January 1939): 243–59.

57   William Lilly, *Annus Tenebrosus or The Dark Year*, 1652 (London, 1652), pp. 36–7.

58   Theodore Spencer, *Shakespeare and the Nature of Man* (New York: Macmillan, 1949), p. 5

59   William Shakespeare, *Hamlet*, I.V.943.

60   A.L. Rowse, *Sex and Society in Shakespeare's Age: Simon Forman the Astrologer* (New Jersey: Chares Scribner's Sons, 1974).

61   Charles Nicholl, *The Chemical Theatre* (London: Routledge and Kegan Paul, 1980).

62   F.E. Halliday, *Shakespeare in his Age* (London: Duckworth, 1956), p. 282.

63   *Julius Caesar*, I, ii, 140–1.

Notes to Chapter 10: The Seventeenth Century: Horoscopes and Telescopes

1   Johannes Kepler, cited in M. Caspar, *Kepler* (New York: Dover Publications, 1993), p. 341.

2   There is no adequate scholarly treatment of Tycho's astrology. For biographies focusing on his astronomy, see John Robert Christianson, *On Tycho's Island: Tycho Brahe and His Assistants, 1570–1601* (Cambridge: Cambridge University Press, 2000); J.L.E. Dreyer, *Tycho Brahe: A Picture of Scientific Work and Life in the Sixteenth Century* (New York: Dover Publications, 1963); Kitty Ferguson, *The Nobleman and his Household. Tycho Brahe and Johannes Kepler: The Strange Partnership that revolutionised Science* (London: Headline, 2002); V. Thoren, *The Lord of Uraniborg: A Biography of Tycho Brahe* (Cambridge: Cambridge University Press, 1990). See also the brief discussion on astrology in A. Pannekoek, *A History of Astronomy* (London: George Allen and Unwin Ltd., 1961), pp. 204–9.

3   Quoted by Owen Gingerich, 'Reflections on the Role of Archaeoastronomy in the History of Astronomy' in A.F. Aveni (ed.), *World Archaeoaastronomy* (Cambridge: Cambridge University Press, 1989), p. 40.

4   The Prutenic Tables were computed by Erasmus Reinhold on the basis of Copernicus's work and published in 1551. See Owen Gingerich, 'The Role of Erasmus Reinhold and the Prutenic Tables in the dissemination of Copernican Theory', *Studia Copernicana* 6 (1973): 43–62.

5   For Tycho's debt to Ficino, see Christianson, pp. 49–50.

6   John Robert Christianson, 'Tycho Brahe's Cosmology from the Astrologia of 1591', *Isis* 59(3) (Autumn 1968): 312–18.

7   *Ibid.*, 'Tycho Brahe's German Treatise on the Comet of 1577', *Isis* 70(1) (March 1979): 118.

8   From the 'De disciplinis mathematicis', trans. in A. Pannekoek, *A History of Astronomy* (London: George Allen and Unwin Ltd., 1961), pp. 205, 206.

9   For Kepler's life and work, see Carola Baumgardt, *Johannes Kepler: Life and Letters* (London: Gollancz, 1952); and M. Caspar, *Kepler* (New York: Dover Publications, 1993). For Kepler's astronomy, see B. Stephenson, *Kepler's Physical Astronomy* (New York: Springer-Verlag, 1987).

10 G.J. Gibbons, *Spirituality and the Occult from the Renaissance to the Modern Age* (London: Routledge, 2001), p. 48.

11 Plato, *Timaeus* 55A-C

12 Johannes Kepler, *Mysterium Cosmographicum: The Secret of the Universe* (trans. A.M. Duncan; New York: Abaris Books, 1981). For discussion, see Judith Field, *Kepler's Geometrical Cosmology* (London, 1988).

13 *Ibid.*; *Epitome of Copernican Astronomy*, books 4 and 5 (trans. C.G. Wallace, in *Great Books of the Western World*, XVI (Chicago: Encyclopaedia Britannica), pp. 1005–85, also *Great Minds Series* (Amerst, NY: Prometheus Books, 1995).

14 Caspar, *Kepler*, pp. 338–9.

15 *Ibid.*, p. 340.

16 *Ibid.*

17 Julius Firmicus Maternus, *Mathesis*, translated as *Ancient Astrology: Theory and Practice*, Jean Rhys Bram (Park Ridge, NJ: Noyes Press, 1975), VI.xvi, p. 195; VI, xxiii, p. 200.

18 For a study of Kepler's astrology, see *Culture and Cosmos*, special double issue on Kepler's Astrology, 12(1 and 2) (Spring/Summer and Autumn/Winter 2009), forthcoming. See also N. Kollerstrom, 'Kepler's Belief in Astrology' in Annabella Kitson (ed.), *History and Astrology: Clio and Urania Confer* (London: Unwin Paperbacks, 1989), pp. 152–70; J.V. Field, 'A Lutheran Astrologer: Johannes Kepler', *Archive for History of Exact Sciences* 31(3) (1984): 189–272; and Judith Field, 'Astrology in Kepler's Cosmology' in Patrick Curry, *Astrology, Science and Society* (Woodbridge, Suffolk: Polity Press, 1987), pp. 143–70.

19 Sheila J. Rabin, 'Kepler's Attitude Toward Pico and the Anti-Astrology Polemic', *Renaissance Quarterly* 50(3) (Autumn 1997): 750–0.

20 Caspar, *Kepler*, p. 339.

21 Kepler to Maestlin, 15 March 1598, letter 89, l. 177, KGW 13, p. 184, cited in Field, *Kepler's Geometrical Cosmology*, p. 127.

22 Claudius Ptolemy, *Tetrabiblos*, trans. F.E. Robbins (Cambridge, MA and London: Harvard University Press, 1940), I.13.

23 Johannes Kepler, 'Johannes Kepler's Tertius Interveniens', (theses 64–9), trans. Ken Negus, *Culture and Cosmos* 1(1) (Spring/Summer 1997): 51–2.

24 *Ibid.*, 'On the More Certain Fundamentals of Astrology', Prague, 1601, trans. Mary Ann Rossi with notes by J. Bruce Brackenbridge, *Proceedings of the American Philosophical Society* 123(2) (1979), Thesis 3: 91.

25 *Ibid.*, Thesis 52, p. 100.

26 *Ibid.*, 'Astrological Prognostications for 1618', trans John Meeks, *Culture and Cosmos* 12(1 and 2) (Spring/Summer and Autumn Winter 2009), forthcoming.

27 For Bodin's own theories, see Jean Bodin, *Method for the Easy Comprehension of History* (trans. Beatrice Reynolds; Records of Civilisations: Sources and Studies no 37, New York, 1945); Bodin, *The Six Books of the Commonweale* (trans. Richard Knolles, London, 1606), facsimile edition, ed. Kenneth Douglas MacRae (Cambridge, MA, 1962); Bodin, *The Six Books of the Comonwealth*, (abridged and trans. M.J. Tooley, London, 1955). For discussion, see Nicholas Campion, 'Astrological Historiography in the Renaissance: The Work of Jean Bodin and Louis Le Roy' in Annabella Kitson (ed.), *History and Astrology: Clio and Urania Confer* (London: Unwin Paperbacks, 1989), pp. 89–136.

28   Johannes Kepler, *The Harmony of the World* (trans. E.J. Aiton, A.M. Duncan and J.V. Field; Philadelphia: American Philosophical Society, 1997), p. 255, n 203.

29   *Ibid.*, p. 278.

30   Kepler, 'On the More Certain Fundamentals', Thesis 68, p. 10.

31   *Ibid.*, Thesis 72, p. 104.

32   *Ibid.*, Thesis 71, p. 104.

33   Michael Hunter and Annabel Gregory (eds), *An Astrological Diary of the Seventeenth Century: Samuel Jeake of Rye 1652–1699* (Oxford: Clarendon Press, 1988), p. 187.

34   Terrie Bloom, 'Borrowed Perceptions: Harriot's Maps of the Moon', *Journal for the History of Astronomy* 9(2) (June 1978): 117–22; Albert van Helden, *The Invention of the Telescope* (Philadelphia: American Philosophical Society, 1977); John D. North, 'Thomas Harriot and the First Telescopic Observations of Sunspots' in John W. Shirley (ed.), *Thomas Harriot: Renaissance Scientist* (Oxford: Clarendon Press, 1974), pp. 129–65; Eileen Reeves, *Galileo's Glassworks: The Telescope and the Mirror* (Cambridge: Harvard University Press, 2008); E. Sluiter, 'The telescope before Galileo', *Journal for the History of Astronomy* 28(3) (August 1997): 223–35.

35   Some argue that Harriot used a 'terrestrial' rather than 'astronomical' telescope. However, Harriot did in fact use a refractor (the only type of telescope invented in 1609) to observe the night skies before Galileo did, thus Harriot may have inadvertently invented the 'astronomical' telescope by turning his 'terrestrial' refractor skyward before Galileo. Harriot's problem is that his records were not published until the late twentieth century. See E. Sluiter, 'The telescope before Galileo', *Journal for the History of Astronomy* 28 (1997): 223–35.

36   See the extract from Bill Shea, 'Melchior Inchofer's "Tractatus Syllepticus": A Consultator of the Holy Office answers Galileo', *Novità Celesti e Crisi Del Sapere Atti del convegno Internazionale di studi Galileiani* Florence, 1984, a cura di P.Galluzi, pp. 283–92 in Nicholas Campion and Nick Kollerstrom, *Galileo's Astrology* (Bristol: Cinnabar Books, 2004)/*Culture and Cosmos* 7(1) (Spring/Summer 2003): 107–9.

37   See the discussion in Marjorie Nicholson, *The Breaking of the Circle* (New York: Columbia University Press, 1962).

38   Dava Sobel, *Galileo's Daughter: a Drama of Science, Faith and Love* (London: Fourth Estate, 1999), p. 30.

39   'Galileo to Monsignor Piero Dini, Florence, 23 March 1615', trans. Julianne Evans, in Nicholas Campion and Nick Kollerstrom, *Galileo's Astrology* (Bristol: Cinnabar Books, 2004)/*Culture and Cosmos* 7(1) (Spring/Summer 2003): 80.

40   Galileo's horoscopes were first subject to an initial analysis by Grazia Mirti and Serena Foglia in the early 1990s. For a detailed analysis, see Bernadette Brady, 'Four Galilean Horoscopes: An Analysis of Galileo's Astrological Techniques' in Nicholas Campion and Nick Kollerstrom, *Galileo's Astrology* (Bristol: Cinnabar Books, 2004)/*Culture and Cosmos* 7(1) (Spring/Summer 2003): 113–44. See also Noel Swerdlow, 'Galileo's Horoscopes', *Journal for the History of Astronomy* 35(part 2) (May 2004): 135–41.

41   Galileo, 'On the Customary Ways of Virginia', trans. Grazia Mirti, *Galileo's Astrology* (Bristol: Cinnabar Books, 2004) *Culture and Cosmos* 7(1) (Spring/Summer 2003): 102.

42   'Galileo to Cristina of Lorraine (in Florence) Padua, 16 January 1609', trans. Julianne Evans, in Campion and Kollerstrom, *Galileo's Astrology/Culture and Cosmos* 7(1) (Spring/Summer 2003): 78.

43   'Galileo's letter to Piero Dini, Rome, 21 May 1611', trans. Michael Edwards, in Campion and Kollerstrom, *Galileo's Astrology/Culture and Cosmos* 7(1) (Spring/Summer 2003): 84–95.

44   Galileo, *Le Opere di Galileo Galilei.*, etc. Tome I. Florence, etc. 1842, p. 123, cited and discussed in Antonio Favaro, 'Galileo, Astrologer', trans. Julianne Evans, in Campion and Kollerstrom, *Galileo's Astrology/Culture and Cosmos* 7(1) (Spring/Summer 2003): 14.

45   Lynn Thorndike, *History of Magic and Experimental Science* (8 Vols; New York: Columbia University Press, 1923–58), Vol. VII, ch. 16.

46   See, for example, J.B. Morin, *Astrologica Gallica*, Book Twenty-One (trans. Richard S. Baldwin as *The Morinus System of House Interpretation*; Washington DC: American Federation of Astrologers, 1974).

47 'Galileo to Elia Didati in Paris, Florence, 15 January 1633', trans. Julianne Evans, in Campion and Kollerstrom, *Galileo's Astrology/Culture and Cosmos* 7(1) (Spring/Summer 2003): 82–3.

48 Antonio Favaro, 'Galileo, Astrologer', trans. Julianne Evans, in Campion and Kollerstrom, *Galileo's Astrology/Culture and Cosmos* 7(1) (Spring/Summer 2003): 16.

49 Bertolt Brecht, *Galileo* (London: Random House, 1999).

50 Colin A. Ronan, *The Cambridge Illustrated History of the World's Science* (Cambridge: Cambridge University Press, 1983), p. 334.

51 S. Kusukawa and I. Maclean (eds) 'Imagineering the Astronomical Revolution', Essay Review, *Journal for the History of Astronomy* 37(part 4) (November 2006): 471.

52 Charles Webster, *From Paracelsus to Newton: Magic and the Making of Modern Science* (Cambridge: Cambridge University Press, 1982), p. 1.

53 Mary Midgley, *Science and Salvation: a Modern Myth and its Meaning* (London and New York: Routledge, 1992), p. 14.

54 Antonio Poppi, 'On Trial for Astral Fatalism: Galileo Faces the Inquisition' in Campion and Kollerstrom, *Galileo's Astrology/Culture and Cosmos* 7(1) (Spring/Summer 2003): 49–58.

55 For a useful summary of Hobbes's ideas and relationship with Galileo, see MacPherson, introduction in Thomas Hobbes, *Leviathan, or the Matter, Forme, and Power of a Common-Wealth Ecclesiastical and Civil*, (ed. C.B. MacPherson; Harmonsdworth, Middlesex: Penguin, 1968).

56 Thomas Hobbes, *Leviathan, or the Matter, Forme, and Power of a Common-Wealth Ecclesiastical and Civil*, (ed. C.B. MacPherson, Harmondsworth, Middlesex: Penguin, 1968), p. 107. See also MacPherson's introduction, p. 29.

57 Thomas Hobbes, 'Philosophical Rudiments Concerning Government and Society, 1651', pp. 10–11, quoted in MacPherson, introduction to the *Leviathan*, pp. 26–7.

58 Hobbes, *Leviathan*, ch. XXVII, p. 234. Hobbes would have reacted in horror to the furore surrounding the greatest eclipse of the republican period (that of 'Black Munday', 29 March 1652), which was to be hailed by republican astrologers such as Nicholas Culpeper as preparing the path for the overthrow of monarchy and the return of Christ to inaugurate the Fifth Kingdom. See Culpeper, *Black Munday*, Catastrophe Magnatum.

Notes to Chapter 11: The Seventeenth Century: Practitioners and Politics

1 Ben Johnson, 'Hymn to Diana', lines 1–7, Arthur Quiller-Couch, ed.; 1919; *The Oxford Book of English Verse: 1250–1900*; http://www.bartleby.com/101/184.html (accessed 23 July 2008).

2 Bernard Capp, *Astrology and the Popular Press: English Almanacs 1500–1800* (London and Boston: Faber and Faber, 1979); Louise Hill Curth, *English Almanacs, Astrology and Popular Medicine, 1550–1700* (London: Palgrave MacMillan, 2008).

3 William Lilly, *Christian Astrology* (London, 1647, facsimile edition; London: Regulus Publishing, 1985).

4 See Derek Parker, *Familiar to All: William Lilly and Astrology in the Seventeenth Century* (London: Jonathan Cape, 1975); Ann Geneva, *Astrology and the Seventeenth Century Mind: William Lilly and the Language of the Stars* (Manchester and New York: Manchester University Press, 1995); and Lilly's own autobiography, *William Lilly's History of His Life and Times from the Year 1602 to 1681* (London, 1715, online at http://www.gutenberg.org/dirs/1/5/8/3/15835/15835.txt).

5 Guido Bonatti, 'The Considerations of Guido Bonatus' in *The Astrologers Guide* (London: George Redway, 1886), no. 7, pp. 6–7; Jerome Cardan, 'Choice Aphorisms from the Seven Segments of Cardan' in *The Astrologers Guide* (London: George Redway, 1886), no 6, p. 74.

6 Keith Thomas, *Religion and the Decline of Magic* (Harmondsworth, Middlesex: Peregrine Books, 1971), p. 757. See also Nicholas Campion, 'Astrology' in *Encyclopaedia of Witchcraft: the Western Tradition* (ed. Richard Golden; San Diego: ABC.CLIO, 2006), Vol. 1, pp. 64–5.

7 Lilly, *Christian Astrology*, pp. 417–20, 442–4.

8 *Ibid.*, pp. 305–7.

9 Thomas, *Religion and the Decline of Magic*, p. 366.

10   Stephen Wilson, *The Magical Universe: Everyday Ritual and Magic in Pre-Modern Europe* (London: Hambledon and London, 2000), esp. pp. 165–214.

11   John Aubrey, *Brief Lives* (London: Penguin, 1987), p. 249.

12   See Derek Parker, *Familiar to All: William Lilly and Astrology in the Seventeenth Century* (London: Jonathan Cape, 1975), p. 134.

13   See William Lilly, *William Lilly's History of His Life and Times from the Year 1602 to 1681* (London, 1715); online at http://www.gutenberg.org/dirs/1/5/8/3/15835/15835.txt; and the discussion in Parker, *Familiar to All*, pp. 131–2.

14   Maurice McCann, 'The Secret of William Lilly's Prediction of the Fire of London', *The Astrological Journal* 32(1) (Jan/Feb 1990): 53–9.

15   Ann Geneva, *Astrology and the Seventeenth Century Mind: William Lilly and the Language of the Stars* (Manchester and New York: Manchester University Press, 1995), p. xv.

16   For esotericism, see Antoine Faivre, *Access to Western Esotericism* (Albany: State University of New York Press, 1994); *Theosophy, Imagination, Tradition: Studies in Western Esotericism* (Albany: State University of New York Press, 2000); and, with Jacob Needleman, *Modern Esoteric Spirituality* (London: SCM Press, 1992).

17   Lilly, *Christian Astrology*, pp. 305–6.

18   Samuel Pepys, *The Diary of Samuel Pepys* (6 Vols; London: HarperCollins, 2000), Vol. 6, p. 369. See also Vol. 1, p. 268.

19   William Lilly, *Annus Tenebrosus or the Dark Year* (London, 1652), p. 21.

20   *Ibid.*, p. 26.

21   *Ibid.*, p. 28.

22   Lilly, *Christian Astrology*, pp. 56, 250, 464–6, 640–2.

23   *Ibid.*, p. 465.

24   For a brief study of Ashmole's use of astrology, see Annabella Kitson, 'Some Varieties of Electional Astrology' in Annabella Kitson (ed.), *History and Astrology: Clio and Urania Confer* (London: Unwin Paperbacks, 1989), pp. 171–99.

25   C.H. Josten (ed.), *Elias Ashmole (1617–1692), His Autobiographical and Historical Notes, his Correspondence, and other Contemporary Sources relating to his Life and Work* (5 Vols; Oxford: Oxford University Press, 1966), Vol. 4, p. 1679.

26   *Ibid.*, p. 1346.

27   For a full treatment of Culpeper's astrological medicine, see Graeme Tobyn, *Culpeper's Medicine: A Practice of Western Holistic Medicine* (Shaftesbury: Element Books, 1997); and, for Culpeper's own work, the *Astrological Judgment of Diseases from the Decumbiture of the Sick* (Tempe, AZ: American Federation of Astrologers, 1959).

28   Nicholas Culpeper, *Catastrophe Magnatum, or the Fall of monarchie. A caveat to magistrates, deduced from the eclipse of the sunne, 29 March 1652* (London, 1652), pp. 55–6. War with the Dutch broke out in July 1652; Culpeper, *Black Munday turn'd white* (London, 1652).

29   John Booker, *Black Munday* (London, 1652).

30   See Joscelyn Godwin, *Robert Fludd: Hermetic philosopher and surveyor of two worlds* (London: Thames and Hudson, 1979); and William H. Huffman (ed.), *Robert Fludd: Essential Writings* (London: Aquarian Press, 1992).

31   Frances Yates, *The Art of Memory* (London Peregrine, 1978), pp. 350–4.

32   Lynn Thorndike, *History of Magic and Experimental Science* (8 Vols; New York: Columbia University Press, 1923–58), Vol. VIII, p. 98.

33   H.P. Blavatsky, *Isis Unveiled* (Pasadena, CA: Theosophical University Press, 1976), Vol. 1, p. 309.

34   Joscelyn Godwin, *Athanasius Kircher: A Renaissance Man and the Quest for Lost Knowledge* (London: Thames and Hudson, 1979).

35   *Isis Unveiled*, Vol. 1, pp. 208–9.

36   See the discussion in Antoine Faivre, *Access to Western Esotericism* (Albany: State University of New York Press, 1994), esp. ch. 2.

37   Blavatsky, *Isis Unveiled*, Vol. 1, p. 221.

38   Jacob Boehme, *The Signature of all Things* (Cambridge: James Clarke and Co, 1969), pp. 34–5.

39   Franz Hartmann, *Jacob Boehme: Life and Doctrines* (London: Kegan, Paul, Trench and Tubner, 1891), pp. 71–3.

40   For a full discussion, see Mary Ellen Bowden, 'The Scientific Revolution in Astrology: the English Reformers, 1558–1686', PhD thesis, Yale University, 1974; and Patrick Curry, *Prophecy and Power: Astrology in Early Modern England* (Oxford: Polity Press, 1989).

41   Francis Bacon, *Advancement of Learning* (London: Dent, 1973), IV.11, XXII.4.

42   See G.J. Gibbons, *Spirituality and the Occult from the Renaissance to the Modern Age* (London: Routledge, 2001), p. 39. See also p. 7.

43   For the argument that modern science emerged out of the occult, rather than reacted against it, see the various papers, especially the Introduction, in Brian Vickers (ed.), *Occult and Scientific Mentalities in the Renaissance* (Cambridge: Cambridge University Press, 1986). See G.J. Gibbons, *Spirituality and the Occult from the Renaissance to the Modern Age* (London: Routledge, 2001), esp. ch. 3; and Charles Webster, *From Paracelsus to Newton: Magic and the Making of Modern Science* (Cambridge: Cambridge University Press, 1982).

44   'Flamsteed to Towneley', 4 July 1678, in Eric G. Forbes, Leslie Murdin and Frances Willmoth, *The Correspondence of John Flamsteed, the First Astronomer Royal*, Vol. 1, 1666–82 (Bristol and Philadelphia: Institute of Physics Publishing, 1995), p. 640.

45   For Flamsteed's attitude to astrology, see Michael Hunter, 'Science and Astrology in Seventeenth Century England' in Patrick Curry (ed.), *Astrology, Science and Society* (Woodbridge, Suffolk: Boydell Press, 1987): 260–300.

46   Michael Hunter, 'Science and Astrology in Seventeenth Century England' in Patrick Curry (ed.), *Astrology, Science and Society* (Woodbridge, Suffolk: Boydell Press, 1987), p. 264.

47   The text was finally published in Hunter, 'Science and Astrology in Seventeenth Century England', pp. 287–300.

48. 'Greenwich: The hospital for seamen', *Old and New London* Vol. 6 (1878):177–90; http://www.british-history.ac.uk/report.asp?compid=45274 (accessed 18 August 2006).

49   For Boyle, see Thorndike, *Magic*, Vol. VIII, ch. 28; and Curry, *Prophecy and Power*, pp. 62–3.

50   Placidus de Titis, *Primum Mobile* (trans. John Cooper; Bromley, Kent: Institute for the Study of Cycles in World Affairs, 1983), p. 1.

51   See Thorndike, *Magic*, Vol. VII, pp. 559–62.

52   René Descartes, *Discourse on Method and the Meditations* (trans. F.E. Sutcliffe; Harmondsworth, Middlesex: Penguin, 1968), Discourse I, pp. 32–3.

53   Anna Marie Roos, 'Israel Hiebner's Astrological Amulets and the English Sigil War', *Culture and Cosmos* 6(2) (Autumn/Winter 2002): 17–43.

54   See Bernard Capp, *Astrology and the Popular Press: English Almanacs 1500–1800* (London and Boston: Faber and Faber, 1979), p. 283.

55   *Ibid.*, p. 207.

56   *Ibid.*, p. 209; see also p. 251.

57   John Trithemius, *The heavenly Intelligences, governing the Orbes under God*, (London, no date).

58   Capp, *Astrology and the Popular Press*, p. 272.

59   Thorndike, *Magic*, Vol. 8, ch. 32.

60   See the discussion in Keith Thomas, *Religion and the Decline of Magic* (Harmondsworth, Middlesex: Peregrine Books, 1971), ch. 22.

61   Patrick Curry, *Prophecy and Power: Astrology in Early Modern England* (Oxford: Polity Press, 1989).

62   Ann Geneva, *Astrology and the Seventeenth Century Mind: William Lilly and the Language of the Stars* (Manchester and New York: Manchester University Press, 1995), p. xv.

63   Thomas, *Religion and the Decline of Magic*, p. 367; Thomas S. Kuhn, *The Copernican Revolution: Planetary Astronomy in the Development of Western Thought* (Cambridge, MA and London: Harvard University Press, 1957); and *The Structure of Scientific Revolutions*, 2nd edn (Chicago: University of Chicago Press, 1970).

64   Capp, *Astrology and the Popular Press*, p. 273.

65 Thorndike, *Magic*, Vol. VI., p. 160.
66 William Shakespeare, *Romeo and Juliet*, Act I, Prologue, line 6. For discussion of *The Duchess of Malfi*, see J.C. Eade, *The Forgotten Sky: A Guide to Astrology in English Literature* (Oxford: Clarendon Press, 1984), pp. 188–9. Eade pointed out that the violent astrological significations given by Webster were impossible for the date given in the text (19 December 1504).
67 John Dryden, *An Evening's Love: or, The Mock Astrologer*, in *The Works of John Dryden*, Vol. 10 (Berkeley: University of California Press, 1970), I.i.116–20.
68 William Congreve, *Love for Love* (London, 1695), II.ii.35–6.
69 Ben Johnson, 'Hymn to Diana', lines 1–7, Arthur Quiller-Couch (ed.); 1919; *The Oxford Book of English Verse: 1250–1900*; http://www.bartleby.com/101/184.html (accessed 23 July 2008).
70 Francis Rabelais, *Pantagruel's Prognostication*, reprinted from the translation of c.1660; Luttrell Reprints, no. 3 (Oxford: Basil Blackwell, 1947).
71 Jonathan Swift, 'The Bickerstaff Papers' in *A Tale of a Tub, The Battle of the Books and Other Satires* (London: Dent, 1970), p. 196.
72 *Ibid.*, p. 198.
73 *Ibid.*, p. 201.
74 *Ibid.*, p. 202.
75 *Ibid.*, p. 200. See also the discussion in Patrick Curry, *Prophecy and Power: Astrology in Early Modern England* (Oxford: Polity Press, 1989), pp. 89–91.
76 Benjamin Franklin, *Poor Richard's Almanack, Selections . . . With a facsimile in reduction of the Almanack for 1733*, ed. Benjamin E. Smith (New York: Century Co., 1898), pp. 216–17. See also the discussion in H.W. Brands, *The First American: The Life and Times of Benjamin Franklin* (New York: Anchor Books, 2002), pp. 124–31. For Richard Saunders, see Thomas, *Religion and the Decline of Magic*, and Curry *Prophecy and Power*.
77 Franklin, *Poor Richard's Almanack*, pp. 216–17.
78 Jacques Casanova, *Memoires*, Romance Books, Vol. 4 p. 12; http://romance-books.classic-literature.co.uk/memoirs-of-jacques-casanova/volume-4a-depart-switzerland/ebook-page-12.asp.
79 Jon Butler, 'Magic, Astrology and the Early American Heritage 1600–1760', *American Historical Review* 84 (1979): 340.

Notes to Chapter 12: The Eighteenth Century: Newton's Children

1 Isaac Newton, *The Principia* (Amherst, NY: Prometheus Books, 1995), General Scholium, Book II, p. 439.
2 T.G. Cowling, *Isaac Newton and Astrology*, Eighteenth Selig Brodetsky Memorial Lecture (Leeds: Leeds University Press, 1977), p. 2; Richard S. Westfall, *Never at Rest: A Biography of Isaac Newton* (Cambridge: Cambridge University Press, 1983), p. 88.
3 The authoritative modern biography of Newton is Richard S. Westfall, *Never at Rest: A Biography of Isaac Newton* (Cambridge: Cambridge University Press, 1983). For a more concise version, see Westfall, *The Life of Isaac Newton* (Cambridge: Cambridge University Press, 1993). For a popular and slightly sensational treatment, see Michael White, *Isaac Newton: the Last Sorcerer* (London: Fourth Estate, 1997). See also Penelope Gouk, *Music, Science and Natural Magic in Seventeenth-Century England* (New Haven: Yale Univerity Press, 1999), pp. 224–57.
4 Alexander Pope, 'Epitaph Intended for Sir Isaac Newton, in Westminster-Abbey', 1730, in *The Complete Poetical Works of Alexander Pope* (Boston and New York: Houghton, Mifflin and Company, 1902).
5 See John North, *The Fontana History of Astronomy and Cosmology* (London: Fontana, 1994), chs 12 and 13.
6 Newton, *The Principia*, Book II, p. 439.

7   See the discussion in G.J. Gibbons, *Spirituality and the Occult from the Renaissance to the Modern Age* (London: Routledge, 2001), pp. 48–9.

8   James Thomson, 'Summer', II.1545–8, cited in Roy Porter, *Enlightenment: Britain and the Creation of the Modern World* (London: Penguin, 2000), p. 135.

9   It was Hawkes who said of Stonehenge, 'Every age has the Stonehenge it deserves – or desires': Jacquetta Hawkes, 'God in the Machine', *Antiquity* 41 (1967): 174.

10 Simon Schaffer, 'Newtonianism' in R.C. Olby, G.N. Cantor, J.R.R. Christie and M.J.S Hodge, *Companion to the History of Modern Science* (London and New York: Routledge, 1996), pp. 610–26. See also Larry Stewart, *The Rise of Public Science: Rhetoric, Technology, and Natural Philosophy in Newtonian Britain, 1660–1750* (Cambridge: Cambridge University Press, 1992); and the discussion in Michael Hoskin, *The Cambridge Concise History of Astronomy* (Cambridge: Cambridge University Press, 1999), ch. 6.

11 T.G. Cowling, *Isaac Newton and Astrology*, Eighteenth Selig Brodetsky Memorial Lecture (Leeds: Leeds University Press, 1977); Betty Jo Teeter Dobbs, *The Foundations of Newton's Alchemy, or the Hunting of the Greene Lyon* (Cambridge: Cambridge University Press, 1975), and *The Janus Faces of Genius: The role of alchemy in Newton's thought* (Cambridge: Cambridge University Press, 1991); Sara Schechner Genuth, 'Comets, Teleology, and the Relationship of Chemistry to Cosmology in Newton's Thought', *Annali dell'Istituto e Museo di Storia della Scienza di Firenze*, 10 (part 2) (1985): 31–65; John Maynard Keynes, 'Newton the Man' in Royal Society, *Newton Tercentenary Celebrations* (Cambridge: Cambridge University Press, 1947), pp. 27–41. Online at http://www-history.mcs.st-andrews.ac.uk/Extras/Keynes_Newton.html; David H. Kubrin, 'Newton and the Cyclical Cosmos: Providence and the Mechanical Philosophy', *Journal of the History of Ideas* 28(3) (1967): 325–46; Newton, *The Chronology of Ancient Kingdoms Amended*, (London, 1728; facsimile edition, London, 1988); Simon Schaffer, 'Newton's Comets and the Transformation of Astrology' in Patrick Curry (ed.), *Astrology, Science and Society* (Woodbridge, Suffolk: Boydell Press, 1987), pp. 219–43.

12 See the brief discussion in Keith Thomas, *Religion and the Decline of Magic* (Harmondsworth, Middlesex: Peregrine Books, 1971).

13 Jim Tester, *A History of Western Astrology* (Woodbridge, Suffolk: Boydell Press, 1987) p. 243.

14 Michael Hunter, *Science and Society in Restoration England* (Aldershot: Gregg Revivals, 1992), p. 19. See also Hunter, 'Science and Astrology in Seventeenth Century England' in Patrick Curry (ed.), *Astrology, Science and Society* (Woodbridge, Suffolk: Boydell Press, 1987), pp. 260–300.

15 Patrick Curry, *Prophecy and Power: Astrology in Early Modern England* (Oxford: Polity Press, 1989).

16 Nicholas Campion, 'Prophecy, Cosmology and the New Age Movement: The Extent and Nature of Contemporary Belief in Astrology', PhD thesis, University of the West of England, 2004, p. 241.

17 Some modern scientists appear to credit Newton with responsibility for modern materialistic, consumerist culture. See, for example, Paul Davies and John Gribbin, *The Matter Myth: Beyond Chaos and Complexity* (London: Viking, 1992), esp. ch 1.

18 G.W.F. Hegel, *Hegel's Philosophy of Mind* (trans. William Wallace; Oxord: Oxford University Press, 1971), p. 38.

19 Cited in Curry, *Prophecy and Power*, p. 124.

20 For Newton's rejection of archetypes, or 'substantial forms', as he called them, see Newton, *The Principia*, 1995, p. 3. For Newton and More, see Rupert A. Hall, *Henry More: Magic, Religion and Experiment* (Oxford: Basil Blackwell, 1990).

21 For Berkeley, see Jonathan Dancy, *Berkeley: An Introduction* (Oxford: Basil Blackwell, 1987) and Anthony C. Grayling, *Berkeley: Central Arguments* (London: Duckworth, 1986).

22 Immanuel Kant, *Universal Natural History and Theory of the Heavens* (Ann Arbor: University of Michigan Press, 1969), p. 145.

23 Curry, *Prophecy and Power*.

24 David Hume, *An Inquiry Concerning Human Understanding* (London: Penguin, 1969); see I.xiv (p. 209) for the rejection of divinity.

25 See Marilyn McCord Adams, *William Ockham* (Notre Dame: University of Notre Dame Press, 1987).

26 Hume, *Human Understanding* p. 176.
27 Bernard Capp, *Astrology and the Popular Press: English Almanacs 1500–1800* (London and Boston: Faber and Faber, 1979), p. 259.
28 Laurence Sterne, *Tristram Shandy* (Ware: Wordsworth Editions, 1996), p. 141.
29 Curry, *Prophecy and Power*, pp. 129, 154.
30 Jon Butler, 'Magic, Astrology and the Early American Heritage 1600–1760', *American Historical Review* 84 (1979): 317–46.
31 Michael P. Winship, 'Cotton Mather, Astrologer' in *The New England Quarterly* 63(2) (June 1990): 310.
32 Michael Quinn, *Early Mormonism and the Magic World View* (Salt Lake City: Signature Books, 1998), pp. 88–92. See also John L. Brooke, *The Refiner's Tale: The Making of Mormon Cosmology, 1644–1844* (Cambridge: Cambridge University Press, 1996).
33 Capp, *Astrology and the Popular Press*, p. 252.
34 *Ibid.*, p. 255.
35 *Ibid.*, p. 261.
36 *Ibid.*, p. 263.
37 See the discussion in Owen Davies, *Witchcraft, Magic and Culture 1736–1951* (Manchester: Manchester University Press, 1999); and Butler, 'Magic, Astrology and the Early American Heritage 1600–1760', *American Historical Review* 84 (1979): 317–46.
38 E.P. Thompson, 'Eighteenth Century English Society: Class Struggle without Class?', *Social History* 3 (1978), esp. p. 156.
39 Curry, *Prophecy and Power*, p. 120.
40 Keith Thomas, *Religion and the Decline of Magic* (Harmondsworth, Middlesex: Peregrine Books, 1971), p. 367.
41 Capp, *Astrology and the Popular Press*, p. 277.
42 Butler, 'Magic, Astrology and the Early American Heritage 1600–1760', *American Historical Review* 84: 340.
43 Curry, *Prophecy and Power*, pp. 122–3.
44 William Stukeley, *Stonehenge: A Temple Restor'd to the British Druids* (London, 1740).
45 William Whiston, *A New Theory of the Earth from its Original to the Consummation of All Things* (London, 1696). For context on Whiston's thought, see Larry Stewart, *The Rise of Public Science: Rhetoric, Technology, and Natural Philosophy in Newtonian Britain, 1660–1750* (Cambridge: Cambridge University Press, 1992), ch. 3.
46 Curry, *Prophecy and Power*, p. 146. For an extended discussion, see also Maureen Farrell, *William Whiston* (New York: Arno Press, 1981), and James E. Force, *William Whiston: Honest Newtonian* (Cambridge: Cambridge University Press, 2002).
47 Comte Henri de Boulainviller, *Histoire du mouvement de l'apogee du Soleil. Ou Pratique des Regles d'astrologie Pour juger des Evenements generaux*, 1711, facsimile edition published by Editions du Nouvel Humanisme, Boulogne-sur-Seine & Garches, 1949.
48 Curry, *Prophecy and Power*, pp. 151–2.
49 G.W.F. Hegel, *Hegel's Philosophy of Mind* (trans. William Wallace; Oxord: Oxford University Press, 1971), p. 39.
50 Franz Mesmer, 'Physical-Medical Treatise on the Influence of the Planets' in George Bloch, *Mesmerism: A Translation of the Scientific and Medical Writings of Franz Anton Mesmer* (Los Altos, CA: William Kauffman, 1980), pp. 1–22.
51 Franz Mesmer, *Mesmerism: Being the Translation of Mesmer's historic* Mémoire sur la découverte du Magnétisme Animal *to appear in English* (London: Macdonald, 1947 [1779]).
52 *Ibid.*, p. 30.
53 Mesmer, 'Physical-Medical Treatise on the Influence of the Planets', p. 7.
54 Maria Tatar, *Spellbound: Studies on Mesmerism and Literature* (Princeton, NJ: Princeton University Press, 1978). p. 7.
55 Gilbert Frankau, 'Introductory Monograph' in Mesmer, *Mesmerism: Being the Translation*, p. 18.

56   *Ibid.*, p. 9.
57   Tatar, *Spellbound*, p. 3.
58   Alphonse Esquiros, *Chants d'un prisonnier*, cited in Christopher McIntosh, *Eliphas Lévi and the French Occult Revival* (New York: Samuel Weiser, 1972) p. 197.
59   Humphry Davy, 'An Essay on Heat, Light, and the Combination of Light', in Thomas Beddoes (ed.), *Contributions to Physical and Medical Knowledge principally from the West of England* (Bristol, 1799), pp. 5–205, cited in Curry, *Prophecy and Power*, p. 152.
60   William Herschel, 1801, in *Philosophical Transactions of the Royal Society*, London, 265; see also 354.
61   Stuart Clark, *The Sun Kings: The Unexpected Tragedy of Richard Carrington and the Tale of How Modern Astronomy Began* (Princeton and Oxford: Princeton University Press, 2007), p. 37.
62   Curry, *Prophecy and Power*, p. 148.

Notes to Chapter 13: The Eighteenth Century: Magicians and Poets

1   John Gage, 'J.M.W. Turner and Solar Myth' in J.B. Bullen (ed.), *The Sun is God: Painting, Literature and Mythology in the Nineetenth Century* (Oxford: Oxford University Press, 1989) p. 39.
2   Jean-Mariem Lhôte. *Court de Gébelin: Le Tarot présenté et commenté par Jean-Marie Lhôte* (Paris: Berg International, 1983).
3   See Margaret C. Jacob, *Living the Enlightenment: Freemasonry and Politics in Eighteenth-Century Europe* (Oxford: Oxford University Press, 1991), esp. pp. 144–51.
4   See Antoine Faivre, *Access to Western Esotericism* (Albany: State University of New York Press, 1994), esp. ch. 3. See also the discussion in Arthur Versluis, *Wisdom's Children: A Christian Esoteric Tradition* (New York: State University of New York Press, 1999).
5   Christopher McIntosh, *Eliphas Lévi and the French Occult Revival* (New York: Samuel Weiser, 1972), p. 41.
6   Joscelyn Godwin, *The Theosophical Enlightenment* (New York: State University of New York Press, 1994).
7   See the discussion on the counter-Enlightenment in Isaiah Berlin, *Against the Current: Essays in the History of Ideas* (London: Pimlico, 1979), pp. 1–24. Berlin takes a generally 'pro-Enlightenment position'.
8   See Thompson's argument in *Witness Against the Beast: William Blake and the Moral Law* (Cambridge: Cambridge University Press, 1993), p. 39.
9   Roy Porter, *Enlightenment: Britain and the Creation of the Modern World* (London: Penguin, 2000), p. 3.
10   See the discussion in Dorinda Outram, *The Enlightenment* (Cambridge: Cambridge University Press, 1995), esp. p. 34.
11   Christopher McIntosh, *Eliphas Levi and the French Occult Revival* (New York: Samuel Weiser, 1972), pp. 22–5.
12   *Ibid.*, p. 26.
13   *Ibid.*, pp. 22–5.
14   See the discussion in Porter, *Enlightenment*, pp. 408–10.
15   See the discussion in G.J. Gibbons, *Spirituality and the Occult from the Renaissance to the Modern Age* (London: Routledge, 2001), ch. 6.
16   Jacob, *Living the Enlightenment*, esp. p. 145.
17   Carl Becker, *The Heavenly City of the Enlightenment Philosophers* (Storrs Lectures), (New Haven, CT and London: Yale University Press, 1932).
18   For Swedenborg as an Enlightenment thinker, see the argument in Wouter J. Hanegraaff, *New Age Religion and Western Culture: Esotericism in the Mirror of Secular Thought* (Leiden and New York: E.J. Brill, 1996). Swedenborg's own writings are extensive, but see, as an example, *The New Jerusalem* (trans. John Chadwick, London: The Swedenborg Society, 1990). For commentaries on Swedenborg, see Michael Stanley (ed.), *Emmanuel Swedenborg* (Berkeley: North Atlantic Books, 2003); Clarke Garrett, 'Swedenborg and the Mystical Enlightenment in Late Eighteenth

Century England', *Journal of the History of Ideas* 45 (1984): 67–81; Colleen McDannell and Bernhard Lang, *Heaven: A History* (New Haven, CT: Yale University Press, 1988).

19 Michael Stanley, 'The Relevance of Emanuel Swedenborg's Theological Concepts for the New Age as it is Envisioned Today' in *Emanuel Swedenborg: A Continuing Vision*, ed. Robert Larson (New York: Swedenborg Foundation, 1988), pp. 354–60.

20 Immanuel Kant, *Dreams of a Spirit Seer* (trans. Emanuel F. Goerwitz; Bristol: Thoemmes Press, 1992), pp. 109–10.

21 Immanuel Kant, *Critique of Practical Reason, Great Books of the Western World 42*, (London: Encyclopaedia Britannica, 1952), p. 360; 'Zei Dinge erfüllen das Gemüt mit immer neuer und zunehmender Bewundering und Ehrfurcht, je oefter und anhaltender sich das Nachdenken damit beschaeftigt: der besternte Himmel über mir und das moralische Gestez in mir'.

22 Kant, *Dreams of a Spirit Seer*, p. 121.

23 Jean-Jacques Rousseau, *The Social Contract* (trans. Maurice Cranston; Harmondsworth, Middlesex: Penguin, 1958), IV.7, p. 181.

24 Isaiah Berlin, *Against the Current: Essays in the History of Ideas* (London: Pimlico, 1979), p. 19.

25 See Alex Owen, *The Place of Enchantment: British Occultism and the Culture of the Modern* (Chicago: University of Chicago Press, 2004), esp. ch. 4. For further background, see also Joshua Gunn, *Modern Occult Rhetoric* (Tuscaloosa, AL: University of Alabama Press, 2003).

26 Anita Brookner, *Romanticism and its Discontents* (London: Viking, 2000), p. 3.

27 Quoted in Ian Wylie, *Young Coleridge and the Philosophers of Nature* (Oxford: Clarendon Press, 1989).

28 William Wordsworth, *The Prelude, Or, Growth of a Poet's Mind (Text of 1805)*, Ernest de Selincourt and Stephen Gill (eds) (Oxford: Oxford University Press, 1989), cited in Roy Porter, *Enlightenment: Britain and the Creation of the Modern World* (London: Penguin, 2000), p. 135. See also lines 401–6: 'Wisdom and Spirit of the universe!/ The Soul that art the eternity of thought,/ That givest to forms and images a breath/ And everlasting motion, not in vain/ By day or star-light thus from my first dawn? Of childhood didst thou intertwine for me/ The passions that build up our human soul.

29 Alan Bewell, *Wordsworth and the Enlightenment: Nature, Man and Society in the Experimental Poetry* (New Haven and London: Yale University Press, 1989). See also L.K. Thomas and Warren U. Ober, *A Mind for Free Voyaging: William Wordsworth at Work Portraying Newton and Science* (Edmonton: University of Alberta Press, 1989).

30 William Wordsworth, 'Evening Voluntaries, XI' in Aubrey de Selincourt (ed.), *The Poetical Works of William Wordsworth* (Oxford: Clarendon Press, 1952–9), Vol. 4, p. 14. See also the discussion in Stephen McCluskey, 'Wordsworth's "Rydal Chapel" and the Orientation of Churches' in Nicholas Campion (ed.), *The Inspiration of Astronomical Phenomena*, Proceedings of the Fourth Conference on the Inspiration of Astronomical Phenomena, sponsored by the Vatican Observatory and the Steward Observatory, Arizona, Magdalen College, Oxford, 3–9 August 2003 (Bristol: Cinnabar Books, 2005), pp. 208–24.

31 See the discussion in Antoine Faivre, *Access to Western Esotericism* (Albany, NY: State University of New York Press, 1994), ch. 4.

32 G.W.F. Hegel, *The Philosophy of Right* (trans. T.M. Knox; London and Oxford: Clarendon Press, 1952), esp. pp. 220–3; and Hegel, *The Philosophy of History* (trans. J. Sibree; New York: Dover Publications, 1956), esp. pp. 79–81, 103–4, 412. See also the discussion in Nicholas Campion, *The Great Year* (London: Penguin, 1994), pp. 360–1, 362–3, 438–40.

33 Johann Wolfgang von Goethe, *Autobiography* (trans. John Oxenford; The Project Gutenberg EBook of Autobiography, by Johann Wolfgang von Goethe, Part the first, First book); http://www.gutenberg.net/dirs/etext04/8tbgt10.txt.

34 Goethe, letter to Schiller, 8 December 1798, cited in Moriz Sondheim, 'Shakespeare and the Astrology of his Time', *Journal of the Warburg Institute* 2(3) (January 1939): 243–4.

35 For this and the following discussion, see Gage, 'J.M.W. Turner and Solar Myth', pp. 39–48.

36 A.M. Jones (ed.), *The Works of Sir William Jones with the life of the author by Lord Teignmouth*, (London, 1807), Vol. 3, pp. 385–6, cited in Gage, 'Turner', p. 42.

37 See Dinah Birch, '"The Sun is God": Ruskin's Solar Mythology' in J.B. Bullen (ed.), *The Sun is*

God: Painting, Literature and Mythology in the Nineteenth Century (Oxford: Oxford University Press, 1989), p. 111.

38   Birch, *Ruskin*, p. 112.
39   Gage, 'Turner', p. 39.

Notes to Chapter 14: The Nineteenth Century: Enlightenment Entrepreneurs

1   William Blake, 'The Marriage of Heaven and Hell', 1793. *Complete Writings*, ed. Geoffrey Keynes (Oxford: Oxford University Press, 1971), p. 154.
2   See Prys Morgan, *Iolo Morganwg* (Cardiff: University of Wales Press, 1975); and G.J. Williams, *Iolo Morganwg. Y Gyfrol Gyntaf* (Cardiff: University of Wales Press, 1956).
3   Bernard Capp, *Astrology and the Popular Press: English Almanacs 1500–1800* (London and Boston: Faber and Faber, 1979), p. 270.
4   Cited in Patrick Curry, 'Ebenezer Sibly', *Dictionary of National Biography*, online edition, (Oxford: Oxford University Press, 2004).
5   Theodor Adorno, *The Stars Down to Earth* (London: Routledge, 1994), p. 119.
6   Owen Chadwick, *The Secularization of the European Mind in the Nineteenth Century* (Cambridge: Cambridge University Press, 1975), p. 88.
7   Ebenezer Sibly, *A Key to Physic and the Occult Sciences* (London, 1794), pp. 1, 130.
8   *Ibid.*, title page.
9   See Roy Porter, *Medicine: A History of Healing: Ancient Traditions to Modern Practices* (London: Marlowe and Co, 1997), and *Disease, Medicine and Society in England, 1550–1860* (Cambridge: Cambridge University Press, 1995).
10   See the discussion in Owen Davies, *Witchcraft, Magic and Culture 1736–1951* (Manchester: Manchester University Press, 1999). See also Ronald Hutton, *The Triumph of the Moon: A History of Modern Pagan Witchcraft* (Oxford: Oxford University Press, 1999), esp. ch. 6.
11   See Wouter J. Hanegraaff, *New Age Religion and Western Culture: Esotericism in the Mirror of Secular Thought* (Leiden and New York: E.J. Brill, 1996).
12   Joscelyn Godwin, *The Theosophical Enlightenment* (New York: State University of New York Press, 1994), p. 116.
13   William Blake, *Complete Writings* (Oxford: Oxford University Press, 1971), p. 865.
14   For Palmer's images of the moon, see Paul Murdin, 'Representing the Moon', *The Inspiration of Astronomical Phenomena: Proceedings of the fourth conference on the Inspiration of Astronomical Phenomena, Magdalen College, Oxford, England*, 3–9 August 2003, special issue of *Culture and Cosmos* 8(1 and 2) (Spring/Summer–Autumn/Winter 2004): 247–70; www.CultureAndCosmos. com.
15   Godwin, *Theosophical* Enlightenment, p. 135.
16   See Patrick Curry, 'John Worsdale', *Dictionary of National Biography*, online edition (Oxford: Oxford University Press, 2004); and Ellic Howe, *Urania's Children: The Strange World of the Astrologers* (London: William Kimber, 1967), pp. 26–8.
17   John Worsdale, *Astronomy and Elementary Philosophy* (London, 1819), p. 47.
18   *Ibid.*, pp. 39, 50, 53.
19   John Worsdale, *Genethliacal Astrology* (London, 1798), p. vii.
20   *Ibid.*, *Celestial Philosophy or Genethliacal Astronomy* (London, 1828) p. 52.
21   *Ibid.*, p. 51.
22   *Ibid.*, p. 53.
23   *Ibid.*, pp. 56–7.
24   See Patrick Curry, *A Confusion of Prophets: Victorian and Edwardian Astrology* (London: Collins and Brown, 1992), pp. 18–19.
25   Anon, 'The Varley Manuscripts', *Modern Astrology*, New Series 19 (1921): 483–7.
26   See Curry, *A Confusion of Prophets*, pp. 46–108; and Ellic Howe, *Urania's Children: The Strange World of the Astrologers* (London: William Kimber, 1967), ch. 3.

27 *Ibid.*, pp. 52–3.
28 Cited in Curry, *A Confusion of Prophets*, p. 76.
29 *Ibid.*, p. 77.
30 Capp, *Astrology and the Popular Press*, pp. 268–9; Maureen Perkins, *Visions of the Future: Almanacs, Time, and Cultural Change* (Oxford: Clarendon Press, 1996), Appendix 1.
31 Davies, *Witchcraft, Magic and Culture*, pp. 231–2.
32 *The Spectator*, 17 February 1894, cited in Davies, *Witchcraft, Magic and Culture*, p. 231.
33 For identification of the first three, see Godwin, *The Theosophical Enlightenment*, p. 142.

Notes to Chapter 15: The Nineteenth Century: Magicians and Sociologists

1 Eliphas Lévi, *Transcendental Magic, its Doctrine and Ritual by Eliphas Lévi*, (Alphonse Louis Constant). *A complete translation of 'Dogme et rituel de la haute magie,'* with a biographical preface, by Arthur Edward Waite (London: George Redway, 1896), p. 1.
2 See the discussion in G.J. Gibbons, *Spirituality and the Occult from the Renaissance to the Modern Age* (London: Routledge, 2001), pp. 129–31.
3 See Arthur John Booth, *Saint–Simon and Saint-Simonism: a chapter in the history of Socialism in France* (Amsterdam: Liberac, 1970 [1871]).
4 Keith Thomas, *Religion and the Decline of Magic* (London: Weidenfeld and Nicolson, 1971), p. 387.
5 Auguste Comte, *System of Positive Polity: or, Treatise on sociology, instituting the religion of humanity* (4 Vols; trans. John Henry Bridges; London: Longmans, 1875), Vol. I, p. 47.
6 Isaac Newton, *The Principia* (Amherst, NY: Prometheus Books, 1995), p. 5.
7 J.T. Merz, *A History of European Thought in the Nineteenth Century* (London: William Blackwood and Sons, 1896), Vol. 1, pp. 341–8.
8 Comte, *System of Positive Polity*, Vol. I, p. 21.
9 *Ibid.*, pp. 23–4.
10 *Ibid.*, pp. 22–4, 28.
11 Max Weber, *Economy and Society: An Outline of Interpretative Sociology* (New York: Columbia University Press, 1968), p. 7.
12 Herbert Spencer, *Social Statistics: or The Conditions Essential to Human Happiness Specified, and the First of them Developed* (London, 1851); see also Theodore M. Porter, *The Rise of Statistical Thinking, 1820–1900* (Princeton: Princeton University Press, 1988).
13 Emile Durkheim, 'Sociologie et sciences sociales' in *Selected Writings*, ed. Anthony Giddens (Cambridge: Cambridge University Press, 1972), p. 54.
14 Max Weber, *The Theory of Social and Economic Organisation* (trans. A.M. Henderson and Talcott Parsons; Oxford: Oxford University Press, 1947), p. 88.
15 Peter J. Bowler, *The Invention of Progress, The Victorians and the Past* (Oxford: Basil Blackwell, 1989), p. 37.
16 Wilbert E. Moore, 'Introduction' in Charles P. Loomis and Iona K. Loomis, *Modern Social Theories* (New York: Van Norstrand Reinhold, 1961), pp. xxii–xxiii. See also the discussion in Ernest Wallwork, *Durkheim, Morality and Milieu* (Cambridge, MA: Harvard University Press, 1972), p. 21.
17 Weber, *Economy and Society*, p. 6.
18 M.A. Quetelet, *A Treatise on Man and the Development of His faculties* (Paris, 1835), trans. R. Knox, Edinburgh, 1842.
19 Alan Leo, *The Complete Dictionary of Astrology*, ed. Vivian Robson (Rochester, VT: Destiny Books, 1983 [c.1900]), p. 8.
20 Christopher McIntosh, *Eliphas Lévi and the French Occult Revival* (New York: Samuel Weiser, 1972), pp. 73–153. See also Jean Pierrot, *The Decadent Imagination 1880–1900*, (trans. Derek Coltman; Chicago: Chicago University Press, 1981), esp. pp. 96–118.
21 Lévi, *Transcendental Magic*, p. 1.

22   Gerard de Nerval, 'Delfica', cited in Christopher McIntosh, *Eliphas Lévi and the French Occult Revival* (New York: Samuel Weiser, 1972), p. 204.
23   Cited in McIntosh, *Eliphas Lévi*, p. 67.
24   *Ibid.*, pp. 128, 167.
25   Honoré de Balzac, *Séraphita* (Dodo Press, 2006), p. 80.
26   McIntosh, *Eliphas Levi*, pp. 197–200.
27   *Ibid.*, p. 202.
28   Arthur Rimbaud, *Complete Works, Selected Letters* (trans. Wallace Fowlie; Chicago: University of Chicago Press, 1966), p. 307.
29   Michael York, *Historical Dictionary of New Age Movements* (Lanham, MD: Scarecrow, 2003), p. 25.
30   McIntosh, *Eliphas Lévi*, p. 205.
31   Archibald Henry Sayce, 'The Astronomy and Astrology of the Babylonians', *Transactions of the Society of Biblical Archaeology* 3(part 1) (1874). See also Noel Swerdow (ed.), *Ancient Astronomy and Celestial Divination* (Cambridge, MA and London: MIT, 1999), pp. 2–6.
32   J.K. Huysmans, *Against Nature* (trans. Robert Baldrick; Harmondsowrth, Middlesex: Penguin, 1959 [1884]), pp. 63–7; Oscar Wilde, *Salomé* (London: The Folio Society, 1957), p. 51. For Huysmans, see McIntosh, *Eliphas Lévi*, pp. 177–95.
33   Wendy Buonaventura, *I Put a Spell on You: Dancing Women from Salome to Madonna* (London: Saqi Books, 2003), p. 33. See also Buonaventura, *Serpent of the Nile: Women and Dance in the Arab World* (London: Saqi Books, 1989), pp. 138–43.
34   Mary K. Greer, *Women of the Golden Dawn: Rebels and Priestesses* (Rochester, VT: Park Street Press, 1995).
35   Max Müller, 'Solar Myths', *The Nineteenth Century* (December 1885): 900–22.
36   McIntosh, *Eliphas Lévi*, p. 165.
37   Isa. 39.1.

Notes to Chapter 16: The Nineteenth Century: The Theosophical Enlightenment

1   H.P. Blavatsky, *Isis Unveiled* (Pasadena: Theosophical University Press, 1976[1877]), Vol. I, pp. 302.
2   For an uncritical biography of Blavatsky, see Sylvia Cranston, *The Extraordinary Life and Influence of Helena Blavatsky* (New York: Jeremy Tarcher/Putnam, 1993). For criticism, see Peter Washington, *Madame Blavatsky's Baboon: A History of the Mystics, Mediums and Misfits Who Brought Spiritualism to America* (New York: Shocken Books, 1993). For important philosophical context, see James Webb, *The Occult Underground* (La Salle, IL: Open Court, 1988). For a summary of the society's history, see Kevin Tingay, 'Madame Blavatsky's Children: Theosophy and Its Heirs' in Marion Bowman and Steven Sutcliffe, *Beyond New Age: Exploring Alternative Spirituality* (Edinburgh: Edinburgh University Press, 2000), pp. 37–50. For a view of theosophy in its wider esoteric context, see Webb, *The Occult Underground*.
3   Joscelyn Godwin, *The Theosophical Enlightenment* (New York: State University of New York Press, 1994).
4   Blavatsky, *Isis Unveiled*, Vol. II, p. 99.
5   Henry Olcott, 'Inaugural Address of the President-Founder of the Theosophical Society', delivered at Mott Memorial Hall in the City of New York, at the first regular meeting of the society, 17 November 1875, Adyar Pamphlets No. 50, Theosophical Society of America, 1975; http://www.theosophical.org/resources/library/olcott-centenary/Ts?Pamphlets?Inaugural-Address.htm (accessed 14 July 2008).
6   Alex Owen, *The Darkened Roon: Women, Power and Spiritualism in Late Victorian England* (Chicago: University of Chicago Press, 1989), p. 240.
7   Margaret C. Jacob, *Living the Enlightenment: Freemasonry and Politics in Eighteenth-Century Europe* (Oxford: Oxford University Press, 1991).

8   For Sepharial, see Kim Farnell, *The Astral Tramp: A Biography of Sepharial* (London: Ascella Publications, 1998).
9   Blavatsky, *Isis Unveiled*, Vol. I, p. 259; Plato, *Timaeus*, 40 C-D.
10 The details are set out in Blavatsky, *Isis Unveiled*.
11 Nicholas Campion, 'Prophecy, Cosmology and the New Age Movement: The Extent and Nature of Contemporary Belief in Astrology', PhD thesis, University of the West of England, 2004, ch. 3.
12 Blavatsky, *The Secret Doctrine*, Theosophical University Press Online Edition http://www. theosociety.org/pasadena/sd/sd1-3-16.htm, p. 634.
13 Campion, 'Prophecy, Cosmology and the New Age Movement', p. 242.
14 Patrick Curry, *A Confusion of Prophets: Victorian and Edwardian Astrology* (London: Collins and Brown, 1992); Ellic Howe, *Urania's Children: The Strange World of the Astrologers* (London: William Kimber, 1967), esp. pp. 57–64; Bessie Leo (ed.), *The Life and Work of Alan Leo* (London: Modern Astrology, 1919).
15 Alan Leo, *Esoteric Astrology: A Study in Human Nature* (London: Modern Astrology, 1913), p. vii.
16 Alan Leo, *The Art of Synthesis* (London: Modern Astrology, 1936) [1st edn. *How to Judge a Nativity*, pt. 2, 1904], p. 2.
17 Alan Leo, 'The Age of Aquarius', *Modern Astrology* 8(7) (July 1911), New Series: 272.
18 Leo, *Esoteric Astrology*, p. v.
19 Blavatsky, *Isis Unveiled*, Vol. I, pp. 302; see also 502 and *The Secret Doctrine*, Vol. I, p. 100.
20 Leo, *The Art of Synthesis*, pp. 30–1.
21 Claudius Ptolemy, *Tetrabiblos* (trans. F.E. Robbins; Cambridge, MA and London: Harvard University Press, 1940), I.11–16.
22 William Lilly, *Christian Astrology* (London, 1647, facsimile edition; London: Regulus Publishing, 1985), p. 93.
23 *Ibid.*
24 Zadkiel, *The Grammar of Astrology* (London, 1849), p. 359.
25 Alan Leo, *How to Judge a Nativity* (London: Modern Astrology, 1922 [1903]), p. 17.
26 Philip Hoare, *England's Lost Eden: Adventures in a Victorian Utopia* (London: HarperCollins, 2005).
27 Bram Dijkstra, *Idols of Perversity: Fantasies of Feminine Evil in Fin-de-Siecle Culture* (Oxford: Oxford University Press, 1986), p. 236.
28 *Ibid.*
29 Jules Lermina, *La Science occulte* (Paris: Ernest Kolb, 1890), p. 3, cited in Jean Pierrot, *The Decadent Imagination 1880–1900* (trans. Derek Coltman; Chicago: Chicago University Press, 1981), p. 105.
30 Edward Lucie-Smith, *Symbolist Art* (London: Thames and Hudson, 1972).
31 See Jean Pierrot, *The Decadent Imagination 1880–1900* (trans. Derek Coltman; Chicago: Chicago University Press, 1981), esp. pp. 105–18.
32 Papus, *Astrology for Initiates: Astrological Secrets of the Western Mystery Tradition* (trans. J. Lee Lehman; York Beach, ME: Samuel Weiser, 1996), pp. 34–5.
33 *Ibid.*, pp. 37–8.
34 See the discussion in Joscelyn Godwin, *The Theosophical Enlightenment* (New York: State University of New York Press, 1994), esp. chs 15–17.
35 Ellic Howe, *The Magicians of the Golden Dawn: A Documentary History of a Magical Order 1887–1923* (Wellingborough: Aquarian Press, 1985); R.A. Gilbert, *The Golden Dawn, Twilight of the Magicians: The Rise and Fall of a Magical Order* (Wellingborough: Aquarian Press, 1983), and *Revelations of the Golden Dawn: The Rose and Fall of a Magical Order* (London: Quantum, 1997); Mary K. Greer, *Women of the Golden Dawn: Rebels and Priestesses* (Rochester VT: Park Street Press, 1995); Frances King, *Ritual Magic in England: 1877 to the Present Day* (London: New English Library, 1972); Israel Regardie, *What You Should Know About the Golden Dawn* (Phoenix, AZ: New Falcon Publications, 1993); Patrick J. Zalewski, *Secret Inner Teachings of the Golden Dawn*, (Phoenix, AZ: Falcon Press, 1988); Ronald Hutton, *The Triumph of the Moon: A History of Modern Pagan Witchcraft* (Oxford: Oxford University Press, 1999), esp. ch. 5.

36   A.E. Waite, *Compendium of Natal Astrology and Universal Ephemeris* (London: Kegan Paul & Co., 1917). See also R.A. Gilbert (ed.), *Hermetic Papers of A.E. Waite: The Unknown Writings of a Modern Mystic* (Wellingborough: Aquarian Press, 1987).

37   Israel Regardie, *The Original Account of the Teachings, Rites and Ceremonies of the Hermetic Order of the Golden Dawn* (St Paul, MN: Llewellyn, 1989 [1937]), p. 447.

38   Patrick J. Zalewskie, *Secret Inner Teachings of the Golden Dawn* (Phoenix, AZ: Falcon Press, 1988), pp. 123, 125, 127

39   See Ronald Hutton, 'Astral Magic: The Acceptable Face of Paganism' in Nicholas Campion, Patrick Curry and Michael York (eds), *Astrology and the Academy*, papers from the inaugural conference of the Sophia Centre, Bath Spa University College, 13–14 June 2003 (Bristol: Cinnabar Books, 2004), pp. 10–24.

40   For Gardner, see Gerald Gardner, *Witchcraft Today: Secrets of the Witch Cult Revealed* (London: Arrow, 1975). For transmission of ideas from the Golden Dawn to Wicca, see Ronald Hutton, *The Triumph of the Moon: A History of Modern Pagan Witchcraft* (Oxford: Oxford University Press, 1999). And for an example of the 'teen witch' phenomenon, see Silver Ravenwolf, *Teen Witch* (St Paul, MN: Llewellyn, 1998).

41   Wilhelm Worringer, 'From Abstraction and Empathy' in Vassiliki Kolocotroni, Jane Goldman and Olga Taxidou, *Modernism: an Anthology of Sources and Documents* (Edinburgh: Edinburgh University Press, 2004), p. 74.

42   J.R.R. Tolkein, *Tree and Leaf* (London: Unwin, 1964), pp. 15–16.

43   Max Weber, *From Max Weber: Essays in Sociology*, ed. H.H. Garth and C. Mills Wright (London: Kegan Paul, Trench, Trubner & Co., 1947), p. 139. See also the discussion in Patrick Curry and Roy Willis, *Astrology, Science and Culture: Pulling Down the Moon* (Oxford: Berg, 2004); Alex Owen, *The Place of Enchantment: British Occultism and the Culture of the Modern* (Chicago: University of Chicago Press, 2004); and David Katz, *The Occult Tradition from the Renaissance to the Present Day* (London: Jonathan Cape, 2005), pp. 110–36.

44   Roy Porter and Mikuláš Teich, *Fin de siècle and its Legacy* (Cambridge: Cambridge University Press, 1990), pp. 222–3.

Notes to Chapter 17: The Twentieth Century: New Age and Ancient Teachings

1   W.B. Yeats, 'The Return of the Stars', cited in Elizabeth Heine, 'W.B. Yeats: Poet and Astrologer', *Culture and Cosmos* 1(2) (Winter/Autumn 1997): 72.

2   In the theosophical astrology with which Yeats would have been familiar a Mars–Uranus conjunction would have been characterized as 'Extremist, enormous latent energy, capable of remarkable expressions, dangerous possibilities. Self-willed, impulsive, uncontrollable. Egotistical, fanatical'; see Alan Leo, *How to Judge a Nativity* (London: Modern Astrology, 1922 [1903]), p. 30.

3   James Webb, *The Harmonious Circle: The Lives and Work of G.I. Gurdjieff, P.D. Ouspensky, and Their Followers* (Boston: Shambhala Publications, 1980).

4   Sigmund Freud, 'Psychoanalysis and Telepathy', 1921, in James Strachey (trans.), *The Complete Psychological Works of Sigmund Freud*, Vol. XVIII (London: Hogarth, 1955), pp. 177–94.

5   See Rudolf Steiner, *An Autobiography* (New York, Multimedia Publishing, 1977).

6   For a full account, see Elisabeth Vreede, *Anthroposophy and Astrology* (Great Barrington, MA: Anthroposophic Press, 2001).

7   Rudolf Steiner, *World History in the Light of Anthroposophy* (London: Rudolf Steiner Press, 1977 [1950]), *The Spiritual Beings in the Heavenly Bodies and in the Kingdoms of Nature* (Vancouver: Steiner Book Centre, 1981 [1951]), *The Reappearance of Christ in the Etheric* (Spring Valley, NY: Anthroposophic Press, 1983); Joscelyn Godwin, *The Theosophical Enlightenment* (New York: State University of New York Press, 1994), p. 345; Richard Leviton, *The Imagination of Pentecost: Rudolf Steiner and Contemporary Spirituality* (Hudson, NY: Anthroposophic Press, 1994), pp. 47–8.

8   Steiner, *The Reappearance of Christ in the Etheric*, p. 15. See also Plato, *Republic* VIII, 546A-B.

9   Alice A. Bailey, *The Unfinished Autobiography* (London; Lucis Press, 1951); John Sinclair, *The Alice Bailey Inheritance: The Inner Plane Teachings of Alice Ann Bailey (1880–1949) and their legacy* (Wellingborough: Turnstone, 1984).

10 Alice A. Bailey, *Esoteric Astrology* (London: Lucis Press, 1973 [1951]).

11 *Ibid.*, *The Destiny of the Nations* (New York: Lucis Publishing Company, 1949), p. 36.

12 *Ibid.*, p. 47.

13 Cyril Fagan, 'Interpretation of the Zodiac of Constellations', *Spica* 1(1) (October 1951): 24.

14 Michael York, *Historical Dictionary of New Age Movements* (Lanham, MD: Scarecrow, 2003), pp. 25–6.

15 Paul Heelas, *The New Age Movement* (Oxford: Blackwell, 1996), pp. 18, 23.

16 Constance E. Cumbey, *The Hidden Dangers of the Rainbow: The New Age Movement and Our Coming Age of Barbarism* (Shreveport, LA: Huntingdon House, 1983).

17 Nicholas Campion, 'Prophecy, Cosmology and the New Age Movement: The Extent and Nature of Contemporary Belief in Astrology', PhD thesis, University of the West of England, 2004, pp. 83–4.

18 York, *Historical Dictionary of New Age Movements*, p. 25.

19 Cherril Smith, 'Art and Theosophy in a Social Context (1875–1925)', *Culture and Cosmos* 12(1) (Spring/Summer 2008). See also Kathleen Hall, 'Theosophy and the Emergence of Modern Abstract Art', *The Quest* 90(3) (May–June 2002): 84–7, 109. For general discussions, see Nadia Choucha, *Surrealism and the Occult* (Oxford: Mandrake, 1991); Paul Waldo-Schwartz, *Art and the Occult* (London: Mandala, 1977); and Sarane Alexandrian, *Surrrealist Art* (London: Thames and Hudson, 1970).

20 Hajo Düchting, *Wassily Kandinsky* (Cologne: Benedikt Raschen Verlag, 1991), p. 58.

21 Wassily Kandinsky, *Concerning the Spiritual in Art* (trans. M.T.H. Sadler; New York: Dover Publications, 1977), p. 13.

22 Robert Hughes, *The Shock of the New: Art and the Century of Change* (London: Thames and Hudson, 1991), esp. pp. 299, 301, 310.

23 *Ibid.*, esp. pp. 202–3.

24 *Ibid.*, p. 313.

25 Herbert Read (ed.), *Surrealism* (London: Faber and Faber, 1937), p. 22; see also, pp. 28, 66–7, 76–7, 100–1.

26 Nicholas Campion, 'Surrealist Cosmology: André Breton and Astrology', *Culture and Cosmos* 6(2) (Autumn/Winter 2002): 52.

27 Raymond Head, 'Astrology, Modernism and Holst's "The Planets"', *Astrology Quarterly* 65(1) (Winter 1994–5): 40–54.

28 Elizabeth Heine, 'W.B. Yeats: Poet and Astrologer', *Culture and Cosmos* 1(2) (Winter/Autumn 1997): 60–75. See also Richard Ellman, *The Identity of Yeats* (London: Faber and Faber, 1964 [1954]); R.F. Foster, *W.B Yeats: A Life*, Vol. I (Oxford: Oxford University Press, 1997); Norman A. Jeffares, *W.B Yeats: A New Biography* (London: Hutchinson, 1988); M.C. Flannery, *Yeats and Magic: The Earlier Works* (Gerard's Cross: Colin Smythe, 1977).

29 Alan Leo, *How to Judge a Nativity* (London: Modern Astrology, 1922 [1903]), p. 50, 238–9.

30 Anne Olivier Bell (ed.), *The Diary of Virginia Woolf, Volume IV: 1931–1935* (London: The Hogarth Press, 1982), p. 257.

31 W.B. Yeats, *A Vision* (London: MacMillan, 1981 [1937]).

32 See Heine, 'W.B. Yeats: Poet and Astrologer': 65–6.

33 Henry Miller, *The Colossus of Maroussi* (London: Minerva, 1991 [1942]), pp. 104–5.

34 Henry Miller, 'The Astrologer Seen Through the Eyes of a Friend' in Sydney Omarr, *Answer in the Sky . . . almost: Confessions of an Astrologer* (Charlottsville, VA: Hampton Roads Publishing Company, 1995), pp. 20–4. See also Sydney Omarr, *My World of Astrology* (Hollywood, CA: Wilshire Book Company, 1965), pp. 120–4.

35 Omarr, *Answer in the Sky*, p. 120.

36   Dane Rudhyar, *The Planetarisation of Consciousness* (New York: Aurora Press, 1977 [1970]), back cover.

37   Louis MacNeice, *Astrology* (London: Spring Books, 1994), p. 12.

38   Jon Stallworthy, *Louis MacNeice* (London: Faber and Faber 1995), p. 162, see also p. 456, 463, 468–9, 482.

39   See the discussion in Spencer, *True as the Stars Above*, pp. 227–33.

40   Al Alvarez, *Where Did It All Go Right?* (London: Richard Cohen Books, 1999). See also Alvarez, 'How Black Magic killed Sylvia Plath', *The Guardian*, G2, 15 September 1999, p. 4.

41   Alvarez, *Where Did It All Go Right?*, p. 203.

42   Ted Hughes, 'St. Botolph's', *Birthday Letters* (London: Faber and Faber, 1998), pp. 14–15.

43   John Etherington, 'Written in Blood', *Apollon* 2 (1999): 61–5.

44   Hughes, 'Horoscopes', *Birthday Letters*, p. 64.

45   Sylvia Plath, *The Journals of Sylvia Plath 1950–1962* (London: Faber and Faber, 1962), 23 October 1956.

46   Campion, 'Prophecy, Cosmology and the New Age Movement', p. 248.

47   Dane Rudhyar, *The Astrology of Personality* (Garden City, NY: Doubleday, 1970 [1936]).

48   *Ibid.*, *New Mansions for New Men* (New York: Lucis Publishing Company, 1938), p. xiii.

49   Wouter J. Hanegraaff, *New Age Religion and Western Culture: Esotericism in the Mirror of Secular Thought* (Leiden and New York: E.J. Brill, 1996), pp. 96–103.

50   Melanie Reinhart, 'In the Shadows of the Age of Aquarius', *The Astrological Journal* 29(3) (May/June 1987): 108–14.

51   Donna Cunningham, *An Astrological Guide to Self-Awareness* (Reno: CRCS, 1978) p. 9.

Notes to Chapter 18: The Twentieth Century: Psychology and the Popular Press

1   C.G. Jung, 'Richard Wilhelm: In Memoriam' in *The Spirit in Man, Art, And Literature*, Collected Works, Vol. 15 (trans. R.F.C. Hull; London: Routledge and Kegan Paul, 1971), p. 56.

2   According to Charles Carter, President of the Astrological Lodge of the Theosophical Society, writing in 1969, 'Dr Jung's open advocacy of Astrology has probably done much to render the subject respectable to our day.' Carter was not wholehearted in his assessment of Jung's influence on astrology's reputation, though. 'But it has to be acknowledged that a great many psychologists regard Jung himself as being something of what they call a "mystic", using that word in a depreciative sense.' See Charles Carter, 'The Astrological Lodge of the Theosophical Society', *In Search* 2(2) (Spring 1969): 13.

3   C.G. Jung, *Memories, Dreams, Reflections* (London: Fontana, 1967), pp. 160–1.

4   As Aniela Jaffe claimed, 'Only since his death have theologians in increasing numbers begun to say that Jung was indubitably an outstanding figure in the religious history of our century.'; Aniela Jaffe, 'Introduction' in, Jung, *Memories, Dreams, Reflections*, p. 13.

5   C.G. Jung, *The Archetypes and the Collective Unconscious*, Collected Works, Vol. 9.1 (trans. R.F.C. Hull; Princeton, NJ: Princeton University Press, 1959), paras 87–110, 115.

6   C.G. Jung, *Psychology and Alchemy*, Collected Works, Vol. 12 (trans. R.F.C. Hull; Princeton, NJ: Princeton University Press, 1963), p.v.

7   C.G. Jung, 'Wotan' in *Civilisation in Transition*, Collected Works, Vol. 10, para 395.

8   The seminal work on Jungian astrology is Liz Greene, *Relating: An Astrological Guide to Living with others on a Small Planet* (London: Coventure, 1977). Greene's *Saturn: A New Look at an Old Devil* (Wellingborough: Aquarian Press, 1976) was the first full application of Jungian principles to an individual planet. Greene relied heavily on Jung but was also influenced by a wider training in psychology, including Freudian theories.

9   C.G. Jung, 'The Structure of the Psyche', *The Structure and Dynamics of the Psyche*, Collected Works, Vol. 8 (trans. R.F.C. Hull; Princeton, NJ: Princeton University Press, 1960), para. 325. He added 'The starry vault of heaven is in truth the open book of cosmic projection, in which are reflected the mythologems, i.e., the archetypes. In this vision astrology and alchemy, the two classical functionaries of the psychology of the collective unconscious, join hands'; Jung, 'On the

Nature of the Psyche', *The Structure and Dynamics of the Psyche*, Collected Works, Vol. 8 (trans. R.F.C. Hull; Princeton, NJ: Princeton University Press, 1960), para. 392.

10 C.G. Jung, Jung to Freud, 12 June 1911, in *Letters 1906–1950*, ed. Gerhard Adler, et al. (Princeton: Bollingen, 1992).

11 Ean Begg, 'Jung, Astrology and the Millennium', *The Astrological Journal* 41(6) (November/ December 1999): 21.

12 C.G. Jung, 'Richard Wilhelm: In Memoriam' in *The Spirit in Man, Art, And Literature*, Collected Works, Vol. 15 (trans. R.F.C. Hull; London: Routledge and Kegan Paul, 1971), p. 56.

13 C.G. Jung, *Mysterium Coniuntionis*, Collected Works, Vol. 14 (trans. R.F.C. Hull; London: Routledge and Kegan Paul, 1963), paras 790–2.

14 C.G. Jung to B.V. Raman, 6 September 1947, Anon, 'A Meeting with B.V. Raman', http://www.wandahl.com/Pages/Articles/MeetingWithRaman.htm (accessed 24 September 2008).

15 C.G. Jung, *Synchronicity: An Acausal Connecting Principle*, Collected Works, Vol. 8: (trans. R.F.C. Hull; London: Routledge and Kegan Paul, 1963), pp. 417–531.

16 *Ibid.*, pp. 417–531. Jung letter to Carl Seelig dated 23 February 1954 (Letters, Vol. 2, p. 109).

17 Jung, 'Richard Wilhelm: In Memoriam', pp. 53–62. See the frontispiece of Margaret Hone's influential, *The Modern Textbook of Astrology* (London: LN Fowler, 4th edn, reprinted 1973, [1951]) for an example of the use of Jung's phrase.

18 Jung, 'Richard Wilhelm', Collected Works (trans. R.F.C. Hull, London: Routledge and Kegan Paul, 1971), Vol. 15, p. 56. See also Jung, *Synchronicity*, p. 6.

19 Edward de Bono, *The Uses of Lateral Thinking* (London: Penguin, 1971).

20 Alexander Ruperti, *Meaning of Humanistic Astrology* (2002), p. 3, http://www.stand.cz/astrologie/czech/texty/rez-ru-a/rez-ru-a.htm (accessed 25 January 2003). See also Dane Rudhyar, *The Lunation Cycle: A Key to the Understanding of Personality*, (Santa Fe: Aurora Press, 1967), pp. 9, 12, 13.

21 Bryan Wilson, *Religion in Secular Society: A Sociological Comment* (Harmondsworth: Pelican, 1969).

22 Dane Rudhyar, *The Astrology of Personality* (Garden City, NY: Doubleday, 1970 [1936]), pp. ix, 3.

23 Nicholas Campion, 'Surrealist Cosmology: André Breton and Astrology', *Culture and Cosmos* 6(2) (Autumn/Winter 2002): 52.

24 Alexander Ruperti, *Cycles of Becoming* (Reno, NV: CRCS Publications, 1978).

25 Jude Currivan, 'Walking between Worlds – Cosmology Embodied in the Landscape of Neolithic and Early Bronze Age Britain', PhD thesis, University of Reading, 2003.

26 Geoffrey Dean, 'A Reassessment of Jung's Astrological Experiment', *Correlation* 14(2) (Northern Winter 1995): 12–22; Frank McGillion and Pety de Vries-Ek, 'A Further Look at Jung's Astrological Experiment in the Context of the Theory of Synchronicity', *Correlation* 14(1) (Northern Summer 1995): 15–25; Steve Strimer, 'Synchronicity and Jung's Astrological Experiment', *NCGR Journal* (Winter 2000/2001): 45–53.

27 C.G. Jung, *Mysterium Coniunctionis, An Inquiry Into The Seperation and Synthesis of Psychic Opposites in Alchemy* (trans. R.F.C. Hull; Bollingen Series XX, Collected Works, Vol. 12 (Princeton, NJ, Princeton University Press, 1983), p. 546.

28 Wouter Hanegraaff, *New Age Religion and Western Culture: Esotericism in the Mirror of Secular Thought* (Leiden and New York: E.J. Brill, 1996), p. 501. See also the critical discussion on Jung's theories in Richard Noll, *The Aryan Christ and the Secret Life of Carl Gustav Jung* (London: MacMillan, 1987), and *The Jung Cult: Origins of a Charismatic Movement* (Princeton: Princeton University Press, 1994), esp. pp. 116–23.

29 Greene, *Relating*, p. 27.

30 C.G. Jung, 'The Sign of the Fishes' in *Aion*, Collected Works, Vol. 9, Part 2, (trans. R.F.C. Hull; London: Routledge and Kegan Paul, 1959), p. 87.

31 'Jung, Astrology and the Millennium': 22.

32 See, for example, James Hillman, *Re-Visioning Psychology* (London: HarperCollins, 1975), and *The Soul's Code: In Search of Character and Calling* (Westminster, Maryland: Random House,

1996); Thomas Moore, *The Planets Within: the Astrological Psychology of Marsilio Ficino* (Great Barrington, MA: Lindisfarne Press, 1990).

33   Isabel Briggs Myers and Peter B. Myers, *Gifts Differing: Understanding Personality Type* (Mountain View, CA: Davies-Black Publishing, 1980); Garry Phillipson and Peter Case, 'The Hidden Language of Modern Management Science: Astrology, Alchemy and the Myers-Briggs Type Indicator', *Culture and Cosmos* 5(2) (Autumn/Winter 2001): 53–72.

34   For 'Oracles to the Vulgar', see Patrick Curry, *Prophecy and Power: Astrology in Early Modern England* (Oxford: Polity Press, 1989), p. 157. For the history and development of sun-sign astrology, see Kim Farnell, *Flirting with the Zodiac: A History of Sun Sign Astrology* (Bournemouth: The Wessex Astrologer, 2006).

35   Rudhyar, *The Astrology of Personality*, p. viii.

36   Cheiro, *Confessions of a Modern Seer* (London: Jarrolds, 1932), ch. 1.

37   R.H. Naylor, 'What the Stars Foretell For The New Princess And A Few Hints On The Happenings Of This Week', *Sunday Express*, 24 August 1930, p. 11.

38   *Ibid.*

39   *Ibid.*

40   R.H. Naylor, 'Were You Born in September?', *Sunday Express*, 31 August 1930, p. 7.

41   Arthur Christiansen, *Headlines All My Life* (London: Heinemann, 1961), p. 65.

42   Theodor Adorno, *The Stars Down to Earth* (London: Routledge, 1994), p. 113.

43   Derek Parker, *The Question of Astrology: A Personal Investigation* (London: Eyre and Spottiswoode, 1970), p. 115.

44   Penelope McMillan, 'Horoscopes: Fans Bask in Sun Sign', *Los Angeles Times*, 5 July 1985, pp. 1, 3, 18.

45   Alexander Ruperti, 'Dane Rudhyar (March 23, 1895 – September 13, 1985): Seed-Man for the New Era', *Astrological Journal* 33(2) (Spring 1986): 55.

46   Anon, 'Personal Forecast', *American Astrology* 1(1) (March 1933): 11.

47   Stuart Sutcliffe, *Children of the New Age: A History of Spiritual Practices* (London: Routledge, 2003), p. 6.

48   Holly Henry, 'From Galactic Expanses to Earth: Virginia Woolf and Olaf Stapledon Envision New Worlds', paper delivered to the INSAP II conference, Malta, January 1999, and *Virginia Woolf and the Discourse of Science: The Aesthetics of Astronomy* (Cambridge: Cambridge University Press, 2003). See also Stephen Kern, *The Culture of Time and Space 1880–1918* (Cambridge: Harvard University Press, 1983), esp. pp. 131–9 for discussion of the implications of changing ideas of space; and Denis Cosgrove, *Apollo's Eye: A Cartographic Genealogy of the Earth in the Western Imagination* (Baltimore: Johns Hopkins University Press, 2001), esp. pp. 176–267, for the implications of modern astronomical discoveries.

49   Arthur Eddington, *The Expanding Universe* (Harmondsworth, Middlesex: Penguin, 1940).

50   Emile Durkheim, *The Elementary Forms of Religious Life* (trans. Karen E. Fields; New York: Free Press, 1995), 'Introduction' and the concluding discussion on pp. 441–2.

51   Campion, 'Surrealist Cosmology: André Breton and Astrology': 52.

52   Dane Rudhyar, *An Astrological Mandala: The Cycle Of Transformation and its 360 Symbolic Phases*, (New York: Vintage Books, 1974), p. 20.

53   Nicholas Campion, 'Prophecy, Cosmology and the New Age Movement: The Extent and Nature of Contemporary Belief In Astrology', PhD thesis, University of the West of England, 2004, p. 148.

Notes to Chapter 19: The Twentieth Century: Sceptics and Scientists

1   Bart J. Bok, Lawrence E. Jerome, Paul Kurtz, 'Objections to Astrology: A Statement by 186 Leading Scientists', *The Humanist* 35(5) (September–October, 1975), p. 4.

2   C.G. Jung, *Memories, Dreams, Reflections* (London: Fontana, 1967), p. 173.

3   Sigmund Freud, 'Psychoanalysis and Telepathy', 1921, in James Strachey (trans.), *The Complete Psychological Works of Sigmund Freud*, Vol. XVIII (London: Hogarth, 1955), pp. 177–94;

Nicholas Campion, 'Sigmund Freud's Investigation of Astrology', *Culture and Cosmos* 2(1) (Spring/Summer 1998): 49–52. See also Frank McGillion, 'The Influence of Wilhelm Fliess' Cosmobiology on Sigmund Freud', *Culture and Cosmos* 2(1) (Spring/Summer 1998): 33–48; David Katz, *The Occult Tradition from the Renaissance to the Present Day* (London: Jonathan Cape, 2005), pp. 146–52; and James Webb, *The Occult Establishment* (Glasgow: Richard Drew Publishing, 1981).

4   Freud, 'Telepathy', p. 184.
5   Bart J. Bok and Margaret W. Mayall, 'Scientists Look at Astrology', *The Scientific Monthly* 52 (1941): 244.
6   Peter Glick and Mark Snyder, 'Self-Fulfilling Prophecy: the Psychology of Belief in Astrology', *The Humanist* 46(part3) (May–June 1986): 20–5, 50; Peter Glick, Deborah Gottesman and Jeffrey Jolton, 'The Fault is Not In The Stars: Susceptibility of Skeptics and Believers in Astrology to the Barnum Effect', *Personality and Social Psychology Bulletin* 15(4) (December 1989): 572–83; Catherine S. Fichten and Betty Sunerton, 'Popular Horoscopes and the Barnum Effect', *The Journal of Psychology* 114 (1983): 123–34; James G. Delaney and Howard B. Woodyard, 'Effects of Reading an Astrological Description on Responding to a Personality Inventory', *Psychological Reports* 34 (1974): 1214; Margaret M. Hamilton, 'Incorporation of Astrology-Based Personality Information into Long-Term Self-Concept', *Journal of Social Behaviour and Personality* 10(3) (1995): 707–18, and 'Who Believes in Astrology? Effect of Favorableness of Astrologically Derived Personality Descriptions on Acceptance of Astrology', *Personality and Individual Differences* 31 (2001): 895–902.
7   Jon D. Miller, 'The Public Acceptance of Astrology and other Pseudo-science in the United States', paper presented to the 1992 annual meeting of the American Association for the Advancement of Science, 9 February 1992.
8   For background, see Ellic Howe, *Urania's Children: The Strange World of the Astrologers* (London: William Kimber, 1967), (republished as *Astrology: A Recent History Including the untold Story of its Role in World War II* (New York: Walker and Company, 1968)); Nicholas Goodricke-Clarke, *The Occult Roots of Nazism: The Ariosophists of Austria and Germany 1890–1935* (Wellingborough, Northants: Aquarian Press, 1985), and *Black Sun: Aryan Cults, Esoteric Nazism and the Politics of Identity* (New York and London: New York University Press, 2002); Peter Lavenda, *Unholy Alliance: A History of Nazi Involvement with the Occult* (London: Continuum, 2002).
9   Adolf Hitler, *Hitler's Table Talk, 1941–1944: His Private Conversations* (trans. Norman Cameron and R.H. Stevens; London: Weidenfeld and Nicolson), 1973, p. 582.
10 *Ibid.*, p. 674.
11 Anon., *The Search for Faith and the Witness of the Church: An Exploration by the Mission Theological Advisory Group* (London: Church House Publishing, 1996).
12 For evangelical critiques of astrology see Peter Anderson, *Satan's Snare: The Influence of the Occult* (Welwyn, Hertfordshire: Evangelical Press, 1988); Doug Harris, *Occult Overviews and New Age Agendas: A Comprehensive Examination of Major Occult and New Age Groups* (Richmond: Reachout Trust, 1999); and Robert A. Morey, *Horoscopes and the Christian: Does Astrology Accurately Predict the Future? Is it Compatible with Christianity?* (Minneapolis: Bethany House Publishers, 1981).
13 Catechism of the Catholic Church, 1994, para. 2116, http://www.vatican.va/archive/catechism/ccc_toc.htm (accessed 15 October 2005).
14 Maximilian Jacobi, 'Astrology', *The Catholic Encyclopedia*, Vol. 2 (New York: Robert Appleton Company, 1907), http://www.newadvent.org/cathen/02018e.htm (accessed 15 October 2005).
15 Rev. Lawrence Cassidy, 'The Believing Christian as a Dedicated Astrologer', *Astrology Quarterly* 64.3 (Summer 1994): 3–13.
16 Theodor Adorno, *The Stars Down to Earth* (London: Routledge, 1994 [1953]). See also Theodor Adorno, Else Frenkel-Brunswick, Daniel J. Levinson and R. Nevitt Sanford, *The Authoritarian Personality*, abridged edition (New York and London: W.W. Norton and Company, 1982).
17 Adorno, *The Stars Down to Earth*, pp. 114–15.
18 For critiques of the theory of the authoritarian personality, see Rodney Stark, 'Atheism, Faith, and

the Social Scientific Study of Religion', *Journal of Contemporary Religion* 14(1) (1999):. 41–62; Ivan D. Steiner, 'Ethnocentrism and Tolerance of Trait "Inconsistency"', *Journal of Abnormal and Social Psychology* 49 (1954): 349–54; Ivan D. Steiner and Homer H. Johnson, 'Authoritarianism and "Tolerance of Trait Inconsistency"', *Journal of Abnormal and Social Psychology* 67(4) (1963), 388–91; Andrew Greeley, *The Sociology of the Paranormal* (London: Sage Publications, 1975).

19   Robert Park, *Voodoo Science: The Road from Foolishness to Fraud* (Oxford: Oxford University Press, 2000), pp. 36, 201.

20   Adorno, *The Stars Down to Earth*, p. 119.

21   *Ibid.*, p. 115.

22   For a discussion of the culture industry, see Dominic Strinati, *An Introduction to Theories of Popular Culture* (London: Routledge, 1995), esp. pp. 61–74.

23   Kieran Flanagan, *The Enchantment of Sociology: A Study of Theology and Culture* (London: MacMillan, 1999), p. 180.

24   Antonio Gramsci, *Selections from the Prison Notebooks* (PLACE International Publishers, 1971); see also the discussion in Patrick Curry, *Prophecy and Power: Astrology in Early Modern England* (Oxford: Polity Press, 1989), pp. 162–6; Barbara Bender, *Stonehenge: Making Space* (Oxford, Berg, 1998), pp. 100, 159.

25   For Hawkins and Thom, see Campion, *The Dawn of Astrology*, ch. 2; see also Alexander Thom, *Megalithic Sites in Britain* (Oxford: Oxford University Press, 1967), and Gerald Hawkins, *Stonehenge Decoded* (New York: Dorset Press, 1965).

26   Bart J. Bok, Lawrence E. Jerome and Paul Kurtz, 'Objections to Astrology: A Statement by 186 Leading Scientists', *The Humanist* 35(5) (September/October 1975): 4–6.

27   Paul Fererabend, 'The Strange Case of Astrology' in Patrick Grim (ed.), *Philosophy of Science and the Occult* (New York: SUNY Press, 1990), pp. 23–7.

28   Richard Dawkins, *Unweaving the Rainbow* (London: Penguin, 1998), p. 121.

29   George P. Hansen, 'CSICOP and the Skeptics: An Overview', *The Journal of the American Society for Psychical Research* 86 (January 1992): 19–63.

30   For Cumbey, see Constance E. Cumbey, *The Hidden Dangers of the Rainbow: The New Age Movement and Our Coming Age of Barbarism* (Shreveport, LA: Huntingdon House, 1983).

31   For a critique of fundamentalist astrologers, see Liz Greene, 'Astrologers Agendas', paper delivered at the Astrological Association of Great Britain conference, Staverton Park, 19–22 September 2008.

32   Edward W. James, 'On Dismissing Astrology and other Irrationalities' in Patrick Grim (ed.), *Philosophy of Science and the Occult* (New York: SUNY Press, 1990), p. 28.

33   Guido Bonatti, *The Astrologer's Guide* (London: Regulus Publishing Co., 1986), para. 7, p. 6.

34   Geoffrey Dean and Arthur Mather, *Recent Advances in Natal Astrology: a Critical Review 1900–1976* (Subiaco, Australia: Analogic, 1977); Hans Eysenck and David Nias, *Astrology: Science or Superstition?* (London: Pelican, 1982); J. Lee Lehman, 'Tiptoeing through the Method: An Historical Review of Empiricism in Astrology, 1990–1991', *Astrological Journal* 36(1) (Jan/Feb. 1994): 60–8.

35   Dean and Mather, *Recent Advances in Natal Astrology*, pp. 544–8.

36   Pat Harris, 'Applications of Astrology to Health Psychology: Astrological and Psychological Factors and Fertility Treatment Outcome', PhD thesis, University of Southampton, 2005.

37   For a comprehensive bibliography of Gauquelin's writings, see Suitbert Ertel, 'Publications of Michel Gauquelin', *Correlation* 11(1) (June 1991): 12–23. His first book, *L'Influence des Astres*, was published in French in 1955, followed by *Les Hommes et les Astres* in 1969. His works in English include *Dreams and Illusions of Astrology* (Buffalo, NY: Prometheus Books, 1969), *Cosmic Influences on Human Behaviour* (London: Futura Publications, 1976), *How Cosmic and Atmospheric Energies Influence Your Health* (New York: Aurora Press, 1984), *Written in the Stars* (Wellingborough, Northamptonshire: Aquarian Press, 1988), *The Cosmic Clocks* (San Diego: Astro-Computing Services, 1988), *Planetary Heredity* (San Diego: Astro-Computing Services, 1988) and *Neo-Astrology: A Copernican Revolution* (London: Penguin, 1991). For a recent summary of Gauquelin's research, including full references to the anti-Gauquelin material, see

Suitbert Ertel and Kenneth Irving, *The Tenacious Mars Effect* (London: Urania Trust, 1996), pp. KI3 – KI13.

38   Michel Gauquelin, *Written in the Stars* (Wellingborough, Northamptonshire: Aquarian Press, 1988), p. 11, citing Breton's 1954 interview with the French astrologer André Barbault (see Nicholas Campion, 'Surrealist Cosmology: André Breton and Astrology', *Culture and Cosmos* 6(2) (Autumn/Winter 2002): 45–56).

39   Michel Gauquelin, *Dreams and Illusions of Astrology* (Buffalo, NY: Prometheus Books, 1969), p. 1.

40   Gauquelin, *Written in the Stars*, p. 42.

41   *Ibid.*, p. 152.

42   Ertel and Irving, *The Tenacious Mars Effect*, p KI 14.

43   Ertel and Irving, *The Tenacious Mars Effect*, pp. KI 17 – KI 23; Patrick Curry, 'Research on the Mars effect', *Zetetic Scholar* 9 (Feb/March 1982): 34–52.

44   Dennis Rawlins, 'sTARBABY', *Fate*, October 1981.

45   Hans Eysenck, 'The Tenacious Mars Effect', review, *Correlation* 15(1) (Northern Summer 1996): 53–4.

46   G. Dean, 'Attribution: A Pervasive New Artefact in the Gauquelin data', *Astrology under Scrutiny* 13(1 and 2) (2000): 1–72.

47   S. Ertel, 'Gauquelin's Planetary Effects – Made up by Superstitious Parents? On Geoffrey Dean's erroneous grand notion', *Astrology under Scrutiny* 13(2) (2000): 73–84.

48   Campion, *The Dawn of Astrology*, chs. 12, 17; Augustine, *City of God* (trans. Henry Bettenson; Harmondsworth, Middlesex: Penguin, 1972); Cicero, *De Divinatione* (trans. W.A. Falconer; Cambridge, MA and London: Harvard University Press, 1929).

Notes to Chapter 20: The Twenty-first Century: Epilogue

1   Freya Mathews, *The Ecological Self* (Savage, MD: Barnes and Noble, 1991), p. 109.

2   Roger B. Culver and Philip A. Ianna, *Astrology: True or False? A Scientific Evaluation*, revised edition (Buffalo, NY: Prometheus Books, 1988).

3   Steven Forrest, *The Night Speaks: A Meditation on the Astrological Worldview* (San Diego: ACS, 1993), p. vii.

4   John Addey, *Astrology Reborn* (London: Faculty of Astrological Studies, 1971), p. 3.

5   Nicholas Campion, 'Prophecy, Cosmology and the New Age Movement: The Extent and Nature of Contemporary Belief in Astrology', PhD thesis, University of the West of England, 2004, ch. 10.

6   These figures are from Campion, 'Prophecy, Cosmology and the New Age Movement, ch. 11.

7   *Ibid.*, p. 231.

8   Harold R. Isaacs, *Scratches on Our Minds. American Images of China and India* (New York: John Day Company, 1958).

9   David Hufford, 'Traditions of Disbelief', *Talking Folklore* 1(part 3) (1987): 19–29.

10   For anecdotes on astrology in twentieth-century film and literature, see Neil Spencer, *True as the Stars Above: Adventures in Modern Astrology* (London: Victor Gollancz, 2000).

11   Ruth Rendell, *Lake of Darkness* (London: Arrow Books, 1981).

12   *Ibid.*, *Thirteen Steps Down* (London: Hutchinson, 2004), p. 44.

13   For the definition of popular culture, see Gordon Lynch, *Understanding Theology and Popular Culture* (Oxford: Blackwell, 2005), p. 2. See also the discussion in John Fiske, *Understanding Popular Culture* (London: Routledge, 1989), esp. pp. 24–5.

14   Dominic Strinati, *An Introduction to Theories of Popular Culture* (London: Routledge, 1995), p. 64.

15   For the following discussion, see Campion, 'Prophecy, Cosmology and the New Age Movement', chs 8, 10.

16   Alex Owen's argument that nineteenth-century spiritualism was a radical form of feminist

spirituality may be applied to contemporary astrology. See Alex Owen, *The Darkened Room: Women, Power and Spiritualism in Late Victorian England* (Chicago: University of Chicago Press, 1989).

17 Shoshanah Feher, 'Who Holds the Cards? Women and New Age Astrology' in James R. Lewis and J. Gordon Melton, *Perspectives on the New Age* (Albany, NY: State University of New York Press, 1992), pp. 179–88.

18 Robert Wuthnow, 'Astrology and Marginality', *Journal for the Scientific Study of Religion* 15(2) (1976): 157–68.

19 For the evolutionist view of astrology as primitive, see Edward Burnett Tylor, *Primitive Culture* (3 Vols; New York: Harper Torchbooks, 1958 [London: Murray, 1871]), Vol. 1, pp. 128–33; and for supporting material on 'primitive thought', see J.G. Frazer, *The Golden Bough: A Study in Magic and Relgion*, abridged edition (London: MacMillan, 1971 [1922]).

20 Herbert Spencer, *The Principles of Sociology*, (New York: D. Appleton and Company, 1904), Vol. 1, pp. 58, 380.

21 See, for example, Ronny Martens and Tim Trachet, *Making Sense of Astrology* (Amherst: Prometheus Books, 1988). For a more balanced assessment, though, see Edward A. Tiryakian, 'Towards the Sociology of Esoteric Culture', *American Journal of Sociology* 78(3) (November 1972): 491–512.

22 Terry Eagleton, *The Idea of Culture* (Oxford: Blackwell, 2000), pp. 49–50.

23 *San Francisco Chronicle*, 2 January 1967, p. 1.

24 Donald T. Regan, *For the Record: From Wall Street to Washington* (London: Arrow Books, 1988).

25 Simo Parpola, *Letters from Assyrian and Babylonian Scholars* (Helsinki: Helsinki University Press, 1993), p. 46; Hermann Hunger, *Astrological Reports to Assyrian Kings* (Helsinki: Helsinki University Press, 1992), p. 320.

26 Danny Penman, 'City looks to the heavens for answers', *Daily Telegraph*, 19 March 2008, http://www.telegraph.co.uk/portal/main.jhtml?xml=/portal/2008/03/19/ftstars119.xml (accessed 16 September 2008).

27 Penny Thornton, *With Love from Diana* (New York: Pocket Books, 1995).

28 Jacob Needleman, *The New Religions* (New York: Dutton, 1977), pp. 191–4; Robin Gill, G. Kirk Hadaway and Penny Long Marler, 'Is Religious Belief Declining in Britain?', *Journal for the Scientific Study of Religion* 37(3) (1998): 512.

29 Bernulf Kanitscheider, 'A Philosopher looks at Astrology', *Interdisciplinary Science Reviews* 16(3) (1991): 259–60; Michael Hill, *A Sociology of Religion* (London: Heinemann, 1979), p. 247.

30 For vernacular religion see Marion Bowman and Steven Sutcliffe, 'Introduction', *Beyond New Age: Exploring Alternative Spirituality* (Edinburgh: Edinburgh University Press, 2000), p. 6; L. Primiano, 'Vernacular Religion and the Search for Method on Religious Folklife', *Western Folklore* 54(1) (1995): 35–56; D. Yoder, 'Towards a Definition of Folk Religion', *Western Folklore* 33(1) (1974): 14.

31 For Wiccan cosmology, see Tanya Luhrmann, *Persuasions of the Witch's Craft: Ritual Magic in Contemporary England* (Cambridge, MA.: Harvard University Press, 1989); Susan Greenwood, *Magic, Witchcraft and the Otherworld: An Anthropology* (Oxford: Berg, 2000); James R. Lewis (ed.), *Mystical Relgion and Modern Wicthcraft* (Albany, NY: State University of New York Press, 1996); Janet Farrar and Stewart Farrar, *The Witches Way: Principles, Rituals and Beliefs of Modern Wichcraft* (London: Robert Hale, 1984), pp. 67–70; Vivianne Crowley, *Wicca: the Old Religion in the New Age* (Wellingborough: Aquarian Press, 1989), p. 107.

32 Rodney Stark and William Simms Bainbridge, *The Future of Religion: Secularization. Revival and Cult Formation* (Berkeley: University of California Press, 1985), p. 34.

33 See Robin Gill, *Churchgoing and Christian Ethics* (Cambridge: Cambridge University Press, 1999). See the discussion in Campion, 'Prophecy, Cosmology and the New Age Movement', chs 8, 10.

34 Bryan Wilson, *Religion in Secular Society: A Sociological Comment* (Harmondsworth: Pelican, 1969), and *Contemporary Transformations of Religion* (Oxford: Clarendon Press, 1979).

35   Theodor Adorno, *The Stars Down to Earth* (London: Routledge, 1994 [1953]), pp. 82–4; Campion, 'Prophecy, Cosmology and the New Age Movement', p. 241: in one survey around 60 per cent of astrologers regarded themselves as 'spiritual but non-aligned'.

36   Campion, 'Prophecy, Cosmology and the New Age Movement', p. 248.

37   Freya Mathews, *The Ecological Self* (Savage, MD: Barnes and Noble, 1991), p. 109.

38   Bowman and Sutcliffe, 'Introduction', p. 11.

39   Rodney Stark, 'Atheism, Faith, and the Social Scientific Study of Religion', *Journal of Contemporary Religion* 14(1) (1999): 56; see also Steven Best and Douglas Kellner, *Postmodern Theory: Critical Interrogations* (London: MacMillan, 1991), pp. 3, 37; Andrew M. Greeley, *The Sociology of the Paranormal* (London: Sage Publications, 1975), p. 7.

40   Dale Caird and Henry G. Law, 'Non-Conventional Beliefs: Their Structure and Measurement', *Journal for the Scientific Study of Religion* 21(2) (1992): 152; J. Milton Yinger, *The Scientific Study of Religion* (New York: MacMillan, 1970), p. 78; William Herbrechtsmeier, 'Buddhism and the Definition of Religion: One More Time', *Journal for the Scientific Study of Religion* 32(1) (1993): 1–18.

41   Geoffrey Dean, Ivan Kelly and Arthur Mather, 'Astrology' in Gordon Stein (ed.), *The Encyclopaedia of the Paranormal* (Amherst, NY: Prometheus Books, 1996), pp. 89–90.

42   Stark, 'Atheism, Faith, and the Social Scientific Study of Religion': 56–7.

43   David J. Hess, *Science in the New Age: The Paranormal, Its Defenders and Debunkers and American Culture* (Wisconsin: University of Wisconsin Press, 1993), p. 36; Paul Heelas, *The New Age Movement* (Oxford: Blackwell, 1996), pp. 23, 34, 138; Robert N. Bellah, 'New Religious Consciousness and the Crisis in Modernity' in Charles Glock and Robert N. Bellah, *The New Religious Consciousness* (Berkeley: University of California Press, 1976), pp. 222–352; John Bauer and Martin Durant, 'British Public Perceptions of Astrology: An Approach from the Sociology of Knowledge', *Culture and Cosmos* 1(1) (1997): 55.

44   Nicholas Campion, 'The Traditional Revival in Modern Astrology: a Preliminary History', *Astrology Quarterly* 74(1) (Winter 2003): 28–38.

45   Steven Best and Douglas Kellner, *Postmodern Theory: Critical Interrogations* (London: MacMillan, 1991), pp. 1–33; Irving Hexham and Karla Poewe, *New Religions as Global Cultures* (Boulder, CO: Westview Press, 1997), pp. 149–51; Frederic Jameson, *Postmodernism or, the Cultural Logic of Late Capitalism* (London: Verso, 1991), p. ix.

46   Patrick Curry, 'Astrology: From Pagan to Postmodern?', *The Astrological Journal* 36(1) (January/February 1994): 69–75.

47   Anthony Aveni, *Behind the Crystal Ball: Magic and Science from Antiquity to the New Age* (London: Newleaf, 1996), p. 303.

48   Robert Hand, 'Foreword' in Olivia Barclay, *Horary Astrology Rediscovered* (West Chester, PA: Whitford Press, 1990), p. 15.

49   Patrick Curry, *A Confusion of Prophets: Victorian and Edwardian Astrology* (London: Collins and Brown, 1992), p. 132.

50   See Henri Corbin, *Mundus Imaginalis, or the Imaginary and the Imaginal*, 1964, http://www.hermetic.com/bey/mundus_imaginalis.htm.

51   Umberto Eco, 'Travels in Hyperreality' in *Faith in Fakes: Travels in Hyperreality* (London: Minerva, 1995), pp. 1–58; 'Dreaming of the Middle Ages' in *Faith in Fakes: Travels in Hyperreality*, pp. 61–85. See also Jean Baudrillard, *Simulacra and Simulations* (Chicago: University of Michigan Press, 1994).

52   Robin Lovitt and Frank E. Reynolds (eds), *Cosmogony and Ethical Order: New Studies in Comparative Ethics* (Chicago: Chicago University Press, 1985), p. 26.

53   As argued by Ann Geneva, *Astrology and the Seventeenth Century Mind: William Lilly and the Language of the Stars* (Manchester and New York: Manchester University Press, 1995), p. xv.

54   C.G. Jung, 'Psychotherapists or the Clergy' in *Psychology and Religion: East and West*, Collected Works, Vol. 11 (trans. R.F.C. Hull; London: Routledge and Kegan Paul, 1969), pp. 330, 336.

55   Peter Berger, *The Sacred Canopy: Elements of a Sociological Theory of Religion* (New York: Anchor Books, 1969). See also the Koran, berating the faithless: 'We spread the heaven like a canopy

and provided it with strong support: yet of its signs they are heedless' (Sura 21.31; trans. N.J. Darwood).

56 Lockard talks of the World Wide Web's creation of 'a new quasi-invisible public architecture and social master narrative': Joseph Lockard, 'Progressive Politics, Electronic Individualism and the Myth of the Virtual Community' in David Porter (ed.), *Internet Culture* (London: Routledge, 1996), p. 230.

Bibliography

Abram, David, *The Spell of the Sensuous* (New York: Vintage, 1997).

Abu 'Ali Al-Khayyat, *The Judgement of Nativities* (trans. James H. Holden; Tempe, AZ: American Federation of Astrologers, 1988).

Abu Ma'shar, *The Abbreviation of the Introduction to Astrology, Together with the Medieval Latin Translation of Adelard of Bath*, ed. and trans. by Charles Burnett, Keiji Yamamoto and Michio Yano (Leiden, New York and Koln: E.J. Brill, 1994).

——*The Abbreviation of the Introduction to Astrology*, trans. C. Burnett with historical and technical annotations by C. Burnett, G. Tobyn, G. Cornelius and V. Wells (Reston, VA: ARHAT publications, 1997).

——*On Historical Astrology: The Book of Religions and Dynasties (On the Great Conjunctions)*, ed.and trans. Keiji Yamamoto and Charles Burnett (2 Vols, Leiden: E.J. Brill, 2000).

Addey, John, *Astrology Reborn* (London: Faculty of Astrological Studies, 1971).

Adler, Margot, *Drawing Down the Moon: Witches, Druids, Goddess-Worshippers, and Other Pagans in America Today* (Boston: Beacon Press, 1987 [1979]).

Adorno, Theodor, *The Stars Down to Earth* (London: Routledge, 1994 [1953]).

Adorno, Theodor, Else Frenkel-Brunswick, Daniel J. Levinson and R. Nevitt Sanford, *The Authoritarian Personality*, abridged edn (New York and London: W.W. Norton and Company, 1982).

Agrippa, Henry Cornelius, *Three Books of Occult Philosophy*, facsimile of the 1651 translation (London: Chthonius Books, 1986).

Ahern, Geoffrey, *Sun at Midnight: The Rudolf Steiner Movement and the Western Esoteric Tradition* (Wellingborough: Aquarian Press, 1984).

Alberi, Mary, 'Alcuin and the New Athens', *History Today* (September 1989): 35–41.

Alexandrian, Sarane, *Surrrealist Art* (London: Thames and Hudson, 1970).

Al-Kindi, *On the Stellar Rays* (trans. Robert Zoller; Berkeley, VA: Project Hindsight, The Golden Hind Press, 1993).

Allawi, Ibrahim, 'Some Evolutionary and Cosmological Aspects to Early Islamic Town Planning' in Margaret Bentley Sevcenko (ed.), *Theories and Principles of Design in the Architecture of Islamic Societies* (Cambridge, MA.: Aga Khan Program for Islamic Architecture, 1988), pp. 57–72; http://archnet.org/library/documents/one-document. tcl?document_id=3776.

Allen, Don Cameron, *The Star-Crossed Renaissance: The Quarrel About Astrology And Its Influence in England* (Durham, NC: Duke University Press, 1941).

Allott, Stephen, *Alcuin of York, c. A.D. 732 to 804: His Life and Letters* (York: William Sessions, 1974).

Alvarez, Al, 'How Black Magic killed Sylvia Plath', The *Guardian*, G2, 15 September 1999.

——'The Varley Manuscripts', *Modern Astrology*, New Series 19 (1921): 483–7.

Anon. *The Search for Faith and the Witness of the Church: An Exploration by the Mission Theological Advisory Group* (London: Church House Publishing, 1996).

——*Ghayat Al-Hakim. Picatrix: the Goal of the Wise* (trans. Hashem Atallah; Seattle: Ouroboros Press, 2002).

Aquinas, Thomas, *Summa Contra Gentiles* (4 Vols; trans. Vernon J. Bourke; Notre Dame: University of Notre Dame Press, 1975).

Aristotle, *Metaphysics* (2 Vols; Vol. 1 trans. Hugh Tredennick, Vol. 2 trans. Hugh Tredennick and G. Cyril Armstrong; Cambridge, MA and London: Harvard University Press, 1933).

——*Meterologica* (trans. H.D.P. Lee; Cambridge, MA and London: Harvard University Press, 1937).

——*Secreta Secretorum* (New York: Da Capo, 1970).

Astell, Ann W., *Chaucer and the Universe of Learning* (Ithaca and London: Cornell University Press, 1988).

Augustine, *Confessions* (trans. R.S. Pine-Coffin; Harmondsworth, Middlesex: Penguin, 1961).

——*City of God* (trans. Henry Bettenson; Harmondsworth, Middlesex: Penguin, 1972).

Bacon, Francis, *Advancement of Learning* (London: Dent, 1973).

Bacon, Roger, *Opus Maius* (2 Vols; trans. Robert Burke; Philadelphia: University of Pennsylvania Press, 1928).

Bailey, Alice A. *The Unfinished Autobiography* (London; Lucis Press, 1951).

——*Esoteric Astrology* (London: Lucis Press, 1973 [1951]).

Baity, Elizabeth Chesley, 'Archaeoastronomy and Ethnoastronomy So Far', *Current Anthropology* 14(4) (October 1973): 389–449.

Balzac, Honoré de, *Séraphita* (Dodo Press, 2006).

Baudrillard, Jean, *Simulacra and Simulations* (Chicago: University of Michigan Press, 1994).

Bauer, John and Martin Durant, 'British Public Perceptions of Astrology: An Approach from the Sociology of Knowledge', *Culture and Cosmos* 1(1) (1997) 55–72.

Baumgardt, Carola, *Johannes Kepler: Life and Letters* (London: Gollancz, 1952).

Becker, Carl, *The Heavenly City of the Enlightenment Philosophers* (Storrs Lectures) (New Haven and London: Yale University Press, 1932).

——*The Declaration of Independence: A Study in the History of Political Ideas* (New York: Vintage, 1958).

Bede, *Ecclesiastical History of the English People* (trans. D.H. Farmer; London: Penguin, 1990).

——*The Reckoning of Time* (trans. Faith Wallis; Liverpool: Liverpool University Press, 2004).

Beer, Gillian, '"The Death of the Sun": Victorian Solar Physics and Solar Myth' in Bullen, J.B., (ed.), *The Sun is God: Painting, Literature and Mythology in the Nineteenth Century* (Oxford: Oxford University Press, 1989), pp. 159–80.

Begg, Ean, 'Jung, Astrology and the Millennium', lecture delivered to the Astrological Association Conference, Plymouth, 9 August 1999.

——'Jung, Astrology and the Millennium', *The Astrological Journal* 41(6) (November/December, 1999): 21–7.

Bell, Anne Olivier (ed.), *The Diary of Virginia Woolf, volume IV: 1931–1935* (London: The Hogarth Press, 1982).

Bellitto, Christopher (ed.), *Introducing Nicholas of Cusa: A Guide to a Renaissance Man* (Mahwah, NJ: Paulist Press, 2004).

Berlin, Isaiah, *Against the Current: Essays in the History of Ideas* (London: Pimlico, 1979).

Berman, Morris, *The Reenchantment of the World* (Ithaca and London: Cornell University Press, 1991).

Bernfeld, Siegfried, 'Freud's Earliest Theories and the School of Herman von Helmholtz', *The Psychoanalytic Quarterly* 13 (1944): 341–62.

Bewell, Alan, *Wordsworth and the Enlightenment: Nature, Man and Society in the Experimental Poetry* (New Haven and London: Yale University Press, 1989).

Biagioli, Mario, *Galileo, Courtier: The Practice of Science in the Culture of Absolutism* (Chicago and London: University of Chicago Press, 1993).

Binsbergen, Wim van, 'The Astrological Origins of Astrological Geomancy', paper read at The SSIPS/SAGP 1996, 15th Annual Conference: 'Global and Multicultural Dimensions of Ancient and Medieval Philosophy and Social Thought: Africana, Christian, Greek, Islamic, Jewish, Indigenous and Asian Traditions', Binghamton University, Department of Philosophy/Center for Medieval and Renaissance studies (CEMERS), October 1996; http://www.shikanda.net/ancient_models/BINGHAMTON%201996.pdf.

Birch, Dinah, '"The Sun is God": Ruskin's Solar Mythology' in Bullen, J.B. (ed.), *The Sun is God: Painting, Literature and Mythology in the Nineteenth Century* (Oxford: Oxford University Press, 1989), pp. 109–24.

Bird, Alison, 'Astrology in Education: An Ethnography', DPhil. thesis, University of Sussex, 2006.

Blake, William, *Complete Writings*, ed. Geoffrey Keynes (Oxford: Oxford University Press, 1971).

Blavatsky, H.P., *Isis Unveiled* (2 Vols; Pasadena: Theosophical University Press, 1976 [1877]).

——*The Secret Doctrine*, Vols 1 and 2, facsimile of the original edition of 1888 (Los Angeles: The Theosophy Company, 1982).

——*The Key to Theosophy* (London: Theosophical Publishing House, 1987 [1889]).

Bloch, George, *Mesmerism: A Translation of the Scientific and Medical Writings of Franz Anton Mesmer* (Los Altos, CA: William Kauffman, 1980).

Boer, Charles, 'Translator's Introduction', in Ficino, Marsilio, *The Book of Life* (trans. Charles Boer; Irving, TX: Spring Publications, 1980), pp. iii–xviii.

Bok, Bart J., Lawrence E. Jerome and Paul Kurtz, 'Objections to Astrology: A Statement by 186 Leading Scientists', *The Humanist* 35(5) (September–October 1975): 4–6.

Bok, Bart J and Margaret W. Mayall, 'Scientists Look at Astrology', *The Scientific Monthly* 52 (1941) 233–44.

Bodin, Jean, *Method for the Easy Comprehension of History* (trans. Beatrice Reynolds; New York: Records of Civilisations: Sources and Studies no 37, 1945).

——*The Six Books of the Commonwealth* (abridged and trans. M.J. Tooley; Oxford: Basil Blackwell, 1955).

——*The Six Books of the Commonweale* (trans. Richard Knolles; London 1606, facsimile edn, ed. Kenneth Douglas MacRae; Cambridge, MA: Harvard University Press, 1962).

Boehme, Jacob, *The Signature of all Things* (Cambridge: James Clarke and Co, 1969).

Boethius, *Tracts and de Consolatione Philosophiae* (trans. H.F. Stewart and E.K. Rand; London and Cambridge, MA: Harvard University Press, 1918).

——*The Consolation of Philosophy* (trans. V.E. Watts; Harmondsworth, Middlesex: Penguin, 1969).

Bonatti, Guido, 'The One Hundred and Forty-Six Considerations of the Famous Astrologer Guido Bonatus' in *The Astrologer's Guide* (trans. Henry Coley; London: Regulus Publishing Co., 1986 [1886]), pp. 1–72.

——*Liber Astronomiae*, Parts 1–IV (trans. Robert Hand and Robert Zoller, ed. Robert Hand and Robert Schmidt; Berkeley Springs: Golden Hind Press, 1994–6).

——*Liber Astronomiae* (2 Vols; trans. Benjamin Dykes; Golden Valley, MN: The Cazimi Press, 2007).

Bonser, W., *The Medical Background to Anglo-Saxon England* (London: Wellcome Historical Medical Library, 1963).

Booker, John, *The Bloody Almanak* (London, 1643).

——*Black Munday* (London, 1652).

Booth, Arthur John, *Saint-Simon and Saint-Simonism: A Chapter in the History of Socialism in France* (Amsterdam: Liberac, 1970 [1871]).

Borchardt, Frank L., 'The Magus as Renaissance Man', *Sixteenth Century Journal* 21(1) (Spring 1990): 57–6.

Boulainviller, Comte Henri de, *Histoire du mouvement de l'apogee du Soleil. Ou Pratique des Regles d'astrologie Pour juger des Evenements generaux*, 1711, facsimile edn (Boulogne-sur-Seine & Garches: Editions du Nouvel Humanisme, 1949).

Bowden, Mary Ellen, 'The Scientific Revolution in Astrology: the English Reformers, 1558–1686', PhD thesis, Yale University, 1974.

Brady, Bernadette, 'Four Galilean Horoscopes: An Analysis of Galileo's Astrological Techniques' in Campion, Nicholas and Nick Kollerstrom, *Galileo's Astrology* (Bristol: Cinnabar Books, 2004)/*Culture and Cosmos* 7(1) (Spring/Summer 2003): 113–44.

Brann, Noel L., *The Abbot Trithemius (1462–1516): The Renaissance of Monastic Humanism*, (Leiden: E.J. Brill, 1981).

Brecht, Bertolt, *Galileo* (London: Random House, 1999).

Broecke, Stephen Vanden, *The Limits of Influence: Pico, Louvain and the Crisis of Renaissance Astrology* (Leiden: E.J. Brill, 2003).

Brooke, John L., *The Refiner's Tale: The Making of Mormon Cosmology, 1644–1844* (Cambridge: Cambridge University Press, 1996 [1994]).

Brookner, Anita, *Romanticism and its Discontents* (London: Viking, 2000).

Brosseder, Claudia, 'The Writing in the Wittenberg Sky: Astrology in Sixteenth-Century Germany', *Journal of the History of Ideas* 66(4) (October 2005): 557–76.

Bullen, J.B. (ed.), *The Sun is God: Painting, Literature and Mythology in the Nineteenth Century* (Oxford: Oxford University Press, 1989).

Buonaventura, Wendy, *Serpent of the Nile: Women and Dance in the Arab World* (London: Saqi Books, 1989).

——*I Put a Spell on You: Dancing Women from Salome to Madonna* (London: Saqi Books, 2003).

Burnett, Charles, *Adelard of Bath: An English Scientist and Arabist of the Early Twelfth Century* (London: Warburg Institute, 1987).

——*Magic and Divination in the Middle Ages: Texts and Techniques in the Islamic and Christian Worlds* (Aldershot: Variorum, 1996).

Burnett, Charles and W.F. Ryan (eds), *Magic and the Classical Tradition* (London and Turin: The Warburg Institute and Nino Aragno Editore, 2006).

Butler, Jon, 'Magic, Astrology and the Early American Heritage 1600–1760', *American Historical Review* 84 (1979): 317–46.

Camden, Carroll, 'Astrology in Shakespeare's Day', *Isis* 19(1) (April 1933): 26–73.

Cameron, Alan, 'The Last Days of the Academy at Athens', *Proceedings of the Cambridge Philological Society* 195 (1969): 7–29.

Campanella, Thomas, *The City of the Sun* (Frankfurt, 1623; trans A.M. Elliot and R. Millner; intro. A.L. Morton; (London: Journeyman, 1981).

Campbell, Bruce H., *Ancient Wisdom Revived: A History of the Theosophical Movement* (Berkeley: University of California Press, 1980).

Campion, Nicholas, 'Astrological Historiography in the Renaissance: The Work of Jean Bodin and Louis Le Roy' in Kitson, Annabella (ed.); *History and Astrology: Clio and Urania Confer* (London: Unwin Paperbacks, 1989), pp. 89–136.

——*The Great Year: Astrology, Millenarianism and History in the Western Tradition* (London: Penguin, 1994).

——'Sigmund Freud's Investigation of Astrology', *Culture and Cosmos* 2(1) (Spring/Summer 1998): 49–52.

——'Surrealist Cosmology: André Breton and Astrology', *Culture and Cosmos* 6(2) (Autumn/Winter 2002): 45–56.

——'Prophecy, Cosmology and the New Age Movement: The Extent and Nature of Contemporary Belief in Astrology', PhD thesis, University of the West of England, 2004.

——'The Traditional Revival in Modern Astrology: a Preliminary History', *Astrology Quarterly* 74(1) (Winter 2003): 28–38; http://www.astrolodge.co.uk/astro/quarterly/traditionalrevival.html.

——*What do Astrologers Believe?* (Oxford: Granta, 2006).

——*The Dawn of Astrology: A Cultural History of Western Astrology*, Vol. 1 (London: Continuum, 2008).

——*Astrology and Cosmology in the World Religions* (New York: New York University Press, forthcoming 2011).

Campion, Nicholas, and Nick Kollerstrom, *Galileo's Astrology* (Bristol: Cinnabar Books 2004)/ *Culture and Cosmos* 7(1) (Spring/Summer 2003).

——*Kepler's Astrology, Culture and Cosmos* 13(1 and 2) (Spring/Summer and Autumn/Winter 2009).

Capp, Bernard, *Astrology and the Popular Press: English Almanacs 1500–1800* (London and Boston: Faber and Faber, 1979).

Carey, Hilary, *Courting Disaster: Astrology at the English Court and University in the Later Middle Ages* (London: MacMillan, 1992).

Caroti, Stefano, 'Melanchthon's Astrology' in Zambelli, Paola, *'Astrologi hallucinati': Stars and the End of the World in Luther's Time* (Berlin and New York: Walter de Gruyter, 1986), pp. 109–21.

Carteret, Jean and Roger Knare, 'An interview with André Breton, April 1954', trans. Morelle Smith in Campion, Nicholas, 'Surrealist Cosmology: André Breton and Astrology', *Culture and Cosmos* 6(2) (Autumn/Winter 2002): 45–56.

Caspar, M., *Kepler* (New York: Dover Publications, 1993).

Cassidy, Rev. Lawrence, 'The Believing Christian as a Dedicated Astrologer', *Astrology Quarterly* 64.3 (Summer 1994): 3–13.

Cassiodorus, *Institutions of Divine and Secular Learning, On the Soul* (Liverpool: Liverpool University Press, 2004).

Cassirer, Ernst, *The Philosophy of Symbolic Forms*, Vol. 2, *Mythical Thought* (New Haven and London: Yale University Press, 1971 [1955]).

Cassirer, Ernst, and Paul Kristeller, *The Renaissance Philosophy of Man* (Chicago: University of Chicago Press, 1956).

Catani, Remo, 'The Polemics on Astrology 1489–1524', *Culture and Cosmos* 3(2) (Autumn/Winter 1999): 16–31.

Chabás, J., and B.R. Goldstein, *The Alfonsine Tables of Toledo* (Dordrecht: Kluwer Academic Publishers, 2003).

Chadwick, Henry, *Boethius: the Consolations of Music, Logic, Theology and Philosophy* (Oxford: Clarendon Press, 1981), pp. 78–107.

Chadwick, Owen, *The Secularization of the European Mind in the Nineteenth Century* (Cambridge: Cambridge University Press, 1975).

Chaucer, Geoffrey, *The Complete Poetry and Prose of Geoffrey Chaucer* (New York: J.H. Fisher, 1977).

Choucha, Nadia, *Surrealism and the Occult* (Oxford: Mandrake, 1991).

Christianson, John Robert, 'Tycho Brahe's Cosmology from the Astrologia of 1591', *Isis* 59(3) (Autumn, 1968): 312–18.

——'Tycho Brahe's German Treatise on the Comet of 1577', *Isis* 70(1) (March 1979): 110–40.

——*On Tycho's Island: Tycho Brahe and His Assistants, 1570–1601* (Cambridge: Cambridge University Press, 2000).

Cicero, *De Divinatione* (trans. W.A. Falconer; Cambridge, MA and London: Harvard University Press, 1929).

——*Republic* (trans. C.W. Keyes; Cambridge, MA, and London: Harvard University Press, 1927).

Clark, Stuart, *The Sun Kings: The Unexpected Tragedy of Richard Carrington and the Tale of How Modern Astronomy Began* (Princeton and Oxford: Princeton University Press, 2007).

Clarke, Desmond, *Descartes: A Biography* (Cambridge: Cambridge University Press, 2006).

Clucas, Stephen (ed.), *John Dee: Interdisciplinary Studies in English Renaissance Thought* (Dordrecht: Springer, 2006).

Clulee, Nicholas H., *John Dee's Natural Philosophy: Between Science and Religion* (London: Routledge, 1989).

Colish, Marcia L., *Medieval Foundations of the Western Intellectual Tradition* (New Haven and London: Yale University Press, 1998).

Comte, Auguste, *System of Positive Polity: or, Treatise on sociology, instituting the religion of humanity* (4 Vols; trans. John Henry Bridges; London: Longmans, 1875 [Paris 1851–4]).

Coopland, G.W., *Nicole Oresme and the Astrologers: A Study of his De Divinacions* (Liverpool: Liverpool University Press, 1952).

Copernicus, Nicolaus, *On the Revolutions of the Heavenly Spheres* (trans. Charles Glenn Wallis; Amherst, NY: Prometheus Books, 1995).

Corbin, Henri, *Mundus Imaginalis, or the Imaginary and the Imaginal*, 1964; http://www. hermetic.com/bey/mundus_imaginalis.htm.

Cornish, Alison, *Reading Dante's Stars* (New Haven and London: Yale University Press, 2000).

Coulston, Charles (ed.), *Dictionary of Scientific Biography* (14 Vols; New York: Charles Scribners and Sons, 1970–6).

Cowling. T.G., *Isaac Newton and Astrology*, Eighteenth Selig Brodetsky Memorial Lecture (Leeds: Leeds University Press, 1977).

Crabtree, Adam, *From Mesmer to Freud: Magnetic Sleep and the Roots of Psychological Healing* (London: Yale University Press, 1993).

Craig, W.J., *The Oxford Shakespeare* (Oxford: Oxford University Press, 1914).

Cranston, Sylvia, *The Extraordinary Life and Influence of Helena Blavatsky* (New York: Jeremy Tarcher/Putnam, 1993).

Culpeper, Nicholas, *Black Munday turn'd white* (London, 1652).

——*Catastrophe Magnatum* (London, 1652).

——*Astrological Judgment of Diseases from the Decumbiture of the Sick* (Tempe, AZ: American Federation of Astrologers, 1959).

Culver, Roger B. and Philip A. Ianna, *Astrology: True or False? A Scientific Evaluation*, rev. edn (Buffalo, NY, Prometheus Books, 1988).

Cumbey, Constance E., *The Hidden Dangers of the Rainbow: The New Age Movement and Our Coming Age of Barbarism* (Shreveport, LA: Huntingdon House, 1983).

Currivan, Jude, 'Walking between Worlds – Cosmology embodied in the landscape of Neolithic and Early Bronze Age Britain', PhD thesis, University of Reading, 2003.

Curry Patrick, 'Research on the Mars effect', *Zetetic Scholar* 9 (Feb/March 1982): 34–52.

——(ed.), *Astrology, Science and Society* (Woodbridge, Suffolk: Boydell Press, 1987).

——*Prophecy and Power: Astrology in Early Modern England* (Oxford: Polity Press, 1989).

——'Astrology in Early Modern England: The Making of a Vulgar Discipline' in Pumfrey, Stephen, Paolo L. Rossi and Maurice Slawinski, *Science, Culture and Popular Belief in Renaissance Europe* (Manchester: Manchester University Press, 1991), pp. 274–91.

——*A Confusion of Prophets: Victorian and Edwardian Astrology* (London: Collins and Brown, 1992).

——'Astrology: From Pagan to Postmodern?' *The Astrological Journal* 36(1) (January/February 1994): 69–75.

——'Astrology' in Boyd, Kelly (ed.), *Encyclopedia of Historians and Historical Writing* (London: Fitzroy Dearborn, 1999), pp. 55–7.

Curth, Louise Hill, *English Almanacs, Astrology and Popular Medicine, 1550–1700* (London: Palgrave MacMillan, 2008).

Danielson, Dennis Richard, *The First Copernican: Georg Joachim Rheticus and the Rise of the Copernican Revolution* (New York: Walker and Company, 2006).

Dante Alighieri, *The Divine Comedy* (3 Vols; trans. Mark Musa; Harmondsworth, Middlesex: Penguin, 1971).

——*The Convivio* (trans. Richard Lansing; 1998); http://dante.ilt.columbia.edu/books/convivi/index.html.

Davies, Owen, 'Newspapers and the Popular Belief in Witchcraft and Magic in the Modern Period', *The Journal of British Studies* 37(2) (April 1998): 139–65.

——'Witchcraft: The Spell That Didn't Break', *History Today* (August 1999): xx.

——*Witchcraft, Magic and Culture 1736–1951* (Manchester: Manchester University Press, 1999).

Dawkins, Richard, *Unweaving the Rainbow* (London: Penguin, 1998).

Drake, Stillman, *Galileo* (Oxford and New York: Oxford University Press, 1980).

Deacon, Richard, *John Dee: Scientist, Geographer, Astrologer and Secret Agent to Elizabeth I* (London: Frederick Muller, 1978).

Dean, G., 'Attribution: A Pervasive New Artefact in the Gauquelin Data', *Astrology under Scrutiny* 13(1 and 2) (2000): 1–72.

Dean, Geoffrey and Arthur Mather *Recent Advances in Natal Astrology: a Critical Review 1900–1976* (Subiaco, Australia: Analogic, 1977).

——'A Reassessment of Jung's Astrological Experiment', *Correlation* 14(2) (Northern Winter 1995): 12–22.

Dean, Geoffrey and Peter Loptson, 'Discourse for Key Topic 2: Some Philosophical Problems of Astrology', *Correlation* 14(2) (Northern Winter 1995/6): 32–44.

Debus, Allen G., *The English Paracelsians* (New York: Franklin Watts Inc., 1966).

Dee, John, *The Hieroglyphic Monad* (London: John M. Watkins, 1947).

——*The Mathematicall Praeface to the Elements of Geometrie of Euclid of Megara* (New York: Science History Publications, 1975).

——*The Rosie Crucian Secrets: Their Excellent Method of making Medicines of Metals also their Lawes and Mysteries* (Wellingborough: Aquarian Press, 1985).

Delaney, James G. and Howard B. Woodyard, 'Effects of Reading an Astrological Description on Responding to a Personality Inventory', *Psychological Reports* 34 (1974): 1214.

Descartes, René, *Discourse on Method and the Meditations* (trans. F.E. Sutcliffe; Harmondsworth, Middlesex: Penguin, 1968).

Dijkstra, Bram, *Idols of Perversity: Fantasies of Feminine Evil in Fin-de-Siecle Culture* (Oxford: Oxford University Press, 1986).

Dixon, C. Scott, 'Popular Astrology and Lutheran Propaganda in Reformation Germany', *History* (1999): 404–18.

Dobbs, Betty Jo Teeter, *The Foundations of Newton's Alchemy, or the Hunting of the Greene Lyon* (Cambridge: Cambridge University Press, 1975).

——*The Janus Faces of Genius: The role of alchemy in Newton's thought* (Cambridge: Cambridge University Press, 1991).

Dryden, John, *An Evening's Love: or, The Mock Astrologer* in *The Works of John Dryden* (Berkeley: University of California Press, 1970).

Duhem, P., *To Save the Phenomena: An Essay on the Idea of Physical Theory from Plato to Galileo* (trans. E. Donald and C. Maschler; Chicago: Chicago University Press, 1969).

Durkheim, Emile, *The Elementary Forms of Religious Life* (trans. Karen E. Fields; New York: Free Press, 1995 [1st edn, *Les Formes élémentaires de la vie religieuse*, Paris: F. Alcan, 1912]).

Eade, J.C., *The Forgotten Sky: A Guide to Astrology in English Literature* (Oxford: Clarendon Press, 1984).

Eagleton, Terry, *Ideology: An Introduction* (London: Verso, 1991).

—*The Idea of Culture* (Oxford: Blackwell, 2000).

Easton, Stewart C., *Roger Bacon and his Search for a Universal Science* (New York: Columbia Univesity Press, 1952).

Eastwood, Bruce S., *The Revival of Planetary Astronomy in Carolingian and Post-Carolingian Europe* (Aldershot: Ashgate, 2002).

——*Ordering the Heavens: Roman Astronomy and Cosmology in the Carolingian Renaissance* (Leiden: Brill, 2007).

Eco, Umberto, 'Dreaming of the Middle Ages' in *Faith in Fakes: Travels in Hypereality* (London: Minerva, 1995), pp. 61–85.

——'Travels in Hypereality' in *Faith in Fakes: Travels in Hypereality* (London: Minerva, 1995), pp. 1–58.

Eddington, Arthur, *The Expanding Universe* (Harmondsworth, Middlesex: Penguin, 1940).

Einhard, 'The Life of Charlemagne' in Einhard and Notker the Stammerer, *Two Lives of Charlemagne* (trans. Lewis Thorpe; Harmondsworth, Middlesex: Penguin, 1969), pp. 49–90.

Ehman, Esther, *Madame du Chatelet* (Leamington Spa: Berg, 1986).

Ellard, Peter, *The Sacred Cosmos: Theological, Philosophical, and Scientific Conversations in the Twelfth-Century School of Chartres* (Scranton and London: University of Scranton Press, 2007).

Epstein, Meira B., *The Correspondence between the Rabbis of Southern France and Maimonides about Astrology* (Reston, VA: ARHAT Publications, 1998).

Epstein, Perle, *Kabbalah: The Way of the Jewish Mystic* (London: Shambhala, 2001).

Ernst, Germana, 'The Sky in a Room: Campanella's *Apologeticus* in Defence of the Pamphlet *De siderali fato vitando*', *Culture and Cosmos* 6(1) (Spring/Summer 2002): 3–10.

——'Astrology and Prophecy in Campanella and Galileo' in Campion, Nicholas and Nick Kollerstrom, *Galileo's Astrology* (Bristol: Cinnabar Books 2004)/*Culture and Cosmos* 7(1) (Spring/Summer 2003): 21–36.

Ertel, Suitbert, 'Publications of Michel Gauquelin', *Correlation* 11(1) (June 1991): 12–23.

——'Gauquelin's planetary effects – made up by superstitious parents? On Geoffrey Dean's erroneous grand notion', *Astrology under Scrutiny* 13(2) (2000): 73–84.

Ertel, Suitbert and Kenneth Irving *The Tenacious Mars Effect* (London: Urania Trust, 1996).

Etherington, John, 'Written in Blood', *Apollon* 2 (1999): 61–5.

Everard, John, *The Corpus Hermeticum; The Divine Pymander in XVII books* (*The Second Book,*

Poemanders, London 1650, trans. John Everard from Ficino's Latin translation); www.levity. com/alchemy/corpherm.html.

Eysenck, Hans and David Nias, *Astrology: Science or Superstition?* (London: Pelican, 1982).

Faivre, Antoine, *Theosophy, Imagination, Tradition: Studies in Western Esotericism* (Albany: State University of New York Press, 2000).

Fanger, Claire, *Conjuring Spirits: Texts and Traditions of Medieval Ritual Magic* (Stroud: Sutton Publishing, 1998).

Farnell Kim, *The Astral Tramp: A Biography of Sepharial* (London: Ascella Publications, 1998).

——*Flirting with the Zodiac* (Bournemouth: The Wessex Astrologer, 2007).

Farrar, Janet and Stewart Farrar, *The Witches Way: Principles, Rituals and Beliefs of Modern Wichcraft* (London: Robert Hale, 1984).

Farrell, Maureen, *William Whiston* (New York: Arno Press, 1981).

Favaro, Antonio, 'Galileo, Astrologer' trans. Julianne Evans, in Campion, Nicholas and Nick Kollerstrom, *Galileo's Astrology*, (Bristol: Cinnabar Books, 2004)/*Culture and Cosmos* 7(1) (Spring/Summer 2003): 9–19.

Feher, Shoshanah, 'Who Holds the Cards? Women and New Age Astrology' in Lewis, James R. and J. Gordon Melton, *Perspectives on the New Age* (Albany: State University of New York Press, 1992), pp. 179–88.

Fenton, Edward (ed.), *The Diaries of John Dee* (Charlbury, Oxfordshire: Day Books, 1998).

Fererabend, Paul, 'The Strange Case of Astrology' in Grim, Patrick (ed.), *Philosophy of Science and the Occult* (New York: SUNY Press, 1990), pp. 23–7.

Fichten, Catherine S. and Betty Sunerton, 'Popular Horoscopes and the Barnum Effect', *The Journal of Psychology*, 114 (1983): 123–34.

Ficino, Marsilio, *The Book of Life* (trans. Charles Boer; Irving, TX: Spring Publications, 1980).

——*Three Books on Life*, ed. Kaske, Carole C. and John R. Clark, *Ficino, Three Books on Life* (Center for Medieval and Early Renaissance Studies, Binghamton: State University of New York at Binghamton, 1989).

——'The Book of the Sun (De Sole)', trans. Cornelius Geoffrey, Darby Costello, Graeme Tobyn, Angela Voss & Vernon Wells, *Sphinx: A Journal for Archetypal Psychology and the Arts* 6 (1994): 123–48; http://www.users.globalnet.co.uk/~alfar2/ficino.htm.

Field, Judith, 'Astrology in Kepler's Cosmology' in Curry, Patrick, *Astrology, Science and Society* (Woodbridge, Suffolk: Polity Press, 1987), pp. 143–70

——*Kepler's Geometrical Cosmology* (London: Athlone, 1988).

Field, J.V., 'A Lutheran Astrologer: Johannes Kepler', *Archive for History of Exact Sciences* 31(3) (1984): 189–272.

Flanagan, Kieran, *The Enchantment of Sociology: A Study of Theology and Culture* (London: MacMillan, 1999).

Flint, Valerie, *The Growth of Magic in Early Medieval Europe* (Oxford: Clarendon Press, 1992).

Force, James E., *William Whiston: Honest Newtonian* (Cambridge: Cambridge University Press, 2002).

Forrest, Steven, *The Night Speaks: A Meditation on the Astrological Worldview* (San Diego: ACS, 1993).

Fowler, Alastair, *Spenser and the Numbers of Time* (London: Routledge and Kegan Paul, 1964).

Frank, Roslyn M., 'Hunting the European Sky Bears: When Bears Ruled the Earth and Guarded the Gate of Heaven' in Koleva, Vesselina and Dmiter Kolev (eds), *Astronomical Traditions in Past Cultures*, Proceedings of the First Annual General Meeting of the European Society for Astronomy in Culture, Smolyan, Bulgaria, 31 August–2 September 1992 (Sofia: Institute of Astronomy, Bulgarian Academy of Sciences and National Astrononical Observatory, Tozhen), pp. 116–42.

——'Hunting the European Sky Bears: Hercules Meets Harzkume', Esteban, César and Juan Antonio Belmonte (eds), *Astronomy and Cultural Diversity: proceedings of the 1999 Oxford VI Conference on Archaeoastronomy and Astronomy in Culture* (Tenerife, 2000), pp. 169–75.

——'Hunting the European Sky Bears: A Proto-European Vision Quest to the End of the Earth' in Fountain, John W. and Rolf M. Sinclair (eds), *Current Studies in Archaeoastronomy: Conversations Across Time and Space* (Durham, NC: Carolina Academic Press, 2005), pp. 455–74.

French, Peter J., *John Dee: The World of an Elizabethan Magus* (London: Routledge and Kegan Paul, 1972).

Freud, Sigmund, 'Psychoanalysis and Telepathy', 1921, in Strachey, James (trans.), *The Complete Psychological Works of Sigmund Freud*, Vol. XVIII (London: Hogarth, 1955), pp. 177–94.

Gage, John, 'J.M.W. Turner and Solar Myth' in Bullen, J.B. (ed.), *The Sun is God: Painting, Literature and Mythology in the Nineteenth Century* (Oxford: Oxford University Press, 1989), pp. 39–48.

Galilei, Galileo, *Dialogue concerning the Two Chief World Systems*, 2nd edn (trans. Stillman Drake; Berkeley: University of California Press, 1967).

——*Siderius Nuncius, or The Sidereal Messenger* (trans. A.V. Helden; Chicago: University of Chicago Press, 1989).

Gardner, Gerald, *Witchcraft Today: Secrets of the Witch Cult Revealed* (London: Arrow, 1975).

Garin, Eugenio, *Astrology in the Renaissance: The Zodiac of Life* (London and Boston: Routledge, 1976).

Garrett, Clarke, 'Swedenborg and the Mystical Enlightenment in Late Eighteenth Century England', *Journal of the History of Ideas* 45 (1984): 67–81.

Gaskoin, Charles, *Alcuin: His Life and his Work* (London: C.J. Clay & Sons, 1904).

Gauquelin, Michel, *Dreams and Illusions of Astrology* (Buffalo, NY: Prometheus Books, 1969).

——*Cosmic Influences on Human Behaviour* (London: Garnstone Press, 1974).

——*The Cosmic Clocks* (San Diego: Astro-Computing Services, 1988).

——*Planetary Heredity* (San Diego: Astro-Computing Services, 1988).

——*Written in the Stars* (Wellingborough, Northamptonshire: Aquarian Press, 1988).

——*Neo-Astrology: A Copernican Revolution* (London: Penguin, 1991).

——*Astrology and Science* (London: Peter Davies, 1999).

Geneva, Ann, *Astrology and the Seventeenth Century Mind: William Lilly and the Language of the Stars* (Manchester and New York: Manchester University Press, 1995).

Genuth, Sara Schechner, 'Comets, Teleology, and the Relationship of Chemistry to Cosmology in Newton's Thought', *Annali dell'Istituto e Museo di Storia della Scienza di Firenze* 10 (part 2) (1985): 31–65.

——*Comets, Popular Culture and the Birth of Modern Cosmology* (Princeton: Princeton University Press, 1997).

Geoffrey of Monmouth, *History of the Kings of Britain* (trans. Lewis Thorpe; Harmondsworth, Middlesex: Penguin, 1965).

——*The Vita Merlini* (trans. John Jay Parry; Bibliobazaar, 2008).

Geoffrey of Tours, *The History of the Franks* (trans. Lewis Thorpe; London: Penguin, 1974).

George, Demetra, 'Manuel I Komnenos and Michael Glycas: A Twelfth-Century Defence and Refutation of Astrology', *Culture and Cosmos* 5(1) (Spring/Summer 2001): 348, 5(2) (Autumn/Winter 2001): 23–51, 6(1) (Spring/Summer 2002): 23–43.

Gibbons, G.J. *Spirituality and the Occult from the Renaissance to the Modern Age* (London: Routledge, 2001).

Gilbert, R.A., *The Golden Dawn, Twilight of the Magicians: The Rise and Fall of a Magical Order* (Wellingborough: Aquarian Press, 1983).

——(ed.), *Hermetic Papers of A.E. Waite: The Unknown Writings of a Modern Mystic* (Wellingborough: Aquarian Press, 1987).

——*Revelations of the Golden Dawn: The Rise and Fall of a Magical Order* (London: Quantum, 1997).

Gill, Robin, *Churchgoing and Christian Ethics* (Cambridge: Cambridge University Press, 1999).

Gill, Robin, G. Kirk Hadaway and Penny Long Marler, 'Is Religious Belief Declining in Britain?', *Journal for the Scientific Study of Religion* 37(3) (1998): 507–16.

Gillispie, C. C., *Pierre Simon Laplace 1749–1827: A Life in Exact Science* (Princeton: Princeton University Press, 1997).

Gingerich, Owen, 'The role of Erasmus Reinhold and the Prutenic Tables in the Dissemination of Copernican Theory', *Studia Copernicana* 6 (1973): 43–62.

Glick, Peter, Deborah Gottesman and Jeffrey Jolton, 'The Fault is Not In The Stars: Susceptibility of Skeptics and Believers in Astrology to the Barnum Effect', *Personality and Social Psychology Bulletin* 15(4) (December 1989): 572–83.

Glick, Peter and Mark Snyder, 'Self-Fulfilling Prophecy: the Psychology of Belief in Astrology', *The Humanist* 46(part 3) (May–June 1986): 20–5, 50.

Godwin, Joscelyn, *The Theosophical Enlightenment* (New York: State University of New York Press, 1994).

——*The Pagan Dream of the Renaissance* (York Beach, ME: Weiser, 2002).

Godwin, Joscelyn and Robert Fludd. *Hermetic Philosopher and Surveyor of Two Worlds* (London: Thames and Hudson, 1979).

Godwin, Joscelyn and Athanasius Kircher, *A Renaissance Man and the Quest for Lost Knowledge* (London: Thames and Hudson, 1979).

Goodman, Linda, *Linda Goodman's Sun Signs* (London: Pan Books, 1970).

Goodricke-Clarke, Nicholas, *The Occult Roots of Nazism: The Ariosophists of Austria and Germany 1890–1935* (Wellingborough, Northants: Aquarian Press, 1985).

——(ed.), *Paracelsus: Essential Readings* (Berkeley: North Atlantic Books, 1999).

——*Black Sun: Aryan Cults, Esoteric Nazism and the Politics of Identity* (New York and London: New York University Press, 2002).

Gossin, Pamela, *Thomas Hardy's Novel Universe: Astronomy, Cosmology, and Gender in the Post-Darwinian World* (Aldershot: Ashgate, 2007).

Grafton, Anthony, *Cardano's Cosmos: The Worlds and Works of a Renaissance Astrologer* (Cambridge and London: Harvard University Press, 1999).

Gramsci, Antonio, *Selections from the Prison Notebooks* (New York: PLACE International Publishers, 1971).

Grant, Edward, *Planets, Stars and Orbs: The Medieval Cosmos 1200–1687* (Cambridge: Cambridge University Press, 1996).

Greene, Liz, *Saturn: A New Look at an Old Devil* (Wellingborough: Aquarian Press, 1976).

——*Relating: An Astrological Guide To Living With Others On A Small Planet* (London: Coventure, 1977).

——'Astrologers' Agendas', paper delivered at the Astrological Association of Great Britain conference, Staverton Park, 19–22 September 2008.

Greenwood, Susan, *Magic, Witchcraft and the Otherworld: An Anthropology* (Oxford: Berg, 2000).

Gunn, Joshua, *Modern Occult Rhetoric* (Tuscaloosa: University of Alabama Press, 2003).

Hahn, R., *Pierre Simon Laplace 1749–1827: A Determined Scientist* (Cambridge, MA: Harvard University Press, 2005).

Hall, A. Rupert, *Henry More: Magic, Religion and Experiment* (Oxford: Basil Blackwell, 1990).

Halliday, F.E., *Shakespeare in his Age* (London: Duckworth, 1956).

Hamilton, Margaret M., 'Incorporation of Astrology-Based Personality Information into Long-Term Self-Concept', *Journal of Social Behaviour and Personality* 10(3) (1995): 707–18.

——'Who Believes in Astrology? Effect of Favorableness of Astrologically Derived Personality Descriptions on Acceptance of Astrology', *Personality and Individual Differences* 31 (2001): 895–902.

Hanegraaff, Wouter J., *New Age Religion and Western Culture: Esotericism in the Mirror of Secular Thought* (Leiden and New York: E.J. Brill, 1996).

Harris, Pat, 'Applications of Astrology to Health Psychology: Astrological and Psychological Factors and Fertility Treatment Outcome', PhD thesis, University of Southampton, 2005.

Hartmann, Franz, *Jacob Boehme: Life and Doctrines* (London: Kegan, Paul, Trench and Tubner, 1891).

Harvey, David Allen, *Beyond Enlightenment: Occultism and Politics in Modern France* (DeKalb: Northern Illinois University Press, 2005).

Harvey, William, *The Circulation of the Blood and other Writings* (trans. Kenneth Franklin; North Clarendon: Everyman's Library, 1993).

Haskins, Charles, *The Renaissance of the Twelfth Century* (Cambridge, MA.: Harvard University Press, 1927).

Hawkes, Jacquetta, 'God in the Machine', *Antiquity* 41 (1967): 74–80.

Hawkins, Gerald, *Stonehenge Decoded* (New York: Dorset Press, 1965).

Head, Raymond, 'Astrology, Modernism and Holst's "The Planets"', *Astrology Quarterly* 65(1) (Winter 1994–5): 40–54.

Headley, John M., *Tommaso Campanella and the Transformation of the World* (Princeton: Princeton University Press, 1997).

Heelas, Paul, *The New Age Movement* (Oxford: Blackwell, 1996).

Hegel, G.W.F., *The Philosophy of Right* (trans. T.M. Knox; London and Oxford: Clarendon Press, 1952).

——*Hegel's Philosophy of Mind* (trans. William Wallace; Oxford: Oxford University Press, 1971).

Heine, Elizabeth, 'W.B. Yeats: Poet and Astrologer', *Culture and Cosmos* 1(2) (Winter/Autumn 1997): 60–75.

Helden, Albert van, *The Invention of the Telescope* (Philadelphia: American Philosophical Society, 1977).

Henderson, John, *The Medieval World of Isidore of Seville: Truth from Words* (Cambridge: Cambridge University Press, 2007).

Henry, Holly, 'From Galactic Expanses to Earth: Virginia Woolf and Olaf Stapledon Envision New Worlds', paper delivered to the INSAP II conference, Malta, January 1999.

——*Virginia Woolf and the Discourse of Science: The Aesthetics of Astronomy* (Cambridge: Cambridge University Press, 2003).

Hillman, James, *Re-Visioning Psychology* (London: HarperCollins, 1975).

——*The Soul's Code: In search of Character and Calling* (London: Bantam Books, 1997).

Hiscock, Nigel, *The Wise Master Builder: Platonic Geometry in Plans of Medieval Abbeys and Cathedrals* (Aldershot: Ashgate, 2000).

Hitler, Adolf, *Hitler's Table Talk, 1941–1944: His Private Conversations* (trans. Norman Cameron and R.H. Stevens; 2nd edn introduced and with a new preface by H.R. Trevor-Roper; London: Weidenfeld and Nicolson, 1973).

Hoare, Philip, *England's Lost Eden: Adventures in a Victorian Utopia* (London: HarperCollins, 2005).

Hobbes, Thomas, *Leviathan, or the Matter, Forme, and Power of a Common-Wealth Ecclesiastical and Civil*, ed. C.B. MacPherson (Harmonsdworth, Middlesex: Penguin, 1968).

Holmyard, E.J., *Jābir ibn Hayyān* (London: John Bale, Sons & Danielson, 1923).

——*Alchemy* (Dover, NY: Harmondsworth, 1990 [1957]).

Hone, Margaret, *The Modern Textbook of Astrology* (London: L.N. Fowler, 4th edn reprinted 1973 [1951]).

Hoskin, Michael, *The Cambridge Concise History of Astronomy* (Cambridge: Cambridge University Press, 1999).

Howe, Ellic, *Urania's Children: The Strange World of the Astrologers* (London: William Kimber, 1967 (republished as *Astrology: A Recent History Including the untold Story of its Role in World War II*; New York: Walker and Company, 1968)).

——*The Magicians of the Golden Dawn: A Documentary History of a Magical Order 1887–1923* (Wellingborough: Aquarian Press, 1985).

Huffman, William H. (ed.), *Robert Fludd: Essential Writings* (London: Aquarian Press, 1992).

——*Robert Fludd* (Berkeley: North Atlantic Books, 2001).

Hufford, David, 'Traditions of Disbelief', *Talking Folklore* 1(part 3) (1987): 19–29.

Hughes, Ted, *Birthday Letters* (London: Faber and Faber, 1998).

Hume, David, *An Inquiry Concerning Human Understanding* (London: Penguin, 1969).

Hunter, Michael, 'Science and Astrology in Seventeenth Century England' in Curry, Patrick (ed.), *Astrology, Science and Society* (Woodbridge, Suffolk: Boydell Press, 1987), pp. 260–300.

Hunter, Michael and Annabel Gregory (eds), *An Astrological Diary of the Seventeenth Century: Samuel Jeake of Rye 1652–1699* (Oxford: Clarendon Press, 1988).

Hutton, Ronald, *The Pagan Religions of the Ancient British Isles: Their Nature and Legacy* (London and New York: BCA, 1991).

——*The Stations of the Sun: A History of the Ritual Year in Britain* (Oxford and New York: Oxford University Press, 1996).

——*The Triumph of the Moon: A History of Modern Pagan Witchcraft* (Oxford: Oxford University Press, 1999).

——*Witches, Druids and King Arthur: Studies in Paganism, Myth and Magic* (London: Hambledon Books, 2003).

——'Astral Magic: The Acceptable Face of Paganism' in Campion, Nicholas, Patrick Curry and Michael York (eds), *Astrology and the Academy*, papers from the inaugural conference of the Sophia Centre, Bath Spa University College, 13–14 June 2003 (Bristol: Cinnabar Books 2004), pp. 10–24.

Huysmans, J.K., *Against Nature* (trans. Robert Baldrick; Harmondsowrth, Middlesex: Penguin, 1959 [1884]).

Ibn-Ezra, Avraham, *The Beginning of Wisdom* (trans. Meira B. Epstein; Reston, VA: ARHAT Publications, 1998).

Ibn-Khaldun, *The Muqaddimah: An Introduction to History* (trans. Franz Rosenthal; London: Routledge and Kegan Paul, 1987 [1967]).

Isaacs, Harold R., *Scratches on Our Minds. American Images of China and India* (New York: John Day Company, 1958).

Isidore of Seville, *History of the Kings of the Goths, Vandals and Suevi* (Leiden: E.J. Brill, 1966).
——*The Etymologies* (trans. Stephen A. Barney, W.J. Lewis, J.A. Beach and Oliver Berghof; Cambridge: Cambridge University Press, 2007).
Izbicki, Thomas M. and Christopher M. Bellitto (eds), *Nicholas of Cusa and His Age: Intellect and Spirituality Essays. Dedicated to the Memory of F. Edward Cranz, Thomas P. McTighe and Charles Trinkaus* (Leiden: E.J. Brill, 2002).
Jacob, Margaret C., *The Newtonians and the English Revolution 1689–1720* (Brighton: Harvester, 1976).
——*The Radical Enlightenment: Pantheists, Freemasons and Republicans* (London: George Allen and Unwin, 1981).
——*Living the Enlightenment: Freemasonry and Politics in Eighteenth-Century Europe* (Oxford: Oxford University Press, 1991).
Jacobi, Jolande, *Paracelsus: Selected Writings* (Princeton: Princeton University Press, 1988).
Jacobi, Maximilian, 'Astrology', *The Catholic Encyclopedia.* (New York: Robert Appleton Company, 1907); http://www.newadvent.org/cathen/02018e.htm.
James, Edward W., 'On Dismissing Astrology and other Irrationalities' in Grim, Patrick (ed.), *Philosophy of Science and the Occult* (New York: SUNY Press, 1990), pp. 28–36.
Jones, Prudence, *A 'House' System from Viking Europe* (Cambridge: Fenris-Wolf, 1991).
——*Northern Myths of the Constellations* (Cambridge: Fenris-Wolf, 1991).
Jung, Carl, 'Foreword' in Wilhelm, Richard, *The I Ching or Book of Changes* (1951), 3rd edn (London: Routledge and Kegan Paul, 1968), pp. xxi–xxxix.
Jung, C.G., *The Archetypes and the Collective Unconscious*, Collected Works (trans. R.F.C. Hull; Princeton, NJ: Princeton University Press, 1959), Vol. 9, Part 1.
——'Flying Saucers: A Modern Myth of Things Seen in the Skies', *Civilisation in Transition*, Collected Works (trans. R.F.C. Hull; London: Routledge and Kegan Paul, 1959), Vol. 10, pp. 307–433.
——'The Sign of the Fishes' in *Aion*, Collected Works (trans. R.F.C. Hull; London: Routledge and Kegan Paul, 1959), Vol. 9, Part 2.
——'Synchronicity: An Acausal Connecting Principle', *The Structure and Dynamics of the Psyche*, The Collected Works (trans. R.F.C. Hull; London: Routledge and Kegan Paul, 1963), Vol. 8, pp. 417–531.
——*Memories, Dreams, Reflections* (London: Fontana, 1967).
——'Richard Wilhelm: In Memoriam' in *The Spirit in Man, Art, and Literature* (trans. R.F.C. Hull; London: Routledge and Kegan Paul, 1971), Vol.15, pp. 53–62.
Juste, David, 'The Catalogus Codicum Astrologorum Latinorum and the Bibliotheca Astrologica Numerica', Paper delivered at the Ancient Astrology Workshop, Warburg Institute, London, 16–17 February 2007.
Kandinsky, Wassily, *Concerning the Spiritual in Art* (trans. M.T.H. Sadler; New York: Dover Publications, 1977).
Kanitscheider, Bernulf, 'A Philosopher looks at Astrology', *Interdisciplinary Science Reviews* 16(3) (1991): 258–66.
Kant, Immanuel, *Dreams of a Spirit Seer* (trans. Emanuel F. Goerwitz; Bristol: Theommes Press, 1992 [1900]).
——*Critique of Practical Reason*, Great Books of the Western World 42 (London: Encyclopaedia Britannica, 1952).
——*Universal Natural History and Theory of the Heavens* (Ann Arbor: University of Michigan Press, 1969).

Kaplan, Aryeh, *Sefer Yetzirah: the Book of Creation in Theory and Practice* (York Beach, ME: Weiser Books, 1997).

Kepler, Johannes, 'On the More Certain Fundamentals of Astrology', Prague, 1601, trans. Mary Ann Rossi with notes by J. Bruce Brackenbridge; *Proceedings of the American Philosophical Society* 123(2) (1979).

——*Mysterium Cosmographicum: The Secret of the Universe* (trans. A.M. Duncan; New York: Abaris Books, 1981).

——*New Astronomy* (trans. W.H. Donahue; Cambridge: Cambridge University Press, 1991).

——'Epitome of Copernican Astronomy', Books 4 and 5 (trans. C.G. Wallace, in *Great Books of the Western World*, XVI; Chicago: Encyclopaedia Britannica), pp. 1005–10085, also Great Minds Series, Prometheus Books, Amberst NY, 1995.

——*The Harmony of the World* (trans. E.J. Aiton, A.M. Duncan and J.V. Field; Philadelphia: American Philosophical Society, 1997).

——'Johannes Kepler's *Tertius Interveniens*' (theses 64–9); trans Ken Negus; *Culture and Cosmos* 1(1) (Spring/Summer 1997): 51–4.

——*Harmonies of the World*, Book Five, ed. Stephen Hawking (London: Running Press, 2002).

——*Kepler's Astrology. The Baby, the Bath Water and the Third Man in the Middle: the First Complete English Translation of Tertius Interveniens and Other Astrological Writings* (trans. Ken Negus; Amherst, MA: Earth Heart Publications, 2008).

Keynes, John Maynard, 'Newton the Man' in Royal Society, *Newton Tercentenary Celebrations* (Cambridge: Cambridge University Press, 1947), pp. 27–41. Online at http://www-history.mcs.st-andrews.ac.uk/Extras/Keynes_Newton.html.

Kieckhefer, Richard, *Magic in the Middle Ages* (Cambridge: Cambridge University Press, 1989).

Kitson, Annabella (ed.), *History and Astrology: Clio and Urania Confer* (London: Unwin Paperbacks, 1989).

——'Some Varieties of Electional Astrology' in Kitson, Annabella (ed.), *History and Astrology: Clio and Urania Confer* (London: Unwin Paperbacks, 1989), pp. 171–99.

Kollerstrom, N., 'Kepler's Belief in Astrology' in Kitson, Annabella (ed.), *History and Astrology: Clio and Urania Confer* (London: Unwin Paperbacks, 1989), pp. 152–70.

Koran (trans. Abdallah Yousuf Ali, no date or place).

Koran (trans. N.J. Darwood; London: Pengun Books, 1990).

Koyré, Alexander, *The Astronomical Revolution: Copernicus, Kepler, Borelli* (trans. R.E.W. Maddison; Itaca, NY: Cornell University Press, 1973).

Kraai, Jesse, 'Rheticus' Heliocentric Providence', PhD thesis, University of Heidelberg, 2001.

——'Rheticus' Poem Concerning the Beer of Breslau and the Twelve Signs of the Zodiac', *Culture and Cosmos* 6(2) (Autumn/Winter 2002): 3–16.

Kristeller, Paul O., *The Philosophy of Marsilio Ficino* (Gloucester, MA: Peter Smith, 1964).

Kuhn, Thomas S., *The Copernican Revolution: Planetary Astronomy in the Development of Western Thought* (Cambridge, MA and London: Harvard University Press, 1957).

——*The Structure of Scientific Revolutions*, 2nd edn (Chicago: University of Chicago Press, 1970).

Kurze, Dietrich, 'Popular Astrology and Prophecy in the Fifteenth and Sixteenth centuries' in Zambelli, Paola, *'Astrologi hallucinati': Stars and the End of the World in Luther's Time* (Berlin and New York: Walter de Gruyter, 1986), pp. 173–93.

Laird, Edgar, 'Christine de Pizan and Controversy Concerning Star Study in the Court of Charles V', *Culture and Cosmos* 1(2) (Winter/Autumn 1997): 35–48.

——'Heaven and the Sphaera Mundi', *Culture & Cosmos* 4(1) (Spring/Summer 2000): 10–35.

Latour, Bruno, *We Have Never Been Modern* (Cambridge, MA: Harvard University Press, 2006 [1991]).

Lehman, Lee J., 'Tiptoeing through the Method: An Historical Review of Empiricism in Astrology, 1990–1991', *Astrological Journal* 36(1) (Jan/Feb. 1994): 60–8.

Lehner, Mark, *The Complete Pyramids* (London: Thames and Hudson, 1997).

LeMay, Richard, *Abu Ma'shar and Latin Aristotelianism* (Beirut: American University of Beirut, Oriental Series No. 38, 1962).

Leo, Alan, 'Introduction' in *Modern Astrology*, 1895, Vol 1. no 1, p. 1.

——'The Editor's Observatory', *Modern Astrology*, 8(3) (March 1911): 89–96, New Series.

——'The Age of Aquarius', *Modern Astrology* 8(7) (July 1911), New Series.

——*Esoteric Astrology: A Study in Human Nature* (London: Modern Astrology, 1913).

——'The Astrological Mind', *Modern Astrology* XI(6) (June 1914): 241–7.

——*How to Judge a Nativity* (London: Modern Astrology, 1922 [1903]).

——*The Art of Synthesis* (London: Modern Astrology, 1936 [1st edn *How to Judge a Nativity* pt. 2, 1904]), p. 2.

——*The Complete Dictionary of Astrology*, ed. Vivian Robson (Rochester, VT: Destiny Books, 1983 [c.1900]).

Levack, Brian P., *Renaissance Magic* (New York and London: Garland Publishing, 1992).

Lévi, Eliphas, *Transcendental Magic, its Doctrine and Ritual by Eliphas Lévi (Alphonse Louis Constant). A complete translation of 'Dogme et rituel de la haute magie,' with a biographical preface, by Arthur Edward Waite* (London: George Redway, 1896).

Lévi-Bruhl, Lucien, *How Natives Think* (Princeton: Princeton University Press, 1985).

Lilly, William, *Christian Astrology* (London, 1647, facsimile edition, London: Regulus Publishing, 1985).

——*William Lilly's History of His Life and Times from the Year 1602 to 1681* (London, 1715).

Lindberg, David C., *The Beginnings of Western Science: The European Scientific Tradition in Philosophical, Religious, and Institutional Context, 600 BC–AD 1450* (Chicago and London: University of Chicago Press, 1992).

Locke, John, *Essay Concerning Human Understanding*, ed. Peter Nidditch (Oxford: Oxford University Press, 1975).

Lovejoy, Arthur O., *The Great Chain of Being* (Cambridge, MA and London: Harvard University Press, 1936).

Lucie-Smith, Edward, *Symbolist Art* (London: Thames and Hudson, 1972).

Ludolphy, Ingetraut, 'Luther und die Astrologie' in Zambelli, Paola, *'Astrologi hallucinati': Stars and the End of the World in Luther's Time'* (Berlin and New York: Walter de Gruyter, 1986), pp. 101–7.

Luhrmann, Tanya, *Persuasions of the Witch's Craft: Ritual Magic in Contemporary England* (Cambridge, MA: Harvard University Press, 1989).

McCann, Maurice, 'The Secret of William Lilly's Prediction of the Fire of London', *The Astrological Journal* 32(1) (Jan/Feb 1990): 53–9.

McCluskey, Stephen C., *Astronomies and Cultures in Early Medieval Europe* (Cambridge: Cambridge University Press, 1998).

——'Astronomies and Cosmologies in the Latin West', *Proceedings of the SEAC Conference*, Granada, 8–12 September 2008, forthcoming, Astronomical Society of the Pacific, 2009.

McDannell, Colleen and Bernhard Lang, *Heaven: A History* (New Haven: Yale University Press, 1988).

McEvoy, James, *Robert Grosseteste* (Oxford: Oxford University Press, 2000).

McGillion, Frank, 'The Influence of Wilhelm Fliess' Cosmobiology on Sigmund Freud', *Culture and Cosmos* 2(1) (Spring/Summer 1998): 33–48.

McGillion, Frank and Pety de Vries-Ek, 'A Further Look at Jung's Astrological Experiment in the Context of the Theory of Synchronicity', *Correlation* 14(1) (Northern Summer 1995): 15–25.

McIntosh, Christopher, *Eliphas Lévi and the French Occult Revival* (New York: Samuel Weiser, 1972).

——*The Rosicrucians: The History and Mythology of an Occult Order* (Wellingborough: Crucible, 1980).

Macrobius, *Commentary on the Dream of Scipio* (trans. W.H. Stahl; New York: Columbia University Press, 1990 [1952]).

MacNeice, Louis, *Astrology* (London: Spring Books, 1994).

Magnus, Albertus, *The Book of Secrets of Albertus Magnus*, ed. Michael R. Best and Frank H. Brightman (Oxford, Clarendon Press, 1973).

Marenbon, John, *The Philosophy of Peter Abelard* (Cambridge: Cambridge University Press, 1999).

Masha'allah, *Book of Nativities* (trans. Robert Hand; Berkeley Springs: Golden Hind Press, 1994).

——*On Reception* (trans. Robert Hand; Reston, VA: ARHAT, 1998).

Maternus, Julius Firmicus, *Mathesis* (translated as *Ancient Astrology: Theory and Practice*, Jean Rhys Bram; Park Ridge, NJ: Noyes Press, 1975).

Mathews, Freya, *The Ecological Self* (Savage, MD: Barnes and Noble, 1991).

Matt, Daniel C., *Zohar: Annotated and Explained* (Woodstock, VT: SkyLights Paths Publishing Co., 2002).

Maxwell-Stuart, P.G. (ed.), *The Occult in Early Modern Europe* (London: MacMillan Press, 1999).

Melanchthon, Philip, 'Initia doctrinae physicae', book 2, in Maxwell-Stuart, P.G. (ed.), *The Occult in Early Modern Europe: a Documentary History* (Basingstoke: Macmillan Press Ltd, 1999), pp. 93–4.

Merkel, Ingrid and Allen G. Debus (eds), *Hermeticism and the Renaissance: Intellectual History and the Occult in Early Modern History* (London: Associated University Presses, 1988).

Mesmer, Franz Anton, *Mesmerism: Being the Translation of Mesmer's historic* Mémoire sur la découverte du Magnétisme Animal *to appear in English* (London: Macdonald, 1947 [1779]).

——'Physical-Medical Treatise on the Influence of the Planets' in Bloch, George, *Mesmerism: a Translation of the Scientific and Medical Writings of Franz Anton Mesmer* (Los Altos, CA: William Kauffman, 1980), pp. 1–22.

Miller, Henry, *The Colossus of Maroussi* (London: Minerva 1991 [1942]).

——'The Astrologer Seen Through the Eyes of a Friend' in Omarr, Sydney, *Answer in the Sky . . . almost: Confessions of an Astrologer* (Charlottsville, VA: Hampton Roads Publishing Company, 1995), pp. 20–4.

Miller, Jon D., 'Scientific Literacy: A Conceptual and Empirical Review', *Daedelus* 112(part 3) (1983): 29–48.

——'The Public Acceptance of Astrology and other Pseudo-science in the United States', paper presented to the 1992 annual meeting of the American Association for the Advancement of Science, 9 February 1992.

Mirandola, Giovanni Pico Della, *Oration on the Dignity of Man* (trans Robert A. Caponigri; Chicago: Gateway, 1959).

Moore, Thomas, *The Planets Within: the Astrological Psychology of Marsilio Ficino* (Great Barrington, MA: Lindisfarne Press, 1990).

Morin, J.B., *Astrologica Gallica*, Book Twenty-One (translated by Richard S. Baldwin as *The Morinus System of House Interpretation*; Washington DC: American Federation of Astrologers, 1974).

Morrall, John B., *Political Thought in the Medieval World* (Toronto: University of Toronto Press, 1980).

Müller, Max, 'Solar Myths', *The Nineteenth Century* (December 1885): 900–22.

Murdin, Paul, 'Representing the Moon', The Inspiration of Astronomical Phenomena: Proceedings of the fourth conference on the Inspiration of Astronomical Phenomena, Magdalen College, Oxford, England, 3–9 August 2003, special issue of *Culture and Cosmos* 8(1 and 2) (Spring/Summer–Autumn/Winter 2004): 247–70; www.CultureAndCosmos.com

Myers, Isabel Briggs and Peter B. Myers, *Gifts Differing: Understanding Personality Type* (Mountain View, CA: Davies-Black Publishing, 1980).

Naylor, R.H., 'What the Stars Foretell For The New Princess And A Few Hints On The Happenings Of This Week', *Sunday Express*, 24 August 1930, p. 11.

——'Were You Born in September?', *Sunday Express*, 31 August 1930, p. 7.

——'What is the Future of Astrology?', *Prediction* 1(4) (May 1936): 151, 157.

Nennius, *History of the Britons* (London: Dodo Press, 2007).

Newton, Isaac, *The Chronology of Ancient Kingdoms Amended* (London, 1728, facsimile edn, London, 1988).

——*The Principia* (Amherst, NY: Prometheus Books, 1995).

Noll, Richard, *The Jung Cult: Origins of a Charismatic Movement* (Princeton: Princeton University Press, 1994).

North, John D., 'Thomas Harriot and the First Telescopic Observations of Sunspots' in Shirley, John W. (ed.), *Thomas Harriot: Renaissance Scientist* (Oxford: Clarendon Press, 1974), pp. 129–65.

North, J.D., *Horoscopes and History* (Warburg Institute Surveys and Texts, XIII; London: The Warburg Institute, 1986).

——*Chaucer's Universe* (Oxford: Clarendon Press, 1988).

——'Astrology and the Fortune of Churches' in *Stars, Minds and Fate: Essays in Ancient and Medieval Cosmology* (London: The Hambledon Press, 1989), pp. 59–89.

——*Stars, Minds and Fate: Essays in Ancient and Medieval Cosmology* (London, The Hambledon Press, 1989).

North, John, *Richard of Wallingford* (Oxford: Clarendon Press, 1989 [1976]).

——*The Universal Frame: Historical Essays in Astronomy, Natural Philosophy and Scientific Method* (London: The Hambledon Press, 1989).

——*Chaucer's Cosmology* in Hetherington, Norris (ed.), *Encyclopaedia of Cosmology* (New York and London: Garland Publishing, 1993), pp. 58–62.

——*The Fontana History of Astronomy and Cosmology* (London: Fontana, 1994).

——*The Ambassadors' Secret: Holbein and the World of the Renaissance* (London and New York: Hambledon and London, 2002).

——*God's Clockmaker: Richard of Wallingford and the Invention of Time* (London: London and Hambledon, 2005).

Notker the Stammerer, 'Charlemagne' in *Two Lives of Charlemagne* (trans. Lewis Thorpe; Harmondsworth, Middlesex: Penguin, 1969), pp. 93–172.

Olcott, Henry, 'Inaugural Address of the President-Founder of the Theosophical Society', delivered at Mott Memorial Hall in the City of New York, at the first regular meeting of the society, 17 November 1875, *Adyar Pamphlets No. 50*, Theosophical Society of America, 1975; http://www.theosophical.org/resources/library/olcott-centenary/Ts?Pamphlets?Inaugural-Address.htm (accessed 14 July 2008).

Omarr, Sydney, *My World of Astrology* (Hollywood, CA.: Wilshire Book Company, 1965).

——*Answer in the Sky . . . almost: Confessions of an Astrologer* (Charlottsville, VA: Hampton Roads Publishing Company, 1995).

Orr, M.A., *Dante and the Early Astronomers* (Port Washington: Kennikat Press, 1913).

Osler, Margaret L., (ed.), *Rethinking the Scientific Revolution* (Cambridge: Cambridge University Press, 2000).

Owen, Alex, *The Darkened Room: Women, Power and Spiritualism in Late Victorian England* (Chicago: University of Chicago Press, 1989).

——*The Place of Enchantment: British Occultism and the Culture of the Modern* (Chicago: University of Chicago Press, 2004).

Paracelsus, *The Hermetic and Alchemical Writings of Aureolus Philippus Theophrastus Bombast*, ed. A.E. Waite (2 Vols; Largs, Scotland: Banton Press, 1990).

Park, Robert, *Voodoo Science: The Road from Foolishness to Fraud* (Oxford: Oxford University Press, 2000).

Parker, Derek, *Familiar to All: William Lilly and Astrology in the Seventeenth Century* (London: Jonathan Cape, 1975).

Partridge, John, *Mikropanastron, or an Astrological Vade Mecum, briefly Teaching the whole Art of Astrology – viz., Questions, Nativities, with all its parts, and the whole Doctrine of Elections never so comprised nor compiled before, &c* (London: William Bromwich: 1679).

Pepys, Samuel, *The Diary of Samuel Pepys* (6 Vols; London: HarperCollins, 2000).

Perkins, Maureen, *Visions of the Future: Almanacs, Time, and Cultural Change* (Oxford: Clarendon Press, 1996).

——*The Reform of Time: Magic and Modernity* (London: Pluto Press, 2001).

Phillipson, Garry and Peter Case, 'The Hidden Language of Modern Management Science: Astrology, Alchemy and the Myers-Briggs Type Indicator', *Culture and Cosmos* 5(2) (Autumn/Winter 2001): 53–72.

Pingree, David, 'Legacies in Astronomy and Celestial Omens' in Dalley, Stephanie (ed.), *The Legacy of Mesopotamia* (Oxford: Clarendon Press, 1998), pp. 125–37.

——*From Astral Omens to Astrology: From Babylon to Bikaner* (Rome: Istituto Italiano Per L'Africa E L'Oriente, 1997).

Plato, *Phaedo* (trans. H.N. Fowler; Cambridge, MA and London: Harvard University Press, 1914).

——*Timaeus* (trans. R.G. Bury; Cambridge, MA and London: Harvard University Press, 1931).

——*Republic* (2 Vols; trans. Paul Shorey; Cambridge, MA and London: Harvard University Press: 1937).

Pliny, *Natural History* (trans H. Rackham; Cambridge, MA and London: Harvard University Press, 1929), Vol. 1, Book II.

Pope, Alexander, *The Complete Poetical Works of Alexander Pope* (Boston and New York: Houghton, Mifflin and Company, 1902).

Popper, Karl, *The Open Society and its Enemies* (2 Vols; London and New York: Routledge, 1957 [1945]).

——*The Logic of Scientific Discovery*, revised (London: Hutchinson, 1972).

——*The Poverty of Historicism* (London and New York: Routledge, 1986).

Poppi, Antonio, 'On Trial for Astral Fatalism: Galileo Faces the Inquisition' in Campion,

Nicholas and Nick Kollerstrom, *Galileo's Astrology* (Bristol: Cinnabar Books 2004)/*Culture and Cosmos* 7(1) (Spring/Summer 2003): 49–58.

Porter, Roy, *Enlightenment: Britain and the Creation of the Modern World* (London: Penguin, 2000).

Poss, Richard L., 'Stars and Spirituality in the Cosmology of Dante's *Commedia*', *Culture and Cosmos* 5(1) (Spring/Summer 2001): 49–56.

Ptolemy, Claudius, 'Centiloquium' in Partridge, John, *Mikropanastron, or an Astrological Vade Mecum, briefly Teaching the whole Art of Astrology – viz., Questions, Nativities, with all its parts, and the whole Doctrine of Elections never so comprised nor compiled before, &c.* (London: William Bromwich: 1679), pp. 305–21.

——*Tetrabiblos* (trans. F.E. Robbins; Cambridge, MA and London: Harvard University Press, 1940).

Pumfrey, Stephen, Paolo L. Rossi and Maurice Slawinski, *Science, Culture and Popular Belief in Renaissance Europe* (Manchester: Manchester University Press, 1991).

Quetelet, M.A., *A Treatise on Man and the Development of His faculties* (Paris, 1835, trans. R.Knox; Edinburgh, 1842, reprint New York, 1966).

Quigley, Joan, *'What Does Joan Say?' My Seven Years as White House Astrologer to Nancy and Ronald Reagan* (New York: Birch Lane Press, 1990).

Rabelais, Francis, *Pantagruel's Prognostication*, reprinted from the translation of c.1660; Luttrell Reprints, No. 3 (Oxford: Basil Blackwell, 1947).

Rabin, Sheila J., 'Kepler's Attitude Toward Pico and the Anti-Astrology Polemic', *Renaissance Quarterly* 50(3) (Autumn 1997): 750–70.

Ramesey, William, *Astrology Restaurata or Astrology Restored: Being an Introduction to the General and Chief Part of the Language of the Stars* (London, 1653).

Raphael, Astrologer of the Nineteenth Century or the Master Key of Futurity (London: William Charlton Wright, c.1825).

Rendell, Ruth, *Lake of Darkness* (London: Arrow Books, 1981).

——*The Killing Doll* (London: Panther Books, 1984).

——*Thirteen Steps Down* (London: Hutchinson, 2004).

Reston, James, *Galileo* (London: Cassell, 1994).

Richardson, J. Michael, *Astrological Symbolism in Spenser's The Shepheadres Calendar: the cultural background of a literary text* (Lampeter: The Edwin Mellen Press, 1989).

Ridolfi, Roberto, *The Life of Girolamo Savonarola* (New York: Knopf, 1959).

Robinson, F.N. (ed.), *The Works of Geoffrey Chaucer* (London: Oxford University Press, 1966).

Roos, Anna Marie, 'Israel Hiebner's Astrological Amulets and the English Sigil War', *Culture and Cosmos* 6(2) (Autumn/Winter 2002): 17–43.

Rousseau, Claudia, 'Cosimo de Medici and Astrology: The Symbolism of Prophecy', PhD thesis, Columbia University, 1983.

——'An Astrological Prognostication to Duke Cosimo I de Medici of Florence', *Culture and Cosmos* 3(2) (Autumn/Winter 1999): 31–59.

Rudhyar, Dane, *The Astrology of Personality* (Garden City, NY: Doubleday, 1970 [1936]).

——*The Planetarizsation of Consciousness* (New York: Aurora Press, 1977 [1970]).

Ruperti, Alexander, *Meaning of Humanistic Astrology*, http://www.stand.cz/astrologie/czech/texty/rez-ru-a/rez-ru-a.htm (accessed 4 October 2002).

Schaffer, Simon, 'Newton's Comets and the Transformation of Astrology' in Curry, Patrick (ed.), *Astrology, Science and Society* (Woodbridge, Suffolk: Boydell Press, 1987), pp. 219–43.

——'Newtonianism' in Olby, R.C., G.N. Cantor, J.R.R. Christie and M.J.S Hodge, *Companion to the History of Modern Science* (London and New York: Routledge, 1996), pp. 610–26.

Schoener, Johannes, *Opusculum Astrologicum* (trans. Robert Hand; Project Hindsight Latin Track, Vol. IV; Berkeley Springs: Golden Hind Press, 1994).

——*Three Books on the Judgment of Nativities* (trans. Robert Hand; Reston, VA: ARHAT, 2001).

Scholem, Gershom (ed.), *Zohar: The Book of Splendor* (New York: Schocken Books, 1963).

——*Origins of the Kabbalah* (trans. Allan Arkush; Princeton: Princeton University Press, 1987).

Scott, Walter (trans.), *Hermetica: The Ancient Greek and Latin Writings which contain Religious or Philosophic Teachings ascribed to Hermes Trismegistus* (4 Vols; Boulder: Shambal, 1982).

Seznec, Jean, *The Survival of the Pagan Gods: The Mythological Tradition and its Place in Renaissance Humanism and Art* (Princeton: Princeton University Press, 1953).

Shea, W.R., *Galileo's Intellectual Revolution* (New York: Science History Publications, 1972).

Sherman, William H., *John Dee: The Politics of Reading and Writing in the English Renaissance* (Amherst: University of Massachusetts Press, 1995).

Shrimplin, Valerie, *Sun Symbolism and Cosmology in Michaelangelo's 'Last Judgment'* (Kirksville, MO: Truman State Univesity Press, 2000).

Shumaker, Wayne, *The Occult Sciences in the Renaissance: A Study in Intellectual Patterns* (Berkeley, Los Angeles and London: University of California Press, 1972).

——(trans.), *John Dee on Astronomy: Propaedemata Aphoristica (1558 & 1568)* (Berkeley and Los Angeles: University of California Press, 1978).

Sibly, Ebenezer, *A Key to Physic and the Occult Sciences* (London, 1794).

——*A New and Complete Ilustration of the Celestial Science of Astrology* (2 Vols; London, 1813).

Silvestris, Bernardus, *Cosmographia*, (trans. and ed. Winthrop Wetherbee; New York: Columbia University Press, 1973).

Sirasi, Nancy G., *Medieval and Early Renaissance Medicine* (Chicago: University of Chicago Press, 1990).

Skinner, Stephen, *Terrestrial Astrology: Divination by Geomancy* (London: Routledge and Kegan Paul, 1980).

Sluiter, E., 'The Telescope before Galileo', *Journal for the History of Astronomy* 28(3) (August 1997): 223–35.

Smoller, Laura Ackerman, *History, Prophecy, and the Stars: The Christian Astrology of Pierre d'Ailly, 1350–1420* (Princeton: Princeton University Press, 1994).

Snyder, C.R. 'Why Horoscopes are True: The Effects of Specificity on Acceptance of Astrological Interpretations', *Journal of Clinical Psychology* 30 (1974): 577–80.

Snyder, C.R. and Glenn R. Larson, 'A Further Look at Student Acceptance of General Personality Interpretation', *Journal of Consulting and Clinical Psychology* 38(3) (1972): 384–8.

Snyder, C.R., Glenn R. Larson and Larry J. Bloom, 'Acceptance of General Personality Interpretations Prior to and After Receipt of Diagnostic Feedback Supposedly Based on Psychological, Graphological, and Astrological Assessment Procedures', *Journal of Clinical Psychology* 32(2) (April 1976): 258–65.

Sondheim, Moriz, 'Shakespeare and the Astrology of his Time', *Journal of the Warburg Institute* 2(3) (January 1939): 243–59.

Spencer, Herbert, *The Principles of Sociology* (New York: D. Appleton and Company, 1904), Vol. 1.

Spencer, Neil, *True as the Stars Above: Adventures in Modern Astrology* (London: Victor Gollancz, 2000).

——'"Hi, I'm Alan, I'm a Leo": The Irresistible Rise of the Sun Sign Republic', paper delivered to the Astrological Association conference, Bath Spa University, 3–5 September 2004.

Spencer, Theodore, *Shakespeare and the Nature of Man* (New York: Macmillan, 1949).

Stanley, Michael (ed.), *Emmanuel Swedenborg* (Berkeley: North Atlantic Books, 2003).

Suster, Gerald, *John Dee* (Berkeley: North Atlantic Books, 2003).

Steiner, Rudolf, *An Autobiography* (New York: Multimedia Publishing, 1977).

——*World History in the Light of Anthroposophy* (London: Rudolf Steiner Press, 1977 [1950]).

——*The Spiritual Beings in the Heavenly Bodies and in the Kingdoms of Nature* (Vancouver: Steiner Book Centre, 1981 [1951]).

——*The Reappearance of Christ in the Etheric* (Spring Valley, NY: Anthroposophic Press, 1983).

Sterne, Laurence, *Tristram Shandy* (Ware: Wordsworth Editions, 1996).

Stewart, Larry, *The Rise of Public Science: Rhetoric, Technology, and Natural Philosophy in Newtonian Britain, 1660–1750* (Cambridge: Cambridge University Press, 1992).

Stoneman, Richard (ed. and trans.), *The Greek Alexander Romance* (London: Penguin, 1991).

Suster, Gerald, *John Dee: Essential Readings* (Wellingborough: Crucible, 1986).

Swedenborg, Emanuel, *The New Jerusalem* (trans. John Chadwick; London: The Swedenborg Society, 1990).

Swift, Jonathan, 'The Bickerstaff Papers' in *A Tale of a Tub, The Battle of the Books and Other Satires* (London: Dent, 1970), pp. 196–226.

Tester, Jim, *A History of Western Astrology* (Woodbridge, Suffolk: Boydell Press, 1987).

Thom, Alexander, *Megalithic Sites in Britain* (Oxford: Oxford University Press, 1967).

Thomas, Keith, *Religion and the Decline of Magic* (Harmondsworth, Middlesex: Peregrine Books, 1971).

Thoren V., *The Lord of Uraniborg: A Biography of Tycho Brahe* (Cambridge: Cambridge University Press, 1990).

Thorndike, Lynn, *History of Magic and Experimental Science* (8 Vols; New York: Columbia University Press, 1923–58).

——*The Sphere of Sacrobosco and its Commentators* (Chicago: University of Chicago Press, 1949).

——*Michael Scot* (London: Thomas Nelson and Sons Ltd., 1965).

——*The Place of Magic in the Intellectual History of Europe* (New York: Ames Press, 1967 [1905]).

Thornton, Penny, *With Love from Diana* (New York: Pocket Books, 1995).

Tiryakian, Edward A., 'Towards the Sociology of Esoteric Culture', *American Journal of Sociology* 78(3) (November 1972): 491–512.

Titis, Placidus de, *Primum Mobile* (trans. John Cooper; Bromley, Kent: Institute for the Study of Cycles in World Affairs, 1983 [1814]).

Tolkein, J.R.R., *Tree and Leaf* (London: Unwin, 1964).

Tylor, Edward Burnett, *Primitive Culture* (3 Vols; New York: Harper Torchbooks, 1958 [London: Murray, 1871]).

Tyson. G.A., 'People Who Consult Astrologers: A Profile', *Personality and Individual Differences* 3 (1982): 119–26.

Vickers, Brian (ed.), *Occult and Scientific Mentalities in the Renaissance* (Cambridge: Cambridge University Press, 1986).

Vladimirou, Andrew, 'Byzantine Astrology in the Eleventh and Twelfth Centuries', PhD thesis, University of Birmingham, 2006.

Voltaire, *Letters Concerning the English Nation* (London: Westminster Press, 1926).

Voss, Angela, 'The Music of the Spheres: Marsilio Ficino and Renaissance Harmonia', *Culture and Cosmos* 2(2) (Autumn/Winter 1998): 16–38.

——'The Astrology of Marsilio Ficino: Divination or Science?', *Culture and Cosmos* 4(2) (Autumn/Winter 2000): 29–45.

——*Marsilio Ficino* (London: Random House, 2007).

Vreede, Elisabeth, *Anthroposophy and Astrology* (Great Barrington, MA: Anthroposophic Press, 2001).

Waldo-Schwartz, Paul, *Art and the Occult* (London: Mandala, 1977).

Walker, D.P., *Spiritual and Demonic Magic from Ficino to Campanella* (London: University of Notre Dame Press, 1975).

Washington, Peter, *Madame Blavatsky's Baboon: A History of the Mystics, Mediums and Misfits Who Brought Spiritualism to America* (New York: Shocken Books, 1993).

Waterfield, Robin, *Jacob Boehme* (Berkeley: North Atlantic Books, 2001).

Webb, James, *The Occult Establishment* (Glasgow: Richard Drew Publishing, 1981).

——*The Harmonious Circle: The Lives and Work of G.I. Gurdjieff, P.D. Ouspensky, and Their Followers* (Boston: Shambhala Publications, 1980).

——*The Occult Underground* (La Salle, IL: Open Court, 1988).

Weber, Max, *From Max Weber: Essays in Sociology*, ed. H.H. Garth and C. Mills Wright, (London: Kegan Paul, Trench, Trubner & Co., 1947).

Webster, Charles, *From Paracelsus to Newton: Magic and the Making of Modern Science* (Cambridge: Cambridge University Press, 1982).

Wedel, T., *The Medieval Attitude to Astrology, Especially in England* (New Haven: Yale University Press, 1920).

Westfall, Richard S., *The Life of Isaac Newton* (Cambridge: Cambridge University Press, 1993).

Willis, Roy and Patrick Curry, *Astrology, Science and Culture: Pulling Down the Moon* (Oxford: Berg, 2004).

Wind, Edgar, *Pagan Mysteries in the Renaissance* (Oxford: Oxford University Press, 1980).

Winship, Michael P., 'Cotton Mather, Astrologer', *The New England Quarterly* 63(2) (June 1990): 308–14.

Wordsworth, William, *The Prelude, Or, Growth of a Poet's Mind (Text of 1805)*, ed. Ernest de Selincourt and Stephen Gill, (Oxford: Oxford University Press, 1989).

Worsdale, John, *Genethliacal Astrology* (London, 1798).

——*Astronomy and Elementary Philosophy* (London, 1819).

——*Celestial Philosophy or Genethliacal Astronomy* (London, 1828).

Wuthnow, Robert, 'Astrology and Marginality', *Journal for the Scientific Study of Religion*, 15(2) (1976): 157–68.

——*Experimentation in American Religion: The New Mysticisms and Their Implications for the Churches* (Berkeley, CA: University of California Press, 1978).

Yates, Frances, *The Art of Memory* (London: Peregrine, 1978 [1966]).

——*The Occult Philosophy in the Elizabethan Age* (London and Boston: Routledge and Kegan Paul, 1983).

——*The Rosicrucian Enlightenment* (London: Routledge and Kegan Paul, 1986 [1972]).

Yeats, W.B., *A Vision* (London: MacMillan, 1981 [1937]).

York, Michael, *The Emerging Network: A Sociology of the New Age and Neo-Pagan Movements* (London: Rowman & Littlefield, 1995).

——*Historical Dictionary of New Age Movements* (Lanham, MD: Scarecrow 2003).

Zadkiel, *The Grammar of Astrology* (London, 1849).

Zalewski, Patrick J., *Secret Inner Teachings of the Golden Dawn* (Phoenix, AZ: Falcon Press, 1988).

Zambelli, Paola, 'Magic and Radical Reformation in Agrippa of Nettesheim', *Journal of the Warburg and Courtauld Institutes* 39(69–103) (1976).

——(ed.), *'Astrologi hallucinati': Stars and the End of the World in Luther's Time* (Berlin and New York: Walter de Gruyter, 1986).

——*The Speculum Astronomiae and its Enigma* (Dordrecht: Kluwer Academic Publishers, 1992).

Zoller, Robert, 'The Astrologer as Military Advisor in the Middle Ages and Renaissance', *Astrology Quarterly* 62(3) (Summer 1992): 33–8, 63(1); (Winter 1992): 15–26, 63(2); (Spring 1994): 35–45, 63(3); (Summer 1993): 16–22.

Index

astrology (*continued*)

   courtly 78–9

   criticisms of 10–16, 28–9, 33, 40, 43,
     51–2, 55, 66, 68–9, 85–6, 95, 99–105,
     113, 126, 134, 165, 169, 178–81, 215,
     262, 265–70, 277

   and cultural theory 268–9

   definitions of 222, 248, 282

   'disguised' 218, 222, 259

   divinatory 101, 104, 113–14

   electional 22, 51, 159

   esoteric 234, 257

   as forbidden knowledge 191

   Hermean 35

   high, middling and *low* 179–84, 206, 216,
     259

   infallibility of 230

   as an intellectual discipline 25

   judicial 33, 39, 49, 52, 54, 56, 63, 69,
     99–107, 113, 125, 139, 150, 156, 163–72,
     175–8, 182–5, 191, 194, 203, 205, 216,
     221, 244

   Jungian 253–4

   Kabbalistic 38

   as a literary device 128–32, 181

   Lutheran 139

   in the media 260–2, 266

   medical 30, 50, 77, 80, 113, 117, 186, 206

   military 20, 138

   natal 23, 32, 51, 63

   natural 13–14, 17, 33–4, 50, 104, 166,
     190–1, 222

   Neoplatonic 89

   Newtonian 185, 218

   19th-Century types of 216

   as an object of ridicule 172–3, 269

   periodic declines in importance of 3, 9, 99,
     168–70, 177–8, 181, 184

   political 109, 143

   popular 23, 25, 34, 68, 84, 126–7, 213–14,
     260–2, 278–9

   practical 95, 100, 156, 240

   propagandistic 96–7, 183

   reform of 106–11, 114–15, 122–3,
     139–41, 148–9, 158, 166, 169, 186, 231,
     272

   scholarly acceptance of 38–9, 43–4, 84

   of the soul 86, 248, 257–8

   superstitious 13–14, 17, 33–4, 191, 284

   technical 35, 94, 106, 168, 212, 253, 256

   testability of 271

   theosophical 230–1, 239

   20th-Century types of 248

   viewed as religion 282, 287

   see also horoscopes and horoscopic
     astrology

'astronomical revolution' 149

astronomy 2–6, 12–13, 21–4, 107–10, 176,
   191, 222

   laws of 150

Athalric 2

Aubrey, John 153

Augustine, St 3, 7, 9, 12–14, 21, 30, 33, 44–6,
   49–51, 55, 73, 80, 86, 89, 95, 104, 111, 267,
   275

Augustus, Emperor 96–7

authoritarian personality, theory of 268

Aveni, Anthony 285

Averroës 44, 46, 54

Avicenna 47, 50, 54, 66

Azriel 36

Bacon, Francis 163–4, 179

Bacon, Roger 51, 53, 58–60, 103

Badelli, Antonio 146

Baghdad 19

Bailey, Alice 239–44, 248, 252, 256, 279–80

Bailley, Edmond 234–5

Bailly, Jean-Sylvain 188

Bainbridge, William Simms 283

Balasi 97–8, 281

Balzac, Honoré de 224–5

Bara, Theda 226

Barrett, Francis 208

Baudrillard, Jean 286

Baumann Jung, Gret 254, 258–9

Bayle, Pierre 168, 191

Bear, the (constellation) 26